Exchange & Production

COMPETITION,
COORDINATION,
& CONTROL

Third Edition

Exchange & Production

COMPETITION, COORDINATION, & CONTROL

Third Edition

Armen Alchian & William R. Allen
University of California, Los Angeles

Wadsworth Publishing Company, Belmont, California
A Division of Wadsworth, Inc.

A Study Guide, by Michael Staten, to accompany
Exchange & Production, Third Edition
is available from your bookstore.

Economics Editor: Bill Oliver
Editorial-Production Services: Douglas Pundick
Designer: Christy Butterfield
Illustration: Miki Greiner
Composition: TriStar Graphics

11 — 93

ISBN 0-534-01320-1

Library of Congress Catalog Card Number: 82-42900

Preface

As its title suggests, this text presents economic principles that explain how our market-directed economy organizes and coordinates production and exchange among competing but nevertheless cooperating people. The book concentrates on what is unfortunately called "microeconomics": the role of markets in which property rights are exchanged and contracts and coalitions are formed to enable greater production and resolution of conflicts of interest. Our premise is that what is called "macroeconomics" cannot be made coherent without these fundamentals.

The third edition of *Exchange and Production* continues to emphasize economic principles. The principles are presented through a series of simple behavioral postulates, and throughout the book the authors demonstrate how these principles explain a wide variety of economic and social phenomena. Although all economics texts use economic principles to analyze a society of scarce resources and unlimited wants, *Exchange and Production* extensively illustrates how the necessity of tradeoffs affects both economic behavior and social behavior.

Note that the book does not attempt to survey the entire range of current economic isssues—such an attempt would be doomed to superficiality and failure. Rather, *Exchange and Production* focuses on teaching principles by repeated appplication to a variety of problems.

A number of changes have been made in the third edition. In the previous editions, demand was emphasized initially and applied solely in the context of a fixed supply; supply and production were sequentially developed later in the book. In contrast, this edition includes the rudiments of production and supply in the first seven chapters. This permits an overview of the operation of a system controlled by the exchange of private property rights in a marketplace. The material that follows explores in greater depth the reasons for and modes of organizing business firms and the rate of output and the amount of inputs hired. Instructors can use the first seven chapters as a demand and supply core and can then select which areas to emphasize from the remaining material.

In addition, new chapters offer more systematic treatment of some pricing tactics, of oligopoly, and of the domestic and political economies. More attention is given to the interaction of the law with economic principles, property rights concepts, public goods, externalities, and opportunistic behavior controls. Recent findings of the meaning and scope of unemployment are included. The monitoring-agency role of unions is more explicitly contained. The role of cost curves, prominent in earlier editions, is reduced and subordinated to greater explanation of the meaning and use of the costs of various acts in the production process. The last chapter, Inflation, has a brief appendix on the money expansion process of the commercial banking system.

The features that aided student comprehension and review—the end-of-chapter summaries and questions—have been retained and updated. And to make the book easier for students to use, a comprehensive glossary has been added, more applications have been included, and the level of exposition and analysis has been simplified, allowing students easier access to the material. The most important new aid for students, however, is the Study Guide, prepared by Michael Staten, of the University of Delaware. This tool offers for each chapter a thorough summary, a list of new terms, and appropriate problems and questions.

Acknowledgment is due to several people. Unnamed as a coauthor of this revision is Arline A. Hoel, whose aid nearly merited that explicit status. Revision of the book's tone was accomplished by Kevin Gleason. Those persons who reviewed the manuscript and contributed valuable suggestions are: Douglas D. Adie, Wheaton College; Edward B. Bell, Cleveland State University; Donald B. Billings, Boise State University; Keith D. Evans, California State University, Northridge; Gerald Flueckiger, Miami University; David E. R. Gay, University of Arkansas; Charles A. Rambeck, Saint John's University. And, of course, the authors acknowledge the important debt to economists of the past two centuries.

Contents

Chapter 1
Scarcity, Competition, and Social Control

Societies have progressed despite almost universal ignorance of economic principles. So why learn them? First, for some people, simply to understand their environment is enough reason. Second, an understanding of economic principles can help people avoid being frustrated and confounded by half-truths and errors about the operation of a private-property, market-directed system, such as the one in the United States. Such half-truths and errors are plentiful. For example: Minimum wage laws help the unskilled and minorities (p. 334); foreign imports reduce jobs in the United States (p. 153 and 304); producers make goods less durable in order to sell more in the future (p. 110); "equal pay for equal work" aids women, minorities, and the young (p. 336); resale of used books reduces authors' royalties (p. 113); strict liability on producers for defective products protects consumers (p. 285); the environment should not be harmed (p. 87); price controls reduce consumers' costs (p. 69); reducing unemployment requires creating more jobs (p. 305); larger incomes for some people mean lower incomes for others (p. 151 and 189); free-tuition education reduces costs to students (p. 69); the military draft is cheaper than a paid-volunteer military (p. 338); inflation is caused by large government deficits, by unions, or by greedy businessmen (p. 405); a reduced supply causes a shortage (p. 61); unemployment is wasteful (p. 371); stockbrokers and analysts can predict which stocks are better purchases (p. 362). These are only a small sample. Undoubtedly you'll detect others after you've read this book.

Third, we would like to say that understanding economics will help you earn more, but as sellers of a service—which is what textbook authors are—we do not promise that economic learning means economic earning, but we believe it does.

The Magnitude of the Task of Economic Control

So large and complex is our economy that it appears incomprehensible: It is composed of 230 million people, in 80 million households, with a labor force of over 100 million (one-third women) and 15 million business units (including over 12 million single proprietorships, 1 million partnerships, and 2 million corporations). These produce, exchange, and consume an uncounted diversity of goods and services worth $3 trillion annually (an average of about $13,000 per person)—close to 25% of the world's total.

Yet no planning agency is in charge of coordinating the economic activities of millions of individuals of different interests and talents in our intricately interdependent society. No one designates who shall produce how much of each good and service and who shall obtain how much of what. For example, no agency plans that food reaches every city—yet food reaches every city. Paradoxically, when a government agency has economic control of some good, such as oil, results have bordered on chaos. (But, as we shall see, it is not correct to believe that all government activity is disruptive and all private activity is ideal.)

Universal Scarcity

Since the fiasco in the Garden of Eden, what we get is by sweat, strain, and anxiety. We want more kinds of goods, and more of them, than we have any realistic prospect of obtaining. That we want more than we have is what is meant by **scarcity**. Even people in the wealthiest societies are in a state of scarcity, and doubtless will remain so despite the fullest use of their productive potential. Despite religious or philosophical exhortations to abandon materialistic desires for more, our wants and goals will remain unfulfilled. The illusion that society was becoming saturated with goods and services was popular in the 1960s. And the opposite illusion (popular in the 1970s) that we were becoming a world of scarcity is equally wrong—because scarcity has been pervasive ever since life began.

Two universal facts about our scarcity are portrayed by the guns-and-butter example in Figure 1-1: (1) In every society production possibilities are limited; (2) production of any good necessitates tradeoffs. For example, our economy could produce a maximum of G guns, if all resources were devoted only to guns; alternatively, if all resources were used for butter, B units could be produced, but no guns would be. Largest feasible intermediate combinations of guns and butter are indicated by the boundary curve between G and B, the **production-possibility boundary**. How big it is depends on people's tastes for leisure and work, methods of organizing joint productive activity, property rights, knowledge, and the stock of productive resources.

The principle of tradeoffs among achievable outputs of goods, illustrated in Figure 1-1, applies not only to guns versus butter but to *all* goods—even leisure versus better grades, more travel versus more safety, or more clothes versus food, to name only a few. Your choice among them can be expressed with that diagram simply by measuring higher grades on the vertical scale and more leisure along the horizontal. You can get *more* of *both* only if you happen to be inside the boundary—that is, behaving inefficiently. If you are on the boundary—that is, behaving efficiently—you can get more of one only by accepting less of the other.

Efficiency: By definition, an economy has organized its resources with **productive efficiency** if it is someplace on the production-possibility boundary. Being on the boundary means that more of any one good can be produced only by having to sacrifice some output of some other goods. If one is on the boundary, that means it is impossible to increase the output of every good at the same time. Then the productive resources are fully occupied, and in their most productive ways. In other words, for *specified amounts of all of the goods except one*, the output of that good is maximized. That is a "constrained" maximum—the maximum output of the one good providing that the specified amounts of the other goods are also produced. Because simultaneous maximizing of the outputs of every good is impossible, we instead think of the maximum output that could be produced of *one* good—under the condition, called a constraint, that specified amounts of the other goods also be produced. Such a **constrained maximum** is called productively efficient, by definition. Obviously, every output combination *on* the production boundary in Figure 1–1 is a *productively* efficient output combination.

But which of all the many different—but efficient—combinations of output, each on the boundary, is "best"? This is a different question, requiring some normative criterion as to how to rank or judge the goodness of each of the different possible efficient output combinations. That one of all the productive efficient output combinations that is deemed best is called the *"economically* efficient" output. All the other outputs on the boundary are not economically efficient, though they are productively efficient. **Economic efficiency**—being at the "optimal" point on the boundary—is, then, a more severe requirement than productive efficiency; it requires defining some appropriate criterion of what is best. Whether or not that can be done is debatable. However, the factors that determine to which combination the economy does tend to move can be analytically explored, and will be.

Growth is represented by an outward shift of the production possibility boundary, for example, to the hypothetical 1987 boundary shown in Figure 1–2. Growth means either that society can produce more per person or that there are more people and hence a larger boundary. Some conditions that aid growth are explored later.

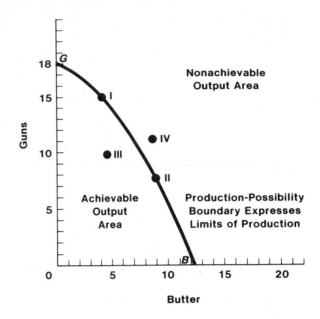

Figure 1-1.

SCARCITY, EFFICIENCY, AND CHOICE ILLUSTRATED BY PRODUCTION-POSSIBILITY BOUNDARY

The curved line portrays limits on the quantities of guns and butter producible in the economy. Any point on the line (for example, I or II) can be produced. No combination of guns and butter outside the curved line (say, point IV) can be achieved by the economy, given its productive powers and the amount of leisure people desire. Less would be produced if the productive resources were unemployed or used inefficiently—as at point III. Society selects a point on the boundary or inside it. Productive efficiency means that the economy is on the production-possibility boundary.

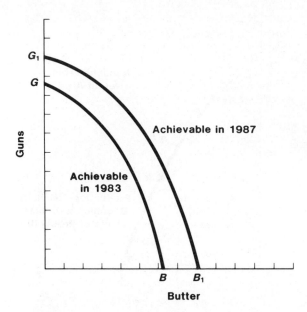

Figure 1-2.

GROWTH OF ECONOMIC
PRODUCTIVE POWERS OF THE ECONOMY

A richer, more productive economy is represented by a
production-possibility boundary that is higher and more to
the right, as for 1987 compared to 1983. Growth can
occur in several ways. A greater production-possibility
boundary is usually induced by a larger labor force.
(But does the output per person increase? That
cannot be indicated by this diagram, which gives
only the social totals.) Moving the frontier outward
involves restricting current consumption by
saving either to create more productive goods
or to invest in knowledge and inventions.

Costs Are the Best of Forsaken Alternatives

The production boundary, which confines us to a choice between more of one good and more of others, conveniently introduces the meaning of an inescapable concept: *cost.* The cost of any chosen act is the most valuable forsaken alternative opportunity. Thus the cost of production of one more unit of butter is the number of guns that otherwise could have been produced. Or, reversing the direction, the cost of another gun is the amount of butter that otherwise could have been produced. This is represented by moving *on* the boundary between points of more or fewer guns and more or less butter. When there are many more than just two goods, many possible combinations of reductions of other goods would enable more of some one good to be produced. Which of the many possible combinations is considered the cost? The answer is: The cost is the combination that is the *most valuable* of those that otherwise could be achieved—the best of the forsaken opportunities. That is why costs are often redundantly called **opportunity costs.** My purchase of a hot dog forsakes my claims to other purchasable goods worth at least as much as the price I pay for the hot dog, say 75¢.

Full Cost: The money spent measures only *part* of the costs. I may have spent five minutes waiting in line, and that time could have been used for something else. Though no extra money expenditure was involved, an opportunity to use some time in another way was forsaken. If the best alternative use of the time was worth the equivalent of what could be bought for 25¢, my "full price" of getting and consuming the hot dog must include the 25-cent value of the alternative use of time.

There are still more costs to consider. Suppose I tarried and joked with the vendor and delayed service to three other people. They lost the opportunity to do what they could have done with that time. If that were worth 5¢ to each of three people in line, the cost (which I do not bear) of my hot dog is 15¢ more, or $1.15, of which I bore only $1.00. And say the seller put onions on the hot dog. In a close conversation with my friends I foul the atmòsphere. With a loss of purer air valued at 5¢, the cost of the purchase *and* consumption of the hot dog amounts to $1.20, of which I bear 75¢ through sacrifice of market-purchasable options and 25¢ worth of time spent in line; 20¢ worth of loss is imposed on other people.Obviously, the full costs are not always fully measured only by the money expenditures, nor borne by the actor.

Many people carelessly talk as if costs are sacrifices only of material things normally bought and sold in the market. However, cost includes every feature in the best of the forsaken options, including forsaken leisure, loss of environmental amenities (views, fresh air, cleanliness), loss of cultural qualities (safety, morality), and loss of any other features to which anyone attaches value.

We caution that "labor, toil, trouble, and pain" are not what is meant by costs. "Bads" associated with an action arc not its costs; they are part of the act. For example, a swimming pool yields the pleasure of swimming and the undesirable consequences of neighborhood children noisily splashing the yard. These undesirable splashes are part of thc act, not part of the costs.

If not all costs are imposed on or borne by the person authorizing an activity (so that some costs are borne by others), the person's choice will be different than if they were. Costs borne by others are called **externalities**. The failure to impose all the components of cost on the decision maker often produces consequences deemed distressing and objectionable—such as "excessive" pollution and "shortsighted" land use or zoning laws. For the moment, however, we assume that full cost is borne by the actor. Later we shall inquire into the conditions permitting, and those preventing, the full cost to be borne and heeded by the actor.

The Problem of Organizing Production

Is productive efficiency achieved in the real world? To think that we simply choose some efficient output combination overlooks the overwhelming task of organizing activities so as to achieve a point on the boundary. But who knows how to make butter, let alone a gun? Who knows how to breed, feed, and milk cows? Does that person also know how to make a modern milk processing plant or the stainless steel, the pumps, and the gases in the refrigerating equipment, the trucks to carry milk, and on and on? Indeed, is there any consumer good that *one* person is able to or knows how to produce? It strains the imagination to think of the number of people, the incredible variety of specialized bits of knowledge, and the technical skills necessary to provide butter for the market. How is the incomprehensible mass of detailed, separately held knowledge, ability, and work of millions of people coordinated?

Methods of Organizing Economic Activity

COMMAND SOCIETIES

In some economies commands are issued through a central command system, as in an army. Everyone is assigned some task by someone ranking higher in the command system. Such a system exists in China. No one is permitted to select his own occupation or place of work. The central authorities, through a system of commands or assignments, decide who does what and where. That system is called Communism in China.

And it is essentially identical to the one used in Russia and almost all other communist countries.

SOCIALIST ECONOMIES

A **socialist** system is one in which income-producing goods (machines, land, buildings) are controlled by government agents and are not exchangeable at market prices, that is, at prices determined by competition among sellers and buyers with their own property. Usually in a socialist economy, people are allowed to select their jobs and places to live, just as you can choose among various government jobs in the United States. In Great Britain, Italy, Sweden, and France more of the economy is socialist-controlled than in the United States. However, in every economy there are some socialist institutions, since every government is essentially a socialist institution.

CAPITALIST OR MARKET ECONOMIES

A widespread system is known as the free-enterprise, private-property—or capitalist—system. It is a system in which people have private property rights to production and consumption goods and over their personal labor services. **Capitalism** (a term coined by Karl Marx) is its standard name. Why? Because market-determined prices of goods reflect the anticipated value of the future as well as the present services from those goods. This reflection of future services is called capitalizing, as will be explained in considerable detail in Chapter 6. Thus, the defining attribute of capitalism is the availability of a market with the right to control and to produce or buy and sell privately owned goods and services in open competition with others.

It is the system that will be analyzed almost exclusively in this book, primarily because it is better understood—not necessarily because it can be proven to be better. The capitalist or private-property system of economic coordination and control was first sys-tematically analyzed by the Scottish philosopher Adam Smith in 1776 in his epic book, *An Inquiry into the Sources of the Wealth of Nations.* Smith saw that system as not chaotic or lacking in coordination and efficiency despite the absence of any central directive authority that consciously planned and directed people. He saw cohesiveness, order, and responsiveness in that system. His basic analytic conception was that people respond predictably to opportunities for gain. He saw that an offer of exchange is a powerful competitive social control, especially "an offer I couldn't refuse." If the bulk of resources is privately owned, coordination of behavior through competition for gains from trade is strongly encouraged.

Adam Smith wrote:
Man has almost constant occasion for the help of his brethren, and it is in vain for him to expect it from their benevolence *only* [emphasis added]. He will be more likely to prevail if he can interest their self-love in his favor, and show them that it is for their own advantage to do for him what he requires of them. Whoever offers another a bargain of any kind, proposes to do this: Give me that which I want, and you shall have this which you want, is the meaning of every such offer; and it is in this manner that we obtain from one another the far greater part of those good offices which we stand in need of. It is not from the benevolence of the butcher, the brewer, or the baker, that we expect our dinner, but from their regard to their own interest. We address ourselves not to their humanity but to their self-love.

We may have benevolence for a circle of friends, but benevolence alone will not induce discovery and exchange of specialized productive activities most beneficial to the unknown masses. An amazing achievement of the private-property, market-exchange system is that it harnesses, *in addition to benevolence*, the powerful motive of self-interest in peaceful, specialized, productive activities that benefit humanity at large, and it suppresses junglelike, parasitic, destructive behavior. Without that peaceful, implicit control and coordination, a few of us would be living in a poverty-stricken, painful, brutish, ignorant Stone Age, and almost all of us would never have experienced life.

Between capitalism and socialism is a span of mixed economic arrangements in which most resources are held as private property, but the state exercises much control over what can be done with them. Laws may prohibit some people from selling certain goods, while politically protecting others who have access to the market. This government-aided "monopolization" by a politically favored group is often called a **mercantilist system**. As we shall see, it comprises a noticeable portion of the American economy.

No society is exclusively capitalist, mercantilist, or socialist. Every society is a mix. In the United States, the roads, postal service, schools, and police are heavily—though not exclusively—socialistic (not exclusively, because we have private schools, private delivery systems, private roads, and private security guards). In predominantly socialist economies, some goods such as furniture, clothes, and cars are privately owned, but most income-producing goods are not.

We will not use the terms *free* enterprise, *free* markets, or *free* society because "free" has no clear meaning that everyone agrees to. We avoid comparing "freer" or "less free" societies and instead investigate differences in cultural attributes, personal behavior, and costs of expressing individual life styles.

Competition, Coordination, and Control

Because of scarcity, **competition** is inescapable—and therefore so is conflict. One means of expressing that conflict is by physical force, or violence, although the "State"—the political authority and its agents and representatives—always claims the exclusive right to use violence, usually with a view to restricting most people to nonviolent modes of competition.

The question is not how to eliminate competition, for as the renowned philosopher and part-time golfer Arnold Palmer recognized, "If you aren't competing, you're dead." The scientific questions are, "What are the permitted kinds of competition? How do they operate? And what are their effects?" The (unanswered) ethical question is, "What is a 'good' competition?" Economics can help answer the scientific questions, but it cannot decide what are the "good" forms of competition.

VIOLENCE AS A FORM OF COMPETITION

Before condemning the threat or use of violence as a means of social control or of getting more goods, note that it is widely practiced and respected—at least, when applied successfully on a national scale. Julius Caesar conquered Gaul and was honored by the Romans; had he simply roughed up the local residents, he would have been damned as a gangster. Alexander the Great, who conquered the Near East, was not regarded by the Greeks as a ruffian, nor was Charlemagne by the Franks. Europeans acquired and divided—and redivided—America by force. Lenin is revered in Russia. So is Franco in Spain, Castro in Cuba, Bolivar in Bolivia, Ieyasu in Japan, and George Washington in the United States. This is not said in defense of all uses of physical force; it is simply an objective statement of fact.

The Supreme Court of the United States, in response to laws passed by Congress, stated that "anticompetitive" contracts or agreements are illegal. But the meaning of "anticompetitive" will not be found in either the Court decisions or the legislation. Are the forbidden forms called "anticompetitive" as a short way of saying they are "anti" the *desired* forms of competition? For example, rival quarterbacks striving for the starting position on a football team could compete by trying to maim each other. If allowed, that kind of competition would eliminate the kind of competition in which they strived to be better passers or signal callers. Members of Congress and justices who talk of "anticompetitive" acts are contributing to confusion; they should say which *kind* of competition is forbidden and which is preferred.

CONTROL BY
RELIGION, LAW, AND OSTRACISM

Formal law and police power are not the only forms of social control. Religious doctrines usually promise punishment or rewards in a next life—a promise to whose effectiveness in controlling human behavior history provides amazing evidence. Social ostracism is also a powerful control, as we learn when snubbed or isolated on the rare occasions of our "uncivilized" behavior. No matter how different among societies or over time, standards of morality and propriety seem essential to the continuance of human society.

Techniques of social control differ in effectiveness. Some can be escaped by migration. Society's intolerance of any behavior can more readily be ignored the less the intolerance is associated with physical government force. When the state and the church operated together, each had greater power than when they operated separately. By definition, government power is less pervasive in a capitalistic, private-property, market-exchange system than in a socialist system. This does not make the private-property, market-exchange system the better one, for you may believe that greater political control over people is desirable.

Controls, Competitive Criteria, and Survival Traits

To distribute 200 Rose Bowl game tickets (or admissions to your college) without selling them, what form of competition would you use? The authors, red-blooded male chauvinists, would award tickets to the 200 most beautiful female applicants. (Why are admissions at your college not allocated that way? Perhaps to some extent they are.) Certainly, a system using beauty is competitive and discriminatory. But *all* competition—like all choice—discriminates; that is its purpose.

If beauty seems a frivolous criterion, consider an alternative: first come, first served. All applicants could run a race, with tickets going to the first 200 at the finish line. Silly? Replace "finish line" with "box office at the Rose Bowl" or "registration desks" for popular college classes or "gasoline stations" during so-called oil shortages, and then ask if it is silly. The only difference is that, in these other instances, there is no single starting time, so some people start earlier and wait at the "finish" line—in rain, cold, and discomfort without benefit to the distributor.

To complicate matters, what is to stop the recipients of our Rose Bowl tickets from passing the tickets to others, according to their own criteria? Or selling them? It is extremely difficult to ensure that one's criteria, selected so reasonably and with the purest of hearts, will be effective throughout the allocative process.

If "first come, first served" were used for allocating food, people who are best able to withstand the rigors of standing in line or whose time is less valuable would have better prospects. They would stand in line up to the point where the cost of so doing equals the value of what is obtained. (Remember the meaning of costs, the best forsaken alternative.) If food, wealth, or social popularity were awarded more to relatively tall people, height would increase over time. And if beauty were the criterion, beauty would be increased. Or if charm and rhetorical ability were important as rationing criteria, as they are in politics, society would be distinguished for its personable, articulate people. If productivity were an important allocative criterion, productivity would be increased and the society would be richer, as would the more productive individuals.

If "fair" competition meant an equal random chance (which it need not), names could be drawn from a bowl (including names of those who did not trouble to apply). Would you want that kind of "equal chance" for your surgeon, mate, juror, waiter, parents, employer, or teacher? But we have selected men for the armed forces that way.

Attributes of Economic Analysis

Three attributes of economic analysis are important: First, economic analysis is solely *scientific*. That is, it helps to explain what conditions lead to what consequences: "If *A*, then *B*." It does not forecast that *A* will occur. And the economist is not ordained to pass final judgment on the desirability of *B*. That is a normative issue. Economics gives no ultimate criteria for determining whether consequences are good or bad, just as chemistry has none for determining whether more rapid oxidation under heat is good or bad. Although scientists (including economists) offer all sorts of ethical assessments, what economic theory says must be distinguished from what an individual economist may prefer. The former is what counts, not the latter. Though the economist may be better able than the noneconomist to discern the consequences of some proposed act, the economist is not superior in evaluating the propriety of that consequence.

Second, economic theory is built on an understanding of some universal traits of hu-

man nature. It is not contended that economic theory has identified (or must identify) *all* the traits that compose human nature. And it is certainly not assumed that all people are exactly alike in every respect. Yet some virtually universal regularities in those preferences or responses yield principles that are powerful in explaining some social phenomena throughout the world. The next chapter describes some regularities of human nature.

Third, scientists, economists among them, achieve understanding of the phenomena they study by constructing and testing theories. Put simply, a theory is a model of the phenomenon being analyzed: a description of the phenomenon that is stripped of all inessential particulars—much like a road map of a city. A theory is a guide to one's analysis. How accurate should a theory be? That is like asking, "How accurate is a road map?" The answer should be, "Good enough for one's purpose." If the purpose is to drive through a town from one end to the other, a crude sketch of a few lines is often sufficient. But one that doesn't show traffic signals, crosswalks, alleys, and street numbers may not be good enough for the police. And a map good enough for them may be insufficiently detailed for a construction firm installing a sewer system; it must show elevations, street widths, power lines, and so on. Like road maps, models or theories of economic phenomena come in various degrees of detail—but all models describing the same set of phenomena are consistent with each other. No map or theory will be perfectly complete in every detail. Some theories, or models, may be so elaborate and difficult to use that the extra trouble and cost of using them is not worth the gain. So ask not, "Is the theory accurate?" but rather "Is the theory good enough for our purposes?" The model, or theory, given in this book is estimated to be good enough—sufficiently thorough in detail and extensive in coverage—for the purposes of the interested student. Someone planning to become a professional economist would later purchase—at higher cost—a more detailed, more elaborate theory.

Some models, then, are useful precisely because they are simpler than others. As we progress through this book our model becomes less simple than it is at the outset. It is probably helpful to suggest at this stage the noteworthy simplifying assumptions that we use now and later abandon.

1. Sellers detect the persisting and the transient changes in consumer tastes or demand for goods costlessly, perfectly, and instantly.

2. Exchangeable private-property rights exist in all goods.

3. No acts of charity occur.

4. No seller affects the total supply enough to affect ones prices or those of other sellers.

5. Full information about the availability, quality, and suppliers of all goods is available costlessly.

6. Contracts for exchange and for joint production effort are costless to form, monitor, and enforce.

7. No one makes long-lived, preexchange investments that have value only when dealing with a particular person. Instead, investments have general values in that they have the same values when any of many other people are dealt with.

What you are going to learn are economic principles and how to use them. The principles in the theory, when brought to the test of usefulness, are far more in accord with actual occurrences than the speculations of "practical men."

Summary

1. Scarcity means that people want more goods and services than are available.

2. The fact that production capability is limited can be expressed by a production-possibility boundary, which indicates the maximum amount of any particular good that can be produced within the constraint that specified amounts of other goods are to be produced. Achieving that constrained production maximum is called technological, or *productive,* efficiency.

3. Achieving the "best" place on the boundary, that is, the best combination of the various production-efficient outputs, is called *economic* efficiency.

4. An opportunity for choice among alternative activities creates costs: The cost of an act *is* the most preferred (highest valued) of the forsaken alternative opportunities.

5. The cost (forsaken option) of an act does not necessarily involve a current expenditure of money, but instead can mean the loss of some opportunities.

6. The costs of an act by one person that are borne by other people are called *externalities.*

7. Scarcity and competition are inseparable. Competition takes many forms. One form is striving to offer people opportunities better than those offered by others. Another is using physical force. All forms of striving to improve one's own situation are competitive, by definition.

8. In *capitalism* the rights to use or alter goods and services are owned by individuals and are exchangeable private-property entitlements.

9. *Socialism* denotes an economic system in which the productive resources are controlled by the government.

10. *Mercantilism* is a system in which government regulates uses of goods and services that are in other respects held as private property.

11. Economic analysis and theory are strictly descriptive and scientific. They provide no bases for moralizing about what might happen, or what is "good" or "bad"—only a basis for discerning what *is*.

Questions

Answers to all questions except those marked with an asterisk are in the Answer section at the end of the book.

1. "If people were reasonable, strikes and wars would not occur." Do you agree? If so, why? If not, why not?

2. a. If there is more than one opportunity to be forsaken, which forsaken opportunity is the cost?
   b. How are values of opportunities measured?
   c. Can there be production without costs?

*3. What is the cost of your college education?

4. "The time involved in purchasing something cannot be considered part of the cost because the time would have passed anyway. Hence to count the value of time as part of the cost of any action is fallacious." Evaluate: What is meant by the value (or cost) of time?

5. Are costs the same thing as the undesirable consequences of some action?

6. What is meant by an equality between private and social costs?

7. Name three honored statesmen who obtained their status by successfully competing in violence and who, had they failed, would have been punished for treason.

8. a. What competition is permissible in politics but not in private business? And the reverse?
   b. What kinds of competition are permissible in seeking admission to college but not permissible for grades in this course?

9. "Governments should monopolize in coercive violence." "Government is a social agency for resolving interpersonal conflict."
   a. Are those two propositions compatible statements of fact?

   b. What evidence can you cite for your answer?

10. What forms of competition are made illegal by laws establishing private-property rights? And socialism?

11. "A more equal distribution of wealth is socially preferred to a less equal distribution." What is meant by "socially" preferred as contrasted to "individually" preferred?

*12. a. What does "equality of opportunity" mean?
   b. How could you determine whether it exists?
   c. Is there equality of opportunity to get an "A" in this course?
   d. How would you make it equal, if it is not?
   e. What is the difference between increasing opportunity and equalizing it?

13. "Under socialism, cooperation will replace competition."
   a. Is the quoted proposition correct?
   b. What evidence can you cite to support your answer?
   c. What is the difference between cooperation and competition?

14. "Food is grown, harvested, sorted, processed, packed, transported, assembled in appropriately small bundles, and offered to consumers every day by individuals pursuing personal interests. No authority is responsible for seeing that these functions are performed. Yet food is available every day. On the other hand, appointed authorities are responsible for seeing that water, education, and electricity are available. In the areas where we consciously plan and control social output, we often find shortages and failure of service. But who has heard of a shortage of restaurants, churches, furniture, beer, shoes, or paper? Is it not surprising that privately owned businesses, operating for the private gain of the owners, provide service to patrons and customers that is as good as, if not better than, what the postal service, post office, schools, and other politically controlled enterprises provide? Furthermore, wouldn't you expect public agencies to be less discriminating according to race and creed than privately owned business? Yet the fact is that

they are not." How do you explain these paradoxes?

15. The economic system is alleged to affect the fundamental social and cultural characteristics in a society. Among these are patterns of speech, expression, religion, travel, marriage, divorce, inheritance, education, legal trials, art, literature, and music.

    a. Are these different under capitalism than under socialism?

    b. Can you cite evidence for your answer?

16. "The free-enterprise, capitalist system is free in that it involves no imposition of force or compulsion." Do you agree? Explain your answer.

17. A historian has said that ships made by the ancient Greeks were of fine quality because they were made by slaves, whose owners therefore spared no labor in making boats. Later, when there was no longer slavery, boats were made in ways that used less labor and were less durable. It is true that ships were later built with less intensive use of labor. Do you agree with the historian's explanation of why?

Chapter 2
Consumer Demand

The Unit of Analysis Is the Individual

To understand the behavior of groups, organizations, and nations we focus on the incentives of their individual members. A business, union, or family aids the common interests of its members, but its actions are the results of preferences and decisions of individuals within those units. Thus, we do not ask, "Why does the U.S. government, or General Motors, or some union, behave as it does?" We ask instead, "Why do the decision makers decide as they do?" An answer is possible because of two principles: First, a person adapts to circumstances so as more fully to achieve his many preferences or goals. Second, although people differ in significant and sometimes intriguing ways, behavior is sufficiently uniform among individuals that it can be largely summarized with a few *behavioral postulates*. To characterize "human nature" so starkly may seem to oversimplify, but our postulates yield an impressive payoff in enabling us to analyze the essentials of complex behavior. (These postulates, however, do *not* mean that all individual choice is only self-interested and self-seeking. They mean instead that, whether or not a choice is made according to self-interest, it is an *individual* who makes the choice.)

Postulate 1

Each person desires many goods and has many goals.

No one wants only one good. We want more of this and also more of that. We want also to accomplish more than one goal.

Postulate 2

For each person, some goods are scarce.

A *good* is anything desired by at least one person. Goods may be either *free* goods or *economic* (that is, scarce) goods. A *free* good is one that no one desires to have more of than is already possessed. The classic example, for most of us, most of the time, is air: No one has to forgo an alternative to inhale. However, air is not a free good to astronauts or deep sea divers; nor is clean air to city residents on smoggy days. An *economic* good is one that a person wants more of than the person now has.

Beware of misleading uses of the word *free*. It does not mean simply anything distributed at a zero money price. On the contrary, some zero-priced goods are scarce, for example, "free" education, "free" public libraries, "free" campsites, "freeways," and "free" beaches. These are scarce even though the money price is "zero." Charging a zero money price does not magically make a scarce good so plentiful that all of us can have as much as we want. Indeed, paradoxically, a zero money price on an economic good, as we shall see, creates what is called a *shortage* of the good.

Hereafter, when we speak of a good, we always mean a *scarce*, or *economic*, good.

Postulate 3

Each person is willing to forsake some of
a good to get more of other goods.

A person is willing to forsake *some* (not necessarily all) of any good if a sufficiently large amount of other goods can be obtained in return. No one steadfastly refuses to give up even the tiniest *portion* of a good no matter what would be obtainable in return.

The amount of a good that a person would be willing to give up to obtain more of some other good is defined as that person's **marginal personal use value** of that other good. The amount of wine a person would be willing to give up to get one more egg is the person's marginal personal use value (measured in terms of units of wine) of that egg. "Marginal" refers to the value of *one more* egg—a marginal egg.

It may be surprising that in economics the personal use value of a good is always defined, measured, or expressed by an *amount of some other good*, as we measured the value of an egg in units of wine. But in economics there is no other measure or kind of value, because no good has an intrinsic, or built-in, value. All values are *relative*.

Although we will generally apply our economic analysis to tradeoffs among ordinary marketable goods and services, it applies as well to tradeoffs among any goals, objectives, ideals, and principles. Each of us on occasion sacrifices or risks *some* small degree of our integrity—our fidelity to an ideal or principle—for some sufficient increase in income or safety or popularity or power. This is a fact of human behavior which economic analysis neither praises nor condemns. (Imagine a world in which no one ever told the slightest lie, or hid the slightest truth, no matter what the resultant gain in security or social pleasantness.) *All* desired entities, conditions, and traits—truth, virtue, health, beauty, safety, responsibility, politeness, decency, self-respect—are marginally substitutable. Goals and ideals, like ordinary goods, are competitive and substitutable in *degrees* of attainability or fulfillment; the tradeoff is between *more* or *less*, not between *all* or *nothing*.

Postulate 4

The more of a good one has, the larger
the total personal use value, but the
lower the marginal personal value of a
unit.

One's total personal value of some specific quantity of a good (not of just one more unit) is measured by the total amount of other goods one would be willing to pay for that specific quantity. A person's experiences, education, and psychological traits affect the person's valuations. But the marginal value depends also on the amount of the good a person already has: *The larger the amount of a good, the larger is its total use value to the person, but the less of other goods is one willing to pay to get an additional unit.* As we have more of any good, additional units can be put to only less valuable, previously unfulfilled uses. Thus, larger amounts increase one's *total* use value but reduce the *marginal* personal value, as Table 2-1 shows.

Postulate 5

Not all people have identical tastes and preferences.

Even people who have identical amounts of the same goods are not likely to place the same personal total and marginal values on them, nor are they likely to feel equally well off: One person's gloried asceticism is another's demeaning poverty.

Postulate 6

People are innovative but consistent.

In hopes of improving their situation, people innovate, trying new things or new ways of doing things. And among the opportunities they discover they will choose consistently in the sense that if situation A is discovered to be preferred to B and B to C, they will, when presented with a choice between A and C, choose A.

NUMERICAL ILLUSTRATIONS

Some of the foregoing can be illustrated with some simple numbers, shown in Table 2-1. Say a person has one unit of a good, X, and would pay $1.00 worth of some *other* goods for one unit of X, rather than have none of it. The total personal value he places on just one unit is *$1.00 worth of other goods*, as the second column in the table shows. If he has two units, his total personal value is larger— $1.90—and the marginal personal value of X

with a *second* unit is 90¢, as the third column shows. (Column 3 is the difference between items in column 2, and column 2 is the *sum* of the items in column 3.) He values having two units rather than only one when a second unit can be acquired by the sacrifice of 90¢ worth of other goods. If a third unit increased the total personal use value of X by 80¢, to $2.70, his marginal use value of X where he has three units is 80¢. Larger amounts of X have a larger total personal use value; but each *increase* in his total use value with each extra unit is successively smaller, decreasing in this example to 10¢ at a tenth unit. It is crucially important always to distinguish between *total* personal use value and *marginal* personal use value at any amount of X. At larger amounts of X, the former always is larger, the latter smaller.

The First Law of Demand

An immediate implication, expressed as the first law of demand, is one of the most useful generalizations in all of economics: The lower the price at which one can buy a good, the more will one purchase, have, use, or con-

Table 2-1

TOTAL AND MARGINAL USE
VALUES OF VARIOUS AMOUNTS OF GOODS

Quantity	Total Personal Use Value	Marginal Personal Use Value
0	0	0
1	$1.00	$1.00
•2	1.90	.90
3	2.70	.80
4	3.40	.70
5	4.00	.60
6	4.50	.50
7	4.90	.40
8	5.20	.30
9	5.40	.20
10	5.50	.10

sume. At a given price per unit, a person will buy as many units as brings the marginal personal use value down to equality with the unit price. And people will tend not to buy units priced higher than their marginal use value. This simple, obvious proposition is illustrated by Table 2-2, which is based on the data in Table 2-1. The quantity purchased at any given price is the quantity at which the marginal personal use value of another unit equals the price per unit. The buyer chooses to buy that quantity at which the last achieved marginal personal use value just covers the existing price. (In the table, the amount purchased at, say, 50¢ could be either five or six units, because the sixth gives no net gain in personal value over price. This is a result of using discrete quantities. We will typically hereafter associate a price with the larger amount—for simplicity and definiteness.)

Demand versus Amount Demanded

Table 2-2 illustrates the *price and demand relationship*: It lists the number of eggs that would be bought and consumed at each

Table 2-2

DEMAND SCHEDULE (PER WEEK)

Price per Egg	Quantity of Eggs
$1.00	1
.90	2
.80	3
.70	4
.60	5
.50	6
.40	7
.30	8
.20	9
.10	10

price under given circumstances. The whole schedule of prices *and* amounts demanded (here number of eggs) at each price is the **demand schedule**. The whole schedule should not be confused with a particular amount demanded at a particular price, because by *demand* economists mean *the whole schedule of amounts and prices*. (If you use this distinction you avoid a lot of misleading terminology and erroneous analysis.) At a price of $1.00, the *amount demanded—not demand—*is one egg a week; at a price of 90¢ the amount demanded would become two eggs a week; at a price of 80¢ the amount demanded would become three eggs a week. But all *amounts demanded* are on the same *unchanged* demand schedule.

Some argue that when the price of a good rises they may continue to consume as much as ever. But, of course, if the price were *much* higher, they would cut down on their consumption. The law of demand does not require that every person reduce consumption of a good with every small rise in its price. The law can be expressed in a way less open to misinterpretation: Whatever the amount demanded at a present price, there is, in that demand schedule, *some* higher price that would make the person reduce the amount demanded. A minor price change may occur without changing the amount the person demands. But certainly there is an upper limit of price change above which the amount demanded *will* be reduced.

Of course, the demand schedule, the amount demanded at any price, depends on many things besides price. A person's demand schedule for, say, gasoline will depend on income, age, health, location, the prices of related goods (for example, automobiles), the prices of public transportation service, and family size, to name a few influences. But the principal factor we shall investigate initially is the price of the good itself, for a reason to be explained later.

Table 2-3   PERSONAL USE VALUES, DEMAND, AND MARKET REVENUE

1	2	3	4	5
		Total	Marginal	Total Market Expenditure
Price (P)	Quantity (Q)	Personal Use Value	Personal Use Value	(or Revenue to Seller)
$1.00	1	$1.00	$1.00	$1.00
.90	2	1.90	.90	1.80
.80	3	2.70	.80	2.40
.70	4	3.40	.70	2.80
.60	5	4.00	.60	3.00
.50	6	4.50	.50	3.00
.40	7	4.90	.40	2.80
.30	8	5.20	.30	2.40
.20	9	5.40	.20	1.80
.10	10	5.50	.10	1.00

Personal Use Valuations and Expenditures

In Table 2-3, which is an elaboration of Table 2-2, the amount demanded by a person is one egg a week when the price is $1.00. We infer that the personal use value of that egg equals at least the value of $1.00 of other things that could have been bought instead. At 90¢ per egg, this person would buy two eggs per week. Because only one could have been chosen but two are demanded at 90¢, the second egg, the marginal egg, must be worth at least 90¢ of other goods that could have been bought instead. A personal value of at least $1.00 on one egg plus at least the 90¢ personal value of the second egg gives a total personal use value of at least $1.90 for two eggs. But the market expenditure required to buy the two eggs is, as column 5 of Table 2-3 shows, only $1.80 (90¢ × 2).

At a lower unit price of 80¢, three eggs would be demanded and consumed. A third egg weekly must have a personal value of at least 80¢; otherwise it wouldn't be purchased. So the *total* use value of the three eggs is $1 + 90¢ + 80¢ = $2.70. But the total

expenditure for the three eggs is only $2.40; (80¢ × 3 = $2.40).[1]

CONSUMER'S SURPLUS

We can now measure the benefit to buyers from purchases in the market. If the price per egg is 80¢, three eggs are demanded each week, according to the demand schedule. To this person one egg weekly has a use value of $1.00, even though its price is only 80¢. The consumer obtains a surplus value of 20¢—a consumer's surplus: the excess of personal valuation (here, $1.00) over the market price (80¢). Similarly, because a second egg could be consumed each week at that same price of 80¢, and because it has a marginal personal use value of 90¢, the consumer would get a

---

[1] Remember that value is not an inherent attribute of a good; thus, we define and measure personal use value in terms of a quantity of other goods that a person regards as equally desirable—here expressed in equivalent dollar values. Remember also that economic goods include *all* things we would like to have—friendships, health, honesty, and the like—and not merely marketable things like milk, shoes, and cars.

Table 2-4 DEMAND, PERSONAL VALUES, MARKET REVENUE, AND CONSUMER'S SURPLUS

1	2	3	4	5	6
Price	Quantity	Total Personal Use Value	Marginal Personal Use Value	Total Market Expenditure or Revenue to Seller	Consumer's Surplus at Alternative Prices
$1.00	1	$1.00	$1.00	$1.00	$ .00
.90	2	1.90	.90	1.80	.10
.80	3	2.70	.80	2.40	.30
.70	4	3.40	.70	2.80	.60
.60	5	4.00	.60	3.00	1.00
.50	6	4.50	.50	3.00	1.50
.40	7	4.90	.40	2.80	2.10
.30	8	5.20	.30	2.40	2.80
.20	9	5.40	.20	1.80	3.60
.10	10	5.50	.10	1.00	4.50

consumer's surplus of 10¢ with that egg. There is no surplus from a third egg at a price of 80¢, because if a third egg is bought per week, marginal personal valuation equals price. The total consumer's surplus is 30¢.

But if the price were lower, say 70¢, consumer's surplus would increase. It would be 10¢ greater on each egg: 30¢ on the first egg, 20¢ on a second, and 10¢ on a third, with zero on a fourth. The amount demanded is that at which the *surplus* of consumer value on the marginal unit is zero. As Table 2–4 shows, the *total* personal use value (column 3) exceeds the *total* expenditures (column 5). The difference between them is the consumer's surplus (column 6).

The concept of consumer's surplus may seem abstract and artificial. But the concept is no more than a formal way to indicate that anyone who buys something believes it is worth more than is being paid for it—else why buy it? If for 50¢ you can buy a Coke for which you would have been willing to pay as much as $1.50, you get a consumer's surplus. That happens with almost everything you buy. Obvious as this notion is, it will later be very helpful in explaining marketing tactics that would otherwise be misunderstood.

Though we do not know the exact demand schedule for any person, we do know a crucial characteristic of the schedule: the *direction* in which price affects the amount demanded. We have already seen that direction expressed in the first, fundamental law of demand: The higher the price, the smaller the amount demanded; or, Whatever the amount demanded of a good at any particular price, a sufficiently higher price will decrease the amount demanded. (Again, a reminder: Price change refers to a *relative* price change, which occurs if all other dollar prices are unchanged.)

Figure 2–1 is a diagram of the demand schedule represented in Table 2–2. Price is measured on the vertical axis and amount of eggs demanded on the horizontal. At each price, the amount demanded is that which makes the buyer's marginal use value equal the price. (Here we show the demand schedule as a straight downward-sloping line purely to keep the arithmetic and the graph simple. Any downward-sloping demand line is permissible for greater realism.)

MARKET VALUE

Total personal use value (column 3 of Table 2–4) should not be confused with *total ex-*

penditure, or **market value** (column 5). We arrive at the total personal use value by adding up successive marginal use values along the buyer's demand schedule. For example, at a quantity of 5, total use value of $4.00 equals marginal use values of $1 + 90¢ + 80¢ + 70¢ + 60¢. But the total market value, $3.00, is the product of the quantity demanded times the price per unit (5 × 60¢). The quantitative relationship among total personal use value, market value, and consumer's surplus is presented in one diagram, Figure 2–2, an elaboration of Figure 2–1.

The Paradox of Value

If we compare Figures 2–3A and 2–3B, it is clear that moving down a demand curve to larger quantities at a lower price has two effects: It increases the total personal use value, and it increases consumer's surplus. But market value need not change invariably in one direction: It may increase, remain constant, or decrease, as the numbers in column 5 of Table 2–4 illustrate. And this variability of market value helps us to resolve a *paradox of value* that long troubled some people: How could a commodity like diamonds be so much less "useful" than a commodity like water and yet be more "valuable"? The paradox arises from confusing total and marginal use values with market values.

Suppose that the commodities in Figures 2–3A and 2–3B are diamonds and water. (For present purposes, it is convenient, though not necessary, for the two demand curves to be identical.) Let the amount of diamonds be sufficiently small that the price and the marginal use value are high—the amount demanded is near the vertical axis. And let the amount of water be so large that the price and marginal use value are low. Then the total personal use value of water (the lined area under the demand curve) can be larger than the total personal use value of diamonds, de-

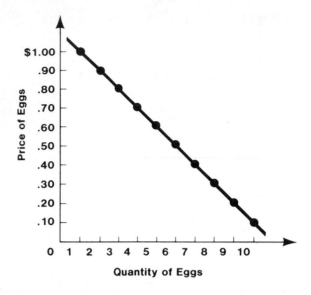

Figure 2-1.

DEMAND FOR EGGS

The dots chart a demand relationship between the price of eggs and the quantity of eggs demanded at each price (see Table 2–2). We connect all of these points on the demand schedule to get a continuous demand curve, as shown by the black line drawn through the dots.

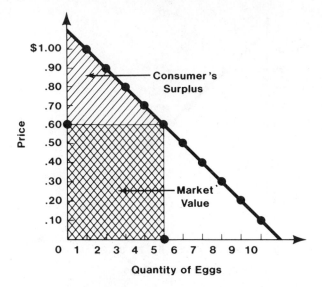

Figure 2-2.

MARKET VALUE, CONSUMER'S
SURPLUS, AND TOTAL PERSONAL USE VALUE

The combined lined and crosshatched areas identify the
consumer's total personal use value, which is divided into
consumer's surplus (the triangular lined area not
crosshatched) and the market value (the crosshatched area). At the horizontal price line, at 60¢,
the quantity demanded is five. The market value is
the total expenditure on the good by the
consumer: the quantity of the good times its
price per unit (60¢ × 5 = $3.00).

spite a very small market value of water and
a very large market value of diamonds.

Needs or Amounts Demanded

Most of us are in the habit of thinking of ourselves as having needs. Some needs are even
claimed to be "vital," "urgent," "crying,"
"minimal," or "critical." Yet, as ringing as
these words can be, they have no basis in
fact. There are no needs as they are commonly thought of, in the sense that there is
no particular amount of a good that anyone
must have. Always, more is better and less is
worse. Always, if the price is higher, people
choose less, because the larger cost (at a
higher price) is greater than the value they
attach to more of this good. They "need"
what they must give up to get more of this
good *more* than they need more of this good.

Imagine a poverty-stricken person. He
says he has the bare necessities. Yet if he
were offered more food in exchange for some
of his clothes, would he refuse on the
grounds that no amount more food would
make less clothing tolerable? Or, on the other hand, would he be unwilling to part with
any small portion of his remaining food for a
lot more clothing or other comforting goods?
Everyone, no matter how poor, will give up
some of one good if offered *enough* of other
goods. All of us, in order to have more of
some other good or service, risk our lives and
safety by traveling at high speeds or by
smoking or doing other things that have a
probability of shortening our lives.

The amount of any good you may say
you need depends on how much of other
things you could get if you forsake *some* of it.
The real question is how much you
"need"—that is, value—more of this good
relative to how much you "need"—value—
more of that. The fundamental law of demand denies that any unique amount can be
regarded as *the* needed amount.

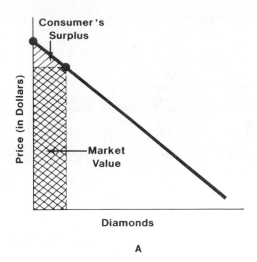

A

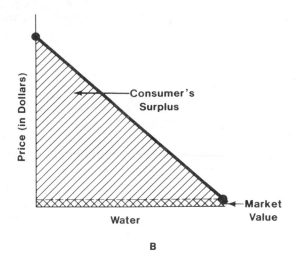

B

Figure 2-3.

TOTAL PERSONAL USE
VALUE AND TOTAL MARKET VALUE

Total personal use value is indicated by both the lined
and crosshatched areas. The total personal use value of
diamonds is smaller than that of water. The total
market value of water can be less than that of
diamonds, as illustrated in the above graphs. The
greater the amount of any good, the greater is
its total personal use value; but the total
market value may decrease.

Marginal Revenue

So far we have used the law of demand to
examine the buyer's behavior. It is instructive also to look at demand from the seller's
point of view. The seller's interest is total
revenue and how that is affected by the price
charged. The buyer's total expenditures on a
good are called *total revenue to seller* (if we
ignore taxes), or *market value.* Because the
price charged affects the quantity demanded
from this seller, and hence the amount sold,
the connection between demand price and
total revenue is not unique. For example, examine the total revenues in the fifth column
of Table 2–5, which is Table 2–3 with a sixth
column added.

At a price of $1.00, one egg would be
sold. The seller's total revenue would be
$1.00. But if the price were 90¢ each for
whatever amount the customer buys, two
eggs would be sold with a market value, or
total revenue, of $1.80. Total revenue is in-
creased by 80¢ (= $1.80 − $1.00). The increase is called the **marginal revenue** at two
units (column 6 of Table 2–5). It is *less*
than the price at which two units are
bought. Why? Because both the first and
second eggs are now purchased for 90¢
each. The seller receives 10¢ less on the

Table 2-5 DEMAND, PERSONAL VALUES, MARKET REVENUES, AND MARGINAL REVENUES

1	2	3	4	5	6
Price (P)	Quantity (Q)	Total Personal Use Value	Marginal Personal Use Value	Total Market Value or Revenue (TR)	Marginal Revenue
$1.00	1	$1.00	$1.00	$1.00	$1.00
.90	2	1.90	.90	1.80	.80
.80	3	2.70	.80	2.40	.60
.70	4	3.40	.70	2.80	.40
.60	5	4.00	.60	3.00	.20
.50	6	4.50	.50	3.00	.00
.40	7	4.90	.40	2.80	−.20
.30	8	5.20	.30	2.40	−.40
.20	9	5.40	.20	1.80	−.60
.10	10	5.50	.10	1.00	−.80

first unit formerly sold for $1.00, which off-sets 10¢ of the 90¢ receipt on the second—giving a marginal revenue of only 80¢. See Figure 2–4.

Though two eggs are purchased at the lower price, *each* egg is priced at less than the former price, $1.00. So total revenue to the seller does not increase by the price of the extra unit sold. Consider what happens if an initial price of 60¢ were cut to 50¢. At the lower price the total market revenue ($3.00) is no larger than at the higher price. At still lower prices, the total market revenue would decrease, because the price received from each extra unit sold is more than offset by a cut in unit price on so large a number of units (already salable at the former price).

In Table 2–5, column 6, Marginal Revenue lists the *changes* in total revenue to the seller when price is changed just sufficiently to induce exactly a *one-unit* change in the amount demanded. (The prices in column 1 of Table 2–5 are those that change the amounts demanded by *one* unit.) Although primarily relevant to a seller's pricing and output decisions, and not very useful in explaining consumer behavior, marginal revenue is an important concept and will be used extensively later.

Price Change versus Other Factors Affecting Demand

If the price of a good changes, the effect on the amount demanded is shown by moving *along* the fixed demand schedule. However, the demand schedule is not always the same. It can *shift* in response to changes in anything other than the price of the good; for example, the consumer's income may have increased. An increase of income can move a person's whole curve upward and to the right so that at any given price more would be demanded than before. Thus, in Figure 2–5, at that price P_1, the amount demanded at the initial income level is Q_1. Say demand increases because the demander's income increases, shifting the schedule to D_2. The demander is then willing to buy either a larger amount (Q_2) at the original price (P_1) or the original amount at a price as high as P_2, to which his higher income has raised his marginal personal use value.

To be sure how changes in demand *schedule* caused by factors other than price differ from changes in *amount* demanded caused by change in price, meditate on Figure 2-6. As in Figure 2-5, we start with demand curve D_1, with a price P_1 and quantity Q_1. If price is reduced to P_3 while the demand schedule is unchanged, we slide down the unchanged demand curve to a larger *amount* demanded, Q_2. Alternatively, suppose price is unchanged when the demand schedule is increased to D_2 (because, say, the demander's income increased). Now the *amount* demanded increases to Q_2, at the old price.

In both cases, amount demanded increased. In the first case, *price decreased* and we moved down the unchanged demand schedule. In the second case, income increased, and the demand schedule shifted; the amount demanded increased even at an unchanged price. Never fail to distinguish between the effect of a *price* change and the effect of factors other than changes in price. The former *moves one along* an unchanged demand schedule; the latter *shifts* the demand schedule.

Meaning of Change in Price and Change in Quantity

MEASURE OF PRICE

The nature and measurement of changes in price and quantity are a little less simple than we have thus far revealed. Say the price of eggs rises from 50¢ to 75¢ a dozen. This is a 50% increase in the *dollar*, or *money*, price of eggs. But suppose the dollar price of everything else also rises by 50%. Though the dollar price of a dozen eggs has risen, it has

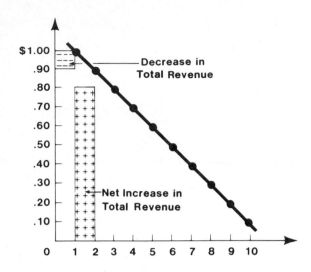

Figure 2-4.

DEMAND FOR EGGS

Because a cut in price is made to sell more units, the extra revenue will be less than the price received on the extra unit sold. The new, uniform price at which an extra unit is sold is lower on *all* the units formerly sold at the higher price. Reduction in revenue on the quantity previously sold at the higher price will offset part of (or possibly more than) the price received on the extra unit sold. As a result, the net revenue increase, called the marginal revenue, from selling one more at the new, lower price will *always* be less than the price received on that extra unit—less by the amount of reduced revenue on all the units formerly salable at the old, higher price.

On any given demand schedule, the marginal revenues associated with each different quantity demanded are indicated by a line under the demand schedule. Calculating the specific marginal revenue schedule requires knowing the demand curve data very precisely—although we know that marginal revenue must be less than the price, as long as the price has to be cut to sell more.

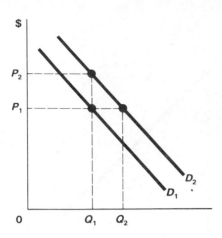

Figure 2-5.

INCREASED DEMAND

Increased demand—a shift to the right (or upward) of a whole demand curve—means more is demanded than before at any given price, or a higher price is obtainable for any given amount being sold, as when Q_1 increases to Q_2 at P_1, or as P_2 is feasible rather than P_1 at Q_1. Increased demand does not mean a movement down along an unchanged demand curve when price falls.

not risen relative to the dollar prices of other goods. The **real price** of eggs—that is, the price *relative* to the prices of other goods— has not risen. (The terms real price and relative price mean the same thing; either can be used.)

If the dollar price of a good changes while the dollar prices of other goods stay unchanged or change in the opposite direction or by a different proportion, then the real or relative price of that good has changed. If the average price of some basket of all other goods rises from $10 to $12.50 (to 1.25 times its former price) when the dollar price of eggs rises from 50¢ to 75¢ (to 1.50 times its former price), the relative price of eggs will have increased to 1.50/1.25 = 1.2— or, by 20%. Formerly one egg had a price equivalent to .05 baskets; now it has a price equivalent to .06 baskets. A rise of 50% in

dollar terms (from 50¢ to 75¢) is a rise in *real* terms (in other goods) of only 20%.

We shall assume (unless explicitly instructed to the contrary) that dollar prices of other goods do not change at all, so every dollar price change of a good changes the real price to the same degree. This assumption spares our analysis needless complications. Real prices are what influence the behavior of people, and under our simplifying assumption that other prices stay constant, a change in the simple dollar price is equivalent to a change in the real price.

Whereas economists speak of changes in the *relative*, or real, price to refer to the price in terms of other goods, they often call the dollar or money price of a good its **nominal price**. This would hardly have to be said if it were not for the current prevalence of inflation. By tending to increase all prices at the same percentage rate, inflation can mask the special factors that are *differentially* affecting the price of goods. During appreciable inflation (such as has been happening since about 1965), a rise in the dollar, or nominal, price of eggs is not necessarily also a rise in the real, or relative, price of eggs. To identify the change, you have to know what has been happening to other prices at the same time—and that is one of the inconvenient consequences of inflation.

The large rise in gasoline prices from 1973 to 1974 from about 40¢ to 60¢ did mean a rise in the price of gasoline relative to other goods. But thereafter, until 1979, the inflation rate raised money prices of other goods more than gasoline prices. From 1974 to 1979 the dollar price of gasoline rose from about 60¢ to 85¢, a rise of 40%, but the prices of other goods in general rose 50%. Thus, from 1974 to 1979 there was a *fall* in relative prices for gasoline from 60¢ to about 55¢—a *fall* of almost 10%. It should have been no surprise that in the late 1970s, after the initial response to the 1973 price jump, the demand for larger, more powerful cars revived—until 1979, when the events in Iran reduced the supply and raised the dollar price in 1980 almost 60%, to $1.20. This increase also raised the relative price in one year by almost 50% because other prices rose only about 10% that year. Since the 1980 leap to $1.20, the rise in the dollar price to $1.35 in 1981 is, when adjusted for 10% inflation of all prices in 1981, an increase in the *relative* price of gasoline during 1981 of about 2%.

MEASURE OF QUANTITY

Another possible confusion—one about the measure of quantity—probably can be avoided merely by calling attention to it. In Table 2–5, the quantity demanded at a price of 90¢ is two per week—which is also a rate of about nine per month or 104 per year. All three quantities express the same rate. We could use a "rate of use" even for durable goods of which a person owns only one item at a time. How can one consume at a rate of more than one car? Replace it more frequently so as to use two per year, or use it more intensively. The principles of demand hold whether *amount* refers to amount owned at any one moment, or to rate of consumption or of purchase, or to frequency of replacement.

Elasticity of Demand to Price Change

How responsive is the amount demanded of a good to a change (either a rise or a fall) in its price? Responsiveness of amount demanded is summarized by the concept **price elasticity of demand**: the ratio of (1) the percentage change in quantity demanded to (2) the small percentage change in the price that induced the increased amount demanded. In Table 2–6, for example, the quantity demanded is increased from one to two, an increase of 100 percent, if the price is reduced from $1.00 to 90¢, a 10% reduction. Putting

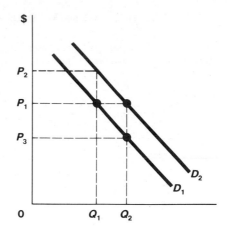

Figure 2-6.

EFFECTS OF PRICE CHANGES
SHOULD NOT BE CONFUSED WITH
OTHER EFFECTS ON AMOUNT DEMANDED

Effects of a change in price are shown by sliding along a given demand curve. Effects of factors other than price are shown by appropriately shifting the whole demand schedule, say from D_1 to D_2. A fall in price from P_1 to P_3 increases the amount demanded from Q_1 to Q_2 without changing the demand schedule. The same increase in amount demanded could be caused by an increase in wealth, or something else, that shifts the whole demand schedule enough to the right to get an increase from Q_1 to Q_2, at the unchanged price.

Table 2-6 DEMAND SCHEDULE, TOTAL MARKET VALUE, AND ELASTICITY

Price	Amount Demanded	Total Revenue	Marginal Revenue	Approximate Elasticity	
1.00	1	1.00			
			.80	10.0	
.90	2	1.80			
			.60	5.0	Total revenue moves opposite to price
.80	3	2.40			change: elastic demand in this range
			.40	3.0	
.70	4	2.80			
			.20	1.5	
.60	5	3.00			
			0	1.0	Unchanged total revenue
.50	6	3.00			
			.20	.75	
.40	7	2.80			
			.40	.6	Total revenue moves in same direction as
.30	8	2.40			price change: inelastic demand in this range
			.60	.4	
.20	9	1.80			
			−.80	.2	
.10	10	1.00			

+100% over −10% gives a ratio of −10. Because the quantity change is in the opposite direction from the price change, the ratio is negative. However, hereafter we will simply ignore the minus sign and refer to the numerical value of the ratio. So the price elasticity of demand in the region of a price of $1.00 for this demand schedule is 10. The demand is called *elastic* at that price if the elasticity is bigger than 1 and *inelastic* if less than 1.

On the same demand schedule, consider a price change from 70¢ to 60¢, a reduction of 14%. The quantity demanded increases from four to five, an increase of 25%. The ratio of the quantity percentage change to the price percentage change is 25/14 or about 1.8. Demand is elastic.

Next, estimate the price elasticity if a change in price from 60¢ to 50¢ induces the quantity demanded to increase from five to six. The ratio of the percentage change in quantity to the percentage change in price is .166/.166, which gives an elasticity of 1. (Note that the marginal revenue is zero; total receipts are unchanged at $3.00.)

Finally, a 33% price reduction from 30¢ to 20¢ induces only a 12.5% increase in quantity sold, from eight to nine units. The elasticity is 12.5/33 = .38.[2] Also, because total revenue is obviously reduced if the percentage increase in quantity is less than the percentage of price reduction, the marginal revenue is negative; in this example it is −60%.

The numerical measure of the elasticity in response to price change depends on the *change* in amount demanded and on the *total* amount demanded. Two diagrams show why. Figure 2–7 shows differences in responsiveness to price. Figure 2–8 shows differences in the initial amounts. Both affect the *percentage* measure of that responsiveness.

Three features of elasticity should be noted:

First, elasticities are not necessarily the

---

[2]Because prices change by rather large percentages in this example, the arithmetic measures of elasticity will differ slightly, depending on the size of the price change. These differences diminish for small-percentage changes in price and quantity. The concept of elasticity is usually referred to in two alternative forms: point and arc. These will be understandable only to those familiar with calculus. Point elasticity is based on continuity of demand and defined as $dx/x \div dp/p$ of the function, while arc elasticity is $\triangle x/x \div \triangle p/p$. Point elasticity is the limiting value of arc elasticity.

same all along a demand schedule.[3]

Second, an elasticity greater than 1 implies that a price cut increases total revenues; that is, marginal revenue is positive. An elasticity less than 1 implies that a price cut decreases total revenue; that is, marginal revenue is negative. If the elasticity is 1, the total revenue does not change. The term *inelastic* is often used in ambiguous ways: Sometimes it means the elasticity is less than "one"; but sometimes it is used even more extremely to mean the elasticity is *zero*—there is no price effect.

Third, and a more subtle point, is that the larger the elasticity, the closer is marginal revenue to price. For example, in Table 2–6, at a price of around 90¢ the elasticity is 10 and the marginal revenue is 80¢, or only about 10¢—or 11%—below the new price. Where the elasticity is 1 (that is, response is called inelastic), the marginal revenue is zero—at the price of 50¢, or 100% below the new price. And where the elasticity is less than 1, the marginal revenue is negative. So low elasticity means that marginal revenue is far below price, whereas high elasticity means that marginal revenue is close to price.[4]

_____

[3] As an aside and to avoid misunderstanding, we note that although the demand schedule has a constant slope, the elasticity changes along it. All along the demand schedule a 10¢ change in price is assumed to make a one-unit change in the amount demanded: The ratio of the *absolute* change in Q to the *absolute* change in P is constant. That is *not*, however, the ratio of the *percentage* changes in P and Q. For example, at two units, the one-unit increase to three units is a 50% increase in amount demanded. But at nine units, the increase of one unit in response to a price cut of 10 cents is now only about 11% in amount demanded. Similarly, the change in price is small or large in relation to the initial price from which the change is considered. What is important is the *percentage* change in amount and the associated *percentage* change in price.

[4] For those familiar with algebra, the exact relationship is: Elasticity = $P/(P-MR)$.

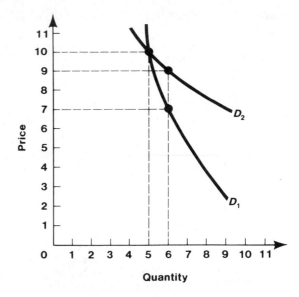

Figure 2-7.

DIFFERING SLOPES AND ELASTICITIES

D_2 requires a price cut of only $1 to sell one more unit, whereas D_1 requires a cut of $3. D_2 is more responsive to price. Its elasticity at that price range is about 2 (a 10 percent cut in price gives a 20 percent change in amount demanded). But D_1 requires a 30 percent cut in price to give a 20 percent increase in amount demanded. Its elasticity is measured at about .66 (= 20/30), less than for D_2. The marginal income at the sixth unit is +$4 (=$54 − $50) for D_2 and is −$8 (=$42 − $50) for D_1.

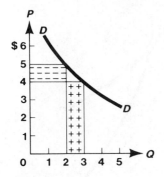

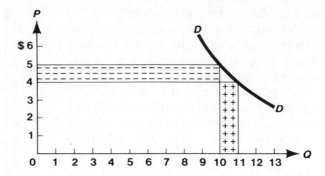

Figure 2-8.

DEMAND ELASTICITIES AND TOTAL REVENUE

The left curve is more elastic, even though in both curves a price drop of $1 induces a one unit increase in amount demanded. On the left curve it changes total sales value from $10 to $12, an increase of $2. Marginal revenue is $2. The $4 price receipt of the third unit is offset by the $1 price cut on each of the two units already being sold. The percentage increase in quantity was 50 percent, while the price decrease was only 20 percent. But with the same sloped curve in the right-hand diagram, the one-unit increase in quantity is only a 10 percent increase in quantity. Total sales value falls from $50 to $44, a decrease of $6. The $4 price receipt on the eleventh unit is more than offset by the $10 loss of revenue caused by the $1 price reduction on each of the 10 units formerly sold at $5. (The marginal revenue at this point is therefore a *negative* amount, −$6.)

The Second Law of Demand

The pattern of response to higher petroleum and energy prices in the 1970s illustrates the second law of demand, which is that the longer the time allowed to adjust amount demanded in response to a price change, the greater is the change in amount demanded, that is, the greater the elasticity. Because the immediate effect of higher prices was so weak, prices had to rise very high to sufficiently reduce the amount demanded. But within a few years people could more effectively and economically switch to energy-economizing equipment, cars, houses, and life styles. Since less hasty adjustments are less costly, prices of energy didn't have to stay so high for the longer run. They began to fall in the late 1970s as the longer-run adjustments were made.

That episode is a typical example of the operation of the second law of demand. The adjustment will be greater after a week and still greater after a month, until eventually full adjustment is achieved. For example, if the price of water were doubled, consumption would immediately decrease some—but would decrease by a great deal more within a few months, after people had more economically made adjustments to their water-using equipment, as we shall elaborate later.

This law is shown by the set of intersecting demands in Figure 2–9. The successive demand curves (1 through 4 and Long Run) show the pattern of responses after price falls from P_1 to P_2. After one day the amount demanded is up to X_1; after two days it is X_2, and so on, until it ultimately reaches the final, long-run adjustment, X_L.

It is not necessary to know the exact quantities and elasticities in all these demand relationships. To draw some important explanations or implications about how our economy operates, we need know only the *direction* and *relative* elasticities of effects. We know that demand curves are (1) negatively sloped with respect to price, and are (2) more elastic for more prolonged price changes.

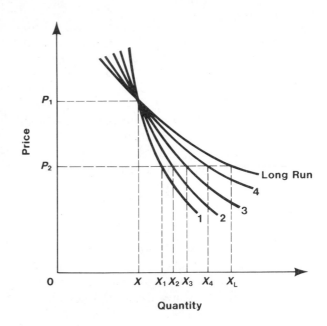

Figure 2-9.

EFFECT OF TIME ON PRICE ELASTICITY OF DEMAND

The longer the time after a price change, the greater the effect on the rate of demand—shown by the flatter, more elastic curves for more elapsed time after a price change.

Illustrations of the Laws of Demand

DEMAND FOR FOOD

If beef prices rise, say in response to a reduced supply, but the demand schedule remains unchanged, people buy less beef and more of other things, because relative to beef, other sources of protein—eggs, poultry, fish, cheese, milk—are made less expensive. Less obvious is that people also substitute some more vacation for less food.

However, we should not speak of demand for "food," since no one buys "food" as such. We buy particular commodities, and our purchases of each of these are affected by price. But even if we do talk summarily of the "demand for food," the law of demand asserts that, with an unchanged demand schedule, a higher price reduces the amount of food demanded and consumed.

DEMAND FOR WOOD

If wood prices rise (relative, of course, to other materials), say because supply is smaller, less wood will be demanded. We substitute plaster, plastics, steel, aluminum, copper, glass, paper, coal, oil, and electricity. You and I may not consciously respond to a 10% rise in the price of wood. But industrial product designers will shift in varying degrees to substitutes. The things we buy will be made with less wood and more of other material. Nor must every person's purchase rate be revised by every price change. Some people are on the margin of choice between one good and another; and, as prices change, they will shift their choices.

DEMAND FOR WATER

Water is an especially subtle, but powerful, example of how the amount demanded responds to price change. Although people cannot live without some water, they do *reduce* (not eliminate) their use of water at higher prices. People in arid regions use less water, not because they don't want or "need" more, but because they don't want so much at such a high price. They *choose* less water and use *more* of other, less expensive, more arid modes of living.

The average per capita daily water usage has varied from 230 gallons in Chicago to 150 in New York City and Los Angeles, down to 120 in San Diego and 110 in Boston. Among the reasons for these differences are differences in industrial uses. Chicago has steel and oil-refining industries that use a great deal of water; New York City businesses—finance, retail, apparel—are light water users. But the cost of water had something to do with determining the locations of those industries.

By the law of demand, if water prices are higher, less water will be used. In New York City, 10% of the total water consumption was estimated to be from leakages in street mains. At higher prices for water, it will pay to reduce that loss. Also, water meters, which make people pay according to use, are not yet universally used. Where they are, people have stronger incentives to conserve

water (by repair and modification of faucets and water-using equipment).

At higher water prices, residences will have smaller gardens and lawns. More sprinklers will be used because they use less water. Gardeners will sweep rather than wash sidewalks. Rock gardens and paved and brick patios will become more common. Automobiles will be washed less often. Water will be softened, because smaller amounts of soft water wash as well. Shower heads will be changed. None of these changes would reflect a change in tastes or desires, but would reflect the higher price of water at which more of other goods must be sacrificed if the same amount of water were to be used. It has been estimated that a doubling of water prices would reduce total domestic water consumption by 10% to 30% within a year. (Translate that into elasticity terms.)

Still more ways of conserving water exist. In many cities, industrial users take about half the water. Their demand is probably more responsive to price than is that of domestic users. Table 2–7 shows great differences in water use even within the same industry. The *maximum* column presents amounts used per unit of output in plants in areas where water is priced low, whereas the *minimum* column shows the smallest amount used per unit of output produced in areas where water costs are high. Note the tremendous range in the first three industries, which happen also to be the heaviest industrial water users. Some industrial firms using water for cooling do not have recirculating cooling units. Some steel mills use 65,000 gallons of water per ton produced, but the Kaiser steel mill (in the Los Angeles area) used only 1600 gallons. One soap plant in the same area has recirculatory cooling towers to reduce water consumption from about six million to less than a half-million gallons per day. At higher water prices, the greater savings on reduced use of water make recycling worthwhile. Clearly, the amount of water

Table 2-7 VARIATIONS AMONG FIRMS AND PRODUCTS IN
INDUSTRIAL CONSUMPTION OF WATER, PER UNIT OF OUTPUT

Product or User and Unit	Draft (in Gallons)		
	Maximum	Typical	Minimum
Steam-electric power (kw-h)	170	80	1.3
Petroleum refining (gallon of crude oil)	44	18	1.7
Steel (finished ton)	65,000	40,000	1400
Soaps, edible oils (pound)	7	—	1.5
Carbon black (pound)	14	4	0.25
Natural rubber (pound)	6	—	2.5
Butadiene (pound)	305	160	13
Glass containers (ton)	670	—	120
Automobiles (per car)	16,000	—	12,000
Trucks, buses (per unit)	20,000	—	15,000

Source: *H. E. Hudson and Janet Abu-Lughod, "Water
Requirements," in Jack B. Graham and Meredith F. Burrill
(eds.),* Water for Industry *(Washington, D.C.: American
Association for the Advancement of Science, 1956),
Publication No. 45, pp. 19–21.*

"needed" varies with price!

There are still more ways to adjust water usage. The largest water user in Southern California is agriculture, which uses approximately 70% of the water—at prices lower than urban dwellers pay, even after the costs of distribution and purification. What would farmers do if the price of water to them reflected its higher alternative use value in cities? Some would go out of the farming business. Higher water prices would reveal that some water to grow watermelons, lettuce, and celery, for example, would be more valuable elsewhere. Less food would be grown in Southern California and more in areas where water is cheaper, and more food would be shipped to Southern California, because shipping products would be cheaper than shipping water. Some areas would decline as people found it preferable to move to places where water is cheaper, or took up tasks that use less water, which is, after all, why the Western deserts are sparsely populated.

When a price rises, how do people discover how to use less? Some people make a living by giving that information: commercial sellers of water-recycling equipment, water softeners, automatic faucets, fertilizers, irrigation and sprinkling equipment, air-conditioning machinery, hardtop patios, chemicals that reduce evaporation, washing machines that use less water, and so on. Every rise in water prices enhances their business prospects. Salespersons make it their business to detect ways in which their equipment is more economical. Teachers may believe that most worthwhile knowledge comes from schools and books, but an amazing amount of information about practical matters is provided by salespersons—because it is to their personal interest to inform potential customers. Though users may not at present know how to alter their use of water, rubber, energy, sugar, steel, or gasoline in response to a price change, were the price to change they would be swamped by salespersons with information about new uses and substitutes.

DEMAND FOR GASOLINE
OR ENERGY (OR ANYTHING)

The gasoline supply to the United States and the world was reduced in 1974 by 10%. Politicians and many business people did not believe that higher gasoline prices would be effective in reducing consumption, and looked for ways to regulate our gasoline-consuming activities. For example, they proposed to prohibit high school students from "waste" driving to school. But as prices of gasoline increased, people themselves in fact decided which were the less valuable uses to be forsaken.

A price rise of about 100%, from 1973 to 1982, has been sufficient to restrict the amount demanded to match the smaller supplies. (The *dollar*, or nominal, price rose about 200%, from 40¢ in 1973 to $1.50 in 1982—but when the 1982 dollar price is adjusted for the effects of inflation on all prices, the 1982 *relative*, or real, price of gasoline is equivalent to about 75¢ in 1973 dollars, or a rise of about 100%.) We reduced driving in larger cars; we reduced speed; we combined more shopping in fewer trips; we turned off the engine more often rather than let it idle; we flew between cities and then rented cars; we drove more in our smaller second car; we tuned our engines better. All that many of us did immediately. And then we purchased smaller new cars.

The same measures are taken with higher prices for heating oil: We wear more clothing, have better-insulated houses, accept lower indoor temperatures, and heat fewer rooms. We were pushed back up the demand schedule as prices rose. The reductions in the amount of gasoline and fuel oil used are the results of a higher price. They are not the results of a reduced demand schedule, nor of politically imposed regulations. Those higher prices revealed that the less valuable former uses weren't feasible with the smaller supply. The market price of the amount actually available provided a common standard of measure against which to test for the more valuable uses.

Was it best to achieve reduced consumption by means of the free-market price that reflects supply and demand? Or is it desirable to compel people to restrict consumption by other means and on some other criterion? Asking people to restrict consumption more than they are induced to do by the market price is to ask them to reduce their gasoline use so that other people can use the gasoline in *lower*-valued uses. Such *required* "conservation" compels diversion to less valuable uses; it is wasteful. It also gives some politicians more power over economic resources and people. We emphasize this effect of nonprice control because market prices are a means of controlling and coordinating people—by competition for scarce resources, an alternative means to the use of political power. Market prices and political power are competing systems for control. The differences in their consequences are enormous, as will be seen later.

Estimates of Elasticities of Demand

We have been fairly adept so far at separating changes in demand from changes in amount demanded. But in the real world matters are rarely so conveniently simple. We can observe a change in price, and we can observe a change in the amount demanded. But how can we be sure that the position of the demand curve has not also changed, because of other independent events? If the curve has shifted, then the observed total change in amount bought will be the result of a change not only in price along a demand curve but also in the position of the demand curve. Exact elasticities of demand, then, are extremely difficult to estimate.

Statisticians have attempted to overcome the ambiguity by separating the effects of these two independent factors, demand shift and price change. One means of recent devise is the *one-year interval of adjustment* elasticity of demand. As measured by this scheme, the elasticity of demand for gasoline in response to a change in its price was recently estimated to be about .1. This means that a 10% rise in price decreases the amount demanded by 1%. (Question: If you were the sole supplier of gasoline in some country and knew that the one-year elasticity of demand for gasoline at present prices was about .1, would you contemplate raising the price by reducing the amount supplied? Would that necessarily be true for a five-year interval of adjustment elasticity of demand?)

Income Effects on Demand

So far we have concentrated on price as a controller of the amount demanded. As emphasized earlier, factors other than price also affect the amount demanded. Changes in income or wealth shift the demand schedule. A larger income will induce more consumption of most goods at the given prices: For example, transportation, food, housing, medical care, education, travel, champagne, and prestige goods increase with income. On the other hand, as income or wealth increases, one's demand for some goods decreases: Candidates might be rump roasts, junk food, hamburger, or small cars. Goods for which demand is greater at higher incomes are called **superior goods**; goods for which demand decreases with increases in income are called **inferior goods**.

INCOME ELASTICITY OF DEMAND

Because demand responds to changes in income, an income elasticity of demand can also be defined. **Income elasticity of demand** is the ratio of the percentage change in amount demanded in response to a percentage change in income. These elasticities are usually positive, unlike the price elasticity of demand, which is negative. Statistical studies indicate that income elasticities of demand are less than 1 for food, drink, clothing, and rental housing, but are greater than 1 for what people typically call luxury goods.

INCOME CHANGES: TEMPORARY OR PERMANENT?

Just as the elasticity of demand in response to a price change depends on the duration of the new price, so does the effect of a change in income: The longer the expected duration, the greater is the effect on wealth and hence on consumption demand. Many people know their earnings fluctuate from week to week and even year to year, probably around some average. They gear their consumption to the anticipated, persisting average. They do not revise consumption with every transient variation in income. Is there a real estate agent who consumes only on the days when a house is sold? Do business people consume only on weekdays when earning income, while consuming at a zero rate on weekends? On the contrary, people adjust consumption rates to a long-run anticipated average income around which temporary variations of earnings are expected. That is why variations in earnings that are believed to be *temporary* are not accompanied by proportional changes in consumption. Unusually high temporary earnings go mostly into temporary accumulation of cash or bonds or repayments of past debts, for example. As a result, current consumption (that is, its demand schedule) does not change in proportion to fluctuations in income. People save in order to smooth over later expected low incomes, and during periods of low earnings they dip into accumulated reserves and inventories.

In Figure 2–10, annual expenditures are charted against that year's income, which

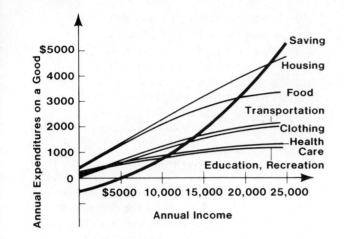

Figure 2-10.

INCOME EFFECT ON DEMAND

The curves show that expenditure rates on general classes of goods and services are related to income—increasing with income but at a lower proportionate rate. Amounts demanded are clearly related to income.

The variation of saving, from negative rates at low incomes to highest rates at high incomes, is deceptive if you think it shows that people whose annual incomes over the years average about $5000 or less do not save. Because incomes fluctuate not unexpectedly over the years, and because a person tends to consume according to his or her longer-run income average, savings will show large residual fluctuations as income fluctuates transiently from year to year.

may temporarily be extremely high or low. But consumption is seen to be relatively insensitive to such fluctuations, so the residual of the current temporary increase in income—savings—is sensitive. But when income is perceived to be lasting or relatively permanent, people adjust their consumption nearly in proportion. In sum, when studying the effect of *current* income, one must be very careful to identify whether current income is mostly temporary or is mostly at the long-term average.

Price Effects on Wealth and Hence on Demand

ENDOWMENT EFFECT

A *price* change in a good causes a substantial change in a person's wealth or income if that good is a substantial part of a person's stock of wealth or source of income. If the selling price of oil rises markedly, the oil-well owner's higher income will increase his demand for, say, a larger house—which uses more oil for heating and air conditioning—as well as his demand for a larger car. Because the oil is sold at a higher price, the owner's income increases enough to shift the demand schedule upward so as to more than offset the effect of the higher price for the oil the owner consumes. On the new, higher demand schedule, the amount demanded increases from what it was on the old low-wealth demand schedule at the old, lower price. (See Figure 2–11.)

The increased price of a good that is both a major source of a person's income and a good that the person consumes has two distinct effects: an **endowment effect**, increasing the person's wealth or income and hence his or her demand for the good, and a **substitution effect**, moving back up along the demand curve. In our example, the substitution effect away from oil in response to the higher price is overbalanced by the greater effect on endowment wealth. So, at a higher price the owner consumes more oil because of the large oil endowment income effect. Unless we separate these two effects of a price rise, we may erroneously suppose a demand schedule to be unchanged when in fact it has shifted because the price change has affected a major source of a person's wealth.

INCOME RELEASE EFFECT

A price change has another kind of effect on demand, called the **income release effect** of a lower price. Even if a particular good is not in a person's source of income, a lower price of that good releases some income formerly spent for the good. Because this released purchasing power is usually small, and of course is distributed over the purchase of all other goods, its effect on the demand for the lower-priced good itself is usually negligible.

Alleged Exceptions to the Laws of Demand

Some people talk of exceptions to the laws of demand. They say people could conceivably be insensitive to price or that they could buy more of some things even when the price rises. Indeed, people conceivably could—almost anything is conceivable. But the law of demand says that actually people are not insensitive to price.

One apparent exception to the law of demand is alleged because observers confuse the relative price with the nominal price: The amount of a good demanded does not fall even though its nominal (dollar) price has risen during a time of inflation, if other nominal prices have risen even more.

Another alleged exception is a prestige or "conspicuous consumption" good—like Mumms champagne, Cross pens, Rolls Royce cars, Orrefors crystal, or whatever the

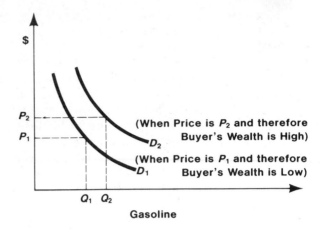

Figure 2-11.

ENDOWMENT AND SUBSTITUTION EFFECTS

Changes in prices of goods that constitute a major source of a person's income or wealth can shift the consumption demand for that good enough to offset the simple price effects of amount demanded (for a given amount of wealth).

"elite" display. Presumably, conspicuous consumption of such goods sheds prestige on the user. Desire for such prestige could *shift* up the demand schedule, but it would not produce a demand schedule that is *sloped upward*. Let the price of the prestige good be even higher, and less of it will be bought. Otherwise what would prevent the price from rising without limit? The prestige effect simply *shifts* its demand schedule *upward*. But the new, higher demand curve still has a negative, that is, downward, slope. The pursuit of prestige is consistent with the laws of demand.

Also cited as contradictions of the law of demand are occasions when a higher price makes the buyer believe the item is better. For example, anyone who proposes to sell something far below its current market price will have more problems making a sale than a seller asking the market price, because an unusually low price immediately stirs doubts about the quality of the item. These are sensible doubts, given the fact that price usually reflects quality. If I offer to sell my nearly new Ford for $4000, a potential buyer will hesitate, suspecting its quality or my ownership. If the buyer can be satisfied that the lower price is not the result of lower quality, he or she will buy the car more readily than if I asked $7000. A good of inferior quality is sold at a lower price because only then will anyone buy it; at the same prices, everyone would prefer the better item. The public's association of higher price with quality is a consequence of the law of demand, not a refutation of it.

Direct Evidence of Validity of the Laws of Demand

Prices of fruits and vegetables are lower during harvest seasons, when the supply is larger, because the greater amount can be sold only at a lower price. If prices of perishable crops did not fall at the peak of the harvest, the first law of demand would be refuted. Likewise, if goods of poorer quality sold for the same price as goods of better quality (assuming everyone agrees on standards of quality), the first law of demand would not be true. Merchants have clearance sales at lower prices to induce you to buy. Someone who seeks your business will lower the price, not raise it. Indeed, in response to several polls and questionnaires in 1974, most people *said* they would not reduce the amount of gasoline they used just because the price went up. They *said* they had to have transportation. (How much? What kind? At what cost?) In fact, their statements, when compared with their behavior, indicated less economic sophistication than their behavior did. Their actual response, as history shows, was to reduce the amount of gasoline demanded at the

higher price, in accord with the first law of demand. Furthermore, the reduction has been greater in the long run, in accord with the second law of demand.

Indirect Evidence of Validity

Often the power of a principle is most clearly corroborated by indirect, unexpected implications. For example, a larger proportion of good-quality California oranges and grapes is shipped for sale to New York while a larger proportion of the poorer-quality fruit remains in California. Are New Yorkers richer or more discriminating? Possibly—but, then, why is the quality *ratio* higher even in the poor districts of New York than in California? The question can be posed for other goods: Why do Asians import disproportionately more expensive American cars than cheaper models? Why are "luxuries" disproportionately represented in international trade? Why do young parents go to expensive plays rather than movies on a higher percentage of their evenings out than do young couples without children? Why are "seconds," slightly defective products, more heavily consumed near the place of manufacture than farther away? Why must a tourist be more careful buying leather goods in Italy than Italian leather goods in the United States? Why is most meat shipped to Alaska "deboned"? The answers all are implications of the law of demand. Let us see why.

Suppose that California grapes cost 50¢ a pound to ship to New York, regardless of quality; that production of grapes is 50% "choice" and 50% "standard"; and that in California the choice grapes sell for $1.00 a pound and the standard for 50¢ a pound. The cost of shipping grapes to New York raises the New York buyer's cost of both types of grapes by 50¢ a pound to $1.50 for choice grapes and $1.00 for standard grapes. One pound of choice grapes in New York costs the same as 1.5 pounds of standard, whereas in California it costs the same as two pounds of standard. New Yorkers have a lower price for choice *relative* to standard grapes, and therefore, in accordance with the first law of demand, consume *relatively* more choice grapes than do Californians. In California, where standard grapes are cheaper relative to choice grapes, a larger *fraction* of grapes consumed should be standard. And it is so.

Pricing Tactics: A Preview

So that you can better understand the explanatory power of the demand schedule, we anticipate some pricing tactics to be explained in more detail later. Suppose a seller knew that a buyer's demand schedule was that in Table 2–2, and suppose the costs of production were 25¢ per egg. This seller could tell the buyer: "You may buy one egg at 99¢. If you do, you may buy a second egg at 89¢. If you do, you may buy a third egg at 79¢, a fourth at 69¢, a fifth at 59¢, a sixth at 49¢, a seventh at 39¢, and the eighth, and as many thereafter as you wish, at 29¢ each." How many will the buyer buy? The correct answer may be surprising.

This customer will buy a first egg, since her one unit is worth at least $1.00, and she can buy it for only 99¢, with a 1¢ gain of consumer's surplus as compared to not buying it at all (although her gain is not as great as it would be were she able to buy each for only 29¢). The second egg has a marginal personal use value to her of 90¢, but will cost only 89¢, giving another 1¢ consumer's surplus. Similarly, each successive additional unit purchased adds 1¢ of use value over the costs, until she has purchased eight units. A ninth would have a marginal use value of only 20¢, but would cost 29¢. Her total consumer's surplus would be only 8¢, 1¢ on each of the eight eggs.

If instead the price had been a uniform 29¢ per egg regardless of quantity purchased, she would still have bought only eight eggs. But her consumer's surplus from this single price would be equivalent to $2.88 (=$5.20 − 8 × 29¢). This is also expressible as the sum of the 71¢ value excess on the first unit (worth $1.00 but purchased for only 29¢) and the 61¢ excess on the second unit (worth 90¢ but costing only 29¢), and so on. The successive excesses are 71¢, 61¢, 51¢, 41¢, 31¢, 21¢, 11¢, and 1¢, which equal $2.88 on the eight eggs. But under a multipart pricing schedule, the seller gets more of the gains from market trade. Who *should* get the gains is unanswerable.

It might at first be surprising that with multipart pricing the buyer still buys the eight units she would have bought at the single low price. Under multipart pricing, her additional cost of $2.80 ($5.12 - $2.32) is a reduction of $2.80 in consumable income that she would have spread over everything else she buys. If she spends about $400 a week on all her purchases, that $2.80 is about a 1% reduction in her consumable income power. Thus she would cut back roughly 1% on all of her purchases—including eggs. She really would buy fewer eggs, because her demand schedule for eggs would have shifted back slightly. Nevertheless, for all practical purposes, this small income effect on her demand for eggs is too small to worry about in most situations.

Thus, whether price is a single per-unit price or a multipart schedule, we once again see that the consumer still buys an amount that brings her marginal personal value down to equality with price of the last unit. Of course, a buyer certainly prefers a uniform, low price, whereas a seller would certainly prefer the multipart price schedule in which only the last unit has a low price. Later we shall investigate circumstances under which some forms of multipart pricing can be employed.

Utility-Maximizing Behavior

The postulates of behavior at the beginning of this chapter are the foundations of what is called a *utility-maximizing* theory of human nature. Saying that a person maximizes utility may seem an elaborate camouflage of our ignorance of why people behave as they do; for whatever a person does, could the person not be said to be maximizing his or her utility? No, because we have specified responses to changes in relative costs and therefore can derive meaningful, refutable implications. The demand relationship is one such validated implication. And we shall give many examples in this book. For the moment, consider an example. Saving lives may be a good. Consider two different situations: In one, you can save a life by jumping into a pond and pulling out a child; in the other, you must jump into a raging torrent with a 99% probability that you will drown. Now, what does our theory tell us? The probability that people will jump into the torrent to save a life is lower than that they will jump into ponds. The analysis *does* rule out some behavior. Not everything is possible under the postulates. Thus they do have scientific meaning and are not mere tautological descriptions.

Summary

1. The unit of economic analysis is the individual, not the institution within which the individual acts.

2. *Postulates of Behavior*:

    1. Each person desires many goods and has many goals.

    2. For each person, some goods are scarce.

    3. Each person is willing to forsake *some* of an economic good to get *more* of some other economic goods.

    4. The more one has of any good, the larger its total personal use value, but the lower is the marginal personal use value.

    5. Not all people have identical tastes and preferences.

    6. People are innovative but consistent.

3. The value of something to a person is the amount of other goods the person is willing to sacrifice for it.

4. Self-interest means that a person values his or her ability to choose among options that affect his or her situation.

5. Demand for a good is the *relationship* of amounts demanded at various possible prices. The term *demand* can be ambiguous: It may refer to either the whole schedule or to only one of those amounts at a given price. This ambiguity is avoided by speaking of *demand* only when meaning the whole schedule and the *amount demanded* when measuring a particular price.

6. Marginal personal value of a good is the change in total personal value associated with an additional unit in the amount of that good.

7. As larger amounts of a good are held, its marginal personal value is smaller.

8. The *amount demanded* of a good, at any price, is interpreted as being the amount at which its *marginal* personal value is brought to equality with the price.

9. The first law of demand states: Whatever the amount demanded at a price, there is a higher price that will reduce the amount demanded.

10. Consumer, or buyer, gain from trade (called consumer's surplus) is the difference between the buyer's total personal value and the market value. Do not confuse the total market value with the total personal use value.

11. The elasticity of demand with respect to price is the ratio of the percentage response in amount demanded to a small percentage

change in price. An elasticity greater than 1 implies that a reduction in price increases total receipts.

12. The greater the elasticity, the closer is marginal revenue to price.

13. Marginal revenue is the change in total revenue when the price on all units is reduced enough to sell one more unit.

14. The second law of demand asserts that the price elasticity of demand for a good is greater in the longer run than in the shorter run.

15. *Need* is a word often used to suggest fixed minimum requirements, when in fact the amount "needed" is variable and depends on the cost.

16. Income, or wealth, affects the demand schedule.

17. An increased demand for a good means that at any price, the demander demands more than formerly, or the marginal personal values have increased, and the demander is willing to pay a higher price (in one form or another).

18. Alleged exceptions to the first law of demand usually result from confusion: Changes in amounts demanded when a price changes are confused with a change in the demand schedule caused by simultaneous changes in nonprice factors; or dollar price changes are mistaken for relative price changes.

19. Not all sellers permit buyers to buy whatever amount they demand at a fixed price. Sometimes a multipart price system permits the seller to get a larger share of the gains from trade.

20. One's wealth can increase so much because of an increased price of some good that is a large part of one's wealth that the demand schedule is raised more than enough to offset the higher price on the amount of that good demanded. This price effect on wealth is called the *endowment effect* of a price change.

21. A lower price to a consumer releases expenditure power that can be spent for all other goods; hence the released expenditure power will probably have insignificant effect in changing the demand for the good whose price was lowered.

Questions

1. "The college football team has a goal."
   a. Is it the social goal of the team, or is it a common goal of each member of the team?
   b. Are you sure that each member has only that goal and not also one of playing more of the game himself?
   c. Is it helpful to talk of one goal being preferred over another?

2. In trying to understand some policy enforced at your college, why is it misleading to ask why the college adopts that policy?

3. If you don't smoke, is tobacco a good? Are purchase and sale necessary for something to be considered a good?

4. "A free good is a self-contradictory concept, because no one wants what is free; otherwise it wouldn't be free. And if no one wants it, it can't be a 'good.'" Evaluate.

*5. Explain or criticize the following statements and questions about the substitution postulate:
   a. "Every student substitutes some romance for grades when dating rather than doing as much studying as otherwise could have been done."
   b. "The substitution postulate says that a student does not seek the highest possible grades."
   c. Does the substitution postulate deny that water, food, and clothing are more basic or more needed than music, art, and travel?
   d. "There is no hierarchy of wants." What does that mean? Can you disprove it?
   e. Is travel in Europe a substitute for formal academic education? for some food? for a bigger house or new clothes or medical

care? For what would it not be a substitute?

f. "I'd like to play poker with you again tomorrow night, but I don't think my wife would like it." Is this consistent with the substitution postulate? Is the wife's welfare being compared with the husband's? Explain.

6. Explain the difference between the statements, "People act in accord with certain fundamental propositions" and "People consult or refer to such propositions for guidance in choosing their behavior."

7. It has been suggested that if a person agrees to let some unknown party choose between two known options for him or her, the person is indifferent between the two options. Do you think that is consistent with the postulates listed in the text?

8. Suppose that I am indifferent if given a choice among the following three combinations of steaks and artichokes:

	Steaks (pounds per year)		Artichokes
Options A:	100	and	30
B:	105	and	29
C:	111	and	28

a. How is my marginal personal value of steak (between options A and B) measured?

b. What is my marginal personal value of artichokes (between B and C)?

c. If the amount of meat in A were doubled to 200, what can be deduced about the amount of meat required in B to make B indifferent with that new A?

*d. Using your answer to (c), compute my personal marginal valuations between the new A and the new B. Is that consistent with the fourth postulate?

9. "All goods or goals are incompatible. And at the same time they are compatible." Can you make sense of that?

10. "It doesn't pay to do your best at any given activity." Explain why.

11. The following is Mr. A's annual demand for pencils.

Price	Quantity	Personal Value Total	Personal Value Marginal	Revenue Total	Revenue Marginal
$2.00	1	2.00	2.00	2.00	2.00
1.90	2	3.90	1.90	3.80	1.80
1.80	3	5.70	1.80	5.40	1.60
1.70	4	7.40	1.70	6.80	1.40
1.60	5	——	——	——	——
1.50	6	——	——	——	——
1.40	7	——	——	——	——
1.30	8	——	——	——	——
1.20	9	——	——	——	——
1.10	10	——	——	——	——

Complete the total and marginal personal use value and total and marginal revenue columns.

12. The demand schedule of question 11 shows that at a price of $2, the annual consumption is 1 unit. At a price of $1.90, the annual consumption is 2 units.

a. Can it be said that this person wants *each* one of those 2 units more than $1.90 worth of any other goods?

b. Note that at the price of $2 the person annually spends $2 on this good, whereas at a price of $1.90 the person spends $3.80, or $1.80 more than previously. Do you still say the person values the extra unit at approximately $1.90, even though he or she spends only $1.80 more?

c. Explain why. In doing so, explain what is meant by *value*.

13. Can Table 2–1 be read as follows? "A person sees a price of $2 and therefore buys one egg. If in the next hour the price has fallen to $1.80, the person dashes out and buys three. If a couple of hours later the price rises to $1.90, the person buys two." If it can't be interpreted that way—and it can't—how is it to be interpreted?

14. For goods like shoes, a persisting rise in price will reduce the number of pairs of shoes a person will want. Because the price at which he can sell used shoes is low relative to the new-shoe price, a person will not sell some shoes in order to reduce his or her stock of shoes. How does the person adjust that stock to the higher cost?

15. Consumption is a rate concept, even though the good being consumed may be held as a stock or finite amount of goods. True or false?

16. To say that a person purchases and consumes water at a rate of 50 gallons per day, or 350 per week, is to say the same thing in two ways. What is the equivalent rate per year?

17. "According to the law of demand, the lower the price of vacations, the more vacations I should take. Yet I take only one per year. Obviously the law of demand must be wrong." Is it?

18. There are three conceptions of the amount demanded: (1) the rate of *consumption;* (2) the quantity a person wants to *buy* in order to increase current stock; (3) the quantity a person wants to *own.* As an example of each: (1) a person may consume eggs at the rate of 6/7 per day (which does not necessarily mean that a fraction of an egg is bought and eaten each day); (2) on Saturday the person buys a half-dozen eggs; (3) the person may own an average of three eggs in his or her refrigerator. Normally, explicit distinctions between rates of purchase and consumption are not necessary because they are closely related. Which of these three measures is a rate of activity and which is a "stock"?

19. Suppose the demand-schedule data in question 11 refer to the number of pencils a person would want to own at each price. The person now owns four pencils.
   a. How many more would he or she *buy* or *sell* at each possible price?
   b. If the equilibrium price in the market turned out to be $1.30, how many would the person want to buy or sell and how many would then be owned—assuming four initially?

20. Explain how each of these is a denial of the law of demand and the basic postulates of economics:
   a. "The budget of the Department of Defense covers only our basic needs and nothing more."
   b. "Our children need better schools."
   c. "Nothing is too good when it comes to education."
   d. "America needs more energy."

21. Why is it nonsense to talk about urgent, crit-ical, crying, vital, basic, minimum, social, or private needs?

*22. A book was entitled *Social Needs and Private Wants.* Would the title have suggested something different if it had been *Social Wants and Private Needs?*

23. Diagnose and evaluate the following news report: "Our city needs more golf courses, according to a report by the National Golf Foundation. Many people do not play as often as they would like because of the lack of courses." Does this differ from the situation of filet mignon steaks, champagne, and autos?

*24. "Californians are crazy. Near a beautiful California beach are a luxurious motel and a state-owned camping area. Despite the luxury of the motel, scores of cars line up for hours each morning seeking free camping sites, whereas at the motel there is hardly a day the rooms are all taken. This shows that Californians prefer outdoor, dusty camps to the luxuries of a motel with pool, TV, room service, and private bath." Do you agree? Explain.

25. Why is the marginal revenue less than price (except at first unit)?

26. An increase in demand is shown graphically by a *demand* curve to the right of, above, below, to the left of, the old demand curve. Select correct options.

27. Which of the following would increase the demand for wigs?
   a. A raise in one's salary.
   b. Higher price of hats.
   c. Having a swimming pool.
   d. Rise in cost of hair care.
   e. Getting divorced.
   f. Number of other people who wear wigs.
   g. Lower price of wigs.

28. Are the following statements correct or incorrect? Explain your answers.
   a. "A 1% fall in price that induces a 3% increase in amount purchased indicates elasticity greater than 1."
   b. "A 1% rise in price that induces a 3% decrease in amount taken indicates elasticity greater than 1."
   c. What is dangerous in asking whether a

1% rise in price induces a 3% decrease in demand?

29. "Elasticity is a measure of the percentage increase in demand for a 1¢ change in price." What are the two errors in that statement?

30. In the graph below, which of the three demand curves has the greatest elasticity at price p_1? At price p_2? Does the elasticity change as the price changes along each curve?

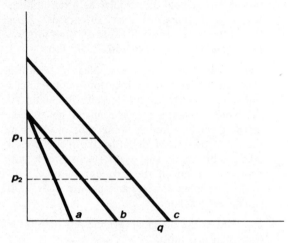

31. a. If the price of gasoline rose 100%, automobile manufacturers would make changes in the designs or operating characteristics of automobiles. True or false?
   b. What effect would that price rise have on gasoline consumption?
   c. Would the effect be more extensive at the end of one year or at the end of three years?
   (This question, which appeared in the first edition of this book, in the 1960s, was criticized then as being absurd—because it contemplated a rise in price as great as 100%. Reality is not absurd!)

32. Explain how what is often called "impulse" buying is consistent with the laws of demand. Explain why habitual buying is also consistent. Suggest some behavior that would not be consistent.

33. Does the demand for children obey the fundamental theorem of demand? The demand by immigrants for entry to the United States? The demand for divorces? The demand for pianos? The demand for a winning college football team? The demand for A's in this course? The demand for appendectomies?

34. a. Does our representing a demand curve with precise numbers mean that people have these numerical schedules in their minds?
   b. What essential property illustrated by the demand-schedule data does characterize their behavior?

35. If the price of candy rises from $1.00 to $1.25 a pound while the price of ice cream rises from 50¢ to 75¢ a quart, in what sense has the price of candy fallen?

36. "If the price of gasoline rose by only 10%, many people would not immediately change their consumption." Explain why this does not refute the law of demand.

37. Economics asserts that people prefer more to less. Yet there are waiting lists of people seeking small apartments in slum areas while bigger, better apartments do not have a list of applicants. How can people want smaller, less luxurious apartments rather than bigger apartments without violating our postulates about people's preferring more economic goods?

38. a. As your wealth or income increases, what happens to your demand schedule for gasoline?
   b. If you owned a dairy farm and the price of milk went up, would you consume more or less milk?

39. Why is it that when a couple goes out, the probability is greater that they will attend an expensive theater if they have infants for whom a baby sitter is necessary than if they are childless?

40. Let P_1 be the domestic price of a higher-quality version of a good and P_2 be the domestic price of a lower-quality version. Let T_1 and T_2 be the transport costs of these goods to a foreign market. Show that if $T_1/T_2 < P_1/P_2$, then *relatively* more of good 1 will be shipped; if the inequality is reversed, relatively more of good 2 will be shipped. "Relative" to what? In your answer, what do you assume about demand conditions in domestic and in foreign markets?

41. A governor of California once asserted that the reduction of Mexican labor in California did no harm, because the total value of the crop harvested was larger than before. Evaluate the relevance of that criterion. (The same was true when the Arabs reduced the amount of oil sold in 1973.)

42. A competing text to this one is claimed by its author to be "invaluable." Does that sound consistent with economic analysis?

*43. You are buying trees to landscape your new home. The following demand schedule characterizes your behavior as a buyer:

Price of Trees	Quantity Demanded
$10	1
9	2
8	3
7	4
6	5
5	6
4	7
3	8
2	9
1	10

The price is quoted at $6. Accordingly, you buy five trees. Then *after* you agree to buy the five trees, the seller offers to sell you one more for only $5.

  a. Do you take it?
  b. Suppose, after you have already agreed to purchase five at $6 each and one for $5, the seller offers to sell you more trees at the price of $3. How many more do you buy?
  c. If the price had been $3 initially, would you have bought more than eight trees?
  d. Suppose you had to pay a membership fee of $5 to buy at this nursery, after which you could buy all the trees you wanted for your own garden at $3 each. How many would you buy? (Assume the price at other nurseries is $4, with no membership fee.)
  e. If you could buy trees at $3 each from some other store without a membership fee, would you still buy only eight trees—saving the $5 for use on *all* your consumption activities?

  f. Now explain why, according to the demand schedule, your purchase of eight trees at $3 each, at a total cost of $24, is a consistent alternative to your purchase of eight trees under the former sequential offers, in which you pay a total of $41 (five at $6, one at $5, and two at $3). (In this example we assume we can slide down an *unmodified* demand curve, because the required modification by the change in wealth is slight.)

*44. If I regard each of the following combinations as equally preferable, which postulate is denied?

	Goods		
	X		**Y**
Options A	100	and	70
B	105	and	69
C	110	and	68
D	115	and	67

*45. Suppose that Mr. A has no preference between A and C of the following three options.

	X		**Y**
Options A	100	and	200
B	110	and	180
C	120	and	160

If he is given a choice among the three options, prove that, according to the postulates, he will choose option B over either A or C. (The proof is easy—but not easy to discover.)

*46. The following alternative combinations of X and Y are all equally valued by Mr. A; that is, he has no preference among them.

  a. What postulate is expressed by there being more than one combination of the same utility to Mr. A?
  b. Do these combinations conform to the postulates?
  c. What postulate is expressed by the negative relationship among the quantities of X and Y in the equally valued combinations?
  d. What postulate is reflected in the changes in X and Y?

Equal-Value Combinations	X	Goods	Y
A	9	and	50
B	10	and	40
C	11	and	34
D	12	and	30
E	14	and	26
F	17	and	21
G	21	and	17
H	26	and	13
I	33	and	10
J	40	and	9
K	47	and	8
L	57	and	7

*47. At a price of $1.00 for X and $1.00 for Y, a person consumes 10 of each. Assume that the price of X rises to $1.50 and the price of Y falls to 60¢. The cost of buying 10 of each at the new prices comes to $21: $15 for the X and $6 for the Y. Explain why an income of $21 at the new prices would be *more* than enough to enable the consumer to achieve the same welfare as before with $20 at the old prices. What principle or postulate of economics did you use in the explanation?

*48. "Economic theory is built on an idealization of humans: We have tremendous computational power, a detailed knowledge of our desires and needs, a thorough understanding of our environment and its causal relationships, a resistance to acting on impulse or by habit." Explain why this statement incorrectly characterizes economic theory.

Chapter 3
Exchange

Trade without Surplus Goods

Trade is commonly believed to occur because people have too much of some goods—that is, they supposedly have a **surplus** of those goods. But this is not so. Trade goes on all the time, but virtually never do we think we have "too much" of things. In fact, trade occurs because participants find it mutually attractive, because people place different *marginal* valuations on *scarce* goods. If my marginal personal value of something you own exceeds your marginal personal value, we would both find it attractive to engage in a sale of some of that good to me, at a price below my marginal personal value and above yours. Demand curve diagrams are a useful way to display this underlying analysis of the reason for exchange. Once you are more familiar with such diagrams you will be able to see some less obvious cases of the same principle—such as the "optimal" number of accidents and "optimal" amount of pollution of the environment, and for that matter the amount of production of any good.

Figure 3-1 shows the marginal personal value graphs for Ms. A and Mr. B. Each at first has 20 eggs per month, but their marginal valuation curves differ. With their present numbers of eggs, Ms. A puts a *higher* value on a marginal egg than does Mr. B (a value of 12¢ compared to 6¢). Our first major principle is that *mutually* advantageous trade opportunities exist when the respective personal valuations *differ* at the initial numbers of eggs. Some eggs will be sold to the person with the higher marginal personal value of eggs, Ms. A, until she gets a quantity of eggs at which her personal valuation decreases to equal that of the increasing marginal use value of eggs to the seller (Mr. B).

Figure 3-1 shows Ms. A's personal marginal value curve for eggs. Its heights, shown by the vertical broken lines, express her suc-

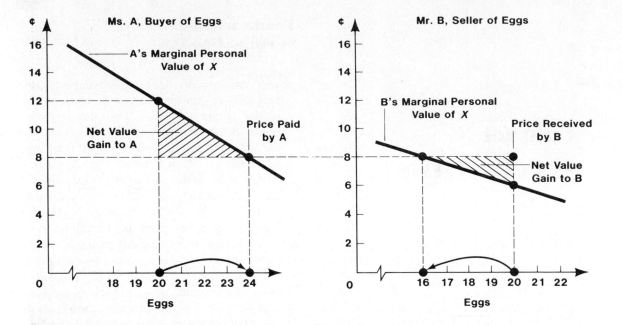

Figure 3-1.

GAINS FROM EXCHANGE

Ms. A is happy to buy some additional eggs at a price below 12¢, and Mr. B gains if he can sell eggs at a price above 6¢. Ms. A gains by obtaining eggs (to 24 per month) for a price of 8¢. Her gain is indicated graphically by the lined area under her marginal value line. When she has bought 4 to have 24 eggs, her valuation of another egg (the twenty-fifth) is reduced to less than 8¢. At a price of 8¢, Ms. A will not choose to buy more than 4 eggs, bringing her total amount to 24. The gain to Mr. B is shown by the crosshatched area above this curve between 20 and 16 eggs. That gain is the amount he is paid in excess of how much the egg he sold is worth to him.

cessive personal marginal valuations of eggs. For example, a twentieth egg per month (instead of only 19 per month) is as valuable as 12¢ more of any other goods. The marginal personal value of a twenty-fourth egg per month is less, only 8¢. (Though we here speak of the value in cents or dollars, it is the alternative goods or services that the money could buy that is the value.)

Both parties could gain by trade at an intermediate price between 12¢ and 6¢ per egg. Ms. A gains by buying a twenty-first egg, which she values at more than 8¢. She also gains on the twenty-second and twenty-third eggs, each of which she values at more than 8¢. Her total gain is indicated graphically by the lined area beyond 20 eggs under her marginal value curve and above the price line. At 24 eggs per month, her marginal personal valuation of eggs is down to 8¢.

Mr. B is willing to sell four to Ms. A at a price of 8¢ each, because he values his forsaken twentieth, nineteenth, and eighteenth eggs each at less than 8¢. His gain is represented by the lined area above his marginal valuation curve and below the price line in the interval of 16 to 20 eggs. Exchange brings the marginal personal values of eggs to both parties to equality, and exhausts the potential gains from exchange.

Although we do not know the particular numerical measures for any person's marginal personal valuation curve, we do know three things about the curve. First, the curve *slopes downward*. That is, as one's holdings of X get larger, there is a decrease in one's marginal personal value for an X: the amount of Y a person is willing to pay for an X.

Second, the *position*, or height, of the whole curve depends in part on how wealthy a person is, that is, how much one has of other goods. Greater wealth is likely to make the curve higher because one is willing to give more of other goods to get a unit more of a given good. In sum, a person's marginal personal value—what one is willing to pay for a unit more of X—depends on (1) the amount of X possessed and (2) one's total wealth. The former determines where one is on a marginal personal valuation curve, while the latter affects the *height* of the whole curve.

With greater wealth or income, the whole marginal value curve shifts upward for *superior* goods and downward for *inferior* goods. (Superior goods, recall, are such things as diamonds, fine wine or imported beer, clothes, food, automotive elegance, and face-lifts; examples of inferior goods may be cheap brands of beer or cosmetics.)

The third thing that we know about marginal personal value curves is that they are *not identical* for everyone, even for people of the same wealth. Tastes or preference patterns differ, and these differences are expressed by different heights and slopes of the marginal personal value curve. (But all such curves, remember, are *downward* sloping.)

To continue practicing graphic analysis, we now use the graphs in a slightly different way: We can also see the gains from trade by superimposing, in Figure 3–2, the two personal valuation graphs of Figure 3–1. In Fig-

ure 3–2 the baseline for Mr. B is turned around to read from *right to left*. The *total* existing number of eggs to both A and B, 40 eggs, is measured by the entire length of the base of the diagram, 0_a to 0_b. The number initially possessed by Ms. A, 20, is indicated by the distance from the left side, 0_a, to X_1, whereas Mr. B's initial 20 eggs are measured by the remainder of the base, from 0_b leftward to point X_1.

Now it is easier to see that the marginal personal value of eggs at the initial point X_1 (where each party has 20 eggs) is greater for Ms. A than for Mr. B. That difference implies that both parties would gain by trade (as measured in *cents*). The gain to Ms. A is her lined area and the gain to Mr. B is his lined area. The exchange benefits the two parties just as much as if there had been a magical, costless increase of goods. This increase is measured by and distributed in accord with the sizes of the lined "gains from trade" areas. Trade is as useful as the creation of more goods.

We cannot generally predict what the sequence of actual trading prices would be, but there are limits to what it can be. It must be between the different initial marginal valuations of the traders. The final price is indicated by the height at which the two valuation curves intersect: In Figure 3–2, 8¢ is the final equilibrium-sustaining price of eggs.

Trade slides each person along his or her own marginal personal valuation curves to where values are equal at the **equilibrium-sustaining price**. The buyer moves down her curve, the seller moves up his curve. *Both* traders gain. Each puts a higher value on what is obtained than on what is given up. When exchange has equalized the buyer's and seller's marginal personal valuations, *no further trade would be mutually desired*. Moving from some distribution point like X_1 to equality at X_3 is often called an *efficient* reallocation of goods; failing to move to equality is called *inefficient*, because both

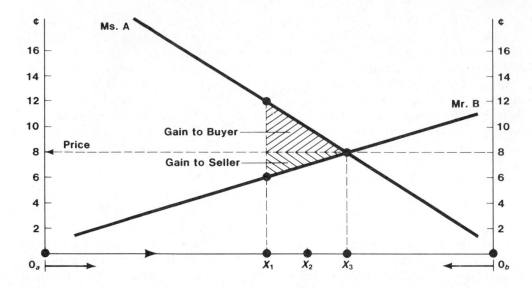

Figure 3-2.

GAINS FROM EXCHANGE:
SUPERIMPOSED MARGINAL VALUE LINES

Reversing and then superimposing the graphs of Figure 3–1 shows the gains from trade more clearly and portrays exchange in terms of a demander and a supplier, with the person with the lower value on eggs being the seller to the demander—the person with the higher value for more eggs. This diagram shows that the supply of eggs to Ms. A is simply to be interpreted as the demand for that good by other people—here Mr. B.

people could be made better off by further trade.

Money, Markets, and Middlemen

Figure 3–2 represents an idealized model of trade for this reason: It deliberately assumes that Ms. A and Mr. B were able to find each other, discover their mutual advantage from trade, and conduct that trade—all without any costs other than the price of the goods actually exchanged. But we know there are substantial costs of finding trade possibilities, of assessing the true characteristics or qualities of goods, and of negotiating exchange contracts and arranging for such legal protections as warranties. These activities are usually performed more economically by the use of money as the medium of exchange and by reliance on middlemen. Middlemen have the effect of increasing the gains from trade, as is shown in Figures 3–3A and 3–3B. If Ms. A's prepurchase search and product inspection cost her the equivalent of 1¢ per unit of the good purchased, her *full* price is 9¢ (8¢ paid to the seller plus the 1¢ of prepurchase costs). See Figure 3–3A. She would then buy only the quantity of eggs that brought her

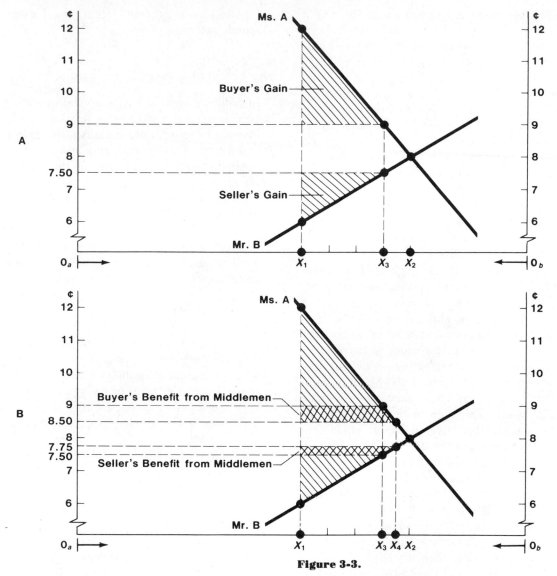

Figure 3-3.

EXCHANGE WITH TRANSACTIONS
COSTS WITH AND WITHOUT MIDDLEMEN

If each unit of X involved a total transaction cost (in addition to its price) of 1.5¢, the lined areas show the gains from the restricted feasible trade. By lowering transactions costs, Figure 3–3B, the middleman allows the trader's gains to be greater than if there were no middleman. The increase in trader's gains is indicated by the double-hatched areas for each trader. More trading will take place with middlemen. Instead of trading from X_1 to X_3 as in Figure 3–3A, trade will increase to X_4.

marginal personal value down to 9¢. And if Mr. B also engaged in some prepurchase search, negotiation, and contract enforcement costs equal to, say, .5¢ per unit of egg, then his *net* realized selling price is 7.5¢, not 8¢. So he would sell only as many eggs as left him with a marginal personal value of 7.5¢.

Of the total potential gain from trade, part is dissipated, or used up, in prepurchase search and negotiation costs, and part is unrealized because of the higher costs of finding and identifying other goods and sellers; the areas with slanted lines in Figure 3-3B show the realized gains from trade; the cross-hatched area shows the amount of potential gain from trade that is dissipated in prepurchase search costs. The rectangular area represents costs of finding and negotiating exchanges. And the triangular wedge with a dotted area is the still unrealized gains from trade that did not occur because of the costs of discovery and performance of 1.5¢ a unit.

If the costs of marketing—which are 1.5¢ for each unit when Ms. A and Mr. B perform their own prepurchase services—could be cut to, say, .75¢, then more trade would occur and both the buyer and seller would benefit, as shown in Figure 3-3B.

To be sure, the *cash* price paid by Ms. A will be higher—say, 8.5¢ instead of 8¢—and the *cash* price received by Mr. B will be lower—7.75¢ instead of 8¢. But the *full* cost (including all the transaction costs) incurred by Ms. A is lower because the payment to the middleman is less than the costs of self-service: 8.5¢ instead of 9¢. And the net value to Mr. B is higher: 7.75¢ rather than 7.5¢.

MONEY

One important way to reduce the costs of finding and negotiating trades is to use money. Its easy recognizability, combined with its portability, storability, and divisibility, induces its use in virtually every trade. No high costs of identifying it or its quality are involved, such as would occur, say, for diamonds, oil, rugs, or eggs.

MIDDLEMEN, WHOLESALERS, AND RETAILERS

In reducing costs of exchange and providing better service, middlemen—retailers, warehousers, salespersons, brokers, advertisers, and a host of other marketing and financing specialists—are as productive as the producers of the eggs and cents. They are not, contrary to common opinion, parasites and cost-increasers.

To make this analysis realistic, consider the costs you would incur if you were to buy a diamond from a person who is not a diamond merchant; or milk from any person on the street who happens to offer some milk for sale, and who is not a reputable grocer or recognized milk seller; or shoes from a stranger who is not known as a shoe retailer. We are accustomed to buying from merchants, whose word about quality we almost unconsciously use as a means of saving on the high costs we would otherwise incur in inspecting and judging the goods—so accustomed, in fact, that we typically fail to realize how the reputation and reliability of an established merchant reduce our shopping costs.

Open Markets and the Costs of Exchange

Competition between middlemen reduces the spread between their buying and selling prices to one that just covers the costs of providing their services at the quality wanted by the consumers. If this spread were larger, more middlemen would be attracted, and they would shave the margin in order to get business. If the spread were too small, some middlemen would lose money and not stay in business. Only those who could provide satisfactory services at the lowest cost would survive. (The spread is reduced by the competition of middleman against middleman, not of consumers or sellers against the middlemen; middlemen do not compete against consumers.)

The spread between buying and selling prices, then, is reduced by the possibility that there will be an unlimited number of middlemen—that is, open-entry market competition among middlemen, or, as we shall call it, **open markets**. Open markets mean that access to markets is open to all people without legal or arbitrary barriers. They do not indicate that there are no costs of providing exchange-facilitating services. A difference between the middleman's buying and selling prices is not necessarily **profit**.

When there are no artificial barriers to exchange—that is, when there are open markets—the price spread is driven down by competition to just cover the costs of a middleman's services: rental costs for space in which transactions can be conducted and goods can be stored for inspection and immediate delivery; costs of record keeping; the cost of inventory, advertising, light, heat, and insurance. The spread between the buying and selling price reflects those costs; in ordinary retailing of most household goods, the spread is that between wholesale and retail prices, and ranges between 15% and 50% of the retail price to the consumer. In part, low-cost discount houses charge lower prices by permitting the consumer to bear directly part of the costs of exchange activities—costs, for example, in the form of the responsibility for collecting information about the item, stricter (or no) return privileges, less credit buying or higher finance charges, less delivery service, less convenience of shopping conditions and location, or slower service because of fewer salespersons.

Restraints on Open-Market Competition

New middlemen would be encouraged to enter the market only if they could compete with those already in it by selling at lower retail prices, or paying higher wholesale prices, or offering better services. But if there were such entrants, middlemen already in the market would object to "unnecessary, inexperienced, low-cost, cut-throat, excessive" competitors. New entrants taking advantage of market competition would eliminate profits, leaving only normal wages for the first middleman—a less pleasant prospect for that person. But open access to markets is not a universal condition. Our initial middleman need not acquiesce to that competition passively. There are several tactics for trying to restrict entry, some crude and some refined.

THREATS OF VIOLENCE AND FORCE

We may as well start with what is sometimes a most effective procedure. A threat to damage the new entrant's person or property is not genteel. But there are threats against anyone who crosses a picket line in seeking work. Here the threat of violence is made by private citizens. But to someone who provides medical, dental, legal, or public utility services without a license, the threat is from government agents—courts and police, who are "legitimate" specialists in applying force. Violence and force or the threat of their possible use are widely applied—sometimes with the help or acquiescence of the state. (We do not suggest that violence is morally right or wrong: Economic analysis has no basis for decreeing that physical coercion is proper in, say, the medical and improper in the labor picket case.)

POLITICAL LICENSING AND SELF-REGULATION

Restraints that keep new, lower-cost, or higher-quality competitors out of the market enable the incumbents to maintain incomes above competitive levels. Whether a law in fact or in guise or intent (it doesn't make much difference which) protects consumers from shoddy products or from unscrupulous, corner-cutting suppliers, such a law permits only "approved" (duly licensed, properly trained, reliable, ethical) traders. The law usually is administered by a state board of regulators staffed by experts, who—naturally—are selected from those already in the business and automatically get licenses under a "grandfather clause," exempting everyone already in the business. These regulators determine when "public necessity and convenience" warrant the entry of more sellers. Because such occasions are rare, incomes of existing sellers are thereby maintained at a level sufficient for the few "respectable" practitioners to enjoy a standard of living they "deserve." Not only middlemen enjoy the protection of restricted entry to markets; many producers and suppliers of goods and services do also. Some examples of enterprises, persons, and institutions so protected are liquor stores, doctors, banks, milk producers, holders of taxi medallions, accredited schools, and morticians. But some consumers do benefit by these restrictions—especially wealthier people, who normally buy from well-established, more expensive firms—whereas poorer people are denied the lower-priced, lower-quality services that would have been provided in an open market.

CARTELS

A group of sellers with the means—often legal—to control what kinds of services existing members may offer and to restrain the entry of new competitors *to the detriment of consumers* is a **cartel**. A cartel is any coalition of sellers that reduces the quantity or quality of output and raises the price, thereby reducing the potential gains to society. A cartel is to be distinguished from other coalitions, such as partnerships or business organizations, that raise the potential gains to consumers by offering increased quantity or quality of output at a lower price. In both the cartel and the business firm, the people who organize and join in the coalition are of course striving to increase their own wealth. What distinguishes a cartel from an ordinary business firm, then, is the difference in its effects on customers. Later we shall investigate the difficulties of creating the conditions under which cartels can be effective. For the moment, it is sufficient to note that to be effective, violators of cartel rules must be detected and punished, sometimes by invalidating their licenses or franchises. But that enforcement is not easy. Agents and spies (sometimes called *commissioners*) are hired to detect illegal acts like price cutting, favors, and special services. Some of our most respected industries are cartels: railroads, radio and television broadcasting, medicine, law; tobacco, butter, wheat, cotton, corn, milk, and peanut production; and colleges with respect to athletic competition.

Cartel members usually must pay for the political power to achieve that legal protection—payments for franchises, licenses or special taxes; purchases of $1000 dinners honoring politicians; charitable contributions to approved public causes; or free services to special groups. (Consult your local politician, state occupational board member, or member of a regulated industry to learn of additional devices.) These payments will just about extract the excess of the anticipated earnings over what could have been earned in an open market—especially after the costs of the legal services involved in obtaining the protective legislation are added in. If politically protected cartels have earnings in excess of competitive returns, is it surprising that many cartels contribute to political parties?

Ethics of Open-Market Exchange

Exchanges occur because transactors expect to be made better off *in their own estimation*. If a consumer enters a transaction using inaccurate and inadequate information, then it is doubtful that the buyer preferred to get what he or she actually got. (Perhaps young people—minors—sometimes make insufficiently informed decisions and therefore are controlled "for their own good.") Conversely, others may know more about consequences, and thereby be in a position to guide the consumer's choices, but may know little about—or disagree with—that consumer's preferences. Medical care, food, pornographic materials, drugs, and education are areas in which minors—and sometimes adults—are prohibited from entering into mutually agreeable exchanges with whomever they please.

Some critics of open-market trade attach more weight to the regrettable consequences of unfortunate choices (unfortunate as defined by the critics and advocates of restraint of access) than to the restraint on gains for those who, if permitted to choose, would make happy choices. Others who make the opposite evaluation favor a larger range of individual responsibility as desirable in itself. Which, if either, view is intrinsically more humane is beyond the scope of economics to say.

Some opponents of open-market trade further contend that many consumers, even when in possession of correct information, make choices that are improper. Such opponents may argue that people "ought" to prefer classical music to pop music, or opera to theater or to TV and movies, or sensible housing to flashy cars. "We" who advocate a tax-supported national theater are saying in effect that taxpayers do not spend their money appropriately; that not enough of them attend the theater, as they "should," to make it self-supporting. "We" are seeking to force others to pay for a theater so that "we" may indulge our tastes at their expense. (Would the issue be changed if "we" were "college teachers" and "tax-supported theater" were "tax-supported college"?)

Freedom: As You Like It

This right to exchange goods in the open market is a basic difference between the capitalist and socialist cultures. We have been careful not to express the matter as "free versus unfree" or "democratic versus undemocratic." You could say that people are freer in Russia, because they are free—that is, prevented—from undertaking the task or risk of making uninformed choices, which they might later regret, just as you and I are freed—prevented—from the risk of hiring a quack to perform an operation or advise us about our illnesses, or from the possibility of buying whole milk with too low a cream content, or from all sorts of possibilities of acquiring inferior things—substandard food, substandard airplane flights, substandard houses. We are protected from our own folly. This may seem an unusual meaning of "free," but it is a widely accepted meaning in Russian *and* American life. But to so use the term "freedom" does not advance understanding. For although one may argue that one's proposed restrictions on other people in fact give them "more freedom," or promote "good" consequences and prevent "bad" ones, different individuals have different notions of what is good and what is bad.

In discussing the arguments for open markets versus those for restrictions on markets we are not speaking of democratic versus undemocratic economic rights. Democracy is a way of *allocating* political power, not a criterion of what is done with it. A dictatorship that is undemocratic could enforce economic and legal rules that are conducive to what some might call a desirable society. A democracy can, if a majority revises various economic and legal rules, produce an "undesirable" society. It is *not* self-evident that democracy is more conducive than any other system to the emergence or continuance of a society that many would call "free," "open," or "desirable." Again, those attributes are not susceptible to objective definition, no matter how many people may believe they are.

Criticisms of Methodology

It is sometimes charged that economic analysis operates on the assumption that people engage in more rational calculation in their economic behavior than they in fact use. Economic analysis does no such thing. Economics does not explain how people *think*; it identifies predictable, observable patterns of responses and behavior. People need not be aware of the principles of economics when they engage in exchange. Sticks and stones, birds and bees obey the law of gravity even though they do not know what it is. Nothing in economic theory rests on any premise that people are logically consistent in their *thought processes*. Instead, it is only the theory and analysis that is logical. And that analysis will be considered empirically valid if the logically implied behavior is in fact observed.

Self-Interest

As we warned earlier, nowhere in this chapter, or this book, is it assumed that people are interested *only* in their own individual wealth or welfare. We assumed instead that a person prefers *command over more* rather than *fewer* goods; we did not assume that the person is oblivious to other people or unconcerned about their welfare. A person may want control over more goods in order to help others. We will later examine situations in which people do engage in charity, are solicitous of other people and consider the effects of their behavior on them, and sacrifice marketable wealth for leisure, knowledge, and contemplation.

Summary

1. For trade to occur it is not necessary that one party have a surplus of some good and another party have an insufficiency.

2. If two persons have different marginal personal valuations of a good, then an exchange can move each person to a preferred situation, provided the costs of negotiating the exchange do not exceed the difference in marginal personal valuations.

3. Goods will be traded from the lower- to the higher-marginal valuing person.

4. Each person will increase or reduce the amount of any good relative to other goods until the person's marginal personal use valuation of the good is reduced or increased to equality with the market price.

5. When every person has the same marginal personal valuation of a good, because that is equated to the market price facing all buyers, the condition is called equilibrium.

6. The general, low-cost recognizability of a commodity enables it to serve as money. In addition, some people specialize in being low-cost middlemen, experts in certain goods, who thereby have the effect of reducing exchange transactions costs.

7. A cartel is a coalition of suppliers organized to reduce the quantity or quality of output, though the value to consumers of the forsaken output or quality would exceed the costs of supplying the good.

8. Economic analysis does not prove that trade is a good thing. It only shows the conditions that lead people, if given the opportunity, to engage in exchange.

Questions

1. Does economic analysis prove that to permit trade is better than to prohibit trade?

2. A parent gives each of his two children some milk and meat. The two children then exchange with each other, one drinking most of the milk

and the other eating most of the meat. If the parent does not permit them to make that exchange, which of the postulates (if any) is the parent denying? Or does the explanation rest on some new postulate not stated in the text?

3. "Trade between the Mediterranean and the Baltic developed when each area produced a surplus of some good."
   a. What do you think this quotation, from a widely used history text, means?
   b. Can you propose an alternative explanation of that trade?

4. Some discount stores advertise that they can sell for less because they buy directly from the manufacturer and sell to the consumer, thus eliminating many middlemen. What is the flaw in this reasoning?

5. "Middlemen and the do-it-yourself principle are incompatible." Explain.

6. It is estimated that 25% of the price a consumer pays for a head of lettuce goes to the farmer; the remaining portion goes to middlemen and distribution costs.
   a. Would you, as a farmer, necessarily prefer to have your percentage raised? Explain your answer.
   b. Would you, as a consumer, prefer to see the farmer's percentage raised? Explain.

7. Which, if any, of the following are compatible with open, or free, markets:
   a. A would-be lawyer must get permission of present lawyers before being able to practice law.
   b. Medical doctors must pass a state examination before being allowed to sell medical services.
   c. Selling is prohibited on Sunday.
   d. Pure food and drug laws restrict the sale of "impure" foods and drugs.
   e. Consumption, manufacture, or sale of alcoholic beverages is prohibited.
   f. Dealers and agents must be certified by the U.S. Securities and Exchange Commission before they can act as middlemen in buying and selling stocks and bonds—that is, before they can be security dealers.

8. You are campaigning for mayor or a seat on the council in your home town, in which the taxi service (or, for that matter, garbage service, milk delivery, electric power, water, gas, and so on) is provided by anyone who wants to operate a taxi business or drive his own cab. You campaign for more government control of taxi drivers in order to ensure better quality of service.
   a. If elected, would you initiate a system of giving just one company the right to perform the service? Why?
   b. If so, how would you decide which company?
   c. In California the right to sell liquor is restricted by the state government to fewer stores than would prevail otherwise. Would you be surprised to learn that the liquor dealers are a political "lobby" and source of "power" in state politics? Why?
   d. What generalization does this suggest about a source of political power?

9. "It is well to remind ourselves from time to time of the benefits we derive from a free-market system. The system rests on freedom of consumer choice, the profit motive, and vigorous competition for the buyer's dollar. By relying on these spontaneous economic forces, we secure these benefits: (a) Our system tends automatically to produce the kinds of goods that consumers want in the relative quantities in which people want them. (b) The system tends automatically to minimize waste. If one producer is making a product inefficiently, another will see an opportunity for profit by making the product at a lower cost. (c) The system encourages innovation and technological change. . . . I regard the preservation and strengthening of the free market as a cardinal objective of this or any Administration's policies." (President J. F. Kennedy, September 1962, speaking to business-magazine and newspaper publishers.) Is it surprising and confusing that while extolling the virtues of an open, competitive economic system, businessmen and politicians restrict markets—for example, by controlling allowable imports of sugar so as to maintain sugar prices in the United States above the open-market level—in order to maintain larger wealth for incumbent businessmen and their employees? A confusion between freedom of competition and freedom from competition is suggested. Why do you think some people praise the private-property, open-market system while attempting to suppress it?

*10. Your college allots you parking space, while a friend is allotted a desk in the library stacks. Suppose you and he would each be better off if you were to trade your parking space for his desk space.

    a. This kind of trading is almost invariably prohibited by the college authorities. Why?

    b. If you were the college president, would you prohibit it?

    c. Would you consider selling parking space to one and all at the market-clearing price, as a downtown parking garage does, or as books and paper are sold in the student store? Why?

11. Suppose it were claimed that a denial of college facilities to some speaker is a denial of the right of free speech. Show how that argument confuses free resources with free speech.

12. Why has gold been so commonly used as money?

Chapter 4
Market Prices as Social Coordinators

The preceding chapter explained the principles governing the consumption and exchange activities between individuals. We saw how price affects the individual's decisions about the amounts that are deemed desirable to consume. We examined as well the ways in which the individual gains from exchange. But a market can consist of millions of individuals. How are all their separate individual decisions coordinated into a consistent whole, rather than creating permanent chaos? What restricts the amounts demanded by the public to the amounts supplied? And how does the amount produced and supplied depend on or respond to the amounts demanded? What, if anything, coordinates the whole economy, so that the constellation of economic activities is not chaotic? When individual demands do fail to be satisfied by existing supplies, what has gone wrong?

In fact, the superficially bewildering economic activities of millions of independent people are guided by a highly ordered set of signals and rewards, though there is no central control and no planning agency such as countries like the Soviet Union and the People's Republic of China, and in our military system, are reputed to have. No national authority computes and rations per capita shares of food, soap, shoes, tires, gasoline, or pencils to individuals.

In this chapter we investigate how individual activities in the system are coordinated, devoting most of our attention to the effects of demand. We study the determinants of market price and we study how that price tends to have two effects: First, it makes the total amount of each good demanded by the community exactly match the total amount supplied; second, it simultaneously enables each person to obtain whatever amount he or she demands at that price. We study how production is organized in more detail in Chapter 7. Here we investigate how the equilibrium-sustaining, or **market-clearing,**

price of each good, reached through market competition, performs all the tasks named in the preceding paragraphs.

Market Demand

We know that more of a good is demanded at lower prices. Lower prices at which we can buy what we demand will enable us to satisfy lower-valued uses, those uses that we consider not worth satisfying at higher prices. And some people who formerly used none at all will find it worthwhile to use some at the lower price. Let us start with a society of four people, A, B, C, and D. Their demands for automobiles are in Table 4-1. (All the automobiles are alike.) The total community, or market, demand follows our first law of demand: Greater amounts are demanded at lower prices. The total amount demanded (also called the market amount demanded) is the sum of the individual amounts demanded at a common price.

For now, we assume that the total amount supplied and available for distribu-

Table 4-1

DEMAND SCHEDULE, TOTAL
MARKET VALUE, AND ELASTICITY

	Quantity of Automobiles				
Price	A	B	C	D	Total (Market)
$1000	2	0	1	1	4
900	2	0	1	1	4
800	2	0	1	2	5
700	2	0	1	2	5
600	3	0	1	2	6
500	3	1	1	2	7
400	3	1	2	2	8
300	3	1	2	3	9
200	3	1	2	4	10
100	4	2	2	4	12

tion is a fixed total, regardless of price. (In Chapters 10 and 11 we investigate how output is determined.) Suppose seven cars exist, all initially owned by A. And suppose, for simplicity, that no person's wealth, and hence demand schedule, is changed significantly by the succeeding sequence of trades.[1] The following is one of many possible exchange sequences. A would sell four cars even if he could get only $100 per car. And he could, because the other people have higher personal marginal use values on a car than he has for four of his seven cars. We can demonstrate this fact in several different ways. For example, if C and D each extravagantly offer $900 for a car, A will delightedly sell one to each. Then B more shrewdly offers only $400 for a car; again, A sells. This leaves A four cars, and B, C, and D have obtained one car each. C then offers to buy another car from A at, say, $300—somewhat less than its $400 value to C—and A sells because he would rather have any amount over $100 than a fourth car. Although D, who has one car, would have paid as much as $800 to get a second car, he initially offers A only $300 for the second car; A will say he has no cars to "spare"—unless he can get $700. B, however, if alerted to this negotiation, would offer his car to D for $600 even though he just bought it. And C, who values his second car at only $400, would undercut B's price by asking for only $500. Neither A nor B would cut their prices that far. So C would sell to D for $500.

---

[1] Throughout this chapter we will operate under one very important assumption: No person ever acts as though the market price could be affected by that person's holding any units off the market. Whatever the amount of the good a seller owns, the seller has too few units to significantly affect the potential selling price by refusing to sell more. Later we shall modify that assumption. For the present we make it because it is often realistic and because it permits us to concentrate on the demand side of the exchange, and the way in which price—however it is determined—controls the allocation of the amount made available.

Thus A ends up with three cars, B with one, C with one, and D with two. Everyone, given his preferences and initial wealth, is content with this pattern of goods; there are no further mutually acceptable revisions. This is the condition of market-clearing **equilibrium**.

At every step in that sequence, both the buyer and seller moved to situations that each valued more highly. Though many other starting allocations and sequences of trade could be imagined, all yield the same final distribution and the same final equilibrium-sustaining, or market-clearing, price, $500: the price that makes the sum of the individual amounts demanded equal to the total amount available. As Table 4–1 shows in the Total Market column, at higher than $500 fewer than the existing seven cars are demanded, and at lower than $500 more than the seven are demanded.

You can better understand the preceding analysis by redoing the problem initially allocating the seven cars among four people in *any* combination. Will the final distribution be the same—in every case—as the present one? Yes. Try it to see why.

Market Supply and Demand: Graphic Interpretation

In Table 4–1, the individual demands for cars at any one price are added horizontally to get the total market, or community, demand. In Figure 4–1 we do the same thing; the total market demand curve is labeled *TT*. The community supply of seven cars is shown by a vertical line, *SS*. It is vertical because, regardless of price, the available amount is fixed at seven. The price at which the community demand intersects the supply line is the price at which the total number of cars demanded by A, B, C, and D—here seven: three, one, one, and two, respectively—equals the number supplied.

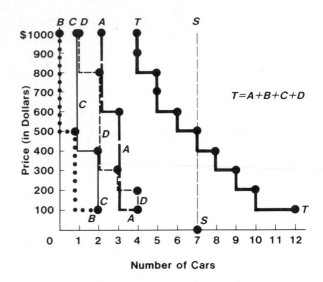

Figure 4-1.

INDIVIDUAL AND TOTAL COMMUNITY
DEMAND CURVES WITH FIXED SUPPLY

The total demand curve *TT* is the sum of the horizontal distances of each of the four individual demand curves at each price. The points are connected by straight line segments. If a fixed number of cars is available regardless of price, the supply curve, *SS*, is a vertical line.

Figure 4–1 shows that at any price above the equilibrium price, $500, the community amount demanded would be less than the number available. If there were a law that cars could be purchased only for a price *above* $500, there would be a *surplus* of cars, with one or more cars being offered for sale but not being demanded. Prices would be less able to allocate the existing supply of goods.

But the surplus would instantly become a *shortage* if the price were somehow restricted to *below* the equilibrium price, say at $300. More cars would be demanded than are available. That is what a shortage is. Consumers would say their needs (at that low price) were not satisfied. Of course, if the price were higher, the "need" for a car would be less urgent than the "need" for the greater amount of other things that the buyer must sacrifice if the car is bought at that higher price. The movement of price to the equilibrium-sustaining price eliminates any apparent surplus or shortage. At that price the total amount that individuals want (or say they need) matches the total available: The market is cleared.[2]

ADJUSTMENTS TO CHANGES IN SUPPLY

We have analyzed how buyers behave to affect price when the total amount supplied is fixed. But what if total supply were reduced? Again there would not be a shortage because a rise in price to a new, higher market equilibrium level would reduce the amount demanded to match the smaller amount supplied. For example, suppose one of A's cars is destroyed by fire, reducing the community supply to six. See Figure 4–2, where this change is represented by shifting the vertical supply line leftward to six on the quantity scale: line S_1S_1 (from S_0S_0). The intersection of demand with the smaller supply now requires a higher equilibrating price, $600. How is the higher price brought about? We assume that A's loss of the car does not reduce his wealth significantly, and that he will seek a replacement. Because no one is willing to sell a car for $500, there would be at that price a shortage, or, to put it in different words, an *excessive amount demanded*. Seven are demanded; six exist. But A, who now has only two cars, still values a third car at $600 (that is, he prefers a third car more than any other things he could get with $600). By offering $600 to purchase a car, A could buy a car (possibly through a used-car dealer) from B, who prefers $600 to his only car.

The destruction of one of the cars and subsequent exchange has benefited B. It may seem unfair that B should gain from A's loss. But to refuse to allow B to make such a gain through trade is also to condemn A to what he considers a worsened situation after the fire, unless you condemn someone else to bear the loss—and *someone* has to bear it.[3] By offering to buy a car for $600 and thereby improving B's situation, A was also able to partially restore his own.

If a price ceiling of $500 had been imposed, B would be prevented from "gouging" A, or, as it is sometimes said, "profit-

---

[2]Had the sale of cars involved used-car dealers instead of only private parties, the sequence of exchanges and prices would have been less erratic and would have converged more quickly at an equilibrium price. Cars could also have been more cheaply and quickly inspected. And when price increased, buyers would probably have complained that used-car dealers had unscrupulously raised prices. Used-car dealers do raise prices—but scrupulously, after demand increases. To replenish their inventories, they must purchase cars at higher wholesale prices. When demand changes, dealers must move *both* their selling, or *retail*, and offer, or *wholesale*, prices; otherwise, used-car lots would either overflow or empty out. Used-car dealers can buy, sell, and survive in business only at wholesale and retail prices that reflect the public's demand for cars.

---

[3]Voluntary insurance is a method for distributing the loss over all consumers, rather than concentrating it on one person.

eering from A's misfortune." We might think we were doing A a favor by putting price controls on the sale of used cars, thereby preventing him from paying more than $500. But at that restricted, low price he cannot get a desired third car, so he is not aided. A shortage would be created—not by the reduction of supply through the burning of a car, but by the prohibition of higher market-clearing prices. To prevent misunderstanding, don't forget that a *reduced supply is not a shortage, nor the cause of a shortage. Shortages are caused solely by restraints on prices.*

To better understand the effect of price controls, consider what happens when the supply *increases*, say, to nine cars, as also shown in Figure 4-2, by a shift of the supply line to the right to S_2S_2. More cars are available than before at each possible price. If the price were now set by law at any price below the new market-clearing price of $300, more cars would be demanded than are available. The typical signs of shortages—waiting lines, outages—will occur, despite an increased supply.

The distinction we're making here is worth the effort to understand because in the real world there are, unfortunately, plentiful instances of shortages being mistakenly attributed to or equated with reductions in supply. For example, the shortages of gasoline and other fossil-fuel sources of energy in the United States during the 1970s occurred not because supplies of oil were reduced but because the price of oil was not allowed to adjust to change in supply by rising to the market-clearing levels—a result of politically imposed price controls on petroleum. If that analysis seems absurd, consider that in European countries, which had no price controls on gasoline, no shortages occurred when the oil supply was reduced. Prices rose to clear the market, so everyone was able to buy the reduced amount they demanded at the higher prices. Only in countries with price controls, such as in the United States, did short-

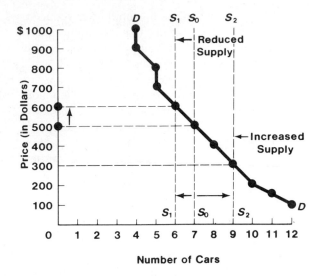

Figure 4-2.

REDUCED SUPPLY RAISES PRICE;
INCREASED SUPPLY LOWERS PRICE

A reduction in supply is shown by shifting the supply curve to the left, from S_0S_0 to S_1S_1. The total market demand line, *DD*, is unchanged. The rise in price from $500 to $600 facilitates the selling and redistribution of cars from those who value a car less than $600 to those who value a car more. If prices could not be raised in response to a reduction in supply, cars would not be reallocated from lower-valuing to higher-valuing users with gains to both buyer and seller.

If supply of cars is increased, as shown by shifting the supply curve to the right, from S_0S_0 to S_2S_2, the total demand curve is again unchanged, and price falls to a market-clearing $300.

ages occur when the oil supply was reduced.

Remember, again, that economic analysis neither condemns nor commends. It only shows how the market system operates and what the consequences of that operation are, and what the consequences are when non-market forces are introduced. It is too early in our analysis for you to draw any judgment as to whether price controls are good or bad—although it may be appropriate to draw a judgment later, when more of their implications are explored.

ADJUSTMENTS TO CHANGES IN DEMAND

Let us return to our initial situation, in which there are seven cars. But now a newcomer, E, joins the community. His added demand increases the community market demand, shown by shifting the aggregate demand line to the right (see Table 4-2 and Figure 4-3). E is willing to pay as much as $900 for a car. How much *must* he pay? No one is willing to sell at the old equilibrium price of $500, but B will sell at $600: He pre-

Table 4-2

CAR-OWNERSHIP DEMAND
SCHEDULES OF A, B, C, D, AND E

Price	Quantity Demanded		
	A,B,C,D	E	Total
$1000	4	0	4
900	4	1	5
800	5	1	6
700	5	1	6
600	6	1	7
500	7	1	8
400	8	1	9
300	9	2	11
200	10	2	12
100	12	3	15

fers $600 to the car. The new equilibrating price (that is, the price at which neither a shortage nor a surplus occurs) is higher: $600. The resulting reallocation of cars is accomplished solely by the force of revised prices in mutually beneficial exchanges.

PRICES AND FIXED SUPPLY

So far in our analysis we have assumed that the supply of cars was simply a given quantity and was not responsive to price. This is why the supply lines in Figures 4-1 and 4-2 are straight vertical lines. It is commonly argued that with such a fixed supply, which is not affected by the price, allowing the price to rise serves no useful function because it doesn't affect the quantity supplied. But our analyses have demonstrated that the higher price has a strong effect in determining who gets what part of the existing supply. Higher prices cause each person to adjust his or her valuation of a prospective purchase relative to other people's valuations. As a result of these innumerable individual decisions, the higher prices restrict the amounts demanded. Market-clearing prices thus are a rationing or allocative device, performing a task that is necessary in every society whether or not the supply is a constant. If price is not allowed to adjust to restrict amounts demanded, some other methods must be used to ration the existing supply among competing claimants. It follows that *if price is restrained below the market-clearing equilibrium, other forms of competition will become more significant.* Political power or other costly means of competition for the goods will decide who gets more and who gets less. Allowing price to respond, even if price has no effect on the quantity, serves a useful function, overlooked by people who think that the only effect of prices is on production rates—an effect that we now examine briefly, and investigate more thoroughly in later chapters.

Production and Supply

PRICE EFFECT ON
AMOUNT PRODUCED AND SUPPLIED

Normally, at higher prices rates of production are higher and amounts supplied are larger. (Remember, when we say that a price is higher or is lower, we mean the *relative* price—that one price, in dollars, relative to prices, in dollars, of other goods and services.) Higher rates of production of any good require more resources. And resources, like goods, remember, are scarce. For example, say we want to expand the national annual output of wheat. The amount of arable land having the best soil composition and located in the best climate is limited, and virtually all of it is already in use. Thus, land more valuable for corn or cattle must be diverted to wheat. Resources that are increasingly more valuable elsewhere must be attracted.

In Figure 4–4 the upward-sloping supply curve (reflecting that higher prices evoke larger rates of supply) means that larger rates of output of the given good require that resources be taken away from successively higher-valued uses elsewhere. Elsewhere, as less of other goods is produced, people are pushed back up their demand curves for those other goods. But if less is produced and supplied, the price of those other goods rises. More resources can be attracted to production of the good only if more is paid for them. So only if the present price of the output of that good rises can the funds be earned to attract resources from other, higher-valued activities.

When the demand for some good (whether it be houses, or computers, or restaurants) increases, usually only small amounts of resources are shifted away from the production of each of all other goods. The reduced amounts available elsewhere in each of many activities are so insignificant and so hard to notice that it is easy to think

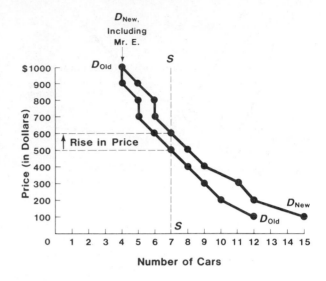

Figure 4-3.

HIGHER PRICE REDISTRIBUTES
CARS IN RESPONSE TO INCREASED DEMAND

The increase in the price of automobiles permits a reallocation of an automobile to E, the higher-valuing person, from B, who prefers $600 to an automobile.

that such reductions don't occur. But the resources must come from somewhere, and because the economy is usually in a state of near-full employment of its resources, there is no waiting supply of idle resources to draw upon in order to increase output.

Higher prices of a good make a larger output more profitable and provide the funds with which to attract resources from production of other goods. Resources are attracted by being paid for at higher prices than in their old uses, where the demand had not increased—or may have decreased. For example, when gasoline became more expensive, people increased their demand for small cars and reduced their demand for larger cars and recreational vehicles. The resulting increased sales and higher prices for small cars encouraged manufacturers to start making more

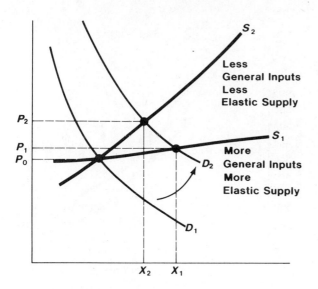

Figure 4-4.

ELASTICITY OF SUPPLY

An increase in demand, as from D_1 to D_2, induces an increase in output, which lessens the amount by which price rises. The elasticity of output is determined by the proportion of generalized and specialized inputs required for production of the good. The curve S_1 shows that more-generalized inputs can be attracted to increase supply of the good by less of a price rise—say to P_1—than can more-specialized inputs, represented by S_2, which require a rise in price to P_2.

small cars and fewer large cars. Resources were attracted to making smaller cars and away from, say, recreational vans. (Not often can such clear, large shifts in demand from one good to other goods be seen so dramatically.) In the market economy, people may buy what they choose and may put their services and equipment to work where they expect the highest resultant income. When consumers' valuations change, and hence demands change, new prices redirect resources toward the higher-valued products and services and away from the less valued.

Figure 4–4 is a demand and supply diagram; it assumes a market economy in which the amount supplied is not fixed. The figure shows graphically how an increase in demand works through price to induce larger rates of output. Say that people demand more meat than before, because they are richer or there are now more of them. The figure shows this change as a movement of the whole demand schedule upward and to the right, from D_1 to D_2. The diagram also shows that the sustainable market-clearing price and output rate are both higher. The increased demand led to increased sales and to a higher output with a new, higher, sustainable, market-clearing price. That higher price restrained the amount demanded below the larger amount that would have been demanded had price not risen, and that higher price also rewarded the suppliers with enough revenue to induce them to increase production and to pay for the increase.

Who Pays a Tax? The Answer by Demand and Supply

The preceding analysis enabled us to grasp the logic by which the market-pricing system operates to relate amounts supplied to amounts demanded. We can improve our understanding and ability to use it by applying it to some frequently posed practical questions, such as who bears a tax. Suppose a

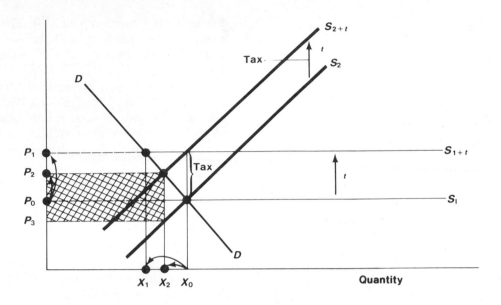

tax is placed on gasoline. Figure 4-5 shows the relationship between **aggregate demand** and **aggregate supply** of gasoline. Say a sales tax of 10¢ per gallon were imposed. The demand schedule—which reflects the value that consumers put on the use of gasoline—is unchanged. However, because of the 10¢-per-gallon tax, at the *old price* the suppliers retain 10¢ less. If suppliers raised the price by 10¢ to as high as P_1 in an attempt to pass the tax to consumers, less gasoline would be sold. In fact, any price higher than initially asked would reduce the amount demanded. Since the price to the consumer now includes a 10¢ tax, the supplier receives less than initially. The price by all sellers cannot be raised by the full amount of the tax without less being demanded. As less is produced, only lower-cost supplies can continue to be produced. With less gasoline supplied because of the lower net-of-tax price to the supplier, a higher consumer price, P_1 (including the tax), is sustained as the new equilibrium price. The difference between P_1 and P_0 (the price paid by the consumer and the portion received by the seller) is the tax the government gets. Part of that tax is borne by the consumer at the higher price P_1 and part

Figure 4-5.

HOW A TAX AFFECTS SUPPLY

A unit tax on a good raises the supply curve by the amount of the tax, t. How much price rises, however, depends on the slopes of the demand and supply curves. If the supply curve is perfectly horizontal, as is S_1, indicating infinite elasticity, the price will rise to P_1 to cover the full amount of the tax. If the supply curve is upward sloping, as is S_2, then price rises to P_2, less than the full amount of the tax. The corresponding supply curves become S_{1+t} and S_{2+t}, respectively.

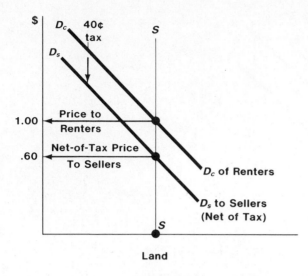

Figure 4-6.

EFFECT OF TAX ON DEMANDS
AND ON PRICE WITH FIXED SUPPLY

Consumers' demand, reflecting use value of land to consumers, stays unchanged despite a tax. But the amount of demand that goes to the sellers as rent falls by the amount of the tax. Consumers' price stays at $1.00 but price received by sellers falls to 60¢ because the vertical supply line represents fixed amount available despite price. If tax is to be paid to government by consumers, consumers' demand is the same as if tax is to be paid to government by sellers. In the former case, buyers pay 60¢ to sellers and 40¢ to government for a total price of $1.00, as before tax. In the latter case, sellers pay 40¢ to government to retain 60¢ of price of $1.00. With vertical supply (that is, total amount available does not vary with price) total price (tax plus proceeds to seller) does not change. What changes is the portion of that $1.00 value that is distributed to the government.

borne by the supplier (the difference between the old price, P_0, and the net-of-tax price, P_3). The difference $P_2 - P_3$ equals the tax per gallon.

We can see now that not all taxes are borne by the supplier, nor are all taxes passed on to consumers, as is often asserted. Who bears the tax in what proportion depends on the supply and demand relationships.

If the supply were fixed and not responsive to price—describable in the graph by a vertical line—then the *buyer's* price would not rise. Only the current owners or suppliers of a good would lose. To see why, consider a tax on land, the total supply of which is fixed regardless of the price paid for land. See Figure 4-6. Suppose a city has many landowners all with uniform land renting for $1.00 per square foot per month. (We assume the land is uniform to simplify our analysis, but the assumption does not change the results.) The city government levies a tax of 40¢ a month per square foot on the land. What happens to the rental value of land? No more land can be produced and none will disappear no matter what the rental income. The supply of land is represented by an unchanged vertical supply line at the existing stock of land. It does not shift or change in any other way when the tax is levied. Nor does the demand to use land by renters shift, because the land use is still worth as much to the renters as before. However, the portion of the renters' demand that accrues to the private landowners is now 40¢ a square foot lower per month. The portion of the demand schedule now going to landowners is 40¢ below the consumers' demand schedule, because the government takes the 40¢ difference. So we draw a new lower demand schedule as seen by the sellers, net of tax.

In effect, the government has made itself the owner of 40% of the value of the land. The landowners cannot increase rents, because the supply is unchanged and so is the users' demand schedule for land. The best the owners can charge is the same market-clearing price, $1.00 per square foot per month with a net of 60¢ after tax. If any landowners tried to raise their rents to recoup part of the rent going to the state, they would find the demand schedule for land to be no different from before: At a higher rent people would want to rent less land. With unchanged demand and a fixed supply of land, any attempt to increase rents will result only in some temporarily unrented land and a return to the equilibrium price as the best of the available opportunities.

WHO DELIVERS
THE TAX TO THE GOVERNMENT?

The question "Who pays the tax?" tends to confuse two separate questions: (1) Who delivers the money to the government? (2) Who bears the corresponding reduction in wealth? Suppose the tax is said to be on the renter rather than the landowner: A renter is now required to pay 40¢ of the unchanged use value to the government. Because the land is still worth only $1.00 to a renter, the renter offers only 60¢ to the landowner. Because every possible renter will behave in this way, the landowner cannot avoid a lower net-of-tax rent. To refuse that lower rent would mean no renter. Because the demand for land is unchanged, the renters are still willing to offer owners (*and the government*) only a total of $1.00 per square foot. If the government extracts 40¢ from the renter only the remainder is available to sellers. Two related demand schedules must be distinguished: the consumer (renter) demand schedule and the *lower* net-of-tax demand schedule seen by the seller after 40¢ is paid to the government. Thus, given a vertical supply line, the people who bear the reduction in wealth because of the tax are the people who own the land at the time the tax is announced.

Our analysis of the effects of taxes on land has been deliberately simple and incom-plete. For example, we have ignored the use of the tax proceeds. If the tax were used to improve roads, schools, or environment near the land and thereby improve its amenities, the use value that consumers put on the land would shift upward. That is, their demand curve would shift upward and to the right. If the renters assessed the value of those improvements to equal the tax cost, the renters' demand for that land would increase by exactly that amount; the increase in rental price would therefore equal the amount of the tax.

WHICH INPUT BEARS THE TAX?

What is meant by saying *the* supplier bears some of the tax? After all, to produce, say, gasoline requires exploring for oil, finding it, pumping it from the ground, shipping it to refineries, refining it, and shipping the gasoline to distributors and then to service stations. Every step requires labor, machinery, natural resources to power the machinery, and money to finance operations. All of these are *inputs* in the production and supply of gasoline. Which input owners suffer the tax? If any input could move or be moved instantly and costlessly to other uses or jobs paying just as much, its owner would not tolerate suffering any loss whatsoever through taxes. But if such moves were costly, the inputs would remain at gasoline production even at a lower income, as long as the decrease in income was less than the costs of moving. The higher the moving cost, the more of an income cut inputs and owners will tolerate in producing gasoline. In technical words, the owners of resources "less mobile, more specialized to gasoline production" will accept a lower wage or income, while the more generalized productive inputs—ones that can move to other work at less cost—suffer less or little loss because they make the move to other, equally high-paying jobs. The wages or prices that keep the more specialized inputs in production of gasoline will be lower—shown by lower costs for smaller rates of output along the supply line.

Furthermore, with lower net-of-tax receipts from gasoline, the suppliers can retain the services of inputs only by paying them less. But the inputs that have the highest-valued alternative options will not accept lower wages. Only those inputs that are less valuable elsewhere will remain despite the lower income. Thus, the costs of the inputs that remain will be lower, at a lower output, than the costs would be at a higher output, which would require bidding more inputs away from other, higher-paying jobs.

These phenomena are described by a supply curve drawn with an upward slope—the normal case. Though we investigate the organization of the productive resources in business firms later in the book, it is sufficient here to realize that the upward-rising supply curve means the resources used are not all identical and have different alternative use values.

If we review our two preceding examples, one with an upward-sloping supply schedule with higher prices and the other with a supply that was vertical and constant (that is, was not responsive to price), we can see that with a rising supply curve, part of a tax is borne by consumers as well as suppliers. The proportion that each bears depends on the price responsiveness of the supply line: The flatter the supply line, the more is borne by consumers and the less by suppliers. If the supply curve were practically a flat horizontal line, the consumers would pay a price higher by almost exactly the amount of the tax.

The change in output and price is also affected by the responsiveness or elasticity of *demand*. The flatter the *demand* curve—that is, the more elastic—the greater will be the reduction in output and the smaller the rise in price. Rather than pay a price that is high-er by the amount of the tax, customers shift more readily to other goods. More of the difference between the new, higher price and the costs of production will be achieved by lower costs associated with much smaller production. This process is directed entirely by market prices, which are in turn set by the demand and supply decisions of people seeking to increase their private wealth. Production responds not only to the values that consumers place on a given output but also on people's willingness to engage in the various types of work that output requires. As you can see, then, it is not a case of what is often simply called "consumer sovereignty," as if consumers' preferences were all that counted. Also influential is the willingness of people to produce what consumers desire. Both producers' and consumers' desires—supply and demand—are involved in determining what gets produced.

Smog Removal and Land Value

Let us suggest another, more startling application of demand and supply principles. If smog were magically removed forever, *at no cost*, from the center of a major industrial city, the value of the land would increase as demand for it increased. The increased demand would enable the landowners thereby to capture the value of the cleaner air. When the tenants began paying a higher rent, they would consume less of other goods because their higher rent left less money for other goods. The renters might be no better off than before, enjoying cleaner air but having less of other goods. Land values would fall in the nearby suburbs because people would no longer have to leave the city for better air.

If, instead of being magically costless, smog removal were very costly because expensive pollution control devices were required, should the landowners bear the costs of cleaning the air? Should they bear the costs of preventing further deterioration? These last two queries are about who *should* do something, so we leave the answers to you.

Rental and Allocation by Consumer Competition

We can get a better appreciation of the effects of competition among demanders if we examine what happens when some people's demands have increased and others' have not. For example, if the demand for rental housing increases, a given tenant's rent will rise. A higher rent will reduce the amount or quality of housing a renter demands; that renter is induced to release some housing to those whose demands have increased. Not owning the house, the renter will not capture the higher market value of the house—nor suffer its loss in value if the demand for housing has fallen.

Figure 4-7 shows the consequences graphically. Curve $D_a + D_b$ represents the community's initial demand for housing space. D_a is the demand schedule for those people whose demands remain unchanged, and D_b is the initial demand by those whose demands increase to D'_b. Initially, the rent is P_1, with X_a the amount of space rented to group A and X_b the amount rented to group B. Then, when group B's demand schedule increases to that shown by curve D'_b, the new total demand schedule, $D_a + D'_b$, intersects the existing housing supply line at a higher price, P_2.

If rents are restrained below P_2, a shortage occurs, as indicated by the distance between the supply line and the new demand curve at every price less than P_2. If the rent were not restrained, it would be bid up to P_2, as those with increased demand offer or tolerate higher rents to get more housing. The housing market would be called "tight" or "strong" or a "seller's market," and the normal buffer vacancies that enable people to locate new rental spaces and move from one to

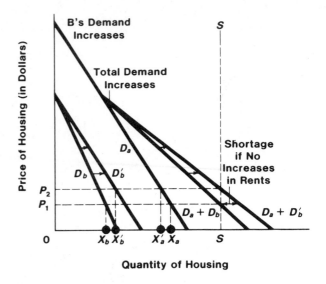

Figure 4-7.

CHANGE IN PRICE OF HOUSING ENABLES REALLOCATION AMONG COMPETING DEMANDERS, FROM A TO B

When demand by group B increases while that of group A does not, the increased total market demand raises the price of housing. Members of group A then demand less. Housing space equivalent to distance $X_b - X'_b$ is transferred from group A to group B, which values it more highly than does group A.

If rentals were held down by law at the old rental, a shortage of housing would appear because more housing than is available is demanded at that old rental. Allowing price to rise would eliminate the shortage: the excessive amount demanded. Miami Beach and, more recently, Santa Monica imposed rent controls when demand for housing increased and rents started to rise. Immediately a shortage appeared. It is proposed that the rent controls be retained until the shortage disappears. Will it?

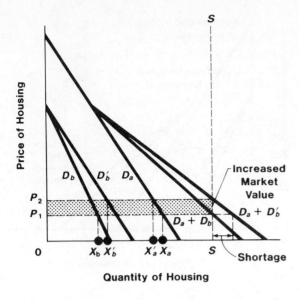

Figure 4-8.

EFFECT OF RENT CONTROL

Shortages are created by rent controls, represented by P_1, the legally restricted price or rent. The result is a transfer or destruction of wealth measured by shaded area.

another with relative ease would temporarily diminish in number. As rents rise, group B, whose demands had increased, obtains a larger aggregate amount, X'_b. Members of group A end up with only X'_a. But each individual in both groups wants less at the higher rent P_2 than he or she demanded at the old rent P_1.

House *owners* receive the increased rent; their houses are worth more. Everyone blames landlords for raising rents. But what enabled them to get higher rents is the *increased demand* by people in group B. Landlords, in effect, tell the A people to meet the competition of the Bs. The Bs and As may be friends and neighbors who complain to each other about "exorbitant" rents, never thinking to blame the competition among themselves for the higher prices.

Price Controls, Shortages, Competition, and Discrimination

So far we have analyzed situations in which prices adjust so that amounts demanded and amounts supplied are made equal. But often you will face a frustrating waiting list or waiting line because a good is out of stock. In other situations, sellers find too few buyers. Is there something wrong with our analysis? How can shortages and surpluses be explained? Do not ask, "What has gone wrong with the world?" The laws of demand have not changed. One possible answer is that the permissible prices may be restricted by law or political controls. (More sources of such events are explored later in this chapter.) In several cities, rent controls limit the rents for apartments; in most cities, water is not priced in accord with demand and supply. In these situations shortages will occur, and there will be queues or rationing, or more discrimination by race, creed, sex, age, and the like.

To see why, we use our housing demand

example. Suppose price controls keep the rent down below the new market-clearing rental.[4] The total amount demanded at that restricted price will exceed the available supply, so a shortage—or what we have also called an excessive demand—develops.[5] Figure 4-8 is based on Figure 4-7. The demands of A and B are shown before and after the demand increase by B. If price is restricted to P_1, B group members will complain of a shortage because they can't get as much space as they demand (or, as they are more likely to say, "need"). There are two other effects as well: (1) a wealth transfer (but not from renters to owners, as would otherwise occur); and (2) an increase in nonprice discrimination.

WEALTH TRANSFER

It is easy to see how the wealth—the increased market value of housing—is transferred when prices are restricted. Suppose a tenant were allowed to sublease to others at uncontrolled rents, even though the rent paid to the landlord were restricted to P_1. It would pay a newcomer, B, to rent space from A, paying a sublease rental to A of P_2. As the diagram shows, B would get more space $(X'_b - X_b)$, which is the amount $(X_a - X'_a)$ given up by A, who would rather have the extra income. And B prefers the extra space to what it costs to get that space. The new increased value of housing services would be captured by the old tenants, a value shown in Figure 4-8 as a shaded area. The owner would get none of it.

This value increase occurs whether or not subleasing is legally permitted. If it is

permitted, both B and A reach mutually preferred positions, but none of the increased value of housing goes to the housing owner. If subleasing is not permitted under the rent controls, the housing space is not reallocated so effectively. But whereas the owners are deprived of the increased value by the legal rent limit, the original tenants get that increased wealth in the form of the more valuable housing space. Hardly anyone has proposed that under rent controls tenants be allowed to sublease at market-clearing prices, despite the benefits that would accrue to tenants. Is it because this would make the wealth redistribution from landlords too transparent to be acceptable politically?

NONMONETARY FULL-PRICE COMPETITION, OR WEALTH WASTAGE

When people value a good at more than the price being asked for it, but are unable to get the amount demanded at that price, the frustrated demanders will compete for more of the goods in nonprice ways. No frustrated demander will idly watch others get something worth more than its money price. *Their marginal personal valuation of another unit of the good exceeds the specified market price. That excess of valuation over price is a measure of how much cost—in addition to that price—they are willing to incur to get another unit.* They will incur new costs, *other than greater money payments to sellers,* to curry the seller's favor. But these extra costs are not a wealth transfer; they eat up that excess value, and are a waste. Some of the nonprice ways in which consumers compete are waiting in line or being put on a waiting list, being nicer to the seller, or accepting a lower standard of service or quality of good. For example, they will stand in line as long as their value of the time in line just matches

[4]In a later chapter we investigate the effects of legally imposed *minimum* prices.

[5]Although the legal maximum price of housing is deemed "fair," some demands are not met at that price. Any person caught in that situation could ask, "What is the meaning of a price at which none of a good is available to a buyer?"

the excess of their personal marginal valuation of the desired goods over its restricted price. Their *full price* (the money price plus the value of the time spent in line or the costs of competing in other ways they choose) for the good will be bid up by competition to match their marginal use value of what they can get.

If you assume that full price exceeds money price only in conditions of restricted prices, then you have forgotten that in Chapter 2 we explained that almost everything you buy has a full cost to *you* that is greater than just the money price—even when there are no price controls. We have generally ignored all but the money price only for the sake of simplicity. And although we later use the idea of full price more extensively, we use it here to show that people are willing to incur a full price equal to the personal marginal use value of the marginal unit they demand. Consequently, even if the money price they must pay is kept low, the full price may not be affected: Buyers will increase their offer of nonmoney components.

Thus, for rent-controlled housing we see longer waiting lists for vacancies, more importance placed by owners on the personal traits and behavior of applicants in determining who gets housing space, and a reduced quality of housing. These nonmoney competitive features become proportionately more important until the full price is equal to what it would have been at the market-clearing price for the good. Thus is it said that price controls do not keep down the full cost to buyers; *instead, they change the way the demanders bear the higher costs, that is, less in money and more in other forms of otherwise undesired competitive activity.*

In sum, restrictions on open-market pricing have these consequences: They (1) make the amount demanded at the money price exceed the amount available; (2) restrain exchange from lower- to higher-valuing users;

(3) reduce the quality of the good; (4) induce wealth-wasting forms of competition; (5) increase nonmonetary discrimination.

Why, then, do any consumers want price controls? For several reasons:

First, some consumers believe—correctly—that if the price were allowed to clear the market their costs would increase. The sellers would gain that greater value. These consumers prefer to take their chances by competing for the price-controlled goods in nonmonetary ways in which they may believe they have a relative advantage; in effect, by being richer (being more willing or able to wait in line; knowing the right people; being of a favored ethnic type; having political power; and the like). If they succeed, they gain the increased value that price controls withhold from the owner. Some people (chiefly the politically strong) find that price controls further enhance their power, particularly when, by weakening the effectiveness of market-exchange offers, political controls decide who gets what goods.

Second, some people do not understand how price controls affect allocation, production, and the quality of products.

Third, many people incorrectly believe that price controls prevent inflation and protect the purchasing power of money. (They do not, as we shall see much later, in Chapter 19.)

Scarcity makes some system of allocation necessary. *Every* allocative system is discriminatory, by definition: To allocate *is* to discriminate. In a capitalist, free-market system the dominant basis of discrimination among people as to who gets what is based heavily on one's productivity, which determines one's wealth, and hence on the amount of money (which, remember, represents claims to other goods) offered in exchange. The analytic question about prices is not whether particular prices are high or low, but how they permit exchange to influence who gets what and who produces what. The private-property system puts *more* goods where there are *more* dollar offers. Everyone can get some of all goods, up to the quantity of each good at which each person's marginal personal value matches its price. Some people feed their dogs while poor children have little milk, because the system permits people individually to decide what to do with their income and wealth. We may wish some people had different tastes and values.

RATIONING BY COUPONS

Some of the wastes of nonprice competition under price controls can be avoided by per capita *rationing*: giving coupons that entitle a person to buy an amount of the good. But not everyone would have equal marginal use values at the amounts they were allotted by the ration coupons. The lower-valuing users would prefer to sell their coupons (rights to buy the good) to higher-valuing people. Therefore, it has been widely proposed that if, at some time in the future, ration coupons are issued for gasoline, they be salable to people who want more of the good and are willing to pay more for a coupon. This arrangement would benefit the person selling the coupon (who values what could be obtained with the money more than what could be had with the coupon) and would for the same reason benefit the purchaser of the coupon.

Such an exchange, however, clearly reveals that the *effective* full price of the good is not being kept down to the official limited price. The transferable ration coupon is worth the difference between the official price and what the free-market price would be. That difference would be offered for a coupon—or would be forsaken by using the coupon rather than selling it. Therefore, the full price for every consumer (money price plus coupon value) equals what the free-market price would be—except that there are extra transactions costs associated with issuance and purchase of coupons.

The 1975 National Energy Act: Erroneous Economics but Good Politics?

Another instructive example of erroneous thinking is the National Energy Act of 1975. Congress mandated a rollback and continuing control of prices of domestic (U.S.) crude oil paid to producers. *Crude-oil* prices were held below market-clearing levels on the assumption that thereby prices would be lower for gasoline, heating fuel, lubricating oil, and other products refined from crude oil. However, keeping the price of domestic crude oil low does not affect the price of the products refined from crude oil. Several presidents, the majority of Congress, Congressional staff advisors, and the National Energy Board (but not the Council of Economic Advisors) erroneously thought that it would.

To see the error, suppose products derived from a barrel of crude oil (gasoline, kerosene, fuel oil, asphalt, plastics, chemicals, drugs, rubber, and the like) are worth $100 at their final free-market prices to consumers. Suppose those final product prices are not controlled by law; they are market-clearing prices. Suppose also that the costs of refining, transporting, and distributing these final products amounts to $66, giving a remainder of $34. Any processor who could convert a barrel of oil into products worth $100 at a cost of $66 would make a profit if a barrel of crude oil could be purchased for less than $34.

Competition among those profit-seeking *refiners* would bid the price of crude oil up to $34 as they competed for the available, underpriced crude oil. The fundamental point is now clear: The price of every productive input is *bid up* to the value of what it is expected to provide consumers; in this way its expected value to consumers determines its costs and its price. In the present example, the $34-a-barrel value of oil comes from the $100 value of the refined products to consumers (minus the $66 of other costs of processing and distributing). Thus, if the legal price of the crude oil were kept down to, say, $10 a barrel, any processor who got that oil for $10 would make a gain of $24 (= $34 − $10) *because the refined products would still sell for $100.* The $100 value of the refined products depends only on the demand for them and their supply. *If the supply of refined products is not changed, then whether the price of crude oil is kept down to $10 by law or bid up to its $34 value* affects only the allocation of that $24 difference; it does not affect the price of gasoline.

For the sake of simplicity, we have assumed that the crude oil will be taken from the ground whether the well owner gets $10 or $24. Although this assumption is not entirely correct, we will hold it for the moment. We shall correct it shortly.

If the supply of domestic crude oil, and hence the supply of its refined products, is not affected by the crude-oil price received by the crude-oil producer, the final product prices will be unaffected by what is paid for the crude oil. This means that the price obtained for *refined* products could not be increased even if the *crude* price were allowed to rise above its legal ceiling of $10 to its market value of $24. To raise the price of the refined products would mean that some amount would not be sold. That is why putting a legal price control on crude oil (or on any *input*) will not—and did not—keep down the price of the *derived final outputs*—gasoline, chemicals, plastics, and drugs obtained from crude oil.

Frequently, since the 1975 National Energy Act was passed, members of Congress and of the administration have erroneously claimed that if the price to American producers of crude oil had been allowed to rise from the legally restricted price of $7 a barrel to the (then) free-market value of $14 a barrel, the price of gasoline refined from that oil would rise about 17¢ a gallon.[6] (Because about 42 gallons of gasoline can be refined from a barrel of oil, a price rise of $7 a barrel divided by 42 gallons of gasoline comes to about 17¢ a gallon.) The error is, of course, in assuming that the cost of making something (rather than the consumers' marginal personal valuations of the available supply) is the basis of its value.

The interaction of demand and supply for any good determines the market value. If more of the good can be produced, people will incur costs to produce more until the costs rise to the product's value. The production costs that it pays to incur are determined by the market value of the good, not the other way around. The value to the consumer is not increased simply because a producer's cost has risen. Not falling into the trap of believing that it is will make you an economically sophisticated person.

To see that costs do not determine value, reconsider the earlier automobile example. If it had cost $100,000 to make those cars, and only seven were available, the price would be unaffected: still $600. The explanation is that only insofar as costs affect the *supply* do they affect price.

Under the National Energy Act's crude-oil price controls, the refiners who were fortunate enough (or politically well enough placed) to command crude oil from a well owner for only $7 were getting oil worth $14 a barrel (disregarding other costs), netting a gain of $7 a barrel at the expense of domestic crude-oil producers. Yet because people persistently think that costs of production determine the price of a good, they believed that the National Energy Act kept down the price of gasoline by limiting the price of crude to refiners. It did nothing of the kind; it had the effect of preventing crude producers from getting that $14 value per barrel. Half of it

---

[6]The error was repeatedly pointed out by many economists—to little practical effect.

remained with the refiners. Such a wealth transfer from one party to another has no effect on the supply, and hence the price of gasoline or any other refined product was unchanged. Economic analysis doesn't enable us to explain why the public and so many politicians expounded that fallacious reasoning.

To correct our artificial assumption that the supplied amount of crude oil was constant, we need only recognize that in fact domestic crude producers would produce more crude at a higher crude price. That would increase the supply of refined products, the prices of which would then be reduced. Far from keeping down the price of refined products, price controls on crude oil actually tend to raise them. But not very much, since prices of refined products already reflect *world* supply and demand. We import crude oil at the world price because that is its value in terms of its refined products at free-market prices after allowing for refining and distribution costs. We also import refined products from foreign crude. For all these reasons, the *supply* of crude oil and refined products to the United States is essentially unaffected by price controls on domestic crude oil.

Refiners can vary the ratios of gasoline, fuel oil, chemicals, and plastics derived from a barrel of crude by adjusting the refining process. The National Energy Act also authorized political authorities to control the proportions of such products refined from the crude. By so doing, the political authorities can determine the relative supply of each type of refined product and hence their relative market prices and values. It was contended by the Act's advocates that this would ensure that not "too much" gasoline is produced at the expense of not having "enough" fuel oil. In accord with the desires of the Act's proponents, controls mandated a reduced gasoline output in favor of more fuel oil for heating. As Ralph Nader, a supporter of such controls, said, "I don't have an automobile." Also, he lives in a city in a part of the United States that has cold winters. Was the National Energy Act a means of transferring economic resources to the benefit of areas of the country like the East, which are colder and more urban and where the automobile is used less, at the expense of the warmer areas where the automobile is used more, as in the West?

Economic Rent

Although for some goods a price may not affect the amount of a good in existence, it does affect assignment to *particular persons and uses*. Any price unnecessary to keeping the good in *existence*, but necessary for *allocation* to highest-valuing users, is called **economic rent**: *economic* to emphasize that it serves an allocative function, and *rent* to indicate that it does not affect the supply.

Willingness to pay is a competitive way of revealing the use value to the demander. If some amount of a good has greater value to one demander than to others, that demander will get it. The entire price or rent of *land* is in excess of the zero amount necessary to keep that land in *existence*. Yet to *compare the values to different users* the market rent is crucial.

But is land rent truly an *economic* rent? Land is surprisingly perishable. Its valuable features include levelness, fertility, and absence of rocks, weeds, and bushes. Any farmer or ecologist knows how fast land can erode or become overgrown with weeds. Goods that have literally *no* preservation or maintenance costs whatsoever are rare—indeed, we can think of no examples. Furthermore, more land can be created and will be created at sufficiently high prices.

LAND RENT—A TAXABLE SURPLUS?

In the belief that payments for some goods are unnecessary to create either the existing or the future supply, some people conclude that the market value of such a good is a surplus that should be taxed. Prominent were the "single-taxers"—followers of Henry George, a nineteenth-century novelist and reformer, who believed that all land rent should be taxed. (Somehow he overlooked equally "pure" economic rents on other resources—for example, beauty and talent.)

Other ideologically motivated advocates of taxing, or nationalizing, land rents are the socialists. The philosophers of the left wing of the British Labour Party argued that land-site values reflect the actions and demands of society as a whole and not the owners of a particular parcel of land. Therefore, the site rent should belong to all the people. But that is true of *every* good, and this argument fails to explain why every person in the society should bear the consequences of changes in value of every parcel of land—even those a person will never see or perceptibly affect. Moreover, some people do not want to carry the risks of losses from all land and instead prefer to hold titles to other goods. Just as people differ in consumption patterns, so people specialize in which goods they prefer to own and on which to bear the risks of changes of value. But socialist doctrine does not permit private-property rights in productive resources. Socialists say that the people should have equal, *non*transferable shares in the value of certain goods—hence those goods are *socialized* (by which is meant the same thing as *nationalized*). That is, their rental value is claimed and distributed by political authorities.

It has been argued that even if land rights were socialized, the *use* of the land would be unaffected, because the government could rent to the highest-bidding user. However, the reward for a private owner to incur the costs, risks, and trouble of discovering and actually putting the land into the highest-valued uses is greater than for a salaried government employee in charge of the socialized land. Thus, the government employee is less likely to find or heed highest market-valued uses. Whether this is good or bad depends in part on whether you think the market-valued uses as revealed by individuals competing in the market are a good or bad criterion. It is not for economists to hazard judgments about that.

Pareto-Optimal Allocations

If the output of goods could be revised or reallocated to make some people better off without hurting anyone else, surely we would say, "Move to the new allocation." Any situation in which a change *must* hurt someone is called a **Pareto-optimal allocation**, after Vilfredo Pareto, the nineteenth-century Italian sociologist and economist who formulated it. Recall our earlier example of a fixed supply of cars: *Given the marginal personal valuations for autos*, the resulting distribution of three, one, one, and two cars to A, B, C, and D, respectively, to each of them is the Pareto-optimal allocation. No subsequent reallocation of a car could benefit either of any two parties. (Try it; it's impossible.) With any other allocation you could find exchanges with a gain from trade shared between the buyer and seller.

None of this means Pareto-optimality is good. Though the Pareto-optimal criterion seems reasonable, it is not universally accepted. Because the concept involves personal judgments, it must rest on the assumption that each person is the right judge of what is best for himself. But acceptance of that is not general. In fact we do not allow children and people legally declared incompetent to make their own choices. Some drugs and literature are prohibited even for adults, though such products have some would-be buyers and sellers.

Summary

1. The market-demand schedule for a good is composed of the sums of the amounts demanded by all people at each possible price.

2. For any good, the total amount demanded and the total amount supplied are made to equal one another by an equilibrium, or market-clearing, price. This price is achieved by the open-market offers and bids among competing buyers and sellers.

3. Shortages and surpluses result from a price being, respectively, too low or too high. Shortages and surpluses are eliminated almost instantly by free-market prices. A reduced supply should not be confused with a shortage, which is caused by price being too low.

4. When demand for a good increases, competition among buyers raises its price. Middlemen or agents transmit the increased demands to potential sellers or suppliers of the good. The higher price paid for the existing amount by those middlemen appears as higher costs to them. The price rise, however, is not caused by the rise in costs, but rather by the higher value placed on the goods by the increased public demand.

5. Though existing prices may have no effect on the currently available amount of some good, the price does affect the distribution of the good. A free-market price will move the goods to their highest-valued users.

6. The supply schedule gives the sums of the amounts supplied at each alternative price. If output rates increase in response to higher prices, the supply curve is upward sloping, from lower left to upper right, with larger amounts at higher prices.

7. The supply curve of a good will be upward sloping if some of the extra inputs required to increase output are more valuable elsewhere—for if they are, they will not work or be put to use here unless paid at least what they could earn elsewhere. The higher the proportion of inputs that have higher-valued alternative uses, the higher the costs of in-creasing rate of output. If the demand (and thus the price) for the product were to fall, these inputs would refuse to work here at lower wages or fees for services, and would leave for the other, higher-paying jobs.

8. How a tax on a good affects its price depends on the slopes of the demand and supply curves. If the amount supplied is fixed regardless of price—that is, if the supply schedule is vertical—a tax will not increase the buyer's price, but will instead be deducted from the seller's price.

9. For a good with an elastic supply schedule—that is, one for which output is not fixed regardless of price—a tax will force resources with use values that are nearly equally high elsewhere to shift elsewhere, rather than absorb the tax by accepting less here. That shift of resources reduces the amount supplied of the taxed good. The reduction enables the supplier's costs to fall and the price of the good to rise. The spread between the new, higher *consumer's price* and the now lower *supplier's cost* will equal the tax.

10. Under price controls, demanders for the good will offer the fixed money price but will also compete with one another by offering more of other costly activities until the *full price* (the money price plus those additional costs) equals the marginal personal valuation. Such nonprice competition is wasteful, because the seller does not value the buyer's nonmonetary competitive activities as much as a direct money receipt.

11. Price controls require that competition for goods be pursued by means other than price. Race, creed, age, sex, and personal characteristics become more important in determining how goods are allocated because they are less capable of being offset by a price difference.

12. Ration coupons may be used in some price-control arrangements, to reduce the nonprice costs to buyers. But if such coupons are salable, they acquire a value equal to the difference between the controlled price and the open-market price, thereby making the

the price paid by consumers the same as the open-market price.

13. If the amount supplied is permanently fixed—that is, unresponsive to any price—all the income received by the seller is called an *economic rent*.

14. Any payment for a good in excess of that required for the *permanent* existence or maintenance is a *pure* economic rent.

15. A *quasi*-rent is the portion of revenue that does not affect the amount supplied now, but will affect the future rate of production.

16. Any allocation of goods among people such that a change to benefit some person would hurt some other person is called a Pareto-optimal allocation. Market exchange at free prices tends toward Pareto-optimal allocations.

Questions

1. The demands to own by A and by B for good X are:

Price	A's Demand	B's Demand	Total Market Demand
$10	0	0 ⁓	_____
9	1	0	_____
8	2	0	_____
7	3	1	_____
6	4	2	_____
5	5	3	_____
4	6	3	_____
3	7	4	_____
2	8	5	_____
1	9	6	_____

a. Complete the total market demand by A and B at each price.
b. If six units of X are available, what will be the resulting allocation between A and B if open-market exchange is used?
c. With six units, if price were legally imposed at $4, would there be a shortage, a surplus, or an exchange equilibrium?
d. If the price were legally imposed at $9,

would there be a shortage, a surplus, or exchange equilibrium?
e. How can there be a change from a shortage to a surplus without any change in supply or demand?

2. In question 1 above, increase the amounts demanded by B uniformly by two units at each price.
a. What will be the new open-market price?
b. What will be the allocation between A and B?
c. If the price is held at the old level by law, will there be a surplus or a shortage?
d. How can that surplus or shortage be eliminated?

3. "The interaction of demand and supply is applicable not only to private-property market exchange but to every problem of allocating scarce resources among competing uses. The usefulness of a resource in any one possible use determines its demand in that use, whereas its usefulness in all alternative uses (against which this particular use must compete) affects the supply of the resource for that use." Are these statements correct?

4. "Competition is never 'buyer against seller,' but always seller against other sellers and buyers against other buyers."
a. Is this true for you when you buy food? Automobiles? Shoes? Sell your labor?
b. Can you cite a case in which it is not true?

5. The first law of demand says that at lower prices, larger amounts of a good are demanded; at higher prices, lower amounts are demanded. The law of market price says that price equates the amount supplied to the amount demanded. Which law holds with fewer exceptions?

6. A distinguished professor of law wrote: "Some people believe that every resource which is scarce should be controlled by the market. And since, in their view, all resources except free goods are scarce, all resources—even rights to radiate radio signals—should be so controlled. But surely some resources are 'scarcer' than others, and thereby possibly merit different treatment. It doesn't advance the argument very much to place a label of 'scarcity' on everything." Would

it be advisable for professors of law to study economics? Why?

7. This chart is typical of scores that have appeared in the last several years in the news media. It purports to predict that supply will fall short of future requirements and demand. On the basis of the analysis in this chapter, why would you say such diagrams are incorrect?

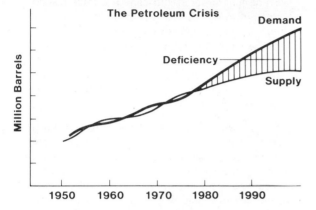

8. When prices on the stock market fall, the financial pages report, "everyone is selling; no one wants to buy." Why is this interpretation incorrect?

9. Which tactic would be more likely to get you a lower price on a new car: going to just one dealer and acting like a tough and aggressive bargainer; or going to several dealers and mildly asking for their selling price while letting it be known that you really intend to buy a car and are shopping around? Explain why. Can you cite any evidence?

10. The Council of Economic Advisers (to the President of the United States) once argued that legally keeping the price that cattle raisers could charge to below the market-clearing level would keep down the price of meat to the consumer. The Federal Energy Agency asserted that holding down crude-oil prices reduced the price of gasoline (made from crude oil). Explain why economic analysis rejects these contentions.

11. "With open-market pricing, housing units are scarce or expensive, whereas with rent control the housing market is characterized by shortages." Explain.

12. Are the words "scarcity," "reduced supply,"

and "shortage" synonyms? If not, what is the difference?

*13. Do you think rent controls would be good or bad for each of the following: (a) a middle-aged couple who do not contemplate moving, (b) a young married couple with two children moving to a new town, (c) a black moving to a new town, (d) a young person receiving a raise in salary, (e) an old person in retirement, (f) a drinker and smoker, (g) a handsome, poised young man, (h) a homely immigrant, (i) a Mormon in a Jewish community, (j) a Jew in a Mormon community, (k) an excellent handyman who likes to work around the house and care for gardens, (l) an old couple who have saved wealth and invested in an apartment house?

14. What does a vertical supply curve imply will happen to the amount supplied when the demand falls? What happens to price? Why?

15. What does an upward-sloping supply curve imply will happen to the output and to the inputs of production if demand and price for that good fall?

16. What does a horizontal supply curve imply will happen to the output of a good and to the productive inputs if the demand for the good falls? If it increases, what happens to price and to the productive inputs?

17. If a tax were placed on the future reruns of the television miniseries *Shogun*, who would bear the taxes; that is, who would be poorer by the amount of the tax collected?

*18. "Price controls give adequate housing to those in the lower-income levels who would otherwise not be able to afford it." Subject this proposition to economic analysis.

19. "In the capitalist system, only money or market-exchange values allocate productive resources." Evaluate.

20. "In capitalism, commercialism dominates and suppresses social, artistic, and cultural values." Evaluate.

21. "Under open-market, private-property pricing, a person is allowed to make any kind of appeal to a seller to get some of the good—even offering money. Under price controls, the buyer

is told that there is one appeal he cannot use—that is, offer of a larger amount of other goods." True or false?

22. At the same price for each, you choose a color television set over a black-and-white set; but when a black-and-white set costs a third as much as a color set, you choose the black and white. In which case are you "discriminating"?

23. Which of the following choices involve discrimination? (a) Cadillac versus Chrysler, (b) Van Gogh versus Gauguin, (c) blondes versus brunettes, (d) beautiful versus homely people, (e) blacks versus whites, (f) Japanese versus Koreans, (g) filet mignon versus hamburger, (h) *all* choices.

24. Collecting data for a cost-of-living survey, you find the following offerings: "List price, $125. Special discount to $90!" "50¢ box of Kleenex for 40¢." "One cent sale. First for $1. Second for 1¢." For each of these cases, which would you report as *the* price? Why?

25. It has been argued that politicians tend to gain from price controls and hence they advocate them. What line of reasoning would support that argument?

*26. The military draft of the U.S. government involved price control—in which the maximum price that could be paid by the military services was set by law. As a result, the number of personnel demanded exceeded the supply *at that price;* but the buyers, instead of accepting the amount sellers were willing to provide at that offered price, resorted to a compulsory draft to satisfy their "excess" of demand. Who gains what by this system of price controls? (Before presuming that military personnel could not be obtained by a wage system, note that the permanent military officers, the leaders, are obtained by a voluntary open-market wage system. So are policemen and firemen.)

*27. Prices (that is, tuitions) charged by many colleges are below the market-clearing price. Without inquiring why, explain how we know the price is that low. Applying the principles of competition, when prices are kept below market-clearing levels, indicate which kinds of nonprice competitive payments or behavior among competing student applicants acquire added influence. Who draws most advantage from these other forms of competition? Indicate (or conjecture) who captures the value of the excess of the market-clearing price over the controlled price of the services of the colleges.

*28. News item: "Seoul, Korea (AP). The city government ordered the capital's 1500 restaurants not to sell any meal containing rice during lunch hours. The measure is designed to encourage the customers to take other food. South Korea is experiencing a serious food shortage because of a poor rice crop." Would open-market prices achieve the same result? How effective will this measure be?

29. "Allowing the prices of goods to rise when more of the good cannot be produced is immoral, because the higher prices do not induce a larger output. They merely give unwarranted profits to those who are lucky enough to own the goods. Either prices should be prevented from rising, or the government should take over ownership in order to prevent unjust enrichment." Do you agree with this analysis? If so, why? If not, why not?

30. Which of the following do you think contain some economic rent? Insofar as any of them contains rent, for what is that rent unnecessary? For what is it necessary?

  a. The wealth of those who owned land in Palm Springs, California, from 1940 through 1975, when land values boomed.
  b. Frank Sinatra's income.
  c. The income of a genius.
  d. The income of oil-well owners.
  e. The salary of the President of the United States.

31. "The rent for land in New York City is not a payment necessary to produce that land. It is a necessary payment to obtain use of the land. From the first point of view, it is an economic rent; from the latter point of view, it is a cost." Do you agree? If so, why? If not, why not?

For Further Study: Futures Markets

After the harvest of wheat, no central planning agency sets limits on each month's consumption to avoid running out before the next harvest. Individual decisions set those limits, each owner of some of that wheat guessing how much to hold back. What guides their decisions? Given that the market value of any stocks of wheat held in the interim will fluctuate, how is that risk borne? Furthermore, if people have different estimates of the appropriate rate of consumption over the year, whose estimate will dominate? How will the various estimates be corrected in order to avoid running out too early or having far too much left over at the beginning of the next harvest? We now explain how. And though we shall speak of wheat, the analysis holds for goods in general.

THE FORECASTER IN COMMODITY MARKETS

After a harvest, farmers, not wanting to hold so much of their wealth in the form of wheat, prefer to sell it, letting someone else bear the risks of forecasting its future value. The millers, who grind grain into flour, don't want to store a year's supply of wheat in advance. Even the consumers refuse to take on this duty. But there is a very simple inducement to someone to store wheat: The price of wheat falls, for the reasons just given: Farmers want to hold less than they have; millers and shoppers want less than the farmers want to sell. This drop in price offers an increased prospect of profit in buying wheat at the lower price, storing it, and selling it later at an anticipated higher price. In a private-property, open-market system anyone may buy wheat at harvest time hoping to profit by selling it later at a higher price. Buying for later resale at an appreciated price is known as **speculation.**

Talents and facilities for storing wheat, and the estimates of future prices and of costs of storing wheat, all determine what the price of wheat will be at harvest. Permitting any or all persons to buy wheat for speculation keeps the price from falling further. And speculators' realized profits, if any, will be smaller. In the United States, anyone can buy and store wheat by telephoning a commodity-market broker who will arrange to have wheat purchased, stored in rented facilities, and insured against theft and spoilage.

CONTROL OF THE RATE OF CONSUMPTION OF STOCKS

Who tells speculators how much wheat to sell each month for consumption? No person does, but something does: the present price of wheat compared to its expected future price.

The relationship between the present, or *spot,* price for wheat and the expected future price affects the rate at which wheat will be sold. The further the present price is below the expected future price, the more will speculators want to hold their wheat, awaiting that future increase in prices. If current consumer demand increases, the spot price will rise and reduce the prospects of profits from continuing to store wheat. Thus, storers are induced to sell more wheat.

There is a market price that closely approximates the expected future price. It is the price of a *futures* contract in the *futures markets:* a standardized type of contract to deliver, say, wheat at a specified future time at a price agreed upon now but to be paid in the future, at delivery. That agreed-to price is essentially a prediction of what the price of wheat will be at that future time. No buyer would make a futures contract now if the price agreed to in it were *greater* than the expected future price. You would not sell a futures contract if the price agreed to in it were *lower* than you expected the future price to be.

FUTURE PRICES AND SPOT PRICES

Suppose it is now September, and you can buy wheat, in 5000-bushel lots, at $5 a bushel for immediate delivery—on the spot. Today's spot price, then, is $5. Today you can also buy a futures contract for delivery of wheat at $5.50 a bushel, payment and delivery to occur next May. That price, $5.50, agreed to now, in September, but to be paid in May of next year, is called the September price of a May futures. The 50¢ difference between the two prices (spot and futures) will, on average, just cover storage, insurance, and interest costs of investment in holding wheat over the interval between harvests.

FUTURE EXPECTED PRICES AND FUTURES MARKETS

The prices in futures contracts, on the commodity futures markets, are reported in the financial sections of major newspapers. In September you may find something like the following for the wheat futures market (which is in Chicago).

Futures Contract Prices of Wheat in May 1983

September 1983 (harvest)	$5.00
December 1983	5.15
March 1984	5.30
May 1984	5.50
September 1984 (harvest)	5.00
December 1984	5.15

These futures prices are predictions of the future spot prices. May is the last month before a new harvest. Obviously the summer harvest cannot be used to increase the amount available for consumption in *May;* if it could, the May price would be pushed down and the September price raised.[1]

---

[1] There is in fact some downward pressure on May prices, for consumers consume less in the expectation of buying and consuming more at a lower price after the new crop is harvested.

Anyone who can make a better prediction of what the price of wheat will turn out to be in the future can quickly reap a fortune. For example, suppose in September 1983 the futures contract price for a May 1984 delivery contract is $5.50. If you believe the price for wheat will go higher than $5.50 before May 1984, you could buy now a May 1984 futures contract, for, say, 5000 bushels of May 1984 wheat at $5.50 a bushel—the wheat to be delivered to you and paid for next May. You nervously wait. If the spot price next May turns out to be higher than $5.50 you can take delivery of the wheat, which you can sell at the higher price, reaping the difference as a profit. (If the price were lower, you would suffer a loss.)

Actually, the seller of the futures contract—who owes you wheat on that contract—could just pay you the profit you made by extending the future spot price more accurately than did that person with whom you made the futures contract. That other party doesn't have to buy wheat to deliver to you—so you could then sell it for your profit. Just paying you the difference is easier.

An important consequence of this speculative activity is that an increased demand for wheat to be delivered in the future pushes up the futures price of a May contract from $5.50 toward that new predicted May price. It also raises the current spot price. How? A higher price for a May futures contract raises the profitability of storing more of the existing wheat for that future time. People who want to acquire wheat now to store until next May drive up its current price. The higher current price reduces current consumption and more can be stored for next May.

But suppose the current price increases for a different reason: Suppose the demand for current consumption increases. The present price of wheat rises. Continued storage will be less profitable—unless it is also expected that the price in the future will increase still further. A faster rate of present consumption will leave smaller stocks and higher prices in the future. Currently, therefore, *futures* prices will be bid up.

What buyers and sellers enter into futures contracts? Millers, who grind wheat into flour, must have sufficient wheat on hand to insure a smooth flow into milling operations. They also want an inventory of flour on hand to make delivery to flour buyers convenient. But having wheat on hand exposes the millers to risks that its market value will decrease, thus offsetting profits from efficient milling and other services. How can they protect their income from the risks of big drops in the price of stored wheat? We give the three main ways possible, and their limitations. Of the three ways, only the third is usually inexpensive enough to be used:

1. Buy no wheat before you need it for milling. Limitation: This method will not permit efficient flow of production.

2. Find someone else to buy the wheat and store it in your place of business; you buy it from the owner as you use it. Any fluctuations in the value of the stock of wheat will be the owner's risk. Limitation: This is not as convenient as the next option.

3. Hedge in futures markets: At the time you buy wheat for later milling, sell a futures contract for the same amount of wheat. If the price of wheat falls in the future, you lose money on the wheat you hold. But because you sold future wheat through a futures contract at a price higher than the price turned out to be in the future, you will make a gain on the futures contract that exactly offsets the loss in the value of the stored wheat. On the other hand, if the price of wheat rises in the future, you will then have to deliver at higher cost than you receive for the contract—giving you a loss on the futures contract exactly offsetting the gain on the value of your stored wheat.

It is worth noting that unless there are large amounts of storable raw materials that are exposed to the risk of price changes it is unlikely there would be enough people seeking to sell futures contracts to maintain a market in such contracts. Futures contracts would not survive if they were only devices for gambling. Cheaper means of gambling are provided by horse races, roulette, craps, athletic events, lotteries, and cards!

ILLUSTRATIVE APPLICATION: COFFEE FUTURES MARKETS

To see how futures markets work, and how they affect allocations for present and future consumption, we apply our analysis to coffee futures. The scenario is only partly imaginary, being based on events of the last several years.[2] The rumor spreads that unseasonably cold weather has damaged some part of the next coffee crop, now blossoming in Brazil. Thus, owners of existing coffee who can store it for next year's expected higher prices can expect greater profits then, or at least greater likelihood that they will make a profit. As more of the existing coffee is withheld for future consumption, the present price of coffee to present consumers will rise.

There is, of course, just as much coffee as there was before the news that the future crop may be smaller. And yet the present price has risen. Consumers demand public investigations. Legislators investigate, and, sure enough, there is just as much coffee in existence now as before the rise, and greedy speculators are accused of driving up the price.

---

[2] In addition to the wheat and coffee markets there are organized open futures markets for at least the following goods: soybeans, oats, corn, cotton, barley, sorghum, sugar, cottonseed oil, soybean oil, hides, lard, eggs (frozen, powdered, and shell), potatoes, frozen chickens and turkeys, silver, tin, rubber, cocoa, platinum, pepper, flaxseed, copper, lead, zinc, wool, pork bellies, orange juice, and foreign monies. (One for onions was outlawed.) Instead of coffee, you could think of any of these goods.

If you were a speculator—and they're people of all types: dentists, carpenters, students—what would you tell complaining members of Congress? Could you defend yourself and claim you deserve not censure but a medal for having benefited all mankind; that you were working for the interest of other people, not against it? Your defense might run something like this: "True, news of the cold weather suggested higher prices next year. I believed that if I bought some of this year's currently stored ˙crop at present spot prices, I could later sell it at higher prices at a tidy profit. No one would sell existing stocks at a price less than could be gotten next year (allowing for the costs of storage, insurance, and interest). However, quite incidentally and unintentionally, my action—like that of many others—enlarged next year's supply of coffee by adding part of this year's stored stocks to next year's reduced harvest. The consumer next year will have more coffee to consume and at prices lower than if we speculators had not carried more coffee from this year over to next year. For that, the consumers should thank us—not condemn us!

"We speculators did not cause the reduced supply of coffee next year. Nature did that. There simply is going to be less coffee next year. The choice facing people is: 'Shall we continue to consume coffee today as if there were not going to be less next year, and then reduce consumption next year by the full reduction in the harvest? Or, shall we start to reduce consumption this year?' The choice is not more coffee rather than less, nor is it lower prices rather than higher prices; it is 'when shall the available coffee be consumed?'

"We speculators enabled people to be better off than otherwise, despite their protestations about the currently higher price of coffee. From the fact that next year's prices are predicted to be higher than this year's, I know that people prefer to give up a pound now in order to have one more next year. It is precisely because of this consumer preference that the futures price for next year's coffee rose over the present price of coffee this year. If our forecast is right, we will make a profit; if wrong, a loss. The profitability of our activity is an acid test that people did want some coffee shifted to the future.

"As speculators, we immediately acted on our prediction of less coffee next year. We are not responsible for that bad event, but we are responsible for anticipating the unfavorable effects of impending events so that people can more cheaply adjust to them—so they will be better off than if news of the coming crop failure were hidden until even more of the current crop was eaten up.

"But what if our predictions were wrong? Suppose only a few buds on each tree were damaged, and the hardier, undamaged buds produced even bigger coffee beans—more than enough to compensate for the reduced number, so that the crop next year will in fact be even larger. Or suppose the cold snap did no damage at all. Or maybe the news about cold weather was simply false. After all, some South American governments have been known to issue false bad news about an impending coffee crop precisely to drive up the spot price of their existing stock. What then?

"The answer is simple. If speculators or people who store coffee make mistakes in foresight, they will lose wealth; they will have paid more for the coffee than they will get when they sell it.

"I will not go so far as to say that any damage done to other people—in the form of higher present prices—by our erroneous forecasts is made up to them by our losses—a transfer of some of our wealth to the rest of society. In part this is correct, but still, perverse forecasts do more damage than our loss of wealth to the rest of society can offset. They do damage in the sense that if our forecasts had been more correct, everyone could have achieved a more desirable adjustment in consumption patterns over time than were in fact achieved. Obviously, the more accurate our forecasts, the better for us and for everyone else. The less accurate they are, the worse for us, and the less helpful to others. However—and this is crucially important—the results are not as bad for everyone else as they would be if everyone had to do his or her own forecasting and storing of stocks for personal consumption, thereby bearing the full consequences of his or her own forecasts—right or wrong.

"Clearly, then, the issue is not whether the forecasts are correct or incorrect in every instance. The issues are instead: (a) What systems exist for making and acting on better forecasts? (b) What systems exist for allocating coffee among people over time and for allocating the risks and consequences of the erroneous forecasts? Any system will have erroneous forecasts, but which one will have fewer of them? And who will bear the major burden of their consequences?"

And so by answering one question our scenario poses new ones, to which we turn.

PRICE-FORECASTING
ERRORS AND RISKS
IN FUTURES MARKETS

Do speculative markets, to which everyone has access, predict future prices more accurately than some other possible scheme? To find an answer, let us look at onions. The organized futures market in onions was abolished by federal law in 1959. Among those who wanted the markets closed were firms that specialize in collecting, storing, sorting, and distributing onions to retailers. Without an open futures market, information about onion conditions is less widely dispersed. Insiders, such as these processors, can benefit by their more exclusive access to information and opportunity to buy and sell onions. How they managed to induce enough members of Congress to vote for that legislation is a question for your professor of political science. However, as it happens, this prohibition provided a fine opportunity to compare the behavior of prices with and without futures markets. The record is clear: With the organized futures markets for onions, the forecasts were more accurate than when they were closed. In particular, with open speculative markets, prices varied less between crops than without them. In other words, the futures prices—the present forecasts of future spot prices—influenced present spot prices more accurately toward reflecting what was going to happen, avoiding the large fluctuations that occur when spot prices respond to unforeseen events.

How should the consequences of forecasting errors be borne? It has been contended that only experts should be allowed to make speculative decisions; this would avoid the errors made by less-informed people. To this there are several considerations. First, if experts are now better informed than the consensus of the markets, they could very rapidly get wealthy by speculating. The experts' superior information would help move the present spot and futures prices in the direction they would have taken if there was a futures market. Second, there is the problem of finding experts. When the government employs a group of specialists in this matter, the specialists are not automatically superior forecasters. The predictions of experts differ.

If, despite these inherent difficulties, a group of experts were responsible for making forecasts and controlling the storage rates, who would bear the losses when the forecasts were erroneous? Shall we require that each and every person, whether voluntarily or involuntarily, shall bear, in proportion to one's taxes, the changing values of the stocks of stored commodities? If the speculative activity is a voluntary arrangement, with open futures markets, those who want to bear more of the risk can hold more of their wealth in the form of stored goods, and those who want to be relieved of those risks can own other forms of wealth. This points up one fundamental feature of a capitalist system: Individuals can adjust their patterns of risk-bearing, as well as their pattern of consuming goods. If you wish to avoid the wealth changes of certain goods, you can own other goods. Although it is impossible to completely avoid risks, choosing among types of risks is possible with open markets and private-property rights. But whether that is desirable, economics cannot say.

Having chosen not to bear the risk of wealth changes in a certain good, a person should not complain if its price later rises. Such complaints would amount to the assertion that insurance is wasted if the disaster that was insured against doesn't happen! (In this case, by not holding goods in advance of use, one has insured against decreases in their value.)

Some people mistakenly believe that speculation can be prevented by legally imposing fixed prices on commodities. But price controls do not prevent shifts in demand or supply. They reduce the opportunity of people to use exchange to adjust their differences in personal values among goods as well as among risks; they create shortages and surpluses, phenomena that do not occur when there are open markets.

SPECULATION UNDER OTHER ECONOMIC SYSTEMS

All societies must decide who will bear the profits and losses; the issue cannot be evaded by abandoning a capitalist system. Only the method of allocation varies from system to system. In a capitalist system, individuals can negotiate among themselves, offering to exchange "this" risk of loss or gain for "that" risk. Just as people negotiate for the particular pattern of consumption goods they shall have, so they can negotiate about the pattern of risks they shall bear. Although the option of bearing no risk at all is open to no one, in a capitalist society risks in one kind of wealth may be exchanged for risks in other kinds of wealth. In a socialist system, risks are not individually negotiable with other people. The risks of value changes in state-owned goods—those owned by the people as a whole—are borne by everyone in the form of the taxes they pay and the kinds and quality of state-supplied services to which they have access.

If you believe a person should have less choice in one's risk patterns, and if you think the people who control the use of goods should not bear the risks, you will prefer to reduce the scope of private property. But if you prefer a wider choice of risk patterns and that those who control use also bear the risks, you will prefer a greater range of private property.

Chapter 5
Information Costs and Achievement of Exchanges

Many prices are fixed, or are so sluggish and unresponsive that we see shortages; commonplace signs are waiting for a table in a restaurant or for a seat on an airplane or at the hair stylist. At other times, sellers often have unused, spare capacity—vacant tables at a restaurant, empty seats on an airplane or at the hair stylist, and unemployment. Why don't prices respond quickly enough to adjust the amounts supplied and demanded to one another? And why don't resources move more quickly to their new highest-valued uses? These real-world phenomena seem to throw our analysis so far open to doubt.

But they do not. The reasons for the apparent discrepancies are some assumptions that we deliberately made to simplify our analysis. These assumptions were:

1. Sellers can detect and respond to persisting changes in demand and supply.

2. For all goods there are exchangeable private-property rights.

3. There is no charity.

4. There are no public goods—goods that can be consumed by some without the supply for others being diminished.

5. No seller has a sufficiently large share of the market to significantly affect the prices at which he or she could buy (wholesale) or sell (retail).

6. It costs potential buyers nothing to obtain full information about the availability and performance of goods and suppliers' services.

7. Contracts can be drawn up, entered into, and enforced costlessly.

These simplifying assumptions permit easy *and valid* exposition of such features of our economy as how gains are obtained from exchange, how demand and supply interact, how price allocates supplies among the many demanders, and why shortages occur and how they differ from a simple reduction in supply. To comprehend many other features of a free-market economy and to understand why prices and resources respond less than instantaneously to changes in supply or demand, we must relax the assumptions and introduce more real-world details. Doing so, however, does not upset any of the results of our prior applications. In this chapter we abandon the first four simplifying assumptions. In later chapters we shall modify the others.

Buffer Stocks, Waiting Lines, and Price Responses to Demand Uncertainty

Every day consumers' purchases fluctuate in random temporary ways. Neither consumers nor suppliers know exactly who will want to buy how much of what, or when. Such information would be so costly to obtain that it is impossible to get. Instead people devise means to adapt to, or accommodate, those transient, unpredictable fluctuations. The main way that suppliers do so is by holding inventories. Consider the options facing a newsstand owner who sells a daily average of 100 copies—but not exactly 100 per day. He could: (1) ask buyers to commit themselves to their demand in advance by reserving a copy; (2) buy fewer than 100 copies and rarely have any unsold copies; (3) buy more than 100 copies and usually have copies left over; (4) buy one copy at a time, ordering each as the preceding one is sold by using a special-delivery service.

The newsstand operator's options are limited by customers' preferences: Customers prefer instant availability from inventories, even at a slightly higher, but predictable, *full price* of the newspaper. (The full price must be higher to cover the costs of the seller's ending up with unsold extra copies.) The higher price to customers may be solely a higher money price, or may take the form of a smaller newspaper or fewer retailers. But this option of higher full price is less costly than the sellers' attempting to obtain complete advance information or making *instantaneous* and unpredictable price adjustments to momentary demand changes. In other words, holding seemingly idle or unemployed inventories can be an economical use of resources.

Sellers don't instantly and temporarily change prices every moment to eliminate all shortages, that is, to instantly clear the market of every excess amount demanded. Imagine a restaurant in which the price of food was adjusted instantly to avoid any waiting. Because prices would be less predictable, planning by buyers would be less useful. Accepting the prospect of having to wait a bit can permit a more predictable price and better consumer planning. If sellers hold inventories or provide greater capacity to handle transient random peak demands, the results are more predictable prices, shorter waiting times, better planning by customers, and lower costs to customers. On the other hand, a sufficiently large reserve capacity to cater instantly to every peak demand would be very expensive.

The value of the waiting or service time is, as we have seen before, part of the *full price*. Some goods require more time for purchase or consumption than do others. Haircuts may cost $10 and about half an hour, whereas one can buy $10 worth of gasoline in about one minute. Thus, the *full* price of the haircut is greater than that of the gasoline. A round of golf may cost $20 and four hours, while $20 of nightclub entertainment takes only one hour. The money price of a trip to

Europe by air may exceed the price of a trip by boat, yet the full price by air may be less because it takes less time.

Some restaurants and stores give quicker service at a higher money price but with a lower full price to buyers who value time more highly. People with high hourly wage earnings (such as surgeons or consulting economists) demand and get quicker service than do people with low hourly earnings. Patients wait to be seen by a doctor unless their time is more valuable than the doctor's. Charity patients wait and wait and wait for doctors' services. The more a buyer rewards the supplier with money in return for not having to wait, the more likely is the supplier to provide reserve capacity, and the market-clearing full price will include a smaller proportion of nonmoney costs to money payments. But it won't necessarily eliminate *all* chance of some waiting time.

Because money and waiting time can be partially substituted for one another as components of the full price, sellers can adjust capacity and techniques to conform to different customers' preferences. Some suppliers offer less risk of waiting but at higher or less predictable prices, whereas others offer more uncertainty about waiting time but at lower or more predictable prices.

Reserve Capacity It is commonly thought that an industry is sick if it has excess capacity that is almost never fully used (for example, barber shops and service stations). But this is not necessarily true. Does Palm Beach have too many hotel rooms because many of them are empty during the summer, or are there too many ski resorts because they are idle most of the time? To understand why some resources are idle sometimes, let us look at rental housing.

An inventory of empty apartments is not necessarily an idle or wasted good. Because housing is produced in advance at a less rapid, and therefore more economical, rate, and because a reserve is held in case demand increases at random times, both holders of housing and consumers economize. Although housing services per unit may be somewhat higher in price (to cover the costs of vacancies the owner is holding), those vacancies allow lower search costs and enable people to move without committing themselves long in advance to moving. We could reduce housing costs by building fewer apartments and thus having fewer vacancies, but that would force people to plan more of their activities well in advance and prevent them from adapting quickly to new situations. (Imagine what it would be like to try to move in a community that had just as many apartments as families so that every apartment was always rented.) On average, the inventory of empty housing that enables people to conveniently search for and move into different housing is small: About 3% of the rent paid by apartment dwellers covers the cost of that vacant apartment space.

Fire escapes, fire hydrants, first-aid kits, and smoke alarms would be wasteful only if complete information about the future—such as whether, or when, a fire or an injury would occur—were free in advance, or if instant production, adjustment, and information were no more costly than slower adjustment or gathering of information. But because instant adjustments do cost more, we reserve what might be miscalled idle resources.

The Illusion That Cost Determines Price

Many prices appear to be set by costs instead of by competition among demanders. To see how appearances can be deceptive let us look at the demand for meat. Suppose that for some reason people's demand for meat increases. At existing prices consumers demand more than they did. As sales increase, butchers' inventories are unexpectedly depleted. Normally, a butcher, like any retailer, carries an inventory larger than the average of daily sales, for the reason we have just examined: to accommodate transient increases in sales without running out of stock or having to raise prices late on days of large demand. Inventories help to assure immediate supply at more predictable prices.

Furthermore, virtually no seller sells exactly the same amount of good day after day. Although the basic consumption demand has not necessarily changed, amounts purchased in any one day vary at random around some stable *average*. Thus, because sellers do not regard every change in sales from one day to the next as a persisting change in consumption rates or demand schedule, sellers will not immediately detect an actual shift in demand. (Because we are looking only at how prices in fact respond to changes in demand, we are deliberately ignoring important ways in which change in demand affects production and employment.)

No butcher knows instantly that the consumption demand has risen for the community as a whole. Any butcher knows only that he or she has sold more meat at the existing price. The increase may be transient, or may represent some other butcher's loss of business. Nevertheless, the butcher will buy more meat than usual the next day to restore the abnormally low inventory, and will buy even more if he or she believes that sales will continue at the higher level. If the aggregate demand for meat has increased, the aggregate of butchers will increase purchases from the packers, the wholesale suppliers, and the increase will persist.

Packers, like retailers, keep inventories as buffers against sales fluctuations. Packers restore their inventories by instructing their cattle buyers (who travel among cattle raisers, fatteners, and stockyards) to buy more than usual. But if all the packers are restoring inventories, not enough cattle are being supplied to meet the increased amount demanded *at the old price*. Some packers can-

not get the amount requested unless they boost their offer prices to persuade cattle raisers to sell steers to them instead of to other packers. Each buyer, although acting independently, offers a higher price along with every other buyer. The cattle raisers let the buyers bid against each other until the price rises to a point where the packers do not want to buy more meat than is available.

We could describe these events graphically by saying that the demand curve for cattle is shifted upward, leading to a higher market-clearing price for cattle. That higher price sends each packer back up along his increased demand curve, so each packer buys less than would have been bought at the old price. The price rises high enough to reduce the total amount demanded to match the amount supplied. Each packer must pay a higher price for cattle to avoid getting less than before. Competition among packers raises the price before cattle production can be increased to meet that new demand. But cattle raisers will then begin to incur greater costs to increase production of cattle up to that amount at which the expected costs match the expected price of cattle. In this way, prices, which depend on demand and supply, also determine how much cost can be incurred to produce more.

Cattle raisers increase their wealth by the higher selling prices. To packers this is a rise in *costs*. Yet the cost to cattle raisers did not increase; nor did the costs of getting cattle to market, of slaughtering, or of distributing meat. The higher price paid by packers to cattle raisers is a result of the increased consumer demand, which is expressed all the way back through to producers, where it becomes evident as higher prices for the existing amount of cattle and for resources used to produce more cattle.

As the price of cattle is bid up (meaning higher *costs* to the packers), packers charge a higher price in order to allocate meat to retail butchers whose demands for meat have increased. Retail butchers, in turn, post higher prices to consumers (which can be sustained only because consumers' demand had initially increased). When consumers complain about the higher price, butchers, in honesty, say that it isn't their fault. The price they pay to get meat has gone up. Every butcher can say, "I never raise prices until my costs go up." And the packers can honestly say the same thing.

Consumers who want to know who is to blame for the higher prices of meat can look in the mirror behind the butcher's counter. They might then say to each other, "If you didn't want more meat, I could have more." The exchange system glosses over this facet of competition among buyers. The buyer-seller negotiations make it appear as if the higher price of meat were caused by the suppliers—the butchers, packers, and farmers—instead of by consumers. For example, in a period of inflation consumer prices appear to rise because costs are rising; but fundamentally what has happened is that a large increase in the money stock has increased consumers' demand for goods, and that larger demand has run up against limited stocks of productive resources with a resultant rise in prices. Inflation is a phenomenon we explore in Chapter 19.

Private-Property Rights

Prices are guides to how goods are allocated only if people have incentives to make offers and to respond to them, as expressed by prices. If exchangeable private-property rights in goods are weak or ill-defined, prices will have less influence.

What do we mean by private property rights? A person's **private-property rights** are the expectation that what one decides to do with certain resources will be effectively carried out, or realized. The greater the probability that those expectations will be upheld (by custom, social ostracism, or government punishment of violators), the stronger are private-property rights. In addition, private-property rights contain the right to exchange use rights with other people. In sum, two essential elements of private property are the right to authorize uses and the salability of that right.

To the extent that rights to goods and services are well defined, enforceable, and inexpensive to transfer (by sale), the market-exchange system, operating through prices, for controlling the use of goods is effective. If, in using my goods, I usurp your authority over your goods, I violate your rights to your goods. I can legally throw a rock through your window or tear down your house and dump garbage on your land if, and only if, I first obtain the rights from you.

In the following sections we will explore some cases in which the rights have not been well defined or, if defined, have not been clearly assigned to particular people, with the result that disputes can arise as to whom the rights belong. Moreover, in some cases those rights, even though well defined and assigned, may be too expensive to enforce in every respect. If I burn garbage or emit smoke, foul smells, or airborne acids over your land, I am using resources whose ownership is not well defined or identified. When I drive my scooter with a blaring exhaust that sends sound vibrations across your property, I momentarily detract from its physical features. When a steel mill uses water and discharges water of lower quality or when a refinery dirties the air, these acts use and change the characteristics of resources that no one seems to own. This is often called "excessive" pollution, "nuisance," "invasion of privacy," "tort," "theft," or an "externality." They all are results of the absence of well-defined, enforceable private-property rights to goods and labor services, which are necessary rights if a market-exchange price system is to operate as outlined in the preceding chapters.

Consider first the problem of defining

or identifying rights. We are slowly learning how to monitor and exchange rights to radio and TV airwaves. Airlines are increasingly able to monitor planes with sufficient accuracy to measure, police, and exchange rights to moving cocoons of airspace. Water is still a relatively expensive item to control in its natural state, though not after it has been captured in reservoirs, canals, or pipes. Since a resource that is not controlled by private-property rights will be less likely to be controlled by market prices and exchange, you can be sure that if the supply of water should fall, say because of a drought in some area, shortages and political control over the use of the water will be increased, rather than letting sufficiently higher market prices allocate the scarcer water, as is done with lumber, meat, and so on. Therefore we forecast with great confidence that in the near future (a decade or so) the supply of water will not increase as rapidly as our growing population, and so the marginal value of water will rise. But it is unlikely that the price of water will be used to allocate and move water from area to area, or be used to control amounts used. Instead, shortages will be created, and political controls on water will be used more extensively than they are now. Like the oil situation of the 1970s, the "water shortage" will be the issue in the 1980s and 1990s—this time a result of a failure to use market prices because of an inability to assign enforceable private-property rights to water.

Where technology and the advance of law have enabled specification of enforceable property rights, exchange through market prices has been more common, even for the control of air, water, streets, airspace, radio and TV frequencies, and that great treasure bed, the ocean floor. As the effective range of surveillance over the ocean increases, greater distances from the shore are being claimed by the nearest country—as has already been done for oil rights hundreds of miles into the North and Caribbean seas. Peru, Chile, Mexico, and Iceland are claiming and selling rights to fish within their claims to the ocean as far as 200 miles from their shores. Such claims give some incentive to conserve ocean resources rather than permit overfishing, just as such rights now do for land use. Wars have occurred as nations attempt to establish their property rights to land and oceans. The status of claims to Antarctica is unclear, and the future will probably see painful attempts to clarify or establish rights.

Nevertheless, though private-property rights may be well defined and assigned to specified persons, making exchanges of rights and collecting payments may be more costly than the value of the use of the resources. For example, the use of some parking spaces costs more to monitor than the value of the parking spaces, with the result that the landowner will have no incentive to rent space for parking. Either he gives away parking rights or lets no one park. Pricing will occur only if devices are available (for example, parking meters with police enforcement) to lower the costs of collection and policing, or if the demand rises sufficiently to raise the exchange value above those costs. For example, where labor to enforce exchanges and to monitor uses is cheaper relative to the value of the land's use, as in Europe compared to the United States, or in U.S. cities compared to suburbs, our analysis would imply that parking attendants are more likely to be used to collect fees and police the space; and that is in fact what happens. To take another example, if theater ushers' wages are high relative to admission values for some theatrical performance, fewer ushers will be used. Seats will more likely be sold at a uniform price and selected first come, first served. In Europe, or in "live" theaters, where wages are lower relative to theater-seat values, a greater variety of seat prices exists. Different quality seats within the theater will be monitored and priced with a higher money price that equilibrates demand with supply. In the full-price equilibrium, money will be more important and nonmoney costs such as waiting will be less.

Parking meters permit cheaper metering and monitoring of street parking, and are more likely to be used where parking-space value is high enough to warrant the costs of installing and operating the meters. As yet, no one has devised an economical way for drivers to use the parking lane as a traveling lane by bidding for that space from those who want to park, and so such transactions do not take place. However, we are not helpless; as the excess of value for driving over parking becomes larger, political controls via legislation are used to prohibit parking in curb lanes during "rush" hours.

At the present time a center of intense interest and great monetary stakes is the use of devices to protect and monitor exchangeable private-property rights to television programs. Economical cables and decoders now permit pricing.

In summary, when cheaply enforceable transferability and well-identified, secure rights do not prevail, the market-exchange and price system for controlling uses of goods is weakened. Other forms of competition and control are more likely. Resort may be made to courts or even to wars. The western states take one another to court in disputes over water from various watersheds, but they don't fight about the use of forest land, oil, iron ore, coal, or other natural resources—because rights to them are privately owned and are transferable. If California, Arizona, Utah, and Colorado were separate nations, the conflict of interests over the water in the Colorado River would not unlikely result in war. Cities upstream dump sewage, and cities downstream bear the consequences; so each city competes for better water by building pipelines farther upstream nearer the source of the purer water.

POLLUTION, SAFETY, AND PROPERTY RIGHTS

More Steel or More Clean Water Analytic attention to the role of transferable property rights will help clarify some current issues emanating from what is called the problem of environmental pollution. Imagine a steel mill making steel and dumping chemicals into a nearby stream, reducing the cleanliness and value of the water downstream. The analysis is clarified in Figure 5–1, which is based on the principles used in Chapter 3 to explain the gains from trade. The heights of the line labeled *DD* represent the marginal values of steel production enabled by use of water. The quantity of water used in steel production is measured along the horizontal axis. But that water could have been used in other ways, with values shown by the line *WW*. Starting from the upper right and going to the lower left, it shows the decreasing marginal values at greater *amounts* of fresher water in nonsteel uses. With maximum steel production and little clean water, the value of the marginal unit of steel is lowest, given by the height of *DD* at the extreme right of the diagram. The value of the marginal amount of clean water sacrificed to make that unit of steel exceeds the value of that marginal unit of steel. An amount of steel production greater than at *X* is not worth the cleaner water sacrificed.

The total use value to consumers of the steel is indicated by the area under the whole demand curve for steel, *DD*, out to whatever is the amount being produced, whereas the total use value to consumers of cleaner water is the area under the demand curve for water, *WW*, reading from right to left. The figure makes clear that maximum production of steel would sacrifice clean water worth more than some of the extra steel. So the steel output that maximizes the value of steel plus the value of water is the steel output *X*.

But how can that amount be achieved in

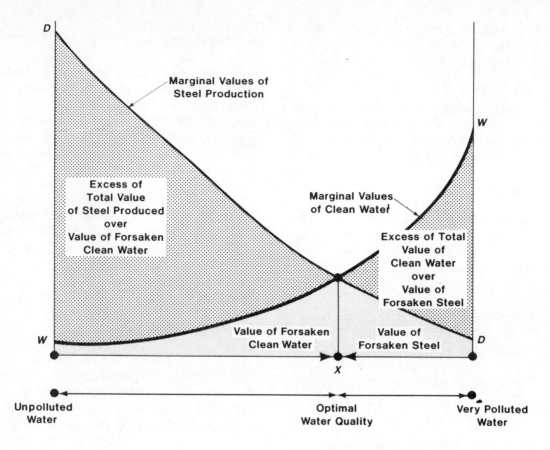

Figure 5-1.

OPTIMAL TRADEOFF
BETWEEN OUTPUTS OF TWO GOODS

More of one good can be produced only if there is less
of another good. That optimal combination is *X*. At any
point to the left of *X* people would be willing to have less
unpolluted water to have more steel; to the right of
X people would be willing to have less steel to
have more unpolluted water.

an economy where the water cannot be
bought and sold in a free market? A government agency may stipulate an allowable maximum amount of discharge of pollutants—in
effect giving the steel consumers the right to
that much clean water. Or the government
could levy a tax—that is, charge a fee—on
the right to discharge chemicals into the
stream. If the price charged exactly equaled
the marginal value of a unit more of cleanliness of water at the intersection of the two
curves *DD* and *WW*, the steel producers
would produce the quantity of steel corresponding to that intersection. It would do so
because its cost of steel now includes the lost
value of the water it dirties—a cost that it
formerly could ignore if no one owned the
stream. In effect, the political authorities
take control of the water and sell its use to
the steel producers at a price (the tax) that

reflects its value as cleaner water. If that fee or price is too low, too much steel will be produced. If it is too high, more clean water will be available than people would want if instead they could have more steel.

Some people complain that such a tax or sale of right for discharging water gives the steel mills a license to pollute. That is correct, and is exactly the same as your getting a "license" to eat meat when you buy meat. The pertinent issue is not what the payment is called, but what the appropriate price is to get the appropriate amounts of steel *and* cleanliness of water.

A third, hypothetical way is to assign private-property rights to the water and permit its owners to sell it to users. The value of cleaner water would be made evident to sellers by the price that consumers offered for different qualities of water. And the value of the steel would be evident by what the steel-mill operators, as middlemen between consumers and water owners, would be willing to pay for different amounts of water for their use. The water owners could simply compare these two values and sell rights to use or pollute the water up to the amount of steel at which the steel mill (reflecting consumers' value of steel) is willing to pay more for the water than the consumers would pay for fresher water. The result will be the situation X—the amount of discharge that maximizes the consumption value of the output of steel plus cleaner water. This result could be achieved *if* private-property rights in water were *cheaply salable* and *controllable*. But they are not.

Another alternative procedure is to permit steel mills to use water but require them to clean it before discharging it so that both more steel and more clean water can be had. However, cleaning the water uses resources that could have been used to make other goods. There is no escape from the need to balance more of this against more of that: We can't have more of everything. Each desired good has a cost—the best alternatives

sacrificed—and to talk and try to act as if that were not true is to make yourself worse off.

Worker Safety   When the government imposes employee safety standards in coal mines or makes the mine operators liable for miners' injuries or loss of health, the supply of labor willing to work at that safer level of work becomes larger and depresses the equilibrating wage. Workers pay for that safety with a lower salary. If the safety levels were a lot lower, the supply of labor would be smaller, and wages would be higher. If workers had the right to renegotiate any politically imposed safety standards with mine operators, they could trade some salary for greater safety, or vice versa, reaching the preferred point—regardless of the initial level of safety.

Allocation under Rights Other Than Private Property: Nonprofit Institutions

Even in the United States, where the economy is predominantly a free market, not all business firms are based on private property. A **nonprofit corporation** has assets (forms of wealth) that are not owned by anyone who can distribute gains to themselves or sell those assets as they can sell private property. All proceeds must be spent in the enterprise to further its specified purposes. Most private colleges are nonprofit institutions, as are many hospitals. Almost all religious and fraternal organizations and unions are nonprofit organizations. In nonprofit corporations the operators have less incentive to heed the marketable value of the enterprise's activities.

Nonprofit corporations—for example, RAND Corporation, Brookings Institution, Harvard University, and nonproprietary hospitals—have incentives to provide services in more expensive, manager-beneficial ways. Costs are higher, because no one could claim the potential savings from lower costs or better operation as effectively as could owners of a private, for-profit organization. Managers are better able to indulge their personal predilections in choosing employees, even choosing those who are less productive over others who could be hired at the same salaries. For example, they might hire prettier secretaries or only members of their own ethnic group, or not hire as many members of the opposite sex. Performance standards for employees, and for their dismissal, are less guided by the market values of services; tenure is stronger than for employees at equal salaries in private, for-profit businesses. Furniture and equipment will be more luxurious. Such are the implications of economic analysis.

Nonprofit institutions and government agencies are less likely to charge market-clearing prices for goods and services. Shortages or surpluses are therefore more likely. So is discrimination among buyers by the use of nonprice criteria. This can be summarized in this statement: The market-clearing *full price* of a nonprofit institution is guided more with a nonmoney price and less with a money price than is a private-property enterprise.

Philanthropy

Every year billions of dollars are donated as philanthropy, or charity. Concerts, museums, and libraries are financed by donors wanting more of the kinds of cultural activity such institutions provide. Almost every college is supported by people who want to give education to young people. Because the tuition price is below the market-clearing price, applicants must compete more on nonprice bases.

An economic analysis of charity or gifts may seem contradictory. How can people give gifts if they are assumed to be selfish? Remember, however, we did *not* assume pure selfishness. Each of us can be, and is, concerned about other people's well-being. I would prefer other people to be richer than poorer, even if it cost me something. The larger my wealth relative to the poor, the greater my willingness to contribute to the poor, just as a larger amount of candy increases my willingness to give up candy for Cokes. This implies that the richer contribute more charity, and they do. Furthermore, I would be induced to give still more by *matching grants*, because each dollar I give up would then direct more than a dollar to the poor.[1]

WHO GAINS WHAT FROM A GIFT

A gift is equivalent to a sale at a price lower than the market-clearing price. The effects are complex but can be seen if we apply our demand theory and personal-value concepts.

Suppose you were admitted to a college that charged a tuition below what it cost the college to provide your education. To analyze the effects on you, use the following five concepts and associated values (the values given are assumed for illustration only):

A. The cost to the college of education = $1000

B. The tuition charged = 700

C. How much you would have spent for tuition at another college if tuition here were full-cost = 800

D. The full personal value you attach to the educa-

---

[1]Income tax deductions for gifts are another way to reduce the donor's costs of giving money to other people—but that also means other taxpayers pay more to offset the donor's reduced tax payments.

tion here at the below-cost tuition college = 1450

E. The personal value you attach to the education you would have obtained if the below-cost tuition had not been available = 1300

Taking these figures, we compute:

1. The cost of the subsidy borne by the subsidizer: A − B = $1000 − $700 = $300

2. The release of cash spending power to the recipient: C − B = $800 − $700 = $100

3. The greater personal value of education to the student: D − E = $1450 − $1300 = $150

Under these circumstances the consumer's surplus achieved by the student who accepts the subsidy is the student's total personal value minus the tuition: $1450 − $700 = $750. The total personal value of the education at the other college minus the full-cost tuition ($1300 − $800) is only $500. So the subsidized education is chosen, because it costs the student $100 less, and also is worth $150 more in educational value to that student.

The total value of the gains to the student in cash and increased education is $250 (items 2 and 3: C − B plus D − E), but this is $50 less than the subsidizer's cost, $300 (item 1: A − B). From the student's point of view, the subsidizer wasted $50 because the student would rather have had a $300 gift in cash to spend than $100 in cash plus $150 in better education. The subsidizer may think the value of the increased education to the recipient is greater than the student does. By that subsidy the donor has induced the student to act in a way the donor prefers. But the student would be made just as well off, *in his or her own way of judging*, if the cash gift had been $250. From the recipient's point of view every gift in kind will involve some waste—if the gift induces the recipient to make life-style changes that would not have been made had payment been strictly in cash.

Compare these results with those for another student with the following preferences. The second student is assumed to value the low-cost education at $1075, and would have spent $1100 on education if the alternative were full-cost tuition, which the student values at $1200. Given these data, we can compute that the student gets a $400 cash release (C − B = $1100 − $700) but a reduction in value of education attained of −$125 (D − E = $1075 − $1200). So the student ends up with less education but more money for other things, a total gain, as valued by the student, of $400 − $125 = $275, which cost the college tuition subsidizer $300—a $25 waste from this student's point of view, though not necessarily in the subsidizer's scheme of things.

The foregoing analysis can be shown to imply that a grant of money is more desirable, dollar for dollar, from the recipient's point of view, than are gifts or subsidies of particular goods. This provokes the question of why so much charity, both private and government, is in "kind" or a subsidy for particular goods—for example, education, food, or housing—instead of cash paid to people who can then buy what they deem most appropriate. Is it that donors want to change the life style of the recipients? Or that recipients can't be trusted to act in ways that the donors consider sensible? Or because the suppliers of subsidized goods are enriched by subsidizing demand for their services? Economic analysis has not yet satisfactorily answered these questions. But the analysis it does provide, as explained by means of the student-tuition example, helps reveal consequences that appear to be widely ignored. We take up a few of these in the following paragraphs; some are intentional and some appear to be unintentional.

FOREIGN AID

Every year the U.S. government grants aid (gifts) to some foreign governments, ostensibly for specific purposes. If the Egyptian government is given $10 million to build a dam, what has Egypt gained? Suppose Egypt had intended to build the dam anyway, financing it by domestic saving. Then the gift for the dam releases some income of the Egyptian government for other things. The gift, purportedly for a dam, is actually usable for general purposes; the Egyptian politicians simply have $10 million more than otherwise. Conceivably, the Egyptian government could lower taxes, thus leaving Egyptians with more income for personal consumption. Or the government itself could spend the extra funds.

UNINTENTIONAL CHARITY

Intent does not necessarily determine what happens. For example, to operate a new television station you must obtain a license from the Federal Communications Commission (FCC). The value of a license is far, far more than its price (which is zero)—often millions of dollars more. Many applicants appeal to the FCC for a license.[2] The law creating the FCC forbids allocating channels first come, first served (although it was done for radio in the early 1920s). Instead, the FCC chooses among applicants. The applicant must show he is "fit" to operate a station and that his community "needs" another station—over

protestations of the owners of existing stations, the value of which might fall. Money that would have been paid to the government under money price competition is instead devoted to other forms of competition for the commission's favor. Because millions of dollars are at stake, millions are spent in the competition.

What criteria do commissioners use for allocating licenses? Respectability, moral reputation, dedication to public service, and education. A newspaper publisher is an attractive candidate for a license, being experienced in collecting and disseminating news. But an applicant who doesn't promise religious programs, and intends to play mainly jazz and Western shows, with few—if any—cultural, political, or news programs or public information, has only a small chance. The applicant must detect the preferences of the commissioners. Although an applicant must not offer outright bribes to the commissioners or their staff, some kinds of behavior favor granting of a license: If in the past the applicant hired some of the FCC technical staff to operate other radio or television stations, or is a former member of Congress or employs one as legal counsel before the FCC, the applicant clearly recognizes able people and could therefore successfully operate a television station. Neither the government nor the winning applicant receives the full value of the broadcast license. Instead, part is dissipated in paying legal fees and publicity costs, in producing the kinds of programs the FCC commissioners prefer, and in paying other expenses incurred while striving for the license. Thus, even though the money price of the license is zero, the full price of getting it is substantial—not to mention the costs of the losing applicants. The same basic story applies to acquiring cable television rights in cities, where the city politicians decide who wins, as you can confirm with almost daily news stories of competitors jockeying for those rights.

The value of the license as a gift can be

---

[2]The number of channels that can be used at one time is not a technologically fixed constant. It depends upon the kind of receivers and transmitters used. More expensive and sensitive equipment greatly increases the number of available channels; and the possibilities with transmission by cable are enormous.

measured in the rise of the price of stock in a company receiving a license. Fortunately for station owners, this wealth gain *is* transferable: They can sell that license to other people. (It's inadvisable to be so crude as to sell immediately the "nude" license alone, without broadcasting equipment.) This analysis does not assume that the FCC commissioners act irresponsibly. They act as responsibly as anyone who is constrained by law to allocate a good by means other than the highest money bid.

There are many more examples of unintentional gifts. Competitive money prices are not used initially to allocate licenses to operate (a) liquor stores; (b) taxis; (c) banks; and (d) sugar-beet, dairy, and tobacco farms. All these rights are salable once they have been awarded. For example, in New York City the "shield," the symbol of a right to operate one taxi, sells for $60,000 or more (in 1982).

NONTRANSFERABLE GIFTS

Some gifts cannot be reallocated or resold: for example, the right to enroll in college or medical school; to enter the United States; to join some unions; to adopt a child; to play golf on a publicly owned golf course; to camp in a national park; or, for children, to ride a school bus for free. When children are given free bus rides to school, who gains what? Lacking free busing, the parents would have either provided transportation for their children or made them walk. Those who are now relieved of buying transportation convert all the subsidy into a general wealth increase. The other parents get a gain not in *general* wealth, but in the *particular* form of better transportation for their children.

To the extent that recipients already purchase the services given to them, gifts might as well be resalable or given as money by the donors. If I am given a case of Coca-Cola each month by some kind-hearted person who thinks I am thereby induced to drink more Cokes, the donor should realize that because I already consume a case a month, I will reduce my buying of Cokes and use the released wealth for other expenditures.

Dollars for What?   Another, perhaps less noticeable, example of substitutability is that in which someone asks for funds for a special purpose. For example, it is common to see a city council raise taxes to finance more police protection, knowing that people want more such protection. But the city council could have reduced expenditures on other activities in order to finance more police protection, and taxes would not have to be increased. If taxes are increased, it is clear that they don't finance more police protection; they enable the other expenditures to continue at higher levels than if the taxes had not been raised. The higher tax, by substituting for funds that could perhaps have been diverted from other activities, is therefore financing more of *all* activities, not just police protection. What the newly collected funds or income are spent for is not indicative of what extra activity is made possible. Money is fungible.

Public Goods

We know that when costs of specifying, enforcing, and exchanging property rights are low enough, prices in market exchanges will direct resources to higher-valued uses and will also equate the amounts demanded and supplied. However, there is a class of goods, called *public* goods, for many of which these costs are prohibitively high. A public good is one which is capable of being used by many persons at the same time without reducing the amount available for any other person. You and I can view a television program without reducing viewing by other people. The total amount produced can be used by everyone. No one's use reduces how much other people can have. Take another example of a public good—an idea; for example, the one that relates the length of the circumference of a circle to the diameter. Once the idea is known, anyone can use it without affecting how much other people can use it. A melody, once created, can be sung by anyone without reducing other people's use. Many inventions are based on ideas which, once discovered, can be used by you without reducing their availability to other people. In contrast, what are called *private* goods are those which we have been analyzing up till now—goods for which use by one person does mean less to others. If I eat a hot dog, no one else can eat it, too. The distinction between public and private goods is not always an all-or-nothing distinction. Some goods are a mixture. For example, a band concert can be heard by many people, or national defense may be provided, but some people will get more than others. If I stand nearer the band at the concert, someone has to stand a little farther away. Both the band concert and national defense have some degree of private and public goods in them. However, in order to simplify introduction to the problem, we shall be assuming purely one or the other.

Just as for private goods, a problem for public goods is to determine how much to produce and who shall pay the costs of production. But unlike private goods there is no point in charging a price just to decide who will get to use it once it is produced, since no person's use affects how much other people can also have. Each can always have all that is produced. Charging a price would be pointless *for that purpose*. On the other hand, there is the task, as stated earlier, of deciding how much of the public good to produce and who will pay the costs. If no price is charged, how will the worth of producing it be revealed? After all, if a person is not threatened with exclusion from use unless he pays, the value to that user will not be revealed or tested. And how will funds be

collected to pay for the costs of production? This is the dilemma: Charging a price for an existing public good is wasteful if that excludes any potential user; but without a price how can revelation of its value be induced, and who will pay?

If it were possible to know how much each person valued its full use, each could be charged a fee less than that full value, and then the person could be allowed to use all that was produced. For example, if I thought some television program could be produced that would be worth $30 to me, and you thought it would be worth $20 to you, the aggregate of the total use value to the two of us would be $50. If the program could be produced for less than $50, it would pay to produce the program. How can a potential producer get you and me to reveal its value to us if we don't have to pay once it is produced? And how could the producer be rewarded? If he could produce the program and then exclude any nonpayer, that would be appropriate so long as he doesn't exclude any viewer by charging more than the program's value to that user—$30 to me and $20 to you. If I were charged more than $30 my viewing would be prevented, and that would be wasteful since no other viewer would have been displaced by my viewing the program. But it is important to be able to exclude nonpayers in order to force them to provide a measure of the value of the public good, but at the same time to charge a price to a viewer that is not so high as to actually exclude him. Neither of these is easy, if indeed possible. Excluding nonpayers of over-the-air broadcasting is difficult; and if that could be done, it is extremely difficult to negotiate the wide variety of prices that would avoid anyone's being excluded.

What has been done in attempts to overcome these problems? Sometimes the government announces a price (tax) for use of some public good and excludes any nonpayers who use the public good. For example, in England a tax on television sets is used which authorizes people to look at programs. Nonpayment by any viewers will mean exclusion from society if they are caught. Presumably the tax excludes so few users that it is a better solution than producing no programs at all. Yet even in this case there remains the problem of knowing which programs are worth producing. One way is to charge on a subscription or program basis, as is done with cable or some over-the-air television signal scrambling systems. Even these systems will exclude and hurt some viewers without thereby benefiting anyone else. However, the relevant alternative is not "perfection," but an action that is better. Maybe someone will find a better solution. Maybe, in the case of television, payment by advertisers is better even though that involves "imperfect" revelation and response to values by many users.

Other alternatives are creation of clubs or smaller groups to jointly finance some public good, such as more police protection for some neighborhood. While some neighbors might refuse to pay (but nevertheless benefit from the extra police protection, given the impossibility of excluding nonpayers from some benefits of the public good), it might be better even for those who do foot the bill, as compared to not having any extra protection at all. We must compare (a)—the value of having the good produced to those who pay as well as to those who don't minus the lost value to any who are unnecessarily excluded—against (b)—the lost value from not having the good at all.

Perhaps the most common device to meet this problem is the use of patents and copyrights for ideas. Patents, which give the inventor the exclusive right to the commercial use of an idea, enable the inventor to charge a price for its use. Though this certainly will restrict its commercial use, it does encourage more creation of such useful ideas. A balance must be considered. Similarly, to encourage the creation of written and musical works, copyrights are given to their au-

thors and composers, giving them the right to charge for their use even though the price charged will somewhat reduce the use of the idea. For example, most American composers of musical works belong to the American Society of Composers and Playwrights (ASCAP). That society helps enforce the copyrights of its members. It monitors all commercial television, radio, and theatrical programs and live concerts to ensure that commercial users pay a fee. This textbook is copyrighted and royalties are received by the authors, if someone buys it. The fact that the ideas are "tied" to a volume of bound paper in the form of a book makes it easier to charge a user of the ideas, because the user has to buy the book. The price of the book really covers a fee for the use of the ideas in the book. Of course, if several people read the same book, rather than just one person, it is difficult to collect a fee from all of them. (But it is not completely impossible if the book is resold from reader to reader, according to the principles explained in Chapter 6 in the discussion of the resale value of a book.) These fees certainly will in some cases dissuade some people from using the ideas, but, as you know, "perfection" is not the relevant alternative. The issue is whether this solution is better than any real alternatives.

Summary

1. Information about buyers' demands and sellers' offerings is not free; nor is the creation and operation of a market.

2. Full price is the money price plus any other costs incurred by the buyer. Not all of the full price necessarily accrues to the seller, though the money price—except for taxes—usually does.

3. Costs of information about buyers' and sellers' offers and the availability of goods are lowered by middlemen and their inventories.

4. Inventories reduce the seller's costs of maintaining a reliable supply and the buyer's costs of collecting information about products. Buffer inventories are not idle, unemployed, or wasteful uses of goods.

5. Transient shifts in demand are more economically met by holding inventories as buffer stocks. Shifts in demand will first become evident through changed inventories and output. Not until the shifts in demand are discovered to be permanent or long-lived will price change.

6. The more specific, secure, and transferable are private-property rights, the lower are marketing and exchange costs.

7. The particular person by whom property rights of a resource are held does not affect how they are used if the rights are cheaply transferable by sale at a price reflecting the highest-valued uses.

8. If private-property rights are too expensive to enforce or exchange, laws or government regulations tend to control uses of goods.

9. Where private-property rights are weak or nonexistent, less of the full price of a good is paid as money. So market values are given less heed in determining production, exchange, and allocation.

10. Use of resources and pollution are curtailed by private-property rights in those resources, because those rights can be sold to permit more or less use of the resource in accord with the resulting values.

11. An economic standard of the appropriate use of any resource is its value in use to the highest-valuing consumers.

12. Philanthropy and charity involve some combination of: (a) gifts in kind—transfers at less than the market price, (b) gifts of general purchasing power, and (c) some waste from the recipient's point of view (though not necessarily from the donor's). The recipient does not necessarily get a net gain because the competition to obtain charity may be equally costly.

13. Public goods are those of which one person may enjoy all that is available without diminishing the amount available to other people. A price could be charged for a public good as long as the price did not restrict consumption unnecessarily by reducing the amount any person would demand to less than the amount available. A price, although not necessary for rationing (because no rationing is needed), would guide production of more or less of the public good. The price relevant for this valuation is the sum of the individual prices charged various users.

Questions

*1. It has been estimated that carrying a spare tire on automobiles costs the public about $150,000,000 or about $5 per car. Is this a wasted or idle resource?

2. You are planning to build an apartment with eight units. You are told you can add a ninth unit for an extra cost of $60,000; if the extra unit is occupied all the time, it will be worth $80,000. If occupied three-fourths of the time you will break even.
   a. Would you build more apartments than you could expect to keep always rented?
   b. Would you consider apartments to be unemployed when not occupied?
   *c. Would you consider every unemployed apartment as a "waste"?

*3. a. Estimate the fraction of your wealth tied up in resources designed to ease your own unforeseeable changing demands or circumstances.
   b. How about the money you hold; items in the medicine cabinet; food kept at home in the refrigerator and freezer and in canned goods; general education? Are these idle, unemployed resources?

4. If there were a cheap enough method of metering the extent of each motorist's use of a street, would such use be more often rationed by a price system? Do you know of any such cases now in use? Name two.

5. Some allege that the number of parking spaces at shopping centers is excessive (that is,

more resources go into the provision of parking space than should). The space that "should" be available is the amount that would clear the market when a charge is levied to cover the construction and maintenance cost of the parking space. However, policing "pay" parking space involves a cost of collecting fees and prosecuting violators. Does that cost mean that it might be "better" to provide "too much" parking space than to provide the "right" amount rationed by price? Explain.

6. A owns and lives in a home near an area in which it is announced a series of 20-story apartments will be built. A sues to prevent the construction, arguing that it will create extra traffic hazards and congestion. In court, A proves the allegation correct. As the judge, how would you rule? Why?

*7. A owns a hillside lot with a beautiful view. B, owner of the lot just below, plants trees that grow up to 50 feet in height and block A's view. A asks B to trim the tops. B refuses. A offers to pay for the trimming. B refuses. A offers $300 in addition. B refuses; B asks for $2000. A sues for $5000 damages to the marketable value of his property.
  a. As the judge, how would you rule?
  b. If A had sued to force B to trim the trees, how would you have ruled?
  c. What will our courts really decide today in such suits?

8. The city of Palm Springs prohibits construction of any building whose shadow will fall on some other person's land between 9 A.M. and 3 P.M. Is that a restriction of private property or a strengthening of it? Explain.

9. A restaurant opens near an apartment building. The cooking smells annoy the tenants and the building owner sues for invasion of property rights.
  a. You are on the jury. Would you find in favor of the restaurant or the apartment owner?
  b. Would your decision depend upon whether or not the apartment owner lived in the affected apartments?

10. "The fact that some airplanes collide is evidence that there is too little air traffic control."

Evaluate. (Hint: What would it cost to avoid all risk of air collision?)

11. A city passed a zoning ordinance prohibiting the owner of a large parcel of land from constructing homes on it because of a fear that the noise of a nearby airport owned by the city would be so disturbing to the new tenants that airport operations would have to be curtailed.
  a. Whose rights were being curtailed by the zoning ordinance?
  b. Under the definition of private-property rights, were the landowner's rights being impaired?
  *c. Can you suggest some other solution to the problem?
  *d. If you were a taxpayer in that town and did not live near the airport what solution would you have voted for?
  *e. If you owned vacant land near the airport, what solution would you advocate? If your vote is different in each case, do you think you are denying the morality of decisions by voting? Why?

12. Ralph Nader has complained that a person who relieves himself in the Detroit River is fined but industries that pollute the same river are not. He says also that muggers are punished but smoggers are not. These he cites as illustrating the inequities and irrationalities of our society and economy in their attitude toward big corporations. What is overlooked in his condemnation?

13. Camping fees in almost all state and national parks are so low that people want more space than is available.
  a. Why is the market price not at a market-clearing level?
  b. How much space would people want at a market-clearing price?

14. Two closely situated golf courses, one privately owned and one publicly owned, are both open to the public.
  a. Which do you think charges the higher price, and which do you think requires less or no advance reservation? Give your reasons.
  *b. Who is benefited in what respects by each course's policy?
  c. As land values in the vicinity of the

courses rise, which one do you think will be converted to housing or business first? Why?

15. Churches are typically nonprofit institutions. Can you think of a problem in allocation of church facilities that is solved without use of the price system?

*16. The college you now attend is almost certainly a nonprofit institution. Are any of its resources allocated at less than market-clearing prices? (Hint: Library facilities? Athletic facilities? Counseling? Course admission? Campus space?) Who gains by the power to select admissible students?

*17. a. Why do college athletic conferences chronically have an enormously larger number of people wanting tickets than are available for the playoffs and important games?
   b. Why are admission tickets for the Masters Golf Tournament (a most prestigious golf tournament) fewer than the number demanded by the public?

18. "When property rights interfere with human rights, property rights have to give in." What do you think this means?

19. "The imbalance between governmentally and privately provided services is evidenced by the fact that the family that vacations in its air-conditioned, power-braked, power-steered car passes through cities over dirty, badly paved, congested streets, not to mention the billboards obstructing the beauties of the countryside. When the family picnics with excellent food provided by private business, they must sit by a polluted stream and then spend the night in a public park that is a menace to health and morals and littered with decaying refuse. Private abundance and public poverty are facts that assail every observant person. A plentiful supply of privately produced goods and a shortage of publicly provided services is inescapable testimony to the lack of a social balance between private and governmentally provided services."

Without trying to prove whether there ought to be fewer or more governmentally provided services, tell why the argument, taken from a popular book advocating more governmentally provided services, is faulty. (Hint: Note the use of the term *shortage*. What does it suggest? How are governmentally provided services rationed?)

20. The *New York Times* sponsors a Christmas charity appeal and gives cash to selected poor families. The *Los Angeles Times* sponsors a charity each summer to send children of poor families to summer camp. To which of these forms of charity would you contribute more? Why? Do you think people who choose the other way are mistaken?

*21. In 1950 many public-welfare and charitable aid organizations refused to help families that owned a television set—no matter how poor the family might be. The welfare workers claimed they were not supposed to finance luxury. What would be your policy for poor families that own big cars?

22. Suppose you are running a university and the faculty is asking for higher salaries, some of which you will have to grant at the sacrifice of buildings and activities. Now, the Ford Foundation gives you $1 million, the income of which is to be allocated exclusively to faculty salaries. Who gains what?

*23. At many colleges faculty members are given free parking space even in areas where parking space is expensive.
   a. Who gains what?
   b. What would be the effect if faculty members could sell their spaces to students?

*24. Immigration-quota rights to the United States are priced at zero instead of being sold at a market-clearing price. Who gains what? Why are these rights not sold at the highest price?

*25. The U.S. Congress has agreements with governments of sugar-producing countries that they will import into the Unite States no more than a specified amount of sugar, thereby raising the price in the United States and increasing the total proceeds to foreign countries. (What is the elasticity of demand for sugar in the United States assumed to be?) Why would Congress agree to a law that raised costs to American consumers? Explain how this could be considered a form of foreign aid that does not appear in the federal government's budget record of taxes and expenditures.

26. There are reputed to be over 100,000 voluntary health and welfare organizations soliciting contributions from the general public, in addition to hundreds of individual hospital-support groups, as well as about 100,000 fraternal, civic, and veteran's organizations and some 300,000 churches that sponsor a variety of charitable activities, not to mention individual charities or gifts. A professor of public-health administration says, "It should not take over 100,000 voluntary agencies to provide private health and welfare services in the U.S." How many do you think it should take? Why?

27. Choose the correct statement: Public goods are those for which (a) several people can simultaneously enjoy the good; (b) it is impossible to exclude some consumers; (c) no consumer reduces the amount of the good available to others by his act of consuming the good; (d) prices should not be charged; (e) the government should provide the goods.

28. A theater performance with several simultaneous viewers is not a public good. Why?

*29. A melody is a public good. What is the best way to induce people to produce melodies?

30. "National defense is shared by everyone. Therefore, it is a public good and should be provided through government taxes and operation."
   a. Does greater antimissile defense for New York City mean greater defense for Houston?
   b. Do more public concerts on the west side of town mean more on the east side?
   c. Does it follow that public goods—those that give benefits to several people without less to anyone else—really do not exist?

31. "Even if it were costless to exclude non-payers from enjoying a public good, it does not follow that nonpayers necessarily should be excluded." Explain why.

32. "Financing public goods by taxes is a means of excluding nonpayers, for nontaxpayers will be put in jail." True or false?

*33. The following is orthodox Chinese Communist (Marxist) economic doctrine: "The goal of socialist production is not profit but the satisfaction of social needs. Goods must be produced as long as they are needed by society, even if a loss is incurred. This follows from the Marxist-Leninist tenet that, contrary to capitalism which seeks maximum profits, the objective of socialism is the maximum satisfaction of the material and cultural requirements of society. This fact gives the Communist Party, as representative of society, the right to determine society's requirements and what the economy should produce."

However, recently the Chinese Communists permitted some Chinese economists to publish the following ideas: "Profits should not be set against the goal of satisfying social needs. The profit level is the best measure of the effectiveness of management. This would mean that no enterprise would operate at a loss because the output would be curtailed unless the state valued its product sufficiently to raise its prices, and no enterprise would try to exceed the output plan at the expense of profits. There would be less need for political participation in enterprise management decisions, if prices were more realistic, in reflecting either market values or costs. The capitalist evil connotations of profits are not present in socialism, because under socialism profit takes on an entirely different character, where it is a good thing." Evaluate the last sentence.

34. "Economic theory is applicable only to a capitalist society." Evaluate.

35. In the 1970s Congress mandated that automobiles emit less exhaust pollution per mile of travel; it also mandated that autos get more miles per gallon. However, the smaller, lighter, less powerful cars that most satisfy these requirements are less safe in high-impact crashes than are larger cars. Is the reduced safety worth the reductions in pollution and fuel consumption?

When Congress earlier mandated safety requirements in cars, the cost of cars rose but there were no fewer accidents, because people drove faster knowing the cars gave extra protection. What is the optimal amount of safety that should be mandated by law?

Chapter 6
Capital Values, Future Yields, and Interest

Most goods are **durable goods**: They yield services not only now but also in the future. Such goods are also called **capital goods**. Apple trees yield future crops; oil wells produce a future stream of oil; land provides the future values of the uses to which it might be put; and automobiles yield travel services for several years. Each future service will have some market value—as, say, of apples from the apple tree have at harvest time. An apple tree will have a value that reflects the anticipated future values of those future apples. The price now of the apple tree is called a *present value*, or a *capital value*, to indicate that it is a price that incorporates in the present value the future anticipated service values. Both terms mean the same thing, so use them interchangeably.

How does the present price of a capital good depend on the future values of its future services? How does the price of an apple tree depend on the expected value of the future apple crops? How does the present value of, say, an acre of land depend on the expected future rents of that land? Or, how does the present value (that is, the price) of a share of common stock in a corporation depend on the expected stream of its future earnings? As we will see, the range of goods to which this question applies is very large and has much personal relevance.

Your first assumption might be that the capital value of a capital good is simply the total value of all those future services. After all, when one buys a tree or an acre of land, what is purchased is simply the right to those future services. Say, for example, an apple tree yields 300 apples each year for 20 years, and in each year every apple is worth 10¢. (We assume for simplicity that no inflation occurs.) The tree would appear to be worth $600 (300 apples at 10¢ per apple in each of 20 years). But that calculated value is too large for two reasons. The first reason is that one must care for the tree and harvest the apples; so if the apples are worth 10¢ each, let us suppose that after the costs of growing and harvesting apples are deducted each apple yields a *net* value of 5¢. That is $15 per year, instead of $30. Over 20 years that would appear to make the tree worth $300 rather than $600. But that, too, is too large a figure. Why is the tree's capital value less than the total of its future apple *net* values? (From now on, we simplify our exposition by ignoring other costs. Whenever we speak of a present or capital value we always mean the *net* value or *net* price over and above all other costs of production.) Let us investigate the second reason why the capital value of a good is not the sum of its future net values, but instead is less.

The Magic of Investment Productivity

Services that are available only in the future (called deferred services) are worth less than the same services available now. Why? Because present goods sometimes can be converted to even more valuable future goods. For example, some things, such as a tree, can grow over time. You have more wood next year than this year, and more in ten years than in nine years. A bushel of wheat can be converted to more than one bushel of wheat by next year.

We don't increase the output simply by saving or not consuming; that would merely not make the future any worse. People who think simply that we should conserve more—that is, consume less—overlook the fact that if resources are put to uses today that *transform* them into productive capital goods, they yield more future services than are given up now. That magic of turning "less now into more later" is called the *net productivity of investment*. In this chapter, we examine how net productivity of investment affects the demand for and prices of capital goods—which almost all our resources are. (We will

not in this chapter explain the factors that affect the rate of investment and its net productivity. That is done in Chapter 17.)

A simple example is, again, a growing tree. Cut it now, or wait and have more lumber next year than you would today. Drink fresh grape juice, or more valuable wine tomorrow. Instead of eating 100 bushels of wheat today, plant them and reap enough next year to pay the costs of all inputs used to make next year's wheat and still have more than the 100 bushels you started with, say 105, giving a net productivity of investment of five bushels, or 5% per year. The yield or gain from the net productivity of investment is called **interest**. Thus the five additional bushels of wheat are the interest on the investment of 100 bushels. **Investment** is that portion of current income that is not consumed and instead is used to create income for the future. Thus the 100 bushels of wheat were an investment. Because they grew to 105, the net productivity of investment, or interest, after allowing for all other costs, is 5% per year ($5/100 = .05$ or 5%).

Interest can be looked at in another way: It is the foreseeable growth in wealth that could be consumed without reducing one's stock of wealth below its initial amount. That is, if we invest 100 bushels and harvest 105, we can consume five bushels—the interest—and replant the other 100 so that our stock of wealth is undiminished. It is expected income from one's wealth. Interest, then, is the same thing as income from capital goods. The basic relationship can be expressed as follows:

(1) $$P(1 + r) = A$$

where P is the present amount invested, r is the annual percentage rate of interest, and A is the future amount. In our example, where the interest or income is $5, this is expressed by:

$$\$100 (1.05) = \$105.$$

Sometimes the interest or income is not

Table 6-1 FUTURE AMOUNT TO WHICH $1.00 NOW WILL GROW BY END OF
SPECIFIED YEAR AT ALTERNATIVE RATES OF COMPOUNDED INTEREST

Year	3%	4%	5%	6%	7%	8%	10%	12%	15%	20%	Year
1	1.03	1.04	1.05	1.06	1.07	1.08	1.10	1.12	1.15	1.20	1
2	1.06	1.08	1.10	1.12	1.14	1.17	1.21	1.25	1.32	1.44	2
3	1.09	1.12	1.16	1.19	1.23	1.26	1.33	1.40	1.52	1.73	3
4	1.13	1.17	1.22	1.26	1.31	1.36	1.46	1.57	1.74	2.07	4
5	1.16	1.22	1.28	1.34	1.40	1.47	1.61	1.76	2.01	2.49	5
6	1.19	1.27	1.34	1.42	1.50	1.59	1.77	1.97	2.31	2.99	6
7	1.23	1.32	1.41	1.50	1.61	1.71	1.94	2.21	2.66	3.58	7
8	1.27	1.37	1.48	1.59	1.72	1.85	2.14	2.48	3.05	4.30	8
9	1.30	1.42	1.55	1.69	1.84	2.00	2.35	2.77	3.52	5.16	9
10	1.34	1.48	1.63	1.79	1.97	2.16	2.59	3.11	4.05	6.19	10
11	1.38	1.54	1.71	1.90	2.10	2.33	2.85	3.48	4.66	7.43	11
12	1.43	1.60	1.80	2.01	2.25	2.52	3.13	3.90	5.30	8.92	12
13	1.47	1.67	1.89	2.13	2.41	2.72	3.45	4.36	6.10	10.7	13
14	1.51	1.73	1.98	2.26	2.58	2.94	3.79	4.89	7.00	12.8	14
15	1.56	1.80	2.08	2.40	2.76	3.17	4.17	5.47	8.13	15.4	15
16	1.60	1.87	2.18	2.54	2.95	3.43	4.59	6.13	9.40	18.5	16
17	1.65	1.95	2.29	2.69	3.16	3.70	5.05	6.87	10.6	22.2	17
18	1.70	2.03	2.41	2.85	3.38	4.00	5.55	7.70	12.5	26.6	18
19	1.75	2.11	2.53	3.03	3.62	4.32	6.11	8.61	14.0	31.9	19
20	1.81	2.19	2.65	3.21	3.87	4.66	6.73	9.65	16.1	38.3	20
25	2.09	2.67	3.39	4.29	5.43	6.85	10.8	17.0	32.9	95.4	25
30	2.43	3.24	4.32	5.74	7.61	10.0	17.4	30.0	66.2	237	30
40	3.26	4.80	7.04	10.3	15.0	21.7	45.3	93.1	267.0	1470	40
50	4.38	7.11	11.5	18.4	29.5	46.9	117	289	1080	9100	50

This table shows to what amounts $1.00 invested now will grow at the end of various years, at different rates of growth compounded annually. For example, $1.00 invested now will grow in 30 years to $5.74 at 6%. In other words, $5.74 due 30 years hence is worth now exactly $1.00 at a 6% rate of interest per year. If you invest $100 now at 10%, you will have $1740 in 30 years. The entries in this table are the reciprocals of the entries in Table 6–2; that is, they are the entries of Table 6–2 divided into 1. Formula for entries in table is $1/(1 + r)^t$.

consumed but is left invested for the next year. For example, for a tree capable of growing for several years at 5% of its size each year, the value of the lumber in the tree would grow to 105 in one year; by the end of the second year it would grow to 110.25, 5% larger than 105, *if none of the lumber were taken from the tree (as consumed income)*. This is expressed by:

$$\$100 \, (1.05) \, (1.05) = \$110.25,$$

or in general form by:

$$P \, (1 + r) \, (1 + r) = A.$$

In three years, if all interest were reinvested without consuming any of it, it would grow to:

$$\$100 \, (1.05) \, (1.05) \, (1.05) = \$115.75.$$

To avoid tedious arithmetic, Table 6–1 shows future amounts to which $1.00 would grow at different rates of interest over various numbers of years. The general formula giving the future amount, A, to which P will grow is:

$$(2) \qquad P(1 + r)^t = A$$

where t is the number of years.

You can now see why 100 bushels of wheat today can be exchanged for 105 next year. You could grow the 105 bushels yourself or lend the 100 bushels to others who can do that and who would be willing to return to you up to 105 bushels in a year. A borrower who has to return less than 105 will be making a profit. (Remember, we assume *no* inflation; the price of wheat is assumed to stay constant over time.) If borrowers or investors compete with one another to get some wheat *now* they would push the *premium* they would offer to pay you (in next year's wheat) up to 5%. For, say, $100 today (assuming a price of $1.00 per bushel) you could get $105 worth of wheat tomorrow, 105 bushels. Expressed in dollars, $100 worth of goods today is worth (is salable for) $105 of tomorrow's goods—even with no inflation.

As indicated earlier, Table 6–1 gives the future amounts to which $1.00 worth of resources invested *now* will grow at various rates of interest and lengths of time (again, this growth has nothing to do with inflation). We now reverse the question and ask how much must be invested now so that it will grow to $1.00 by some specified future time at a specified interest rate.

WHAT PRESENT AMOUNT WILL GROW TO A SPECIFIED FUTURE AMOUNT?

This is an important question because very often the future amount to be received is known and one wants to estimate a reasonable present value that might be offered to buy it. Table 6–2 shows what *present* amounts would grow to $1.00, at different lengths of investment and interest rates. For example, to buy something that will be worth $1.00 10 years from now, if the rate of interest in the interim is 10% per year, the present price (to be paid now) is only $.385, which is in the column for 10% and the row for 10 years.

This can be expressed as follows:

$$(3) \qquad \frac{A}{(1 + r)} = P$$

where P is the present price to be paid now for the future amount, A, to be received in *one* year with r as the rate of interest. Inserting the numbers in our example gives:

$$\frac{\$1.00}{(1 + .10)} = \frac{\$1.00}{(1.10)} = \$.909$$

as the present price, or capital value, of $1.00 *deferred* one year at a 10% rate of interest. (Try to remember to use this terminology.) The present value of the deferred $1.00, being less than $1.00, is sometimes called a *discounted value*; the term simply indicates that the present value is less than the future amount. Because the present value can be obtained by dividing by 1.1 or by multiplying by 1/1.1 or .909, this process of deriving the present (lower) value of a future larger amount is called discounting for time, or just plain *discounting*. (Note that its meaning is entirely different from that of a discount price in a retail store.)

If the date of future receipt of the dollar were to be deferred two years, that is, to be two years away, the discounting appears twice. Therefore the formula for the present value of something deferred two years is:

$$P = \frac{A}{(1 + r)(1 + r)}$$

or, at 10% interest rates:

$$\$.826 = \frac{\$1.00}{(1.10)(1.10)} = \frac{\$1.00}{(1.21)} .$$

And for an A 10 years away the formula is:

Table 6-2 PRESENT VALUE OF A FUTURE $1.00: WHAT A DOLLAR AT END OF
SPECIFIED FUTURE YEAR IS WORTH TODAY AT ALTERNATIVE INTEREST RATES

Year	3%	4%	5%	6%	7%	8%	10%	12%	15%	20%	Year
1	.971	.962	.952	.943	.935	.926	.909	.893	.870	.833	1
2	.943	.925	.907	.890	.873	.857	.826	.797	.756	.694	2
3	.915	.889	.864	.840	.816	.794	.751	.711	.658	.578	3
4	.888	.855	.823	.792	.763	.735	.683	.636	.572	.482	4
5	.863	.822	.784	.747	.713	.681	.620	.567	.497	.402	5
6	.837	.790	.746	.705	.666	.630	.564	.507	.432	.335	6
7	.813	.760	.711	.665	.623	.583	.513	.452	.376	.279	7
8	.789	.731	.677	.627	.582	.540	.466	.404	.326	.233	8
9	.766	.703	.645	.592	.544	.500	.424	.360	.284	.194	9
10	.744	.676	.614	.558	.508	.463	.385	.322	.247	.162	10
11	.722	.650	.585	.527	.475	.429	.350	.287	.215	.134	11
12	.701	.625	.557	.497	.444	.397	.318	.257	.187	.112	12
13	.681	.601	.530	.469	.415	.368	.289	.229	.162	.0935	13
14	.661	.577	.505	.442	.388	.340	.263	.204	.141	.0779	14
15	.642	.555	.481	.417	.362	.315	.239	.183	.122	.0649	15
16	.623	.534	.458	.394	.339	.292	.217	.163	.107	.0541	16
17	.605	.513	.436	.371	.317	.270	.197	.146	.093	.0451	17
18	.587	.494	.416	.501	.296	.250	.179	.130	.0808	.0376	18
19	.570	.475	.396	.331	.277	.232	.163	.116	.0703	.0313	19
20	.554	.456	.377	.312	.258	.215	.148	.104	.0611	.0261	20
25	.478	.375	.295	.233	.184	.146	.0923	.0588	.0304	.0105	25
30	.412	.308	.231	.174	.131	.0994	.0573	.0334	.0151	.00421	30
40	.307	.208	.142	.0972	.067	.0460	.0221	.0107	.00373	.000680	40
50	.228	.141	.087	.0543	.034	.0213	.00852	.00346	.000922	.000109	50

Each column lists how much a dollar received at the end of various years in the future is worth today. For example, at 6% per year a dollar to be received 10 years hence is equivalent in value to $.558 now. In other words, $.558 invested now at 6%, with interest compounded annually, would grow to $1.00 in 10 years. Note that $1.00 to be received at the end of 50 years is, at 6%, worth today just about a nickel. And at 10% it is worth only about .8 of one cent, which is to say that 8 mills (.8 of a cent) invested now would grow, at

10% interest compounded annually, to $1.00 in 50 years. Similarly $1000 in 50 years is worth today $8.52, and $10,000 is worth today $85—all at 10% rate of interest. *Forty years* from now (when you are about 60) $10,000 would cost you now, at 10% rate of growth per year, about $221. (See the entry in the column headed 10% and in the row of 40 years.) Formula for entry in table is $1/(1 + r)^t$. (No inflation is involved.)

$$P = \frac{A}{(1 + r)^{10}},$$

which at 10% is:

$$1/2.59 = .385.$$

The farther away the deferred future amount, the lower its present value.

$$(4) \quad P = \frac{A}{(1 + r)^t}$$

It is possible to ask the question, "What must be the rate of interest to be able to invest $1.00 today and get $1.10 in one year?" The general formula for one year is in general

$$(5) \quad r = \frac{(A - P)}{P}$$

To find the interest rate for investments lasting longer than one year is not so easy, but if you use Table 6–2 you'll be able to approximate your answer. Specify the present amount to be invested today to grow to $1.00. Then find that number in the row for the number of years the investment persists. For example, if you were to invest 25¢ today to get $1.00 after 10 years, what would the annual rate of interest have to be? Looking in the row for 10 years, the number closest to 25¢ is in the column for 15%.

Illustrative Uses of Capital Value Principles

LENDING IS BUYING DEBT

We are ready to act like financial experts and interpret some economic events. You may have noticed that we referred both to valuing a claim to $100 to be delivered in one year and to investing now for a future return. Buying a claim to something in the future is the same as *lending*. To lend now *is* to buy a claim for some amount in the future. When I lend you $100 to be repaid with some interest in one year, I have bought your debt of $100, and you must repay me for doing so. When I lend $100 expecting $100 plus $5 interest in a year, I buy now, for $100, a claim to $105 deferred one year—called the *future amount*. When a loan is made, the amount borrowed, or loaned, is called the *principal*. The principal, then, is exactly what we were calling the capital value (or present value, or price) of a claim to a future receipt.

Consider the following common situation. Almost every Thursday the U.S. government borrows money for short periods—say, one year. It does so by auctioning what it calls Treasury certificates or **Treasury bills**. These are **promissory notes**; that is, they are promises to pay $10,000 in one year.

There is no *explicit* interest. But suppose a successful bidder gets one for $9000. What is the *implicit* rate of interest? (See formula 5.) The $1000 excess to be received in one year is 11.1% of the $9000, so the implicit rate of interest is 11.1% per year:

$$11.1 = \frac{(\$10,000 - \$9000)}{\$9,000}.$$

The rate thus calculated is commonly called the *Treasury bill rate*. Treasury bills, or T-bills, as they're called, are offered by many savings and loan banks as intermediaries. Even though no interest is stated in these U.S. Treasury loan contracts, there is interest in fact. Whenever the present price is less than the promised future amount, the difference is interest. (There is virtually no risk of nonpayment with U.S. Treasury certificates. But if the promise of a future amount were very risky, the difference between present price and future amount would represent also a return for risk.) You should now be able to understand that the higher is the *current* price of the Treasury certificate, the lower is the implicit interest rate.

INTEREST IS THE PRICE OF EARLIER AVAILABILITY

Interest is often called the price of money. That is a misleading way of saying that the rate of interest is the price of *borrowing* money. You borrow money to buy other resources *earlier*—earlier than if you had to save from your own income. Interest is really the price of getting goods earlier, and is paid for out of the services or growth provided by having the goods. But almost everywhere and always there are laws against usury, which is an ambiguous pejorative—that is, condemning—term for interest. Most often **usury** means too high an interest rate, but sometimes it means any interest whatsoever. Early Christian dogma condemned usury. The strict Muslim interpretation of the Koran prohibits interest in any form—a problem for some Arabs who run businesses. In Communist doctrine interest is called exploitation. Yet all opponents of usury reinterpret their doctrines to admit interest. The early Christians let the Jews collect interest. The Communists cleverly call it by another name, an "efficiency index." The Catholic Church called it simply a discount, with no explicit interest, as our government does now on U.S. Treasury certificates.

MONETARY AND NONMONETARY SERVICE IN INTEREST

Some capital goods such as paintings and houses yield a stream of nonconsumable services. Others may yield no interim consumable services; instead they improve, or ripen, or mature with age, and therefore increase in value. In any case, for every capital good, over the year, the value of whatever may be its consumable service flow plus the change in its own value will turn out to be virtually the same *percentage of capital value* for *all resources* (per dollar of capital value) and also will equal the market rate of interest (virtually the same because some allowance for a real difference is necessary). No one would want to own the resource or good that failed to do so. The present price of such a good would fall sufficiently to make its yield a larger percentage of that new, lower price—and hence equal to the percentage return on other capital goods.

As an example, the price of a bottle of wine yielding no service until it is consumed would have to rise over time at the rate of interest every year, or else no one would want it since it gives no consumable yield in the interim except a capital value rise. If someone believes the wine will be worth $100 in 10 years, when it is ready for drinking, its present price would have to be low enough so that the difference between it and $100 would represent an increase in value

obtained by any investment for 10 years at the market rate of interest. From Table 6–2, if we multiply by 100, it can be seen that the present value would be $38.50 (the entry for 10 years and an assumed 10% annual interest rate: .385 × 100). This present value is also called its *discounted* value.

No matter what resource you consider, its capital value change *plus* its net service flow during a year must be expected to equal the (risk-adjusted) rate of interest—where, as we must hasten to generalize, the service value is comprised not only of the salable services but also of the value of any income or nonmonetary personal services derived from it in the interim. If a tree yields no service in the interim other than increasing in wood content, its value as a tree must rise at the rate of interest, as does the price of any other good that has no service value while it is being held. But say the tree also yields a service while standing, by giving shade and beauty, as paintings give pleasure, or a house gives shelter, or a stock pays dividends. Then it is the sum of (1) the increase in the price *plus* (2) the values of marketable and nonmarketable services or income to be derived from it over the year that add up to a percentage return matching the rate of interest. If the percentage were greater than the interest rate, the resource would be underpriced in that at that low price it would yield a higher rate of return than others, so that you could make a profit buying the underpriced resource. Since there aren't many, if any, people persistently finding such cases, it is safe to deduce that resources are in fact priced to yield virtually the same expected, average return over time (allowing for risk). That is a fundamental and universally observed result of competition in the demand and supply for capital goods. That is what is meant by "clearing the market for capital goods." At that price, the expected net percentage yields are the same for all resources and are equal to the rate of interest.

Annuities

So far we have treated investments as yielding a single final value some time in the future. But as we have indicated, most capital goods yield a stream of future outputs or services—like apple trees yielding apples every year, or a machine tool yielding a series of future services over its life. If we take the whole series of future yields over the life of the good and treat the services in a year as, in effect, a payment once a year, the services can be called an **annuity**. The services coming from a machine or house will, we assume, get the same dollar rental or value every year. As we have learned, the present price paid for a claim to the service to be delivered, say, exactly 10 years from now, and which will at that time be worth $1.00, will today be worth much less. Therefore, the present price of a machine that yields future services is the *sum* of *discounted*, that is, *present*, values of all the future values of the future services.

If a machine is expected to yield services worth $1.00 at the end of *each* of the next four years and no longer, and if the pertinent competitive rate of interest is 10% per year, then the four $1.00 rental values will be discounted back to a present value:

$\dfrac{\$1.00}{(1.10)}$ = $.909 = the present value of the $1.00 of services rendered at the end of the first year

$\dfrac{\$1.00}{(1.10)^2}$ = .826 = the present value of the second year's dollar services

$\dfrac{\$1.00}{(1.10)^3}$ = .751 = the present value of the third year's dollar services

$\dfrac{\$1.00}{(1.10)^4}$ = .683 = the present value of the fourth year's dollar services

$\overline{\$3.17}$ = present value of the whole four-year stream and hence of the machine.

The longer the series of yields, the great-er the present value of the machine because more terms are included. For example, if the machine were twice as durable and gave eight (instead of four) years of service worth $1.00 in each year, its capital value would be computed simply by extending the series over eight terms:

$\dfrac{\$1.00}{(1.10)^5}$ = $ .621 = present value of fifth year of service

$\dfrac{\$1.00}{(1.10)^6}$ = .564 = present value of sixth year of service

$\dfrac{\$1.00}{(1.10)^7}$ = .513 = present value of seventh year of service

$\dfrac{\$1.00}{(1.10)^8}$ = .467 = present value of eighth year of service

$\overline{\$2.165}$ = present value of last four years of service

$+\underline{\$3.17}$ = present value of first four years of service

$\$5.335$ = present value of eight years.

Notice that the second four years add only $2.165 to the present capital value, less than the $3.17 of the first four years.

In general, the following annuity formula holds:

Present Value =

$$\frac{A_1}{(1 + r)} + \frac{A_2}{(1 + r)^2} + \frac{A_3}{(1 + r)^3} + \frac{A_4}{(1 + r)^4} + \cdots$$

where A_1, A_2, A_3, A_4 are the future amounts at the end of years 1, 2, 3, 4, and so on to the end of the series of future amounts.

The more future terms there are in an annuity, the greater the present value, even though more distant terms have smaller present values because of the discount effect. This is an extremely important truth, which we soon apply to several problems.

Suppose, to push things to an extreme, the machine were permanent and gave $1.00 of services every year forever. At 5% interest rates, what would it be worth now? The answer is $20, the sum of that infinitely long series of diminishing *present* values. If it seems odd that an infinitely long series could add up to only $20, consider this analogy: You invest $20 in a bank paying 5% interest. Every year you get $1.00 interest. Take it out—which makes it the equivalent of a service—and repeat the next year. Every year forever $1.00 can be taken out and there is still $20 left over. The same idea is expressed by the statement that the present value of a *perpetuity* (an infinitely long annuity) of $1.00 a year has a present value of $20, if the interest rate is 5% per year. If the interest rate were lower, say 3%, then the present value of a perpetuity of $1.00 a year would be $33.33 (3% of $33.33 will yield you $1.00 every year, without requiring you to diminish the initial investment value of $33.33).

From Table 6–3, you can see that the first 50 years of a series of receipts (a 50-year annuity of $1.00 a year) has a present value of only $18.30 at 5% interest. The entire *subsequent* part of an infinitely long series of $1.00 receipts, beginning *after* 50 years from now, is worth *today* only about $1.70 (that is, $20 − $18.30). Small present investments can yield amazing amounts in the *distant* future.

Before applying our analysis, we show how to get an answer to a common question: How much must be paid each period for a stated number of periods (as with an installment plan) to repay some amount borrowed now?

REPAYING A DEBT BY INSTALLMENTS

The annual payments on a loan must be large enough to pay interest and to repay some part of the principal, the amount borrowed. The calculation can be worked out easily by using the data in Table 6–4, which shows how much must be paid each year to cancel a debt of $1.00 at various rates of interest and numbers of years. Simply multiply that entry by the size of the debt, and that gives the amount that must be paid annually, with the *first payment being made a year from now* (*not* right now), to repay the debt plus interest during the interval.

For example, to repay a debt of $10,000 in 10 years at interest rates of 10%, the entry in Table 6–4 is .163. This has been rounded from .1627. (We use the more accurate figure.) The amount each year is 10,000 times larger, $1627. It is instructive to realize that although the annual payment is fixed, payments in the early years are made up mostly of payments of interest and only a small part is repayment of some of the principal borrowed. As time passes and the principal is being repaid with the installments, the amount due gets smaller and hence the interest due gets smaller, so that a larger portion of the uniform later payments of $1627 is repayment of principal. (In the first year, interest is $1000 and $627 is for repayment of principal. In the last year only $180 is interest and the remainder, $1487, is repayment of principal.)

Applications and Examples

To better understand the investment principles just investigated, consider a few common applications.

1. EAT YOUR CAKE AND HAVE IT, TOO

Some colleges lend students money for tuition without interest for four years. Should you borrow? Of course! Put the money in a savings account paying, say, 8% per year. Each year draw out the interest and throw a party. At the end of four years, you can draw out the $1000 plus the last year's interest, re-

Table 6-3   PRESENT CAPITAL VALUE (PRICE) OF ANNUITY OF $1.00, RECEIVED AT END OF EACH YEAR

Year	3%	4%	5%	6%	7%	8%	10%	12%	15%	20%	Year
1	0.971	0.960	0.952	0.943	0.935	0.926	0.909	0.890	0.870	0.833	1
2	1.91	1.89	1.86	1.83	1.81	1.78	1.73	1.69	1.63	1.53	2
3	2.83	2.78	2.72	2.67	2.62	2.58	2.48	2.40	2.28	2.11	3
4	3.72	3.63	3.55	3.47	3.39	3.31	3.16	3.04	2.86	2.59	4
5	4.58	4.45	4.33	4.21	4.10	3.99	3.79	3.60	3.35	2.99	5
6	5.42	5.24	5.08	4.92	4.77	4.62	4.35	4.11	3.78	3.33	6
7	6.23	6.00	5.79	5.58	5.39	5.21	4.86	4.56	4.16	3.60	7
8	7.02	6.73	6.46	6.21	5.97	5.75	5.33	4.97	4.49	3.84	8
9	7.79	7.44	7.11	6.80	6.52	6.25	5.75	5.33	4.78	4.03	9
10	8.53	8.11	7.72	7.36	7.02	6.71	6.14	5.65	5.02	4.19	10
11	9.25	8.76	8.31	7.89	7.50	7.14	6.49	5.94	5.23	4.33	11
12	9.95	9.39	8.86	8.38	7.94	7.54	6.81	6.19	5.41	4.44	12
13	10.6	9.99	9.39	8.85	8.36	7.90	7.10	6.42	5.65	4.53	13
14	11.2	10.6	9.90	9.29	8.75	8.24	7.36	6.63	5.76	4.61	14
15	11.9	11.1	10.4	9.72	9.11	8.56	7.61	6.81	5.87	4.68	15
16	12.6	11.6	10.8	10.1	9.45	8.85	7.82	6.97	5.96	4.73	16
17	13.2	12.2	11.3	10.5	9.76	9.12	8.02	7.12	6.03	4.77	17
18	13.8	12.7	11.7	10.8	10.1	9.37	8.20	7.25	6.10	4.81	18
19	14.3	13.1	12.1	11.2	10.3	9.60	8.36	7.37	6.17	4.84	19
20	14.9	13.6	12.5	11.5	10.6	9.82	8.51	7.47	6.37	4.87	20
25	17.4	15.6	14.1	12.8	11.7	10.7	9.08	7.84	6.46	4.95	25
30	19.6	17.3	15.4	13.8	12.4	11.3	9.43	8.06	6.57	4.98	30
40	23.1	19.8	17.2	15.0	13.3	11.9	9.78	8.24	6.64	5.00	40
50	25.7	21.5	18.3	15.8	13.8	12.2	9.91	8.25	6.66	5.00	50

An annuity is a sequence of constant amounts received at annual intervals. This table shows with each entry how much it takes today to buy an annuity of $1.00 a year at the rates of interest indicated. For example, an annuity of $1.00 a year for 20 years at 6% interest could be purchased today with $11.50. This amount would, if invested at 6%, be sufficient to yield some interest which, along with some depletion of the principal in each year, would enable a payout of exactly $1.00 a year for 20 years, at which time the fund would be completely depleted. And $1000 a year for 20 years would, at 6% compounded annually, cost today $11,400, which is obviously 1000 times as much as for an annuity of just $1.00. Formula for entry is $[1 - (1 + r)^{-t}]/r$.

pay the $1000, and spend the last year's interest for a graduation gift.

If you apply the concepts we've been developing, you see that if you borrow $1000 you are receiving an $80 four-year annuity. At 8% interest, its present value is $264.80 (= $80 × 3.31): See Table 6-3. This means that borrowing $1000 at *zero* interest for four years is equivalent to getting a gift of $264.80 upon entrance to college. $1000 now is a claim to a lot more real goods and services than is $1000 four years hence—even if there is no inflation of any prices.

2. SUPPRESSION OF IMPROVEMENTS?

You manufacture for 50¢ and sell for that price a light bulb that lasts one year. You then invent a light bulb that lasts two years and gives the same light for the same rate of power usage. How much could you charge for this new bulb, if buyers value a light

Table 6-4   UNIFORM ANNUAL PAYMENTS TO BE PAID AT END OF EACH YEAR PER $1.00 BORROWED NOW

Year	3%	4%	5%	6%	7%	8%	10%	12%	15%	20%	Year
1	1.03	1.04	1.05	1.06	1.07	1.08	1.10	1.12	1.15	1.20	1
2	.524	.529	.538	.546	.552	.562	.578	.592	.613	.654	2
3	.353	.360	.368	.375	.381	.388	.403	.417	.439	.474	3
4	.269	.275	.282	.289	.295	.302	.316	.329	.350	.386	4
5	.218	.225	.231	.238	.244	.251	.267	.278	.299	.334	5
6	.185	.191	.197	.204	.210	.216	.230	.243	.265	.300	6
7	.161	.167	.173	.179	.186	.192	.206	.219	.240	.278	7
8	.142	.149	.155	.161	.168	.174	.188	.201	.223	.260	8
9	.128	.134	.141	.147	.153	.160	.174	.188	.209	.248	9
10	.117	.123	.130	.136	.142	.149	.163	.177	.199	.239	10
11	.108	.114	.120	.127	.133	.140	.154	.168	.191	.231	11
12	.101	.106	.113	.119	.126	.133	.147	.162	.185	.225	12
13	.0943	.100	.107	.113	.120	.127	.141	.156	.177	.221	13
14	.0885	.0943	.101	.108	.114	.121	.136	.151	.174	.217	14
15	.0840	.0901	.0982	.103	.110	.117	.132	.147	.170	.214	15
16	.0794	.0862	.0929	.0990	.106	.113	.128	.143	.168	.211	16
17	.0758	.0819	.0885	.0961	.102	.110	.125	.140	.166	.210	17
18	.0725	.0787	.0855	.0925	.0990	.107	.122	.138	.164	.208	18
19	.0699	.0763	.0826	.0901	.0971	.104	.120	.136	.162	.207	19
20	.0671	.0735	.0800	.0877	.0943	.102	.118	.134	.161	.205	20
25	.0575	.0641	.0709	.0781	.0855	.0935	.110	.128	.155	.202	25
30	.0510 •	.0578	.0649	.0724	.0806	.0885	.106	.124	.152	.201	30
40	.0433	.0505	.0581	.0666	.0752	.0840	.102	.121	.151	.200	40
50	.0389	.0465	.9546	.0632	.0725	.0820	.101	.120	.150	.200	50

An annuity is a sequence of annual amounts received at annual intervals for a specified number of years. The entries in the table give the possible annuities of various lengths, for various interest rates, which have a present value of $1.00. For example, for $1.00 present value or cost, at 6% interest, one can receive an annuity for *one* year of $1.06, or of 54.6 cents for each of two years, or 37.5 cents for each of three years, or 28.9 cents for each of four years.

Another way to use the data is to treat annuities as payments. For example, a debt of $1.00 can be paid off, at 6% interest, with $1.06 in one year, or 54.6 cents annually for two years, or 28.9 cents annually for four years, or 10.2 cents annually for 20 years.

bulb's services at 50¢ during each year of service? Assume the rate of interest is 10%. Because the second year of service is over a year away, they will offer you *now* 45¢ more for the new, improved bulb. This value is obtained by discounting the second year's value, 50¢, by .909 (see in Table 6–2 where the 10% column intersects the row for one year: .909), which gives 45.45¢. See also Table 6–5.

So you could sell a two-year bulb for about 95¢ now. A three-year bulb would sell now for the present value of three years of service. The third year's 50¢ service value is worth *now*, paid two years in advance, 41.30¢ (computed by dividing 50¢ by (1.10)²; or look in Table 6–2 for the discount factor where the 10% column and the row for two years intersect: .826 multiplied by 50¢ gives 41.30¢). Therefore, three-year bulbs would sell now for $1.37 (50¢ + 45.50¢ + 41.30¢).

These computations of course influence your behavior as a producer: You would produce the three-year bulb and sell it for $1.37

Table 6-5 LIGHT-BULB PRICES DEPEND ON LENGTH OF BULB LIFE*

One-year bulb: One sold each year at price of 50¢

Years	1st	2nd	3rd	4th	5th	6th
Service value:	.50	.50	.50	.50	.50	.50
Price:	.50	.50	.50	.50	.50	.50
Cost:	.50	.50	.50	.50	.50	.50
Profit:	0	0	0	0	0	0
Present value of profits:	0	0	0	0	0	0

Two-year bulb: One sold every two years at price of 95.45¢

Years	1st	2nd	3rd	4th	5th	6th
Service value:	.50 .4545	.50	.50 .4545	.50	.50 .4545	.50
Price: Present value of bulb's service	.9545		.9545		.9545	
Cost:	.50	0	.50	0	.50	0
Profit:	.4545	0	.4545	0	.4545	0
Present value of profits:	1.14	0	.3756	0	.3104	0

Three-year bulb: One sold every three years at price of $1.37

Years	1st	2nd	3rd	4th	5th	6th
Service value:	.50 .455 .416	.50	.50	.50 .45 .42	.50	.50
Price:	1.37	0	0	1.37	0	0
Cost:	.50	0	0	.50	0	0
Profit:	.87	0	0	.87	0	0
Present value of profits:	1.52	0	0	.65	0	0

*Each bulb costs 50¢ to make; the service value of each type of bulb
is 50¢ per year; the interest rate is 10%.

rather than sell three one-year bulbs for 50¢ each, even though it meant selling fewer light bulbs, as long as the cost of producing a three-year bulb is less than nearly three times the cost of producing one three-year bulb.[1] You'll get the equivalent of $1.37 in either case, but if the cost is less than $1.37

for a three-year bulb you'll make money producing it, despite fewer sales, because you're selling at a higher price and incurring a cost that is less than proportionately higher.

The important conclusion is that it does *not* pay to suppress improvements just to sell more old units, because the selling price of the better ones will be more than proportionately higher, and the costs won't. Only if the costs of producing better goods were disproportionately higher—in which case they could not be considered better—would it not be profitable. Despite popular charges to the contrary, it doesn't pay to suppress known inventions that reduce the cost of maintain-

[1]"Almost" because you would be able to produce two of the one-year bulbs *later,* and therefore the present value of those later costs is less than 50¢ each. Their present cost is 50¢/(1 + r) and 50¢/(1 + r)². If r = 10%, the present value of costs is 50¢ + 45¢ + 41¢ = $1.36.

ing the same quality or improve quality at the same cost.

3. FORCED OBSOLESCENCE?

Another surprising application of this same point is to textbooks. If a text can be resold and used by a second student, the *initial* sale price of the book, just like that of the light bulb, will include the second student's use value, adjusted to present value terms. Suppose, for the sake of simplicity, that there were no costs of arranging a resale of this text to the next student. If both students value their use of the book at $5, the publisher could have sold the new book for $9.55.[2] The first student would be willing to pay $9.55 for the book knowing that it can later be sold for $5 to the second student—for a net use cost of only $5 to the first student. (Remember, $5 a year from now is equivalent to $4.55 now.)

Suppose the author gets 15% of the sales value: That's 15% of $9.55 rather than 15% of two successive $5 books. So, the two-life book (costing less to make than two one-year books) would sell new for $5 plus $4.55 (the present value of the second year's $5 value discounted at 10% interest rates), or $9.55, which is worth two $5 receipts, one coming now and the other in a year. Clearly, it is an efficient used-book market that permits this.

Just as you are willing to pay more for a Volkswagen because of its high resale value, you will pay more for texts that can be resold. Killing the resale value of a book (or automobile or refrigerator or TV set), either by abolishing used-book markets or by quickly issuing new editions, profits neither authors nor publishers—a fact seemingly unknown to many authors but known to publishers.

---

[2]Assuming an interest rate of 10%, $9.55 = $5.00 + $4.55.

4. THE COST OF BORROWING IS NOT THE SUM OF REPAYMENTS

Many people calculate the cost of borrowing as being the sum of all the future interest. They are wrong to do so because payments at different times are not equivalent claims to consumption power. Payments nearer the present are claims to greater consumption power. The correct method, then, is to convert all the payments to equivalent consumption values as of any common time—say the present—before adding.

To see why, one must remember the meaning of cost—the sacrificed alternatives. Consider two alternative methods of repaying a loan of $4. In method A a $1.00 payment is made at the end of each of five years. In method B only two $2.25 payments are made over the next two years. It might seem that method A costs a total of $5 and method B only $4.50. But B involves repaying *earlier*. Table 6-6 shows the two plans and their differences. If interest rates are 10%, repaying by method A gives the borrower more consumption power than does repaying by method B. Instead of paying the first $2.25 to the lender under method B, the borrower could pay $1.00 under method A and invest the $1.25 remainder at 10%. The $1.25 grows in a year to $1.37, from which the second $1.00 installment payment can be made. The remainder, 37¢, plus the $2.25 invested at that time (instead of being paid as under method B) totals $2.62, which grows in the third year to $2.88. From this the third $1.00 installment payment can be made. The remaining $1.88 will grow to $2.06 in the fourth year. After the fourth $1.00 installment payment is made, $1.06 is left, which grows during the fifth year to $1.17, leaving, after the fifth and final $1.00 installment payment, a surplus of 17¢. That 17¢ is how much more consumption the borrower would have given the lender under repayment method B; using method A the borrower keeps that for himself or herself.

But recall our main point: Although the five $1.00 payments under method A appear to make up a larger sum than the two $2.25 payments under method B, the sum under A is really smaller when the timing and interest growth are properly measured.

The preceding involved a lot of tedious calculation. A simple way to find the cheaper method is to compute the present value of each payment scheme. The *present value*, at 10% interest, of the series of five $1.00 payments is $3.79: That is the amount today that, at 10% interest, will enable you to pay $1.00 in each of the next five years. The present value of the shorter, two-term $2.25 payments is $3.90—some 11¢ more costly. That 11¢ is the difference *now*; the 17¢ difference calculated above was the difference five years from now. At 10% rate of interest per year, 11¢ will grow in five years to 17¢. Nickels and dimes—but on a $400,000 loan the difference would have been $11,000 now and $17,000 five years from now.

To ensure that you thoroughly understand what is happening, and why the interest rate is crucial, suppose the rate of interest were only 5% per year. Then the present value of method A, $4.33, would be *bigger* than that of method B, $4.19. At 5%, then, it pays to repay in two $2.25 installments under method B. The reason for the difference is that with so low a rate of interest (growth of present values to future values), an earlier expenditure or sacrifice of consumption power won't so quickly or likely exceed later, deferred purchasing power. At low rates it pays to defer more and pay more in the future.

5. PAY NOW OR PAY LATER

Consider a lesson from the early 1970s, when energy prices were still controlled and were therefore unable fully to influence uses of energy. At that time, and still today, lower-priced air conditioners were made with less-costly cooling systems that require more electrical energy to operate than higher-priced models having the same cooling capacity and useful life. Several legislators proposed prohibiting the sale of air conditioners using more electricity. But prohibition of those high-energy users could be wasteful. Why? Table 6–7 shows hypothetical data for air conditioner A, cheaper to buy but using

Table 6-6 COMPARISON OF TWO METHODS OF REPAYING (10% INTEREST RATE) $4 DEBT

	Year-End Number				
	1	**2**	**3**	**4**	**5**
Method B payments	−$2.25	−$2.25	—	—	—
Method A payments	−$1.00	−$1.00	−$1.00	−$1.00	−$1.00
Extra payment in B:	1.25 grows to	1.37 −1.00			
		.37 +2.25			
		2.62 grows to	2.88 −1.00		
			1.88 grows to	2.06 −1.00	
				1.06 grows to	1.17 −1.00
			Excess cost of method B over method A =		.17

Table 6-7 ENERGY COST EXAMPLE

Machine	Purchase Cost	Annual Energy Cost in Each of 10 Years	Present Value at 6% of All Costs
Energy user A	$ 60	$25	$ 60 + $184 = $244
Energy saver B	$100	$20	$100 + $147 = $247

more electricity, and for air conditioner B, higher priced but energy conserving. Only purchase price and annual energy costs differ.

Some people might argue that you would save $5 a year for 10 years with machine B so that the energy saving of $50 in 10 years exceeds the $40 higher production cost. But you should spot the error: You must not add up that series of $5 annual energy savings, because each occurs at a different time in the future. It is their *present value* that must be computed.

For each machine the *present value* of the total outlays, present and future, for the next decade is shown at a 6% rate of interest. The *present value* of all outlays for air conditioner A (lower in price but higher in energy use) is *lower* than that for B (higher in price but lower in energy use). The difference in present values, $3 (= $247 − $244), is what would be saved in total resource value over that interval, counting all costs—materials, labor, and energy. Why? The difference in purchase prices, $40 (= $100 − $60), would earn, at 6% interest rate, the equivalent of an annuity of $5.43 each year for 10 years—which is more than the extra $5 cost of energy for the high energy user.[3] In this example, the lower-priced machine uses a lower total value of *all* resources (of various kinds and at various times). It is wasteful to save energy worth less than other resources thereby used up.

This example illustrates two economic principles: First, it is incomplete analysis, and hence incorrect analysis, to try to economize on only *one component* of costs—for example, energy. The value of the energy saved is only $4 per year, but it comes at a $5.43 cost of other resources annually. *Minimizing* the cost of some *one* input always increases the costs of some other inputs by more than the savings in the minimized input. *Maximizing* the output per unit of any *one* input of production has the same negative effect, increasing the costs for other inputs by more than the gains. Such technological output–input ratios (or *technological* efficiencies, as they are called) are misleading for making decisions.

The second economic principle is that of capital valuation, the only correct way to compare costs: Before expenditures at *different times* can be added they must be converted to contemporary values as if they all occurred at one common time. Costs are sacrifices of other goods; a proper measure that finds the lowest capital-valued cost means the *least* sacrifice of other goods. That is also all that is meant by *efficiency*: There is no waste.

6. HONOR THY PARENTS

Your parents, having reached age 70 with savings of $50,000, plan to retire on that

---

[3]Either Table 6-3 or Table 6-4 can be used to calculate the 10-year, 6% annuity purchased with the $40. In Table 6-3 the present value of an annuity of $1.00 per year is $7.36. Because here we save $40 on the principal, divide $40 by $7.36 and obtain the yearly return of $5.43. In Table 6-4, the 10-year annuity purchased with $1.00 is 13.6¢ a year; with $40, we purchase 13.6¢ × $40 = $5.44, which is more than the savings in energy costs.

fund. They want to use it at a rate that permits them to draw out the largest possible uniform amount each year for 15 years. After that, if they are still alive, you will shoulder your moral responsibility and take care of them financially. How much can they spend each year for 15 years? The question can be rephrased in the terms we've been using: What 15-year annuity is equivalent to a present value of $50,000? If you get 10% interest per year, the present capital value of a 15-year $1.00 annuity, as seen in Table 6-3, is $7.60. Since there is now $50,000 in the fund, $50,000/7.60 = $6570, the amount of each annual payment. (This is an approximation, because $6570 is really the amount that could be spent at the *end* of each of fifteen years, not *during* each year; but the difference is slight.) If they want to use up the fund in 10 instead of 15 years, they can get $8140 (= $50,000/6.14) at the end of each year. If they earn only 4%, they can get a 15-year annuity of only $4500 (= $50,000/11.1).

7. WHO CARES ABOUT DISTANT FUTURE YIELDS?

Does the private-property, capitalist system fail to heed the values of future generations? No. It heeds the perceived distant future values as well as it does the near-term expectations. It does so because the anticipated future value of a good and its present value are related in such a way that the present value steadily rises at the interest rate to that future value at that future date.

Figure 6-1 shows the path of the gradually increasing capital values of a resource, a live tree, that will yield a single service, lumber, at some one future date. The figure shows both the value of the wood if it were cut down and used as lumber at any given year, and the time path of the value of the tree if left standing. When the two values come together it pays to cut down the tree. For all earlier intervals the tree is worth more alive because the wood is growing faster than the rate of interest. So it pays to plant trees if the initial year's value exceeds the costs of planting the tree. The vertical value scale is logarithmic; that is, a constant slope represents a constant *percentage* rate of growth. As time passes and we approach that future date, the present capital value rises toward that anticipated future value, and *rises at the market rate of interest*. Consequently, the date at which you might invest in that resource has no effect on your realized rate of return. If you invest in the first year, or any year, you will get the same annual percentage rate of growth, as long as beliefs about the future value of the lumber don't change.

You can expect the same rate of return—the rate of interest—whether you invest in a new or an old resource. You could get 10% per year whether you buy a lot of young trees for $1000 or one tree nearly ready to cut for $1000. They are equally profitable. What ensures that equilibrium? People don't give away opportunities to get more than the rate of interest—that is, profitable opportunities. If a young tree were priced so low that people expected to get a higher return over its life than 10% per year, everyone would want to buy it; if it were priced too high, the return would be smaller, so no one would want to buy it: The price would adjust. *Every* durable good whether new or old will be priced on the *expectation* of the same interest rate of return.

So young trees would be valued high enough to make it worthwhile to plant them and not cut them, for if they were cut down before their growth rate fell to the rate of interest, the extra value of lumber from the tree would be sacrificed. If the value of a live tree exceeds that of its lumber, it should not be cut. That excess value is simply the discounted value of the future lumber growth of the tree that is greater than can be obtained in any investment in anything else—the rate of interest. When the growth rate of lumber

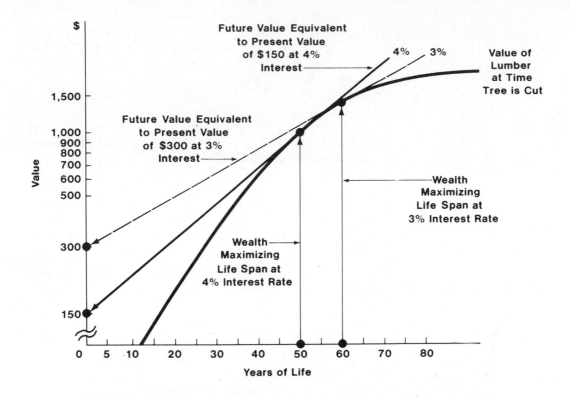

Figure 6-1.

GROWTH OF CAPITAL VALUE OF A TREE:
OPTIMAL CUTTING TIME DEPENDS ON INTEREST
RATE AND PATTERN OF GROWTH OF LUMBER VALUE

The dollar values are given on a logarithmic scale. As the
two interest curves and the lumber-value curve show, at
a 3% interest rate the tree should be felled in its sixtieth
year and at a 4% interest rate in its fiftieth year. These
are the wealth-maximizing life spans. Cutting the tree
down any later will yield *less* lumber value than would
cutting at these optimal times and reinvesting in new
trees, which would grow faster than a 60-year-old
tree and faster than the interest rate.

in the standing tree no longer exceeds the interest rate and falls below it, the value of a
live tree will rise less than the rate of interest; the tree's value will not grow thereafter
as much as investments in other things. To
preserve the tree solely for more lumber
would be wasteful, since the lumber can be
used more productively for investment that
will get at least the rate of interest—which is
now more than the live tree can do.

Contrary to the common belief that the
capitalist market system undervalues the future, the future is valued and valued no higher for one resource than for any other. Any
owner of a standing tree will lose wealth if it
is cut while the value of its lumber grows
faster than the rate of interest—which is the
rate of net productivity on other resources.
People have been misled probably because
many resources—natural ones especially,
such as trees, buffalos, whales, or lakes that
no one owned—have not been subjected to a

market evaluation so as to prevent overconsumption.

What is true for things like trees that render their services all at one end point is true for goods that yield a continuing stream of services, like machine tools, land, houses, art, gold, oil wells, or common stocks and bonds. It is a fact that the expected rate of return on all those is the same—*if* one corrects for degrees of risk. A slightly higher expected rate of return will induce people to own riskier assets. It is remarkable how small a premium will induce people to bear greater variability of potential outcomes, that is, risk. One reason is that risky assets can be owned jointly with other assets that tend to reduce the risk of the combined set.

8. ARAB OIL POLICY: IS OPEC FRIEND OR FOE?

Since 1974 the common assumption has been that Arab oil producers colluded to raise prices, because the world demand for oil had less than unitary elasticity. (Remember the definition and significance of this from Chapter 2.) But another explanation is possible. The Arabs might have begun to suspect in about 1973 that prospective future supplies of petroleum would not satisfy future amounts demanded at current prices, and that even without any Arab conspiracy to reduce output, the competitive market price would be as high as $30 a barrel in 1985. Thus, assuming a 10% interest rate, a barrel of oil 10 years prior, in 1975, would be worth about $12. Such a *new* projection of the future energy situation and consequent future value of petroleum would mean that no producer would extract oil in 1974 unless it could be sold for almost $12—instead of the 1973 price of $3.

Under this interpretation, the Arabs have done us a service: By preventing excessive consumption of oil in low-value (that is, less than $12) current uses, they preserved more for the higher-valued uses in the future, as conservationists contend should be done for beaches, forests, and other natural resources.

This brief scenario illustrates how the present price of a durable good depends on the expected future use values of that good. The price *now* will rise (and curtail current consumption) if the expected future value suddenly rises until the new current and newly perceived future values differ just enough to cover the expected costs of storage and interest. Whether the forecasts of future oil supplies and demands are correct—or more realistically, how small their error is and in what direction—is unknown. But any person or agency that can systematically do better than open-market competition could get enormously rich by buying those resources at what they "know" are excessively low prices.

9. RANDOM PRICE CHANGES AND STOCK SELECTIONS

According to the preceding principles, because the present values of resources reflect anticipated future values from earnings, rentals, or sales, every resource should be priced to reflect the same expected rate of return: the market rate of interest. An underpriced asset would give a higher rate of return than other assets, so people would drive up its price as they competed for that bargain; conversely, an overpriced asset, one priced higher than the discounted (at the rate of interest) value of the anticipated future rentals and receipts, will yield less than the rate of interest. So no one would want to hold it at that price, and its price would fall. The price of every resource must be such that the expected return is at least as good as on any other asset, and that rate of return is the market rate of interest.

The preceding principles have some very powerful and surprising implications. For example, they indicate that the *past* path of prices of some resource is irrelevant in predicting whether it is now underpriced or overpriced relative to future yields or prices. If in the past month the price of some share of common stock on the stock exchange has fallen drastically while another has risen considerably, which is the better buy? The past prices do not tell you which. One price has fallen just far enough to give an expected future growth that just matches the currently perceived future prospects of the stock that has risen. The currently perceived future expected average gain from each stock is the same for all stocks.

We have just seen how economic analysis says that prices are set in open markets. What are the facts? Do past paths of stock prices indeed give *no* clue about which stock offers greater prospects of a gain? Yes. All corporate stocks are currently priced in the stock market so as to offer the same expected future gain, and the *past* prices add no information that will help make a more accurate selection of which one can be expected to rise more than the other. The price will change by more than the normal rate of interest only if there is some change in knowledge or belief about the future. But those changes are by definition not predictable—or they would already have influenced the current stock price. The stock price will vary in the future *at random* around the same expected average rate of return. There is an equal chance that it will go up enough to give a gain more than the rate of interest or will go down by an offsetting amount. Prices *will* change, but the path or sequence of changes will be at random around an average expectation equal to the rate of interest.

No price patterns are known that allow anyone to make profits predictably, though a lot of people chart prices in the futile hope that they can thereby beat the market. (The person doesn't exist who systematically or reliably does so; at least such a person hasn't been identified.) You might as well pick stocks at random and hold them without continually trying to revise your holdings. (Later, in Chapter 17, we present some more details about common stocks and how much they vary randomly.)

Stockbrokers and investment counselors have begun to realize these facts and now offer portfolios (sets of stocks) that essentially encompass the diverse range of stocks on the exchanges. These are called indexed funds because they are "indexed" to or representative of the whole market. Indexing avoids fruitless and expensive research to pick better stocks, as if the counselors could reliably beat the best of the rest of the world. In effect, these counselors simply buy a set of stocks and hold them, buying or selling stocks only if the flows of funds in or out do not match. All this is exactly what the preceding principles of capital values imply for a market in which anyone who wants to buy or sell is entitled to do so at whatever prices he or she negotiates.

What then can "your" stockbroker tell you? Only what any other stockbroker can tell you: what are common, preferred, and participating preferred stocks, bonds, treasury bills, and the like; where the stock markets are; how to place an order to buy or sell most cheaply and conveniently; where to have your securities held; how to collect your dividends; how to handle some tax matters. But for learning which stocks are more likely to give a gain, or whether the market is likely to be rising or falling and other such forecasts—plug your ears. (Remember: If they could predict better, they'd be too rich to bother with customers.)

10. HIGH AND INCREASING CALIFORNIA LAND VALUES?

Some desert land in California is nearly worthless, but some along the coast is astonishingly expensive. The puzzling facts are that land values keep rising in California more rapidly than elsewhere, and, still more puzzling, that land in California with annual rents of $10 a square foot sells for $180 a square foot—far more than land of the same current rent in the Midwest, which sells for only $100. How can land prices in California for land of the *same current rental* or service value be so much higher *and* continue to rise more steeply than land elsewhere? Why hasn't the prospect of a more rapid increase in California's population adjusted the present California prices upward once and for all? Are people continually being surprised and revising their expectations, and hence prices, upward, whereas in the Midwest forecasts are more accurate? No, it all makes perfect sense, if you keep in mind the distinction between *present value* and *future rents* of a parcel of land. The explanation rests on the expectation that population will rise more rapidly in California, which implies increasingly higher *future annual rents* than will occur in the Midwest where rents won't rise at all. Say two pieces of land for sale have the same present rent: The price of the land with rising expected future rents will exceed the price of the land with constant expected future rents. Furthermore, its value will rise faster (at the interest rate) over time than the Midwest land as those higher future California rents get closer in time.

Table 6–8 gives an example: Both parcels of land have the same first-year rental of $10 per square foot, but one parcel draws a constant rent and the other has a rental rising in four years to $20, at which it then stays constant. At a 10% rate of interest, its present value is about $179 per square foot or 17.9 times the first-year rental, whereas the present value of the constant-rent land is only $100, 10 times its first and constant annual rent. Which investment is the better one? And in the first year, when the rental values are the same, which is the cheaper one to buy for the first year's service?

The answer is that both have the same cost for a first year's rental and both are equally profitable investments. In California land value rises during the first year to $187, a gain of $7.90. In the Midwest land value doesn't rise. In both places the rent is $10.00 in the first year. If you buy land in California, you must invest $79 more, which could have earned 10%, or $7.90. So in California during the first year you get three things: a $7.90 capital gain, plus a $10 rental income, minus $7.90, the forgone interest on your greater investment of $79—all of which adds up to the $10 cost of a first year's rental of equivalent land in the Midwest. The capital value gain exactly matches the lost earnings on the extra $79. You don't make any profit on the California land just because it rises in

Table 6-8   ASSUMED FUTURE RENTALS AND CAPITAL VALUES OF MIDWEST LAND

Year	California		Midwest	
	Assumed Rentals	Value of Land at Beginning of Year	Assumed Rentals	Value of Land at Beginning of Year
1	$10.00	179	$10	$100
2	12.50	187	$10	$100
3	15.00	193	$10	$100
4	17.50	197	$10	$100
5	20.00	200	$10	$100
6	20.00	200	$10	$100
7	20.00	200	$10	$100

value; you just get interest on your larger investment paid for that larger future rental stream. It doesn't cost any more to occupy the land in the first year even if the purchase price of the land is higher than that of other land with the same initial rent. The results are the same for every year in the future until one stops growing in rental value relative to the other. Only people who bought land *before expectations* changed about future increasing population density will have made a profit on California land.

An exactly analogous situation is a growth stock such as Xerox, which started at a high price and increased in price by a higher percentage because it had *earnings that were expected to increase*, whereas some other stock with the same current earnings was expected not to grow in earnings. Each stock has equally good profit prospects for exactly the same reasons as just explained for land prices. Just change the words "land" to "stocks" and "rents" to "earnings." If the stocks weren't equally good prospects, who are the fools selling the stock with a better prospect of a gain, and who are the fools buying the stock with a poorer prospect? Economic analysis doesn't rely on the assumption that all people are fools. It assumes that people don't want to give away profitable prospects, and that there are enough people to prevent detectable underpricing or overpricing.

11. IS BORROWING AT HIGH INTEREST RATES MORE EXPENSIVE DURING INFLATION?

None of the preceding analysis and applications assumed a continuing inflation of prices. **Inflation** is a rise of *all* money prices at the same percentage rate. Inflation is examined in detail in Chapter 19. Here it suffices to say simply that inflation is induced by increasing the national supply of money faster than the stock of real goods. The more rapid increase of the money stock induces an inflation of money prices of goods. The value of money falls; or, put another way, market-clearing prices go up. In later chapters we will examine why the money supply increases so much faster than the supply of goods.

How *does* inflation affect the rate of interest? To emphasize the relevance of the question, let us investigate whether inflation's effects on interest rates make it more expensive for young people to buy houses or condominiums (apartments that are bought rather than rented), as is often contended.

If lenders and borrowers expect inflation to continue—say at the rate of 10% per year—lenders will insist on being repaid more dollars, to compensate for the reduced purchasing power of the dollar when it is later repaid, and borrowers will be willing to comply. Thus, if the *real* rate of interest—the rate in the absence of inflation—were 5%, then with an expected 10% inflation the lenders would be able to get a rate of interest in *money* terms of about 15%. And you, to borrow, would be willing to pay 15% per year. The reason is that what you buy with the borrowed funds of, say, $100 will be worth 10% more dollars in a year, so you give up only 5% in real terms when you pay 15% in money while getting 10% higher dollar value in your investment. You have a real cost of only 5%.[4]

It is true that a $15 interest payment is greater than a $5 interest payment. But we should be clear about what that extra $10 (or extra 10%) represents. It is not an interest payment to the lender. The reason will be

_____

[4]For one-year loans, the relationship between the promised *real* interest rate r and the promised nominal money interest rate, R, if the price level is *anticipated* to increase at the rate of p percent a year, is:

$$(1 + R) = (1 + r)(1 + p) = 1 + r + p + rp.$$

If we consider rp to be negligibly small, then $R = r + p$. In Israel, where inflation has exceeded 100% per year, interest rates of over 100% per year are common.

clear if you think ahead to the time the debt comes due, say in 10 years. At that time what you have bought now, say the condominium, will have risen with 10% annual inflation to over twice its original value—indeed, to about 2.6 times its initial value. If inflation is correctly anticipated, what you bought for $100 will be worth $260 in 10 years. But all you must repay at that time on your debt is the principal dollar amount of $100, $160 less than if you were to repay an amount *really* worth as much as you borrowed initially. That would have given you a gain of $160. However, it is that $160 which you are paying for with the extra $10 payments in the $15 "interest." Of that so-called interest of $15, about $10 is an earlier repayment of some of the debt. When the debt is finally due, all you have to pay is $100 despite the fact that all prices are 2.6 times higher (as, on average, will be your income and everything else you own) than if there had been no inflation and all prices were the same as initially. In full effect, you borrowed $100 and ended up with something worth $260 after paying 5% real interest. You are no richer in real terms. Instead of repaying the lender $260 at the end of 10 years to compensate for the effect of inflation on the principal due, you have been paying back some of the principal earlier in those $10 extra payments that were included in the $15 inflation-adjusted interest. The inflation-adjusted interest has two components: a payment of interest in real terms plus a repayment of part of the principal earlier than if there had been no inflation, for in the absence of inflation the borrower could have paid only interest for the life of the loan and repaid the principal in a lump sum at the end. The money would give the lender the same purchasing power as it had when it was loaned out.

A borrower who did not want to repay a debt so fast with such large early payments could borrow $10 more every year to pay that higher interest. But in 10 years that borrower

would owe $160 more on that extra debt, a total of $260 instead of the initial $100. In real terms that is the same as if there had been no inflation and people paid only true interest until the debt was due, at which time they repaid the same real principal.

Alternatively, instead of going deeper into debt (in nominal dollar, but not in real, terms), the borrower could agree to repay 5% every year on a *principal* that *increases* at 10% per year. In that case the payments for interest would be $5 the first year instead of $15, and $5.50 in the second year instead of $15, and $6.04 in the third year, and so on, until in the tenth year the interest (the *real* interest) would be 5% of $260, or $13. In this case the real interest keeps a constant purchasing power, but the debt owed will have increased to $260 at the end of the term, which will have the same real purchasing power as the initial $100—and the house will be worth $260. You could sell it and pay off the $260 debt at the end of 10 years.

What if the inflation rate proves to be a lot less than expected? Then a borrower owes more than was borrowed in real terms. What if the inflation is higher than expected? The borrower will get a bonanza. And that is the trouble with an inflationary situation. Predictions of the future become more critical and add to our uncertainty and hesitancy to borrow and invest. But that is another story best put off until later.

When this was written, in 1982, the *monetary* (nominal) rate of interest being negotiated on first class (AAA) long-term industrial and U.S. government bonds was around 11%.[5] If currently negotiated *nominal* interest rates incorporate anticipations of inflation of about 5% to 7%, the promised real rate is about 4% to 6%—not a very unusual real rate on very safe investments, judging from the past century of experience. (What

[5]In the financial community, the most secure bonds are given the rating AAA, called triple A, and successively less-secure bonds are rated AA, A, and B.

the actually *realized* real rate will be depends on what the actual inflation rate happens to be over the life of the bond.) Failure to distinguish between the nominal rate of interest (which *includes* adjustments for anticipations in inflation) and the real rate of interest is widespread and a source of great confusion in the political arena and the news media alike. You should now be able to avoid such confusion.

Wealth, Interest, Income, and Profits

Physical **wealth** is the current stock of economic goods. The *market value* of that physical wealth is the sum of the market values of the individual goods. *Wealth* is used sometimes to mean the market value of the goods and at other times to mean the collection of the goods. (Remember also the still greater *total personal use value*.)

STANDARD INCOME

If the physical stock of wealth is put to its highest-valued uses, in exactly one year it will be expected to be larger by the rate of interest. During the year society could have consumed that increase in wealth and still have the same initial amount of wealth at year's end. This market-forecasted sustainable rate of increase in wealth is called **standard income**. If wealth is $100 and the rate of interest in the economy is 10%, then the foreseen, permanently sustainable annual standard income is $10 per year. By definition, standard income, wealth, and the rate of interest are related as follows:

$$I = W \times r$$

where I denotes standard income, W is the market value of physical wealth, and r is the annual rate of interest. If you know the value of any two of these, you can determine the third.

SAVING

Saving is the nonconsumption of standard income. Saving (that is, not consuming) some of that income enlarges wealth because the saving is added to the wealth. If you invest the saving, you'll get even more wealth; you'll get interest on the investment. If you consume more than your standard income, that is, *dissave*, you will have less wealth at year's end than you started with.

PROFITS AND LOSSES

Wealth may surprisingly increase by more than expected. If that gain in wealth is not accounted for by receipt of interest or investment of savings out of standard income, there is a **profit**. For example, assume there is no inflation and that wealth would grow, with no saving and no investment, in one year from $100 to $106 because the interest rate is 6%; the standard income is $6 per year on that wealth. But if the market value increased by more than the savings (that is, to more than $106), or to over $100 if all the $6 standard income had been consumed, the net gain is called *profit*: the change in wealth not accounted for by investment of savings of standard income.

Suppose an asset has a market value of $150 at the beginning of a year and $200 at the end. At an interest rate of 6%, the predicted value would have risen to $159 (= $150 × 1.06) *if all* of the interest (standard income) were saved. The unpredicted increase in value, $41 (= $200 − $159), would be profit. Alternatively, if *none* of the standard income had been saved, the value would have been expected to remain at $150. Then, all of the $50 increase (to $200) would have been profit. In general, profit equals the value at the end of a period minus initial value and minus the saving out of the predicted interest (standard income).

If your wealth today is $100 and there is unexpected good news about future yields or demands for the services of the goods you own, the market value of the goods will instantly jump to, say, $120. Your $20 increase in wealth value that was unpredicted by the market is a **capital gain**, or *profit*. Now you foresee that you can get $2 more standard income per year every year thereafter: $12 per year instead of $10. That profit can be expressed either as a wealth gain of $20 or an increase in the standard income flow of $2 per year.[6]

We commonly express this ambiguously by saying that any rise in wealth that is unexpected by the market is a profit, and any fall is a loss. Of course, it is possible that some person with confidence or foresight or luck bought the wealth and then got a profit when it rose more than the rate of interest could account for. The fact that the buyer had been able to buy at a price that yielded a profit demonstrates that the growth was not fully or accurately expected by other people, that is, by the market.

Capital Values, Property Rights, and Care of Wealth

Changes in anticipations of future events affect present prices of goods, or assets. In the stock exchange these revisions are made especially apparent, because the price of a share of common stock—a share of ownership in a business corporation—is the capitalized present worth of the anticipated series of future earnings. If it is newly anticipated that higher taxes will be placed on cars or that gasoline prices will rise more than formerly expected, the value of General Motors stock will drop now, imposing a loss of wealth on the *current* owners of resources specialized to General Motors' production of cars, that is, the stockholders.

Both private-property rights and capital-

goods markets (in which ownership of assets can be bought and sold) are essential foundations of the market system for organizing economic activity; if the rights or the markets or the prices are suppressed, the resulting system will lead to actions that appear to be wasteful or shortsighted, especially in the way things are consumed and maintained and in the kinds of investments. The homeowner who can resell a house will maintain and repair it now even though the repairs may not yield better housing now. The owner will do so because the present market value of the house anticipates the lower future maintenance costs that result from the present repairs. The value of the house is thereby maintained.

This might suggest that tenants would not maintain the premises they rent. And the owner, who is not blind to this possibility, takes selective, contractual precautions. Rental contracts provide incentives for appropriately careful use of the property by tenants. The owners will be more careful in selecting tenants, avoiding unreliable ones, unless housing laws force the owner to be less discriminating.

The effects of different types of property rights are illustrated by the modern business enterprise. The owner is influenced by all anticipated effects, present and future, that change the present capital value of the enterprise. Foreseeable developments and consequences of present acts will be capitalized into the owner's resources, which are more specialized to this firm in their usefulness and value than are its employees, who are therefore less motivated by the foreseeable long-run consequences to the enterprise. To make employees' actions more responsive to the total span of effects, two claims systems are sometimes added to the wage system. One is a *stock option* for managers and employees who have the most influence on the long-run effects and wealth of the firm. These people have rights to buy shares of stock at preassigned values. Because the

---

[6]More detailed exposition of the sources of profits and other meanings of the term are given in Chapter 9.

long-run anticipated effects of their actions are capitalized into the present value of the shares of stock, those employees will pay more heed to their long-run effects than they would without stock options. In the second system, *profit sharing*, managers and employees share the annual earnings of the firm. "Profit sharing", that is, sharing in some of the profits, does less than the stock option to emphasize the future effects of present behavior since current earnings do not include changes in the capital value of the firm. Because current accounting earnings do not include the *wealth* effects of the longer-run implications of present events, earnings fail to direct full attention to all the wealth-changing consequences of current employee behavior. We will analyze the organization of firms in more detail in Chapter 9.

Summary

1. Capital goods render services now and in the future. The current price of a capital good is the sum of the value of current services and the present values of the future expected services.

2. Earlier availability of services is typically more valuable than their later availability because appropriate investment and use of current services makes possible a net increase in future services.

3. In addition to being the time premium paid for borrowed wealth, the *interest rate* is a measure of: (a) the relationship between present amounts of a good and the amounts of future goods for which the present amount can be traded; (b) the maximal growth rate of wealth; (c) the price of earlier relative to later availability; and (d) the rate of standard income relative to wealth.

4. The cost of borrowing is not the sum of the interest payments, but is instead the present value (discounted values) of the future interest payments, because, even with zero inflation, earlier payments are greater sacrifices

of consumption potential than are later payments of the same dollar amount.

5. The higher the rate of interest, the lower will be the present value of a future service.

6. $P(1 + r)^t = A$ is a way to summarize the relationship among present value, P, rate of interest, r, time, t, and future amount, A.

7. Under private-property rights, foreseeable changes of the future value of services from some existing good are capitalized by a change in the *current* price of the good. Those wealth changes are incurred by the owner of the good at the time the future consequences of any act are *foreseen*, rather than when and if they later occur.

8. The maturity date of any good (that is, the date at which it is consumed) affects its *present* value but not the rate of return on its *current* value. There is thus as much incentive to invest in slowly maturing goods as to invest in rapidly maturing goods, because their anticipated future value is competitively bid into their current price.

9. Producing shorter-lived goods in order to sell more replacements is not profitable because the sales prices of shorter-lived goods are proportionally less than those of longer-lived goods, and extra costs of replacement are incurred.

10. The nominal rate of interest has normally been between 2% and 4% per year on secure capital. But if inflation is expected, the *nominal* interest rate includes a premium to cover the expected rate, to compensate for the depreciation of the money in which debts will later be repaid.

11. Physical wealth is the current stock of economic goods.

12. The market value measure of that wealth is the sum of the marketable values of the goods.

13. Standard income is the highest market-forecasted sustainable rate at which wealth increases. Standard income is equal, by defini-

tion, to the market value of wealth multiplied by the rate of interest.

14. Saving is the nonconsumption of standard income.

15. Profit is any increase in wealth in excess of that from savings out of standard income. It is the growth of wealth in excess of that implied by the rate of interest. Losses are a failure of wealth to increase by the rate of interest.

16. Because there is no universal standardized terminology, often what is here called standard income is elsewhere called profit.

Questions

1. You invest $350 today. At the end of one year you will get back $385. What is the implied, or effective, rate of interest?

2. How much will $250 grow to in three years at 7% compounded annually? How long will it take to double?

3. At the end of a year you will get $220. At a 10% interest rate, what present amount will grow to that amount? In other words, what is the present value of $220 deferred one year at 10%?

*4. In what sense is interest the price of money? In what sense is it not the price of money?

5. What is the present value of $2500 due in five years at 8%?

6. What is the present value of $2500 due in 10 years at 8% per year?

7. What present amount is equivalent to $1000 paid at the end of each of the next three years at 8% interest? That is, what is the present value of a $1000 three-year annuity at 8% interest?

8. You borrow $1000 today and agree to pay the loan in five equal annual installments at 10% interest. Using Table 6-4, determine the amount of each payment, the first payment to be due in one year.

9. If you can borrow $1000 from your college at a 5% interest rate for six years, what is the pres-ent value of the "gift" to you, at the market rate of interest of 10%? (Hint: Each year you can earn $100 by investing now at 10%. Which would you rather have—an outright gift of $300 or that loan?

10. You buy a house by borrowing its full price, $80,000. Your annual installments in repaying the loan are $9440 for 20 years at 10%. (Do you agree?) Check with Table 6-4.
   a. At the end of the first year, how much of the house's value is yours; that is, what is your equity? (Hint: On $80,000 the interest for the first year at 10% is $8000, but you paid $9440 at the end of the first year.)
   b. At the end of twenty years, assuming the house is still worth $80,000, what is your equity?

11. Two refrigerators are available for purchase. One costs more to buy but less to operate.

	Purchase Price	Annual Operating Cost in Each of 10 Years
A	$400	$100
B	$340	$110

Which is the cheaper source of refrigeration over a 10-year period?

*12. If the value of your buildings or common stock should fall, how can you tell whether there has been a rise in the rate of interest or a fall in anticipated future net receipts? (Hint: Look at the bond market. How will this help give an answer?)

*13. Which do you think will have a bigger influence in revising your annual *consumption* rate—an unexpected gift of $1000 or an unexpected salary increase of $50 per month? (Hint: What is the present value of each at, say, 10% per year?) Why did the question say *"unexpected"* gift and salary increase?

14. You receive word that the value of a building you own has fallen from $10,000 to $5000. One possibility is that the interest rate has risen to twice its former level. A second possibility is that the building has been damaged by a fire. In either event your wealth is now $5000. Do you care which factor caused a decrease in your wealth? Why?

15. Mr. A has an income of $10,000 per year. At Christmas an aunt unexpectedly gives him $5000 in cash.

    a. What is his income during that year?

    b. Is the $5000 gift a part of his income?

    c. How much is his annual rate of income increased by the gift (at interest rates of 10%)?

16. Estimate the present value of your future earnings. Project your earnings until age 65. Then obtain the present value of that projection, at 10% interest. Are you now worth over $300,000?

17. Time Fiber Corporation common stock sells at a price 80 times as great as the accountants' reported current annual earnings. The stock of Allegheny Ludlum Corporation, a steel producer, sells at less than 10 times its reported earnings. Assume that the same accounting principles are used in each firm. What do you think will happen to the price of each firm's stock if in the next reporting period each firm reports earnings that are *unchanged* from the preceding period? Explain. (What would the price–earnings ratio be in some year of losses?)

18. If your income from nonbusiness wealth is $500 a year, what is your nonbusiness wealth at 10% interest?

19. If you consume all of your income for two years, what will be your wealth at the end of two years, if it is $1000 now with 5% interest?

20. You contemplate purchasing a house in a new suburban development. You may buy the house for $40,000, but title to the land will remain with the developer and you must pay $1000 per year for land rent, and at the end of 50 years the developer will get the house. You estimate the land is worth $15,000, and that in 50 years the house will be worth $40,000. Or you may purchase the *land* and the house now for $65,000. At 6% interest, which is cheaper?

21. "The employees of the South Bend Lathe Co. were able to buy the entire common stock (and hence ownership) of the company for $10 million in cash. The employees used a federal government plan known as Employee Stock Ownership Plan, or ESOP, whereby the ESOP employee group was able to borrow the full purchase price of $10 million, of which $5 million was lent by the U.S. government to the ESOP for 25 years at 3% annual interest, and the other $5 million was obtained from Indiana banks at 4 percentage points above the prime rate (then at about 9%)." In effect, the $5 million loan from the federal taxpayers at 3% for 35 years was a gift of how much in present- value terms? (Use 10% as the relevant cost of interest, even though the employees must pay 4% above the prime rate which ranged around 7% to 8% in 1976.)

*22. Do you know of any products that have become more expensive over the past several centuries or decades because of the exhaustion of cheaper ores or resources from which that product is obtained? Is it true for copper, iron, oil, tin, diamonds, coal?

23. A retired person has $100,000 to invest in stocks and expects to get an income of about $10,000 a year (if interest rates are 10%). If you advise purchase of stocks that pay out no earnings as dividends, the person complains there will be no income. How would you explain that there *is* an income of 10%?

*24. a. A family with the 1980 median income of about $21,500 buys a house at the median price of $51,920. Suppose no inflation were anticipated and in fact none occurs, so the family can borrow at 3% interest. Suppose the family expects its real income to rise at 3% per year for the next 30 years. This family borrows the entire price of a house and agrees to make an annual mortgage payment of $2627, which will extinguish the debt in 30 years. (Verify this by reference to Table 6-3. Two-figure accuracy is as close as you can expect.) That mortgage payment will be a decreasing fraction of the family's rising real income.

    b. Suppose instead a correctly anticipated inflation of 8% per year occurs. The family borrows $51,920 at 11% to buy the house. Annual dollar income will rise at 11% per year for the next 30 years. The price of the house now is $51,920 but its value will rise at 8% more than if there were no inflation. The family in this inflationary world must repay each year about $5900 (which can be verified by interpolation for 11% in Table 6-3). This is 27.6% of the family's current income of $21,500 compared to only $2627, or 12% of income, with no inflation. For this reason it is argued that anticipated inflation makes buying a home very difficult for young families. Yet we observe them buying homes. Why? Are they confused? Look ahead a few years. What is called interest now also includes an earlier repayment of the debt. Note that the annual payments are *constant* whereas the future income and the value of the house rise enormously in 20 or 30 years, at which time the mortgage payments are a very small fraction of an equivalent *real* amount of debt. In effect, the higher repayment schedule under anticipated inflation is really an earlier repayment of the principal. The real borrowing costs

are spread differently over time, being earlier under inflation. To avoid earlier repayment the family could borrow some more every year to make those larger repayments, thereby deferring more of the repayment of the total combined debt to the future so as to even the burden over time rather than concentrating so much in the earlier years.

*25. In April 1981 Congress passed a law reducing income taxes to take effect six months later, in October 1981. It was argued that, having more income left after taxes, people would begin spending more in October, increasing the demand for consumer goods. Others argued that the six-month delay between the law's passage and its going into effect would have no influence on consumers. They would increase their spending as soon as the law was passed, in April. How could the latter prediction be correct?

Chapter 7
Production with Specialization

So far we have been investigating how a private-property, market-pricing system allocates consumer goods. But before goods can be allocated they have to be produced. How are our diverse talents and efforts directed toward production? We ask again: Must a central planning agency collect data, make overall plans, and then issue directives or general instructions? Again the answer is, No, there is another way to organize the production that a society undertakes.

It was first presented by Adam Smith in 1776, in his book, *An Inquiry into the Nature and Causes of the Wealth of Nations*. He recognized that altruism, an unselfish desire to help other people, could not alone solve the problem of directing our energies to the most useful tasks. It could not alone tell us what to produce and in what quantities. For example, which of all the other people should one aid the most in one's production choices? Some selection must be made; discrimination is inescapable. Smith recognized that if another force, *personal self-interest*, were allowed to operate, individual efforts and talents could be efficiently coordinated to produce the most highly valued products. That was a startling proposition. It strongly influenced the writers of the Constitution of the United States. That it is a valid proposition under appropriate conditions has since been established—a feat for which economists have won Nobel prizes.

In this chapter we see how specialization of production (or what is also called "division of labor"), wherein people produce some goods that they sell to others in exchange for the goods they want to consume, can result in a larger total output than if people self-sufficiently produced only what they consumed. We examine how that specialization is directed and organized and how it determines people's incomes. In the next chapter we investigate a second source of larger output: teamwork organized and controlled within the modern business firm. Actually, because business firms also specialize in production, the system relies on a combination of specialization and teamwork.

In economics we distinguish among three kinds of productive situations: The first, in which the amount of goods is fixed and cannot be added to regardless of the price incentive to do so, is called the **market period**. When the period being analyzed is one in which more can be produced and supplied to consumers using the current stock of productive resources, it is called a **short-run period**. A **long-run period** is one in which the supply of productive goods—machines, labor, and the like—can be altered in response to price.

Production and Exchange

Production occurs when the physical characteristics of resources are improved. Although we commonly think of production as changing the form of material—from ores to steel, from steel to cars or I-beams—production also includes improving the time of availability or location of a good. Moving water from a well into a house is productive, as are carrying coal from a mine to a furnace; tilling the soil, planting seeds, or caring for the crop; harvesting, cleaning, grading, transporting, preserving, and distributing the crop to retail stores; or advertising, wrapping, and delivering a good to the consumer's home. Production may also be of music, films, and other forms of entertainment.

Gains from Specialization and Cooperation: A Simple Preview

The source of gains from cooperative specialization can be suggested by a very simple example, which will help in understanding a later explanation that is both more precise and more general. Suppose I could type 6 letters or make 100 bricks in an hour, whereas you could type 12 letters or make 150 bricks. You are twice as good a typist and 1.5 times better at brick making than I am. You can do more of either than I can in the same time. Suppose we want to build a brick wall *and* type some letters. Who should make the bricks? Assume both kinds of work are equally distasteful (see Table 7–1). If the wall will have 600 bricks in it, it would take me 6 hours and the sacrifice of 36 letters not typed. My cost of making bricks is .06 letters per brick. It would take you only 4 hours with the sacrifice of 48 letters. Your brick-making cost is .08 letters per brick. I should make the bricks because I can do so more cheaply, at .06 letters per brick, forsaking only 36 letters for 600 bricks. That's the cost if I make the bricks. In the 4 hours it would take you to make 600 bricks, you could have typed 48 letters; that is your total cost of 600 bricks (at .08 letters per brick). I am the lower-cost maker of bricks.

Even though you can make more bricks per hour than I can, you can also type better. But your superiority at brick making over me is lower than your superiority at typing over me. If you type and I make bricks, we will

Table 7-1 SPECIALIZATION AND MARGINAL COSTS DIFFERENCES

	Product (Per hour)			Marginal Cost of	
	Letters		Bricks	Letters	Bricks
I	6	or	100	16.67 Bricks	.06 Letters
You	12	or	150	12.5 Bricks	.08 Letters

have the most letters typed *and* have the bricks. In one 8-hour day we can have the 600 bricks plus 108 letters (= 96 + 12). But if you make the 600 bricks, we will have only 96 letters (= 48 + 48). In other words, when I make the bricks, we sacrifice the fewer letters, 12. That is, we minimize the costs.

To better understand this, consider that although you have an *absolute* advantage over me in numbers of bricks and letters, specialization must be considered. What should be compared is not the absolute number of bricks that you or I can make per hour, but rather (a) my brick-making ability *relative* to my typing with (b) your brick-making ability *relative* to your typing. In more familiar terms, we must compare my marginal costs of bricks with your marginal costs of bricks—because costs are the most highly valued of the sacrificed alternatives. By making this comparison we discover the **comparative advantage** of each use. Because of your absolute advantage, you will certainly be richer than me, because you can produce more than I can per hour of either bricks or letters: You have an absolute advantage in both. But absolute advantage determines wealth, not costs: Be-

cause I am a lower-cost maker of bricks, I have a comparative advantage in bricks, as you have in typing. I will be richer making bricks than if I type, whereas you will be richer if you type than if you make bricks.

This example illustrates, first, the *reason* for specialization in production and, second, why and how costs determine specialization. We now show how specialization in production to increase physical output can be *directed* by market prices.

Specialization, Marginal Costs, and Trade

Corporations, labor unions, credit buying, suburban shopping centers, trading stamps, discount houses, factories, and all the other institutions through which economic activity is conducted help the organization of production in a private-enterprise society; they do not obstruct it. A television set is a complicated mechanism, yet it is built up of a chain of relatively simple principles. Once these principles are grasped, the method by which

Table 7-2   DAILY POTENTIAL OUTPUTS AND COSTS OF PRODUCER A

Output of X	Total Cost	Marginal Cost	Average Cost	Value of Other Concurrent Output
0	0	0	0	$14.50
1	$ 1.00	$1.00	$1.00	13.50
2	2.10	1.10	1.05	12.40
3	3.30	1.20	1.10	11.20
4	4.60	1.30	1.15	9.90
5	6.00	1.40	1.20	8.50
6	7.50	1.50	1.25	7.00
7	9.10	1.60	1.30	5.40
8	10.80	1.70	1.35	3.70
9	12.60	1.80	1.40	1.90
10	14.50	1.90	1.45	0

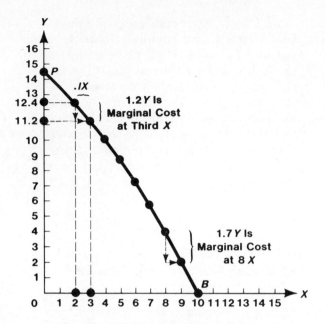

Figure 7-1.

TOTAL PRODUCTION POSSIBILITY OF
PRODUCER A FOR PRODUCTION OF X AND Y

For any output of X, the height of the line measures the
maximum feasible output of Y. The larger the output of X,
the smaller the feasible output of Y. The steepening
slope at larger X shows that greater and greater
sacrifices of Y are required for each extra unit of X
produced. That is, at greater outputs of X, the
marginal cost of more X increases.

TV operates can be said to be understood.
Similarly, on the surface the economic system
looks enormously complicated and confusing.
And without a validated theory, it is. But if
one has a validated theory, bewilderment is
replaced by confidence as complexity is reduced to sequences of simplicity. So in this
and the next chapter, do not think the exposi-
tory simplicity means that the principles developed are too simple to be applicable to the
real world. They *are* applicable, and like all
theory and analysis, their ability to be expressed simply while being accurately descriptive is a virtue. This simplicity enhances
the understanding of the way the economic
constellation operates. It is not a disordered
collection of uncoordinated activities.

Whether we pair the United States and
Britain, Atlanta and Baltimore, American
Airlines and United Airlines, or any two people called A and B, the methods of coordinating specialization of production are the same,
as is the source of gains from trade. International, interregional, interfirm, and interpersonal trade rest on the same principle.

Before we can see how specialization is
organized in a large decentralized market
economy, we must adjust our earlier example
a bit. We had assumed that each person's
marginal cost of bricks, or tradeoff rate, was
constant. Whether I worked a few or many
hours each day making bricks, the number of
letters I could have typed instead *per brick*
was a constant, .06 letters per brick. We now
abandon the assumption that the marginal
cost is constant. Typically, the tradeoff rate
depends on how intensively we engage in an
activity. For example, say a farmer can produce eggs or wine. If all the land is devoted
to grapevines, 1000 gallons of wine can be
produced but no eggs. Producing some eggs
will require sacrificing some land now given
to vines. Initially the land least appropriate
for vines will be used, but if more and more
eggs are to be produced annually, land successively better for grapevines must be transferred to chickens, and the extra amount of

wine sacrificed for the extra eggs will be larger. In economic jargon, the marginal cost of eggs is higher at greater rates of production of eggs, because smaller and smaller amounts of appropriate resources are left for further expansion of production.

A Two-Person Economy

Let us look at a simple two-person, two-commodity model. The two persons are A and B. A's production capability is shown in Table 7–2. A's resources could produce, at most, 10 X daily, or if all resources were devoted to production of something else, A could produce daily other services or goods worth $14.50. To simplify matters we will refer to the other possible products as Y, and measure them in dollars, as if each Y were worth $1. We can produce combinations of both X and Y, as indicated in the table. For example, A could produce 1 X daily and $13.50 of Y; or 2 X daily and $12.40 of Y. Notice that A's marginal costs of producing X are greater at larger rates of production of X.

The production capabilities of A, shown in Table 7–2, reveal that if 1 X is produced daily, $1 of Y will be sacrificed daily. A's cost of 1 X is $1. To produce 2 X daily rather than only 1 X daily will cost A an extra sacrifice of $1.10 Y daily. The $1.10 *increase* in *total* cost is called the *marginal cost* at 2 X. **Marginal cost** *is the increase in total cost between outputs differing by one unit of output* (here X). The cost increase is not necessarily constant regardless of total output. An increase in output from 5 X to 6 X will raise the total costs from $6 to $7.50, so the marginal cost at 6 X (or "of the sixth X," as it is sometimes called) is $1.50. The concept of marginal cost is extremely important and should be learned well. Also, once the meaning of cost is understood, it is easy to see that *minimizing* the *cost* of any output is the same as maximizing the value of the other output one can also produce.

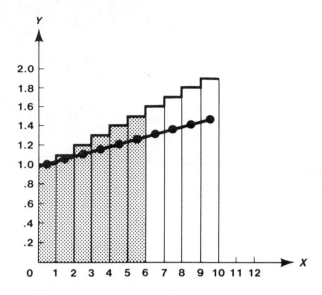

Figure 7-2.

A'S MARGINAL AND AVERAGE COSTS OF PRODUCING X

Bars show marginal costs; the connected dots show the average cost at each output, based on data in Table 7–2. Accumulated areas of bars to any output of X represent the output of other goods forsaken to produce that amount of X. A major purpose of this figure is to emphasize the difference between the concepts of marginal and average costs.

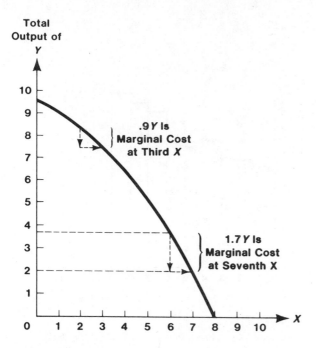

Total
Output of
Y

Figure 7-3.

TOTAL PRODUCTION POSSIBILITY OF B

Taken from data in Table 7–3. For any specified amount of X (on horizontal axis) the curve shows the maximum of Y achievable (on vertical axis). The more of X that is produced, the less of Y that can be produced.

Figures 7–1 and 7–2 list A's production possibilities and the implied marginal costs. By definition, the marginal costs at 1 X and at 2 X add up to the total costs of producing 2 X. And the first three marginal costs at 1, 2, and 3 add up to the total cost of 3 X (which should now be obvious, if you understand the meaning of marginal costs).

In Figure 7–2 producer A's marginal costs are shown by the bars above the quantities 1, 2, 3, and so on. The increasing heights depict higher marginal costs at larger outputs. The total cost at 10 units of X would be $1.90 (of Y) *more* than the total cost of 9 X. That means the marginal cost at 10 is $1.90. The total area of all the marginal cost bars from zero to any output of X represents *total* costs for that output. For example, the *total* cost of producing 6 X is measured by the area of *all* the marginal cost bars up to and including 6 X, representing a total cost of $7.50 (which is the value of other potential goods and services forsaken). The *average* cost at six units of X is $7.50/6 X = $1.25 per X; average costs are indicated by the dotted line in Figure 7–2. To see how average, total, and marginal costs are reused mathematically, consider the following analogy to successive test scores during a semester. Your total

Table 7-3 DAILY POTENTIAL OUTPUTS AND COSTS OF PRODUCER B

Output of X	Total Cost	Marginal Cost	Average Cost	Value of Other Concurrent Output
0	0	0	0	$9.60
1	$ .50	$ .50	$ .50	9.10
2	1.20	.70	.60	8.40
3	2.10	.90	.70	7.50
4	3.20	1.10	.80	6.40
5	4.50	1.30	.90	5.10
6	6.00	1.50	1.00	3.60
7	7.70	1.70	1.10	1.90
8	9.60	1.90	1.20	0

score accumulated to any test is the sum of the successive test scores. If the successive scores for the tests increased, as our marginal costs do, your average score per test would also be increasing. The current average of all the tests taken would be less than the score on your most recent test, because of your good fortune in having successively higher test scores (or your bad fortune in having started so low).

The productive capabilities of our second producer, B, are summarized in Table 7-3 and Figures 7-3 and 7-4. Like A, B's marginal costs of X increase as the output of X increases. B differs from A in two significant respects:

1. B is not as productive as A in producing X or anything else.

2. B's marginal costs of X start lower at small outputs of X, but they increase more rapidly.

Achieving Production Efficiency by Equalizing Marginal Costs

Suppose A is living in isolation and is self-sufficient, making 2 X and $12.40 worth of Y each day, and consuming only what is produced. (To simplify, assume Y is always worth $1, so the quantity of Y is equal to its dollar value.) The meaning of self-sufficiency is: Each person consumes only what he or she produces. Specialization, however, means that one consumes less of some goods than one produces and more of others. Table 7-2 shows that A can produce 2 X and $12.40 of Y. Notice that A's marginal cost of making a second X daily is $1.10 of Y.

Next, B, who is also self-sufficient, is also making 2 X (at a marginal cost of 70¢) and $8.40 worth of Y. Certainly A is richer than B, for although each has 2 X, A has more Y ($12.40) than does B ($8.40). There is no way A and B could have more Y, given that each

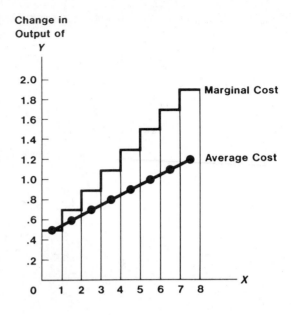

Figure 7-4.

B'S MARGINAL AND AVERAGE COSTS OF PRODUCING X

Bars show marginal costs, and dots in each bar show average cost at that output, for data from Table 7-3. Note that the accumulated areas of the bars to any output represent total cost—the total alternative output sacrificed. As the output of X increases so does the marginal cost.

Table 7-4   GAINS FROM SPECIALIZATION AND TRADE IF MARGINAL COSTS DIFFER

Before Specialization

	Produces		Consumes	
Person	**X**	**Y**	**X**	**Y**
A	2 and 12.4		2 and 12.4	
B	2 and 8.4		2 and 8.4	
Total	4	20.8	4	20.8

After Specialization

	Produces		Consumes		
Person	**X**	**Y**	**X**	**Y**	
A	1 and 13.5		2 and 12.5		A produces 1.1 more Y and spends only 1Y to buy 1X from B, gaining .1Y.
B	3 and 7.5		2 and 8.5		B produces 1X more (at cost 0.9Y) but sells the 1X to A for 1Y, also gaining .1Y.
Total	4	21	4	21	

Gain from specialization is .2Y.

must produce and consume 2 X to remain self-sufficient.

However, because their marginal costs differ at their current output of X, you and I can see that if A and B were not self-sufficient, but instead each produced more of some good to sell to the other in exchange for some of the other good, both could be richer and better off. If you can't see that right away, as very few people can, we remind you that the idea was first formulated only in 1776, several thousand years after people began specializing.

The crucial feature is that if A and B are producing outputs at which their *marginal costs are not equal,* they should revise their outputs to make them equal. Let us see why. The marginal cost at 2 X is $1.10 for A and only 70¢ for B. By producing one fewer X, A could save enough resources to instead produce $1.10 more of Y. (Be sure to check the arithmetic by referring to the data in the tables. This may be tedious, but it is very important to work through the numerical details to ensure understanding. This is a place where words alone are not sufficient to make

an idea crystal clear.) Since B's marginal cost of producing X is less than A's, B could produce another X by giving up less than $1.10—in fact, only 90¢, which is B's marginal cost of a third X. Thus, by producing one X fewer, A could produce 1.10 Y more while B produces an offsetting X with a marginal cost of only 90¢ of Y. As a result a 20¢ amount more of Y ($1.10 − 90¢) would be obtained. A and B together would still have a total of 4 X, but their total Y would be 20¢ *larger,* $21 (= $13.50 + $7.50) instead of only $20.80 ($12.40 + $8.40). They could divide that 20¢ larger output of Y. Table 7–4 summarizes the initial and final situations.

Specialization is now occurring because A is producing only 1 X but consuming 2 X, and is producing 13.5 Y but consuming less than 13.5 Y. If the two persons want an output of 4 X with the maximum possible amount of Y, the best way is for A to produce 1 X and B to produce 3 X. There is no other way to do so and have more Y. Indeed, any other arrangement would be worse, in that less than 21 Y would be produced.

What may at first be surprising is that though A can produce more X in one day than can B—10 compared to 8—B produces the increased amount of X. But as we saw in our earlier example of letters and bricks, being able to produce more X does not make A a lower-cost producer of X. We do not measure absolute advantage but *comparative* advantage: What counts is one's ability at producing X. The marginal costs of X measure how much "better" A is at producing X than is B. For output rates of 1 X, 2 X, or 3 X daily, the marginal costs for B are less than for A. If only 1 or 2 or 3 X are to be produced, B can do it better (that is, more cheaply) than can A.

If given amounts of X are to be produced, the production-possibility boundary for Y is listed in Table 7-5. (Recall from Chapter 1 that the production-possibility boundary shows the largest combined amounts of goods that can be produced with available resources.) Suppose A and B want more than 4 X—say 6 X. B should produce 4 X and A should produce 2 X. Each would be producing at the same marginal cost. If B produced all 6 X, the marginal cost of the fifth and sixth would exceed A's marginal costs to produce one or two. The total cost would be $6 worth of Y. So somehow B should be induced to produce 4 X and A to produce 2 X, for a total cost of only $5.30 ($3.20 for B and $2.10 for A). If 7 X were desired, B producing four and A three would be cheaper than any other possible assignment. (Try to get seven units in a cheaper way; you can't.) Table 7-5 gives the best way for all other totals of X.

The producers should *always keep the marginal costs as close as possible to equality so that one won't have a lower marginal cost for another unit than any other party is incurring at his or her output of* X. Table 7-5 shows the amount of X that should be produced by A and by B for each social total of X such that the remaining output of Y is maximized. In other words, the X is produced with the minimum sacrifice of Y, which is to say the X is produced at the minimum total cost. Remember that the minimum total cost is merely another way of saying maximum value of other feasible outputs.

DIAGRAMMATIC ANALYSIS

By looking at Figure 7-5 we can see how equating marginal costs has the effect of minimizing costs. This figure shows two producers' generalized marginal cost curves, MC_A and MC_B. (They are smoothed for the sake of graphic clarity.) As the figure shows, if each person produces equal amounts (X_a and X_b), B would have a lower marginal cost than A. Therefore, if B expanded production of X (to X'_b) and A reduced production by the same number of units (to X'_a) B's margin-

Table 7-5

TOTAL EFFICIENT OUTPUTS OF
Y AND X BY PRODUCERS A AND B

X	Y	Y's Produced by A and B	Marginal Cost of X
0	24.10	= 14.50 + 9.60	0
1	23.60	= 14.50 + 9.10	.50
2	22.90	= 14.50 + 8.40	.70
3	22.00	= 14.50 + 7.50	.90
4	21.00	= 13.50 + 7.50	1.00
5	19.90	= 12.40 + 7.50	1.10
6	18.80	= 12.40 + 6.40	1.10
7	17.60	= 11.20 + 6.40	1.20
8	16.30	= 11.20 + 5.10	1.30
9	15.00	= 9.90 + 5.10	1.30
10	13.60	= 8.50 + 5.10	1.40
11	12.10	= 8.50 + 3.60	1.50
12	10.60	= 7.00 + 3.60	1.50
13	9.00	= 5.40 + 3.60	1.60
14	7.30	= 3.70 + 3.60	1.70
15	5.60	= 3.70 + 1.90	1.70
16	3.80	= 1.90 + 1.90	1.80
17	1.90	= 1.90 + 0	1.90
18	0	= 0 + 0	0

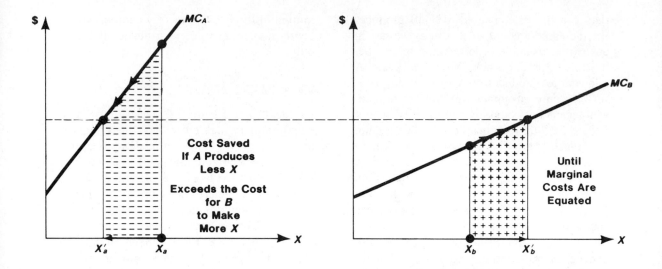

Figure 7-5.

GAINS FROM PRODUCING
AT EQUAL MARGINAL COSTS

A and B produce the same amount of X ($X_a = X_b$).
Marginal cost for X_a is greater than marginal cost for X_b.
If A reduces output, to X'_a, by as much as B expands, to
X'_b, the total costs to both producers will be reduced, as
can be seen from the fact that the extra cost to B
(area occupied by plus signs) is less than savings of
costs by A (area occupied by cross-hatching) over
quantity $X_a - X'_a$. Total amount of X is the same as
before. Total costs of that output are
minimized because marginal costs to A are
now the same as for B.

al cost of producing more X would be less than the marginal cost that A avoids by reducing the output of X by a matching amount. The *total* output of X would be the same, but the total cost is lower (that is, more of other goods are available). The shaded area under the marginal cost curve MC_B represents the increase in cost with B's expansion of output while the *larger* shaded area for A shows the larger saving in cost when A reduces output of X by a matching amount. If producers of X are at outputs with unequal marginal costs, the total cost will be reduced if the one producing at lower marginal cost expands production and the one producing at higher marginal cost reduces production. When the producers' marginal costs are equal (which does not mean that their outputs are the same), the total cost is minimized.

COORDINATION BY AUTHORITY

A central planner or dictator who knew every producer's marginal-cost curve could calculate the output for each producer at which all producers' marginal costs are equated. Doing so would achieve the lowest total cost. The planner would first add the marginal-

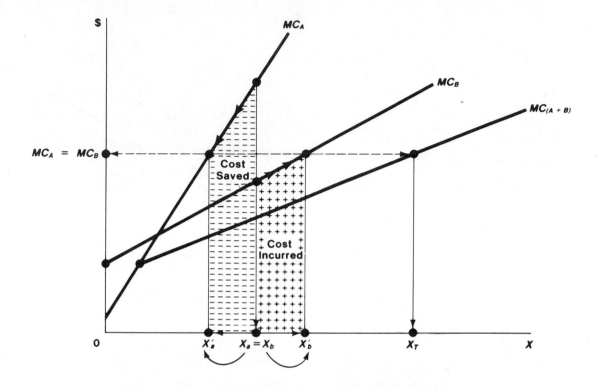

Figure 7-6.

MAXIMUM EFFICIENCY OF AGGREGATE SUPPLY
AT EQUAL MARGINAL COSTS FOR ALL PRODUCERS

When all producers' marginal costs are equal — that is,
$MC_A = MC_B$ — at outputs X'_a and X'_b, then aggregate
supply, X_T, is most efficient. Note that A's and B's
marginal costs are *not* equal at equal outputs; that
is, when $X_a = X_b$. When A's and B's marginal
costs differ, aggregate supply is not at its
maximum and aggregate cost is not at its
lowest.

cost curves of all producers horizontally, as
in Figure 7-6. (We continue to use two producers, and we ignore the question of how
the planner would obtain all that necessary
information.) The result is the extreme right-
hand curve, MC_{A+B}, called the *industry supply* curve. It is the *sums* of the horizontal distances of all the individual outputs with
equal marginal costs. For any total desired
amount of X, on the horizontal scale, the dictator notes the height on the supply schedule. That is the minimum cost of producing X for each producer at that desired total output. For example, if a total of
X_T units is to be produced, the amounts that
A and B should each produce are indicated
where the horizontal line at that marginal-
cost height intersects the two individual marginal-cost curves. That indicates X_a by A and
X_b by B. Any other output quotas totalling
X_T would be more costly, because one pro-

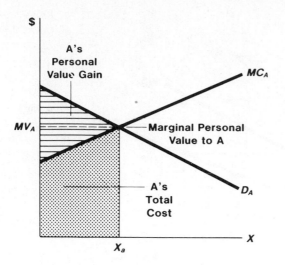

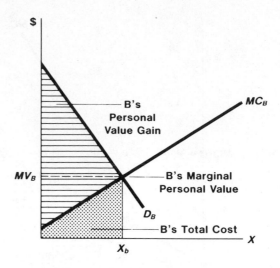

Figure 7-7.

INDEPENDENT, SELF-SUFFICIENT EQUILIBRIUMS

Person A self-sufficiently produces X_a. His total personal value of X_a is the area under his demand curve D_A and exceeds his costs (the area under the marginal-cost curve). The net total personal value to him of X_a is the horizontally lined area. His personal marginal value at X_a is MV_A. Person B also self-sufficiently produces quantity X_b and gets the net total personal value shown by the horizontally lined area. Her personal marginal value at X_b is MV_B.

ducer would have a higher marginal cost than the other.

PRODUCTION INEFFICIENCY BY AUTHORITY?

From 1974 to 1980, a U.S. government energy authority ordered all oil refineries to reduce their production of gasoline by *the same proportion* of their output and to produce more heating fuel. (Crude oil, remember, can be refined into heating oil and gasoline in varying proportions.) We can use earlier figures for graphic interpretation by calling heating oil X and gasoline Y, and A and B two different refiners. The data in Tables 7–2 and 7–3 will illustrate the consequences of such a government order. To simplify the arithmetic, assume that a 50% reduction is required. Refiner A cuts back from 1 X to 0.5 X; B cuts back from 3 X to 1.5 X. They would then produce 2 X at a total cost of $1.35 (= 50¢ cost to A plus 85¢ cost to B). With a little calculation we can see that if, instead, B produced 2 X and A cut back to no X, the total cost of 2 X would be only $1.20, a social saving of 15¢.

Why did the energy board use an inefficient method that had the effect of making marginal costs unequal? One possible reason

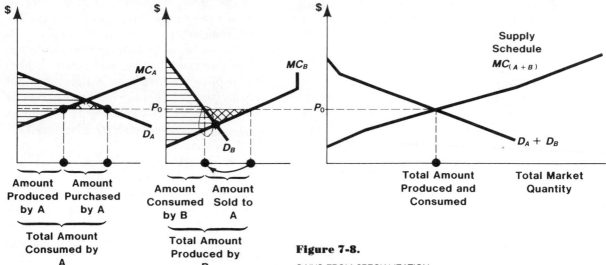

Figure 7-8.

GAINS FROM SPECIALIZATION
AND EXCHANGE WITH INTERDEPENDENCE

is ignorance on the part of the energy board. Another answer might have been, "We did not know the cost or production-possibility data for *each* refinery. Therefore we used a fair method." Fair, maybe; inefficient, certainly. Or the authority may respond that it used political vote-getting considerations. Ask your political scientist why.

PRODUCTION EFFICIENCY BY DECENTRALIZED COORDINATION

An alternative to data-collection and central planning is quicker and, in addition, determines the production of heating oil and gasoline in closer accord to consumers' valuations of gasoline and fuel oil, and of the costs of production. That method, which is not centrally directed, is the price-directed market-exchange system. Adam Smith aptly dubbed it the "invisible hand"; by this he meant that by pursuing one's own self-interest, one is nevertheless led to efficient output decisions.

To see how it works, assume, instead of an economic dictator, a capitalist system in which everyone (here, producers A and B) lives self-sufficiently, with private-property rights in productive resources. Everyone pro-

Trading between A and B as in a market results in larger output of X and other goods and gains to A and B over their self-sufficient, independent status. The extreme right-hand panel is Aggregated Demand and Aggregated Supply (marginal costs). Price is P_o, at which A buys all his consumption of X and B produces more X than when self-sufficient and sells some to A.

The gain to A is the ability to buy more at a lower price and to save production costs by purchasing at a lower price some that was formerly produced by himself at a higher marginal cost. Similarly, the gain to B is comprised of the ability to sell more at a price greater than her costs of production as well as selling some at a price greater than those units of the good are worth to her in personal consumption.

A produces less of X and more of other things, while B produces more of X and less of other things for a larger total social output with larger total personal values. For person B, the gain in the crosshatched area is comprised of two types: The left part is gain from selling some to A at a price greater than its value to B, and the right part is gain from transferring resources to producing more units of X, which are sold to A at a price greater than cost to B, which cost is simply the (lower) value of other output forsaken.

The gains to all parties from using the market rather than being self-sufficient are the crosshatched areas. Note that X is now produced at equal marginal costs by both A and B, which is also equal to the market price. Result is efficiency in production. No other "assignment" of production quotas to A and B would be efficient for this particular *total* output of X.

See Fig. 7-9

duces as much of each good as is worth producing for *one's own* consumption. Figure 7-7 shows the situation: A's marginal costs of producing X and his demand for that good. He produces an amount of X at which its marginal personal value to him falls to his marginal cost of producing X, which, remember, rises: More X would cost him more than they are worth to him. He self-sufficiently produces only what he consumes. Similarly, B produces an amount of X at which her demand and marginal-cost lines intersect.

Each would stay self-sufficient if they could not communicate and exchange in a market. But if they can, they will discover that A has a higher *marginal* personal value for X than does B. This would be revealed to B if A offers B more for an X than that X is worth to B. We can best see this by combining the two demand curves under self-sufficiency, in Figure 7-7, into an aggregate, or market, demand curve, and also by combining their marginal cost curves into an aggregate, or market, supply curve; Figure 7-8 does both these things. These aggregate demand and supply curves are horizontal summations of the individual demand curves and the individual marginal cost curves (which are in effect supply curves). Study Figure 7-8 and the caption carefully. It summarizes the process and the effects in ways that make matters clearer.

If these two people trade with each other, the total of the amounts demanded and supplied by each would be equated by a market price at the intersection of the aggregate demand and supply curves. At that price, B would be induced to produce more X than she consumes—selling some to A—and A would produce less X than he consumes—buying the difference from B. (A pays with the other goods he produces.)

Their self-interest has the effect of directing their outputs to the intersection of the demand and supply curves; that change in output is guided by the market price. B

will get profits by producing some more X, which she can sell to A at a price greater than their marginal cost to B. Similarly, A has the incentive to shift from production of X to other goods and to purchase the X from B at a price lower than his marginal costs of making those X. Figure 7-8 emphasizes the output results for A and B. Figure 7-9 probes into more detailed effects. They warrant careful study.

When each person's output is such that all producers' costs are equal, that total amount of X is being produced with minimum total cost. The various producers of X can bring their marginal costs to equality in the market system if, in pursuit of profits, each producer looks at a common market price and individually adjusts its output of X to bring its marginal cost of producing X to equality with that common, perceived price.

For each person giving up self-sufficiency in our example the cost of living is lowered and *output* consumption increases. Market prices serve as both coordinating guides and incentives to producers in affecting what and how much they produce—as well as the amount they consume. At the equilibrium free-market price the aggregate amounts produced equal the amounts demanded—without a central, all-knowing authority. The institutional features for such a system of control and coordination are (1) an accessible, reliable *marketplace* in which (2) *prices* of *exchangeable* goods are *revealed*, with (3) *private-property* ownership of resources.

You may think that all this seems a tediously involved way to say that whoever can produce one good at lower cost should do so and sell some to other parties in exchange for what others can produce at lower costs. The reason we did not put it that way is that the meaning of *lower cost* is usually misunderstood. Some people think it means lower *average* cost, and that leads to error. To see why, reexamine the data in Tables 7-2 and 7-3. To produce 6 X, A should produce 2 and B should produce 4. Although B's (80¢)

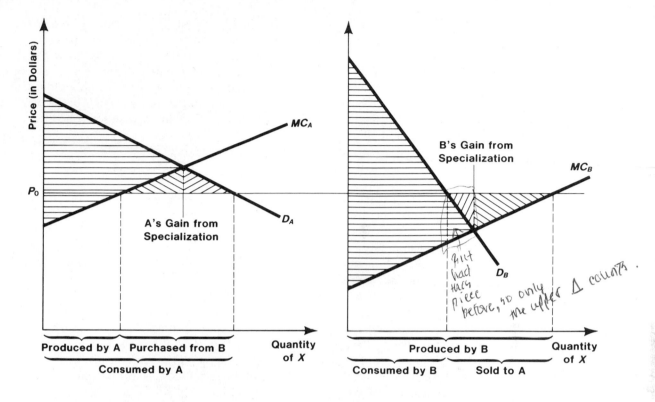

Figure 7-9 graph labels:
- Left graph: Price (in Dollars), MC_A, P_0, A's Gain from Specialization, D_A, Produced by A, Purchased from B, Consumed by A, Quantity of X
- Right graph: B's Gain from Specialization, MC_B, D_B, Produced by B, Consumed by B, Sold to A, Quantity of X

(handwritten note on right graph:) just had half piece before, so only the upper △ counts.

average cost of producing those 4 X is lower than A's (which is $1.05), it would not be efficient (that is, it would *increase total* costs) if output of X were increased by B and decreased by A. It is marginal, not average, cost that is decisive in determining efficient output assignments. Always precede the word *cost* with either *total, average,* or *marginal* if you want to increase your chances of correct economic analysis.

Some Misunderstandings of Costs

If the preceding exposition were so perfect as to be thoroughly understood, the following comments would be unnecessary reviews. See if they are.

1. TIME IS NOT A COST

The person who specialized in producing X was not the person who could produce the

Figure 7-9.

FURTHER DETAILS OF GAINS FROM SPECIALIZED PRODUCTION AND EXCHANGE

This enlargement of the left-hand and center graphs in Figure 7–8 shows two sources of gains to A and B. A gains by being able to buy more at a price that is below the value of the extra amounts purchased and consumed; he also gains by being able to reduce his output of X and produce other goods while purchasing the displaced X at a price lower than his own marginal costs of producing that amount had been. These two gains are shown as the adjoining lined triangles.

B gains from two sources. The increased output of X is sold at a price that exceeds her marginal costs of production, and some of X that B formerly consumed is sold at a price that exceeds its personal value to B when consumed by her. These two areas, for A and B respectively, are shown as adjoining lined triangles.

most X. B, who specialized in X, could produce only 8 X whereas A could produce 10 X daily. Or, it might be thought that since A could produce an X in less time than could B, A must be the lower-cost producer of X. Not so. Cost is *not* measured by time used. No one *saves* time; it is merely used for something else. The forsaken best alternative *use* of that time—not the time itself—is the cost. The *value* of the time used is pertinent—and that value differs among people according to the value of what they would otherwise have produced in the time involved. One person whose time is worth $10 an hour because he or she can produce $10 of Y in an hour, or can produce 5 X in an hour, has a marginal cost of $2 for each extra unit of X produced. Another worker whose hourly services are worth only $4 an hour in making other things and who can produce only 1 X in an hour, incurs a marginal (and average) cost of $4 for an X. But suppose our first person, who could produce 5 X in an hour, could produce $50, instead of $10, worth of other goods in that hour; then his or her marginal cost of an X is higher, $10, rather than only $2, though the time used is the same! The marginal costs of our two producers now are reversed. So beware of measuring costs simply by hours of time: What is critical is the *forsaken output value* which is measured by multiplying the number of minutes of time used by the value of the best alternative use per minute. Thus, when people say that labor in Asian countries is less costly than American labor because the Asians earn very low wages per hour, it's because they have low productivity at other tasks also.

2. EVERYONE HAS A LOWER MARGINAL COST IN SOME ACTIVITY

Lower marginal cost producers of X will, by definition, necessarily have higher marginal costs of producing other goods. To say that

my marginal cost of producing X is *higher* than yours is to say that my marginal cost of producing the other good, Y, is *lower* than yours. Since, by the definition of costs, one is the reciprocal of the other, each producer must have some output at which his or her marginal costs are lower than someone else's.

3. QUALITY AND COST ARE DIRECTLY PROPORTIONAL

Costs can be reduced by lowering quality. Quieter, smoother, faster, more comfortable, safer, prettier, more versatile kinds of travel are more expensive. Yet people value such qualities in an automobile. Thus, lowering a car's cost per mile makes sense *only if every other* aspect of the product and its quality of performance is left unchanged. It is not necessarily sensible either to reduce cost by lessening the quality of the good more than the cost saving, or to increase quality regardless of the increased cost. (How do you reconcile this consideration with Congressional legislation requiring more miles per gallon in automobiles or more insulation in homes to reduce energy costs?)

Differential Earnings, Ricardian Rents

Although everyone may be producing outputs at which marginal costs are equal, the *average* costs per unit of output may *differ*. For example, Tables 7–2 and 7–3 show that if A is producing 2 X while B is producing 4 X, each has the same marginal cost, $1.10 (the increment to total cost for the marginal unit being produced). But their average costs at those outputs are different: $1.05 for A and 80¢ for B. If the price to consumers were $1.10, A's net earnings would be 10¢ (= 5¢ × 2) and B's net earnings would be $1.20 (= 30¢ × 4). A superior producer like B (that is, the one with larger net earnings) will soon receive offers for other services from other producers because they expect that he or she could do the same for them. But they would have to bid at least as much as those earnings of $1.20. Competition to buy or hire the services of that superior talent will raise its price or salary up to that value. The owner of the superior resource gets the value of its superior productivity.

People sometimes make the mistake of confusing this differential earning from superior productive power with a *monopoly return*, a return gained by excluding competitors. Especially fertile land is superior, but we do not call it a monopoly. We do not call the higher differential earnings of a superior surgeon a monopoly return, for it is not caused by an artificial, contrived restraint that prevents other people from offering their services to the public. In honor of a "superior" early English economist, David Ricardo, who first made this distinction, the differential earnings of superior productive talent are often called **Ricardian rents**.

More Producers: Net Gains or Transfers?

Just as two people gain by specialization and exchange between themselves, the entry of a third person into specialization enables the *three* people to produce a larger output than the total of the three if the third were not allowed to also specialize and trade with the first two. To illustrate, suppose a new immigrant, C, enters the society, with the productive capabilities described in Table 7–6. In every output rate C is less capable than A or B, and will be poorer. But C's marginal cost pattern for producing X differs from theirs; it starts lower, and does not go as far before reaching C's maximum potential of 5 X.

The results can be analyzed by examining Figure 7–10. C's market price exceeds the marginal costs at the initial output of X, as panel C shows. Therefore, it is profitable for C to produce some more X to sell to A and B. In the extreme right-hand panel marked Total, the intersection of the new aggregate supply and demand curves, which now include C, is at a larger output of X. The new equilibrium price of X will be lower: P_n instead of P_O.

Party A gains by being able to buy more X at a lower price, and also by releasing some resources from production of X to other, higher-valued uses. However, as a large producer and seller of X, B loses, suffering a lower selling price of X. This loss to B is a *transfer* to customer A, because A's purchase price of X is lower. B can offset some of the loss by being able to produce other goods with resources formerly used to produce the X that was displaced by C's competition.

Table 7-6 DAILY POTENTIAL OUTPUTS AND COSTS OF PRODUCER C

Output of X	Total Cost	Marginal Cost	Average Cost	Value of Other Concurrent Output
0	0	0	0	$4.50
1	$ .30	$ .30	$.30	4.20
2	.90	.60	.45	3.60
3	1.80	.90	.60	2.70
4	3.00	1.20	.75	1.50
5	4.50	1.50	.90	0

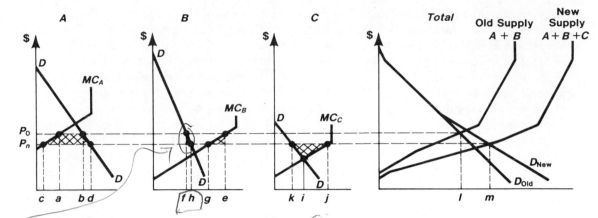

a = amount produced by *A* before *C* entered the market.
b = amount consumed by *A* before *C* entered the market.
c = amount produced by *A* after *C* enters the market.
d = amount consumed by *A* after *C* enters the market.
e = amount produced by *B* before *C* enters the market.
f = amount consumed by *B* before *C* entered the market.
g = amount produced by *B* after *C* enters the market.

h = amount consumed by *B* after *C* enters the market.
i = amount produced and consumed by *C* before *C* enters.
j = amount produced by *C* after *C* enters the market.
k = amount consumed by *C* after *C* enters the market.
l = total amount produced and consumed before *C* entered.
m = total amount produced and consumed after *C* enters.

yes √2

Figure 7-10.

A NEW PRODUCER ENTERS THE MARKET

When C enters the market, the price is greater than his marginal cost at his existing output, *i*. So he increases his output of *X* to *j* to make some profits. The new market-supply curve is shown in the right panel. The intersection of the new supply and demand curves will be at a larger output and a lower price, since C initially had lower marginal personal value for the amount he produced before joining the market. The benefits to A are indicated by the crosshatched area, representing his lower cost of purchase of the former amount of *X* he consumed, plus his ability to buy more at that lower price (the right-hand tip of his crosshatched area) and the gain from release of resources from some production of *X* for his own use to other more valuable production (the left-hand tip of his crosshatched area).

B, the larger producer of *X*, suffers a loss of income as a large seller of *X* because his selling price falls as C enters and expands the supply. B's loss is only partly reduced by his ability to transfer some resources to other output (the right-hand crosshatched triangle under his marginal-cost curve over his reduced output of *X*) and by his ability to consume more at the lower price (the left-hand crosshatched triangle).

C, the new entrant, gains as shown by the cross-hatched area in his panel of the diagram. C gains by ability to produce and sell more *X* at a price greater than his cost and to sell some of the *X* he formerly consumed at a price higher than that *X* was worth to him.

It is important to note that the gains to A are in large part simply a transfer (or retention) of income formerly spent in buying *X* from B. Hence the major part of the gain to A is a transfer from B and not a true social gain. Conversely, most of the loss imposed on B is not a true social loss but is that transfer to A. Most of the actual gain resulting from C's entry is obtained by C, though some is obtained by A and B as explained above. *Moral and caution:* Do not add transfer gains to some consumers to the social gain consequent to entry of new producers, for that would over-count the social gain; nor subtract the loss to former producers now partially displaced by the new entrants, for that is not a social loss, but merely a transfer.

That resource transfer permits some true social gain, which others, like party A, share in through the lower prices of goods now more abundantly produced. Nevertheless, the major part of the *increase* in the social output resulting from C's entry (above the former social total of A and B *and* C when C had no access to the market of A and B) accrues mostly to C.

There are, then, several consequences of C's entry into the market:

1. C, the newcomer, obtains most of the total gain in output.

2. Consumers of what the newcomer produces gain because its price falls; they keep some of their income that formerly went to the higher-price suppliers.

3. The prior producers of the good produced by the newcomer lose some income to their customers (this is the transfer counterpart of 2).

4. Some social gain is provided everyone by the release of some resources by former producers of *X* to other output.

It is important to recognize that the total increase in output is large enough to make everyone better off. It would be possible to transfer some income to B from the beneficiaries, A and C, which would make B better off while also leaving A and C better off than before C entered the community. For example, a tax or fee imposed on the newcomer, C (paid out of C's gain), and distributed to B would leave everyone better off than if C had not entered the community at all. But rarely are such taxes or fees imposed on new entrants. *Always* the admission of newcomers increases the social total above what it would be if they were excluded from the market, and they usually capture much (although not all) of the gain.

The newcomers would be exaggerating their contribution if they thought that they created all the gains to the consumers of *X*, because, as we have seen, part of the gain to those consumers is an *income transfer*, through lower prices, from the old producers to the consumers. Do not overlook this distinction between the *real output gain* (most of which is captured by the newcomers) and the *transfer of income* from old producers to consumers of goods produced by newcomers.

INCREASED DEMAND ATTRACTS HIGHER-COST ENTRANTS

The entrant, C in our example, had lower costs than existing producers. But even higher-cost producers can enter if there has been an increase in demand for the good. The increased demand will sustain a higher price even though a larger amount is supplied—some by the newcomer and some by the existing firms that expand in response to the higher demand. It is important to note that this increased output can be sustained in this case only because of the initial increase in demand for the good. As in the preceding case, consumers will benefit from the larger output provided in part by the newcomers and in part by the expansion of existing firms, all of which keeps prices lower than they otherwise would have been. The existing producers will argue that they could have provided the increased output to satisfy the increased demand, and they could have—but only at a higher price.

An example of this is the creation of new motels in growing, more populous areas, keeping motel rates and profits to existing motel owners lower than otherwise. The same holds for restaurants, gasoline stations, or grocery stores—indeed, every service. On a larger, more spectacular scale, when the demand for smaller cars increased because of higher gasoline prices, existing producers of smaller cars (Toyota, Nissan, Volkswagen, Fiat, and so on) would have obtained higher prices and profits if General Motors, Ford, and Chrysler (higher-cost producers of smaller cars) were not allowed to enter into small-car production. Another example is provided by "blue jeans." When that demand jumped, the initial makers (Levi's and Lee) benefited, but the entry of new producers attracted by the increased demand, higher price, and profit prospects benefited consumers—not Levi Strauss or Lee.

Short-Run Price and Output Adjustments; Input Specificity

The full adjustment of output and price is not as direct as outlined in the preceding explanation. On the way to that final long-run adjustment there is often some temporary overshooting of price and output. Price may temporarily fall below the ultimate new level, with the output temporarily larger. These transitional deviations are not the result of mistakes; they occur because some inputs are "specific" to certain tasks. They are not instantly and costlessly mobile and capable of shifting or being converted to other equally well-paying tasks. For example, grapevines cannot be converted to apple trees, or wine presses into chicken coops. Almost all productive resources have some degree of specificity.

To see how this affects the transition, reconsider our initial example of the entrant with lower costs (not the one who enters because demand has increased, our second example). When the lower-cost entrant produces, more is supplied and the price falls. Existing producers who were just breaking even will not cover their costs. Rather than accepting lower wages or rents some of the inputs of the initial firms will switch to other work.

However, not all inputs can switch instantly at no transfer cost to other equally well-paying jobs. So if the value of their services falls in their current jobs, they will continue to work there because doing so is still more valuable than their next best options.

Even if their earnings here fall far below their replacement or initial creation costs, they may nevertheless be better off than in their next best opportunity. Their initial creation costs are irrelevant. But in time, as enough of these specific resources wear out and are no longer worth replacing, the total output will fall and price will readjust upward to the new long-run equilibrium, which is lower than before the lower-cost entrants appeared, but higher than during the transition. It is the durability and costly mobility or nontransferability of some existing inputs that cause the overshooting in the transition.

Excellent examples of these transitional prices and values of specific resources are common. The entry of jet engines to compete with existing propeller-driven airplanes caused a drastic reduction in the value of those planes. The microwave transmission system increased the supply of communication channels and lowered the value of existing wire communication systems. The entry of new motels affects the values and replacement of older motels. The 16-bit microprocessor in microcomputers lowered the value of the prior 8-bit microprocessor. In each case the temporarily larger supply from both new and old sources depressed the price below the level that would persist after the older, less economical items were no longer worth using. If the new entrant complains and interprets the drastic, temporary fall in price as "predatory" or "cutthroat" pricing by the existing producers, remember the preceding analysis.

However, suppose the initiating factor were an increase in demand, instead of the entry of new, lower-cost producers. Even here, the transition adjustment of price involves some "overshooting." The increased demand will raise prices higher than will persist after the output is expanded, because when new entrants are attracted their larger supply will pull prices back down from their short-run higher level. This happens because the supply cannot be expanded instantly.

Some resources must be transferred to this new activity. But some resources have enough specificity or immobility so that it is not possible to move them or create new ones instantly and costlessly. So in the interim, after demand has increased but before the amount supplied has increased much, prices will tend to move in the short run to higher levels, to clear the market. Then as resources shift and output expands prices will move back a bit toward the long-run equilibrium level, which is higher than before the initial increase in demand started the adjustment.

Monopoly Restraints

You can now see why existing producers, such as B in our preceding example, who foresee loss of wealth, seek laws prohibiting or restricting entrants into "their" businesses. Such restrictions can take any of several patterns. Immigrants would be opposed by those with whom they are likely to compete, just as doctors trained abroad are restricted from practicing medicine in the United States, or Mexican seasonal labor is kept out of U. S. lettuce, tomato, and grape fields to protect local lettuce and grape pickers. Existing producers might persuade legislators to pass laws prohibiting sale of the product by any new suppliers: Taxi companies in most cities manage to have the city government exclude new entrants; cattle raisers prohibit importation of foreign meat; sugar-cane and auto producers get quotas on imported sugar or autos from foreign producers; American textile workers prohibit (or place a tax, called a tariff, on) the importation of textiles from Korea or Taiwan to protect the incomes of resources specialized in domestic textile production. These restrictions are usually imposed by force of the argument that they protect the American standard of living from competition that drives down wages. But do they? *Some* American *producers* are protected—those specializing in producing the goods in this country—but consumers are prevented from having more goods at lower prices. As we have seen, the consumer's standard of living is reduced by more than the protected American producers' standard is maintained. The result is a net social loss.

Artificial, contrived restrictions to protect existing producers and resources from the entry of competing newcomers are called **monopoly** restraints; they protect the wealth of existing producers. Frustrated would-be entrants must turn elsewhere and produce something of less value. This loss of potential value of output is called *monopoly distortion* or *monopoly inefficiency.*

If every producer had this protection, wouldn't we all be richer, given that every consumer is also a producer? No. The social loss from each such restriction is greater than the gains to the existing producers. (It's the reverse of the net gains from new producers, discussed above.) Everyone would be worse off. But the effect might be quite subtle, because whereas the gains of each particular restriction are concentrated in a small group—and usually are a substantial portion of their income—the losses, on the other hand, are so dispersed as to be too small per person to make it worth the person's incurring the costs of trying to prevent each of them.

As stated earlier, our three-person model applies much more broadly to the real world. It contains the basic explanation of all international trade. Therefore, you may consider person A to be in America, B in Great Britain, and C in Canada. Or let A and B be two people in America and C be a person in Canada. Then if C trades with A and B—thus conducting international trade—exactly the same principles and results as in the example will occur—with gains to C and to at least one of the persons A or B (the United States). In our example it was A, the large consumer of the good produced by B and also imported from C, who gained and B who lost when C was allowed to trade with them; but remember that the gains to A and C exceeded any loss that might have been imposed on B.

To avoid a loss, it would pay B, as explained earlier, to restrict the right of C to trade with A. This could be done by placing a quota on the amount of C's goods that could be imported to the country in which A and B lived, or by banning those imports outright, or by imposing a tariff on the good. These would reduce the extent of such trade, reducing the gains to A and C while protecting B, but at a loss to A and C that exceeds the advantage to B. (A tariff also might be imposed to raise revenue for the government, without regard to whether it protected or hurt anyone.)

In any case, the analysis in this chapter is the basic explanation of all trade, be it interpersonal, interregional, or international. The major difference between trade across and trade within national boundaries is that international trade involves two kinds of money, and thus financial arrangements must be made to enable payments in the appropriate money. These arrangements constitute the world of international finance.

Obstacles to Coordinated Specialization: Absence of Markets and Transferable Property Rights

As we have seen repeatedly, a free market cannot operate unless private-property rights and market prices are the prevailing features. If no one owns the rights to a good or a resource, there is no way that voluntary exchange and prices in the market can protect those goods and make users heed the highest use value of that resource—as we do for things we own, like our labor, eggs, wine, cotton, and the like. For example, suppose that in producing X, people are using or polluting some water or air or disturbing the neighborhood. If those valuable forsaken goods are not fully owned and priced and salable in a market, their value is not impressed on those who use them. Even if revealed fully in offered market prices, the responsible party would ignore them unless required to compensate those who had the rights to forsaken output or quality. If no one owned the rights to those resources, no one could make the user pay a price equal to the cost. But if the user had to pay that cost he would have to give *full* weight to the value of the goods sacrificed in making more X.

The problem is not that markets or market prices are inherently misleading, but rather that property rights, and our legal system of enforcing them, are incomplete, or the costs of making contracts too high: Transferable property rights over some goods are not sufficiently defined or enforced so as to prevent excessive use in less valuable ways, such as by excessively polluting air or water or by excessive noise. Furthermore, people are not always honest. They promise one thing and do another, if it suits their interest. We all shirk a bit, and sometimes place our own interest over that of other people. We can act opportunistically and with guile. Enough people are sufficiently dishonest that we use locks and safes and extensive provisions for enforcement of contracts and penalties for nonperformance. Because procedures have been devised to control such deviant behavior, specialization, exchange, and cooperative work can be advantageous. But it hasn't been easy. In later parts of this book we have occasion to consider some such arrangements that would otherwise seem unnecessary and wasteful.

Are Specialization and Efficient Production "Good"?

For all its benefits, specialization might seem to increase the risks over those of self-sufficiency: If other people's demands or supplies should change, some specialists will lose some value of their investment in specialized goods and training. They will become poorer than if they had specialized in something else, or possibly even poorer than if they had been more self-sufficient, like the farmers of olden days. But too much should not be made of this point, for the losses of investment in certain specialized machinery and skills are the consequence of imperfect foresight, not of specialization. Even a self-sufficient hermit who must invest in productive skills for his own personal use can imperfectly forecast his own future demands.

SPECIALIZATION, ALIENATION, SOCIALISM, AND INTEREST GROUPS

Karl Marx asserted that a system of specialization of production and market exchange "alienated" producers from understanding their social role and interrelationships with other people. Each worker–producer was said to feel he or she was producing solely in response to impersonal market prices rather than to satisfy others' or their own human wants and values. (According to economic analysis, of course, prices reflect just such human desires and values.) Marx contended that producers come into social contact with one another primarily through exchange of their products; as a consequence, "persons exist for one another merely as representatives of, and therefore as owners of, commodities. The process of production has the mastery over man instead of being controlled by him."[1]

To eliminate alienation and the alleged "mastery of production processes over man," Marx advocated control of production and distribution by centralized authorities in accord with a central plan, as if society were a single huge factory. Marx called for socialism, that is, government ownership of all the productive resources. He believed this would eliminate alienation, although he did not explain how.

A second, but discredited, contention is that centralized government control of productive resources gives a higher output, with more rapid growth. The useful question is, "What is the right amount of alienation (or sweat or toil or injuries) in view of what we get from bearing those risks and ills?" If you can find a way to reduce alienation or work *without* reducing productive output through specialization, fine and dandy. But everything is a matter of degree—with tradeoffs.

Reprise and Preview

So far the general economic forces controlling and directing the economic activity of people in a capitalistic, private-property system have been the subject of our attention. An overview of the skeleton of forces that operate has been presented. For that system to operate more effectively several institutions and arrangements have evolved: For example, business firms of large size and with a corporate structure have become dominant forms of enterprise; labor unions exist; advertising and marketing arrangements of a complex nature have sprung up; a money and banking system involving complicated lending and borrowing arrangements is common; governments actively regulate, tax and spend. Of interest is the resultant pattern of incomes and earnings over one's lifetime and across members of the society. On the basis of the preceding basic analysis we can proceed to inquire into the role of these auxiliary institutions and arrangements and to study with more perception the factors affecting incomes, jobs, inflation—in sum, a large variety of economic events.

You could choose in which order to study the remaining chapters, in large part in accord with your own interests. For example,

---

[1] *Capital*, Vol. 1 (New York: Modern Library, Random House, 1959), pp. 93, 97.

if inflation is still a persisting phenomenon as you read this, you might skip immediately to that chapter, because it is relatively simple and does not require much from the intervening chapters. However, we have presented the material in a sequence of chapters which permits successive application of principles to sequentially more involved issues or events. Thus the exposition of the determination of wages and incomes comes after a more extensive explanation of the ways in which productive activity is organized and the demand for personal services made effective—the topic of the next chapter.

Summary

1. Specialization is the production of more of some goods or services and less of other goods or services than a person consumes.

2. The cost of any act is the forsaken alternative output. The marginal cost is the change in total costs consequent to producing one more unit—a marginal change in output. Having a comparative advantage means having a lower marginal cost of production.

3. Output is defined to be efficient if it is impossible to increase the output rate of any good without reducing others. No central planning and directive agency is necessary to efficiently organize specialization in production.

4. The gains from specialization are distributed as lower buying prices to consumers and as profits to producers. The latter are dissipated by competition, as lower prices to consumers and larger wages or prices for the responsible resources.

5. Anyone who can produce more will be richer, but will not have lower costs in all possible activities. Total output potential determines wealth, not costs.

6. Producers do not have identical marginal cost schedules. Efficient total production of a good by several producers requires that all producers' rates of output be such that their marginal costs are equal or as nearly equal as possible.

7. The total output from all producers of a good at any given price forms one point on the aggregate market supply schedule, which is made up of all the outputs so obtained at every possible price.

8. Efficient supply under a capitalist system requires a market in which price can be determined and revealed to all potential producers.

9. New producers in a market, by lowering the market prices of goods they produce, enable the consumer to buy more and transfer income from prior producers of that good to consumers. The transfer of income by lower prices from prior producers should not be counted in the net *social* gain of income from having more producers. Although the net social gains are more than large enough to permit, in principle, full compensation to prior producers, such compensation rarely occurs.

10. Because productive inputs are specific to a good or must incur costs in moving or being converted, transitional, short-run adjustments in price or output overshoot the longer-run equilibrium.

11. By preventing some potential producers from producing higher-valued goods for the market, contrived monopoly restraints can increase the wealth of existing producers, but only by *transferring* wealth from consumers and also by reducing total output value.

12. The analysis of this chapter presumed low transactions and information costs, and secure private-property rights.

13. Because not all producers have identical marginal cost schedules, each producer will always have a lower marginal cost at some rate of production for some good. No one, by definition of costs, can have lower costs for every good.

14. Never does a newcomer eliminate all jobs for present producers, forcing them into a state of prolonged unemployment. Instead they are forced to shift to next best paying tasks, as, for example, were American car producers by imports of Japanese and German cars. Always, productive tasks remain at which the foreign importers are more costly producers.

15. More-productive inputs obtain higher incomes, called Ricardian rents, because they produce more, not by restricting entry by competitors.

16. Specialization can cause "alienation." But as always, the question is not whether such ill effects can or should be eliminated, but what is the appropriate amount, given the gains in productivity from specialization.

Questions

1. Smith's production possibilities are indicated by the following table:

Alternative Daily Production Possibilities by Smith's Resources

Oats		Soybeans
10	and	0
9	and	1.0
8	and	1.9
7	and	2.7
6	and	3.4
5	and	4.0
4	and	4.5
3	and	4.9
2	and	5.2
1	and	5.4
0	and	5.5

   a. What is Smith's marginal cost schedule for producing oats if soybeans are worth $50 a bushel?

   b. If the price of oats is $20 a bushel, how many bushels should he produce to maximize the value of his outputs?

2. "Cost is an opportunity concept and exists wherever a choice exists." Explain.

3. "A firm's costs for material, labor, and equipment are simply measures of the highest-valued alternative output producible by those resources." True or false?

4. Why are costs not measured in terms of labor hours?

5. What is meant by efficient production?

6. a. For producers A and B in the text, how many units of output of X should each produce if a total of 6 units is desired?
   b. Did your solution have A's and B's marginal costs equal?
   c. What would the price of X have to be to induce a total output of 6 units?

7. The following questions involve the production data of the two people given in Tables 7–2 and 7–3.
   a. If the price of an X were $1.10 and the price of a Y were $1.00, what should each person produce in order to maximize personal wealth?
   b. Would the resulting assignment of tasks be efficient?
   c. If the price of an X is $1.60 and the price of a Y rises to $2.00, how much X would each produce in order to maximize personal wealth? (Hint: Recompute costs of X.)

8. The production-possibility schedules are:

Mr. A			Mr. B		
X	and	Y	X	and	Y
5	1.5	0	3		0
4	1.4	1.5	2		1
3	.9	2.9	1		2
2	.7	3.8	0		3
1	.5	4.5			
0		5			

   *a. Convert these two production possibilities into marginal costs of X.
   b. Who profitably produces some X at its lowest price?
   c. Who would profitably produce some Y at its lowest price?
   d. At what ratio of the price of X to the price of Y would Mr. B switch from pro-

duction of all *X* to production of some *Y*?

9. "It is better to buy from a firm that is losing money than from one that is making a profit, because the former firm is charging too low a price while the latter is charging more than costs." Evaluate.

10. A prime minister of an emerging country once bragged that he was going to make his country self-sufficient and independent of foreigners. Do the principles of this chapter suggest anything about how you as a native of that country might have been affected? Explain.

11. Which of the following are differential earnings from superior productivity and which are from monopoly sources?
    a. Johnny Carson's income
    b. Bob Hope's income
    c. Kareem Jabbar's income
    d. Jack Nicklaus's golf earnings
    e. Brooke Shields' income
    f. TV station owner's income
    g. Senator Edward Kennedy's income
    h. McDonald's income
    i. Holiday Inn's income

12. In the discussion in this chapter let Mr. C be a resident of Japan and the others be residents of the United States. Mr. A is a tuna-boat owner and fisherman; B is an American worker in any other American industry. Let *Y* be "tuna" and *X* be "other products." Mr. A persuades his congressional representative to induce other House members to pass a law prohibiting the importing of Japanese tuna—product *Y* produced by Mr. C. Who gains and who loses by a tariff or embargo on Japanese tuna? (This example captures the essence of the purposes and effects of tariffs and embargoes.)

13. The three-person problem can also be interpreted as a case in which admission to the market for sale of *Y* requires a license from the state, and this license is given only if the current output from those now in the production of *Y* is deemed "inadequate to meet current demands." Who gains and who loses? Can you give some real examples of this situation?

14. Would the three-person new-entrant problem also serve as an example of the effect of ap-

prenticeship laws, which prohibit a person from acting as a "qualified" carpenter, meat cutter, or the like until he or she has served a specified number of years as an apprentice? Explain.

15. In California it was proposed that the state should finance the education of more doctors because the costs of educating them would be exceeded by their value as measured in lower costs to patients. Explain why this comparison does not in fact determine whether the costs of the education would result in a social gain.

16. "The increased output of specialization is distributed as profits and as a lower price to consumers." What determines the portion of each?

17. What is meant by a subsistence or self-sufficient economy as contrasted to a specialized, interdependent economy?

18. Does efficient production assume that perfect knowledge exists? Explain.

19. When a group of Russian officials touring American farms asked who told the farmers how much to produce in order to supply the appropriate amounts of goods, the farmers said that no one told them. But the Russians were convinced the farmers were concealing something. What would you have told the Russians?

20. "It's wrong to profit from someone else's misfortune."
    a. Explain why, if that were taken literally, we would *all* be poorer.
    b. Does the doctor profit from your illness? The farmer from your hunger? The shoemaker from your tender feet? The teacher from your ignorance? The preacher from your sinfulness?

21. A capitalist system presumes enforcement of certain institutions or rules. What are they?

22. The following remark is commonly made about some rich people: "He is an independently wealthy man." From what is he independent? Does his wealth not depend upon other people's demands?

23. a. Do you think specialization will be carried to greater extent in a large city or a small one?
    b. Why?
    c. Give examples.

*24. Mexico, like almost every other country for that matter, prides itself on being independent in the production of various goods. Does that make its citizens richer or poorer?

25. Evidence of the very great extent of specialization of knowledge is provided by Albert Einstein's assertion just prior to his death (*Socialist International Information*): "The economic anarchy of capitalist society as it exists today is in my view the main cause of our evils. Production is carried on for profit, not for use." What was Einstein's error in economic analysis?

26. A steals from B successfully.
　　a. Is that production? Why?
　*b. If you say "No, because someone is hurt," what would you say about the case in which a new invention displaces some other producers?
　*c. Are there some kinds of production that you think should not be allowed?

27. Several years ago India proposed to build a steel mill and asked the U.S. government to finance the project. In support of India's request, John Kenneth Galbraith, then the American Ambassador to India, wrote: "Although it would be a large mill, there is no doubt that the steel is needed. While the plant would be costly, it would soon pay for itself in the imports that it would save. To import a million tons of steel products would cost the Indians about $200 million. The proposed mill with an annual capacity of 1 million tons would cost $513 million to build. Three years of operations would thus recover the dollar cost of the mill and more. Since India combines her pressing need for steel with an equally acute shortage of dollars, the economic attraction is obvious. She could not, in fact, afford to import the steel that the mill could supply." Explain what is wrong with every sentence except the third and fourth.

28. "Every profit represents the gain from moving resources to higher-valued uses." Do you agree? If so, why? If not, why not?

*29. Dr. John H. Knowles, President of the Rockefeller Foundation, said after a trip to China in 1976, "China is now able to meet all of its energy needs and is even in a position to export." Is that a meaningful or correct statement? If so, does it mean China is better off than if it imported sources of energy? Why?

30. In 1980 English newspapers boasted that England was self-sufficient in crude oil because of its production in the North Sea. Is that cause for congratulations?

Chapter 8
Production by Firms

Joint Production

In the preceding chapter we analyzed a model, a simplified explanation, showing how specialization enables output to increase, and how specialization is coordinated in a market-directed, private-property economy. For the sake of simplicity each of the producers in the model operated alone in producing their output. But another major source of larger output is teamwork, in which people coordinate their specialized activities. This is done in an organization in which one party (typically the owner) directs and monitors the other members (employees), without their buying and selling among themselves, as if in a marketplace, their component elements that create the firm's products, the value of which is instead divided among the team of members. Why the productive effort is organized as teamwork, and why payments are made the way they are, is part of the subject of this chapter.

We again formulate a model in which only the crucial organizational features are made explicit. We ignore features that are for the time being irrelevant, such as whether the enterprises are small or large, unionized or nonunionized, conglomerate or single-product, local or multinational, new or old, retailing or manufacturing, corporation or proprietorship. We pass over such administrative problems as how to select personnel, how to plan production schedules, how to arrange for purchases and storage, how to keep tax and accounting records, how to persuade politicians on proposed legislation or regulation, and an incredible array of tasks that occupy a businessman's time.

To isolate essential problems that occur in teamwork and how they can be handled, imagine an island, Fishland, where 1000 similar people do nothing but fish from the shore, each catching four fish daily. Thus, the *social total*—that is, the amount taken in

Table 8-1   CATCH OF FISH ON BOARD*

Number of Men on Board	Total Catch (on Board)	Marginal Product (on Board)	Average Product (on Board)	Net Social Marginal Product	Social Total (Shore Plus Boat)
0	0	0	0	0	4000 + 0 = 4000
1	6	+ 6	6	2	3996 + 6 = 4002
2	16	+10	8	6	3992 + 16 = 4008
3	24	+ 8	8	4	3988 + 24 = 4012
4	30	+ 6	7.5	2	3984 + 30 = 4014
5	34	+ 4	6.8	0	3980 + 34 = 4014
6	36	+ 2	6	− 2	3976 + 36 = 4012
7	36	0	5.14	− 4	3972 + 36 = 4008
8	32	− 4	4	− 8	3968 + 32 = 4000
9	27	− 5	3	− 9	3964 + 27 = 3991
10	21	− 6	2.1	−10	3960 + 21 = 3981

*Anyone fishing from shore catches four fish, and there are 1000 people.

by the economy as a whole—is 4000 fish. A boat is found; some can now fish on the ocean. Everyone is interested only in how many fish are caught; fishing from shore or from a boat is equally pleasant or arduous. Table 8-1 gives the various quantities of fish that can be caught. The discoverer of the boat uses it alone and catches six fish, two more than from shore. The social total is two fish larger, as shown in the rightmost column of Table 8-1. If another person joins the first on the boat, the pair can catch a total of 16— 10 more than with only one person on the boat. So with two people, the **marginal product** on board is 10 fish. Because we must subtract the four fish the second person would have caught from shore, the *social total* is six fish greater than with only one person on the boat, and eight more than without the boat. Who gets the extra 8 fish? If the two people share the boat catch equally, each get four *more* than the shore fishers. No one else is affected.

As Figure 8-1 and Table 8-1 show, a third person could profitably fish from the boat, increasing the boat total by 8 to 24 fish. (Check the numbers in the table and figure to make sure you understand.) The social total increases by four: the difference between the marginal product on the boat and the forsaken four fish that the third person could have caught from the shore. If a fourth person joined the crew the marginal product *on the boat* would be six, which exceeds the forsaken four fish from the shore, giving a *social* marginal product of two. With four people the total product on the boat is 30; subtracting 16 forsaken fish from the shore (four for each person who shifted to the boat) yields a *social total* gain of 14 fish.

WHAT IS A MARGINAL PRODUCT? WHO PRODUCES IT? WHOSE IS IT?

When we use the expression *"marginal* product of an input," we do not mean how much *that* input produces. What we mean is the *change* in the *total* catch of fish that results from having, say, three units of labor instead of only two on the boat. According to Table 8-1, the marginal product with a third unit of labor (as compared to two units of labor) when used jointly with the boat is eight fish. Those eight fish are not caught by the third laborer. Instead, that eight is the *increase in the total* catch when three laborers are used instead of two, along with the boat and equipment. (If a basketball team used six players instead of five, should the sixth player claim to have produced the extra points? All that can be validly asserted is that six produce more than five do, and the increase is what is meant by the marginal product *at* six people—which is thus more accurate than speaking of the marginal product of the sixth person.)

To produce any good, more than one kind of input is used. Say a tree and a power saw and I make lumber. How much of the lumber did I make? How much did the power saw make? With teamwork by joint resources it is as meaningless to ask what is produced by *each* input as it is to state that a person is paid according to his or her output. Instead, we can ask what determines the payment (that is, the price) for services of an input.

If we want to achieve the *social maximum* output—that is, with no waste of resources—then the optimal number of people fishing from the boat is four or five: five because the marginal product, four fish, with a fifth crew member on the boat would exactly offset the lost marginal product, four fish, from the shore. For the sake of convenience in arithmetic, whenever two such numbers are equivalent, we continue to arbitrarily use the larger. Maximizing the *social output*, then, requires that the boat crew be enlarged to that size at which the marginal product on board decreases to that on the shore. In Figure 8-1 the marginal social gains are the areas of plus signs in the first four marginal product bars. If too many were on the boat—say, six—the result would be a smaller social total.

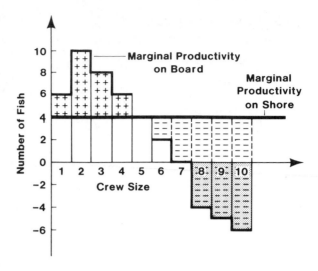

Figure 8-1.

MARGINAL PRODUCTS ON BOAT

The vertical bars represent the marginal product (in fish) on board the boat. The horizontal line at 4 fish is the marginal product (in units of fish) on the shore. The areas occupied by plus signs denote the gain by having fishermen on the boat; the areas marked with minus signs are the social losses of having too many people fish on the boat. The shaded bars below zero represent reductions in the total productivity of those on board combined with there being fewer people fishing on shore.

Control, Property Rights, and Incentives

We now come to the first point of interest in developing our model to more accurately describe the real world: How many people *will* be allowed on the boat, and who gets the output?

SCENE 1: SHARE AND SHARE ALIKE

In the first scene of our Fishland saga, assume that the discoverer of the boat determines how many persons can be on board, and decides that all those on board will divide the total catch equally; that is, each will get an equal per capita share. Our discoverer will allow only one or two other people, for then the *average* (the equal per capita share) that each person gets is at the maximum: eight fish. The discoverer will not tolerate a total of four people on board because even though the social total would increase by 2 fish, the average (which each gets) would fall from 8 to 7.5—fewer fish for the discoverer. If we change the rules and allow all three of the crew to decide whether any more will be allowed to join, the outcome is the same: No, because another person reduces the average to be shared from 8 to 7.5 for four people.

This is a characteristic result for socialist firms, in which the incumbent workers share the net income equally and newcomers are admitted only by permission of the existing group. It is also a trait of many labor unions and professions: Longshoremen, electricians, musicians, doctors, lawyers, and a vast host of other unionists and professionals admit new members only by permission (granted through certifying boards) of the present members. One would therefore expect the effect on the *average* of benefits to the existing members to be the criterion determining whether new members can be added.

However, if a new member paid an entry fee to be shared by present members, the number of new members admitted would be drastically altered. How does the entry fee make a difference? If it nearly equals the excess of an entrant's per-share production within the organization over what he or she could earn without membership, payment of that excess to existing members will enable them to divide it among themselves and get a still larger average. The lower average they otherwise would get is more than made up for by their share of the entry fee paid by the newcomer. (Look at the data in Table 8–1 to check this. Unless you do, you may find it hard to understand the following example.) For example, a fourth person on the boat could pay a daily entry fee of 3 fish to the first three members, leaving the fourth person a net daily take-home of 4.5 fish (from the per-capita share of 7.5 fish) and giving them an extra fish each; that added to their new 7.5 average gives them 8.5 fish, half a fish more than before.

In general, any newcomer who can get a marginal catch bigger on the boat than on the shore would be willing to offer almost all of that excess to the existing crew to be divided among themselves. The total available to them, and hence *their* average, is bound to increase. The prior members, who decide to let new members buy their way in, have in effect become the controlling owners maximizing their incomes. Some unions have a very large entry fee; some country clubs charge a large entry fee. These can be regarded as a way for new members to buy their way into a group and compensate its prior members for the lowering of their average of amenities derived from their membership in the club.

SCENE 2: PRIVATE PROPERTY

As scene 2 opens, we change arrangements: The boat is *owned* by its finder. Instead of having to share the catch, the owner now seeks solely to maximize personal wealth, that is, the number of fish the owner gets to keep. The owner hires a crew and keeps all the fish in excess of the wages paid to the crew. How much will they be paid? How many will be hired? How much will the owner gain?

Because crew members are not slaves, they must be paid enough to attract them from their next best opportunity, which is catching 4 fish on the shore: They must be paid at least 4 fish per day. Thus, the boat owner will hire as many people as have a marginal catch, or product, on the boat that exceeds the wage that each must be paid. As the crew gets larger, the marginal product, after an initial rise, declines until with the fifth crew member the marginal product is down to almost as low as 4 fish. That is very little more than can be caught on the shore, and just enough to attract a person away from shore fishing. This is portrayed in Figure 8–1. (Remember, whether four or five crew members are hired is here unimportant; either number is an answer to our problem.) Certainly more than three will be hired, but not as many as 6. Neither of those crew sizes would maximize the boat owner's gains. A crew size is selected that maximizes the boat owner's gain (14 fish) and also happens to maximize the *social* total (14 fish)!

That coincidence between maximum private and maximum social gain is not accidental. People with private-property rights who seek profits in an open-market system will maximize the social total in many situations. What those situations are we will see later. Here, we will show that this double result is possible, that it is not a contrived quirk of our special example, and that it happens without the profit seeker's intent or a central directive authority.

SCENE 3: BOAT RENTING

As scene 3 of Fishland opens, the boat owner, having decided to retire, now rents the boat to any group that forms a crew. How large a group will be on board and what rent will be obtained? (For simplicity, assume the owner stays on shore and there catches four fish while the boat renters are at sea.) Again, four or five people will be the crew and they will offer a rental of up to 14 fish. The total catch with 4 on the boat is 30 fish, which is 14 more than they would have caught from shore. Competition among all people to form crews and to rent the boat will force the winning crews to pay up to 14 fish in rent and be left with incomes of at least four fish per person! A three-person crew could not pay that much rent; they catch only 24 fish, only 12 more than they could have caught from shore. If they paid 14 fish in rent, they would each have only 3 1/3 fish. Nor could a six-person crew pay that much rent. The highest rent can be paid only by a four- or five-person team. (Table 8–1 shows that a fifth person has a marginal product of four fish, exactly what would have been caught on shore: Adding a fifth gives neither an increase nor a loss.)

The highest rental value of the boat is 14 fish per day, exactly the maximum gain in fish that can be caught through use of the boat. Essentially, all of it is paid to the boat owner. Again, the owner's personal income has been maximized, as has the social income. (In Figure 8–1 the gain obtained by the owner is the area occupied by plus signs out to where the on-boat and on-shore marginal products are equal.) Our analysis has assumed that a boat owner who maximizes income will (by definition of a maximum) limit the crew to that size beyond which the marginal product of another input does not exceed what the input could earn elsewhere.

A crew size can be achieved that maximizes both the social total and the boat owner's wealth if someone has the right to: (a) determine how many are employed on the boat *or* charge rent for the boat, and (b) keep the net receipts. (We shall later see some conditions in which private gains and social gains diverge.)

We can summarize the main lines of our analysis and their implications in the **marginal productivity theory** of demand for inputs: The demand for productive inputs depends on the marginal products; inputs will be demanded up to that amount at which their marginal product falls to equality with the wage or price of the input. Because the marginal products decrease at greater input, more inputs are demanded at lower wages, and fewer at higher wages or prices. This theory is used extensively later.

Employees or Renters? The arrangements in scenes 2 and 3 are virtually identical: Instead of saying the boat owner hired the crew as in scene 1, we could say the boat was hired by the fishermen as in scene 2. In scene 1 the crew is paid a bit over 4 fish to work on the boat and the owner keeps the remainder of the total catch, a net of 14 fish. In scene 2 the crew pays the owner 14 fish as rental and each has a little over 4 fish left. There is *no* difference in this example between renting the boat and being hired by the boat owner as employees!

Is there, then, no difference between Macy's hiring clerks as *employees* and the clerks paying the owners of Macy's *rent* for its building and facilities (and inventory-use costs) out of the total daily sales—leaving the clerks with the same income in either case? There indeed is no difference, *if the anticipated output performance of the inputs can be predicted with certainty.* But if mistaken estimates of the anticipated product are made, someone must bear the consequences.

In our fishing example, uncertainty about the catch makes the difference between renting and hiring: The catch can vary because of (a) natural hazards, events beyond human control, or (b) behavior of the fishermen, such as shirking and negligence. Natural hazards make for no great difference

to the renter or the employee. In both cases the owner bears the natural variations: The rent will be adjusted each day in response to past and hence future expected changes. Furthermore, the owner can take out insurance against that kind of natural hazard.

The major and significant difference to the owner between hiring workers and renting a productive facility comes from the second factor: the difference in the incentives to shirk or be negligent under the two systems, a matter we will take up shortly. First we move to scene 4, and we assume again that the catch is still certain.

SCENE 4:
THE BOAT AS COMMUNAL PROPERTY

The boat owner has been expropriated: The boat is now communal, or public, property. Anyone and everyone can board the boat, just as they can use the streets, parks, and beaches. People crowd onto the boat until the *average* catch (which each gets) matches that on shore. Eight people will be on board with four fish each to take home.

It is easy to see why that happens, if you again examine the data in Table 8–1. With each person on board *sharing equally* in the catch, people crowd on so long as the *average* catch exceeds their individual catch on shore. So a sixth, seventh, and eighth person will go on board; the sixth because the average catch is then 6 fish; the seventh because the average is 5.14; the eighth because the average is 4. Every person's share in the catch—the average—is reduced as more people crowd on board. But each newcomer ignores the external harmful effect on other people. With eight persons on board no one else would gain by joining the crew.

Notice the full consequences. A sixth person on board causes a social loss of two fish: the marginal product on board, two, minus the forsaken marginal product, four, on shore. A seventh causes a loss of four fish: the marginal product on board, zero, minus his sacrificed marginal product, four, on shore. An eighth causes a social loss of eight fish. The total social decrease caused by the sixth, seventh, and eighth persons is 14 fish (= 2 + 4 + 8), which cancels the social *gain* of 14 fish from the first four or five people. The potential gain formerly obtained and received as larger income by the owners is entirely dissipated by overcrowding the boat. *No one* is better off than before the boat was found. What happened to the extra 14 fish? They aren't caught, because there is congestion on board instead of the optimal number of people.

Congestion is shown graphically in Figure 8–1. The social gain, indicated by the plus-marked area, represents the *marginal products on board* in excess of the *marginal products sacrificed on shore*. It is maximized at 14 fish with five people on board. With more people, the marginal product on board will decrease to less than what is sacrificed on shore, out into the region where there is a shaded area below the line representing marginal product on shore and above the line representing marginal product on board, which is below the shore marginal product when more than five people are on the boat. Unrestricted communal access is common for highways, beaches, sidewalks, parks, air, rivers, lakes, oceans. The reason for the congestion should be obvious: the absence of property rights with which to exclude an excessive number of people. With communal or public property, no one has adequate incentive to heed those effects of congestion. They are left "external" to each person's interests, and are often called externalities.

So as the curtain falls on scene 4 a government agent is appointed to control the number of people allowed on the boat.

SCENE 5: GOVERNMENT CONTROL

The last scene opens with the government agent being told to maximize profit from renting the boat. The 14-fish rent (the social gain) is, then, supposed to go to the government and be distributed however the authorities see fit. It would appear that the only difference between this and the system of private-property rights in the boat is in who gets the 14-fish gain. However, this is not quite correct.

What will the government agent lose by taking life easier and not charging the right fee? The loss is imposed on the public as a whole. But who in the public or government has an incentive as strong as a private owner to detect managerial opportunism, or shirking and negligence, or lost rental value? A political authority suffers less loss of potential personal wealth than a private owner does in being less attentive to nonownable gains. The authority would permit more people on board if that enhanced his or her popularity and hold on political office. On the other hand, the authority might allow too few on board because that permits shorter working hours (such as by closing on holidays and earlier in the afternoons) and not operating the boat as fully as needed to maximize profits.

But when was a government agency supposed to maximize *profits*? It is usually, or always, given the mandate, or goal, to "maximize public welfare and benefit." (The agency might be a nonprofit corporation operating or overseeing hospitals, colleges, or the postal service.) How is "maximize public welfare" interpreted? In our example, is it by maximizing the number on board, or the catch on the boat, or the social total of the catch?

That goal is sturdy and widespread, because its ambiguity permits wide latitude of interpretation and hence of measuring performance. It is commonly the mandate of government authorities who control access to the television and radio airwaves, air space for airplanes, postal service, highways, national and state parks and beaches, airports, harbors, and schools. It is even applied to federal forests, offshore oil, and land. Zoning commissions that control the use of land (such as in determining how congested it can be) are similarly instructed to maximize "public welfare and usefulness." But hardly any government authority is instructed to maximize profits: not the postal service, or the water, electricity, gas, or bus company. All are instructed to "serve the public," or "break even." Sadly, no validated theory of political behavior exists with which to predict what is likely to happen.

CONTROL OF OPPORTUNISTIC BEHAVIOR

Not all people are always perfectly honest. People act opportunistically, or negligently, or cheat and shirk if they can get away with it. A person often delivers less than another person believed was promised and is paying for, possibly because the second person honestly expected more than the first had honestly promised or was capable of delivering—or because the first person was deliberately cheating. It makes no difference; one of the parties is deceived and believes less should be paid. Furthermore, the *anticipation* of opportunism induces people to make precautionary contractual arrangements to avoid later misunderstandings, disputes, and losses.

To be a potential victim, a person must have made some kind of commitment of specialized wealth to the other party in such a way that the other party's behavior affects the first person's subsequent wealth. The specializer is then not in a position to say, "No matter what you do, I can go elsewhere to associate with someone else and be just as well off there as I am here with you. If you try cheating, I can leave with my wealth at no loss." An economist would say that the first party's wealth is not entirely "salvageable" elsewhere; it will be lower if the second party doesn't behave as expected. At the

other extreme, the resources of the first party are completely "generalized" if his or her wealth is not dependent on any other *specific* persons.

If all possible contingencies could be foreseen, and the performance of each party perfectly measured, and any deviations could be corrected by costless, perfect enforcement, then simple but lengthy and detailed contracts would avoid all disputes and losses. But that is not possible. Alternative arrangements have evolved. To see some we visit Fishland II.

FISHLAND II

The catch by any crew on the boat will depend on more things than we have so far considered in Fishland I. For example, if every crew member were to share equally in the day's total catch, regardless of how many fish any individual caught, certainly each would secretly relax and work less cleverly and diligently, because for every fish not caught only a fraction of the loss is borne by the shirker. Part of the loss is borne by others in the crew, while the shirking member gets all the benefits of shirking. Thus, share and share alike in Fishland II tends to be less productive than it was presumed to be in Fishland I.

If, contrary to fact, shirking could be detected instantly and costlessly, it would be eliminated, because any benefits to the shirker would be canceled by punishment or a reduced reward. Everyone on a team wants to reduce the possibility of shirking by other team members. Crew members will seek methods that tend to reveal and punish shirking, thereby reducing its incidence even if it involves submitting themselves to the same discipline. The problem is *how* to effectively restrain that shirking and opportunism, that is, how to monitor behavior.

One way is to have a monitor detect what each person does and adjust the person's pay accordingly. But the monitor can also relax and be less diligent. It would not be wise for the crew to hire a monitor for a salary that is paid even if the monitor relaxes, unless someone could monitor the monitor. But who monitors the monitor who monitors the monitor . . . ?

There are some reliable monitoring devices. First, let the monitor not be hired for a salary but be given the remainder, or residual, of the catch after everyone else is paid the promised amounts. The monitor is the residual claimant: the recipient of the profits or losses after the promised payments. Who will this monitor be? Whose wealth is most affected by the quality of monitoring? The crew members will not lose much because they can earn almost as much elsewhere. What about the boat owner? If the catch is small, and if all crew members must be paid what they can get elsewhere, the owner of the boat, which can earn almost nothing elsewhere, will suffer the reduced value if fewer fish are caught. The owner who loses from ineffective monitoring has incentive to insist on good monitoring. It is therefore not surprising that the monitor is, or is responsible to, the owner of the resources most highly specialized to the team's activity—in our case, the boat. The boat owner will be the "monitor," the "employer," or the "boss."

A second means of controlling a monitor is competition from potential monitors who offer to displace less effective monitors. Within the firm anyone who sees a shirking or ineffective monitor will have incentives to displace that monitor, as may anyone outside the firm who is aware of the less diligent activity (just as purveyors of watches, automobiles, tires, or shoes seek to offer customers better opportunities, thereby displacing less effective producers). Potential replacements who detect shirking will offer to work to better standards or for lower wages. Competitors have incentives to detect and evaluate performances and to persuade potential customers (that is, employers) that the alternatives they offer are superior.

Failing a technique for monitoring it, shirking can be adapted to by paying each member a smaller wage to offset anticipated but undetectable shirking. Money wages will be smaller if various kinds of behavior—personal use of company phones, longer coffee breaks, tardiness, and the like—are tolerated by the employer. If the average extent of such fringe "benefits" is correctly estimated, the average wage will be correspondingly lower. If deviations from the average are excessively difficult to detect, *some* employees can benefit from excessive *undetected* shirking.

INTERSPECIALIZED RESOURCES AND COMMON OWNERSHIP

One especially important source of opportunistic behavior is worth examining. We will illustrate, at first, with a simple example. Suppose someone invents a power winch to help pull in fishing nets faster and thus catch more fish. Suppose the boat owner agrees to lease it from the inventor, who installs it on the boat—a rather costly operation since it must be securely fastened to the boat deck. The catch of fish increases, but so does opportunism: The boat owner slyly conjectures that even if faced with a refusal to pay all the promised rent, the winch owner could not effectively respond by threatening to take the winch off the boat. The winch is worthless elsewhere. Removing it would make the winch owner worse off than accepting the lower rent. In economic language, it has no salvage value in any other use. It is *specific, or specialized, to that boat*, which means it is more valuable on that boat than anywhere else. The boat owner is opportunistically expropriating some of the value of the winch specialized to his boat.

The winch inventor-owner should have anticipated this possible behavior, say by refusing to invest in making and owning a winch specific to and installed on a boat owned by someone else. The winch owner should have made the boat owner buy and pay for the winch as it was being created and installed on the boat. Or the winch inventor and the boat owner should have formed a partnership with each having equal rights in the value of the combined boat and winch. When the winch and boat are owned in common, what earnings come from one owned resource go to the other. How the earnings are assigned to one resource or the other makes no difference. So we would expect *interspecific resources*—that is, resources specialized to one another, like the winch and boat—to be produced and owned in common. The ownership of the winch and boat should be integrated to avoid the possibility that the value of one of the interspecific resources could be expropriated by the owner of the other interspecific resource. And typically they are so owned.

To be thoroughly realistic, imagine building an oil refinery to be supplied by one crude-oil pipeline. After the refinery is built, what would prevent the pipeline owner from asking a higher price for the use of it? The refinery owner would have to build another pipeline or shut down or relocate the refinery—no cheap task. The owner of the existing pipeline could threaten to expropriate an amount up to the costs of building a new pipeline or an amount equal to the lost value of the refinery if it were shut down or moved. On the other hand, the refiner would threaten not to pay, and the pipeline could not be removed.

Because both pipeline and refinery builders know these possibilities in reality, prior to building either they form one company to own both; or one party builds and owns both. In either case, highly interspecific resources are owned in common, because otherwise the difference between (a) the value *with* the resource to which a given resource is interspecific and (b) the salvage value of that given resource is liable to be

expropriated by opportunistic action.[1]

By contrast, generalized resources, which can easily move to other tasks with little or no loss of value, are less likely to be owned in common with the specific resources. Thus, in Fishland II, the fishing lines could easily be transferred to the shore and earn no less than on the boat. They would not be owned in common with the boat. The crew members could also fish from shore; they need not own the boat. But if some person had skills so specialized to the boat that only this person knew how to operate or pilot the boat and thus could threaten to expropriate some of its value, this operator would very likely have to be an owner of the boat. But if good substitutes were readily available, it would be less important that the pilot or operator then have ownership of the boat.

Like machinery, people can become interspecific to varying degrees. For example, an employee who purchases a house near his or her place of employment would face a large loss through moving costs if he or she later decides to move to a new employer. Or the prospect of such costs might induce the employee to accept a lower wage or go without a raise as a condition of keeping his or her job and avoiding that moving cost. A sec-

---

[1] Another example or two should reveal the importance of specialized resources in our economy. Railroads don't rent the land on which they place tracks. Imagine the expropriation of value by a landowner who says, "Pay more or remove your tracks." And you don't find banks renting safes. Imagine a safe owner being told by the bank, "I'm sorry, but we can't pay as much rent any more. Take away your safe embedded in concrete in a deep basement." Or, if a newspaper reporting staff and a printing press were owned separately, with only one printing press in town, imagine the reporters telling the printing press owner they can only pay less rent. Can the owner take away that heavy, installed, expensive-to-move press? Or, reversing the threat, imagine the press owner telling the reporters, "Pay a higher rent this afternoon, or I won't print your paper." Two-sided symmetric threat possibilities are foreseeable; as a result, initial investment in *all* interspecialized resources will be by *one* owning group.

retary may have invested in learning some special skills useful only to the present employer. Because that knowledge is worthless elsewhere, the secretary would not risk that initial investment without some assurance of job and pay conditions. Seniority and tenure rights help serve that purpose, as do rights to pensions and insurance and job priorities in the event of temporary recessions. As we shall see in more detail later, unions act as agents to help deter opportunistic expropriation of the value of employees who have become more specialized to the firm. (Sometimes unions achieve the reverse effect by protecting employees who shirk or otherwise reduce the welfare of other employees.) The monitoring function of unions may be their most important function, more important than any ability to raise the wages of members above open-market competitive levels.

A most common instance of interspecific resources is marriage: Two people become interspecific to each other and to their offspring. Although such arrangements are not central to economic analysis, they indicate that interspecificity of resources can also apply to people; and although people do not own each other, what might appear to be unusual or otherwise inexplicably restrictive contracts or arrangements may be the means of restricting potentially exploitive behavior.

Substitution, Complementarity, and the Demand for Inputs

An important principle illustrated in our model of teamwork on the fishing boat is that the greater the quantity of capital equipment or machinery available, the larger will be the total output. The boat is a capital good that enhances output, as are nets, power lines, navigational equipment, and the like, working in ways that are complementary to human labor. That is, these capital goods, when used with human labor, increase

the output, but in very special ways. To simplify our exposition of how they do so, we shall reduce the variety of types of inputs to two, called *labor* and *capital*—or *factors of production*, which means any productive resources.

Labor includes an extremely large variety of different personal talents; capital includes an uncountable variety of machinery and nonhuman devices. But capital is more generally interpreted to include also the environment and the resources of the whole economy: The transportation system, the education and technology of co-workers, the effectiveness of the market in facilitating specialization and exchange, the honesty of the populace and the extent to which contracts are honored—all of these are examples of *cooperative resources*. If you moved the carpenters of any small U.S. city to India, Morocco, Brazil, or Indonesia, their marginal productivity would be a lot lower simply because there is less jointly available capital per person in the form of education, formal vocational training, and general sophistication of the technology. A richer country with lots of capital equipment and stable, market-facilitating institutions is a more efficient place for a given amount of labor. Although the productivity of the American carpenters would be lower in such underdeveloped countries as those just named, the average productivity would be greater than for most natives of those countries—a consequence of the greater education of the Americans.[2]

---

[2]Warning: The word "capital" often also refers to values of past investments in enhancing knowledge, abilities, and talents of people. In fact a large portion of our capital is in human form. Undoubtedly a major portion of the advance of our present and future wealth and income is based on increased human capital. Nevertheless, in the present chapter we shall use the terms labor and capital to denote human and nonhuman capital respectively—without implying that the quality of labor is not heavily dependent upon investment in improving human abilities.

Like the fishing boat, capital in general increases the total output available with some given quantity of labor. In our example, the social output jumped from 4000 fish without the boat to 4014 fish with the boat—a gain of 14 fish. Does it follow that having even more capital (more boats, or more equipment) will increase the output? Yes. But a more subtle and very important question is, "What does having more equipment do to the *whole schedule of the marginal product of labor?*"

Let us interpret this question carefully. It asks what happens to the whole schedule of marginal products (increases in the number of fish caught) at different crew sizes, if a boat has more equipment, as compared to one without that extra equipment. For a constant amount of equipment on the boat, the marginal products of labor, after an initial rise at small amounts of labor, gradually fall and ultimately even become negative. If there is more equipment on the boat, the whole schedule of marginal products of labor might be shifted upward. In that case (1) the total product is larger (more fish are caught) at each crew size, *and* (2) at any given crew size the marginal product (the increase in catch) at any amount of labor is bigger than on a boat less well equipped.

However, suppose the new capital were a power winch that pulled the nets with less labor and greater speed. This might *twist* the marginal product schedule, having a large effect on the output with only one or two crew members, while the fourth and fifth now don't add as much as before. Although this new equipment strongly raises marginal productivity for small crews of fewer than three laborers, it *lowers* the marginal products for crews larger than three. The winch could be called a labor-saving device. It raises the labor marginal product schedule upward at small crews but lowers it at larger crews, so that although *total* product is larger, the *marginal* product is smaller at the original crew size.

A word processor may raise the total output of two secretaries who formerly used typewriters, but it may lower the marginal product of a second secretary because the first one can now work so fast with the word processor and get so much done that the remaining tasks are low-valued. The second typist now *adds* little value. But it is possible that the word processor may be so effective that even the second secretary's marginal product is higher than before. It depends on the particular circumstances. The new equipment may result in more labor being hired because the marginal productivity schedule in the firm is raised even at the initial amount of secretarial labor. (Although obviously we should not speak of just one kind of capital good, for simplicity we here continue to do so.) Thus, in summary: More capital goods increase the *total* product at the initial amount of labor input; but an increase in one kind of capital may increase the *marginal* product of labor at the initial amount of associated inputs, whereas an increase in another kind of capital may decrease the marginal product of labor.

CAPITAL SUBSTITUTION AND LABOR SAVING

Capital is always a substitute for labor, in the sense that with more of the capital equipment one could use fewer units of labor for the *same total* output. In this sense, *substitution* states that a *given output* could be produced by any of a variety of techniques that use different ratios of inputs of capital and labor, that is, different production techniques. Capital and labor are substitutable in that an increase of one can be used as a substitute for a reduction of the other while maintaining the same total output.

THE DEMAND FOR PRODUCTIVE INPUTS

The downward-sloping marginal product schedule tells us, first, that at lower prices of an input, more will be employed; and, second, that the quantity of each input that maximizes the firm's wealth is that at which the marginal product of that type of input is brought to equality with the input's price. No extra inputs would be used if they increase total product value less than its costs, and no input is left unused that would add more value than its costs. Because different inputs are marginally substitutable, it follows that if the price of one input rises, less will be used, and some quantity of another or others substituted. The conclusion is: first, that a lower price of one kind of input increases the amount demanded of that input, and may reduce the amount demanded of another or other inputs; but, second, that the *ratio* of the two amounts of input will be increased toward the cheaper input.

Obviously, if you were labor you would like to be in a situation with a lot of capital—if more capital raised the whole marginal productivity schedule of your type of labor—but with less of the other jointly used input if that lowered the marginal productivity curve of your kind of services.

SPEED OF SUBSTITUTION

Substituting and altering inputs are costly adjustments. One must learn of new inputs and feasible combinations of new ones or of new and old; one must make decisions and see that they are carried out; one must rearrange inputs and schedule the timing of new inputs. How quickly these steps of substitution are carried out in response to new prices depends on the costs of adjustment. As in consumers' behavior, the demand for inputs is more elastic the longer the time since the price change. And differences of elasticity can be represented by differently sloping demand curves for different intervals after a price change. The *immediate* period may show little response to prices, because quick changes are more expensive. Because many input adjustments are made only after a sub-

stantial interval, those affected usually fail to recognize the changes as consequences of the input price change.

An example is what happened when the wages of Chicago elevator operators rose. Wages had been $1 to $1.25 an hour, until a minimum wage of $2.40 an hour was imposed for operators in downtown (though not suburban) buildings. With two shifts of operators, the higher wage raised the cost of a manually operated elevator to about $10,000 per year. Owners of some of those buildings then found it profitable to use automatic elevators, each of which cost about $8000 a year to operate. When the elevator operators were discharged several months after they had started being paid $2.40 an hour, they were not likely to understand that it was a result of the higher wage, since that had been initiated a long time before. They blamed it on automation.

INPUT SUBSTITUTION
BY PRODUCT SUBSTITUTION

Substitution among inputs also occurs because of the choices consumers make among goods. More of the consumer goods that use more of the cheaper inputs will be supplied. Those product prices will fall. If the price of unfinished plastics falls relative to glass, the price of plastic containers falls; consumers buy more plastic containers, and plastics are thereby substituted for glass, affecting the demand for inputs in glassmaking. As another example, higher wages for carpenters will induce contractors and homeowners to use more power saws and more standardization with less carpentering service. Wood-paneled walls will be displaced by plaster, and some wood window frames by steel and aluminum.

Competition tests and *favors the adoption* of the more appropriate existing techniques by yielding greater profits and growth—whether or not a given individual producer adjusted to the new price situation consciously. All a producer has to do is happen to be nearer the better combination of inputs. It is irrelevant whether they got there because management calculated marginal productivities through extensive research and testing, with the advice of astrologers and consulting economists, or because of sheer luck. Being there is sufficient. Nor need a producer imitating the successful firms know marginal productivities of various inputs. All one need know is what techniques succeeded best.

DERIVED DEMAND
FOR PRODUCTIVE RESOURCES

You should be able to see by now why the demand for an input is called **derived demand**. The marginal product value is *derived* from the value the consumer puts on the final product. If consumers' valuation of that product rises, demand for the inputs will rise. The term *derived demand* emphasizes this dependence of the demand for an input on the value of the product to the ultimate consumer.

MONETARY AND
NONMONETARY VALUES
OF MARGINAL PRODUCTIVITY

The fact of marginal value productivity is true in every economy. In a capitalist economy, the increase in marketable wealth belongs to an identifiable owner. However, if there were no owner—no one who was able to keep the increase—the selection of inputs would be more influenced by the nonmarketable productivity. More congenial colleagues might be employed by such an operator if the gains of hiring lower-salaried workers who were equally productive of *marketable* values of goods could not be retained. For example, a legal limit on income or a heavily taxed income would induce employers to

hire employees with more nonmonetary appeal to them—good looks, or shared race, ethnic background, religious affiliation, and the like. Production will be less closely oriented to market-valued demands. Because government agencies are not privately owned or profit-seeking, their managers are more influenced by the nonmonetary attributes of inputs. If an organization's rules only mildly penalize people for not increasing marketable wealth, those responsible for its productivity will be less influenced by market values. The generalized marginal-productivity principle (that is, monetary plus nonmonetary effects) is the one that should be used when analyzing any situation.

Nothing in the foregoing analysis implies that being less responsive to monetary value is undesirable. One's assessment depends upon whether one prefers the economic, cultural, and political attributes of a private-property, open-market system or the same attributes of some other system. Some people may think they could achieve their idea of a better way of life through nonmarket types of competition for resolving conflicts of interests in the presence of scarcity. For example, people with certain kinds of personalities may find competition for political power more favorable to them than market competition.

CONSUMPTION
VALUATIONS, EFFICIENCY,
AND RESOURCE SUBSTITUTION

The principles explained in this chapter involving substitution among inputs, plus the principle explained in the preceding chapter involving production responses to consumers' demands and to changes in costs, can be applied to clear up a very common misunderstanding. You have probably read complaints that sprawling suburbs and highways are using up the prime agricultural lands. You have heard celebrities telling you to conserve energy. You will see stickers on refrigerators and television sets stating the electrical operating cost. You will hear Boeing express pride in the fuel efficiency of its new airplanes. Congress has legislated regulations about the miles per gallon that American-made (but not foreign-made) automobiles should deliver. All these examples reflect a basic misunderstanding of costs. What is the error?

First, resources are used to serve people, not merely to be "saved." The question is, "What is the best rate and way to use them?" The question is not, "What is the way to not use them?" We strive to use productive resources in ways that maximize our welfare now and in the future. If you remember capital value theory you will recall that values of future uses are included in the present prices of goods.

The second error is to forget that there are many ways to produce something. It is inefficient to use more insulation or aluminum instead of steel to make refrigerators or cars if the value of the electricity or gasoline thereby saved is less than the value of products that could otherwise have been produced with the extra aluminum or insulation. Life is a choice of more of this versus more of that, not less of this. An automobile labeled fuel efficient because it gets higher mileage than some other cars can be more expensive than the value of the fuel saved. When you buy a stereo system and are told the speaker is very energy efficient in converting much of the electric power to sound, you should ask how much it cost in other resources to economize on that electrical power. Did it cost $100 of other resources to save $10 of energy? Making a house more energy efficient to save, say, $100 a year in fuel may cost far more than the savings. Concentration on one particular input as a criterion of how or what to produce is a sure way to increase your costs—that is, reduce your welfare.

Nevertheless, technological efficiency is commonly invoked as the criterion in legislation, even if implementing the criterion does not increase social welfare, as witnessed by the recent laws mandating energy saving. Technological efficiency—minimizing the cost of one particular input of production or operation—does not accurately reflect full costs, as does economic efficiency. If the costs of substitute inputs are less than the savings in fuel costs, people will use some of them whether or not legislation is passed—unless you assume that consumers, salespersons, and producers have forgotten how to seek profits or increase welfare.

Why that kind of legislation or compulsion? One possibility is that forcing you to consume less of some good releases more of it for someone else—in less valuable uses (otherwise no legislation would have been necessary). Or perhaps a tax on gasoline is not really meant to promote its conservation but rather to collect more taxes for some special benefit (for example, aqueducts in the Southwest, urban mass transit in the East, or research grants to professors of economics in the Midwest). If you find our amateur political analysis obnoxious, no matter. The point is that you have to guess why it is legislated, if it reduces the aggregate value of potential output and consumer welfare.

Returning to the examples for a last time, consider the argument that houses and highways should not be built on prime agricultural land. What is the proposed better alternative? Is it to use land less desirable for housing and transportation, which is also less desirable for agricultural uses? We could put houses on mountaintops or in swamps and make the quantity of housing smaller, less desirable, and more expensive in order to keep food more plentiful. But the value of the extra food that is forsaken when houses and highways *are* put on prime land is *less* than the value of the housing, living, and transportation convenience. If prime agricultural land is less valuable for crops than for more housing and transportation, it is harmful to human welfare not to use prime agricultural land for more housing and highways. Think it over. The two basic propositions are, first, that it is not resources themselves that are critical, but what can be done with them; and, second, that because inputs are substitutable, one should know what value of consumption output is lost by saving one input and using more of some others—as one must because you can't produce more by using fewer inputs.

Summary

1. Teamwork, or joint, coordinated effort, is another source of increased output over effort by a single person.

2. Teamwork is not easily monitored by market forces, so the performance of each team member is internally monitored.

3. One measure of the performance of each input is marginal product: the increase in total output when a new unit of input is added to the team.

4. The systems of property rights, reward, and of membership control determine team size. Under some systems, such as joint sharing with entry controlled by existing members, teams can be too small, because members are excluded who would have had a marginal product greater than in any other activity. Or uncontrolled entry can result in teams that are too large, the marginal product of the added input being less than it would be elsewhere, thus reducing total community output. A private-property arrangement can result in a team size that maximizes total community output.

5. A business firm is a team to which some of the inputs are specialized. A specialized input is one the value of which will be reduced if the team effort fails to produce the anticipated value of output. Generalized resources will not fall in value, because they can transfer to other activities or teams with no loss of income or reduction of productivity.

6. Owners of the specialized inputs—that is, of the firm—will be the monitors, or supervisors, because they have the most to lose or to gain from the effectiveness of the monitoring.

7. All the specialized resources used in a team will tend to be owned by the same people, to prevent potential disputes over division of receipts among these resources, the alternative market values of which are not high enough to protect them from opportunistic behavior by the owners of the other resources to which they are specialized.

8. The demand for any resource is derived from its marginal productivity schedule: Lower prices for that input increase the amount of the input demanded by the firm.

9. Marginal productivity includes nonmonetary forms of productivity, such as contributions to congeniality, pleasantness, and environmental amenities.

Questions

1. What is the measurement problem in joint teamwork that is not present in specialization of the type examined in the preceding chapter?

2. a. Why is zero congestion wasteful?
   b. What social institutions prevent too much congestion and achieve optimal congestion?
   c. What *is* "optimal" congestion?

*3. Cite examples of privately owned overcongested resources, and some that are undercongested. Can you explain why each occurred? Cite examples of government-controlled overcongested resources, and some that are undercongested. Can you explain why each type occurs?

4. Which of the following are examples of excessive congestion?
   a. traffic jams
   b. crowds at public parks in summer
   c. air traffic at J. F. Kennedy airport at about 5 P.M.
   d. pollution of rivers
   e. deer hunting on opening day

f. public tennis courts on Sunday afternoon
g. full house in a movie
h. CB radio bands
i. sidewalks at Christmas time
j. New York City subway at rush hour
k. buzzards eating a dead deer
l. residential crowding in a large city
m. customers in a store during a sale

5. Suppose in the fishing boat example in the chapter people discovered how to make boats that were good for one day and that cost the equivalent of two fish. Assume all property is privately owned, and there are 1000 people.
　a. How many boats would the community use each day?
　b. What would be each person's income?
　c. What would a boat's selling price be and how many boats would a boat maker have to make per day for it to be worthwhile to do so?

*6. For what events is the distribution of risk the same in socialist and capitalist systems? (Hint: How about divorce, cancer, baldness, homeliness, having children all of the same sex, being left-handed?)

7. How does socialism differ from capitalism in distributing profits and risks of losses?

8. If the boat owner, in the example in the text, were to employ the fishermen at a promised wage of 4 fish per day, the owner would bear the risk of the day's catch. But suppose the fishermen rented the boat from the boat owner for a fixed daily fee of, say, 14 fish. If the day's catch on board is less than enough to pay the rent and still leave at least 4 fish per fishermen, the renters will have lost. The risk is borne by the renters, not by the boat owner, who was promised 14 fish no matter what the catch. Is that correct?

9. a. What is meant by specialized resources?
　*b. What are some of the specialized resources in a gasoline station, a restaurant, a bank?
　c. Who will tend to own specialized resources? Why?
　*d. A bank that uses a computer system for its record keeping typically rents the computers but owns the tapes on which the data is stored. Why?
　*e. Will contracts involving joint use of specialized resources or skills differ from those for resources not specialized to each other? Why? People are resources, too. Is there any greater specialization of resources between a husband and wife than between a male and female sharing living quarters? Give examples.

10. Some mining areas are isolated and all employee housing is owned by the mining company. These are called company towns. Often they are criticized as means of extracting higher rents for housing from the employees. Criticize that kind of argument. Then, from the principle of specialized resources, show how employees benefit by having housing owned by the mine owners.

11. The FCC says rights to use the radio-frequency spectrum should be assigned to permit maximum usage.
　a. Explain why that statement as it stands is meaningless and useless.
　*b. Would it have been meaningful to say rights should be assigned to achieve efficient use? What would be the criterion of efficiency?

12. According to the analyses developed in this chapter, resources will be employed in amounts at which marginal value product is not less than price. That also determines their earnings (price times the number of units employed).
　a. Who makes up the difference if promised earnings exceed the value of output?
　b. If the promised earnings are less than the total value of output, who gets the difference?
　c. What forces revise payments toward equality with value of output?

13. "If a firm uses resources efficiently, a change in their prices will induce a change in the relative amounts employed." What will induce that change—some directive from a central planning agency, the social consciousness of the employer, or what?

14. "Even if only one combination of productive inputs could be used to produce some good, there would still be substitution among productive resources in response to changes in their prices." Explain what that substitution is and how it would be induced.

15. Who is substituted for whom when a firm uses one typist, an electric typewriter, and a copying machine rather than two typists and two manual typewriters? This is called a substitution of capital for labor. Why is that misleading?

16. "The advent of the one-man bus involved more capital equipment: an automatically operated coin box and a door-control device—to name two of the capital goods that replaced the conductor."
    a. Is this a case of capital replacing labor? Where?
    b. Is it a case of labor replacing labor? Where?
    c. Is it a case of no substitution for labor at all, but instead a job revision with a greater total output? Where?

*17. "Invention and the lower cost of power in the home have replaced the domestic servant by capital equipment. Without that machinery more people would be working in homes as servants. But the replacement of domestic employees by capital has not led to the replacement of labor. The released labor is used elsewhere."
    a. Can you suggest where?
    b. Who was aided and who was hurt by the use of the vacuum cleaner, washing machine, water heater, forced-air furnace, garbage disposal, automatic oven, electric mixer, and refrigerator?

18. The electric refrigerator replaced the iceman with capital. Did eliminating the job of the iceman reduce the total number of jobs? Explain.

19. "Automation does not mean there will be more people than jobs available. It does not mean fewer jobs for unskilled people—in fact a person can be less skilled if all he has to do is punch buttons, pull triggers, and turn steering wheels, compared to driving a team of horses, shooting a bow and arrow, or wielding a chisel." Do you agree? If so, why? If not, why not?

20. "A molecule of sugar is composed of a fixed ratio of atoms of hydrogen, carbon, and oxygen; it follows that there is no substitutability of inputs in the manufacture of sugar."
    a. Do you agree? Why?
    *b. Is the reasoning in the preceding question applicable to every other kind of good that can be manufactured—whether or not the good is composed of a fixed ratio of components? For example, is the reasoning applicable to making gasoline, running a railroad, operating a bus, building a house, or selling groceries?

21. Assume that wage rates of gardeners were to double because of reduced supply of gardeners, with an unchanged demand.
    a. What substitution for gardeners would occur?
    b. Where or from whom could you learn about the available substitution techniques?

22. There are two kinds of economic efficiency—one of cost minimization and one of profit maximization. In what sense is profit maximization a more general criterion of efficiency?

23. In Iowa the yield of wheat is 30 bushels per acre; in Washington it is 50 bushels per acre. Which is better?

24. Jet engines are given an efficiency rating according to the thrust generated per pound of engine weight. Explain why that is an inadequate measure of efficiency.

25. Steers can be bred with such superb qualities that they will sell for about 50% more per pound than the standard steers raised for meat. Which type should the farmer raise? Give the answer in terms of technological versus economic efficiency.

26. A high-fidelity stereo sound system is called efficient if it uses a low amount of electric power per decibel of sound generated. Why is that technical efficiency not an adequate efficiency criterion for choosing among sound systems, even if the quality of the sound were the same?

27. A water-storage facility is needed, and engineers, asked for advice, propose a dam and attest to its efficiency.
    *a. If they attest to its technical efficiency, does that still leave open the question of its economic efficiency? For example, if

the value of the water stored is less than the cost of impounding and distributing it, is the dam, though it may be technically efficient, an economically efficient one?

b. This problem extends the notion of economic efficiency beyond the selection of the cheapest way of doing something. Economic efficiency is extended to include what?

Chapter 9

Business Firms: Ownership, Control, and Profits

The Business Firm

All business firms are created for essentially one purpose: to increase the wealth of their members. And all such firms share the characteristic of being made up of a group of resource owners who bind themselves by contracts and undertake to share in some way the results of their work. Usually the owners of the inputs whose values are most dependent on—or specialized to—the outcome will be called the owners and employers.

If the firm succeeds or fails, the owners of specialized resources receive the gain or incur loss, whereas the owners of generalized resources can more easily move to other firms or kinds of employment paying as much as was expected in the first firm. Because owners of the specialized inputs have more of their inputs' values dependent on the firm's success, they demand more responsibility for directing, managing, or monitoring the firm's activities; they are the employers or bosses.

UNCERTAINTY AND CONTROL

Before there can be teamwork there must be a team; someone must select its members. Someone must then direct their activities and monitor their performance and make adjustments in pay or assigned duties according to how they perform. All these tasks are done without perfect information. On the other hand, people contemplating joining a team must try to identify their best abilities and the team's best activities. For example, students elect a field of specialization to master in their studies; but after graduation they must then estimate where in that field their talents are most valuable. Which final products are most valuable to which consumers? Sampling and researching the desires of the nation's consumers is very costly. Furthermore, consumers themselves don't know what they will demand in the future.

One source of predictions and advice is a specialist in making forecasts, particularly one whose wealth is significantly affected by the accuracy of the forecasts. A person who puts his money where his mouth is is essentially a specialist in conveying to productive resources predictions of the values consumers place on given products—predictions backed by the predictor's wealth. Employees, in effect, ask the employers (1) to predict which products will be most valuable to produce, (2) decide the best way to undertake teamwork to produce the goods, and (3) see that the team works effectively. Employees, in short, ask employers to deal with the uncertainty of the market and to direct and monitor the productive teamwork.

RISK ALLOCATION BY INSURANCE

There are essentially two sources of uncertainty: the possibility of uncontrollable events, and the unpredictability of human behavior—especially in the quality of attention, care, efforts, and diligence. The distinction is not as sharp as it might at first seem. Our life expectancy and the likelihood of our remaining in good health are far from entirely prey to uncontrollable luck and random events. Some people work as test pilots, firefighters, and police officers rather than as retail clerks or engineers. Although there is much we cannot control, we can control our choice of activity. Moreover, though we cannot control the odds that earthquakes, hurricanes, or torrential rains and floods will occur, we can control exposure to those risks by not living in California or Florida, or in river-bottom lands. Those who live in such places in effect deliberately choose to bear those risks. They can take more expensive precautions by the kinds of houses and other structures they build. The fact that the land rents are lower than they otherwise would be

is a way of compensating people in advance for the risk of future disaster.

An *individual's* risk of severe loss can be reduced if it is shared with a large group of persons, each of whom absorbs a tiny fraction of the loss. This is the principle behind **insurance**: Each person makes a small annual payment, or insurance *premium*, to a fund to compensate whoever experiences the disaster. Life, fire, accident, and theft are typical categories of insurance.

Insurance, paradoxically, may increase the probability of the disaster. Insurance, like any safety-enhancing device, tends to make each person act less carefully by freeing the person of the prospect of bearing that severe loss. Drivers with auto-accident insurance drive a bit less carefully, as persons with theft and fire insurance may be less cautious in their behavior. To overcome this tendency the insurance group will insist that each member take protective measures: install prescribed locks on doors, install sprinkler systems, submit to building inspections, use better electrical wiring, receive no police citations for driving fast, and the like.

If people could not be induced to act more carefully, insurance would not be available. The event insured against would occur so often that those paying insurance premiums would find the costs prohibitive. That is why you can't get insurance against going broke as a businessperson.

RISK ALLOCATION BY OWNERSHIP

Many hazards are not formally insurable, that is, by purchase of an insurance policy: You can't buy insurance against your oil wells going dry, or not finding gold on your land, or people's tastes and demands shifting away from your services, or divorce, or dull children, or marital infidelity. Yet you can insure against some of these events. For example, you can transfer the risk of an oil well's unexpectedly drying up by selling the well to someone else. You will get the present value of oil that other people *expect* is there. The new owner, not you, bears the loss if the well later dries up, and gets the profit if it lasts longer than you expected. With salable private property, risks can readily be transferred to the more willing, optimistic people who accept your offer of sale. By renting some goods and owning others one can make wealth risk-bearing less dependent on consumption patterns.

In some countries, some farmers (called *ejidos* in Mexico) can sell the crop from the land but cannot sell the land or borrow against its value. (If they could borrow against it, they could then default on the loan, letting the lender take the land, thus circumventing the ban on sale of the land.) They have only *usufruct* rights: rights to what they grow on the land. Such restrictions weaken incentives to improve or invest in the farmland, because the resulting capital values cannot be realized by those most optimistic or willing to bear them, the farmers who invested in improving productivity of the land.

The bearing of risks could be assigned by the political system. Because a socialist economy is based on a political allocation of risk bearing, one of the issues debated between proponents of private-property and socialist systems is the relative merits of their respective risk-distribution institutions. A crucial element of ownership is bearing the uncertainty of the future value or productivity of the resource that is owned. The owner, by definition, bears that risk. For government property no member of the public can avoid bearing that risk. Whatever your attitudes toward the risks of owning various resources, you can't sell your interest in, say, Yosemite National Park, the postal system, or the Tennessee Valley Authority. Shares in public or government property cannot be traded, except by geographic mobility (by moving to another county, state, or country). You gain or lose as the tax laws and distribution of government services decide.

In addition to insurable risk or that which is selectively borne by choice of what kind of goods to own, another source of variations in the result of productive venture is the difficulty of controlling actual performance of the team or input members. They may be malingerers who cheat or shirk on the promised activity, or they may honestly contend they are providing more to the group than they are being given credit for. In particular, if it is difficult to correctly measure each person's production so as to know what was contributed to the group's result, some method of approximating that worker's productivity and of paying for it from the proceeds of the group must be found. But detection and control of shirking and detection of actual productivity are difficult in many situations. The group may then agree to have a supervisor or monitor to observe their behavior and pay in accord with the observer's evaluation. This is a task different from that of deciding what should be produced and how it should be produced. We call these latter tasks direction, leadership, or entrepreneurship, especially if new ventures are involved. The tasks of entrepreneurship (leadership) and of monitoring the work of several inputs is conducted in the enterprise called the business firm.

The Corporation

Business firms commonly assume one of three forms of ownership: individual proprietorship, partnership, or corporation. In the individual **proprietorship**, the owner is responsible for all debts of the firm, usually to the full extent of the owner's wealth. That is called unlimited liability. Also, the firm ceases to exist at the death of its owner. A **partnership** is joint ownership by two or more people. Each partner usually has unlimited liability for the entire firm and can individually make commitments binding the other partners. The partnership terminates if any member withdraws or dies. In the dominant contractual form of the firm, the **corporation**, several people jointly own its specialized resources. They are called the **stockholders**, because their ownership is evidenced by shares of common **stock**. Their liability is limited to what is already invested, and the firm continues to exist despite the death of a stockholder or the sale of stock to new owners.

Almost 90% of commercial and industrial sales are made by corporations; partnerships and individual proprietorships account for the remainder. But in numbers of firms, the proportions are reversed: Of the approximately 15 million business firms in the United States, 12 million are individual proprietorships (mostly in retailing, construction, real estate, insurance, wholesaling, and farming), whereas about 1 million are partnerships and 2 million are corporations (in manufacturing, wholesale and retail trade, and finance). Typically proprietorships are small and corporations much larger.

In the United States the market-generated national income is about $3 trillion (about $13,000 per capita). Each of the 10 largest corporations has from 100,000 to 600,000 employees. The 100 largest industrial corporations employ over 8 million people, or about 10% of all employees. Each of the top 50 corporations exceeds $1 billion in sales annually, with assets of about the same value.[1] Though business firms are much larger than 50 years ago, it is no harder to organize a new business, because people are wealthier. Thus, organizing a $500,000 capital fund for a new business venture would be no harder than gathering $10,000 was 50 years ago. Each year for the past 50 years, new firms

have been organized at a ratio of about one new to ten existing firms. Half the new firms are terminated in five to ten years because of losses. The net earnings of successful corporations equal about 5 to 6% of the U.S. national income. The net earnings yield a return, on average, of about 10 to 15% on the stockholders' invested capital and about 5¢ per dollar of sales.

A few hundred large corporations produce nearly half the value of final industrial output, and account for about 75% of national income. This fact must be interpreted carefully. For example, General Motors buys components from thousands of smaller firms. When these parts are assembled into a Chevrolet, should it be said that General Motors *produced* the Chevrolet, or that, rather, it designed and assembled it? Thousands of firms were involved in designing and providing parts and equipment to that giant assembly line known as General Motors. If we take into account only the final assembler, we might say that General Motors sells (produces?) 100% of these Chevrolets. If we take into account all its suppliers, then over one thousand firms produce those cars. What, then, does General Motors contribute in that productive sequence? Does it determine prices, styles, quality, and employment policies for other producers? Is there less response to consumer demands than if there were scores of assembly firms in place of one General Motors? Does General Motors make wages, prices, or total output any different from what they would be if there were a hundred firms all responding to the same market forces? We will investigate possible answers to these questions in our later analysis.

TRANSFERABLE CONTINUITY

The distinctive characteristic that makes the corporation a superior way of organizing economic production is its transferable continuity. The corporation is not terminated by a

---

[1]In 1980 Exxon had about $80 billion in sales, followed by American Telephone & Telegraph, General Electric, Mobil, Ford, Standard Oil (California), Gulf, and International Business Machines.

change of owners. Furthermore, transfer of shares by sale, gift, or legacy requires no permission of other owners, whereas in a partnership, every change requires agreement of all the partners. Shares of common stock in many corporations are usually sold in a stock market, such as the New York Stock Exchange, the American Stock Exchange, and several local exchanges. Shares of lesser-known corporations are sold by private negotiations, often through a geographically dispersed but close-knit set of stockbrokers known as the *over-the-counter* market.

That independent salability, which enables the venture to continue beyond the life or participation of any particular persons, has an important consequence: The distant future effects that are expected to accrue from current acts can be more completely capitalized in present market values of the salable shares of common stock. For this reason, current investment opportunities that will take a long time to pay off will be heeded, because the current salability of rights in those future effects enables current stockholders to immediately reap the foreseeable benefits through the changes in present capital value (price) of the shares of common stock—as explained in Chapter 6. Managers would be less responsive to long-run effects if they did not own salable rights to those effects or were not responsible to people who own them.

SEPARATION OF OWNERSHIP FROM CONTROL, OR EFFICIENT SPECIALIZATION IN OWNERSHIP RIGHTS?

Ownership of goods means the right to: (a) select uses of the goods; (b) transfer those rights to a good to other people in exchange for rights to other goods; and (c) bear the changes in their usefulness or market values, whether caused by physical changes or changes in market price.

The form that ownership in a corpora-

tion takes leads to a crucial question: To get the maximum benefits of property rights, must all owners of goods exercise all these rights themselves, or is it sometimes more efficient to use agents to exercise some of these rights? The latter course can indeed be more efficient because people differ in their talents. We have already seen some of the benefits of specialization. Yet the objection might be raised that the owner's and agent's *interests* would differ. In this particular case, even if interests differ, the benefits of specialization in exercising ownership rights can exceed the costs of satisfactorily controlling the agent's behavior. Therefore, delegating the components of private-property rights to one or more agents does not necessarily separate ownership from control or, as often alleged, reduce corporate economic efficiency. Instead, it allows *specialization* in the exercise of the separable duties of ownership to yield superior economic results. For example, it is commonly argued that if a corporation has thousands of stockholders no one of whom owns a majority of the stock, then the managers and directors rather than the stockholders control the corporation (whereas the stockholders bear the risk of changes in the value of its assets).[2] Directors are chosen by stockholders in one-vote-per-share, not one-vote-per-person, elections. Directors, then, are agents of stockholders and are authorized to make contracts (that is, to authorize operations) for the stockholders. Thus, it behooves director-managers to act with appropriate attention to stockholders' interests.

Potential conflicts of interest between agent and owner occur within the corpora-

---

[2]Let us compare the numbers of stockholders and employees (in parentheses) of several corporations as of 1980: General Motors, 1,350,000 stockholders (800,000 employees); General Electric, 530,000 (400,000); General Tire, 52,000 (40,000); General Foods, 97,000 (48,000); General Mills, 29,000 (50,000); General Telephone, 500,000 (200,000).

tion as they do in every group. The more diffused the stockholdings and the larger the corporation, the higher is any one stockholder's cost of policing the corporation's internal management as thoroughly and effectively as in a small proprietorship. Though this problem resembles that of the taxpayer whose cost of policing government employees is ludicrously higher than any potential gain, there is a difference. Unlike the taxpayer, the shareholder in a capitalist corporation has a salable share in the capitalized present value of the foreseeable future consequences of present actions. Shareholders therefore have more cause to monitor corporate action. Finally, any possible effects of dispersion of ownership would not necessarily impose losses on stockholders, for they can discount those anticipated effects into their lower initial purchase price of the stock.

Still another potent force makes managers responsive to stockholders' interests: competition among potential managers. Management is not a monolithic bloc of shirkers protecting one another from discovery and penalty. Each has a personal interest that puts him or her in competition with the others—and not only others in his or her own corporation. Any manager who tolerates management or employee behavior that impairs stockholders' interests sacrifices opportunities to attract better offers from other corporations. And such offers are a source of rapid promotion. We advance by appealing not only to our current employer's and customers' interests but also to the interests of other potential employers. People have interest in excelling and in letting others know of their excellence. This holds for managers, too.

Competition disciplines stockholders also. If all the present stockholders are lax in monitoring and exercising control, performance will lag and the value of the stock will fall. The lower price will entice other people to buy a sufficiently strong block of the stock and remove the existing management. In the financial news, and sometimes in the general news, you can find evidence of such behavior: You will hear of "takeovers," offers by one corporation to exchange some of its shares for those of the acquired—or merged—corporation, in order to improve the management in the acquired company. If the performance of management improves, it will result in a rise in the stock price, thereby rewarding all the stockholders. Present members of the management staff who can't earn as much elsewhere often do not approve of raiders and seek to frustrate takeover attempts by persuading regulators and legislators to enact regulations and laws prohibiting such offers or takeovers. (Some Securities and Exchange Commission rules make takeovers more difficult; to whose benefit we leave to your analysis.)

Government-operated firms, nonprofit firms, and profit-limited enterprises (such as some public utilities which are not allowed to exceed some specified rate of profit) permit more departures from market-value discipline, because consumer market demands become less influential and the performance of managers is not subject to being tested by the value of corporate stock. Yet popular allegations abound—although they are not borne out by economic analysis or evidence—that the large, for-profit corporation with thousands or millions of stockholders is run inefficiently, to the harm of the stockholders, and is not responsive to consumers' valuations of the corporation's goods and services.

Fundamental Sources of Profits

A successful firm is one that creates a value of output that exceeds what the members believe they could have earned elsewhere. It has a profit; but because success is copied, this is temporary. The rest of the world catches on and competes for responsible but currently undervalued resources, thereby bidding up the input prices (and hence costs) to more fully reflect their now more accurately foreseeable values. This converts the profits into higher wages, rents, or purchase prices of those inputs. The larger output from more firms brings down prices of the final products. Can profits persist? The answer requires a deeper understanding of why profits occur and how they are reported.

As we have emphasized in earlier chapters, foresight is imperfect, and changes in market values are inevitable in all economic systems. (A change from a capitalistic to a communist, socialist, or feudal economic system will not prevent profit and losses; it will change only the determination of who bears them, because certainly no earthly revolution will remove uncertainty.) Innovative activities and extraneous events alike can have unforeseen results. Because the effects of those new, unforeseen circumstances were, by definition, not captured in the prior price, the values of the pertinent assets change (for had the results been foreseen, the price of resources would already have been at that new higher or lower value).

If future prospects now appear, say, better than formerly anticipated, the price of shares of stock in the corporation is bid up as outsiders try to buy a share of those improved prospects. The price will be driven up to whatever level makes the anticipated returns bear just the normal rate of interest on the new stock price. That higher price gives to the existing stockholders the value of that larger future stream of earnings (larger than other people formerly expected).

However, if that profitable innovative action was the result of some employee's superiority—formerly unanticipated by potential employers—in ability to make good decisions or investments, such superior ability will, once revealed, bring a higher salary to the superior employee, and a smaller rise in price of the firm's common stock.

PROFITS OF LABOR

Wages are the earnings for human services; **rent** is payment for services from inanimate goods. The long future flow of a person's wages has a present capital value (as explained in Chapter 6). The present value of your long sequence of future wages may be $500,000. If you have an accident and suffer reduced prospective future receipts, the present value of your wages will fall, say, to $200,000, a loss of $300,000.

The capitalized value of nonhuman wealth is more clearly measurable because most inanimate goods can be bought and sold, whereas a person is not bought or sold. Typically only a person's current services are sold. If one could literally sell all future services now, one could capitalize and convert (or "cash in") any profit to other forms of wealth. But because no person can, we bear the risk of the future value of our labor services.

RICARDIAN DIFFERENTIAL OF SUPERIOR ABILITY

In a sense, all profits—or values—are values of people rather than of inanimate goods. Goods and resources are valuable only because of how people use them. People with superior talents know better than others how to use resources to make them more valuable. Inputs of unequal abilities will generally draw unequal earnings. The earnings of the person of superior ability are called the **differential earnings**, or (as defined earlier) *Ricardian rents*, of superior talent. (The latter term distinguishes such rents from *monopoly rents*, which are enhanced earnings to some sellers who have managed to prevent other people from competing with them and bidding up the prices of inputs and lowering consumers' prices.) For example, there is certainly some large Ricardian rent in the higher incomes of Frank Sinatra, Jack Nicklaus, and Kareem Jabbar, to name only a few.

How quickly and accurately is the superior ability of a person, asset, or enterprise recognized and converted to a higher price, rent, or wage for its services? As quickly as the most optimistic people are willing to bid up the price or wage or rent in their belief that the superior ability is really there and not a one-time lucky experience. The ability to distinguish between luck and true superior ability can be crucial to one's wealth. One of the authors made a hole-in-one the first time he played golf. No one immediately offered him a professional contract; 30 years later he got his second hole-in-one. An author who writes one successful novel has no certainty of writing another one as good. Such instances as holes-in-one and the one successful novel are examples of the *regression phenomenon*: the tendency of good luck to be followed by, or regress to, normal luck (which does not mean bad luck). To fail to account for the phenomenon is to commit a *regression fallacy*. The market does not commit regression fallacies.[3] People recognize

___

[3] An example of a regression phenomenon is the following: Of 100 identical salespersons, some would have more sales in one week by good luck and others would have fewer sales by bad luck. In the next week they would more likely have their usual luck and would make a number of sales nearer their long-run average. That is, both the very lucky and the unlucky in the first week tend to *regress* toward their longer-run average—because they cannot continue to have unusually good or bad luck. This tendency to *regress* toward the long-run average after unusually good or bad luck is called the regression phenomenon. It assumes that the differences in performance in the first week were at least partly affected by transient luck.

One of the notorious ways of taking advantage of this is to invite people to take some performance test—say, a reading test—and to tell those who score below average to take lessons in reading improvement. After the lessons their test performance will on average improve because their performance on the first test was due partly to unusually bad luck. Their performance on average would have improved whether or not they took reading improvement lessons.

that great success is often accidental, and do not see every instance of success as promising equal future success. On the contrary, later performance will probably regress toward true ability. In the interim, a truly superior resource, be it a person or a nonhuman asset, will be temporarily undervalued but ultimately will rise in value. Anyone who knows which resources are currently undervalued can make a fortune hiring or buying them at the current undervalued market prices.

As an example, if General Motors hires a superior designer, the increased value of the cars at first shows up as a profit to GM. But GM cannot continue to purchase the designer's superior services at less than they are revealed to be worth, unless *all* other potential employers remain ignorant of the designer's ability—and the designer will not let that happen. As other employers bid for the designer's work, they drive up his or her wage until it matches the high value of the superior ability. Thus are the costs of that designer's services raised to all who thereafter buy them.

Barriers to Entry or Filters?

The difficulty that other firms have in trying to copy a first firm's success is often attributed to "barriers to entry." The term suggests that the first firm is somehow unfairly restraining other firms from entering the market, but this need not be so. Features of the open market itself make the entry of other firms more difficult. First, because everyone *else* knows about the first firm's success, the costs of buying the resources or hiring the people have been bid up; instead of profits, only normal rates of return can be expected by new firms.

A second feature of the market is that reliable prepurchase information about a good is not costless to create and transmit, and customers cannot detect the quality of a new supplier's goods costlessly prior to purchase. Hence consumers sensibly and economically use past experience to predict future performance. Doing so is cheaper than treating every new seller equally, for though some may be better, some will surely be worse. Consumer knowledge of the quality of goods from existing suppliers is a useful, desirable "barrier" to new, untried candidates. If experience were of *no* predictive value whatsoever, then no "barrier," or, to put it more accurately, no *filter* device, would be available. Life would be more costly for consumers. A filter is a barrier to inferior alternatives and protects consumers from the higher costs of continual trial and error. It is, then, *not* a cost-increasing barrier. It would pay to eliminate it *only* on the premise that every new supplier were *probably* as good as present sellers. And that premise is false.

Imagine that General Motors were to secretly produce some cars for me that were exactly like their own but had my name on them. The public would not know the cars were really the same GM product. How many cars would I sell? At what price? With what confidence for consumers? *Known*, consistent, proven performance at some level of quality—not necessarily at the highest level but at a predictable level—is what influences consumers. For example, the names Trave-Lodge and Intercontinental are equally reliable predictors, or filters, one of a medium quality and price and the other of a higher quality and price. Both names are valuable to consumers as cheap identifiers of reliable suppliers.

The information value of a brand name or trademark reflects the *past* reliable services and products supplied under the name or trademark. The investment in creating that reliability is what the firm is getting a return on, a return on investment in what is called an intangible (because, unlike goods and machinery and the like, it literally cannot be touched or seen). But it is an intangible that, like knowledge, is valuable. When Standard Oil, New Jersey, changed its public trade name to Exxon from Esso (to avoid legal conflict with other Standard Oil companies), and when Datsun changed its name in the United States to Nissan, they took great pains to make clear that the new name was merely replacing the former name, and was not the name of some new company. To have used the new names without indicating which companies they represented would have failed to transfer to them the consumer's valuation of the Esso and Datsun names as predictors of a quality of service.

The value of a firm's name is often called **goodwill**. Although goodwill is hardly ever fully entered in accounting records, it is revealed in the market value of the common stock of the corporation. If one could subtract the sale value of all the other assets of the corporation, the remainder would be goodwill.

Another feature of the market that encourages would-be entrants to see barriers to entry is that large initial investments must be made in capital equipment. These large investments are often necessary for low-cost production. If customers were willing to pay higher prices to newcomers who have higher costs of production per unit because they haven't made large initial investments that enable much lower operating costs, newcomers could enter with less risk. But the "barrier" is the customers' current preference for lower-cost suppliers of proven reliability who made a high initial investment successfully. If a newcomer could be sure of success in attracting customers, the initial investments would not restrict entry at all. But of course new entrants *cannot* be sure of success. Thus, it is the customers' knowledge of present suppliers and unwillingness to promise to buy from unproven newcomers that is the "barrier." It is often claimed that the large initial investment is a "barrier" that allows existing firms to make larger profits than if the initial investment were smaller. This is a misunderstanding.

To better see why, we must separate two kinds of entry investment activities. One is the cost of expensive long-lived equipment that may or may not later be salable if the business is not a success; the other is the *trial* cost, the cost of *trying* to create a successful firm: the cost of searching, testing, and judging, and trying to assemble the appropriate team of inputs in that firm. The trial cost (which is not part of the later costs of operating a proven successful firm) can be very high and is not recovered if the search and assembly does not result in a successful firm.

A large trial cost and a large investment cost in equipment can separately or together deter entry. Because the cost of a trial is large, the successful new firm is expected to earn enough to have induced people to make those trials with uncertain outcomes: To be in equilibrium it must be earning a return in excess of depreciation, wages, and other continuing costs. That "expected excess" is the "premium" that covers the expected costs of failed searches.

If you must pay $1.00 to make a trial, all of which you lose if the trial is unsuccessful, then how much must you expect to receive on the successful trials if you are to break even? If half the trials are unsuccessful, then you must get back $2.00 on each success. Clearly, if the trial cost of entry into some business is high, successes must pay more than the operating costs if entry is to be induced, though the successes receive what seem to be extra-large profits.

And so it is in various industries. Those with a larger forfeitable initial investment, whether in trial costs or in equipment with little salvage value elsewhere, show greater rates of profits for the successful firms than in industries where initial forfeitable investments are small. The larger profits of the successful firms encourage those discouraged by the large forfeitable investment costs to

believe that the successful firms are earning so much because they have somehow thrown up barriers to subsequent entry. But this misreads the situation: The high investment costs do not *enable* larger profits for the successful firms; rather, the larger profit prospect for successes must be present to offset the higher initial trial and investment costs that would be lost by unsuccessful entrants.

Because of interdependencies among the appropriate team members, the value of all the inputs *as a team* can exceed the sum of the values each member would have with some other employer. Since a firm has to pay in wages and rents to each team member only what each person or piece of equipment could have earned elsewhere, it follows that if the group as a team is superior, then the team—the firm—is worth more than the salaries and rents of all the member inputs. The successful "firm" is worth more than the sum of the separate input values.

An example of the implications of the difficulty of assembling a well-coordinated team of inputs is provided by the fact that some established business firms that want to get into another line of business will buy out a firm already successfully operating in that line of business. Why didn't the firm seeking entry hire away the pertinent workers and buy similar equipment? It is difficult to know exactly which of the inputs form the critical group in that production team. So the new entrant might buy the whole firm, thereby acquiring a team already successfully assembled without going through the more expensive process of trial and error in assembling a new team itself.

Business Profits

The excess of the value of the firm over the costs paid to its separate members might be called profits. But as we have seen, the term "profit" can mean many different things. You may recall that by *profit* an economist means an increase in wealth above that accounted for by savings of the interest (income) of one's wealth. That interpretation was explained in Chapter 6. But the term is used more loosely to mean other things as well. Each year business firms report their profits. According to our rigorous definition given above, that should be the change in the firm's stock values over the interval in excess of interest on the value of the stock. But the firm might report a profit during a year in which the price of the stock fell. Then the stockholders have had a loss. The stock price fell because during the year future prospects became bleaker. If you recall the meaning of an annuity given in Chapter 6, it is possible for the first term in the annuity to be a positive amount, but for the terms to unexpectedly become smaller so that the present value of that sequence drops. That is why a firm can be earning income this year, but enough less than expected so that its stock price falls. Was there a profit? It all depends on what you want to mean by that term. If profit is to be used to measure a change in one's wealth, there has been a loss.

ACCOUNTING DATA

We now consider how difficult it is to compute earnings from accounting data as reported by some business firms. Financial accounting data provide a record of the amounts of money spent or committed to future payment, and the goods and services obtained in exchange. All past expenditures and receipts are included in the accounts, but only *some* of the future commitments for expenditure and foreseeable future receipts are included. Prospects of receipts are excluded, with very good reason, as illustrated by the following scenario.

With $31,000 I buy land and oil drilling equipment ($10,000) and pay wages ($21,000) to myself and the drill workers. In a year I strike oil. What should my accountant do? Record an estimate of the present value of the unknown amount of uncaptured and unsold oil? If I could now get $100,000 on the market for the land and oil rights, then *whether or not* I sell, my wealth has increased to $100,000 plus any resale value of the drilling equipment (say it has depreciated to $6000, down $4000 from its initial price of $10,000). There was $31,000 invested initially, so with a 10% interest rate, interest costs would be $3100 (.10 x $31,000). My wealth is $106,000 ($6000 in equipment + $100,000 in the market value of the land and oil rights). Because I have no liabilities, my wealth gain (my profit) is $71,900 (= $100,000 value discovered − $21,000 wages − $4000 depreciation − $3100 interest).

However, the accounting records will show a negative income or *loss* of $41,000 during the year! We used up $4000 of oil-well equipment and $36,000 for all wages and $1000 for interest, but we have sold no oil. The accountant is unwilling to record a value of the prospective *future* oil sales, because the oil has not yet been sold at a definite price. If the oil is to be valued, *accounting custom* dictates that it should be valued at the cost ($41,000) of finding it, which is called its *book value*. If we didn't understand the custom, we might think the $41,000 represented the *market* value of the oil field, but the usual accounting convention is to *not* record any value over costs (or at most only up to a formal, or nominal, $1) until there is a sale and receipt. Also, a zero (or $1) valuation is adopted if the asset is not a physical, tangible thing but is instead an idea, design, patent, new product, trademark, reputation, "quality assurance," or personality.

For example, the value of the name "Kodak" was established by a consistently reliable product; the name identifies a product of reliability. How should that expensively created, fragile, valuable reputation, the name "Kodak," be valued? At the advertising cost? At the cost of having created reliable products? At zero? Or at an estimate of its assurance value to future customers? Convention prefers the zero or $1 value—false though that value certainly is. Regardless of accounting convention, we know that the prospect of future sales is part of the value of a firm. Ford has no contract with future customers for sales of Ford cars next year. Nor does any firm have such a contract with the public for its product. Nevertheless, people believe that Ford will have sales next year, and they back that belief by buying common stock in that corporation. They pay for, or bet on, the *prospect* of successful *future* operations. In fact, the market price of almost every good is a present bet about future prospects.

What about *my* labor services in the oil venture? These should be counted. Say they would amount to $30,000 per year if I worked full time on the oil venture. These implicit costs total $30,000. I worked only half time on the oil venture, so my labor costs are $15,000. Total wages are $41,000. After all that, if I still have achieved a surplus of product value, I have a profit. That surplus occurred because I was able to produce more than the *market* (that is, everyone else) expected I could produce with those resources. It is a pure profit: something the market did not expect to occur, for if it had, others would have kept me from buying those services so cheaply by bidding up their price.

When you read that some enterprise has "net earnings" or "income" or "profits" of some amount or percentage, you must investigate in each case how they counted the costs of interest on their investment and their implicit wages. Usually, the reported net earnings are the net *before* that implicit interest on the investment is deducted—and sometimes even before the owner's implicit wages.

If you examine the annual reports of business firms, you will find assertions like: "We have started production on a very promising new product. We are currently operating at a loss, but we expect in a year to be covering costs and making profits." If that statement were taken literally, one would wonder why they hadn't waited until next year to start operations. Translated into our terms of economic analysis it means: "At the present time the *current* rate of sales is less than current investment and expenditures; but the present investment expenditures on materials and equipment and training will bring larger future receipts that will exceed future outlays. We believe the new product will promise a net flow of future receipts that will increase our wealth. In fact, the investing public is now of the same opinion, and that is why the market value of our shares of common stock has increased during the current year. So we really had a profit. Hooray!"

Misdefinitions of Profits

DIFFERENCE BETWEEN WHOLESALE AND RETAIL PRICE

Sometimes the difference between the price that a retailer pays for goods and the selling price is called profit. More normally, that difference is called *markup*, to indicate how much above the wholesale purchase price the selling price must be to cover all the retailer's many costs, such as for space, shelter, management, sales clerks, inventory for display and immediate delivery, record keeping, security, insurance, advertising, taxes, light, heat, fixtures, breakage, pilferage, packaging, returns, employee training, and many other costly activities. Yet some people say that the sale of a good at a markup of 100% (of the wholesale purchase price, or 50% of the retail price) represents a profit of 100%. Even Congressional reports have said so. Sometimes the owners even fail to include in costs an estimate of their own labor services, so that what may appear as "profits" is merely wages for personal labor.

Another error in computing profits by subtracting costs from earnings is to count all costs except taxes, thus calculating "profits before taxes." Remarkably, a government agency has used this concept, apparently unaware of its implications. It suggests that taxes are not really a part of costs—that they are payments for no service. It is difficult to believe that the government agency would want to suggest that taxes are merely tribute collected from profits. One would hardly be more surprised if a labor union published a graph of "profits before wages" as if wages were not costs.

Measuring profits or **earnings** as a *percent of a firm's sales* is very misleading for two reasons. First, a person who invests $1 to produce some product in one day and sells it for $1.01 (a rate of 1% on sales), and then repeats the action every day for a year, will have had sales of $368.65 in the year with *net earnings* of one cent each day, or $3.65 throughout the year. That sum is 1% of sales per year, but it is a very large return of 365% per year on the initial $1 investment. Second, a very small margin of earnings on sales will not necessarily be wiped out by a slight rise in costs, for the price may also rise, depending upon general supply and demand conditions such as we have already analyzed. Some businesspersons use the small size of their margins of earnings on sales to indicate that they are not earning "excessive profits." Whatever the facts, "excessive profits" is simply a pejorative term suggesting that profits are larger than someone thinks they should be.

Summary

1. A capitalistic firm is a group of resource owners bound by contracts wherein: (a) the inputs cooperate in joint, or team, production; (b) one central party has contracts with the owners of the other joint inputs; (c) the central party owns the inputs whose values depend most specifically on the group's performance; (d) the central party holds the residual claim beyond obligations specified in advance; (e) the central party can sell its position; and (f) the central party directs the choice of productive activity of the team.

2. The person called the firm's owner predicts for the owners of jointly used inputs the best use values of their services to consumers.

3. The corporation is like a partnership in that it can be an association with several joint owners. But it is unlike a partnership in that any member of it can sell his or her shares to anyone else without prior approval of existing shareholders and the corporation can continue, whereas a partnership is terminated if any member leaves.

4. Directing and controlling effective teamwork require effective monitoring and revision of contracts and duties. Joint ownership of resources that are specialized to one another reduces opportunistic behavior.

5. Teamwork is monitored by agents of owners of the resources most specific to the activities of the team.

6. Specialization of activity in directing and monitoring activities and in risk bearing is often misleadingly called separation of ownership from control, whereas it is specialization in the exercise of ownership rights.

7. Because common stocks readily reveal in their price the present capital value of the corporation, the corporation's current decisions and operations tend to be made in the light of their foreseeable consequences.

8. Stock markets help capital value effects to be detected or revealed, thereby enhancing the usefulness of the corporate form in controlling resources and production.

9. Bearing the uncertain consequences of any action is called risk bearing.

10. Though many future events are completely uncontrollable, the consequences of such

events are not. Hence a distinction between unavoidable risk and avoidable risk is of dubious use.

11. Insurance distributes risk among a class of people, each accepting a definite cost in order to compensate those who would suffer a large loss if the uncertain event occurred and they were not so protected.

12. Ownership of private-property rights has an essential feature: risk bearing. Risks from some specified events can be shared through insurance, but any unspecified, uninsured risks are by definition borne by the owner.

13. Imperfect foresight into the future value of any productive resource will result in losses or profits to that input as the future is revealed. This is true for labor, capital goods, and owners of a business organization. Usually the gains or losses to individuals from their labor services are called simply changes in wages, even though those changes are profits and losses.

14. Innovative activity may result in greater profits or losses. Therefore, some profits or losses occur because of superior or lucky (or inferior or unlucky) innovative activity. Distinguishing superior ability from luck is not always possible. As superior skills are discerned, superior inputs will obtain higher contractual incomes and less in the form of residual profits.

15. Competition among firms for resources producing output of a value in excess of what is being paid them will bid up their prices to match the value of their product.

16. When the future is more clearly perceived to promise more valuable consequences than were formerly anticipated, the present value of the relevant capital assets is driven up by competition to acquire them. That increase capitalizes the future profit stream into higher present values and yields the new buyers at the higher prices just the normal predictable rate of return.

17. The source of superiority of successful firms if often misleadingly called a barrier to entry by inferior actual or potential competitors.

18. Accountants keep records of past expenditures and revenues. Attempts to deduce profits from accounting records can be very misleading, because they record historical values, not present market values of existing resources.

19. Monopoly rents, increases in income obtained by restricting competitors, are often also called profits, misleadingly.

Questions

1. A friend of yours, a brilliant engineer and administrator, is operating a business. You propose to bet on its success and offer your friend some money to expand its operations. A corporation is formed allotting you 40% and your friend 60% of the common stock. You invest $30,000. This is often described as separation of ownership from control, because you don't have the majority vote. Would you ever be willing to invest wealth in such a fashion—that is, give up control while retaining ownership of 40% of the value of this business? Why?

2. Is it a disadvantage of the corporation that not every stockholder can make the controlling decisions? That the control is dispersed? That some people who own less than half of the corporation can make controlling decisions?

3. A criticism of the modern corporation is that the management or directors, by virtue of their central position, are able to collect proxies (rights to cast votes of stockholders) from the other stockholders, and as a result the management is in a powerful position and cannot be easily dislodged. It has been said that "the typical small stockholder can do nothing about changing management and that under ordinary circumstances management can count on remaining in office; and often the proxy battle is fought to determine which minority group shall control." Take the assertions as being correct.
   a. Does it follow that stability of management in "ordinary circumstances" harms stockholders?

b. Does it follow that a typical small stockholder "should" be able to turn out management?

c. If a minority group succeeds in swinging voting decisions, does this mean that a minority controls or that a majority controls through the leadership of a minority group? Is this to be interpreted in the same way that political parties consisting of a group of organized politicians have elections to see which minority group shall control the government? Why or why not?

4. "Very few corporations lose wealth, and still fewer go broke." Do you agree? What evidence can you cite?

5. a. In analyzing the behavior of corporation management and directors, why is it pertinent to distinguish between nonprofit or publicly regulated, limited-profit corporations on the one hand, and private for-profit business corporations on the other?

b. Which do you think would be more marked by self-perpetuating management and stockholder lethargy? Why?

*c. Which do you think would show more discrimination in employment practices according to race and religion? Why?

6. Joseph Thagworthy has a stable of race horses and a breeding farm. The two, although operated as a business, lose him over $50,000 annually. Yet he continues year after year because he enjoys the activity more than if he spent a similar sum for travel or conventional types of consumption activities.

a. Would it be correct to say that he is maximizing his wealth in that business?

b. Do you think an increase in the losses would induce an increase in that kind of activity? What does economic theory postulate about that?

7. An engineer devises a way to make a new product that is very much in demand. The process requires the engineer's continued attention along with a lot of machinery useful only in this process. If a business firm is started to use that engineer's process, who will own the firm—the engineer or an investor who hires the engineer?

Why? If the firm uses the services of a secretary and a security guard, are they as likely to be owners of the firm as is the engineer? Why?

8. A young college teacher hits upon a sparkling teaching style and is rewarded with a higher salary. Has she had a profit? Explain.

9. "Under a socialist system, profits and losses are eliminated." Comment.

10. "Paper profits and losses are not real profits and losses." Do you agree? If so, why? If not, why not?

11. The process whereby secret information is revealed by the stock market is exemplified by the following episode: On March 7, 1954, the *New York Times* reported a test in which a new bomb of enormous force had been exploded on March 1, 1954. On March 31, 1954, Atomic Energy Commissioner Strauss reported publicly for the first time the nature of the new bomb and its dependence on lithium. Weeks prior to his announcement, the price of the stock of Lithium Corporation of America, one of the producers of lithium, increased substantially. How is this rise in price consistent with the fact that everyone connected with the corporation and the test really kept the secret?

12. General Electric and Xerox each sold their computer subsidiaries to Minneapolis Honeywell because the subsidiaries were unable to avoid losses. Why would anyone *pay* for a business that is *losing* money? It should have a negative value. One would think that General Electric and Xerox would have to pay someone to take on a business that is losing money. Explain the behavior of these firms. Can you find some explanation that doesn't make the buyers foolish companies? If your explanation makes the buyers look sensible, is it consistent with General Electric and Xerox selling their computer divisions rather than continuing with them?

13. "Capitalism encourages deceitful advertising, dishonesty, and faithlessness." Do you agree? If so, why? If not, why not?

14. Suppose it were true that rich people got rich exclusively from profits. Suppose further that those who received the profits were no smarter, no more foresighted, no nicer, no harder

working, no more productive than other people. Does this mean that their profits are "undeserved" and that the rich people performed no service?

15. Taxes are often levied on corporations. What in fact is being taxed?

16. "Big profits are made by successful firms in large capital investment industries. This shows that large capital investments restrict entry and permit firms already in business to make larger profits because of the high costs of entry." True or false?

*17. Our laws and customs reflect the assignments of risk bearing. A person who owns land as private property must bear the consequences of changes in the value of that land if people move away or no longer value that location so highly. Similarly, if he catches cold or breaks his leg or becomes hard of hearing and can no longer earn so large an income, he must bear the consequences.

    a. Would you advocate that people bear the wealth losses to their private property re-

gardless of cause (aside from legal recourse to violators of property rights)?

    b. Would you want a homeowner to bear the consequences of a meteorite's falling on his house? Fire from using gasoline in the house? Flood damage to houses near rivers? Income loss from cancer? Blindness?

    c. Who do you think should bear the loss if the individual does not?

    d. Why would you draw the line differently in different cases? What is the criterion you used?

    e. In each case, do you think people's behavior would be affected according to the risk bearing involved?

    f. Would you allow people to agree to take on certain risks in exchange for not bearing other risks, if two people could make a mutually agreeable partition and exchange of such risks? How would that differ from a system of private-property rights?

For Further Study: Interpreting Financial Statements

Business firms periodically (commonly every three or six months and annually) issue financial reports of their activities and current status. Reproduced below is a slightly simplified balance sheet reported for the United Mining Corporation for March 31, 1982. A *balance* sheet presents a listing and cost valuation of a company's assets, liabilities, and ownership structure. *Assets* are the resources owned by the corporation. There are always claims held by other people against a business; these claims are called *liabilities*. The net value of these assets—that is, the value after liabilities are subtracted—is called *equity* or *net worth*.

    The basic definition is:

$$\text{Assets} - \text{Liabilities} = \text{Equity},$$

which can be rewritten:

$$\text{Assets} = \text{Liabilities} + \text{Equity}.$$

The firm's balance sheet presents items classified as assets on the left side and liabilities and equity on the right side. What do the listed items mean?

ASSETS

Assets are divided into several categories and are grouped separately as either *current* or *long term*. Current assets are made up of:

    Cash. The amount of money held, including checking accounts.

    Accounts receivable. These are the past sales yet to be paid for by customers; charge accounts or credit extended to customers allowing them, usually, 30 days to pay.

Reserve for bad debts. Very likely some customers will fail to pay their debts. To express this fact and to estimate the expected amount of receivables that will become "bad," the accountants subtract an amount called a "reserve for bad debts" or "doubtful accounts." This is called a "reserve" because it expresses a "reservation" or "qualification" about the value of the receivables. Reserves in accounting statements do *not* represent collections of money or assets that have been reserved in the sense of being set aside. In bookkeeping, the word *reserve* almost never denotes a setting aside of cash or actual reserving of assets. It is almost always used to express explicitly a reservation or adjustment in the stated value of some asset or liability.

Unbilled costs. The corporation is making some products to custom order; and, as gradually completed, the corporation records the incurred costs as claims accruing against the customer, for which a bill will be submitted upon completion and delivery to the customer.

Inventories. The corporation refines ores. This is the value of ore removed from its mines and not yet sold, plus any other unsold products. In general, this records values of products or raw materials on hand.

Prepaid expenses. The corporation has paid in advance for some goods and services yet to be obtained—just as when you prepay a magazine subscription, you would record that asset as a prepaid expense in your personal balance sheet.

Marketable securities. These are typically U.S. government bonds or notes payable in the near future, common stocks of other companies, or bonds of other companies. In all cases, these securities are saleable on bond or stock exchanges.

Long-term assets are made up of the following:

Investments. This corporation owns some stock of another company. Usually, the particular investment is identified in footnotes that accompany the balance sheet.

Plant and equipment. This is the origi-

United Mining Corporation
Balance Sheet, March 31, 1982
(in Thousands of Dollars)

Assets		Liabilities	
Current		**Current**	
Cash	$1,929	Accounts payable	$11,923
Accounts receivable	4,669	Notes payable	2,358
Reserve for bad debts	−600	Accrued liabilities,	
Unbilled costs	13,335	future production	10,200
Inventories	7,515	Current liabilities	24,481
Prepaid expenses	756		
Marketable securities	5,577	**Long Term**	
Current assets	33,181	Long-term debt	48,623
Long Term		Minority interest	3,974
Investments	9,334	Long-term Liabilities	52,597
Government contracts	18,244	**Equity**	
Plant and equipment	69,877	Preferred, convertible stock,	
Less reserve for depreciation	−7,000	10,000 shares (5%, $100)	1,000
Other	538	Common stock (20¢ par)	
Goodwill	100	5,175,000 issued	1,035
Long-term assets	91,093	Capital surplus	28,658
Total assets	124,274	Retained earnings	18,538
			47,196
		Liability + Equity	124,274

nal amount paid for the physical property—mines, mills, smelters, and the like—of the corporation. Sometimes this is the *cost of replacing it,* especially if there have been drastic changes in costs of this equipment since purchase.

Reserve for depreciation. The property, plant, and equipment have been used and partly worn out. An estimate of the portion of the plant so consumed is called depreciation or reserve for depreciation. Subtracting depreciation from the initial price gives the "book" value of equipment. (See above: *Reserve for bad debts.*)

Other assets. These can be almost any kind of asset—mines, land, buildings, claims against others, and the like. Usually footnotes to the balance sheet will give clues.

Goodwill. Patents and trademarks are often given some small or token estimate of value and called goodwill. Sometimes the continued success of a company is reflected in certain intangibles, for example, its greater income, because it is known to supply good, reliable products.

LIABILITIES

Liabilities are conventionally categorized into *current* and *long-term* liabilities, with the former usually representing claims that must be paid within a year.

Accounts payable. The corporation has purchased goods and equipment for which it must yet pay. The amount still due is recorded.

Notes payable. The corporation has borrowed, and the amount due is shown. This item may also include any long-term debt that will fall due within a year.

Accrued liabilities. At the present moment (the end of the month), the corporation has accrued obligations to pay taxes or wages. For example, if wages are paid on the fifteenth of the month, then at the end of the month it will owe about half a month's wages, to be paid in two weeks.

Long-term debt. The corporation has issued bonds to borrow money. In the present instance, these will run until about 1995. Bonds are the paper record of indebtedness of the firm to the bondholders.

Minority interest. The corporation is the primary owner of a subsidiary company, the entire value of which has been recorded among the assets. However, because this corporation is not the sole owner, it has recorded here the ownership rights of the other owners. This recorded *minority interest* offsets part of the value shown on the asset side. Usually every balance sheet has footnotes giving further details. A footnote in this report would tell us that the subsidiary company, which has a recorded value of about $14,700,000, is all included in this corporation's reported property, plant, and equipment ($69,877,000) on the asset side. $3,974,000 of that belongs to other people—the subsidiary company's other owners, the *minority interest.*

EQUITY OR OWNERSHIP

Many firms include many different items under *Equity.*

Preferred, convertible stock. Preferred stock is a term for what is simply a debt of the company, probably issued by the firm to borrow investment funds. It is called *preferred* stock because its holders, in the event of bankruptcy, have a preferred claim against the company, prior to that of the common stock holders. This might have been called bonds of $100 denominations paying 5% per year—except that preferred stock often differs from a bond in that if the $5 "interest" or "dividend" on the stock is not paid, its holder cannot institute legal foreclosure proceedings against the company. The holder simply has preference to the earnings, if any, for payment of interest before any dividends can be paid to the common stock holders. Sometimes the preferred stock is "cumulative," which means that if any arrears of unpaid dividends accumulate, the common stock holders cannot take any dividends until they are paid. And, as here, the preferred stock may be *convertible:* The preferred stock holder has the option to exchange (convert) it into common stock at a preset exchange rate. In the present instance, the exchange rate is 10 common for one preferred stock (information usually given in a footnote to the balance sheet). Thus the present preferred convertible stock has a par of $100 with 5%; it pays $5 preferred dividends each year (if earned) and may be converted to 10 shares of common stock.

A person who buys a share of preferred, convertible stock for $100 has some hope that the common stock will rise above $10 a share; converting to 10 shares will then give the holder more than $100. As the price of a common share approaches $10 in the stock market, the selling price of preferred convertible stock will rise above $100, reflecting both the current value of the preferred "dividends" due and the present values of further future possible rises in the common stock price. A purchaser of *convertible* preferred common stock is in fact a partial common stock holder or owner. A purchaser of nonconvertible preferred stock is simply a creditor of the company.

Finally, some preferred stocks (and bonds) are "callable"; that is, the company has the option to pay them off prior to their due date. A $100 callable preferred stock will usually be callable at some price slightly above $100, but the premium diminishes as the due date approaches. The owner of a callable, convertible, cumulative, preferred stock (of $100 par value, at 5%, convertible at $10, and callable at $105 within five years) will collect $5 a year in dividends, if earned; $105 may be offered for the stock, which the holder must take or convert to common stock (10 shares because at $10 per share they will equal the $100 par value of the convertible preferred share). As you can see, all sorts of terms are possible in a "preferred stock."

The remaining three items show the equity, the ownership rights of the stockholders, which usually is expressed in three parts: *common stock, additional paid-in capital,* and *retained earnings* (sometimes the last two are combined and called simply *capital surplus*). We already know that equity, by definition, equals the difference between assets and liabilities (including preferred stock as a liability). In the present instance, if we subtract the liabilities (current plus long term) from the assets ($124,274,000 − $77,078,000), we get $47,196,000, which is the *book value* of the common stock holders' equity. How was it attained? Initially, when the stock was issued, $29,693,000 (= $28,658,000 + $1,035,000) was paid into the company. The figure recorded for legal and tax purposes is $1,035,000 as the *initial par value* and $28,658,000 as the *additional amount paid* originally for that stock. This division is of no economic significance and reflects some technically legal quirks. We mention it here to avoid any impression that the par value reflects some currently relevant economic value.

What happened to that $29,693,000? It was invested and spent (along with proceeds of loans) for property, wages, equipment, and the like, and at the moment the results of that activity are shown as assets on one side and as incurred obligations on the other.

Retained earnings. The corporation has *invested* $18,538,000 of its earnings to purchase new equipment and facilities. It may also have paid out some of the earnings as dividends to common stock holders, but we can't tell from the balance sheet data. If it had losses, they will reduce this figure.

Such is what the balance sheet record of this corporation indicates. If we divide the recorded *book value* of the ownership, $47,196,000 (= $1,035,000 + $28,658,000 + 18,538,000), by the 5,175,000 shares outstanding, it comes to about $9.12 a share.

It is tempting to conclude that a share of common stock is worth about $10; but don't

United Mining Corporation
Income Statement, Year Ended March 31, 1982

Sales		$83,261,000
Costs and Expenses		
Costs of goods sold (labor, materials, power)	$67,929,000	
Depreciation of equipment and depletion of ore	4,599,000	
Selling and administrative	6,079,000	
Interest on debt	4,105,000	
		82,712,000
Operating net income		534,000
Share belonging to minority interest		111,000
Federal Income Tax		25
Net earnings		422,075
Earnings per share		$.08

yield to that temptation, or else you are rejecting everything you have learned in this book. Why? Because the figures in the balance sheet's asset column are the historical outlays for the equipment (adjusted for depreciation). They do not tell us what the company will do in the future. How do we know that the mine—which *cost,* say, $1,000,000 to find and develop—is not going to yield $100,000,000 in receipts, or maybe nothing?

None of this is revealed by the balance-sheet asset records—unless the corporation directors decide to make a prognosis of that future receipt stream, discount it into a present value, and record it under "goodwill" or "profits." But they don't do this, simply because they know how unreliable that is. Instead, they issue a report of operations and events along with their balance sheets. For example, this corporation once reported: "The outlook for widespread civilian and military use of uranium improved greatly during the past year. The capability of the industry in the free—world countries, based on currently known or reserve information, is estimated to be about 20,000 tons annually, in the face of a projected annual amount demanded of 40,000 tons, excluding military purchases." But the directors did not foresee the rejection of a proposal to build another nuclear-powered aircraft carrier or the cur-

rent fear of nuclear hazards. All the directors could do was report what was then known and make some clearly labeled forecasts, which other people can accept, reject, or revise at their own risk.

The recorded book values measure only the past costs of accumulating the assets—adjusted by a formal depreciation method. They are *not* measures of what the assets would sell for now if disposed of piecemeal because the company was to be liquidated. Nor is it a measure of the value of the company's future net receipts from its business operations. The present value of its future earnings may be far above the costs of the assets it uses. An excess of stock price over book value is an indication of profitable prospects; it is not an indication of deception of the stockholders. Nor is a stock price below the book value any evidence that it is a safe investment in the sense that if worse came to worst the company could sell off its assets and collect enough to pay each stockholder the book value. The book value is a measure neither of the piecemeal disposal value nor the value of the going enterprise as a whole. It is instead merely a formalized means of indicating the past dollar measure of costs of the owned assets, adjusted for depreciation by some formal method that often bears little if any relation to the future earnings prospects or the decrease in current market demand for those assets.

At the time the balance sheet situation is disclosed the company also issues its *Income Statement,* a statement of its receipts and expenditures during the year ending at the date of the balance sheet. It reported net earnings of $.08 per share of common stock for the year ending March 31, 1982. That is less than 1% per year on the value of a share of stock, hardly a return competitive with yields available on secure bonds or on common stocks (around 12%). Why the difference? The current earnings may grow to large earnings in the future. It is the present value of all those future earnings that is reflected in the stock price.

The present value of the stock of a company with expectations of rapidly rising future earnings will be high relative to current reported earnings. Stocks should not be compared by looking at only their current earnings. A company with negative earnings this year but with superb prospects of large positive earnings in the future could be worth more than one with positive earnings this year but no prospects for future earnings growth. The ratio of stock price to *current* earnings is a highly misleading basis for comparing two stocks—although many people naively use that ratio.

Chapter 10
Price Takers' Supply and Price Response to Consumer Demand

In preceding chapters we assumed each seller's price was set in the market and could not be affected by any individual seller's offering of a larger or a smaller supply. Such sellers are called **price takers**, because each must take the market price as given by outside forces. For example, farmers producing wheat, corn, or soybeans sell such similar goods that, at any slight difference in price among sellers of one of those goods, the buyers will switch to sellers whose price is lowest. Each buyer knows that the product of each supplier is the same, regardless of who the supplier is. That is why at the slightest difference in price, the price taker will lose all his sales. And the seller won't accept a lower price, because he can sell all he can produce at the market price.[1]

In another kind of situation, the seller can get a higher price than that of the rest of the suppliers in the market, albeit by having fewer customers. Such sellers are called *price searchers*, because they must search for the best price to charge (a task we will explore in the next chapter).

Fortunately, for many economic phenomena the price taker model (see Figure 10-1) gives just as accurate implications and predictions as does the price searcher model. Indeed, some economic phenomena are unaffected by whether the suppliers are price takers or price searchers. In this chapter we examine the price taker and its applications. In the next chapter we analyze the price searcher model and its applications.

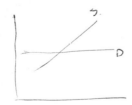

---

[1]Recall from Chapter 3 that elasticity of demand is a measure as a percentage of how the amount demanded responds to a small percentage change in price. As seen by the price taker, the demand is infinitely elastic, because the slightest rise in the asking price would wipe out all sales, and the slightest cut would increase the amount demanded far beyond anything that supplier could contemplate supplying. The response measured in the percentage change in amount demanded is indefinitely large.

Table 10-1 MEASURES OF PRODUCTION COST·

(1) Number of Units	(2) Total Constant Cost	(3) Total Variable Cost	(4) Total Cost	(5) Marginal Cost	(6) Average Constant Cost	(7) Average Variable Cost	(8) Average Total Cost
0	$1	0	$ 1	—	—	—	—
1	1	$ 9	10	$ 9	$1.00	$9.00	$10
2	1	17	18	8	.50	8.50	9
3	1	23	24	6	.33	7.67	8
4	1	27	28	4	.25	6.75	7
5	1	34	35	7	.20	6.80	7
6	1	47	48	13	.16	7.83	8
7	1	69	70	22	.14	9.86	10

·*Simplified cost data to illustrate relationships among classifications of costs and how price will affect more profitable output. Total cost (column 4) is sum of constant cost (column 2) and variable cost (column 3). Marginal cost is change in total cost—due entirely to change in total variable cost. Last three columns are costs per unit of output.*

Marginal Revenue Equals Price

The best way to describe a price taker's situation is in terms of its marginal revenue. This seller supplies more units, but does not thereby cause the market price to be lowered. There is no reduction of price on any of the units sold. The extra, or marginal revenue to that seller as a result of selling that one more unit is the price received on a unit. (You will refresh your understanding of marginal revenue if you review the discussion of it in Chapter 3.)

By way of contrast, if a supplier who is a price searcher (discussed in the next chapter) offers additional units to customers, the result is a significantly lower price. The price falls not just on the additional units offered but on *all* units offered, including those formerly for sale at a higher price. Thus, the necessary reduction in the market price if one more unit is to be sold partly offsets the revenue from the sale of that additional unit.

The *marginal* revenue, the *net increase* in revenue of selling one more unit, is therefore less than its price: It is lower by the decrease in revenue caused by the reduction in the price of *all* the units sold.

The market price is an easy and excellent measure of a price taker's marginal revenue on a marginal—that is, extra—unit of output, because the price doesn't change if the one seller offers more or less. The seller thus *takes* price in two senses: First, price is not affected by the seller's output; and second, the price is a good measure of the seller's marginal revenue.

How is a price taker's output rate determined? To answer that we must recognize how the cost is related to rates of output. Table 10–1 shows a greatly simplified but adequate relationship between cost and outputs.

Column 4 lists total production cost; column 2 shows a *constant* cost of $1 per day that remains unchanged regardless of the rate of operations (for this reason it is also called a *nonoperating* cost).

The term *constant cost* tends to confuse

costs of two very different kinds: (1) those which do not vary even if the rate of output changes (and are avoidable only if the firm terminates its business); and (2) those which are the *past* costs of *past* acts. For example, the past purchase price of equipment that exceeds the present resale value is a *past*, or *sunk*, cost. It is not a cost of any present or future action or production, unlike the constant-rate continuing costs. Knowledge of past costs tells you (too late!) only what was the cost of a past decision and is irrelevant to any future action (except for tax calculations). By constant cost we mean the first sense: a cost being incurred at a constant rate.

The *variable*, or *operating*, cost, listed in column 3 of Table 10–1 depends on the output rate. (Note that total cost is simply the total of the variable and constant costs.) Column 5 gives the *marginal* cost, the *change* in total cost when output is *one* unit larger. Finally, the last three columns give *average* costs (per unit of output) for each of three different costs: Column 6 gives average constant cost per unit of output; column 7 gives average (per unit) variable cost; and column 8 gives average total cost.

Figure 10–2 shows graphically how the average total cost per unit and the marginal cost are related. Notice the shape of both curves. They *may* fall at first, *may* have a nearly flat portion (possibly over a large range of outputs), but ultimately, for larger output rates, certainly *will* rise until an upper limit to the productive capacity is approached (at which point the cost increase becomes practically infinite). Nothing about the actual shapes in any particular real situation should be inferred from the shapes of curves used here. The shapes may vary from firm to firm, but one important *logical connection* between marginal and total costs always holds: The marginal cost curve cuts the lowest point of the average cost curve. This connection will be used later in our analysis.

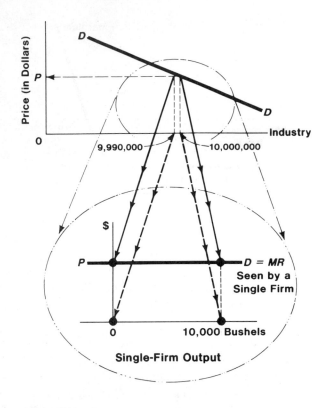

Figure 10-1.

DEMAND AND MARGINAL REVENUE SITUATION DEFINING A PRICE TAKER

DD is the demand facing the whole industry. With the industry supply the price is determined. Each firm takes that market price as the only price at which it can sell, for either or both of two reasons: First, a firm is so small that any reduction in its output would change the market price by only a trivial amount, and the firm, being so small, would have a marginal revenue essentially equal to price. Second, if a firm did cut output to raise price, other firms would expand and restrict the price rise. Competition from other sellers makes the existing market price the only price worth contemplating and makes marginal revenue practically equal to price. All this is often summarized by saying that the individual firm sees the demand for its product as essentially a horizontal line at the market price, with marginal revenue equal to price.

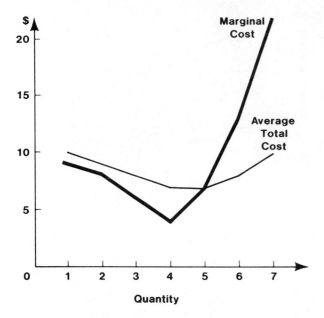

Figure 10-2.

MARGINAL AND AVERAGE TOTAL
COSTS AT DIFFERENT OUTPUTS

Where marginal cost is less than average total cost,
average total cost will decline, but where marginal cost
has increased to above the average total cost,
average total cost will increase—which happens at
the largest outputs of producer's capabilities.

WEALTH-MAXIMIZING OUTPUT

What rate of output will maximize a price taker's profit, or wealth value of the inputs? Answer: a rate of output beyond which the marginal costs exceed the market price. For example, if the price is $13, the profit-maximizing rate is six units daily, as shown in Figure 10-3. The total cost of six units (from Table 10-1) is $48; total revenue is $78. The difference is $30 (the *operating* profit is $31, with $1 of constant, or nonoperating, costs). Producing one more unit daily (seven per day) would increase the total cost by a marginal cost of $22 but would bring in marginal revenue (extra receipts) of only $13, the unchanged price. To produce fewer than six units at a marginal cost below price would forsake potential profits. Profit is maximized at that rate of output at which marginal cost and marginal revenue are equal—which, in the price taker's case, means they are equal to the unchanged price.

If the market price were higher, say, $22, seven units would maximize profits at $84 ($154 − $70). If the price were only $7, no profit would be possible. A price taker's *output response* to a market price is shown by that producer's *marginal cost* curve. That upward-sloping curve says that a higher market price would induce a larger rate of supply (see Figure 10-4).

How low would the price have to go to stop this firm from producing? If the price were above average variable costs, the firm would continue to produce, at least temporarily, because getting any income over the variable cost is better than immediately shutting down: The price at least covers the unavoidable costs that continue even if the producer shuts down temporarily. (In Table 10-1, the lowest average variable cost is $6.75 at an output of four units. Any price above that would cover the operating costs.) If the price stays below the lowest *total* cost *per unit*, $7, it will ultimately pay to shut down when the equipment wears out; it wouldn't pay to buy new equipment or renew contracts.

QUASI-RENTS

We have ignored the initial investment in equipment that enabled the firm to operate with the costs given in Table 10-1. It is reasonable to assume that, if the producer had made a large investment in facilities, the subsequent operating costs, say, labor, might be smaller, whereas a smaller investment may have resulted in larger operating costs. Assume that for the data in Table 10-1 to apply, an initial investment of $10,000 was made in equipment and that, for the contemplated expected economic life of the equipment, it would take revenue of about $10 a day over the future life span to recover that initial investment. That $10,000 is sunk and gone, and is irrelevant for any costs of operation once the investment is made. It doesn't appear in future production costs, and the investor hopes to recover it from future revenue, taking a loss if he does not.

In our example, we have already seen that if the price were $22 the firm would have covered its continuing plus variable costs of $70 a day, with an excess of $84. Allowing $10 for recovery of the prorated investment cost, that is $74 a day as a profit stream.

But if the price were only $7, it would pay to produce only five units. The excess of revenue over continuing costs would then be zero ($35 − $35), which would leave nothing toward recovery of the initial investment. The initial investment would be a total loss. But the producer is not losing on the continuing and operating costs, though the investment has been lost. The price could fall even farther before the firm would suspend production. Suppose the price were only $6.80. It would pay to produce four units with a total revenue of $27.20, covering the variable costs of $27 and still leaving 20¢ toward covering part of the continuing costs (these, remember,

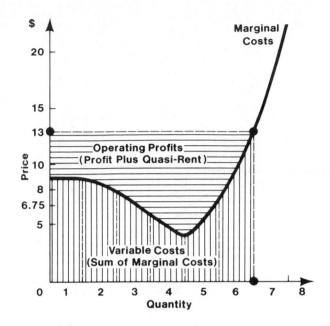

Figure 10-3.

MARGINAL COST, PRICE,
AND PROFIT-MAXIMIZING OUTPUT RATE

Since the sum of the successive marginal costs equals the total of variable costs, the area shown under the marginal cost curve represents total *variable* costs. Since each unit is sold at the market price, the rectangle under the price line represents total revenue. The area above the marginal cost curve and under the price line is a measure of "operating" profits (called "operating" because the constant costs, which are not included in the marginal costs, must be subtracted from that profit area to show true profits) This diagram is designed to show the determination of output that maximizes profits, so no matter whether the constant cost is small or large, both the operating and true profits, after subtracting the constant costs, would be maximized where the area above the marginal cost line and below the price line is maximized. If the constant costs were so large as to exceed the operating profits at the price assumed in the diagram . . . the firm would shut down operations.

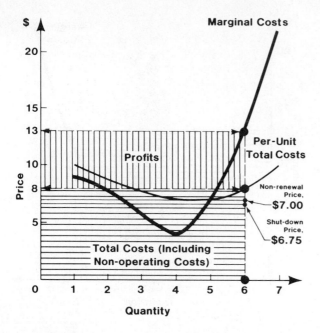

Figure 10-4.

OUTPUT, PRICE, COST, REVENUE, AND PROFITS

This diagram shows graphically the measures of profits and total costs at the profit-maximizing output when price is $13. The total costs are the rectangle over the base of 6 units of output and an average cost of $8, for a total cost of $48. Total revenue minus total cost is the profit (the rectangle above the cost rectangle). So long as price exceeds $6.75 (the lowest per-unit operating costs), production would continue because at least some portion of unavoidable, constant costs were being covered . . . thereby minimizing losses. Ultimately, when equipment or contract renewal was required, operations would terminate unless expected price was at least $7.00—to cover all future expected costs.

continue whether or not the firm temporarily suspends production; examples are night watchmen, land rent, and some administrative office staff). If the price fell so far that total revenue didn't match even the variable operating costs, let alone any part of the continuing costs, the firm would suspend production, at least temporarily.

The circumstances of the preceding example can be described in terms of the concept *quasi-rent*, which is defined as the excess of revenues over the total of its variable operating costs plus the continuing costs at a constant rate per day (even if the firm suspends operations). Quasi-rent can be assigned to recovering some or all of the initial investment cost in the equipment. It is what the equipment can now earn and becomes a measure of its value. That excess over the variable operating and continuing costs would induce the firm to continue to operate.

Almost every business has made investments in durable resources. The firm will find it better to operate than to shut down, even though market price is driven so low that the revenue covers only the variable operating costs, leaving practically nothing to cover any continuing costs and nothing toward recovery of past investment costs. Often these past investment costs are mistakenly added to the present costs to make up so-called full costs. But, clearly, such full costs have nothing to do with costs of present production, nor with whether or not it pays to produce, given that the past investment in equipment has been made. An investor in a new business would certainly hope to recover all the costs—the full costs; but once the investment is made, recovery is not necessary for use of the equipment. Recovery only makes the initial investment profitable. As for future investments, it is the prospect of future revenues that counts, not revenues on past investment. Later, we shall make use of the concept of quasi-rent in explaining some competitive pricing tactics that are widely misunderstood, even by the business managers who act in conformity with the exposition given above.

Market Supply: Aggregated Supplies from All Firms

The total amount of a good supplied to the market is the sum of the outputs of all the producers, as explained in Chapter 7. To refresh understanding, in Figure 10-5 the *marginal costs* for two firms are portrayed. The total supply curve of this product is obtained by *adding the output (horizontal distance on a graph) of each firm's marginal cost curve at any common price that is above the lowest average variable cost of that firm.* The resulting curve, *SS*, is the industry- or market-supply curve. If the price were $2, the maximum wealth or profit outputs of firms A and B would be X_A and X_B. At prices below $1.30, firm B would immediately shut down, but A would not shut down unless prices were as low as 85¢. These lower limits are the lowest average variable costs—the only costs that are incurred by *operating* with existing equipment.

Figure 10-6 shows the total market–demand curve (*DD*) intersecting the *industry-*supply curve (*SS*) at the price of $2. Outputs by firms A and B are indicated by the distances OX_A and OX_B. If the market demand increases, shown in Figure 10-6 as a shift to the right of the *DD* curve to D_1D_1, the price will be bid up (if no laws prevent price changes). The increased demand schedule sustains a higher equilibrium price, which in duces existing firms to produce greater, and more profitable, outputs at higher marginal costs.

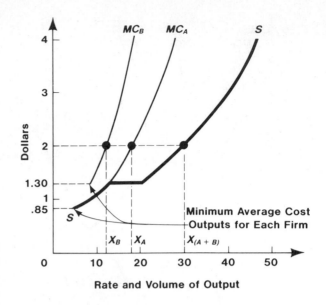

Figure 10-5.

TOTAL SUPPLY FROM A TWO-FIRM INDUSTRY

If price faced by these producers were $2, output would be 11 by producer B and 19 by producer A, for a total of 30. The horizontal sum of the individual marginal cost curves is the total industry supply (where no producer would produce at a price below his lowest average variable cost). Can you also see that if the two producers were producing outputs at which marginal costs were not equal, the producer at the output with the higher marginal cost should reduce his output, and the one at an output with lower marginal costs should correspondingly expand?

Only two firms are shown here. In fact, there are probably scores of producers in most industries, each with some marginal cost curve. All would be summed to get the industry-supply curve, and each firm would take the price in the market as the price that it regards as unaffected by its own output rate. We show only two firms to keep the diagram from becoming cluttered. The basic principle illustrated is that the amount supplied is determined by market price and marginal costs within each firm, with output being adjusted to that at which marginal cost equals price.

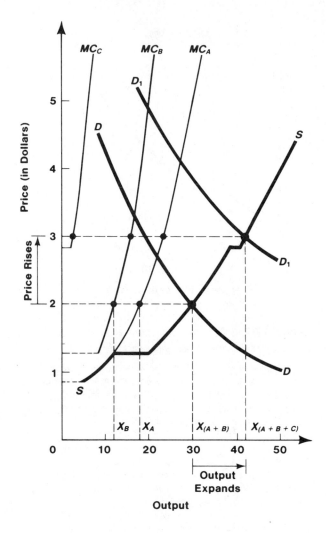

Figure 10-6.

DEMAND, SUPPLY, AND PRICE
TAKER'S DETERMINATION OF OUTPUT

As market demand increases, new firms are attracted by
higher prices and wealth prospects. At a price of
approximately $3, Firm *C* will be able to produce
profitably. Supply of output by industry shows increased
output with higher price beacuse of (1) increased output
by each firm, which increases output to point where
marginal costs equal price, and (2) increased number
of firms as price rises above anticipated minimum
average costs of new potential firms. *SS*, the supply
line, is the horizontal sum of the three firms'
marginal cost lines, above their minimum
average cost points.

Long-Run Supply
Response: Entry of
New Firms and Equipment

The longer a high demand and high price are
expected to persist, the greater the numbers
of new producers attracted into the market
and of existing firms expanding their facilities. Because every firm finds it profitable to
expand its output to that at which its long-
run marginal costs are expected to equal the
higher price, all firms will operate at uniform
marginal costs, though possibly at different
output rates. Firms with the highest minimum of average costs will be regarded as
marginal, or fringe, firms, because if demand
falls, the lower price will force them to shut
down first. (If demand stays high, or if they
learn how to reduce their costs, these firms
become recognized as established firms and,
in turn, look on firms with still higher costs
as the new marginal, or fringe, firms.)

The principle applies to all firms, even
of the simplest type. At big football games,
the fees for parking near the stadium are
higher, and high-cost parking lots are opened
as more local residents rent space in their
driveways and yards. These fringe operators
are disliked by the established parking lot operators. They appear when demand and
price are high. Charter airlines appear in the
summer. Likewise, seasonal variations in demand are met by temporary entrants in construction, harvesting, summer resorts, auto
rentals—indeed, in every industry. When
the demand for buildings or farm products
increases, the number of building contractors
and farmers increases, as does the output of
each group.

But suppose suppliers and customers are
prohibited from raising prices when demand
increases. Then higher-cost suppliers are discouraged from producing. If prices were allowed to rise, new, higher-priced fringe operators would contribute to lower prices. They
increase the amount supplied and reduce *full
prices* below what they otherwise would

have been. For example, in Washington, D.C., hundreds of people with full-time jobs elsewhere become taxi drivers during rush hours; steel mills operate their more costly blast furnaces only during times of peak demand for steel; barber shop chairs that are idle most (but not all) of the time represent high-cost, but *not* excessive, capacity; some firms, when demand warrants it, use second and third shifts, though they raise the cost of production. The amount supplied keeps the price lower than it would have been. Later, if demand falls, the lower price makes it unprofitable to maintain so high a rate of production. Then all firms reduce output, and some withdraw from that business. The displaced resources regretfully and grudgingly revert to their next-best sources of income (which served as a measure of their costs of being used in the first industry).

ELASTICITY OF SUPPLY

How steeply can a long-run supply curve rise? It can be *vertical*, as for land and for goods of which there is a fixed total supply. (The pricing of such goods was analyzed in Chapter 4.) Or it can be virtually horizontal, that is, infinitely elastic. In the latter case, the long-run rate of output can be increased to as much as is demanded at a constant marginal and average cost of producing more. Say, for example, that in a large country the stock of resources doing all kinds of other work is so large that the production of one good could be increased by switching away a very small fraction of resources from other tasks. Then the unit costs of getting a sufficiently greater amount of resources into this activity may be essentially constant. If so, then larger output rates in one firm or industry do not cause detectably higher resource prices and higher average costs. This situation is called *constant average (and marginal) cost of production*. Each unit costs the same over the range of output sufficient to satisfy the increased demand at the old price.

To be sure you understand, consider what would happen if demand for that product fell. If in the long run the productive inputs are perfectly mobile—that is, they could shift to other jobs and earn just as much as they did making this product—workers would not be willing to stay at this job unless they continued to be paid at the same wage rates: Were there any attempt to maintain output by cutting wages or payments to inputs, those inputs would leave rather than accept a lower wage. They would not accept a lower income than they could get elsewhere.

Obviously, in the short run the marginal cost curves will not be horizontal: That is, resources would not *instantly* leave for other jobs at the slightest threat of any cut in their wages or rents. There are moving costs, and quick adjustments cost more than less hasty ones. Those inputs with higher transfer costs would accept some temporary wage cuts or unemployment. But in time they would move. That is why long-run supply is *more* elastic than short-run supply in response to price.

Increasing output quickly costs more than increasing it more slowly, as Figure 10-7 shows. There are two supply curves: S_1 for an early, faster increase; S_2, for the later, more gradual increase. When demand increases from D_1 to D_2 price (P_1) rises at first toward P_2 along the short-run supply curve. The long-run equilibrium price is P_n, in conformity with the long-run supply. We cannot predict the exact timing or transition path of price adjustment to P_n. That depends upon the size of inventories and cost of faster relative to slower supply adjustment.

ADJUSTMENTS WITHOUT
FULL INFORMATION ABOUT COSTS

No one need have full information about market demands or about costs of all possible output programs in order for supplies to re-

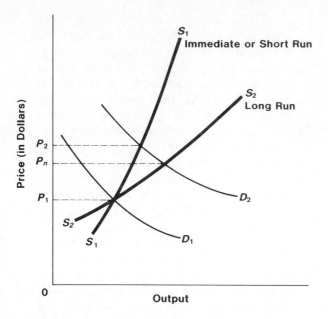

Figure 10-7.

ADJUSTMENT OF SUPPLY TO SHIFTS IN DEMAND

Starting at the initial equilibrium situation, with price p_1, as demand increases, its intersection with supply will slide along S_1, the intermediate, or short-run, supply response which shows increased production from existing firms. In time, new firms will be attracted or new productive equipment will be installed by incumbent firms, and outputs will be more responsive, as indicated by the long-run supply curve, S_2. The short-run supply curve is the summation of the incumbent firms' marginal-cost curves. The long-run supply curve is the sum of the amounts firms (including new firms and new equipment) could persistently produce at each price without losses.

spond to demand. Of course, many producers, by compiling data with which to estimate costs, increase their probability of being near the wealth-maximizing output. They know that when demand rises and permits a higher price, an expanded output becomes more profitable, even if they may not know exactly how much larger the output should be. All the market forces are now more favorable to enlarging output or to sustaining one that had been too large. Even if (as does not in fact happen) every firm picked outputs at random, those which had picked larger outputs would now be more profitable and would grow more than those which had picked smaller outputs. (Witness the growth of Sears relative to Ward's after World War II. Sears chose expansion as potentially profitable; Ward's chose not to expand. Neither knew in advance which was going to be appropriate.) Later, other producers will imitate the more profitable ones, not because they have been exhorted to do so to promote national or social interest, but because they see that changing production in the indicated direction will increase their personal wealth.

ABSORPTION OF PROFITS
BY HIGHER-VALUED INPUTS

Figure 10–8 helps us analyze more effects of market competition. For firms A and B, marginal cost curves (*MC*) —curves showing how supply responds to price—are shown for prices at which the firm would produce some output. Also shown are average cost curves (*AC*). Firm B is only breaking even, because the price is at the lowest level that induces it to produce. Firm A is making a profit; at the output at which its marginal cost equals the market price, its average cost is lower than price. A marginal firm, by definition, is one that is barely covering its costs. Notice, nevertheless, that both firms are operating at outputs that are marginal in that they break even on the marginal unit of output, because their

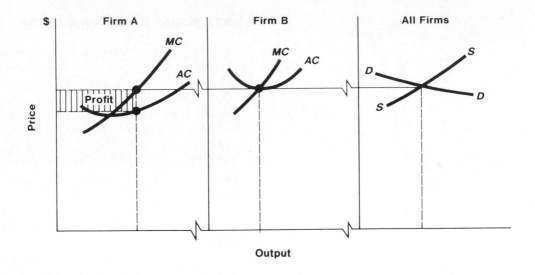

selected outputs are those at which their marginal costs are equal to the market price.

At this point in our analysis you may wonder why one firm, here firm A, has lower average costs. And why doesn't firm B find the reason and copy it? If a particular input is responsible—say, more efficient workers or equipment—why doesn't firm B bid it away and enjoy those lower costs? It will, but firm A will also compete to keep that input. The price (be it wages or rent) of the formerly undervalued input will be bid up, raising the costs to firm A and exhausting its profit. In the long run, after other firms have detected the responsible superior, but underpriced inputs, and have bid up their prices, all firms will have similar costs and will just break even. Firm A has had lower costs simply because it had been able to get inputs at prices that *no one* else then thought were more valuable than that price. No one else confidently predicted, and then backed the prediction with money, that the value of those inputs would ultimately prove to be higher. So some firms have lower costs only until other firms learn their secret and bid up the prices of the responsible resources. In the long run, profits will be competed to the responsible inputs as they are paid what they are now believed to be worth.

Figure 10-8.

HOW DIFFERENCES IN PROFITS ARE ELIMINATED BY COMPETITION FOR INPUTS

Differences in profits are the result of errors in forecasts of future values of inputs. As true values are revealed, competition pushes prices of inputs toward that value which exhausts the profits. Firm A, showing lower average costs, will have its costs of using inputs increased as other firms compete for the responsible inputs. Or they may copy techniques that enable lower costs, until the altered supply lowers market price to the same costs that all firms have. If not imitable, differential productivity of profits will be imputed to the responsible resources that enabled profits. Their values will be bid up to values that include their superiority value, thereby meaning higher costs for any user.

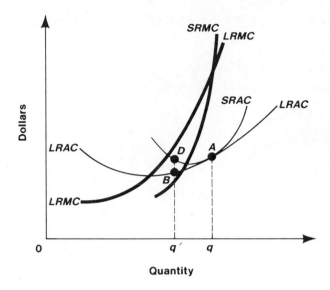

Figure 10-9.

SHORT- AND LONG-RUN
AVERAGE AND MARGINAL COSTS

A change from the output, for which existing facilities are optimal, to, say, q', will raise average costs to D, above, B, what costs would have been if existing equipment had been optimal for new output, q'.

Short Runs and Long Runs

Warning: Economists use the expressions *short run* and *long run* in two different senses without explicitly distinguishing between them. *Short run* can mean an immediate and quick adjustment to a new, possibly long-lasting situation, or it can mean a short-*lived* activity, the starting time of which doesn't matter. In our preceding analysis we meant *both* immediate and temporary, but neither meaning requires the other. *Long run* can mean a later, ultimate effect, or it can mean a long-*lasting* activity, the starting time of which, again, doesn't matter.

Again, initiating a new production program *quickly* is more costly than is a more gradual adjustment, as Figure 10–9 shows. (Of course, the quicker may prove to be more profitable.) The figure exposes in a highly stylized way the logical relationships among marginal, average variable, and average total costs. In fact, the particular shapes of the related curves depend on the particular production techniques, equipment, and quantities of output involved. Each case is unique, but the logical interrelationships are the same for all. The long-run, average cost curve, *LRAC*, shows the average cost of producing each possible output *if* the producers *initially chose* the most appropriate (lowest cost) production technique for that output. The selected output q, for example, would have resulted in average costs equal to the height qA on the curve *LRAC*.

If, after starting at q, the producer decides to change the output, the average costs for sustaining that new output will be higher than if that other output had been the initial one. Changing output, for example, to q' from q, affects average costs of production as shown by the height $q'D$ on the *SRAC* curve moving from output q. That curve shows short-run (quick adjustment) average costs of revised outputs starting from q. If, after equipment is altered, that new program is continued indefinitely, then future costs become the low-cost, long-run average cost (*LRAC*) of producing at q'.

For outputs larger than the initial planned output q, a short-run (quicker adjustment) marginal cost exceeds the long-run (gradual expansion) marginal cost. But if outputs are reduced to less than existing equipment is best suited for, the costs are not as low as they would be with more extensive adjustment in production techniques. Reducing output hastily does not lower costs as much as does reducing output in the long run. In economic terms, *the elasticity of supply changes in either direction is greater for a long-run adjustment period than for a short-run adjustment period.* Here the two senses of *long run* apply: Less rapid adjustment is less costly; and a production program of longer duration is less costly per unit than one of shorter duration.

Consequences of Wealth-Maximizing Response to Market Demand

WHAT IS THE APPROPRIATE PRICE RESPONSE?

If price should fall in response to a persisting decrease in demand or overexpansion of capacity, some firms will shut down, the earliest ones to do so being those with higher average variable costs—*not* those which are poorer or smaller or which have less money on hand. Whether rich or poor, a firm shuts down not when cash is exhausted but when continued operation at low prices reduces wealth more than would shutting down.

Prices can fall below the long-run average costs. The lower prices may be adequate to cover only short-run, temporary operating costs with *existing* capacity. Prices that temporarily fall below long-run costs are often incorrectly called *predatory* prices. When prices fall, it is not because some firm is trying to drive out other firms in order to later raise prices *above long-term* costs. Instead, the reduced demand means consumers are refusing to buy at a price that covers the costs of permanently keeping all the existing producers in that industry. Consumers are forcing some producers and equipment to move from an activity which is now less valuable to other, more valuable activities. If waste is to be avoided, reduced demand necessitates reductions in output and in productive facilities. Market prices are cut temporarily until either demand later increases or, if demand does not later increase, enough productive facilities are used up and not replaced. In the latter case, as output falls, prices rise to just cover the long-run average costs from new facilities. They do not rise above those costs.

WHAT IS THE APPROPRIATE OUTPUT?

In Table 10-1, although the wealth-maximizing output at a price of $10 is five units, this producer could produce as many as seven and still cover total costs—but the profits would be lost. We might think that producing five rather than seven is socially wasteful, because the price exceeds the average costs for the extra units. But thinking so would be incorrect analysis, for the *marginal* cost is the cost of the extra output, and beyond five units of output it exceeds price. Thus, to produce the sixth and seventh units would use resources (the marginal costs) that are worth at least $13 in uses elsewhere but that consumers value in more of this good priced at only $10. That value is less than the value ($13) of other goods that would be forsaken. Therefore, the price-taking, wealth-maximizing producer is not underproducing by holding the output rate to five units; producing more would erase that producer's profit and wastefully use more resources that are worth more than the extra output is here.

Thus, the product's price measures its value; the marginal costs measure the value of forsaken output. The logical implication, then, is that wealth-maximizing price takers maximize the social value of resources. Ironically, this implication was developed by socialist theorists, who asked what "should" be the output. Using the criterion that resources should provide the greatest value as judged by consumers, they deduced that producers seeking to maximize their wealth with open access to markets gave precisely that result. Everyone was embarrassed—the socialists because they had provided an argument for private property and market prices, and the capitalists because, much as they would have liked this justification of their activity, not all of them could claim to be selling in, or even defending, open markets.

CONSUMER DEMANDS
DETERMINE VALUES AND USES
OF PRODUCTIVE RESOURCES

When market demands increase (say, for sports cars, computers and computer programs, wigs, colored tennis balls), the prices of the materials used in producing those goods respond. The profits of those who first got those inputs at the old wages or prices show that the old valuations of the input are too low. As new facilities are built that can use those inputs, the new, greater demand for them will bid up their prices until no sure prospects of future profit remain. The profit is absorbed into the higher values of inputs: Profits, then, lead to higher costs.

If I discover oil on my land, competition by other people for my land raises its value. The cost of my using that land is now higher. Anything that becomes more valuable also becomes, by definition, more costly to use, because the user must forsake the greater value that could have been obtained by selling the good to someone else at that new, higher value.

Desire for greater wealth directs resources to the uses consumers value most by making it more costly to employ in less-valued uses.[2] The more quickly, completely, and broadly do producers learn of the market's revaluation of assets, the more fully and quickly will they direct resources toward the new, highest valued uses.

To adjust to revaluations by consumers, producers must put resource uses and values through a gigantic web of substitutions. For example, if the demand for wheat increases, more wheat can be produced only if resources are taken from the production of other goods (by resource owners seeking greater wealth). Land transferred to wheat is taken from oats and corn, and as the supplies of land for those uses falls, reducing the outputs of those goods, their prices increase a bit. As their prices rise, other land will then be shifted to corn and oats—land formerly used for, say, cotton, barley, cattle grazing, or parks, or potentially useful for housing or industrial sites. Also, labor and other resources are diverted to wheat. Laborers who would otherwise work as cattle raisers, carpenters, or gas station attendants switch to wheat production. And their places are partly filled from still other occupations. The substitution and shifting is broad and extensive. The many ultimate economy-wide effects are so diffused as to be hardly noticeable among the many other everyday events that influence the output of any other particular good. For this reason, we are sometimes misled into thinking

---

[2]In Chapter 8, where we defined the cost of a given use of resources by one person as the highest *alternative* forsaken value of output of those resources, we seemed to exclude the value of their *present* use. But we now see that a more general conception of costs consists of imputing to a given resource a market value that reflects its highest possible value in *any* line of activity, including the present one. Costs of resources in a particular occupation stem not only from *alternative uses* but also from alternative *users*. Even if my land is good only for oil production (that is, it has no alternative uses), it still has a value, which must be taken into account, because other users will bid for it.

that more of a good can be produced without producing less of some other, be it leisure or lingerie.

EFFECTS OF A TAX

In Chapter 4, the effects of imposing a tax were outlined. Here, now that we have learned about marginal cost curves and the process of competing market values of resource services into the prices of those resources, we can use the diagrammatic approach to more clearly deduce the price and output effects of a tax on the production of a good.

Tax on All Producers in an Industry: Price and Output Effect Suppose manufacturers are taxed 50¢ on each deck of playing cards they produce. Each firm's marginal and average costs are increased by 50¢. Summing the new, higher marginal cost curves over all the firms that would produce cards yields a higher cost-supply curve or a lower output curve, as seen in Figure 10-10. Before the tax, the consumer's price was 75¢. If that price were to persist, each producer, now operating with a higher marginal cost schedule, would reduce output from X_1 to X_2. But the old price would not persist for long: The reduced *industry* output (on the new, smaller market-supply curve) would result in a higher price, which would cover part of the tax and induce each firm to reduce output less, only to X_3 instead of X_2. Our first conclusion is that the higher tax raised costs. But a higher price can be sustained *only if the supply to the market decreased*. Always, an effect on price depends on an effect on aggregate *supply*. Only because the higher tax moved the aggregate supply curve back to the left—to a smaller sustained production at each price—could a higher price be sustained. The same analysis could be used for anything that raised the marginal costs of production, such as higher wages for labor or higher prices of material, power, or transport.

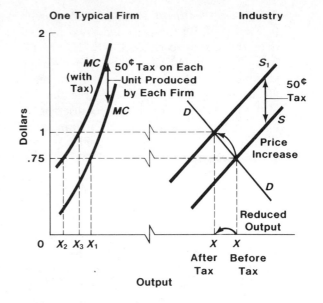

Figure 10-10.

EFFECT OF TAX ON OUTPUT AND PRICE

Tax is levied on output of playing cards of all firms in industry. Supply curve shifts upward to incorporate taxes of 50¢ per unit. This reduces output at the old price, and the price moves up to $1. Higher price results from the smaller supply function. Unless tax affects supply curve, price cannot be affected. Price rises by less than tax because, at smaller output, marginal and average costs are lower. Part of tax is revealed as a higher price to consumer and a smaller rate of consumption; another part is reflected in reduced wealth value of resources specialized in production of this taxed good. Tax is borne by consumers and by owners of capital goods and labor services specialized to this industry.

Effect on Wealth of Productive Resources

In Figure 10-10, the price increased by less than the tax on each deck—by 25¢, to $1 from 75¢. The output was reduced by each supplier firm's moving back down that marginal cost curve that is higher by the amount of the tax. Output is reduced, because not so many resources are now as valuable in making playing cards as they are elsewhere.

We can see that the total tax receipts (tax per deck times number now produced) come in part from a higher consumer price and in part from a lower value of, and thus payments to, those resources that were more useful in manufacturing the taxed good. Clearly, the taxes are not all borne by the consumer in higher prices and fewer decks of cards; part is borne by the owners of the resources specialized to card production, which are by definition less valuable elsewhere. The incomes to specialized resources (which could be machines, people, or even land) fall by the amount of their former excess value in card production over their salvage value in alternative uses.

But reductions in output and in the value of resources are not the only adjustment. In the long run, the equipment specialized to producing cards will wear out and not be replaced, further reducing output, as Figure 10-11 shows. When a final long-run adjustment is achieved, the price of cards will be sufficiently high to cover the tax and the new full cost of production, including the cost of installing and maintaining new specialized equipment.

Old versus New Card-Making Resources

There are two separate effects on value that should not be confused: (a) the effect on the value of specialized resources *existing* at the time the tax is imposed, and (b) the effect on the value of newly producible resources. The value of *old* equipment will reflect the lower capital value of the future receipts *net* of the taxes that must be paid when using the old equipment. A wealth loss occurs only to the owners of the specialized resources *existing at the announcement* of the tax, not to those who later may buy or create new card-making equipment. (The supply curve of old, existing equipment is *vertical*, that is, fixed.) Hence all changes in the net value of its services are capitalized into current capital values and are borne by the current owners—as for land (discussed in Chapter 4).

Tax on One Firm or on All Producers?

Suppose the tax had been levied on *just one* producer of cards. If that producer's output is only a small part of industry supply, the industry supply does not shift by a perceptible amount. Price is not significantly affected unless *market* supply is affected. No one producer can recoup part of the tax by a higher price. The unaffected supply from other producers is large enough to satisfy demand at the existing price.

The greater the number of suppliers who are taxed, the more the tax will reduce market supply. To raise the costs of just one supplier, who makes a small part of the total supply, will affect the total supply by a negligible amount, with no appreciable effect on the price.

SICK INDUSTRIES

Certain industries are commonly called "sick": They allegedly have an excessive number of firms; the number is "excessive" because most of the firms lose wealth. As rapidly as some lose and leave, new ones enter—with the same risk of mortality. There seems to be no long-run adjustment that makes the industry profitable, or at least eliminates loss. The more commonly cited examples of sick industries are the operation of small groceries, bars, restaurants, or night clubs; coal mining; retail gasoline sales; textile manufacturing; and farming.

What, according to people who make this argument, causes some industries to be

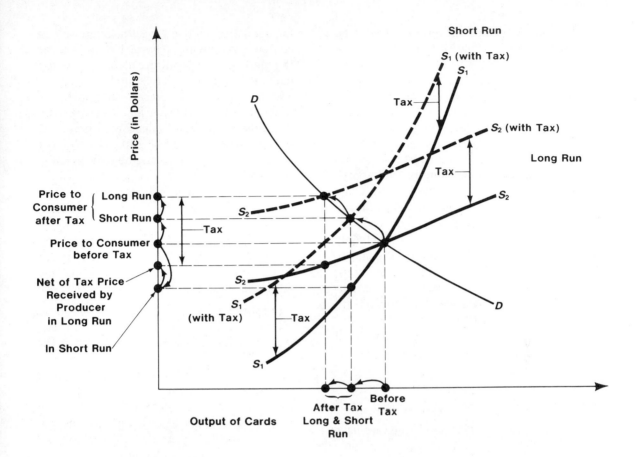

Figure 10-11.

HOW A PER-UNIT TAX AFFECTS OUTPUT
AND PRICE IN THE SHORT RUN AND LONG RUN

The more time allowed after a tax is imposed or cost is increased, the greater will be the effect on the amount supplied (reflecting withdrawal of resources from the industry). In any event, the higher input price or tax results in higher price to consumers, smaller rate of card consumption, and reduced income and wealth to owners of productive resources specialized to card production. The diagram shows price and output effects but *not* the *wealth* effects.

"sick"? They point to a long-term decline in demand, the tendency of people to overestimate their ability, plain ignorance about how to run a business, or the low cost of entering the business. But these explanations do not hold up under closer study by economic analysis.

First, all firms in an industry could be losing wealth when demand is falling unexpectedly. There is nothing "sick" about adjustments to a decreasing demand. Second, all proprietors could be willingly losing wealth if the business provides a sufficient amount of nonmonetary satisfaction, as is said to be the case for horse racing, novel writing, acting, or owning baseball clubs. One person grows orchids, makes money, and considers it a business; another grows orchids and loses money but regards it as a hobby or consumption activity. Everyone could lose money (relative to what he or she could earn elsewhere) if this business operation were more pleasant. These considerations help to explain why some "firms" can run at a "loss."

Third, there is a more powerful consideration: In some industries the profits may be large for only a few, with the rest losing money. In acting, writing, painting, and sports, only a few persons make a big success, while the vast majority of entrants never make enough to cover the cost. Nothing in economic analysis says that an industry in which only a few make fortunes should not have too many "failures." These failures (or is it more accurate to call them nonsuccesses?) entered hoping they would succeed, and they often remain despite years of frustration and disappointment. On average, half of all new firms, in all industries, fail to survive to their fifth year!

ACTIONS AND COSTS

So far in our analysis in this chapter, we have deliberately used simplified types of outputs and simplified measures of those costs. We now modify one oversimplification: The *full* costs of any present action are more than just the best, forsaken alternative, *current* uses; they include the *future* forsaken uses as well. The more complete costs of an act are therefore measured by the consequent reduction in the *present value* of one's wealth: the loss of present value of the present and *future* forsaken alternatives. (We examined the concept of present, or capital, values in Chapter 6.) Before interpreting this statement with an illustration, we must state precisely what the act is that we are measuring the costs of. Too often this is left ambiguous—with resulting confusion about what are "the" costs.

Costs of Acquisition   Normally, the purchase price of an asset is called its cost. But we know that the cost of an act is the result-ing reduction in one's wealth. Suppose you contemplate buying a Ford. Let us analyze the pertinent expenditure data in the top half of Table 10–2. The purchase price is $8000. The immediate resale value would be $7400. If you kept the car for two years without using it, its resale value would be $5000. If you drove the car, say, 10,000 miles per year, the resale value would be only $4400 in two years.

Let us now look at the bottom half of Table 10–2. What is the cost of *acquiring* title to the car? It is $600, the difference between the initial price and the *immediate* resale value. But once the car is acquired, this cost is sunk, or fixed, and irrelevant to any future decision.

Continuing Possession   Once title to the car is acquired, what is the cost of simply possessing it for two years without using it? It is the difference in its value now and its resale value in two years, $5000. But do not subtract $5000 from $7400! They are values as of *different* dates, and (as you recall from Chapter 7) they must be converted to contemporaneous values. We must convert the $5000 as of two years hence to a present value. At a 10% annual rate of interest (using Table 6–1), the present value of $5000 deferred two years is .826 × $5000 = $4130. Subtracting this from $7400 gives 3270, the cost of two years of possession without use.

To be still more realistic, assume that taxes and insurance must be paid if the car is possessed. At the *beginning* of each year, $400 is paid to cover the year's tax and insurance, whether or not the car is operated. Converting these two successive annual payments to present values gives $400 + (.909)$400 = $763.60, the present value of taxes and insurance if the car is possessed for two years. *Once the car is already acquired*, the cost of keeping it two years is $3270 + $763.60 = $4033.60. The cost of *acquiring* and *keeping* but not using the car for two years is $600 + $4033.60 = $4633.60, which we round to $4634.

Operating Cost But you are not running an auto museum. You want to use the Ford. Other outlays, listed in Table 10–2, will be made for repairs, gasoline, and the like. We assume that they are paid at the *end* of each year, as if they accumulated on a credit card. Since we cannot properly add outlays now to outlays a year later without adjusting for timing, we convert all outlays to present values. They sum to $2066 [= ($1000 × .909) + ($1400 × .826)]. If the car is used, its resale value will depreciate more, to $4400 at the end of two years (compared to $5000 if not used). The extra depreciation at the end of two years (at a 10% interest rate) is $600,

which has a present value of $496. Adding this $496 to $2066 gives $2564 as the present-value measure of costs of *operations*.

The cost of operation would vary according to the actual use of the car (here, an assumed 10,000 miles per year). You can see why this figure is sometimes called the *variable* cost: It varies with, or depends on, the amount of performed service. The constant cost, the cost of possession, $4634, is independent of the mileage performed. (And although it is also commonly called a *fixed* cost, it is not a *sunk* cost of a past act.) The sum of $2562 and $4634 is $7196, the total cost, measured in capital value, of acquiring,

Table 10-2 EXPENDITURES AND COSTS FOR ACQUISITION, POSSESSION, AND OPERATION OF CAR FOR TWO YEARS

	Expenditures			
	Now	End of First Year	End of Second Year	Present Value
Purchase Price	$8000	—	—	$8000
Resale Value				
Not driven	7400	—	$5000	4130
Driven 20,000 miles	—	—	4400	3634
Tax and insurance	400	$ 400	—	764
Gas, tires, repairs	—	1000	1400	2066

	Costs	
1. Acquisition	$8000	
	−7400	
		$600
2. Possession for two years; zero mileage (that is, without operation)		
Current resale	$7400	
Final resale (present value)	−4130	
Depreciation	3270	
Tax and insurance	764	4034
Acquisition and continued possession without operation		$4634
3. Operation (20,000 miles in two years)	$4130	
(Extra depreciation because of mileage)	−3634	
	496	
Gasoline, oil, tires, etc.	2066	
Operation		$2562 (13¢/mile)
4. Total costs of acquisition, possession, and operation		$7196 (36¢/mile)
5. Driver labor cost ($1000 per month)		$21,720
		$28,918 ($1.45/mile)

possessing, and obtaining 20,000 miles of service from that car over two years. These distinctions are important for answering such questions as whether to enter a given business, and, once you are in a business, how far prices can be cut if demand falls short of expectations. If this car were to be used purely for personal uses, we could ignore the cost of the driver. But if it were used as a taxi, the annual labor cost of having a driver might be $12,000, or $1000 per month. The present value of that series of payments over two years, at a 10% interest rate, is about $21,720. (This computation of capital values involves a bit more arithmetic than used so far, because receipts were previously assumed to be annual rather than monthly.)

We can now summarize the classification of acts and their costs for the two-year, 20,000-mile output program of activity:

Acquisition: $600 or 3¢/mile.

Operation of car: $2562 or 12.81 cents/ mile.

Each of these costs has more than one name, which requires that they be kept straight. We list their most common names:

Acquisition cost ($600): sunk; fixed.

Possession cost ($4034): overhead; constant.

Operating cost ($2562), or, including labor for a taxi ($2562 + $21,720 = $24,284): direct; operating; variable.

Especially ambiguous are the terms *fixed*, *constant*, and *variable*. When you see one of these terms, you have to deduce from the context what specific activity or cost is meant. Or else ask the user.

DIMENSIONS OF OUTPUT

We now consider an important distinction mentioned briefly before. *Larger output* can mean one of two things: either a faster rate of production for any unit of time (such as per day) or a larger *total* amount produced (regardless of the rate of production per unit of time). Larger output can also mean both things simultaneously: If annual production is increased from, say, 10 units to 15, a larger volume is produced at a faster *rate* (15 units per year instead of 10 per year).

Both components of output—rate and total volume—help producers choose the appropriate production technique. Suppose General Motors decides to produce 150,000 units of a new economy car during the coming two years. Having planned a *volume* of production for the two years, it has also necessarily picked an implied rate of production, that is, 75,000 per year over two years. Of the many different production techniques that could yield that output, the producer wants the one that costs least. After a production technique is selected, time will be needed to assemble or adjust existing equipment, raw materials, and labor to it. The more rapidly that is done, the more expensive it is. Thus, the producer is concerned with several dimensions of output: its *volume*, its *rate*, and the *duration* of its *adjustment* period.

First Production Generalization

The greater the planned volume of production at an unchanged rate of production, the lower will be the average unit cost of output.

This generalization, commonly known as the *economies of mass production*, says that if automobiles are produced at a constant *rate* (say, five per day), the larger the total number of that model cars produced at that rate, the lower their average cost. Of course, producing a larger volume at a constant rate requires more time. Two main factors contribute to economies of mass production: First, large-scale (that is, large-*volume*) production techniques are not mere duplications of small-scale production methods. Producing only 10 cars would be cheaper using a custom workshop technique, but producing thousands of cars would be cheaper on an assembly line. The cheapest technique of painting one car is to use a spray gun, of painting 1000 cars, to set up a paint bath into which the cars are submerged. But one could not construct a 1/1000 portion of a paint bath unit to paint one car. The second factor in economies of production is that the more an activity is repeated, the more likely will better ways of doing it be discovered and mastered. Improvement and learning by experience are evident in managerial functions, production scheduling, job layouts, material-flow control, and manual dexterity. The rate of learning is usually greatest at first and then diminishes as it approaches a plateau.

Second Production Generalization

For a given volume of production, the faster the rate of production, the higher will be the total, average unit, and marginal costs.

A higher rate of production requires more input *in a given period of time*, which increases costs. Bringing in more resources leaves only successively more costly resources available for this kind of work. And less time is available for the best methods to be identified. Furthermore, resource owners insist on higher pay for overtime as more leisure is sacrificed. Thus, even when the total volume of output is not changed, a higher rate of production increases total costs.

Some producers plan production in terms of definite lengths of time, so a larger *volume* of production during the period will require a higher *rate* of production. For example, a doubled volume in a fixed time requires a doubled rate of production. The net effect on costs is impossible to generalize. Information about each situation must be had.

Another source of confusion in measuring output is the fact that many dimensions of output are variable. What is the output of a restaurant? Is it number of customers served, tables available, amount of floor space, items on the menu, number of waiters, speed of service, quantity of food per serving, or the waiting time for a table? An airline may measure its supply by speed of planes, seats per plane, customer miles, number of planes, flights per day, cities serviced, and the like. Which would you think an airline meant when it said it increased its output? In every case, we must identify the dimension of output or supply that is of interest, and we must consider how varying *that* dimension affects cost—and how the demand for that particular dimension is expressed in a market price. Diagrams and tables showing "Output" or "Supply" may make it seem deceptively easy to identify and measure the dimensions of output. But it is a lot harder to know what is pertinent in a given situation.

JOINT PRODUCTS WITH COMMON COSTS

Many production processes yield several different products at the same time; such products are called *joint products*. Beef and hides are joint products of cattle. A few other joint products are cotton yarn and cottonseed oil; kerosene, fuel oil, and gasoline; and butter and milk. They are interdependent in supply. Producing more of one generally involves producing more of the other. More beef also yields more hides; more cotton yields more cottonseed oil. On the other hand, for a barrel of oil to yield more gasoline, there must be less fuel oil or kerosene produced.

For joint products, a higher price for one will lead to an increased output of the other: A higher price for cotton will induce a larger output of cotton and, thus, more cottonseed.

Yet, even for these joint products, more of one can mean less of the other. Meat, hides, and fat are joint products, but they are substitutes in that different breeds of cattle yield different ratios among them. By selecting different breeds and slaughtering at different ages, one could change the ratio and get more hide and less meat or vice versa. Likewise, gasoline, kerosene, and fuel oil—all refined from crude oil—can be obtained in different ratios by different refining methods. If only one of the joint products is of primary economic interest, the other is often called the *by-product*.

Impossibility of Apportioning Costs of Input Common to Joint Products If two products are produced jointly with a common input, the cost of the common input cannot be allocated to each of the joint products. Because hides and meat are produced from one steer, the feeding and care of the steer is a common input, or a common cost, to both products. What portion of the feed cost is the cost of the hide and what portion is the cost of the meat? If an airplane carries passengers and cargo, what portion of the common input's costs of jet fuel, of labor, and of facilities is the cost of each? Common input costs can't be allocated, so one cannot tell what the "cost" is of each product. Calling one product the by-product and assigning all the common costs to the "basic" product is simply a play on words masking an arbitrary allocation. Things seem to fall apart at the "joints." But there is no problem. How much of each joint product to produce, or the ratio in which they should be produced, can still be determined. For that we use marginal cost.

Measuring the *marginal* cost of changes in output rates of the joint products does not require any allocation of common costs. To discover the wealth-maximizing price and output mixture requires knowing only the *changes* in total cost and total revenue that follow from changes in output. If the marginal cost (including any *increase* in the total of unallocable common costs) is less than the marginal revenue from that extra output, that increase in output will be profitable; otherwise, it will not.

DEPRECIATION, OBSOLESCENCE, AND RESOURCE USES

Depreciation is the predictable, anticipated reduction in the value of a resource as it suffers predictable deterioration from use or from aging. Depreciation is a cost, even though it is neither a current expenditure nor an obligation to spend. The value of an asset falls when it is used, so by that use the owner is forsaking the alternative use values.

In contrast to depreciation are the *unexpected* reductions in value caused by *unanticipated* developments unrelated to use, usually because of a new, superior competing product. This reduction is called *obsolescence*. Unexpected improvements in competing resources or products do not necessarily idle the old assets. Instead, the value of the older existing machine falls enough to reflect the lower value of its continued use in the face of competition by the unexpected new input. Old propeller-driven airliners suffered a loss of value (a sunk cost) when jet engines became unexpectedly available, yet they still fly economically.

To illustrate, let us suppose several things: Some existing machine can produce 500 units of X before it falls apart; it depreciates in proportion to its use. Associated costs for materials and labor are 20¢ per unit of X; the product sells for 30¢ per unit, so the non-machine costs are covered by a margin of 10¢ per unit. The machine is then worth $50—500 units of potential output yielding 10¢ each over other costs—ignoring interest discounting for simplicity.

As luck would have it, a new machine is *unexpectedly* introduced. (We stress *unexpectedly* because if the new machine had been anticipated, the existing one would have already been worth less than $50.) The new machine produces 1000 units before it falls apart (its investment per unit of output is 10¢ per unit), while its associated labor and material costs are only 16¢ per unit, a total of 26¢. As the new machine starts supplying more output to the market, the product price falls toward 26¢ per unit. The new machine would sell for $100 because it yields a net price over its nonmachine costs of 10¢ a unit. If the old machine still has 500 units of service left, its value, which was $50, would fall to $30 (equal to 500 units times 6¢, the excess of the product's new lower price, 26¢, over its 20¢ of nonmachine costs). It has suffered an obsolescence of $20. If the price of the product falls to 20¢, that excess of price over nonmachine costs is wiped out. There is nothing left over the associated input costs to give any value to the old machine, and it will be retired from use.

DEMAND FOR INTERDEPENDENT PRODUCTS

You may have heard that demands for some goods are not heeded because the goods must be used jointly with some other good that would first have to be produced by someone else. With that kind of reasoning, Congress enacted a law requiring every manufacturer of television sets to sell *only* sets that receive all 83 television channels, from 2 to 84. Presumably that law was passed because there was not enough market incentive to make all-channel sets, and until sets were made to receive all 83 channels, there would be insufficient incentive to telecast on the higher-frequency channels. A vicious circle?

The notion that the demand for such products goes unheeded is supported by neither historical facts nor economic analysis. Production and sales of automobiles, radios, and TVs did not wait for the construction of gas stations or radio or TV stations. Nor did FM receivers wait for FM transmitters; in fact, they became widely used despite laws restricting FM broadcasting.[3] Stereo records and stereo players, frozen foods and home freezers, color television sets and color telecasting—all these pairs had different independent producers on each side.

How does a market economy overcome this vicious circle whereby *neither* of two interdependent products is produced because *each* requires that first the other be produced? The answer is that the vicious circle isn't there in the first place. Product interdependencies are not ignored. Specialization implies that producers rely on other people to produce jointly used products as they mutually and independently seek opportunities to increase their wealth. In fact, jointly used goods will be more effectively produced if specialization *is* permitted than if one firm must produce both of the interdependent products. Why, then, the belief that the open market is not itself sufficient inducement to produce jointly used products? It comes from the mistaken notions that output must be carried out on a large scale from the beginning, and that people are unwilling to invest now in anticipation of future receipts, *implying that present capital values are irrelevant.* But these suppositions are disproved by events every day. A factory is built and others quickly build homes and stores in the area. Only the person who ignores the incentives and exchange opportunities in a marketplace will fail to see the coordinated anticipatory activity.

---

[3] No law required—until 1974—radio manufacturers to make only FM–AM combination radios. As the design technology improved in the 1950s, FM sets became easier to tune, cheaper, and more reliable. Transmitters "magically" increased in number. For a long time, the Federal Communications Commission *prohibited* color television broadcasts until it could decide on the "best" kind of color system. And when it decided, it chose wrong! Fortunately, the Korean War forestalled production until the superiority of the electronic scan system became more obvious. (Guess who lobbied for FM–AM radio receiver requirements in 1974?)

DEVELOPERS AND SPECULATORS: RISK-BEARING PREDICTORS AND REPRESENTATIVES OF FUTURE CONSUMERS

An especially instructive, yet misunderstood, example of anticipating and representing future market demand for goods that are as yet unproduced and undemanded is the speculative land and housing developer. Future renters and buyers usually do not order construction of their future homes. Instead, speculative (that is, acting on foresight) developers build in the expectation of those future demands. Suburban developers are charged with being interested in a quick dollar—a true charge. But to earn that quick dollar they must have accurately predicted future demands (for, say, houses, condominiums, and apartments) and made a timely response to supply the product. The anticipated future demanders will move to the area. But if you could ask them if they would demand those new buildings in the future, they could honestly say they don't know what their future demands will be. Dress manufacturers design and make dresses months in advance of customers' demands, and hence they are speculative clothing developers. Similarly, land developers are agents for expected but unidentified future buyers. Competition among current anticipators of the future demands of those unidentified people establishes current capitalized value of that latent future demand. Speculative developers do not drive up land values; it is the anticipated future demand, which they are revealing as a present value, that establishes the current land values. (Understanding capital values improves your ability to interpret some economic activities.)

Some Pricing Tactics

Economic principles can explain some widely used pricing tactics that are commonly misunderstood by the public, as is evidenced by allegations made in lawsuits about their undesirable effects on prices. Careful economic analysis, however, often shows that those pricing tactics are not correctly interpreted.

BASING POINT PRICING AND THE PHANTOM OF "PHANTOM FREIGHT"

Recently, in the southeastern United States, a jury awarded over a billion dollars to customers of local suppliers of plywood. The suppliers were alleged to have conspired to overcharge their customers by including, in the price of plywood produced in the Southeast, an amount to cover "phantom freight," as if that plywood had been shipped thousands of miles—from the Northwest, the dominant source of plywood.

Some facts are necessary to properly assess this case. First, most domestic plywood comes from the Northwest, primarily from Washington and Oregon. Second, because of competition among suppliers in the Northwest, the prices in any city in the country will be the market-clearing price in that city. Third, no Northwest supplier will ship to any city that does not yield, after freight costs, a net price, called a *mill net price*, that matches the mill net price from shipping to every other city in the United States. That is, after subtracting the cost of freight to each city, the producer would get just as high a mill net price in New York City as it would in Los Angeles.

For example, if freight from the Northwest costs $10 a ton to New York and $6 a ton to Los Angeles, the price in New York will be $4 higher than in Los Angeles and $10 higher than in the Northwest. If the national demand for plywood is such that the price in New York is $100 per ton, the price in Los Angeles will be $4 less, or $96. From each city the mill net price is $90.

Now suppose the demand for plywood increases in Los Angeles, raising the price there to, say, $150 per ton. More plywood would be shipped there instead of to New

York, while the reduced supply in New York would raise the New York price. The larger supply to Los Angeles will have reduced its price rise to, say, $140, while the market-clearing price in New York will have risen to $144, $4 more than in Los Angeles. And always the Northwest suppliers would be receiving the same, uniform mill net price from each city, now $134 ($10 less than the New York price and $6 less than the Los Angeles price).[4]

How would the Northwest suppliers quote their prices to customers? In New York a supplier could say, "The price is $4 more than in Los Angeles, or $1 more than in Chicago, or 30¢ more than in Pittsburgh," and so on; in Los Angeles the supplier could recite a similar sequence of complicated alternatives. But the simplest, most direct way is to say, "The price is the Northwest base price (the mill net price) plus transport to your city." That is *basing point pricing*, with the site, here in the Northwest, of the dominant supply to the entire United States being the *basing point*.

Derived Demand

The price at the basing point, the Northwest, is not arbitrarily set first and then a freight charge added to it. Instead, the demand in each city attracts a supply from the Northwest until the price in each city is that city's market-clearing price. Thus, the basing point price, or mill net price, is *derived* from the market-clearing price in each city. The prices in all the cities will differ from one another and be tied together by the difference in the cost of transport from the prime source of supply, the Northwest. They will all rise and fall together, while keeping that relationship among them. Obviously, quoting a basing point price does not mean *setting* or *fixing* a price. That price reflects the pattern and levels of *competitive market prices*, by which each consumer in each city is competing for plywood against every other consumer in every other city, and every supplier is competing against every other supplier, and all the suppliers in a given location are receiving the same mill net price from every customer.

Derived demand for productive inputs is very important: The consumer valuation of a good determines the value that can be earned by (imputed to) its productive inputs. Competition among profit-seeking suppliers to obtain those inputs drives up their purchase or rental price until that price absorbs the value of their services. The more plentiful any input, and hence the more of the final service or good produced with a lower resulting market value, the lower the derived value of the input. The value of any resource above any other resource is determined by both the degree of its superior productivity and its supply relative to demand.

COMPETITIVE INPUT VALUATION AND RICARDIAN RENTS

That greater value and higher income to productive resources is called *Ricardian rent*, because the value from their services is greater than the value from other, less productive resources. The jury's decision in the case against the plywood suppliers showed a failure to recognize the action of derived demand on the values of superior productive resources.

Before applying the concept of Ricardian rent to plywood pricing, we first use it in simpler situations where the implications are easier to see. Suppose you are a surgeon who

---

[4]A more general, but here unnecessary, statement refers to mill net *marginal revenue*, rather than mill net price. We are simplifying our example by assuming that the marginal revenue in each city is equal to the price. The distinction between the two measures will be significant for other issues discussed in later chapters.

can remove an appendix as safely as any other surgeon but in half the usual time. Suppose the standard fee for an appendectomy is $500. What price could you get for your services? Would it be the standard fee? Or would it be half as much, because you take only half as long? The answer is that you would get as much as people would offer *for the service*; your service is as good as any other surgeon's, if not better. Other surgeons get $500 for the same service, so you could not get more and you would not have to accept less. (The example could as well be of an auto mechanic who can replace a transmission twice as fast as other mechanics and gets twice the hourly wage rather than charging the customer half.)

Your fee would not be lower, because your larger supply of services (that is, the same service in half the time) does not increase the market supply enough to affect prices noticeably. For a half-hour's work you would get what other surgeons got for an hour. You are twice as productive as they are, with the same fee but twice the income. That higher income resulting from your superior productivity is Ricardian rent. In other words, the basing point price, $500, is the fee of other surgeons—the dominant supply.

Now we come to the point of this analogy. Because you spend only half the time that other surgeons spend on the surgery, I might say, "You are getting paid too much. For a half-hour's work you are paid what other people get for an hour's work. I contend you are getting paid for 'phantom time'—for an extra half-hour that you didn't work." I am assuming that your time is no more valuable than any other surgeon's—an obviously false assumption. A surgeon is paid for what is accomplished for the patient, not for how long he or she takes to do it. Your services per hour are more valuable than others', and you are paid exactly what a half-hour of your time is worth. You are not overcharging the patient when you

charge $500. Value is not derived from *labor time*. To believe that it *is* is to commit the error in the *labor theory of value*: failing to recognize that though the final product may have the same value, its productive inputs can have different productivities. Competition for the superior productive input will raise its value to that of its output (competition from other inputs will keep it from being even higher). Its superior productivity will be converted into a higher income for that input. This, again, is the law of derived demand: the absorption, through competition, of the value of the final product by its productive inputs. Superior inputs get higher incomes, Ricardian rents of superior ability; their customers don't get lower prices.

Derived demand explains the differences in incomes of superior lawyers, painters, computer programmers, lands for growing wine grapes, salespersons, musicians, and so on and so forth. The high incomes received by Moses Malone, Liza Minnelli, Reggie Jackson, Ben Vereen, John McEnroe—each of whom can produce a more valuable consumer service in the same time than the rest of us—are not the result of overcharging for a deceptive phantom time.

Now let's apply these competitive market principles to the plywood markets. A new source of supply developed in the Southeast, obviously nearer than the Northwest to southeastern customers of plywood. Because its location eliminates transport costs to the Southeast, it is a superior source to southeastern customers. At what price, then, will the plywood produced in the Southeast be sold there? No matter where it is produced, it will get a competitive price that clears the market in which it is sold, even though it doesn't have to be transported so far—as faster surgeons or mechanics get the same price per unit of output service as other surgeons and mechanics even though they don't work as long. Any timberland located closer to the consumer will get a rent equal to the transport cost avoided. The owners of the southeastern timberland get a larger portion of the market price because their land is nearer the consumer. The price of plywood in the Southeast will not fall until increased production—no matter where it occurs—increases the *total* U.S. supply and lowers prices in all cities. (Remember that the prices in *all* cities are tied together by differences in transport costs.)

Not until the total U.S. supply increases enough to significantly lower prices in *all* parts of the United States will southeastern producers' incomes be reduced. People will bid more for southeastern land on which to grow pine trees, or for the existing plywood-making machinery. They will bid up to the savings in transport costs from the superior (that is, nearer-to-market) location of that land or machinery. The timberland owner and the owner of existing, installed plywood-making machinery get a Ricardian rent, a return for superior location, until enough other people imitate them.

Why, then, the jury's verdict against the southeastern suppliers? Apparently the jury was confused by the way prices are quoted: A "Northwest base price plus transport" suggests that the Northwest price is set *first* and then the price in each city is determined by adding on transport costs. But no matter how a price is *expressed*, we have seen how competitive forces actually set it: In any city the market price, out of which producers get their mill net price, is the price that will attract enough supply to satisfy the amount demanded at that price. The price in any city must attract supply away from other consumers throughout the United States. No matter where the plywood is produced, the *differences* of prices (more accurately of the marginal revenues) among all cities will match the transport cost differences among those cities, but the *level of prices* in those cities will be as high as necessary to equate the total amount demanded nationally to the total amount supplied nationally. The land and machinery located close to the customers in the Southeast would be highly demanded, with the result that it would become very valuable—exactly as the high price of land in New York City is related to the high hotel and office rentals there, or as the fees to New York lawyers are the same whether the (equally good) lawyers were born in New York or incurred transport costs to come there from Seattle.

Review and Prologue

It is worth emphasizing that the analytical model used so far—the price taker market— is adequate to permit reliable analysis of many economic phenomena: response of production to present and anticipated consumer demand; effects of taxes on product prices and on earnings of inputs; the means of risk bearing; the role of property rights, and of specialization, in production; capital valuation of assets; the reason for "excess" capacity and buffer inventories and some forms of unemployment; effects of price controls; the meaning of costs and the distinctions among marginal, average, total, variable, and sunk costs; the different roles of marginal and average costs in determining output; the difference between long-run effects and short-run effects; international trade; the measurement of costs in terms of present, or capital, values; why prices that appear to be below costs may in fact be above costs; the distinction between monopoly rents and Ricardian rents of differential ability; and how profits are obtained and then absorbed by superior inputs and resources. The price taker model could explain such things as inflation, international finance and foreign exchange rates, the money system, business fluctuations that create recessions, and so on. However, many other important phenomena are not adequately explainable by this model. For some of those, the price searcher model—the topic of the next chapter—is appropriate.

Summary

1. A *price taker* is a seller who cannot change the market price by changing the amount offered. That market price is one at which all of the price taker's supply can be sold.

2. The price taker's marginal revenue is equal to the price of the product, because the price is constant regardless of how many units the price taker offers for sale.

3. *Constant cost* can mean either a cost that occurs at a constant rate per unit of production, or a cost that is sunk, that was incurred in the past and is no longer pertinent to any present or future decisions. The two are very different: The first is a true cost of some possible act; the second is merely a reference to a past cost of a past act.

4. Variable costs are those that change if the rate of output changes; they increase with larger output.

5. Marginal cost is the increase in costs when the output rate is increased by a unit.

6. The wealth-maximizing output rate of a price searcher is that rate at which the marginal cost is brought up to equality with the price.

7. Any income received by some resource in excess of its operating costs but that does not cover its original (sunk) costs of production is called a quasi-rent. Whether a quasi-rent is received or not, the resource will continue to be available—until it wears out, at which time it will be replaced only if a quasi-rent is expected.

8. The price takers' market price is determined by the supply and demand in the market for that good. The supply in that market is the aggregate output from all the price takers at each possible price—output rates at which their individual marginal costs are equal.

9. An output at which marginal cost equals price is often considered optimal in that the value of the extra output to consumers, measured by its price, just equals its marginal cost.

10. The long run for the industry is that in which all entrants who could earn a profit, or the competitive rate of interest, on their investments have entered into production. The market price will be equal to the costs of entering and producing that product.

11. Any producers who think their long-run per-unit cost is less than the long-run price have miscalculated their costs by undervaluing some resource. If other people could identify the resource responsible for those low costs, they would compete for it and bid up the price, and hence its value and cost, until that former miscalculated or misforecasted value is corrected upward to eliminate the profit prospect. This higher value of superior ability is called Ricardian rent to superior producers.

12. If demand falls, resources specialized to this product will fall in value to what they are worth in their next-best activity. The resource owner will accept a lower reward, at least down to that next-best alternative, rather than not produce. When this price fall of existing resources is brought about by a new supplier's increasing of the aggregate supply, which lowers the equilibrium price, it is sometimes called predatory pricing under the mistaken impression the existing resource is trying to drive the new one out, whereas in fact the increased supply from the new one is driving down the best price available to the existing resource.

13. The effects of a tax on the production of a good depend on how readily the productive resources can shift to making other goods at no less reward. If they can, the resources lose nothing, and consumers must pay the full amount of the tax; moreover, the smaller supply of the taxed good would raise its equilibrium price. If any existing resources cannot make such a shift, they will have to take a loss in order to retain their jobs, which remain better than any other option. In that case, consumers do not have to pay all the tax.

14. A tax on just one or a few suppliers of a

good will not increase the price, because they cannot affect the total supply enough to affect price.

15. The cost of any act requires a careful statement of exactly what act is being costed. Typically, the costs of obtaining title or possession or of operating some resource should be clearly separated. And since these acts continue over an interval of time, their cost is best measured in capital value terms.

16. A firm's output can be measured as rate or speed of output or as total volume. Thus, these two possible meanings must be carefully distinguished when referring to a "larger" output.

17. Two generalizations can be made about costs. First, the faster the rate of production of any good, the higher the costs of whatever amount is produced. Second, the larger the amount that is produced at any given rate, the lower the total cost per unit of output.

18. If some costs are incurred to produce two products jointly, only the marginal costs of each of the joint products can be defined. Any costs that are common to both outputs cannot be separately assigned.

19. Depreciation of a resource is the predicted reduction in value as the resource is used or ages. Obsolescence is the unexpected decrease in value because of new, unexpected developments. Sometimes obsolescence refers to the reduced value that was *expected* to occur because of new, better products. However, any *anticipated* effect would already have been computed into a lower present price of the resource.

20. Some products are interdependent in that the demand for one depends on the supply of another. Nevertheless, each can be produced independently insofar as the producers anticipate that effect and invest in production of one of the goods, knowing others will also invest in the other good. The anticipated future effects are capitalized into present values of the currently produced resources that yield these interdependent products.

21. Developers, as speculators, are making investments for which they expect sufficient demand from future consumers to make the investments profitable. Some may buy a resource and prevent it from being used wastefully now, because they are betting it will be more highly demanded in the future.

22. A classic example of misunderstanding of business practices is the common belief that basing-point pricing, with what is called "phantom freight," is a payment for services not provided. In fact, what is called "phantom freight" is the higher value of more productive resources—usually those that save transportation costs and thereby are paid for the costs they avoid, as a form of Ricardian rent because of superior ability or location.

Questions

1. You own 1000 shares of General Electric common stock. If you try to sell some, you find you can get a price of $61½ per share for all 1000 shares. If you offer only 500 shares, you can get a price of $61⅝—12½ cents more per share. If you sought a price of $61¾, you would sell nothing. Compute your marginal revenue as best you can with the given data. Is it close to the price? Is the elasticity of demand for your shares high or low?

2. In a price takers' market, does the marginal revenue of each seller approximate the average revenue (price)? Why?

3. Most elementary arithmetic books contain the following type of question: "Mr. Black, the grocer, can buy bread for 15¢. What price should he charge to make a profit of 50%?" Without worrying why Mr. Black should be content with 50 instead of 500% profit, wherein does this question ignore a basic economic fact of life? Suggest a formulation of the problem that will enable students to learn how to manipulate percentage calculations without being taught erroneous economics.

4. Explain why the marginal cost schedule above the lowest average variable cost is the supply schedule of the firm in a price taker's market.

*a. What is the supply schedule of the firm in Table 10-1?

*b. If price were $22, what would be the rate of profits?

c. How low a permanent price would make this firm stop production permanently?

d. How low could price be temporarily without making this firm suspend production?

5. "Marginal costs serve as a guide to how much of a good to produce, while average costs help indicate whether to produce the good at all." Explain.

6. Are there short-run and long-run costs for a given output program, or are there two different contemplated output programs, each with its own cost?

*7. If in some industry there were 100 firms exactly like the one whose cost data are given in Table 10-1, what would be the industry supply schedule—assuming a price takers' market?

8. The following describes the market demand in the price takers' market for 100 firms each with costs given in Table 10-1.

Demand Schedule

Price	Quantity	Price	Quantity
28.00	450	19.20	810
26.00	500	18.40	850
24.00	560	17.60	900
23.00	610	16.80	950
22.00	660	16.00	1000
21.00	710	15.20	1100
20.00	770	14.40	1200

a. What will be the equilibrium price?

b. What will be the rate of output at that price?

c. If price is somehow kept below that equilibrium, what will be observed in the marketplace?

d. At the equilibrium price of the current problem, will new firms be attracted to producing this good?

e. If new firms can enter this business, each one having the same cost conditions as firms already in the business, to what value will the market price move? (Hint: In the long-run supply curve, price will equal average cost of each firm, including entry of new firms. Assume all firms are identical.)

f. As new firms enter, what will happen to the output of the existing firms?

g. What will happen to the costs of the firms whose minimum average cost curves were lower? (Hint: What happens to the profits of those lower-cost firms?)

9. Suppose the average cost per unit of output in producing an X is $5, where cost is interpreted as the highest sacrificed alternative use value. And suppose, if these resources were to be used elsewhere, their sacrificed value of output here is $6. What will make these two different "costs" of the same resources converge to the same value?

10. "The open-market, capitalist system is a system of consumer sovereignty. Consumer preferences determine what shall be produced and how much shall be produced." Evaluate.

11. Question eleven deleted.

12. A tax of 1¢ is levied on each pound of peanuts grown by farmers.

a. What effect will this have on the output of peanuts?

b. How will it induce that effect?

c. What will happen to the price of peanuts?

d. Will the land on which peanuts are grown fall in value—in view of the facts (i) that peanuts are grown from plants that must be seeded every year, and (ii) that the land can be used for other crops?

*e. What will happen to the value of *existing* machines used for harvesting, shelling, roasting, packaging, and crushing peanuts? Why?

*f. Explain why these changes in value will not be permanent even though the tax is permanent.

*g. Does the temporary drop in value mean that the wealth-reduction effect of the tax is only temporary? Why or why not?

h. The proceeds of the peanuts tax are used to finance purchases of this book for free distribution to college students. Who is paying for the books so distributed? (The answer is *not* that those who lost wealth from the revised valuation of existing resources are paying for books. That loss of wealth is not offset as a gain to anyone else.)

*i. Who gains what as a result of the tax and expenditure of the proceeds?

13. Suppose that the tax in the preceding problem is levied against only one producer of peanuts.

a. What will happen to the price of peanuts?

b. To the output?

c. To the wealth of the various peanut producers?

d. Whose wealth will be affected by this tax?

14. Pittsburgh put a 20% tax on gross receipts of private commercial parking-lot operators while exempting competing publicly operated lots. In 1975 the U.S. Supreme Court held the tax constitutional even though its enforcement may destroy particular businesses. The Court also concluded that, in any event, a shortage of parking spaces in Pittsburgh would enable private lot operators to pass the 20% gross receipts tax on to their customers. The burden of the tax thus will fall upon customers. Is the Court's economic analysis correct? Explain.

Firm A		Firm B		Firm C	
Output	Marginal Cost	Output	Marginal Cost	Output	Marginal Cost
1	$1.00	1	$ .20	1	$ .10
2	1.10	2	.40	2	.15
3	1.20	3	.60	3	.20
4	1.30	4	.80	4	.25
5	1.40	5	1.00	5	is impossible
6	1.50	6	1.20		
7	1.60	7	is impossible		
8	1.70				
9	1.80				
10	1.90				
11	is impossible				

15. Above are shown marginal cost data for three firms, A, B, C, constituting the entire industry producing X. Each firm acts as if it were a price taker.

*a. Compute the supply schedule of this industry. (Hint: At each possible price indicate the amount that would be most profitably produced by each firm. The sum of those amounts gives amount supplied by the industry at each price.)

b. What is the general rule used to derive the supply schedule for an industry comprised of price takers? How does wealth-maximizing behavior by each firm yield that?

c. The amount supplied at each price by the *industry* in the above example is produced efficiently. What does that mean?

16. Using the same numbers as in question 15 for firms A, B, and C, reinterpret them as follows: The "output" is now clean water. Each firm produces steel; it uses water and changes the chemical content. To "produce" cleaner water requires some special cleaning action or the reduction of production of steel. Mill A could clean *one* of the 10 gallons of water it uses, abuses, dirties, or pollutes at a cost of $1.00. It can do so either by cleaning the water after it is used or by reducing the output of steel in order to not dirty that one gallon of water. In either case the cost of getting that clean gallon is $1.00 of what could otherwise have been produced—in line with the general definition and meaning of costs. Similarly, a second gallon per day could be cleaned or not be dirtied at a cost of $1.10 more. The marginal cost of a second gallon of clean water is $1.10. Similarly, the marginal costs of producing more gallons of clean water are given by the remaining data for this mill and for the other mills in the appropriate columns. It is important to understand that, by *not* using water (or by not abusing it), the mill is in effect producing clean water at a sacrifice of other goods (steel) that could be had if the water were in fact used. Or if more steel is produced and the water used and dirtied, then the costs are the costs of removing that dirt. If the water is not dirtied (and the steel not produced), then the value of the steel forsaken (net of the other costs that are also involved in making steel) is the cost of having more clean water.

    a. The problem is as follows: If cleaner water is worth 75¢ a gallon, how many gallons of clean water should be "produced" or not polluted by these steel mills? Which mills?

    b. If each mill were required to pay 75¢ for each gallon of water that it polluted, how many gallons would each mill use and clean before discharging water? Or how many gallons of clean water would each mill not use that it otherwise would have?

    c. If, instead of a pollution fee of 75¢, polluting water were simply made illegal, would that be better or worse? In what sense? Assume clean water is worth 75¢ a gallon no matter how much is involved here.

    d. Would it be better (than a pollution fee of 75¢) to tell each mill that it must clean up 20% of its discharged water? Or that each must discharge at least two gallons of clean water?

    e. What is the principle for the efficient amount of clean water?

    f. If someone owned the rights to the water and could sell it to users, would that affect the amount of polluted water?

    g. Is pollution to be interpreted as any use of a resource without compensation to the resource owner, or is it "excessive" use—beyond what would be used if compensation were required?

17. You have a machine that will produce Xs at a cost of $1.00 each (the sum of the labor and materials worth 70¢ per unit and depreciation of machinery of 30¢ a unit). The Xs sell for $1.00 each. The machine, which is worth $300, is useful only for producing X. Someone invents a superior machine that requires only 40¢ of labor and materials to produce an X. That new machine is put to use and the total supply of X increases. Because the demand is unchanged, the price of X falls.

    a. How far would the owner of the first machine be able to cut price before shutting down production?

    b. If the new machine could produce 1000 units—each worth 90¢—before totally wearing out, what would it be worth new? (Assume a zero rate of interest.)

Chapter 11
Price Searchers

Suppose a market in which products and suppliers are heterogeneous, that is, the same good offered by different suppliers can differ greatly in the number and combination of features, the quality of materials and workmanship, availability, and the like. Suppose also that there are costs to the consumer in obtaining prepurchase information about goods and suppliers, and costs to consumers and suppliers in negotiating and enforcing contracts. Finally, suppose that there are economic advantages to producing on a large scale, or volume. To analyze such a market we cannot use the price taker model; we must use a different model: the *price searcher*.

Market-Power Price Searchers

The corner grocer, filling station owner, druggist, clothier, restaurant owner, and General Motors—all face a demand schedule such that they could raise their price per unit of a good without losing all their customers. Why wouldn't such firms lose every customer if they raised their price? Why would a price cut not attract all customers from the other sellers?

PRODUCT INFORMATION IS NOT COSTLESS

No one knows everything about all goods. Seeking prepurchase information about their existence, location, ultimate performance, or the asking prices by different sellers is not costless. Shoppers squeeze bread, smell cheese, heft oranges, sniff perfume, shake walnuts, pick grapes, slam car doors, bounce on mattresses, try on clothes, feel cloth, but still they are not sure. They read advertisements, ask for warranties, rely on the seller's reputation and maker's brand name, use return privileges, and sample and select from inventories.

Because prepurchase information about a good is not costless or perfect, a buyer who sees identical goods available at different prices will not automatically buy the lower-priced one. There is good reason to have doubts about whether goods are really identical: Such doubts prevent gullibility. Buyers sensibly do not switch immediately to any seller who asks a lower price for what is claimed to be the same good. Some of us sensibly don't incur the costs to find out whether every lower-priced version really is equal. We weigh the costs and benefits of reducing our ignorance and decide that there is an optimal, or acceptable, degree of ignorance. The lower the cost of information, the more we want it; the more it costs, the less we require. That is simply an application of our first law of demand. Why else do we not acquire the information that would turn each of us into first-class physicists, physicians, and mechanics?

Because not every consumer has the same tastes and no consumer knows costlessly the exact qualities of every good offered by every supplier, some suppliers will find that a slightly lower price does not attract all consumers away from other suppliers of essentially similar products, nor does a slight rise in price drive away all consumers. Some sellers, then, see a demand for their products that is negatively sloped with respect to price.

The fact is that seemingly similar goods from different suppliers *are* different. Fully informed customers will prefer one over the other and will not be willing to shift to a less desired product at the slightest increase in price. Not all customers will shift from beer to champagne at the slightest rise in the price of beer or fall in the price of champagne. And some would not shift from Bud to Coors if the price of Coors were slightly lowered, nor from Apple to Radio Shack computers if the price of the Apple were retained.

BRAND NAMES: REDUCING PREPURCHASE INFORMATION COSTS

One economical source of prepurchase information about the qualities of products is a familiar brand name, with which the reputability of the maker is associated. If a new or unknown producer claims its product is just as good, can you be sure? Kodak, American Express, Howard Johnson's, and Holiday Inn are names that identify goods and services of verified, predictable standards of quality—not necessarily of the highest quality, but of *predictable* quality. For example, one well-known brand of canned food offers riper, tastier, and better-quality goods than does another brand, which sells for less. Both brand names are reliable predictors of different levels of quality. You may think the difference in quality is not worth the cost—but then you aren't the only consumer. Many agricultural products such as lettuce, potatoes, tomatoes, squash, and onions typically have no brand name, because their quality is relatively easy to detect at time of purchase.

More recently, as labeling has become cheaper and shoppers' time has become more valuable, reliance on brand names as a means of indicating quality has increased. More commonly, the reputability of the *retailer*—whether for diamonds or meat—helps identify the expected quality of unbranded goods. The more difficult it is to predict the quality or performance of a good, and the more serious the consequences of deviations from the quality expected, the more one will rely on the reputation, the brand name, of the maker or the retailer.

A supplier has an incentive to produce goods of reliable, predictable quality insofar as the firm's performance will later be associated with its name and thereby bring it repeat or new customers. (If you doubt this, try buying goods in communist countries where stores and products are unbranded and goods are sold simply as stockings, pickles, bread, or canned soups. One such experience will give you a profound understanding of the value of brand names to both consumer and producer.)

Price and Marginal Revenue of a Price Searcher

A seller whose price depends on the amount offered, that is, whose price will fall if more is supplied and rise if less is supplied—is often said to be a **price searcher** with *market power*. The market power consists of the seller's ability to affect his selling price by changing the supply. How significant is the seller's market power? It is not limitless: If demand is sufficiently low or the seller's costs sufficiently high, that market power will not guarantee that costs are covered, much less that there will be a profit. Nevertheless, the price searcher faces a larger range of possible prices than the price taker. Such a seller must *search* to find what price and quantity are most profitable.

Suppose a total daily supply of 20 gallons of unusually good drinking water comes from one well. (To keep the essentials clear, we assume at first that there are no costs of bottling and selling the water.) Assume the demand for that water is the schedule in Table 11-1 (shown as a graph in Figure 11-1). By supplying only 3 gallons the well owner could get a price of $18 per gallon, with a total revenue of $54. Or, by announcing a price of $17, the seller would sell one more gallon. The total revenue is then $68, only $14 more for selling one more gallon and not $17 (the price per gallon), because, to sell one more gallon daily, the seller lowered the price on *every* one of the 3 gallons formerly sold at the higher price. That gives back $3 to existing customers. The *increase* in revenue, the marginal revenue, is only $14, even though the fourth unit sells for $17. In deciding how much to sell, the seller looks at *marginal revenue*, not simply at price.

Selling 10 (or 11) gallons daily (10 × $11 = $110) would maximize the owner's wealth.

Offering more than 11 gallons would reduce total revenue: The marginal revenue would be negative. Offering less, say, 9 gallons, would raise the price to $12 per gallon but would reduce total revenue to only $108.

The seller refuses to sell more than 11 gallons even though its marginal cost is zero (remember, we are assuming production is costless), which is less than the value to the customer of the unsold water—measured by *price*, not by the marginal revenue. Any excess of price over marginal cost (which is here zero) is evidence of waste in that the consumer values the available but *unused* gallons at more than their cost. This discrepancy between price and marginal cost occurs because the seller heeds marginal revenue rather than the price—which is greater than the marginal revenue. If demand is such that

Table 11-1

DEMAND FACING PRICE SEARCHER

Price	Quantity	Total Revenue	Marginal Revenue
$20	1	$ 20	$ 20
19	2	38	18
18	3	54	16
17	4	68	14
16	5	80	12
15	6	90	10
14	7	98	8
13	8	104	6
12	9	108	4
11	10	110	2
10	11	110	0
9	12	108	− 2
8	13	104	− 4
7	14	98	− 6
6	15	90	− 8
5	16	80	−10
4	17	68	−12
3	18	54	−14
2	19	38	−16
1	20	20	−18

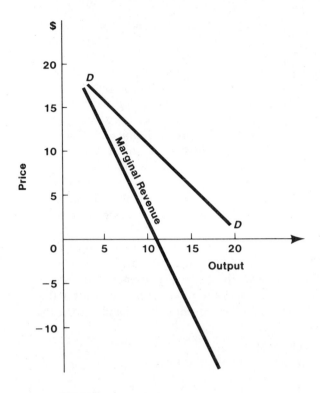

Figure 11-1.

DEMAND SCHEDULE FACING A PRICE SEARCHER

The "marginal revenue" indicates how much the seller's total receipts *change* when he sells one more (or one less) by appropriately changing his selling price on all the units he offers for sale. At any number of units sold, the marginal revenue is less than the price (unless only one unit is sold). It is the lower line, the marginal revenue, that the price searcher concentrates on. But we call him a price searcher because he must search for the optimal (the profit-maximizing) price for his wares. And he can come closer to finding that price if he has a good estimate of his marginal revenue.

to sell more the seller must cut the price on all units, including those which were already selling, then marginal revenue is less than price. However, if price could be reduced on *only* the additional units sold while *the first 10 gallons maintained their old, higher price,* the seller's marginal revenue would equal the price. Later we shall investigate some ways of doing that. In fact, a reason for explaining the price searcher's marginal revenue is to convey an understanding of certain pricing and sales tactics, some of which have at times been declared illegal despite their enhancing output.

PRODUCTION COSTS

Although we now abandon the simplifying assumption that there are *no* costs of production, the preceding implications remain unchanged, as we now illustrate. Table 11–2 shows the daily costs of production as do the

Table 11-2

TOTAL, AVERAGE, AND MARGINAL COSTS AT DIFFERENT OUTPUTS (PLUS CONSTANT COST OF $26)

Output	Total Cost	Average Cost	Marginal Cost
0	$ 30	—	—
1	$ 37	$37.00	$ 7
2	$ 45	22.50	8
3	$ 54	18.00	9
4	$ 64	16.00	10
5	$ 75	15.00	11
6	$ 87	14.50	12
7	$100	14.28	13
8	$114	14.25	14
9	$129	14.33	15
10	$145	14.50	16
11	$162	14.73	17
12	$180	15.00	18
13	$199	15.30	19
14	$219	15.64	20
15	$240	16.00	21
16	$262	16.38	22

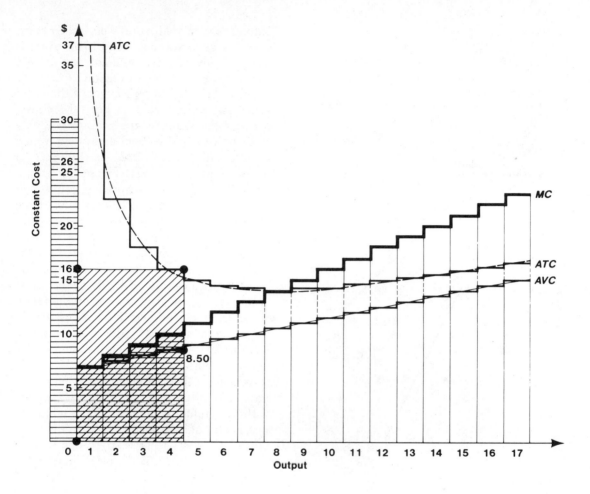

Figure 11-2.

RELATIONSHIPS AMONG CONSTANT COST,
AVERAGE TOTAL COST (*ATC*), MARGINAL
COST (*MC*), AND AVERAGE VARIABLE COST (*AVC*)

The average total cost (*AVC*) is equal to the sum of
the average variable cost (*AVC*) plus the average
constant, or fixed, cost, which diminishes
as the fixed cost is spread over a larger output, resulting
in a lower fixed cost per unit of output. Note that the
marginal cost (*MC*) curve cuts the *ATC* and *AVC* curves
at their lowest points.

cost curves in Figure 11-2. We assume a constant cost of $30 per day regardless of output. The average cost and marginal cost curves are labeled *ATC, AVC,* and *MC.*

We assume that the demand conditions from Table 11-1 are fully known to the seller (an assumption we later abandon). Figure 11-3 plots these with the cost curves of Figure 11-2. The demand curve and its marginal revenue curve are *DD* and *MR.* The output that maximizes the firm's profit is five units, each sold at a price of $16, with an average cost of $15. The total profit is $5. Producing and selling a larger output (say, six units) would lower the price on all units, reducing the total profit. The output program of five units is profit-maximizing; at larger

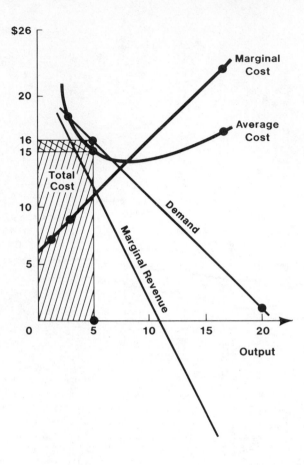

Figure 11-3.

PRICE SEARCHER'S
PROFIT-MAXIMIZING OUTPUT AND PRICE

The difference between price and average total cost at
the selected output indicates the profit per unit. Total
profit is that difference multiplied by the amount of
output. At the profit-maximizing output, though
marginal revenue is equal to marginal cost,
price is greater than marginal cost.

outputs (six units or more) marginal costs exceed marginal revenue. And price exceeds
marginal cost, with a resultant loss in consumer value, as shown in Figure 11–4.

Any price could be charged if the seller
were willing and able to bear the consequences. For example, at a price of $18, only
three units would be sold and profits would
be zero. At a price of $12, nine units would
be sold with a loss of $21. The seller couldn't
stand that. Market demand and cost conditions, along with a desire for wealth, force
the seller toward the profit-maximizing price
of $16, for which the seller searches.

It is not uncommon for lawyers to say
that a price searcher has "market power" in
that the price can be set by the seller. However, there is, in fact, very little discretion
available, since the demand and cost conditions determine what is the profit-maximizing (or loss-minimizing) price. The price
searcher who is setting a price is really
searching for that optimal price. (One should
not, as is often done, confuse "searching"
with "determining.") This supplier refuses to
make extra units at a cost less than their value to consumers (that is, the value to consumers as measured by the price—not by the
marginal revenue of the seller). By heeding a
marginal revenue that is less than price, the
seller underproduces this good, in the sense
that the value of the extra product would
have exceeded the costs of producing it. This
loss or waste is called *monopoly distortion*—
not, however, because of a contrived restriction on other potential suppliers (which is
what *monopoly* most commonly means), but
because economists call *any* price searcher a
monopolist.

Demand Changes and
Effects on Output and Price

For price searchers, the effects of a change in
demand or costs are basically similar to those
for price takers. Increased costs will raise the

cost curves and reduce the supply, resulting in higher prices; increased demand will tend to result in increased output at a higher price.[1]

SHORT-RUN RESPONSE

Suppose demand increases. The profit-maximizing price and output are higher, producing larger profits. But which increases first, price or output? And by what process? Earlier we explained how a changed demand impinges on sellers: Retailers keep buffer inventories to stabilize prices and provide quick availability of goods. A *persisting* higher demand will reduce those retailers' inventories. As retailers attempt to replenish them, wholesalers' and manufacturers' inventories will decrease. When manufacturers' inventories fall, they will increase production. To do so requires that they employ more resources, which they obtain by offering higher wages, with higher costs and higher prices. Economic analysis has not adequately identified all the factors that will explain precisely the speed of response of output relative to price. But one factor that makes the output typically rise *before* prices is the difficulty of getting reliable signals that quickly distinguish persisting from transient demand variations.

When demand fluctuates transiently around some long-term average, market price will not do the same. Changing price instantly in response to every transient demand fluctuation would lose a retailer customers. Sellers instead provide steady, predictable

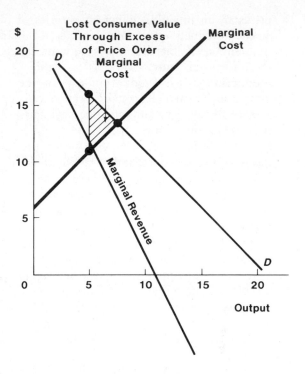

Figure 11-4.

LOSS IN CONSUMER VALUE FROM EXCESS OF PRICE OVER MARGINAL COST

Restricting output to where marginal cost equals marginal revenue loses some excess of consumer value over cost of production.

---

[1]We say *tend* to result in a higher price and larger output, because if the demand increases but at the same time becomes twisted toward significantly greater elasticity, the increased demand may then result in larger output and a lower price. Conversely, if the demand increase is associated with a twisting of the curve toward significantly less elasticity, a smaller output and higher price may result. These appear to be highly exceptional cases and will therefore be ignored. And in any event, although they may occur in the short run, the long-run tendency is toward the normal result.

prices by maintaining buffer inventories of finished products or standby capacity to fill transient, reversible differences between the rate of current purchases and the steadier production rates. Production can in the meantime be carried on more economically at a relatively constant rate that maintains those buffer inventories.

The cheaper it is to provide stable, predictable prices and reliability of supply by buffer inventories and reserve production capacity, the more likely a demand increase will affect output before price. The more costly are such inventories or adjustments of output, the more likely a demand increase will affect price before output. This distinction is especially important in the analysis of effects of aggregate, national demand changes. A *general, economy-wide demand increase or decrease for all goods* will increase or decrease output and employment before prices.

LONG-RUN CAPACITY RESPONSE TO DEMAND CHANGES

When demand increases, existing firms expand. But they cannot conceal their increased wealth for long. Sales personnel know who is doing well; the word gets around. Other firms imitate this firm. Managers leave and organize their own company, taking part of the company's know-how. Hundreds of firms have been created by former employees of older computer companies. If the production of electronic organs, of pianos, of Cokes, or of Arrow shirts becomes more profitable, other suppliers or former managers will produce close substitutes and dissipate the profit of the first producer. Competing producers bid up prices of responsible resources: assemblers, supervisors, designers, production engineers, salespersons, managers, and research staff. Formerly undervalued inputs are paid more, absorbing the profits into costs. This is as true for land, buildings, and labor—whether the labor be that of plumbers, managers, or teachers—as it is for resources owned by a business. Even the business owner's own services must be valued at a higher figure, because the more such a person can earn elsewhere for those superior services, the higher are his or her costs of continuing in the present business. Thus, after disequilibrating shocks and changes in demand and supply conditions, events tend toward the zero-profit, long-run equilibrium. But each new event changes the situation, so there are always some new instances of profit and loss as profits and losses of older events are being competed away. The zero-profit equilibrium for price searchers is shown in Figure 11–5.

If demand falls, the direction of adjustments in price and output are reversed. Values paying for resources in current uses fall, according to how immobile or specialized they are. Resources will be shifted to where their service values are not so low. All resources whose values are affected will be poorer, because consumers' demands for their prior services are lower. To keep them at their old jobs at the former income would require compelling consumers to continue to buy things they no longer value so highly. And that can't be done in a private-property system. But it can be done if sufficient political authority can be exerted to control what consumers can or must buy or support by special taxes to subsidize the less demanded producers—a topic we shall explore later.

Seller's Search for Wealth-Maximizing Price, Output, and Quality

If people had better knowledge of future demands and costs, outputs would be adjusted toward their wealth-maximizing levels more quickly. Profits or losses would be smaller, because the future use values of resources would be more correctly figured into current values.

The revaluation process and search for future higher-valued products are characteristics of a world of *uncertainty, partial ignorance, and costly information*, which is *not* to be confused with stupidity or irrationality. Producer-sellers must feel like gamblers at the racetrack: A horse will win, but *which one?*

Consider the problem faced by a company that proposes to design a jet airliner it believes will be a good replacement for the Boeing 737. What price and what scale of production should it plan? This is precisely the kind of question faced by Lockheed with its L-1011 and by Douglas with its DC-10. Boeing had earlier calculated sufficiently well to get a profit on the 737. How close it was to *the* profit-maximizing price no one will ever know, but the demand for the Boeing 737 did lie above the cost curve for a region that Boeing managed to find. If the demand curve for the L-1011 ever did lie above its cost curve, Lockheed wasn't able to find where. If management had known, they would have saved their stockholders millions of dollars. Apparently Douglas was no luckier with its DC-10.

Ford misjudged the demand for the Edsel and lost millions but guessed right (that is, profitably) with the Mustang. General Electric invested in computer design and production and produced poorer stockholders. Chrysler designed automobiles in the 1950s for which the demand curve was under the average cost curve and lost at least $100 million. Not even the alleged consumer manipulations by advertisers could adequately sway buyers.

On the other hand, Kodak sacrificed large profits in grossly *under*estimating the enormous demand for its Instamatic cameras. Hewlett-Packard underestimated the demand for its hand-sized electronic computers, although they made some profits. Not only the giants display uncertainty, ignorance, and error. The grocer, druggist, and clothier must decide what products to stock. Farmers must guess next season's price in selecting what

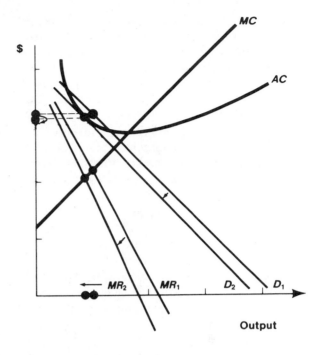

Figure 11-5.

LONG-RUN EQUILIBRIUM

Profits to some firms induce other firms to enter into competition. The effect is to divert some sales from the initially profitable firms, reducing demand for their output from D_1 to D_2 (at the same time that increased competition for inputs drives the firms' costs up). The combined downward shift in demand and upward shift in costs eliminates transient profits (at which demand curve is tangent to average cost curve). Price is then equal to average cost (and marginal revenue equals marginal cost).

crops to plant now. Students must select careers. Only in knowing the *present* marginal revenue does the price taker have an advantage over the price searcher.

Consumers reliably reveal their demands only after they are actually offered new goods. Producers propose; consumers dispose. Transistor radios were invented and produced without consumers giving potential producers advance orders. The same is true for many, many products: stereo and quadraphonic sound systems, video recorders, electronic musical instruments, power steering, computers, miniskirts, automatic transmissions, color television, Frisbees, instant coffee, frozen foods, credit cards, electronic watches, cordless electric knives, no-iron fabrics, synthetic fibers, stretch clothes, coin-operated–dry-cleaning machines, water-based paints, fiber-point pens, and so on. In each case, the hope of greater wealth provoked someone to risk wealth in producing some new item.

Survival of Best of Actual Activity

The preceding discussion has profound implications that should not be overlooked. Business people are investors who do not read tables of known costs and demand schedules to select their wealth-maximizing output. Instead they willingly invest and risk their wealth in estimating or trying production techniques, products, and outputs, hoping they really will have sufficiently low costs and high demands to yield a profit. If you ask them about marginal costs and marginal revenues, they are likely to wonder what you are talking about. To invest in exactly the best production technique or the most profitable product, let alone the most profitable price and output, is a gamble.

What the principles of economic analysis do is show how underlying factors deter-

mine what can or cannot continue to be done profitably. We can discern in what direction new input prices and demand would affect the profitable output. Competition between suppliers with different production techniques eliminates the poorer and retains the better. Untested techniques or products may be still better, but we won't know. (If you think other techniques should be tested, who should bear the risks of failure?)

Economic analysis does not assume that the producers zero in on exactly the best production opportunities and achieve maximum profits. Economic analysis uses the maximum profit and wealth *criterion*, because the closer a business firm is to that output and price, the more profitable it will be, the more rapidly it can grow, the more wealth it will create, and the more wealth society will permit it to control. What we are able to do by economic analysis is to reveal how external events affect demand and supply conditions, and how the competitive process selects *surviving* firms and products.

Monopoly: Open- and Closed-Market Price Searchers

The price searcher is often said to be a *monopolist* because he or she is faced with a negatively sloped demand, meaning that at every amount sold, marginal revenue is less than price. However, as suggested earlier, monopoly has another, very different meaning. It is the condition of a seller who is protected by *legal sanctions* from any other supplier whose offerings would reduce the demand for the protected seller's goods. (This topic is treated in Chapter 13.) Such monopolists have *both* a negatively sloped demand curve and legal protection from potential competitors. Only when both conditions are present do we use the term monopoly. By contrast, we use the term *price searcher* to describe any seller (a) with a *neg-*

atively sloped demand curve (that is, with a marginal revenue significantly below price) and (b) *without* legal restrictions on competitors. The effects of restrictions are very different from the effects of differences in tastes and of products of different sellers not being exactly the same, as we shall see later.

Some Price Searcher Pricing Systems

Price searchers, as we have seen, are sellers who face a *negatively sloped demand*, with respect to price, *for their products*.

And so do protected monopolists, as we have also seen. However, though price searchers and monopolists have negatively sloped demand schedules, their effects on the opportunities of customers are different. The differences lie in the fact that, by definition, the monopolist has managed to have restrictions imposed on competitors. Although both the price searcher's and monopolist's price depends on that supplier's output, the pricing arrangements can differ. Thus, every negatively sloped demand must be examined to see whether it results from diversity among products and sellers, and the existence of information costs to consumers, or whether it results from restrictions imposed on potential competitors.

MULTIPART PRICING TO ONE CUSTOMER

Some selling devices and pricing systems allow sellers to reduce the price on only the extra units, rather than on *all* units sold. We now examine some devices designed to increase the seller's profits and some that also lead to expanded output. Although we try to identify their side effects, these are of no consequence to the seller and are beyond the scope of economic analysis to determine whether they are "good" or "bad."

Table 11-3 presents the demand schedule of one customer facing a seller. Column three is the seller's total revenue at each possible price; column four is the marginal revenue. Column five, which gives the customer's *total personal use value* at each quantity, is important in this pricing tactic, called two-part, or block, pricing. For simplicity, we assume the marginal cost of production is constant at 30¢.

Table 11-3   DEMAND OF ONE CONSUMER

Price	Quantity	Revenue	Marginal Revenue	Consumer's Total Personal Value
$1.00	1	$1.00	$ 1.00	$1.00
.90	2	1.80	.80	1.90
.80	3	2.40	.60	2.70
.70	4	2.80	.40	3.40
.60	5	3.00	.20	4.00
.50	6	3.00	.00	4.50
.40	7	2.80	− .20	4.90
.30	8	2.40	− .40	5.20
.20	9	1.80	− .60	5.40
.10	10	1.00	− .80	5.50

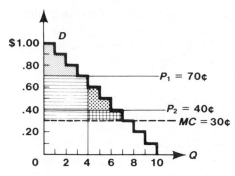

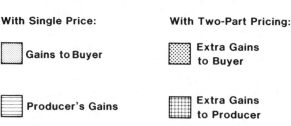

Figure 11-6.

EFFECT OF MULTIPART PRICING ON DISTRIBUTION
OF GAINS OF TRADE BETWEEN BUYER AND SELLER

If seller could charge a single price to the buyer, who
could then buy any amount at that price, the price would
be 70¢, and the gain to the buyer would be the shaded
area above that price and under buyer's demand line.
(This price cold be charged because marginal revenue
crosses and falls below marginal cost of 30¢ beyond four
units. Compute the marginal cost and verify.) If seller
could then charge a lower price, say, 40¢, for any
additional units, on the condition that the first four are
sold at 70¢, the seller could sell three more units for a
total of seven, getting additional profits of 10¢ on each,
while the buyer gets the extra personal value under
buyer's demand line and above the price of those
three units. (Can you construct another set of prices
that would get the same output but with almost all
the gains going to the seller? Hint: Try setting the
first price at 99¢ and then construct a series
of prices for subsequent amounts.)

If the price is set at 70¢, the price that
maximizes the seller's profits ($1.60), the
amount demanded and supplied (four units)
equates marginal revenue and marginal cost
(30¢). But suppose it were possible to cut the
price *only* on extra units sold, not on all, so
that the first four units continue to sell for
70¢ each, but the customer can buy *more* at
a bargain price of 40¢ each. Hence the term
two-part, or **block, pricing.** The customer
would buy three more at 40¢ each, giving the
seller a net gain of 10¢ (40¢ − 30¢) on each
of the extra three units sold, raising the seller's total profits by 30¢, to $1.90. The buyer
also benefits by getting three units more.
The buyer values them successively at 60¢ +
50¢ + 40¢, though paying only 40¢ each—a
gain worth 30¢. (The customer and seller are
indifferent as to whether the third 40-cent
item, the seventh in total, is purchased.)

As Figure 11–6 shows, this two-part, or
block, pricing system improves the seller's
situation, because lowering the price *only* on
extra units causes no loss of revenue on the
former rate of sales. Such a loss would have
offset part or all of the revenue from the extra units sold. Certainly this two-part price
schedule is better for both buyer and seller
than a single price at 70¢, even if it is not as
good for the buyer as a single low price of
40¢ on all units—but the seller would not
agree to such a price, anyway.

Consider a multipart price schedule in
which *every* unit has a different price. Start
at the first unit and go right down the demand schedule as follows: The price is 95¢
for the first one, 85¢ for the second, 75¢ for
the third, and so on down to 35¢ for the seventh, and last, unit, barely over its marginal
cost. The buyer, *given no other way of buying this good,* would reluctantly agree, because that is better than not buying at all.
Now the seller has captured almost all the
total use value of the product, gaining all the
area under the demand schedule and above
the marginal cost. The seller nets 65¢ (95¢ −
30¢) on the first one, 55¢ on the second,

down to 5¢ on the seventh. The total daily net is $2.45 (= 65¢ + 55¢ + ... + 5¢). The seller (assuming he or she knows the buyer's personal valuation schedule) has managed to get from the buyer almost all that each unit is worth. Because of these greater gains from exchange, the seller's earnings are larger: $2.45 instead of the $1.90 from the two-part schedule. The buyer's gain is only 5¢ on each of the seven, totaling 35¢: less than the 90¢ consumer's surplus at the single 70-cent price. This per-unit, block-pricing system is a neat one if the seller can use it. You may believe you've never seen such a system in actuality, but it's no different from charging a fixed price of $4.00 for a *package* of seven, because you must buy seven or none.

How Should the Gains of Greater Exchange Be Shared? Whenever it takes the form of two-part pricing or the price differs per unit, multipart pricing increases the extent of beneficial trade and gives more of the gains to the seller. But economic analysis cannot answer the question about distribution of gains, whether the producer or the consumer should get more of the gain. Yet some people argue that there is a proper division, which occurs if every seller and buyer acts as a price taker. For example, if there had been only a single price equal to *marginal cost*, more of the total use value would have gone to the consumer and less to the producer. Of course, no price searcher would have set a single price at its marginal cost. If a single price had to be set, it would be one at which the seller estimates that the marginal cost would be matched not by the price but by the marginal revenue at the amount demanded.

Because the price of extra units exceeds their marginal cost, the seller would like to sell more, but not if the price on all units already saleable also has to be cut. At the best *single* price (70¢ in our earlier example) the seller's profits would be $1.60; but by using two-part pricing and producing more

until the value, or price, of the last unit sold was closer to marginal costs, the seller got a profit of $1.90. This was obtained because the extra units could be sold without the prices on the units already salable having to be cut. The per-unit, multipart pricing system yielded profits of $2.45. (And, as we shall see later, if a good were to be sold at a single price equal to the marginal cost of 30¢, *with a tie-in of something else* priced as high as $2.80, then as much of the good would be produced as if the seller were a price taker selling at a price equal to the marginal cost.)

Why the division of gains associated with a single price that equals marginal costs *should* be right and proper has never been demonstrated. Although that output results in the efficient amount of production and exchange of this good, so does multipart pricing, if the last price equals marginal cost. The two pricing systems differ only in how they divide the gains from trade between buyer and seller.

Multipart Pricing Does Not Imply Subsidies among Customers If a seller offers different multipart pricing schedules to different customers, it does not necessarily follow that the high-price customers are paying for, or subsidizing, the services to the low-price customers. However, in some cases, public regulatory commissions require that a good or service be provided to some customers at prices below the seller's marginal costs. The costs must then be subsidized by some other source, such as by taxes or monopoly rents earned in sales to other customers. For example, mail service to many rural areas is at prices below costs, and the difference is covered by funds from other sources. No private producer would persistently sell to customers at a price below cost. (Giveaways and free trials do not contradict this statement. They communicate information about products to potential customers, and so are an investment that the seller hopes to recover in future business with customers who liked the product they sampled.)

Feasibility of Multipart Pricing Multipart (block) pricing is feasible only if two conditions are satisfied: (1) The seller must be a price searcher; that is, the demand for the seller's products must have a sufficiently negative slope, so that marginal revenue is significantly below price; and (2) customers must be unable, either by law or because it is too expensive, to engage in **arbitrage**—buying a good at a low price and selling it to others at a higher price for a profit.

The term *cream skimming* is often used to describe the tactics of a competitor who undercuts the high-price units of a seller who is (a) using a multipart pricing schedule or (b) charging some buyers more than others. (Without such pricing, there would be no higher-price customers.) Almost every public utility offers successively lower prices for higher rates of use. Electricity, gas, and water users who are given lower prices on successively larger blocks of power are facing a multipart, decreasing pricing schedule. The utility company is getting more revenue from the customers than it would get at a single price. (Ever try to resell power and water?) Xerox offers lower prices for larger volumes of use, charging a high price for the first batch of copies and successively lower prices for successively larger batches. Lower prices for large blocks sometimes reflect higher setup costs for small runs, but that is not the case for any of the examples cited.

Is there anything inefficient about a multipart pricing system? There can be, if some customers pay higher *last* prices—that is, *marginal prices*—than do other customers. The lower–last-price buyers would use the electricity, gas, or water in less valuable ways than would the higher–last-price buyers. For example, if I, as a householder, pay 10¢ for a kilowatt hour, whereas you (industry) pay only 6¢ for your last kilowatts of power, that

power is worth more if used by me than if by you. My extra uses are more valuable than yours, which create a social waste of about 4¢ per kilowatt hour. Such a waste is not created by every multipart pricing schedule, only by one in which we are not both getting marginal units at the same marginal price.

A power company using multipart pricing could try to tailor a separate multipart price schedule for each customer, so that every customer's power use brought marginal personal value down to the seller's marginal cost of producing power for that customer, say, 6¢ per kilowatt hour. Although the schedules could differ among buyers, every schedule would end with units sold at a price equal to the buyer's marginal cost. There would then be no waste—no uneconomic restriction of output—although some or all buyers of electric power would pay more than if all buyers paid a single price equal to marginal cost.

Why do government-owned or -regulated public utilities use multipart pricing? The municipally owned utility company is part of the government and can use multipart schedules as a taxing device to appropriate some of the gains from trade. Privately owned, for-profit utilities are likewise encouraged to use multipart pricing schedules, because their larger earnings can be absorbed by higher taxes on utilities. Governments prevent competition that would foil these pricing methods.

TIE-INS

Division of Consumer's Surplus A tie-in is an offer to sell a good at a given price on the condition that the buyer also buy another good at a stated price. As an example, let us look at what at first may seem an absurd situation. We use the demand situation described in Table 11–3. Suppose, as before, the seller can produce units at a marginal cost of 30¢. Suppose, further, that the seller sets a single price of 30¢ on each unit sold but refuses to sell any unless the buyer agrees to also buy something else—say, yesterday's newspaper, at the "exorbitant" price of $2. This tie-in may seem like a ridiculous offer, but if the buyer were faced with the option of getting none or buying the good at 30¢ per unit, on the condition that some worthless thing also be bought for $2, the buyer would agree rather than get none. The buyer would buy up to eight units and get a consumer's surplus of 80¢ [= $5.20 − (30¢ × 8) − $2]. Refusing to buy yields no benefit—no consumer's surplus.

The tie-in can be profitable because without it the total value to the buyer ($5.20) exceeds the cost at 30¢ each by $2.80 [= 5.20 − (30¢ × 8)]. The buyer would have gotten a consumer's surplus of $2.80. So we know the seller could have asked as much as $2.80 for a worthless tied-in item, making a total price of $5.20, which is what the buyer will pay for eight rather than have none at all. In a tie-in, then, the prices of the items are separately meaningless. Only the *sum* of the two prices is relevant, and only that is compared to the buyer's *total personal valuation* for the two items.

Why discuss these apparently different ways to accomplish the same thing—getting as much as possible from the buyer? It is important to see that multipart pricing and tie-ins are essentially the same, because the U.S. Supreme Court, misled perhaps by their superficially different forms, has frequently claimed that they have different effects. They thus have declared one form, multipart pricing, legal and the other form, tie-ins, illegal. For example, it was argued in the Court that tie-ins extended a monopoly in the tying item (the good demanded by the buyer) into the market for the tied item (the old newspaper in our earlier example). But it does nothing of the sort. It merely uses the tied item as a vehicle for collecting more of the total consumer use value of the *tying* item. The tied item need not be something of no value to the consumer (like our old, worthless news-

paper): The seller might just as well have insisted that the customer buy the same number of Cokes he or she normally buys, but now from *this* seller at a price sufficient to capture the same amount of total consumer use value, $2, as the tying item. The seller would then be buying Cokes from the Coca-Cola Company at the normal price and selling them to the customer for the payment of the $2 consumer's surplus of the *tying* item. Thus, tie-ins do not necessarily extend any monopoly into the market of the tied item.

Interbuyer Discrimination One use of tie-ins is to enable sellers to calculate the different total personal use values of their various customers for the tying good, so that they, the sellers, can try to capture more of it than they could get with a single price to all buyers. That is, each seller must identify the different areas under the different demand curves of its customers. For example, IBM has patents on a valuable computer and special abilities to produce and service it. IBM is a price searcher. It faces a negatively sloped demand for its products. To capture more of the total use value of its products and services to different customers, IBM must solve two problems: First, how can it learn each user's total personal use value for IBM computers, so that it knows the unique fee or price appropriate to each user? Second, how can it prevent arbitrage (resale of machines among customers), which would upset a differential fee system?

There may be a way. Of IBM's customers, suppose A has a very high demand for a computer and B has a low demand; that is, A places a high value on it, B a low value. If each customer's demand for some *other* good is highly correlated with its demand for the computer, a solution may be available. Suppose A is a large firm and B is a small firm; A uses a lot more machine punch cards in its computer than does B. If, as a prior condition to renting computers to customers, IBM required each customer to buy all their punch cards from IBM *at a higher price than they would otherwise pay*, the customer would agree rather than not have an IBM machine at all. How much more would the customer be willing to pay to get an IBM machine? Obviously, up to an amount that equals the firm's *total use value of the computer* (the area under its demand curve for the computer over the price of the computer). If the computer's value to the customer is correlated to the number of cards the customer uses, then by requiring the customer to buy all its punch cards from IBM at a price higher than the market price, IBM would have measured and captured, indirectly, some of the consumer's surplus of total use value of the computer. This tie-in arrangement favors the sellers if the assumed correlation of tied to tying item is correct and strong enough. Tie-ins, then, distribute more of the gains of specialization and trade to the supplier.

IBM's tie-in scheme does *not* create any monopoly rent in cards: The higher card price extracts from the buyer more of what the *machine* is worth. Nor is IBM monopolizing or driving any card producers or sellers out of business. IBM could simply have bought from existing suppliers the cards that it sold to its customers. It should be noted that there are other purposes of tie-ins, such as assuring proper machine servicing and maintenance, which a company might consider inseparable from its reputation for producing reliable, superior machines. In fact we do not *know* what motivated IBM in its tie-in arrangements.

Expenditures made solely to capture more of the consumer's surplus might be regarded as wasteful, because they affect only the distribution of wealth rather than production. If so, it should be carefully noted that the Court does not declare it illegal to get a larger share of the product value from the buyer by using superior bargaining tactics, supplying more information about alter-

natives, and the like. Apparently, the Court has been misled by differences in the *forms* of such tactics and has failed to see that they all—those declared legal and those declared illegal alike—have the same *effect*.

Quality Protection Gasoline stations often must buy tires, batteries, and accessories from gasoline producers if they are to get gasoline; computers and software are often tied in; Xerox and A. B. Dick mimeograph each require purchase of their own ink, stencils, and paper for their machines, claiming that they are more appropriate. And they might be right: Inferior ink and materials can foul up the machine, and if these items are supplied by different suppliers, the user will not know who is responsible for a malfunction. No one supplier will accept such responsibility unless that supplier alone supplies all the interrelated components.

Circumvention of Price Controls Another use of tie-ins is to overcome price controls. During price controls on gasoline, sellers often required that to get gasoline you had to buy a lube job. Thus, despite the limit on its price, they captured more of the value of the gasoline. (They did not monopolize the lube business.) Still another tie-in can be identified: Many retailers pay rents on their buildings and land that are a percentage of their retail sales. A retailer with big sales, who is therefore presumably a higher valuer of the premises, pays more than a retailer with smaller sales, who is presumably a lower valuer of the premises. This tie-in of rent to sales might be a way for the owner to capture more of the renter's value of the premises, but it might also be a way of sharing risk in the value of the premises. In either case, the owner of the premises could have achieved the same effect by requiring the retailer to also buy from the owner all the wrapping paper, or delivery service, or credit servicing, or any other goods or services that are correlated with the amount of sales. Yet that tie-in scheme would probably be declared illegal, whereas basing rent on percentage of sales is legal and extremely widespread.

Free Services   Recall the price searcher earlier in this chapter who has a demand curve with a marginal revenue that is less than the price, at that output at which marginal cost equals marginal revenue. This seller would like to sell another unit, if the price could be cut on the *extra unit only*, but not on any of the units already salable at the current price. One way to do so is to offer the buyer of that extra unit a gift of something else—without offering that gift to the other buyers. The gift cuts the net price to the buyer by the amount of its value to that buyer. The seller gets less, the price minus the cost of the gift; but as long as that net price exceeds the seller's marginal cost, the seller will make some extra income. So the seller tries to find new customers by the device of offering them, and *only* them, a *free* tie-in.

We can illustrate: Table 11-4 repeats the numerical demand data from Table 11-1. At an output of five units the price is $16, the marginal revenue $12, and the marginal cost $11. Suppose a hotel operator (the seller) can attract a sixth customer from the local airport, without cutting the $16 price on rooms to other customers, by offering the new customer a free ride from the airport. Assume the customer would pay only $15 for a room if he or she had to pay the $2 taxi fare to the hotel, for a total of $17. With this special offer, the customer pays $16 to the hotel and gets something worth $17: the hotel room, which, remember, is valued at only $15, plus the $2 taxi ride. All customers pay $16 for a room. The seller's marginal revenue by getting another occupant with this offer is $14, instead of $12, because the price of $16 was not cut to any other customers. After deducting the cost of the taxi, the hotel owner has $14: a gain of $2 over the $12 marginal cost of a room to the sixth customer. The gains to the sixth customer ($1) and to the

seller ($2) total $3, which is exactly the formerly wasted difference between the $15 value of the extra unit and its marginal cost of $12. Although all current customers do not get these "free" services, they also do not pay extra for the new customer's use of them. The new one pays a lower price—but pays enough to cover marginal cost.

Other means of accomplishing the same thing include free parking, free credit cards, free delivery, free warranties, return privileges, the extra time of clerks and larger inventories for "picky" and "choosy" customers, advertising, loss leaders, giveaways, and trading stamps. "Free" services do not necessarily raise consumers' costs. Whether they do depends upon how many of the old customers use them. If *every* old customer used

Table 11-4

DEMAND FACING PRICE SEARCHER

Price	Quantity	Revenue	
		Total	Marginal
$20	1	$ 20	$ 20
19	2	38	18
18	3	54	16
17	4	68	14
16	5	80	12
15	6	90	10
14	7	98	8
13	8	104	6
12	9	108	4
11	10	110	2
10	11	110	0
9	12	108	− 2
8	13	104	− 4
7	14	98	− 6
6	15	90	− 8
5	16	80	−10
4	17	68	−12
3	18	54	−14
2	19	38	−16
1	20	20	−18

every free service with *every* unit purchased, the effect would be equivalent to a price cut on every unit sold, and this scheme would not work.

PRICE DISCRIMINATION AMONG CUSTOMERS

Another means of increasing a seller's profit, one entirely separate from tie-ins, is for a seller to equalize the marginal revenue from all its customers. Suppose a seller has two separate classes of customers, A and B, with two different demand schedules, shown in Table 11-5. The supplier can make six units at a constant marginal cost of $6 a unit and a total cost of $36., At the same price to both classes of customer, $8, A buys five and B buys one, yielding $48 in sales revenue and $12 in profits.

The supplier can do better if: (1) the customers with different demands can be identified; (2) the supplier accordingly charges each class of customer a different price; and (3) each customer finds it too expensive to resell the goods to other customers. Only thus can the seller practice **price discrimination**: selling at different prices to customers with different demands in order to bring marginal revenues into equality. In our example, the supplier should set a price of $9 to class-A customers, who buy four, and $7 to class-B customers, who buy two. The total revenue is $50. Costs are $36 and profits $14—$2 more than with a uniform price. At those two different prices, the *marginal revenues from each class of customer are equal*, at $6, and are equal to the $6 marginal cost (see Figure 11-7).

If you think our seller could increase revenue by selling fewer units to the $7 customers and the same number more to the $9 customers, you are forgetting our assumption here that the price must be cut (to $8) on *all* units. Selling one more unit when *all* units are at a lower price, $8, increases sales receipts by only $4, the marginal revenue. But the marginal revenue in the B market is $6, which adds $2 to total revenue. That explains the difference between the total revenues of $48 from a uniform price and $50

Table 11-5   PRICE DISCRIMINATION BETWEEN TWO SEPARABLE CUSTOMERS

| | Customer A | | | Customer B | |
Price	Quantity	Marginal Revenue		Quantity	Marginal Revenue
$12	1	$ 12		0	$ 0
11	2	10		0	0
10	3	8		0	0
9	4	6		0	0
8	5	4		1	8
7	6	2		2	6
6	7	0		3	4
5	8	− 2		4	2
4	9	− 4		5	0
3	10	− 6		6	−2
2	11	− 8		7	−4
1	12	−10		8	−6

from discriminatory prices (at equal marginal revenues). Clearly, it is not prices but marginal revenues that the seller compares in the quest for greater earnings.

Price discrimination among customers can be tried by any seller whose customers are identifiably different and who find it too expensive to resell to each other. Those sellers who are at the clearest advantage are legal monopolies, for they are protected by law from other sellers who might cut price, and even from customers who might try to resell: railroads, milk producers, the postal service, and the telephone company, to mention a few. In each of these cases, although the costs of service to each buyer are the same, the price charged depends upon who the customer is or what the item is that is to be shipped by rail or post.

Legally protected monopolies are not necessary for all kinds of price discrimination. Some motels charge lower prices to commercial than to noncommercial clients for exactly the same rooms and services. Because commercial travelers have more knowledge of alternatives, their demands are more elastic, more sensitive to any one seller's price; thus the marginal revenue from them is closer to price. It is also probable that, in any country, native residents pay less than tourists do for many goods. Rich persons usually pay more than others for surgical services (which are not resaleable), but on the other hand they may get superior service. Lawyers sometimes charge different fees for the same service to different customers. (But again, are the services the same?) The matter of quality difference is difficult to settle and should make one cautious in gauging what is happening. Hertz and Avis have discounts to special customers. Colleges give larger scholarships (tuition price cuts) to the better students, who are also sought by other colleges—that is, students whose demand for a particular college is more elastic. Does your college bookstore give a discount to faculty but not to students?

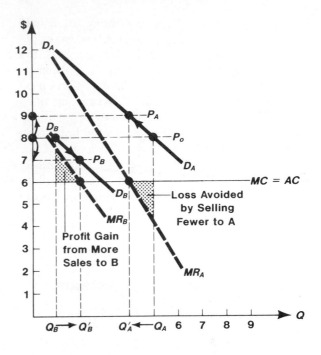

Figure 11-7.

PRICE DIFFERENTIATION BY
EQUALIZING MARGINAL REVENUE

Any seller, whose uniform price (P_0) to different buyers results in unequal marginal revenues among buyers, could increase profits by changing prices so as to make all marginal revenues equal, as seller has done, above, by raising the price to class-A consumers to D_A and lowering the price to class-B consumers to P_B. The two shaded areas show the gains from selling more at P_B and the marginal losses avoided by selling fewer at D_A than were sold at P_0. This price differentiation is called price discrimination. If it is to be successful, lower-price buyers must not be able to resell to higher-price buyers.

In any event, price discrimination does not require legal restrictions on actual or potential competition from other suppliers. If a supplier were able to separate its customers only by some legally imposed restriction on their right to buy from other suppliers or to resell to each other, then the excluded potential suppliers would be prevented from using their resources in the ways of highest value to the public. That effect of a legal restriction should not be confused with, or attributed to, price discrimination, which may occur without legal restrictions on other people.

Effects of Different Pricing Systems

Because consumers would buy more of a good if the producer charged a price equal to marginal cost, the producer seeks to make sure that marginal revenue, not price, equals marginal cost. The producer, then, does not produce enough to bring its value to consumers, its price, down to the marginal cost. Is there, as there seems to be, a social loss, or waste? That underproduction, called **monopoly distortion**, would be a genuine waste only if there were an economically worthwhile way to avoid it. If it were the result of a legal monopoly, presumably a change of the law could repeal the monopoly. (But what is the cost of getting the law changed? And what were the reasons for the legal monopoly?) Often, even where there is no protected monopoly, information costs, transaction costs, and economies of scale may be involved. Because no economically efficient alternatives to these are known, the underproduction is not a waste or an inefficiency; like wintry cold, it is economically unavoidable.

If two customers face different prices, and one is prevented, by other than economic costs, from buying in the lower-price market, there is an *allocative* distortion among

customers. Both the lower- and the higher-paying customers would be better off if the amount supplied could be reallocated by the lower-paying customer reselling to the higher-paying. But if they could in fact resell, no one would pay the higher price, so the seller could no longer sell at different prices.

As we have seen, one possible way to overcome both of these sources of monopoly distortion—price discrimination and prices that exceed marginal cost—is multipart pricing, wherein the seller's marginal revenue on the last unit sold to each buyer is equal to *both* the selling price and the seller's marginal cost. Such multipart pricing affects the distribution of the gains from specialization and trade.

PRICE DISCRIMINATION?

We should recognize by now that the terms *discrimination*, *monopoly*, and *competition* can be readily misunderstood. Yet the Robinson-Patman Law of 1938 prohibits "price discrimination" if it tends "to create a monopoly, lessen competition, or injure competitors." We should not be surprised that the confusion created by that terminology has occasioned considerable and continuous legal action that has raised costs to business firms and their customers.

Another classic example of misinterpretation of "discrimination" is that in which a railroad charged more to ship goods from New York to Denver than for the longer distance from New York to San Francisco. This seems discriminatory against people in Denver. Why did those rates exist? The railroads from New York to San Francisco had to compete with transport by water via the Panama Canal. There was no low-cost competition to Denver.

What a seller can get for his or her product depends not on what it costs, but on what the interaction of amount supplied and market demand determines the price should be. The supply of cheaper transportation to

San Francisco from New York is much larger than to Denver at any given price. Nature discriminated in providing a superb harbor at San Francisco and none at Denver. To correct this "injustice," the law compelled railroads to charge no more to Denver than to San Francisco. Unable to raise the San Francisco rail rate because of competition from the cheaper water transport, railroads had to lower the rate to Denver. Had Denver instead been the destination of most freight, its rate would not have been cut. Then the San Francisco rate would have been raised, because the railroads would have preferred to lose some of their small San Francisco revenue rather than reduce the larger Denver revenue. In that event, fares would still have been equal in dollar price, but San Francisco would suffer in the cause of the equality.

Sometimes, joint products (those having common inputs and hence inseparable costs) sell for very different prices. Long-distance telephone demand is higher in the daytime than at night, so night phone rates are lower because, although the supply is constant, demand is smaller. If night demand were the larger, night rates would be higher than day rates. The relative level of rates depends upon the relative size of the demands to be rationed.

Is it "fair" that night workers are able to make long-distance calls more cheaply? That theaters should charge less for matinees than for evening performances? That paintings involving the same production costs should sell for different prices? These disparities arise because of differences in the demand for the good or service, reflecting differences in availability, convenience, or, as perceived by the buyer, in quality. Why doesn't the person paying a higher price instead buy in the lower-price market? Because using the lower-price market is not worth the sacrifices (like moving to San Francisco from Denver, or working nights rather than days in order to save on long-distance calls).

Summary

1. *Price searchers* face steeply negative demand schedules in response to price; thus, marginal revenue is significantly less than price. Some producers are price searchers because of economies of scale in production, administration, and marketing, or because of differences in tastes and the costs of ascertaining the characteristics of goods from other suppliers.

2. Brand names on products reduce information costs to consumers by indicating quality.

3. Inventories, price stability, price-searching activity, and advertising are typical features of price searchers' markets.

4. Because of transiently fluctuating demands, price searchers keep inventories to assure a predictable price and ready supply.

5. A seller who perceives marginal revenue significantly below price will produce only to where marginal cost equals marginal revenue rather than to where it equals price—its value to consumers. This is called monopoly distortion (in that the marginal cost of another unit is *less* than its value to consumers).

6. Though price searchers may "administer" their prices, the sustainable price is determined by demand and supply conditions, not by the seller's arbitrary decision.

7. Because sellers who are protected by contrived restrictions on competitors are typically like price searchers in having a marginal revenue less than price, price searchers are sometimes called monopolists. However, the presence of restrictions in one case and absence in the other is an important distinction that prevents one from concluding that the two must be essentially similar.

8. Some price searchers can use pricing devices that are not usable by price takers and that tend to overcome the so-called underproduction by price searchers who sell only an amount at which the marginal cost equals

the marginal revenue, rather than the higher price. These include price discrimination, multipart pricing, tie-ins, and giveaways, which often are used in order to achieve sales to customers who value the product at more than the marginal costs.

Questions

*1. a. Can you suggest some goods for which the brand names are of no significance? What about sugar, flour, soap, aspirin, tires, dog foods, bread, milk, soap, corn flakes, cigarettes, canned peaches, banks, beer?
   b. Obviously you will not agree that all these are examples of goods whose brand names are insignificant. Are any? If so, do you purchase without regard to brand?
   c. If not, what do you mean by an insignificant difference?
   d. What makes you prefer one brand over another at the same price?
   e. Can you name any good and two of its brands for which you believe *no* one in his or her right mind could have a "good" reason for preferring one over the other?

2. Answer the following questions concerning the demand schedule below.
   a. Complete the data for total revenue, marginal revenue, and average revenue.
   b. What happens to the difference between selling price and marginal revenue?

Price	Quantity	Revenue		
		Total	Marginal	Average
$20	2	$40		$20
19	3	57	$+17	19
18	4	72	+15	18
17	5	—	—	—
16	6	—	—	—
15	7	—	—	—
14	8	—	—	—
13	9	—	—	—
12	10	—	—	—
11	11	—	—	—
10	12	—	—	—
9	13	—	—	—

c. How many units would you want to produce and sell if you could produce as many as you wanted at an average cost of $8 per unit and if you wanted to maximize your net receipts? (Hint: What is marginal cost?)
d. What price would you charge?
e. Could you charge $18 if you wanted to? What would be the consequences?
f. What are the consequences of charging $14?

3. On a television interview a prominent theatrical producer expressed delight that tickets for his play had been sold out for the next four months. Explain why he might have cause to be very sad, rather than happy.

*4. Change the data in Table 11–1 as follows: From every indicated "quantity purchased" at each price, subtract 6. If the new number is negative, simply call it zero.
   a. Recompute the total and marginal revenue.
   b. What is the new wealth-maximizing output for this producer if he has zero costs?
   c. What is the new wealth-maximizing output for this producer if his marginal cost is $8 at every output?

5. Is it true that for some products you prefer one brand over the other if both have the same price, but if there is any price difference between them you will take the lower-priced one?
   *a. If this is true for some goods, does it suggest something about the basis for or "strength" of your preference?
   b. Would you say that you "discriminate" among brands?
   c. Is that "justifiable" discrimination?

*6. Two brands of bacon, one nationally known and the other a local store brand, sell for $1.79 and $1.39, respectively, in the local store. Both are in fact of the same quality and are packed by the same packer. Noting this fact, a television commentator says that when you buy the more expensive brand you are paying for the advertising. Explain why consumers who buy the more expensive brand are not paying for advertising.

*7. In France, Italy, Spain, and Hong Kong, individual bargaining over the price of a good is commonplace.

a. Would you prefer that custom to be more common in the United States than not bargaining?

b. But on second thought, can you name three goods that are commonly purchased in the United States by bargaining?

c. How would you explain the simultaneous presence of two different customs?

*8. Compare and evaluate the following two assertions:

a. "Advertising and brand names create impressions of differences among competing brands where no significant difference really exists. As a result, because of consumer ignorance, sellers face a less elastic demand and can raise price without losing all sales to competitors. Creation of impressions of significant product differentiation by advertising is a social waste."

b. "Advertising and brand names permit customers to know more surely, cheaply, and fully the differences among various products. Otherwise, customers would select blindly, letting the price difference be their only reason for choosing one over the other, much as people would choose purely on the basis of price among superficially identical goods. By identifying products and their makers more fully prior to purchase, brand names and advertising permit customers to be more, not less, discriminating about qualities with less costly investigation into product details. Hence advertising and brand names that make demands less elastic because they identify more fully differences in product and quality assurance are a social benefit."

9. "General Electric announces a new 11-inch, 12-pound portable television for $99.50." "Papermate pens are sold at an announced price of $2.00." "Sunbeam appliances are sold at retail prices set by the manufacturer." Explain why the above statements do not imply price setting by the seller. That is, explain why the prices were not instead, say, three times as high.

10. Using the data of Tables 11–1 and 11–2, suppose that your costs of production are changed by a reduction in the cost of materials or labor so that at every output your marginal costs are $5 less.

a. What will this do to the marginal cost schedule?

b. What will be your wealth-maximizing price and output?

c. What are your profits?

11. Suppose a $5 tax is levied on your business—an annual license tax of a flat $5 regardless of how much you produce.

a. What will be your price and output?

b. What is the amount of your profits?

12. As a superior student you provide a tutoring service. The higher the price you decide to charge, the fewer the hours of work you get.

a. Are you a price taker or a price searcher?

*b. Assume that your time, when you are not tutoring, is worth an equivalent of $2 an hour. The daily demand for your tutor services is not perfectly predictable; it varies at "random" around a mean rate of daily demand which depends on the price you can charge. If, at the price you charge, you find that all your available time is always used, and there are occasional applicants whom you must reject because you are fully booked up, do you think you are charging the wealth-maximizing price? Explain.

*c. If you are charging a price at which you occasionally have idle time, are you charging too low a price?

*d. Given a fluctuating demand, how can you be sure that you have charged the "right" price?

13. In what sense can the marginal cost curve of a price searcher be considered a supply curve?

14. Let the demand schedule of question 2 represent the characteristics of the demand for your service as a gardener, and suppose you sell in a price-searchers' market.

a. What price should you charge per garden to maximize your daily net receipts if the "cost" of caring for a garden is zero?

b. If your time is worth the equivalent of $3

per garden maintained, what price would you charge?

  c. Is this the "highest" price the traffic will bear, the highest price possible, the lowest price possible, or a "reasonable" price?

*15. "Much advertising is deceitful, dishonest, misleading, fraudulent, and disingenuous. Therefore, it should be subject to government regulation." If you accept that conclusion, would you accept the same conclusion for daily conversation, political talks, lovers' pleadings—which are subject to the same charges? Explain why or why not.

16. The makers of the better hearing aids try to give their retail agents territories that are relatively large so as to separate their customers. They also state the price at which agents must sell. This use of exclusive selling territories and of "price fixing" has usually been called illegal—though more recently the courts have begun to declare them legal. What would justify the courts' saying the practices are legal? If General Motors has a policy of territorial protection for its dealers, how might that be justified as "socially desirable?"

17. "Decades ago there were scores of producers of goods; today there are a few large firms, so consumers now have fewer sources of supply. This is one of the disadvantages of large firms." Evaluate.

*18. The average number of newspapers in a city has decreased to virtually one or two, from the four or five from a couple of generations ago. Has this reduced the number or quality or variety or raised the costs of sources of news to a person in a city with fewer newspapers? As a mental exercise try to formulate an argument that the decrease in the average number of papers in a city is the result of an increasing number and variety of alternative news sources. What are you inclined to believe—with your slight evidence?

19. Price discrimination between two markets consists of selling in one market at a price below that of another. That is also called "dumping" into the low-priced market—a very misleading term. The actual purpose is simply to equate

marginal revenues, as explained in the text. Yet some observers allege the reason is that the seller is trying to drive some other competitor in the class-B market out of existence so this seller can later raise prices. No such objective is involved. Finally, it is argued that the seller must be selling below cost in the class-B market, or else how could the seller's price be lower and still cover transport costs?

  a. Show how.

  b. Show that even if it cost 25¢ to ship a unit of the good from the factory—located where all the class-A customers are—to class-B customers, profits for the producer would increase despite the fact that the selling price is $2 less for class B customers than for class A.

  c. Would the seller ever sell at a price below costs—marginal costs?
  Note: Just a few examples of "dumping" favorable to American consumers are Belgian glass; Japanese, German, and Italian cars; Polish golf carts; Korean textiles; Japanese steel; and tuition grants by colleges.

20. Some colleges charge high tuitions, but at the same time they give a large number of tuition fellowships ranging from full tuition payment down to practically nothing. If you apply the principles of discriminatory pricing techniques of an earlier chapter, can you show that tuition grants are a form of discriminatory pricing of education? Does that make them undesirable?

21. An attempt to impose losses on competitors in order to achieve a monopoly position with subsequent "above-competitive" prices would be a predatory action. A case frequently alleged to be a predatory action involved Rockefeller's Standard Oil Company in the nineteenth century, when Standard's low prices in selected local markets were interpreted as devices to bankrupt smaller refiners. Would this be an intelligent tactic—that is, wealth maximizing—even if no law prohibited it?

22. You are a producer of computers, but to distribute them to the public you first sell them to a distributor who in turn retails them to the public, whose demand for the computer is given by the data in Table 11–1. The retail distributor may choose the reselling price to the public that is best for the distributor. As the producer, you have a uniform marginal cost of production of $4 each, regardless of how many you produce.

    a. Show that the price you should charge the distributor is about $12.50. How many will the distributor buy at that price, and what retail price will in turn be charged?

    b. Show that you, the distributor, and the public could be better off if you required the distributor to not charge the public over $13. According to the law a retail price limit is illegal as being presumably anticompetitive because it does not allow the distributor to decide what price to charge for what he or she has bought from you. Who loses because of that interpretation of the law? (The situation described in the example is faced by some newspaper publishers.)

    *c. Can you think of any of several other products for which this example helps to explain why some firms tend to be vertically integrated (that is, where a firm does manufacturing, distributing, and retailing)? (This is not the only reason for vertical integration.) The problem illustrated in this question is known as the problem of "successive monopoly."

23. Suppose you, the seller, have six units of a good available. At any price you ask of A you must let him buy all he wants, and you must permit B to have all she wants at the price you ask of B; but the price asked of A and B can be different.

Units Demanded			Marginal Revenue	
Price	A	B	A	B
$10	1	0	$10	0
9	2	0	8	0
8	3	0	6	0
7	4	0	4	0
6	5	1	2	6
5	6	2	0	4
4	7	3	−2	2
3	8	4	−4	0
2	9	5	−6	−2
1	10	6	−8	−4

    a. What price should you charge A, and what should you charge B, if you want to maximize your revenue?

    b. If you charge the same price to both buyers, what is your best price and revenue?

    c. Suppose you can produce this good at a cost of $2 for each unit you make. How many should you make, and what price should you charge to A and what to B in order to maximize your net earnings? How many will A buy, and how many will B buy? What will be your net earnings?

    *d. Construct an example of *multipart pricing* with *different sets* of prices to each buyer, so as to get still more revenue than with the preceding policy. Why do you think this kind of multipart plus discriminatory pricing is relatively uncommon? Can you give some examples of it? (Hint: Check the water, telephone, gas, and electric rates charged in your community; what prevents new sellers or customers from reselling to each other in all these cases?)

*24. You invent a photocopy machine. You know that the average cost of making the machine is $1000 and that its operating costs are 1¢ each time the machine is used. You could sell the machine for, say, $2000, letting users pay the 1¢ operating costs. On the other hand, if you can discriminate among customers, and charge some a higher price than others, you can make still more money. In order to make discriminatory pricing effective, you must not sell machines to the users, for they could then resell them from the "low-priced" to the "higher-priced" customers and undermine your attempt to get more revenue. Suppose, however, you rent the machine to each user at a uniform fee but charge 3¢ each time the machine makes a photocopy.

    a. Would that achieve your purpose? Explain.

    b. Selling at different prices is illegal; 3¢ per copy is legal. Why?

    c. Is this kind of "discrimination" good?

Chapter 12
Competition among the Few

Coalitions, Collusion, Cartels, and Firms: An Exercise in Names

If the owners of the entire supply of resources used in the making of a product could agree to restrict the output of the product, they would reap greater income. For reasons we examined in Chapter 9, this increase in income is called *monopoly rent*. (Recall the example, in Chapter 11, of the ten water sellers: Each sold one gallon of water at a price of $1 a gallon; but each would be made wealthier by cutting output in half and selling only half a gallon at $5 a gallon. Without that agreement among all suppliers of the good there would be no monopoly rent, because each independent seller would heed only its own marginal revenue in determining its output, and therefore price, and would ignore the *industry's* marginal revenue.)

The terminology can be confusing. An agreement or coalition that results in smaller output, lower quality, or higher prices is commonly called a *collusion* or *cartel*. Both terms are pejorative: They express a normative judgment that such a coalition is improper, "antisocial," or "anticompetitive." That normative judgment is based on the effect of a cartel: Because the colluding suppliers' gains through transfer of income to them are less than the loss to the rest of society, the sum of total personal use values over the entire number of consumers and producers is reduced. However, a coalition that results in a better product or lower price, thus yielding a gain to both consumers and producers—a net social gain—is deemed desirable by our social standards and laws. Such a coalition is not called a collusion or cartel, but is instead often called a *firm*. You should be alert, then, to distinguish terms that reflect economic analysis and those that express normative judgments.

We now investigate some conditions that affect the viability of effective collusions or cartels. We say "effective" because undoubtedly many attempts to create productive cartels don't succeed at all.

Collusion among Producers

Producers who eliminate competition in the open market do not eliminate competition itself. It simply relocates and changes form. Collusion, for example, causes competition to shift from the marketplace to the conference tables of the firms, where it must be decided how the potential gain will be divided among the firms of the cartel, and how cheating can be prevented and loopholes in the agreement identified and closed. (And, of course, at the conference table, each firm looks for other ways of cheating and undiscovered loopholes that it may use.) Thus, whether a proposed cartel is open or secret, it faces formidable hazards, even aside from the consequences of violating any legal prohibitions. We look at several problems of forming an effective cartel.

1. Who are the significant potential suppliers? Are their products and services identical? Are there other goods or services sufficiently similar to yours that some degree of substitution can occur if you raise your prices? For example, in trying to organize doctors, what would you do about interns, chiropractors, registered nurses, druggists, dentists, and drug companies? All are substitutes for some medical service. If all doctors raise their fees, people will seek more aid from their druggists and use self-prescribed drugs. Or if you are a steel producer, what would you do about suppliers of aluminum, brass, plastics, wood, and concrete, all of which are to some extent substitutes? And what about firms that make steel for their own use and could expand and sell steel to other steel users? Firms that are not brought into the collusion will profit and grow under the cartel members' umbrella of higher price and restricted output. Actual or potential outsiders can nullify, or cancel the effects of, the collusion.

2. Suppose, however, you decide not to include all the suppliers in your industry in your cartel. Say you include only the 10 major steel companies. Of the more than 1000 companies producing thousands of kinds of steel in the United States, these 10 produce 90% of the total output. The rest, even including new entrants, will not grow rapidly enough to upset your plan too quickly, or so you hope. Your problems are not solved, for not even all of the 10 participants will agree about the best price or what their share of sales should be. That depends on the relationship of cost to output in each firm, the elasticity of demand, and each firm's estimates of its prospects for growth. Lower prices are more advantageous to lower-cost firms with prospects of growth than to higher-cost, smaller-output firms. Many explorations of and attempts at collusion never pass this obstacle. And we haven't even mentioned the foreign producers who sell steel in the United States.

3. Controlling competition in *all* its forms is prohibitively expensive. Each cartel member will be alert to the gains from those forms of competition that are not controlled by the cartel, for example, quality, delivery charges, warranty and repair services, credit, allowances on turn-ins, and trial and refund privileges. Even when a federal regulatory agency enforced the former U.S. domestic airline cartel, there was inadequate control of competition in the quality of airline attendants, the quality and types of service, types of planes, and other fringe benefits to passengers. Unless such kinds of competition are controlled by some enforcement technique, the potential gains from a cartel will be dissipated.

4. Finding and using secret competitive tactics, or tactics no one thought to prohibit, is potentially very profitable. The probability of a firm's success in this is inversely related to the cartel's ability to control and standardize products and fringe services. In any event, there must be some technique available for enforcing the output and performance agreement, and for punishing violators. Some forms of cheating could be controlled if all the colluding members pooled their output and sold it through a single central sales agency, then split the proceeds (which is essentially how the lemon, milk, and raisin cartels—to name but three—work effectively). An alternative safeguard would be to assign each buyer to one seller. This would reduce the incentive for price cutting—though it would not entirely eliminate it, for by cutting prices you would enable your customer to undersell its competitors, thereby increasing your customer's volume of sales and hence the demand for your goods; in this way you indirectly take business from your fellow conspirators.

5. Within the cartel there will be competition among firms over the shares of sales allotted each member. Younger, growing firms will want an *increasing* share.

6. If expanding or creating new production facilities requires large investments, potential new competitors will be dissuaded from quickly entering the business. This fact would appear to make effective collusion more likely, but there is a counterforce. If existing, colluding firms also have such expensive facilities, and if new entrants do appear, the colluders will lose their own large investment value—and this loss of value will continue after the collusion has ended.

These inherent contradictions and hazards to effective collusion explain why many exploratory attempts are never carried through and why many actual collusions never become effective. Proposals are discussed and agreements reached, only to be left ineffective by these hard, competitive realities.[1]

THE MYTH OF THE OPEC CARTEL

Let us apply these principles to investigate what is often alleged to be the most effective cartel of all: the Organization of Petroleum Exporting Countries (OPEC). In the process we will see that the supposition that OPEC is a cartel is very weak, and that instead OPEC exemplifies an industrial situation in which there is a *dominant firm*.

In 1973 OPEC was supposed to have reduced its oil output to obtain higher prices. The largest producer, Saudi Arabia, cut its output and raised its prices. At the same time, all the other suppliers also took advantage of the higher prices. The smaller sellers expanded their output but not enough to offset Saudi Arabia's reduction. (Obviously, Saudi Arabia was not willing to cut its output to the point where prices would be as high as the smaller producers wanted them to be.)

OPEC did satisfy one essential condition of an effective cartel agreement: Its members controlled enough of the *resources capable of producing this good* to raise its price. It was not possible to find (let alone produce) sufficiently large amounts of petroleum to quick-

---

[1]A favorable occasion for collusion, in open markets, is that of sales to government agencies through sealed bids. Accusations of collusion made against sellers of meat, flour, water, pipe, steel, office furniture, cement, milk, and banking services have all involved such sales. The government solicits bids from several sellers and opens them all at one time. No rebidding is allowed (in sharp contrast to, say, the purchase of a car by a private party who solicits bids from various sellers and gives each a chance to undercut the others). If there is collusion, and if any colluding sellers do not bid as agreed, the others will find out immediately because all bids are revealed. It does not seem accidental that most cases of established effective collusion have been on sales to government agencies or government-regulated public utilities selling through sealed bids.

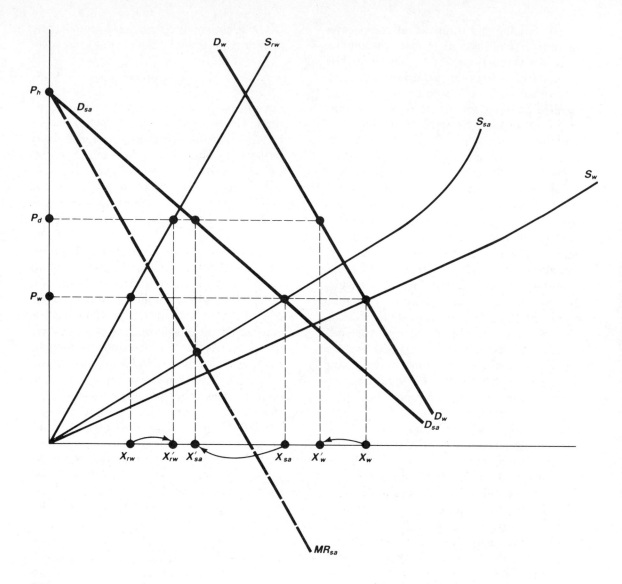

Figure 12-1.

THE PRICE AND OUTPUT EFFECTS
OF A DOMINANT FIRM

If one producer—here Saudi Arabia—holds a dominant
share of the actual and potential facilities for producing
some good—here petroleum—it may act as a price
taker and sell whatever amount the world demands at
the prevailing market price. In doing so Saudi Arabia
would be ignoring the effects of its actions on the world
price of oil, P_W, at the intersection of the world demand
and supply curves D_W and S_W. Saudi Arabia would be
supplying X_{sa} and the rest of the world's smaller

producers would be supplying X_{rw}. However, Saudi Arabia
may recognize that it could set a price, P_d, and let the
rest of the world's smaller producers supply whatever
amount, S_{rw}, they can produce profitably at that price.
The unfulfilled amount demanded by consumers is then
supplied by the dominant firm. The world demand is
shown as D_W. At any price the amount supplied by the
smaller producers, S_{rw}, is subtracted from the world
demand, D_W, leaving a demand, D_{sa}, facing the dominant
firm, Saudi Arabia. The wealth-maximizing price for Saudi
Arabia is P_d, that price at which its marginal revenue
curve, MR_{sa}, crosses its marginal cost of producing oil,
S_{sa}. At P_d the world demands the amount X'_w, of which
X'_{sa} is supplied by Saudi Arabia and the rest, X'_{rw}, is

ly fill the gap. In contrast, for many other goods such as steel, drugs, or automobiles, new facilities could be created quickly enough.

The Dominant Firm Situation OPEC is not a cartel because only one producer, Saudi Arabia, cut its output to raise prices. There is no evidence that it made any agreement to cut output only on the condition the others also do so. The evidence is rather that Saudi Arabia decided alone to cut output, although the other oil suppliers also reaped the benefits of a higher price and a larger output. Saudi Arabia controls enough of the existing *and potential* sources of oil to reap a benefit from a higher price, despite producing less. Such a situation is often the result of there being a **dominant firm** rather than a cartel. But such a firm must control not only the current supply but also the *sources of potential expansion in the near future.*

A diagrammatic analysis using demand and supply curves will help make the analysis coherent. In Figure 12–1, D_w is the world demand for oil and S_w is the world supply, which is the sum of the supplies from Saudi Arabia, S_{sa}, and from the rest of the world, S_{rw}. Notice that the Saudi Arabian supply is a large portion of the total supply. This assumption is important.

The world market price of oil, P_w, is that price at which the amount demanded equals the amount supplied, that is, where the world demand and world supply lines D_w and S_w intersect. Let us assume that this is the initial condition, the one in effect before

1973. Suppose that at that time the Saudi Arabian princes contemplate their own marginal revenue at that output. They deduce their marginal revenue from their demand curve by noting how much of their oil would be demanded at each possible world price. Figure 12–1 shows how to define the demand for Saudi Arabian oil. At each possible price, subtract from the world's amount demanded the amount supplied by the non-Saudi portion of the world. What remains is the amount that the non-Saudi suppliers could not supply: It is the amount that would be demanded from Saudi Arabia, and in Figure 12–1 it is the line D_{sa}. That amount equals the horizontal distances between the world demand, D_w, and the supply from the rest of the world, S_{rw}. For example, if the price were as high as P_h, all the world demand would be provided by the other suppliers and none by Saudi Arabia. At lower prices, more will be demanded but less will be supplied by the rest of the world, so some will be demanded from Saudi Arabia. Thus does the demand for Saudi Arabian oil depend on world demand and non–Saudi Arabian supply.

Now we ask: What is the marginal revenue curve to Saudi Arabia? Because the demand for its oil slopes downward, its marginal revenue, the line MR_{sa} in Figure 12–1, is less than price. At any amount supplied by Saudi Arabia, the height of that marginal revenue line shows how much money Saudi Arabia gets by producing one more barrel (or forsakes by producing one less).

What should Saudi Arabia do if it were initially selling in a market at which the price was P_w? At that price and output, X_{sa}, Saudi Arabia would have a marginal revenue far below its marginal cost and possibly even negative, as suggested in the diagram. By cutting its output it would avoid sales of oil at a marginal cost that exceeds its low marginal revenue. And it would increase its profits by ceasing to produce more than its wealth-maximizing output, X'_{sa}, which is the

supplied by the rest of the world. This price would maximize Saudi Arabia's profits even though, being the dominant firm, it supplies less, X'_{sa}, than before, X_{sa}, at the lower price, P_w. The other producers all expand from X_{rw} to X'_{rw} and also enjoy higher prices than before. Although the rest of the world's suppliers have increased output, that new world price, P_d, is sustained because of the dominant firm's reduction of output. And total output, from all suppliers, is smaller, now being X'_w instead of X_w.

intersection of its marginal revenue line, MR_{sa}, and its marginal cost of producing oil. That implies a higher price, P_d.

So it is plausible that in 1973 Saudi Arabia, recognizing itself to be the dominant present and potential future supplier, saw also that its marginal revenue was low. It knew that because of its dominant position it could sell less to get a higher price and higher total revenue. Other supplying countries couldn't expand enough in response to the higher price to offset Saudi Arabia's effects. Thus, Figure 12–1 describes the logic of the *dominant firm* situation. Is it an accurate story of what happened? No one knows.

Remember, some of the members of OPEC are at swords' points. At OPEC meetings the smaller suppliers always agitate for higher prices. They want Saudi Arabia to cut output more so that their unchanged output will get still higher prices. But Saudi Arabia has already set its output, and hence its price, to maximize its *own* earnings: Further cuts in output and increases in price would reduce its income. You can see now why Saudi Arabia can pose as the "moderate" seeking to avoid "excessively higher prices" to "protect the consumer nations" against the desires of the "hawks," or "anti-consumers." Those who attribute benevolent motives to Saudi Arabia simply miss the point that it is in Saudi Arabia's *economic* self-interest to be more "moderate" than the other producers.

NEITHER DOMINANT FIRM NOR CARTEL?

If the preceding analysis is not enough to make you doubt that OPEC is a *cartel*, another line of analysis may thoroughly undermine your confidence in knowing with certainty why oil prices rose so much in the early 1970s. When the Persian Gulf oil fields were first explored, about 50 years ago, the exploring companies were granted 50-year concessions: During that time they could produce and sell all the oil they extracted if they paid a royalty to the granting governments. Because no one knew what other arrangements would be made after expiration of the 50-year concessions, the oil companies had an incentive to extract oil more rapidly than if they owned the underground oil, because they would lose the rights to any unextracted oil after 1980 (*if* there were no political revolutions sooner, as there were). The absence of secure property rights reduced the incentive to conserve for the future, and incentives for overly rapid extraction were made even stronger when, in the 1950s, the Iranian government prematurely terminated its agreement, increasing the likelihood that other Middle Eastern governments would do so as well. Thus, in the 1960s more crude oil was extracted, and at lower prices to consumers, than if the oil companies had secure rights to *future* extracted oil. The governments that had granted the oil concessions saw that such rapid extraction was reducing the stores of underground oil and, responding to the incentive to conserve oil for higher future values, terminated the contracts. The reduced output of oil appears to be what caused the price to rise in the early 1970s. These events did more than reaffirm control of output by owners instead of by others not acting in the owners' interests, as the following analysis demonstrates.

Many have argued that in the years 1970 to 1973 the governments in those nations possessing significant stocks of underground oil began to be aware of the following developments: The rate of exploration for oil had fallen sharply from what it had been in earlier decades; the rate of successful explorations had also fallen; and as the wealth of the developing nations was increasing, so was their demand for gasoline and petroleum products. Suddenly the future promised to be quite different from what had formerly been expected. In particular, this revised perception of the future implied a substantially higher *fu-*

ture value of oil than had been anticipated before 1970.

If you owned an oil well and you saw the future value of oil being revised significantly upward, what would you do if you had been allowing someone else to pump your oil at an unrestricted rate? If you kept the oil in the ground, it could be sold later at a much higher price than formerly anticipated. The 1970 price of about $3 a barrel was lower than the newly anticipated future price discounted to a *present value* by the compounded rate of interest. (Remember what the principles of capital value say about the relationship of present to future values.) With a *real* interest rate (that is, one in the absence of inflation) of about 3%, oil worth $3 in 1970 would be pumped out only if the price in 1980 were not expected to have risen by more than 3% per year compounded for 10 years—that is, about $4 (= $3 × 1.34).

Suppose that in the early 1970s people began to believe that the future value of oil (disregarding inflation) would be higher than the formerly anticipated $4 1980 value and might be as high as, say, $15 (in fact, it turned out to be $30). Then the price of oil should have jumped in about 1972 to approximately $11 (= $15/1.34). In this analysis, that jump in price would have occurred not because of a cartel or a dominant firm situation, but because the world began to perceive a new future. The new, higher price forced consumers to cease consuming oil as if it would remain cheap and plentiful in the future, and to conserve more for the revised, higher-valued future uses. Our analysis is not affected in the slightest by the fact that the owners of the oil were Arabians and were opposed to Israel and to recent military actions in which it was involved, or that they also were made much richer by the new outputs and prices.

EVIDENCE OF A CARTEL

So we leave you with a conundrum. What is the most valid explanation of the steep rise in oil prices in the early 1970s? Is OPEC a cartel, as it is commonly thought to be? Or does that common perception mask a dominant firm situation? Or does it mask instead a situation resulting from the oil-producing nations' simultaneously realizing that future oil values had risen and resuming control of their property to reduce output and raise prices?

That the prices of several firms in an industry behave simultaneously in the same way, or that one firm shows price leadership, is evidence neither for nor against the existence of collusive agreements. What *is* evidence is the existence of costly enforcement techniques: The costs incurred to enforce restrictions and prohibitions are evidence that a collusion is sufficiently effective to make it worth those costs of enforcement. The techniques of enforcement can take various forms. There may be restrictions on new investments by colluding firms and penalties for noncompliance. Or members of an industry may police themselves or submit to regulation by an industry association; in either case they may also be subject to state laws or state-enforced standards. Members who do not comply are denied the right to do business, such as by revocation of licenses or special privileges for "unethical" behavior.

But strangely enough, in some circumstances each of these techniques assures consumers better service, by keeping some firms from a "free ride" on the prepurchase, useful investments of *other* suppliers of the good, thereby destroying the incentive of those other suppliers to make the useful investment in the first place.

A strong implication of the foregoing is that an agreement would be most effectively formulated and enforced by an organization, membership in which is a prerequisite for investing in the industry. The organization may provide special advantages, such as qualifying its members for government subsidies or tax favors; pooling patent rights; conferring rights to do business with the government; exempting members from strikes by unions; controlling the entry of newcomers by licensing policies; or protecting investments in prepurchase service. For example, the American Medical Association gives its members sufficient privileges (such as access to certified surgical hospitals) to enforce its prohibition of certain types of competition.

Similarly, from the turn of the century up until World War II, business firms in Germany were compelled by the state to belong to chambers of commerce as a condition of the right to engage in business. Prohibitions of types of market competition could be enforced by expelling any firm in violation from the chamber, and thus from the market. It is no wonder that in those years Germany had many effective cartels. In Switzerland this arrangement was used by Swiss watchmakers before the coming of the electronic watch.

An alternative to forming a cartel is to get laws passed to regulate the industry in the "public interest," to eliminate quackery, shoddy merchandising, dangerous products, or disorderly pricing. In administering such laws the regulatory agency enforces what is essentially cartel behavior. Examples of such agencies are the Securities and Exchange Commission, the Interstate Commerce Commission, the Federal Communications Commission, the Civil Aeronautics Board, the Food and Drug Administration, the National Labor Relations Board, the U.S. Department of Agriculture, state liquor control boards, and public utility commissions. In the next chapter, some effects of these agencies are examined in detail.

MERGERS

Another kind of action by firms that superficially appears to be an ideal vehicle for collusive action is the **merger**, whereby two or more firms become joined under one owner-ship. The idea is simply to merge with your rivals into one big firm and then control output to increase profit, which is then divided among the merged firms. Such a tactic must first surmount the problem of deciding who pays how much to whom in the merger agreement. But supposing this can be resolved, is the merger worthwhile? The most serious impediment to its effectiveness is the ability of other producers to create new supplies. If merged firms reduce output and try to raise prices, other firms will enter the industry. The merged firms may make more money for a few years, but the entrance of new firms assures that later earnings will be smaller than otherwise. If this consequence is foreseen, the immediate net effect may be a *loss of present wealth*, a lower value of the common stock.

There is at least one way to test whether mergers have effects similar to those of cartels, or have instead increased consumer benefits: Compare what happens to the stock values of the merged firms with what happens to those of the unmerged, competing firms. If the merged firms act as a cartel, the unmerged firms reap benefits under the umbrella of higher prices. If the merger instead improves the quality of the product or results in lower costs and lower prices, then the stock price of each merged firm should rise relative to those of other firms in that industry. The evidence that has been collected seems to indicate that the latter has happened: As judged by their effects on stock prices, mergers seem on average to have reduced costs and improved services.

Mergers can be profitable because they make better operation of a marginal firm possible or bring it superior management. Mergers and takeovers—by stock purchases, exchange of stock, or direct purchases of assets—often represent competition among managers and investor-entrepreneurs for control of firms that can be improved.

We started this chapter by examining cartels—in which joint coordinated controls or restraints are used to restrain market competition among a group of suppliers. We also examined the dominant firm situation in which no joint coordinated controls are involved, and we briefly discussed mergers. We now consider *oligopolies*.

Oligopolies

Our analysis in earlier chapters of how firms respond to market forces assumed first that each firm was a price taker, taking the market price as given by outside forces. We then introduced situations in which the firm did not have an automatically given market price for its products. Instead it had to search for its best price. That firm was called a price searcher. It had a demand schedule facing it rather than a market price. It had to ascertain and set the best price in the face of that demand schedule. We also assumed the firm would seek the best price along that demand schedule—its wealth-maximizing price. But in finding that price, the firm acted as if its actions would not significantly and directly affect the output or demand facing other firms. Or, if the actions of other firms were affected, there was not sufficient feedback to make our first firm significantly alter its demand schedule. The firm was assumed to be relatively independent of any feedback caused by effects of its actions on other firms. In many situations, however, what one firm does will affect the behavior of other firms enough that the first will anticipate that response in making its initial decision. A significant interdependence may exist. If firm A were to raise its price, firm B might respond with a price or output change that would affect the profitability of firm A's initial contemplated action. If so, what would be firm A's initial action? What will such recognized and significant interdependence do to the firms' pricing and output response to consumer demands? Will the preceding basic principles derived from the price tak-

ers' and the price searchers' situations still hold? Such a situation is an **oligopoly**—each firm's action is influenced by the anticipated response of other firms. This can happen when a relatively small number of firms selling the same goods affect one another.

However, it is important not to confuse this with another phenomenon that superficially appears similar, one called *price leadership. Price leader* is the name attached to whichever firm is the first to reliably detect a change in demand or supply conditions that implies a higher or lower sustainable market price. Thus, if demand should increase for the kind of product made by several firms, the market price will have to be higher to ration the amount supplied and to maintain a higher rate of output. But who will be the first seller to recognize that a changed rate of sales, for example, reflects a persisting rather than temporary increase? If you recall our earlier example of the meat market (Chapter 4), a persisting changed demand was finally verified at the general cattle auction. In some industries with only a few firms, there is no general auction market to reveal changed demands so clearly. When sales increase, sellers wonder whether the increase is temporary or persisting. Which will be the first and surest to detect a real persisting change and not be misled by a passing fluctuation? Which seller will the other sellers regard as the one with the most reliable information to detect such changes earlier and more surely? This is not a case in which the firm that is more informed is worrying about the response of the other firms, as in an oligopoly. The firm is instead trying to ascertain whether market conditions of demand or supply have changed in a lasting manner, so that a new market-clearing price is called for, whether or not other firms realize that yet. Any delay in adjusting price or output to a persisting change in demand or supply will increase costs to firms trying to quickly restore depleted inventories, to buyers suddenly facing outages and failure of supply, or to suppliers finding inventories getting too large because of continued overproduction when demand has not, in fact, increased. There is no point delaying one's response to a known, long-lasting change in demand or supply conditions. On the other hand, an adjustment of price to every slight deviation in sales rates or inventory depletions will, if the changes are really temporary, lead to incorrect prices as misleading signals about new persisting values and output rates and, consequently, what costs are worth incurring in producing the good.

All sellers and buyers desire quick information about exactly what changes (temporary or persisting) in demand or supply conditions have occurred. Who is most likely to keep best informed and have the greatest incentive to correctly detect those conditions? The bigger a firm is, the more it has to gain by detecting these changes quickly. Also, the bigger it is relative to total sales of other firms, the more likely its observed sales rate will be a true measure of what is happening in general. Thus, one would expect the biggest firm to be the leader in knowledge and in the incentive to detect and respond to changed conditions. It will be known as the price leader. But this is far different from implying that this firm is selling at a collusive price. The analogy of a faster, stronger hound in a pack of hounds chasing a fox is appropriate. It will be the first, not in directing where the fox will go, but in following the fox and thus leading all the other dogs. That is a price leader—the first and most reliable respondent to market conditions. A firm that leads a group of firms into a collusion or cartel is in a different situation.

Now we know that what is often called price leadership does not necessarily involve any collusion, tacit or explicit, and may not be at all pertinent to oligopolistic interdependence. But we return to the question of what happens in oligopolistic situations and how

we know one when it is seen. The answers to both these questions are not satisfactory, since not much is known. Scores of alternative models or possibilities have been conjectured by economists, but none have been well validated. This does not mean that no oligopolies have been identified. It means instead that we just don't know whether oligopolistic situations yield results significantly different from the ordinary price taker, price searcher, or dominant firm situations. Lots of people have strong opinions based mostly on personal impressions rather than on reliable evidence.

The Law and Market Competition

The Sherman Antitrust Act of 1890 prohibited "combinations or conspiracies to restrain trade" and "monopolizing." Because the act did not define "monopoly" or "restraint of trade," it was left to the U.S. Supreme Court to interpret them. A meaningful start was made in the *United States* v. *Addyston Steel Pipe* decision in 1899. The Court, recognizing that contracts, by definition, constrain each party to do certain things and restrain them from doing others, stated that so-called restraints were not necessarily in and of themselves undesirable: Restraints could, and often do, have desirable effects. The Court said that restraints were lawful if they were ancillary restraints to the main purpose of lawful business contracts or were necessary to protect one of the parties' contractual rights. For example, a contractual clause between two partners restraining one partner from doing business separately in the same business would be a legitimate restraint. Since 1899, the courts have often looked for the *reason* for contractual restraints. They have not declared any restraint to be illegal *per se* without first ascertaining its purpose and effect. This criterion became known as the "rule of reason": That is, the restraint was judged according to the reasons for it and whether it was "socially useful" in its effects.

Nevertheless, the courts—state, federal, district, and appellate—spawned an enormous body of interpretations and judgments without great uniformity or consistency. Almost any term in a contract that was alleged in one decision to be "monopolistic" or "anticompetitive," and thus illegal, has been found in another decision to be legal. The Supreme Court has tried to bring some order to the application of antitrust law by resolving the inconsistencies and ambiguities among the different courts and cases. But so far the task is beyond its capabilities. In fact, the task is practically impossible: Not enough is known about certain business practices, contractual clauses, and methods of organizing joint cooperative efforts to discern in each case exactly what their effects are. The sophistication of economic analysis is not yet up to that task.

For example, courts have interpreted monopolizing to mean the act of "raising prices or excluding competition," or the "power to control prices and exclude competition." A good test of how well you have learned the elementary principles of economics is how quickly and thoroughly you can see the ambiguity in those words. Raising *whose* prices? Yours or other sellers'? Raising them above what "right" level? Does producing a better product and getting a higher price mean you are *controlling* its price? What determines what the price can be? Does "exclude competition" include doing so well that some competitors go out of business? A producer's doing a better job induces customers to exclude less satisfying competitors, and that is precisely what competition is supposed to do. These judicial pronouncements provide no better guide as to what acts would get one convicted for the crimes of "monopolizing" or "restraining trade" than would legislation that declared all acts offensive to the "public interest" to be felonies.

In another effort to reduce ambiguity, the Clayton Antitrust Act (1914) prohibited both "price discrimination" and mergers that "reduce competition" (but exempted labor unions, insurance companies, and farmers from antimonopoly laws). In response to complaints by some businesspersons against competitors, the 1914 Federal Trade Commission Act was passed; it declared some marketing tactics illegal and created the Federal Trade Commission (FTC) to administer it and the Clayton Antitrust Act. The FTC was to investigate businesses and stop "illegal" or "unfair" practices by issuing "cease and desist" orders. Not surprisingly, what is and is not an "unfair" practice cannot reliably be determined in advance by anyone in business or by anyone else. As we have already seen, price discrimination, especially if sporadic or the result of sellers' groping for the new, competitive prices, can increase the efficiency of resource use.

Mergers have also come under attack, despite the evidence that many mergers have enhanced the economic efficiency of firms in the market, with benefit to consumers and producers. The practical problem is to find ways of knowing which merged firms will have the effects of a cartel. The judicial decisions and commission actions show little evidence of economic understanding, in part because there is so little validated economic analysis from which to make reliable inferences.

Common Misinterpretations of Modern Business Actions

A few misinterpretations of business activity are sufficiently common and popular to deserve evaluation.

ARBITRARY ADMINISTRATION OF PRICES

A modern myth has grown up about modern markets, because when the prices of each seller in an industry change, they change at about the same time, and the largest firm usually seems to be a price leader, that is, the first to change the price. These facts have been used to support the myth that big firms administer or set prices by some undefined process sometimes called "tacit collusion" or "shared monopoly," to the harm of consumers, who must be protected by government intervention. U.S. Steel, General Motors, and the large drug companies are said to set their prices by administrative decision. And so they do, just as Alcoa announces the price of its aluminum and RCA decides the price of its radios and television sets. But what determines those prices and whether they will stick?

As we know, the price searcher cannot set its price at will, if wealth maximizing is the goal, for too high a price will mean *less* wealth. General Motors could raise the price of its cars by producing fewer. Other producers would gleefully fill the void, and GM stockholders and employees would lose. The ability to temporarily raise the price should not be confused with the incentive to do so, or with the permanent ability to do so without losing wealth.

Describing sellers as those who use their "market power" to "set prices" or who "search for the wealth-maximizing price" in the light of market demand, is a matter of semantics. Call prices "monopolist-administered" if you want to suggest that the seller is a selfish, noncompeting, economic royalist. Otherwise, call them "market-revealed, demand and supply–determined prices." Neither self-restraint nor concern for interests of other people determines prices. It is the effect on one's own wealth that restrains.

All prices are administered in the sense that each person decides at what price to sell *in light of the market demand*. Sellers may appear to be colluding because they often act similarly, but they do so in fact simply because they are all subject to similar market forces.

SIZE, CONCENTRATION, AND PROFITS: SALES OR RESOURCES?

Another misunderstanding of the market is the notion that big firms make bigger profits because they are big, rather than that firms with better products or lower costs become big firms. Bigness itself does not increase the probability of making profits. General Motors has earned profits in the capital-value sense during many years and has had losses during many years. But some very large firms have lost wealth in many years (Braniff, Singer, Ward's), and some very small firms have had spectacular growth (Hewlett-Packard, Texas Instruments, Xerox, Southwest Airlines).

Related to this notion that size and profits are related is the notion that concentration of an industry in a few firms increases profits; for example, if 90% of an industry's sales are made by, say, the four largest firms, rather than, say, 20 firms, industry profits are alleged to be increased. The conclusion is then suggested that the more concentrated the industry and the more effectively prices are kept up, possibly by advertising, collusion, and barriers to entry, the greater are profits—not a very sound conclusion.[2]

First, those concentrated sellers do not necessarily own the same large percentage of resources capable of producing those products. One income tax firm, H & R Block, does about 40% of the income tax preparations that are done commercially, yet it has an insignificantly small fraction of the resources that could quickly provide those services if it should raise its price above its competitors' costs. Block's high earnings come from superior or lower-cost service, not from

---

[2]In the photocopy business, Xerox has made enormous profits. It and a couple of other copier manufacturers have a very large share of the market. (But have they a large share and large profits because they developed superior products? Unusually superior products can explain several cases of high concentration and large profits.)

control of supply. Having a large fraction of *sales* of a product or service should not be confused with having a large fraction of the input *resources*.

If collusion and restrictions on the entry of new firms were a source of higher profit rates, they should be enjoyed by every firm in the industry, the smallest as well as the largest, for all firms would benefit from the collusive actions. What are the facts? The best available evidence (which supplements earlier studies that were less detailed, comprehensive, or rigorous) is that in any industry the largest firms have lower operating costs and are more profitable than the smaller firms, no matter what the degree of concentration in that industry. That is what one would expect if firms that supplied better products, or products at lower cost, *grew* in size and became the major suppliers. Concentration is the result of growth of superior, lower-cost firms.

Some products such as automobiles, electric turbine generators, computers, and airplanes are much cheaper to make, distribute, and service in a volume that is a large percentage of the market demand. That the same industries in different countries tend to be the concentrated industries suggests that larger firms are more appropriate for certain types of activity, rather than that some superior firms become abnormally large.

It is often suggested that because a few large corporations produce a large share of the U.S. output, competition must be weaker than it used to be, and consumers have a smaller range of purchase options. That reasoning is false. Consumers now have *more* alternative suppliers: If there were 1000 small towns and 10 sellers in each town, there would be 10,000 different business firms, but each buyer would have only the 10 in his or her town from which to choose. With cheaper and faster transportation and communication, the total number of business firms could be cut to, say, 40 firms. If each firm and consumer were able to trade in half of all the

markets, each buyer would now face, on average, 20 possible sellers. Transportation and communication have so improved that today the average consumer undoubtedly has more options from more suppliers than the consumer did a few decades ago. What counts is not the number of firms in the whole economy but the number of firms seeking to serve a consumer.

Perhaps one of the most interesting examples is provided by the U.S. automobile industry. For the past 75 years, the number of suppliers of automobiles to the American consumer has been virtually constant at about 10. The first to be large, Ford, was outgrown by General Motors in the 1920s. Ford had been the first to standardize a few models designed for the mass consumer, with no custom features to appeal to a smaller class of buyers. Ford enabled the consumer to reap the advantages of a large *volume*, but large volumes prevent a large number of such large producers. From the 1920s onward, three or four mass-production suppliers were sufficient to provide about 75% of the cars demanded by the American public, who preferred the lower price of more standardized cars to the higher prices of more specialized, distinctive cars.

The number of producers was large only during two transient intervals: The first was when automobiles were first produced and producers had not yet learned that consumers would prefer mass-produced, standardized cars at lower prices. That interval ended by the 1920s. The second began after World War II, when the government, which had created assembly facilities for war production, gave those facilities to new or smaller companies, such as Kaiser, Hudson, Packard, and Studebaker; these companies used the facilities to produce cars and sell them at prices that did not reflect the full costs of continued production. When the facilities wore out, the firms could not survive on that small-scale production.

In the past thirty years, as the world market for cars has increased, foreign mass producers such as the Japanese and Germans began to sell a standardized car in several countries, thereby obtaining the lower costs of large volume. By contrast, the French, English, and Italians were making more unusual, custom-type cars. As the costs of international shipping declined, the foreigners could produce at very large volume and sell in the United States at prices competitive with the American cars designed only for the domestic market. These new foreign suppliers to the United States reduced the number of American suppliers but increased the total number of suppliers to the American consumer. That there are thus more suppliers in the 1980s can be explained by the high *international volumes* of production, which imply lower costs per unit.

ABSENCE OF PRICE COMPETITION?

It has commonly been argued that an *oligopoly*—an industry, remember, of a very few interdependent sellers—is characterized by *weak price competition* or by *tacit collusion* among sellers. Although the two terms have never been clearly defined, the context suggests that any one seller is aware that if one firm cuts its price, others will quickly match it, and everyone's profits will take a beating. So instead, each firm holds its price at some "reasonable" level.

You must not confuse what makes those few sellers charge nearly the same price with what determines its *level*. A common price can mean simply that it is not profitable to charge a lower, or a *higher*, price than other suppliers are charging. A nearly identical price—or indeed an identical price—among all sellers could as well have been arrived at through independent competition as through a collusive pact. Hence it is not useful evidence of either.

One reason why the number of firms is thought to be inversely related to the degree of price and quality competitiveness is that in some industries the one major firm has a patent or is a government-regulated public utility (such as water, power, taxis, railroads) protected by law from the entry of other firms. In these cases the absence of market competition is incorrectly attributed to the *fewness* of firms. The correct interpretation is that the existing firm is protected by law.

PRICE FIXING?

Some manufacturers set a price at which the retailer is supposed to sell. Often such a manufacturer is accused of "price fixing," of acting "monopolistically" or "anticompetitively" or in "restraint of trade." Whatever those undefined terms are supposed to mean, consider the following facts.

Consumers cannot always judge the quality of a good before they buy it. A new food-processing machine has to be demonstrated. A watch may have to be repaired, a computer may malfunction, an income tax preparer may overestimate your taxes. You won't know ahead of time, and you may not even know afterward. If a manufacturer's product is sold under one brand name but by many *independent retailers, each of whom provides prepurchase information or affects some relevant attributes of the product or service*, the manufacturer can induce retailers to provide that service only by preventing customers from using it for free. For example, say one retailer invests in providing customers the desired prepurchase information and quality-assuring services, such as by advising them on appropriate goods, maintaining a larger inventory for better selection, and the like. If other retailers could sell the good at a discount, consumers could use the first retailer's investment to learn about the good or to service it, regardless of where they bought it. Conscientious retailers would be unwilling to help customers learn about that manufacturer's product unless customers and other retailers could be prevented from that free use of the first retailer's investment.

What can the manufacturer do? First it can prohibit sales by discount houses. And it can permit a retail price sufficiently above wholesale costs and those of providing the customer service that the retailer foresees attractively large profit premiums as long as it sells that manufacturer's products. Now, notice the retailer's position. A manufacturer that detects a retailer failing to perform its obligations toward the manufacturer and customers can cease selling the product through that retailer, depriving the retailer of the present value of the premium stream. Dishonesty by the retailer costs him more than it is worth. Clearly such price fixing is to the public's advantage in obtaining prepurchase information about desirable goods.

It used to be argued that imposing minimum retail prices would be a mistake: A manufacturer should want retailers to charge the lowest possible price above the wholesale price. That argument was advanced several years ago, before economists realized that because retailers share duties with manufacturers in providing product quality and service for a product sold under a manufacturer's brand name (like McDonald's, Kentucky Fried Chicken, Coors), it would pay retailers to cheat on those duties for the sake of a short-lived gain. One way to achieve self-enforcing contracts with retailers is to offer that premium of the assured higher price, the present value of which would be lost by a retailer caught cheating. Thus, the higher retail price, or lower wholesale price, is the best means of enforcing the retailer's obligations. Therefore, manufacturers who set prices at which retailers can sell may be benefiting themselves, consumers, and retailers all at the same time.

We said *may* be benefiting, because not every case in which the retail price is fixed by a manufacturer has that effect. Nevertheless, the opposite charge, that price fixing is necessarily harmful to the consumer, is not correct—despite the fact that the U.S. Supreme Court declared price fixing *per se* illegal.

PRICE RIGIDITY

Many people, lawyers and members of congressional committees among them, argue that more concentration of the output of an industry in a few large firms raises prices or makes them less flexible. Evidence does not confirm the charges. Indeed, the number or size of firms in a price searcher industry shows no connection with the flexibility of prices.

What then is the evidence for the argument? The price of automobiles was reported to be stable and invariant because the list, or recommended, price announced by the automobile companies stayed unchanged throughout the model year. But one of the first things a person learns in shopping for a car is that the list price is, at most, the selling price only at the beginning of the model year. "Special" deals are offered to everyone who states the intention to shop around.

Although the catalogue prices of the thousands of varieties of steel may not change for many months, extensive studies of actual contract prices of steel show that the actual prices are highly variable from day to day. Discounts for cash payment vary; speed of delivery and special services vary from week to week; quantity discounts are common. A steel purchase is a complex transaction.[3]

---

[3]One factor that tends to relate high concentration in a few firms to price rigidity is a statistical artifact. The smaller the number of firms, each with equally flexible or frequent price changes, the fewer the *total number* of price changes; this *frequency* of recorded price changes merely reflects the number of *different* seller's prices to count. So one would *see* more changes if there were more sellers, even though the flexibility of any one seller's price is the same and is equally responsive to demand changes, regardless of degree of concentration.

The current assessment of the charge of price rigidity in concentrated industries was summarized by a president of the American Economic Association:

> Economists have long struggled to find a rational explanation for prolonged price rigidity, which is in general as inadvisable for profit-maximizing monopolists as it is impossible for "price taker" industries. Putting aside minor or special circumstances (the cost of a price change; the procedural delays in cartel or public regulation), they have failed to discover any such explanation. It appears that the real world has been equally remiss in supplying the phenomena they were seeking to explain.[4]

ADVERTISING: EDUCATION AND INFORMATION

In a world of specialization, communication is necessary and takes several forms: education, news, and advertising. Information of interest to only a specialized group is disseminated to that group. A new drug or TV set would be reported as news in a merchandiser's trade journal, such as *Variety, Electronic Products*, or *Textile World*. To convey information to a small number of unidentified persons within a large group is often more expensive, per person, than general advertising, even though in both cases there are many uninterested recipients. But such advertising is not wasteful unless there is a cheaper way to identify in advance the few to whom it should be directed.

Does advertising create differences in consumers' tastes to make consumers responsive to product differentiation? Although any one of us can be misled by advertising, it is another matter to show that consumers' tastes are formed by advertising or that people are misled more than if there were no advertising. Advertising is a means of communicating the existence of suppliers and the characteristics of goods. The greater our awareness of alternative products and their availability, prices, and characteristics, the less will sellers of inferior products retain customers. A seller's long-term survival rests on continued consumer acceptance—at least for products that continue under the same brand name. We therefore expect a positive correlation between a seller's *continued* advertising and quality of product and profitability: Good products make advertising more profitable.

We do not assume, however, that advertisers are any more honest than anyone else. They are less honest the less they are penalized by competitors for their dishonesty. The issues are: What reduces the costs of discovering more complete and accurate information, and what raises advertisers' losses if they are dishonest? To prevent fraud and theft we rely to some extent on legal actions but also on ourselves, purchasing locks, safes, walls, cash registers, fences, and grills, and hiring private security guards. We are wary of falsehoods and misleading statements. And we rely on the self-interest of one seller to unmask discreditable competitors, as one newspaper staff's self-interest in its incomes induces it to reveal any lies and errors published by its competitors. Advertising is a means of providing and testing information. Its usefulness does not rest solely on the notion of advertisers' honesty and goodwill but also on the opposite assumption that information disseminated by self-serving competitors renders dishonesty more discoverable and self-defeating, thereby helping the public discover the truth more cheaply and surely.

Advertising under Communal Property Rights Much of the criticism of advertising

---

[4]George J. Stigler, "Administered Prices and Oligopolistic Inflation," *The Journal of Business of the University of Chicago*, Vol. 35; No. 1 (January 1962), p. 8.

on radio and television, and of the programming itself, is really criticism of how television and radio programs are paid for, and of the politically imposed limit on the number of stations and on over-the-air and cable channels for pay-TV. Theaters rarely show commercials, because the paying patron guides the producers' decisions about what is desired. Pay-television gives viewers more program control. (Imagine what you would experience in movie theaters if theater owners could not charge admissions.) Specialized programs on pay-TV appeal to smaller, specialized groups because a minority could concentrate its "dollar votes" on preferred programs. If newspapers could not be sold, they would have even more advertising, as evidenced by the ratio of advertising to news in neighborhood throwaway newspapers.

Billboards and roadside advertising seem to run a close second to TV commercials as objects of criticism. (What about bumper stickers and advertising on cars, buses, and taxis?) However, it is not necessarily the advertising itself that is objected to, but rather its being thrust upon people in undesired places, circumstances, and ways. Roadside signs are a prime example. Because roads do not have private owners, there is less reward to anyone to meet the demand for roads without signs. It is simply technically impossible to bring the uses of such resources under the control of the normal market operation of the private-property system. And that, of course, is a reason for using nonmarket, political controls.

Advertising Controls or Censorship Fear that advertising will mislead people suggests that political authorities should decide what is permissible advertising. We do engage in censorship: We expose our children to censored ideas when we control what the schools teach them. The continued vitality of a culture requires that its customs, taboos, and values be passed on to succeeding generations. This censorship applies to children, and all parents have a large say in it. We censor our children's channels of communication *because* they are children—and this is the crux of the question whether the content of advertising should be subject to political control. Are we to apply to adults the reasons for censoring children's communications? Each of us may differ in our judgment. We may not like the way others behave when exposed to ideas and persuasive thoughts. But there is no dispute that political control of advertising content is political censorship, in the sense that it places prior restrictions on what can and cannot be publicly said. The dispute is how much censorship is good or bad. Economics has no answer.

Summary

1. The terms *collusion* and *cartel* are applied to coalitions of producers or sellers that have the effect of reducing the social sum of benefits to consumers and producers, because the gains to the producers are less than the losses to the consumers.

2. A cartel's effectiveness depends in part on the extent of its ability to prevent outside resources from competing against it. If no outside resources are capable of producing an effective substitute for the cartel's product, the cartel is more likely to be effective.

3. The *dominant firm* situation requires not only that one firm be the largest of current producers, but that it also have a sufficiently large portion of the present *and known future resources* for production of the good.

4. Use of the term *price fixing* to denote a manufacturer's setting the price of its good to the retailer can produce misunderstanding. By setting the price, a manufacturer can ensure that retailers provide services desired by consumers.

5. More highly concentrated industries—industries composed of or dominated by a few large firms—do not yield higher profits by virtue of the large firms' greater control or

larger share of the supply of productive resources. Instead, more efficient and therefore more profitable firms grow and tend to become major suppliers to a larger portion of the consumers, leading to greater concentration.

6. In some industries the technological characteristics of production, distribution, and product service favor economies of scale, leading to larger firms. Such concentrated industries do not imply that the market power of the larger firms brings larger profits.

7. From currently available evidence (little of it reliable), laws meant to broaden market competition and to restrain undesirable tactics by some sellers or buyers have had results which can be called counterproductive or beneficial according to one's political values.

8. Advertising is a means for lesser-known and well-known firms alike to make more widely known the availability of their wares and their characteristics. Advertising lowers consumers' costs of acquiring information about available goods and services and prices.

9. Communal property is sometimes used by advertisers, because there are no means of pricing and controlling the use of that property.

Questions

1. Suppose there are 10 identical producers of the good being sold in the market characterized by the total market demand given here. Each producer has *zero* costs of production for 20 units; no producer can produce any more.
   a. If all are selling in a price takers' market, what is the price and output?
   b. If all sellers could reach an effective agreement to restrict output and raise price, what price should they select?
   c. What will be each seller's output and revenue?
   d. How much would each seller gain by the effective agreement?

Demand Schedule

| | | Dollar Value of Daily Revenue | | |
Price	Quantity Demanded Daily	Total	Increment	Marginal (for Unit Increase in Quantity)
$1.00	56.52	$56.52	0	0
.95	62.25	59.14	$2.62	.46
.90	68.39	61.55	2.41	.41
.85	74.65	63.45	1.90	.30
.80	81.36	65.09	1.64	.24
.75	88.17	66.13	1.04	.15
.70	95.45	66.82	.69	.09
.67	100.00	67.00	.18	.03
.65	103.00	66.95	−.05	−.02
.60	110.67	66.40	−.43	−.05
.55	118.60	65.23	−1.17	−.15
.50	127.01	63.51	−1.72	−.18
.45	135.72	61.07	−2.44	−.28
.40	144.48	57.79	−3.28	−.37
.35	153.76	53.81	−3.98	−.43
.30	163.07	48.92	−4.98	−.53
.25	172.92	43.23	−5.69	−.58
.20	182.79	37.16	−6.07	−.61
.15	193.21	28.98	−8.18	−.78
.10	203.92	20.39	−8.59	−.81
.05	214.62	10.70	−9.69	−.91

*e. How much money would it be worth to each seller to seek means of reaching and enforcing that effective agreement?
*f. How much would you gain if you as *one* seller succeeded in staying outside the agreement or in secretly breaking it while all others raised the price and reduced their output?

2. The first case prosecuted under the federal laws against collusion to raise prices involved steel pipe sold to the U.S. government. More recently, an electrical-equipment industry's collusion, which sent some business leaders to jail, was also against the government. What explanations are there for the fact that a majority of prosecuted cases involve collusion against the government?

*3. Assume that all existing firms producing a commodity were successfully and effectively to collude to restrict output and raise prices. What open-market forces would operate to obstruct the effectiveness of the collusion?

4. What are the differences among collusion, cooperation, and competition? How would you define collusion between two people so as to exclude partnerships and corporate, joint ownership from the concept? What are the undesirable consequences that distinguish desirable coalitions from cartels?

5. The National and the American Baseball Leagues are two separate leagues of 12 franchised teams. To prevent competition among teams for *new* players, a draft (similar to that used in the football and basketball leagues) has been adopted, wherein each newcomer from a high school is assigned to a particular team. Under this agreement, or assignment, no other team owner will be allowed to sign that newcomer.

   a. Who benefits from this arrangement? Who suffers?

   b. Does this system exist in sports and nowhere else?

Chapter 13
Restricted Access to Markets

People and firms do not passively submit to open-market competition. As we saw in the last chapter, competing firms may investigate the possibilities of collusive action among themselves. They often attempt, sometimes successfully, to obtain politically enforced restrictions against potential competitors. Competition moves from the marketplace to the political arena, where rivals strive for political power. The difference between these two types of competition, one for market offers and the other for political power, is the essential difference between capitalism and socialism. (Remember, nothing in economic analysis enables us to draw conclusions about the propriety of competition for political power.)

Political Restraints on Consumers' Market Access

Often when producers are legally restrained from making and selling a product or service to consumers, the restrictions, called *producer controls*, are justified as protecting consumers. But it can be convincingly argued that many such restrictions are imposed to protect certain producers from other producers who could otherwise benefit customers. Thus, some restrictions on producers in fact restrict consumers. We now examine some producer controls.

PROTECTION OF OR FROM COMPETITION?

One of the principal effects of political regulation of business has been to confuse protection *of* competition with protection *from* competitors. For example, the Federal Trade Commission has responded to complaints of business firms against one another. When firms complain of "unfair," "destabilizing," "disorderly," and "cutthroat" competition, generally it is because their competitors are more successfully catering to buyers' preferences.

The price searcher and the protected monopolist differ from each other in that the latter is protected from actual or potential competitors by restrictions, whereas the price searcher is not so protected. A protected market keeps some resources from moving to their most valuable uses, because the protected sellers price, marginal revenue, and marginal cost are greater than some outsider's marginal cost would have been. The result is a more severe distortion of output than would be produced by a price searcher, because no seller is restricted from offering wares in any market.

How are market entry restrictions obtained? We now investigate some of the various techniques.

ADVERTISING RESTRICTIONS

Advertising, again, is a means of informing potential buyers of the existence of a seller and the availability of its goods. Any obstacle that either prevents a seller from informing potential customers about offers or increases the costs of informing them will protect better-known sellers. If General Motors wanted to restrain the growth of American Motors, Volkswagen, or Toyota, it should seek to prohibit advertising. Holiday Inn, a nationally known motel chain, is favored by bans on local highway advertising. The American Medical Association, American Bar Association, and American Dental Association used to prohibit advertising. Examine the yellow pages of the telephone directory and compare the advertising in various professions. Would you regard restrictions on advertising as helpful to consumers or new suppliers? In many states and cities, advertising the price's of gasoline or reading glasses or contact lenses, for example, is illegal or severely restricted. Prices there are higher. Restrictions on advertising also increase the costs to consumers of gaining information.

SANITATION AND HEALTH STANDARDS

Laws prohibit the sale or use of foods and drugs that the U.S. Food and Drug Administration officials deem unfit. By establishing and enforcing standards of cleanliness, government agencies reduce the individual's costs of collecting information. But cleanliness is not costless. Some consumers prefer cheaper goods even though they are produced in less sanitary conditions, such as are, say, imported dates. As an example, the government refused to allow the sale of a cheap, high-protein, biologically sterile, powdered food because it was said to be filthy, being made from *whole* fish. Yet people eat whole oysters, and pigs and chickens are converters of garbage, insects, and worms. No one objects to more cleanliness if its cost is not excessive. But a high-priced barbershop that uses a fresh protective apron for every customer will find itself underpriced by one that reuses the apron with a new piece of paper around each customer's neck. The higher-priced shop would do well to insist on higher standards of cleanliness to keep out lower-cost competitors. A requirement of higher standards is a restriction on consumers—usually poorer people—who can afford only lower-quality, cheaper service. Insisting that all but higher-quality goods and services be prohibited is like permitting only Rolls-Royces and banning VWs. Which is better for the poor and for the rich?

Until about 1950 margarine could not be sold in some states; it was an inferior substitute for butter. And in many areas it could be sold only as a *white* spread—even though butter is artificially colored and flavored. Major milk-producing states had the strongest bans on margarine. (Do you suspect milk producers are big political campaign contributors?)

QUALITY CONTROL

Codes in every city control the types and grades of materials that can be used in the construction of buildings. New York City's building code was overhauled only after 30 years, long delaying the use of new, better, cheaper construction methods. The rapid growth in the use of mobile trailer homes as permanent residences in the last several years can be explained partly by the fact that they are not covered by local building codes. Now, under pressures from the building trades' unions, codes are being expanded to include mobile homes.

It is commonly believed that "Bad goods drive out the good."[1] And the remedy is that bad goods must be prohibited. But that common belief is incorrect. When *both quality and price* are permitted to be determined in open-market competition, neither drives out the other. Instead, the prices reflect the difference in quality. Yet to assure higher quality, the medical profession restricts entry into the market by state licensing laws administered by state licensing boards made up of licensed doctors. The medical profession emphasizes that it has brought the United States the highest quality medical care *for those who can afford it*. If a law permitted the sale of only Rolls-Royces, Cadillacs, and Lincolns, we could certainly have the best-*quality* automobiles in the world—and the most pedestrians. Some people would live longer and be in better health if medical aid and hospitals were available that embodied less expertise and skill, and thus were lower in price, because at the present time less knowledgeable or helpful substitutes are used instead, such as nurses, druggists, midwives, books, self-medication, faith-healers,

friends, and hearsay remedies. (Indeed, in nineteenth-century France there was such medical aid in the person of the *officier de santé*, or health officer, a licensed practitioner without an M.D. degree.)

It is hard to know when people who profess to be acting only to protect other people are being sincere and when they have ulterior motives. (For example, do you regard the remainder of this paragraph as sincere?) Like health, wealth can be ruined by carelessness. A broken leg can be reset; a broken budget can't be. Wealth, like health, must be protected from personal ignorance. If a person invests $1000 in some business and loses it, the person's family suffers. Therefore, before making *any* investment, every person ought to be required to consult a licensed, certified economist, who would prescribe how wealth should be invested. Without this safeguard millions of people every day make foolish investments and irrevocably lose their wealth and harm their families. Many people follow the advice of economic quacks—stockbrokers, politicians, friends, and writers of tip sheets. They overinvest without consulting economists, who could prevent their going too far into debt or buying in the wrong area or taking the wrong job or the wrong kind of insurance.[2]

---

[1]This old saying, known as Gresham's law, describes the consequence of not allowing prices to reflect differences in quality. Keeping the prices of higher-quality goods below their market level reduces incentives to produce those goods and increases incentives to produce low-cost, inferior goods.

[2]There have been signs of progress in recent decades toward serious agreement with this facetious argument. In 1964 the Securities and Exchange Commission issued a report evaluating the securities and stock market dealers' practices. In the covering letter the chairman of the committee says: "Under existing Federal law there is a right of free access and unlimited entry into the securities business for anyone, regardless of qualifications, except those excluded on the basis of prior securities violations. The steady growth in the very numbers of investors and participants, according to the report, has made this concept obsolete.... Greater emphasis should be given by the Securities and Exchange Commission and the exchanges and associations of security dealers to the concept of suitability of particular securities for particular customers." Can you imagine what this would do for economists' incomes?

Regulations and restrictions are often sought by already well established suppliers who would benefit by restraints on lower-cost or lower-quality suppliers. But lower-quality and lower-cost suppliers are not undesirable or wasteful. They provide otherwise unavailable services to less affluent people. While it would be desirable that the less affluent have better-quality services, the issue here is not better quality versus lower quality, but lower quality versus none.

Even with an issue that appears as clear-cut desirable as restricting premature introduction of new drugs, one must measure the costs against benefits. What is given up? Availability of newer and more effective drugs is delayed so that people are denied sooner relief or even the saving of their lives. Although there are benefit's in avoiding losses from what prove to be harmful drugs, there are losses from the delay of what prove to be better drugs. Tradeoffs are inevitable. Unfortunately, several studies have indicated that the increased delay of certain new drugs has caused more loss than have too-early introductions.

A very simple example of very great delay (too long?) has been that involving permission to sell UHT milk in the United States (UHT milk is treated so as to remain drinkable for months without refrigeration). Though it has been sold in Great Britain for many years with an excellent record, only now can it be sold in the United States. Several drugs for heart disease have been treated similarly. We repeat that the point is not the wisdom of restrictions but the weight attached to the two types of error—too late with too much prolonged, avoidable suffering and death, or too early with otherwise avoidable suffering and death.

Similarly, according to studies, compulsory safety devices for passenger cars resulted in less careful driving with more accidents and injuries to pedestrians. But that should not be surprising. The increase in the number of fatalities and injuries is not the crucial test of the desirability of such laws on safety. For example, when airplanes were riskier and fewer people flew, fewer were killed. Now that airplanes are safer, more people fly, and consequently a larger number are killed in airplane accidents (although the incidence of fatalities *per passenger mile* is far lower than formerly). Unless you believe that the increased availability and lower cost of flying was not beneficial, you cannot conclude that the increased incidence of accidents and amount of damage that are consequences of more comprehensive safety requirements are not worth the gain.

PROTECTION OF EMPLOYEES, MORALS, AND SERVICE STANDARDS

Laws prohibiting sales during evenings and Sundays are alleged to protect the health of employees, the morals of the community, and the quality of service. As the Supreme Court has affirmed, Sunday selling diverts people from rest and violates what most Christians call the Sabbath. But no employees work 24 hours. Sunday and evening buying is a convenience to many shoppers. Of course, consumers *could* do all their shopping between 3 P.M. and 7 P.M. on Mondays, Wednesdays, and Fridays. Any store able to reduce its costs and its prices enough by keeping such hours could survive with consumers who prefer the lower prices at those days and hours—except that there aren't enough people with such preferences. "Blue" laws, laws regulating behavior on Sundays, are often supported by retail stores that use more labor service relative to capital than do the discount houses that are, or would be, open evenings and Sundays. The extra labor hours add more to the total costs of conventional department stores than to those of the discount houses.

It is sometimes argued that entry into an industry must be restricted so that the overall industry output cannot exceed one that allows adequate prices and profits. Otherwise, the argument goes, some firms will go out of business, and when demand later increases there will not be enough firms. This reasoning is known as the *orderly market* argument. For highly seasonal products, such as milk, if the price fluctuated from troughs in June (when the supply is greatest) to peaks in November (when supply is smallest), dairy farmers would be driven out of business in June and few would be in business in November to provide an adequate supply of milk. Also, when prices are high, fly-by-night producers will enter and "skim the cream," only to leave when demand and prices fall. The "responsible" year-round producers will not survive. Therefore, controls should be placed on entry so that irresponsible, short-term producers cannot undermine the long term stability of the industry. (This argument was also the basis of regulation of domestic U.S. air carriers, until 1978. What followed the removal of those controls requires no telling here.)

Can you spot the analytic errors in the orderly market argument? First, seasonal variations are no surprise. Retail stores predictably do about half their business in the Christmas season. They are not bankrupted by the summer low-sales months—just as they are not by low Sunday sales. Yet some milk producers allege that there must be controlled entry to assure "adequate" supplies in all seasons. Controlled entry achieves that with a *uniform year-round high price*. During the high-production season, the "excess" milk (which would not be "excess" if its price were allowed to fall in that season) is diverted to cheeses (or is bought by the government and exported, at a loss of $1 billion in 1981). In California the number of commercial milk cows is so restricted by law (because at the high milk prices dairy farmers would find it profitable to have more cows) that the value of having another cow (beyond the limited number) is worth more than $2000, a measure of the contrived monopoly rent. The situation is similar in every major metropolitan area, where federal and state laws permit dairy farmers to enforce controls. It is well known that dairy associations pay part of their monopoly rents to politicians for laws to enforce restrictions on supply.

The argument for orderly markets contains two basic misconceptions. First, it assumes that changes in demand whether unanticipated or cyclical and thus anticipated, are viewed by *every* producer as permanent changes. Second, it argues that increasing supplies drive down prices, thereby reducing supplies, thereby in turn driving prices up; it thus confuses a movement *of* the supply curve with a movement *along* an unchanged supply curve as price and output fall in response to a demand curve decrease. See Figure 13–1.

Using the rationale of maintaining an orderly market, the Interstate Commerce Commission regulated truckers, with the result that monopoly rents went to the favored trucking companies and the Teamsters Union. Farm price-support laws, such as in wheat, cotton, and tobacco, control the entry of new producers into those markets. Farm marketing boards for raisins, peaches, sugar, rice, oranges, and lemons, to name a few commodities, control the *salable* output of those crops in the *name* of orderly prices but in the interest of greater wealth for the current producers. Imports of sugar, peanuts, and rice are restricted so the domestic price of those goods will be high enough to increase the value of domestic resources specialized to those products. We investigate a few examples.

Import Quotas Rights to import some sugar from lower-priced foreign markets to high-

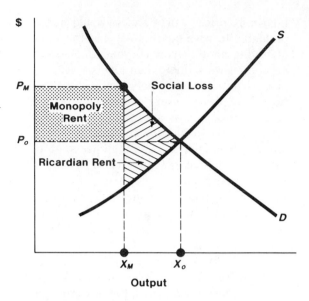

Figure 13-1.

MONOPOLY RENT FROM RESTRICTIONS ON OUTPUT

When the output of a good is reduced, as from X_0 to X_M, by restrictions on entry to a market, the price is raised from P_0 to P_M. Protected suppliers receive a higher income at a smaller output: The *monopoly rent* is that portion of income represented by the rectangular area between the old price P_0 and the new price P_M extending out to the monopoly output quantity X_M. The area below P_0 and above the supply curve S is *Ricardian rent,* the return to the superior productive inputs. The area defined by P_0, the demand curve D, and outputs X_M and X_0 is the *social loss* from restriction of entry, because otherwise output worth more than its cost would have been produced. However, the monopoly rent is *not* such a loss: It is a transfer of income from the consumer to the protected supplier. As we shall see, competition to achieve protected monopolist status entails costs up to that amount of transferred income, and thus wastes resources.

er-priced U.S. markets are called **import quotas**. Those valuable rights are granted by a sugar quota board of the Department of Agriculture. Successful applicants are selected by several criteria. Is your country friendly? Is it behaving properly? Are you a deserving recipient of this favor? Who is the lawyer or representative arguing your case? A former member of Congress? If this suggests favoritism and potential for scandal, that's life.

Tax-Subsidized Price Supports and Surpluses A major political means of avoiding the effects of market forces on income and wealth has been much used by farmers, particularly producers of milk, corn, soybeans, wheat, and rice. A look at a historical instance will demonstrate the motives for seeking protection and how that protection works. After World War II the demand for wheat fell. Distressed wheat farmers, seeking to avoid losses and the need to reduce output, succeeded in persuading the government to enact legislation instituting *price supports.* For every crop covered by such laws there is a price, the **parity price**, which the law seeks to achieve. The parity price is nearly always higher than the market-clearing price. At that higher parity price the public demands less of the good than is supplied, creating a surplus. The government then steps in and, not literally but in effect, buys the unsold crop. It does this by lending the farmer money, using the unsold crop as security on the loan. If the farmer doesn't repay, the government keeps the unsold crop, thus, in effect, buying the crop to support the parity price.

The government makes these loans (or purchases, if you will) out of tax revenues, which denies taxpayers the right to withdraw from these high-priced markets. In 1965 the total accumulated stocks of government-held crops had cost the taxpayers over $5 billion, including some $1 billion a year for storage.

Economic analysis does not support the popular claim that surpluses exist because production exceeds demand. As has already been well established throughout this book, demand is not fixed: The amount demanded depends on the price. The American public (not to mention the enormous population of the rest of the world) would happily have consumed all the current U.S. farm output if government policies had not kept prices well above their market-clearing levels. Indeed, in the 1970s, when several countries suffered repeated large-scale crop losses because of severe weather, and when inflation caused open-market prices on the world market to rise above the parity price, the surplus almost disappeared. But recently, larger U.S. harvests and a higher parity price have threatened to create new surpluses.

If we seem to be condemning the farmers' actions, rereading what we have said will show that there is no suggestion of impropriety. Farmers are not unique in attempting to avoid market forces. We are examining agricultural cases because they are relatively simple.

Holding Crop off the Market[3]   At one time lemon growers tried to raise their prices by each withholding some output from the domestic market. But some growers stayed out of the agreement and sold *all* their crop at the raised prices. Furthermore, some superior producers could make more wealth if there were no such artificial restrictions. How could they and other producers be controlled? In 1941, a law was enacted permitting a majority of the growers of any agricultural product to compel *all* growers of that product to withhold part of their crop from the market.

How can a group of growers control each producer's sales? One way, as indicated earlier, is to set up a central sales agency that pools all the output and decides what portion of each producer's output goes to several outlets: to be sold at high prices as fresh fruit in domestic markets; to be destroyed; or to be sold at lower prices as concentrates or flavorings in domestic and foreign markets. Because of the artificially maintained high prices, growers produce ever-larger outputs, requiring that the proportion of lemons authorized for domestic sale as fresh fruit be steadily reduced over the years: from 90% of the total crop in 1942, the program's first year, to less than half the total crop today.

The program's unintended effect has been to encourage each grower to create larger groves to compete for a larger share of the limited sales. As a result, farmers are no better off now than they were before the program. They have dissipated the monopoly rent in the costs of larger groves. Without this scheme, there would have been fewer producers, with lower costs, selling a large share of their fresh lemons at lower prices. There is a social waste as well, measurable as the loss of forsaken crops, such as avocados, grapefruit, or macadamia nuts, or of land for residential housing.

PRODUCTION CONTROLS

An alternative method of keeping the price above its market-clearing level is to limit production to as much as can be sold at the desired price, in effect, again, a parity price. This method is tidy, eliminating both low prices to the producers and potentially embarrassing surpluses. One way to control production in agriculture is to assign each producer a maximum allowable acreage that can be planted, say 80% of a farmer's available land (obviously the farmer will pick the best 80% and pour on the fertilizer). The farmer will even receive payment, called a conservation payment, for keeping land idle. Those who do not restrict their acreage will not be allowed to sell at the parity price. In fact, in

---

[3]The following analysis is applicable with minor variations to many products, including milk, eggs, wheat, cotton, tobacco, peanuts, rice, raisins, corn, and oranges.

the case of tobacco a prohibitive tax of 75% of the value of the crop is levied on such excess acreage. Land licensed for tobacco growing is marked as such and is policed by helicopters. There is no tobacco surplus, because the price goes to whatever level will clear the market of the *licensed* (untaxed) output. The output-control technique used for tobacco has been extolled by recent U.S. presidents as deserving application to other crops. You can see why. This system is called self-policing; a voting majority of the growers authorize's and enforce's the acreage-reduction scheme on all producers.

The best U.S. lands for cotton production are in the West. But because the farms there are larger and fewer than elsewhere, these lower-cost producers are outnumbered. To cut back the use of older, more costly lands is obviously not acceptable to the eastern majority. Instead, everyone is cut back by the same percentage of the acreage that has been in use in the past few years. This ingeniously reduces the newer acreage by a bigger percentage than the old, because the farther into the past the base is extended, the smaller it will be in a recently expanding area (as, conversely, it will be for older areas that are *declining*). Consequently, the votes in favor of acreage-restriction schemes fall dramatically as one moves into the newer, larger, better western farms.[4]

When applied to farming, production control promotes greater use of fertilizer and other jointly productive resources to increase yield per acre; production becomes more intensive. As the output per acre skyrockets, acreage must be cut back more than had been expected, because farming has become "surprisingly productive."

Public Utilities

In certain industries, such as electricity, gas, water, sewage and railroads, it may be that the cost of serving the public is lower if only one firm operates. Larger output may be available at lower costs per unit of output. Such an industry called a decreasing-cost industry, or sometimes, a **natural monopoly**, suggesting that one firm can provide the supply at lower total cost than if the total output were produced by several smaller firms.[5]

Because of the absence of competition, such natural monopolies are commonly subjected to government controls over prices, investment, output, and profits. So, too, are legal monopolies, firms that, by law, are the only ones allowed to produce a good or service for the market. Regulation of these matters is performed by regulatory commissions. If the monopoly firm fails to make a profit, the stockholders bear the losses. They may then sell their stock at a loss to new buyers who expect to do better. Or the service will either come to an end or be subsidized by taxes (as are Amtrak, most city bus lines, and most rapid transit systems).

No one firm, monopoly or not, will capture all the knowledge, talent, and skill applicable to the production of its goods and services. Thus, prohibiting new entrants

---

[4]We interject an ironic note. Although we call the western lands better, some are so only because of federal irrigation projects that keep water prices substantially below the costs—the difference being made up by taxes on the rest of the country. Thus farmers in the Southeast pay taxes to enable water to be sold at below cost to their competition in the western desert areas. And to protect themselves from the consequent lower prices, they appeal for more taxes on consumers to finance "loans on unsold cotton"; finally, they appeal for federal regulations restricting production of cotton on those very western lands for which they have paid taxes to help irrigate at less than cost.

[5]Technological advances in electronic communication have altered the presumption that telephone service can be provided more cheaply by one central supplier. Similarly, close substitutes for railroads have eroded the presumption that there is only one supplier of transport services.

reduces the likelihood that new or improved products or lower-cost methods of production will be discovered and tested. Moreover, innovations that would lower costs would be slow to be adopted; for although a protected monopolist has as much to gain from lower costs as any other firm, it is the regulatory commission that decides how any increased profits would be distributed, or whether they would be allowed. If profits to the utility are restricted its incentive to lower costs is removed. Nor can members of the regulatory commission directly capture the gains of lower costs; as a result, they, too, will be less motivated to lower costs than if they owned the protected public utility.

Other industries that are not natural monopolies, in that their marginal costs do not decrease as output increases, are sometimes nevertheless made into *contrived* monopolies by law and are called public utilities. Examples are taxi services, radio and television broadcasting, and garbage-collection services.

WHOSE "UTILITY" IN PROTECTED PUBLIC UTILITIES?

Let us examine an instructive example of the incentives for creating regulatory agencies and the consequences of such agencies. In 1887 the Interstate Commerce Commission (ICC) was established to regulate the railroads. What was the basic problem? By 1880 too many railroads had been built; for example, seven tracks ran between Omaha and Chicago. Although the initial investment costs of building a railroad are high, subsequent operating costs are low. Railroads could cut prices far below the long-run total average costs. And this some railroads did: Rather than shut down because prices did not cover past investment costs, they dropped their prices to the marginal costs of operation with existing equipment. Other railroads sought to prevent this price cutting, which usually involved secret price dis-

counts. Shippers who did not get the lower freight rates demanded that the government prohibit secret price cuts. Even the railroads wanted—*as a group*—to avoid price competition.

In the absence of regulation, prices would have remained low until some rails and equipment wore out, at which time only those railroads with more heavily used routes would have been maintained. However, the law passed in 1887 establishing the ICC also required railroads to charge "just and reasonable" rates and to publicly post those rates. Thus, the railroads could do what they had unsuccessfully sought to do by private collusion—to prevent individually advantageous but mutually disadvantageous secret price cutting.

The ICC became the vehicle for maintaining an effective cartel in transportation. ICC regulations imposed legal price collusion (much as if General Motors, Ford, Chrysler, and American Motors had a federal agency that excluded imports and also helped them mutually set prices at which all their cars could be sold). In 1920 the ICC was additionally empowered to control the entry of new competitors and the addition of new routes, thus further protecting the existing railroads. Unfortunately for the rails, other forms of transportation were developing— autos, trucks, airplanes, and barges. Because of the high rail freight rates, trucks and barges took much of the business. So the ICC was charged with regulating them, too. The ICC now must approve interstate rates charged by the highway transport industry, waterways, pipelines, and railroads. (State and local agencies control intrastate and local fares.) Regulations and restrictions on competition among these services has eliminated cheaper services that would have saved more than an estimated $5 billion *annually*. (Add to these lost savings the nearly $100 million in annual expenditures by the ICC.)

Regulatory agencies were also set up for

airlines (Civil Aeronautics Board), for radio and TV (Federal Communications Commission), and for energy (Federal Energy Agency). All were set up in the belief that open-market competition in these industries is unfeasible or in some way inappropriate. After the airlines were deregulated by the Carter administration, the results exposed and removed many of the stultifying effects of regulation.

Patents and Copyrights

Patents and copyrights are legally granted exclusive rights (that is, a protected monopoly) to the commercial use of certain goods or ideas.[6] Others can produce these goods and services only under license from the patent holder, the patentee. For example, the principle of Polaroid film is patented; Polaroid Corporation, the patentee, can license others to produce and sell that film. The patent, given for a period of years, usually 17, is occasionally renewable for 17 more. The potential income from patents and copyrights is intended to induce the discovery and application of new, useful knowledge. If others could use a new, valuable idea without paying, there would be less incentive to discover and develop inventions. Even though many people try to invent or do research without that incentive, the prospect of gain will attract more thought and resources.

Of the value of an invention, what is the appropriate share that should go to the inventor? And what is the appropriate method of collecting that share of the value? The absence of clear-cut criteria for answering these questions provokes dispute about how long a patent should be protected and what kind of

pricing and use of the patent should be allowed.

SUPPRESSION OF NEW IDEAS?

Sometimes an inventor discovers a new idea that makes obsolete an idea on which the inventor has a current patent. What is the likely effect? Does the patent system cause new ideas to be suppressed? Say I owned a cable pay-television system and then discovered a cheap way to eliminate the cables: Would I use or suppress the wireless system? What I would do depends upon the relative costs. Since the wires are already installed, the cost of their continued use is low until they must be replaced. If producing and installing the new system costs less than continuing to use the existing system, I would immediately abandon the old system. Otherwise, I would delay using the new system until the old had to be replaced or repaired at a higher cost than that of installing and using the new. This delay in introducing a new idea is sometimes regarded as "unjustified." But in fact it reflects the truly lower cost of using up existing equipment first.

For example, it is a commonplace of modern folklore that gasoline producers have a new fuel or carburetor that would enormously reduce the demand for gasoline, but to protect their wealth they have withheld the device. Is this likely? If the device or idea were patented, it would be public knowledge; but there is no patent record or any other evidence of such a device. And if the invention were not patented, then any other person who knew about it could manufacture the device and earn an enormous fortune—more than the existing companies could make by withholding it. Therefore the invention could not be kept off the market if it really was cheaper. And it would not be used if it did not save costs. In sum, if such a device did exist, it could be made and sold at a price reflecting the value of the gasoline saved, a net profit to the owner, whether or

---

[6]Patents do not prevent other people from using some idea or device if they use it for themselves and not to produce something for *sale* to other people; only commercial use is forbidden.

not the producer is now an oil or auto producer.

NONPATENTABLE RESEARCH AND DEVELOPMENT

There is no generally accepted rule for deciding what kinds of exploratory activity should be given patent and copyright monopolies. Supermarkets, self-service gas stations, drive-up windows in banks, colored soaps, open-all-night stores, discount houses, metal tennis rackets, and a host of cost reductions and quality improvements are not subject to copyright or patent. Nevertheless, much research and development is conducted without the incentive of patents or copyrights. Most firms have to derive their profits from being first to offer a new product, grabbing a larger share of the market than they will have after their competitors come in.

PATENT POOLING

Another piece of erroneous folklore is that several inventors will pool their related patents simply to monopolize some general field of research. Each inventor grants the other a right to the use of any future related patents. However, there is another possible explanation. Pools or mutual sharing of related patents from continuing research are a way to encourage *more future research*. Many patents are so closely interrelated and interdependent that it is impossible to easily identify infringements. Many products are based on a series of patented advances in knowledge. The problems of getting and maintaining agreement among each of the patentees for manufacturing such products would obstruct the incentive to discover future related improvements. It would be next to impossible to collect royalties for such ideas if everyone were fighting over what part of what device reflected this patent and what part that. So agreeing to pool any future *related* inventions under one ownership

is a way to induce the continued discovery of related ideas.

Monopoly Rents: Creation and Dissipation

The effect of legal barriers to entry in a market and of some methods of maintaining "orderly" markets is to increase the wealth of those already in the market when the protective scheme goes into effect. That increase in wealth is *monopoly rent*; *monopoly* because it is derived from restricting access to the market, and *rent* because it does not induce an increase in supply. Monopoly rent is not a profit achieved by transferring resources from lower- to higher-valued uses.

What happens to monopoly rent? By way of answer we examine the production-control scheme whereby tobacco farmers are *licensed* to use a certain acreage for crop. The monopoly rent was obtained by those who owned the land at the time the scheme was started. The value of the licensed land is the value of the tobacco crop after all other costs of production (labor, equipment, fertilizer, insecticides, management, taxes, and the like) are subtracted. Suppose that that net revenue from a licensed acre is $400 for each crop year. Recall from our earlier capital value analysis that an annuity of $400 per year at a 10% interest rate would have a value of about $4000. Suppose also that land of the same kind *without* a license yields a net revenue of $100 annually and has a value of $1000. The difference, $3000, is the capital value of the monopoly rent.[7] When the licensing scheme is revealed, the favored acre rises in value, and its owner captures the higher wealth. The owner can farm the land for the annual higher-income stream, rent it

---

[7]These are realistic values. Recall that the monopoly rent is about $2000 per cow in the dairy industry in California.

out for the higher rent, or sell the land and the license.

The purchaser of the licensed land gets no *gain* because of the higher purchase price, $4000: $1000 for the land and $3000 for the license. The income from tobacco production on that land equals a normal competitive return on that $4000 purchase price. If the license to grow an acre of tobacco could be sold "bare"—that is, was transferable to any given acre of land—for, say, $3000, it would pay owners of less appropriate land to transfer their licenses, acre for acre, to more appropriate land. If such transfers were legal, the total costs of the produced tobacco would be lower, regardless of who captures the monopoly rent. Why are such transfers not legal? Some political observers have suggested that the sale of bare licenses would expose the monopoly rents provided to the tobacco landowners (just as they *are* exposed in the sale of bare licenses for liquor stores, taxi franchises, and radio and television stations).

Although widely favored politically because there is no surplus, the kind of production control that the licensing of tobacco growing accomplishes has three affects: (1) It reduces consumption below what it would have been with open-market competition; (2) it yields monopoly rents, but only to the owners of licensed land, not to the tobacco growers (unless they happen also to be the owners); (3) it wastes resources by preventing highest valued uses of them.

COMPETITION FOR MONOPOLY STATUS

People compete to acquire the status of a politically protected monopoly. Bribes, political contributions, payment of higher taxes, and the costs of public-relations counsel and lawyers to obtain rights, licenses, franchises, or exclusive authorization are the forms such competition commonly takes. They tend to absorb all the monopoly rent. These perva-sive payments to both political parties have been publicized by several congressional investigating committees.

If entry into some industry, profession, or labor union is restricted so that members receive some monopoly rent, would-be entrants will spend money competing to obtain some of those monopoly rents. These candidates try to acquire whatever qualities they believe the authorities require as their standard of admission. The long waiting lists of applicants to medical schools suggest that medical earnings are composed partly of a monopoly rent. But it is questionable whether that monopoly rent is captured by the entrants as increased wealth. For example, say you pay the costs of becoming qualified for admission to medical school and finally to practice. If the net capital value of the high but short-lived income you will have eventually earned in your career is measured, starting from the date you decided to train for admission to medical school, you may discover that it is merely equal to the average income of all college graduates.

The owners of a protected monopoly cannot count on getting all the monopoly rent as a net gain. In some states liquor licenses are worth an average of over $40,000, though issued for a minor sum (about $2000 in Florida). Taxi licenses are worth about $50,000 in New York. In many states entry into the savings-and-loan banking industry is subject to the approval of state officials. In California permission to open a bank once exceeded $50,000 in value, measured by the immediate rise in the price on the stock of groups obtaining permission. Part of the protected monopoly rent of television is taken not necessarily in the form of money but in the form of power to dictate programming. Television stations are requested to provide free coverage of the political campaigns, especially national ones, of major-party candidates. They are also required to broadcast the kind of programs that FCC authorities think appropriate. (Newspapers, which do not have to apply for a license, not surprisingly act in ways that television cannot.)

In Turkey and India (the only two countries for which careful estimates have been made) monopoly rents to parties favored with monopoly status—such as by licenses to import goods, to build a factory, or to open a business—equal about 7% to 12% of national income. The cost of competition to get those rights absorbs the prospective monopoly rent. If import licenses for raw materials are given in proportion to the size of one's factory, a would-be entrant will overbuild the factory. People compete by bribing officials or promising to hire them after they leave government service, or by hiring their relatives or locating firms in the capital city, and the like. The winners are not necessarily any richer after paying those costs.

Summary

1. Governments often restrain the right to produce or consume some kinds of goods and services. These restraints are sometimes imposed to protect consumers thought to be inadequately informed. Restrictions on advertising; impositions of standards of sanitation, health, and quality; and regulation of working hours and conditions are examples. These can sometimes help less informed consumers. But they also can protect some sellers from competitors who otherwise could cater to consumers' demands, whether well informed or not.

2. Attempts to make markets "orderly," or impose import quotas, or support prices by agreeing to control or withhold goods from sale are devices to protect producers' interests at a cost to consumers exceeding the benefits to the producers.

3. Public utilities are examples of *natural monopolies:* productive enterprises that have costs that decrease as output increases, so that one producer could serve all consumers at a lower cost than could several producers.

4. Public utilities are regulated by government in the expectation that the prices will be lower and service better than if unregulated.

5. Patents and copyrights are devices to give an inventor or author enforceable private-property rights in the product. Whether or not that also gives monopoly rents depends on how closely substitutable are other products.

6. Withholding the use of a patented idea in order to protect inferior ideas or techniques is not a profitable tactic for an inventor, and the older, inferior product could not successfully compete with the new idea or technique that was really cheaper or superior.

7. Resources protected from competition by other resources with a resultant higher market value collect a *monopoly rent,* which is essentially a wealth transfer of some of the consumer's surplus to the supplier through a higher price. In addition, the resulting smaller output destroys some of the potentially higher-valued use of some resources that must be used in less-valuable ways because they are prohibited from competing with the protected seller.

8. Prospects of monopoly rents through government controls on competition will induce costly competition to obtain such controls. The costs will tend to match that prospective gain, resulting in no net social gain but, instead, a social loss because of the distorted resource use.

Questions

1. European coal producers pool their sales through a central agency.
   a. Why is that essential for an effective policing of the collusion agreement among the producers?
   b. Why haven't some coal producers stayed out of the agreement and taken advantage of the opportunity to sell more coal at the price maintained by the "cartel," as it is called?

*2. Suppose you could live in a society in

which trademarks were not protected by law and anyone could imitate the trademark.

    a. As a consumer, would you prefer to live in that world or in one where trademarks were exclusively reserved for a particular manufacturer as part of his property? Why?
    b. As a producer, which would you prefer?

*3. Milk delivery is sometimes called inefficient because when several firms deliver milk to homes, there is duplication of delivery trucks and labor.

    a. For standard items such as milk, would you prefer to live in a community with one centralized delivery service controlled by a regulatory commission to ensure low price and adequate quality, or in one where anyone who wants to deliver milk can enter the market? Why?
    b. Apply your analysis of the preceding problem to the case of garbage collecting. Would you feel differently about that?
    c. How about mail service? Newspapers? Electric power?
    d. If your answers differ, what factor makes you change your preference?

4. It is probably safe to say that a majority of the faculty at any college contends that students are not competent to judge the quality of the instruction in various courses and hence should not be relied upon as evaluators of instructor competence.

    a. What do you think?
    *b. At the same time, it is probably safe to say that a majority of the faculty thinks its students have come to that college because the students can tell good colleges from bad. Do you see any inconsistency in this pair of beliefs? Explain.

*5. European countries import inspected frozen fresh meat from Argentina. But the United States limits imports of fresh meat, because some other countries have hoof and mouth disease (a rapidly spreading disease that kills cattle, although it does not endanger human life). Whom does the import limitation benefit and whom does it hurt? How?

6. Texas, which has the legal right to subdivide itself into seven states, surprises us by doing so. One of the new states, Texaseven, with no college in its boundaries, decides to give to every high-school student a four-year annual grant of $1500 to be applied to education costs at the college of his choice anywhere in the world.

    a. Would you consider that new state to have the finest or the worst educational system in the world?
    *b. Why is that method not used more widely, despite its temporary wide use immediately after World War II as an aid to veterans?
    *c. Why is it opposed by the officials of most state universities?

7. Read the first quotation in footnote 2, p. 285.
    *a. Why has the growth in numbers of investors made open markets for security dealers and for investors an obsolete concept?
    b. If you were a black, a Jew, or an immigrant, would you find this development to your advantage? Why?

8. Tentatively classify the following, on the basis of your present information, as (a) price takers, (b) closed monopolists, or (c) open monopolists. (Remember, market closure does not necessarily convert a price takers' to a price searchers' market.)

Electric company
City bus line
Airline
General Motors
  Corporation
Corner drug store
Prescription
  pharmacist
U.S. Steel
  Corporation
Lettuce grower
Electrician
Elizabeth Taylor

9. "Retail grocery stores are monopolies." In what sense is that correct and in what sense is it false? "The medical profession is a monopoly." In what sense is that true and in what sense false? Which kind of monopoly implies a higher price?

*10. The market for economics professors in most colleges is completely open. No legal requirements about training or prior experience exist as a condition of teaching. A majority of the profession has opposed certification—under which a certification board, consisting of professors, would administer standards of competence. Consider the following:

a. If all present college professors were automatically certified (under a kind of exception called a "grandfather clause"), but all new entrants had to obtain certification by passing certain tests, would the market be open or restricted?

b. If the number of professors admitted were controlled by the board of college professors, which is what would happen, do you think they would restrict entry to the "needed" numbers and would keep out inadequately trained people in order to protect students? Would this have any effect on the wages of college professors? What would be the effect on the number of professors?

c. Similar systems of certification (or admission or licensing or self-policing) are used by doctors, lawyers, pharmacists, architects, dentists, morticians, butchers, longshoremen, psychiatrists, barbers, and realtors, to name a few. What do you think it implies about the wages in these professions relative to wages in an open market? What does it imply about the quality of those who actually practice the professions? About the quality and quantity of services provided the community? Is there a difference between the quality of competence of those certified and the quantity of service obtained by the public as a whole?

11. Diagnose and explain the various features reported in the following news story: "An attractive brunette seated in a rear row gave an excited whoop when her name was called Wednesday during a drawing at the County Building. She had good reason to be elated. For $2000 she had picked up an on-sale liquor license with a market value of about $40,000. She was one of 54 persons who had applied for the 25 new on-sale licenses to be issued in the county this year by the Alcoholic Beverage Control Board. A drawing was used to determine who would get the new on-sale licenses, which permit sale of drinks on the premises. An applicant must have had a premise available and must operate the business for two years before he can sell the license."

*12. Gulf Oil, Baxter Laboratories, Richardson-Merrell, Levi Strauss, and Tenneco are a sample of many American firms that made payments to foreign government officials to conduct business abroad.

a. Who extorted payment from whom, or who bribed whom?

b. How is that activity different from paying franchise fees or taxes to do business abroad?

c. Why don't the foreign governments use explicit license fees and taxes rather than insist on covert payments to government officials and their relatives?

d. Almost all the payments made by the companies were to government officials and their relatives. Would it be safer to simply put the official's relatives on the payroll and let him neglect his work?

e. The press called this corporate bribery. What would you call it?

13. As determined by congressional action, radio and television networks are not required to give "equal-time" rights to any political parties other than the Republican and Democratic parties.

a. Would you consider this a collusion by the two major political parties against the many smaller political parties?

b. Why are newspapers not required to give equal-space rights to the two major political parties? (Hint: The answer is *not* that radio space is limited or a natural resource that "belongs to the people.")

14. Why, despite so much political campaigning against "monopolies," do politicians create closed markets or closed monopolies?

*15. The judicial council of the American Medical Association recommended that it be considered unethical for a doctor to own a drug store in the area in which he practices medicine. It also recommended similarly for ophthalmologists who dispense eyeglasses for a profit. "Any arrangement by which the physician profits from the remedy he prescribes is unethical," in the opinion of the council.

a. Who do you think would benefit if this recommendation were adopted by the American Medical Association and made effective?

b. If it is unethical for a surgeon to profit from the remedy he prescribes, should any surgeon diagnosing a patient be allowed to perform the recommended operation?

c. Should a building contractor be allowed to have any interest in a lumber company? Should any teacher be allowed to use his own textbook? Should a doctor be allowed to own a hospital? Or own an undertaking business?

d. As a patient, would you prefer to deal with doctors who are prohibited from ownership of drug stores? How would this help you or hurt you?

16. The U.S. postal system is a monopoly. No one else may institute a competitive system of transporting personal messages for pay.

a. Why do you think it has remained a monopoly?

*b. The prices charged are uniform despite vast differences in costs of service to different patrons. Why is this kind of discriminatory pricing practiced for mail but not for food, clothes, or dancing lessons?

*17. Why do union officials object to admitting that their power rests on a closed monopoly, while at the same time opposing any legislation that would destroy that monopoly power? Answer the same question when applied to the American Medical Association.

*18. Moving companies are regulated by the Interstate Commerce Commission; their rates per pound are legally set. Explain why that would entail prohibition of making binding bids, prior to moving, as to the cost of the move? In what manner will they compete for business?

19. Is it possible for an economy to be such that everyone is a closed monopolist yet everyone is poorer than if there were no restrictions on the open market? Explain.

*20. When seeking a replacement for a retiring member of a regulatory board, President Johnson said that he wanted a strong man of action to help strengthen the board, because he had noted that even the regulated industry didn't like weak regulatory boards. Why do you suppose the regulated industry likes a strong regulatory board? (Hint: Who is regulated for whose benefit?)

21. A liquor-retailing license in Florida was recently sold for over $110,000. The seller was the person who initially got the license from the state at a cost of $1750.

a. Did the subsequent buyer get a profit in the form of a monopoly rent?

b. Did the initial licensee get a profit in the form of a monopoly rent?

Chapter 14
Income from Personal Services

Productive Resources and Incomes

Almost 80% of the market value of output in the United States is paid for current human services and is called *wages* and *salaries*. The other 20% is for payments to owners of nonhuman resources. The names of those payments depend on what the good is and whether it is rented out or used by the owner. (See Table 14-1.) For resources other than money the payments are called *rents*; for money, they are called *interest*. If used by the owner, rather than rented to someone else, the service value is called *implicit rent*. For resources owned by owners of business firms the income is called business *earnings* or *net income*; sometimes it is also called *profits*. Any of that income paid from the firm to its owners (stockholders) is called a *dividend*.

In Chapter 6 we defined *standard income* as being equal to the *interest* on total wealth. So, according to that interpretation, the earnings—composed, as just noted, of wages, rents, interest on money, and profits—from the entire stock of human and nonhuman capital could be called *interest*.

Table 14-1   CLASSES OF U.S. INCOME EARNINGS

Resources from Which Services Come	Form of Payment for Services	Percent of National Income
Human	Wages, salaries	80%
Nonhuman		
Used by nonowner	Rent earnings,	2%
Used by owner	Implicit rent, net income, profit, dividend	13%
Deferred current consumption to produce future income	Interest	5%

Almost all productive resources (also called *capital goods*) have been produced with the past investment of human labor and intellectual services. Though some resources, such as land, minerals, and water, are not of human creation, their usefulness is often the result of past labor. Students purchase services from teachers to create more productive powers in themselves, a form of human capital: Educating a person is a form of investment in a capital good.

The labor services that made capital goods were paid for *at the time of their making* by someone who hoped to recover more than those costs from the later enhanced production, whether the capital goods be animate or inanimate. The person paying the wage is called an investor, a speculator, or, more inclusively, a **capitalist**. A completed machine is usually used jointly with more labor. The *current* labor and machine yield a product selling for, say, $100. That is expected to cover those *current* labor-service wages of, say, $80. The remaining $20 is for "capital depreciation and profit." Of that, say $15 is for repayment to the person who earlier paid the wages for the labor used to make the machine.[1] This would leave something to cover the interest on that investment for the earlier labor. Only if there is a remainder after that in excess of any value of the investor's own labor services will the investor have a profit.

Although *capital* includes people as well as nonhuman goods, we see the values of *non*human wealth more easily and clearly, because rights to those *goods* are bought and sold, whereas people normally sell only current *services*. Nevertheless, some *indicators* of the values of human wealth do exist. One is life insurance. The amount of insurance a person buys is correlated with the present value of the services that can be sold in the years remaining.

If a person could literally sell claims to future services now, one could immediately exchange claims to future earnings for other forms of wealth. But as it is, a major portion of one's wealth is tied up in one's *potential* labor services. This is a disadvantage that free people must live with. Each of us, whether we want to or not, must bear the risk that unforeseen developments may reduce the value of our human wealth. Occasionally, some people manage to sell rights to some of their future labor services. Classic examples are professional athletes who receive "bonuses" for signing to play exclusively for some ball team.

Most economic production is done in business firms. If the firm has a single proprietor as the operator, income would include wages for the operator's services, though it is sometimes called "profits" to indicate that the amount received for those labor services is a residual, rather than guaranteed as for the employees. As explained earlier, there is expected some interest on investments of earlier services in the firm and, finally, possibly some profit.

Supply of Labor

Of over 160 million able-bodied adults (that is, persons over the age of 16) in the United States, about 100 million (roughly 60%) are in the labor-market force—employed or seeking appropriate employment for money wages. This *labor-market participation rate* has remained close to 60% for the past century. Table 14–2 shows the participation rates by age for males and for females in

---

[1]If the machine lasts four years and was created a year ago with $60 of labor services, the depreciation would be roughly equal to about $15 (plus interest on the advance) for each year's full service—in effect, the value of past services now used up.

Table 14-2 LABOR-FORCE PARTICIPATION RATES, BY AGE AND SEX
(PERCENT OF POPULATION IN EACH CATEGORY)

Ages	1980 Male	1980 Female	1960 Male	1960 Female	Ages	Female Single	Female Married	Male Single	Male Married
16–17	52%	45%	46%	28%	16–19	54%	48%	61%	94%
18–19	74	62	73	51					
20–24	86	68	89	46	20–24	75	60	81	96
25–34	94	62	96	36	25–44	80	56	88	97
35–44	95	61	96	43					
45–54	90	57	94	49	45–64	66	45	68	85
55–64	73	41	85	37					
65–over	20	8	32	11		14	7	17	23

Source: U.S. Department of Commerce, *Statistical Abstract of the United States.*

1960 and 1980. Almost 80% of the males are in the labor force, down from about 90% a century ago. Decreases in participation by teenagers and those aged over 65 were almost exactly offset by increases by females. Almost 50% of women (and about two-thirds of single women) are now in the labor market, over twice the rate in 1900, probably reflecting increased education for women, the availability of ready-cooked and processed foods and of appliances permitting more substitution of capital goods for household labor, better pregnancy-prevention techniques, and increases in wages. The decreased participation rate of both men and women older than about 50 is a result of Social Security payments for those not working at those ages. Figure 14-1 relates labor-force participation to age and gender; Figure 14-2 relates participation of men and women to marital status.

Although the preceding data refer to people working in the labor market for money wages, perhaps the largest class of workers are women managing households as wives and mothers. Something like 30 to 50 million women are heads of households. It is regrettable that economic analysis and official data have not been directed more fully to measur-

ing the magnitude of their contribution to the national income. Typically, national income measures marketed products and services and hence does not include the value of the services of a head of household. Nevertheless, the value of such services in managing and performing the various activities of a household (acting as chefs, purchasing agents, nurses, decorators, social service workers, secretaries, gardeners, tailors, chauffeurs, maids, psychiatrists, and so on) were estimated to average close to $12,000 per family head in 1980, totaling roughly $500 billion—equal to about one-third the measured national marketed income.

Of the 110 million people in the labor-market force, over 45 million are in nonmanufacturing, or *service*, industries; about 30 million are in manufacturing; less than 5 million are in agriculture; 2.5 million are in the military; and about 5 million are at any given moment temporarily between jobs and unemployed. (Over 5% of those in the work force hold two jobs.)

Figure 14-3 shows employment by type of final product. Figure 14-4 shows the distribution by type of labor skills or tasks.

About 24% of those in the labor force

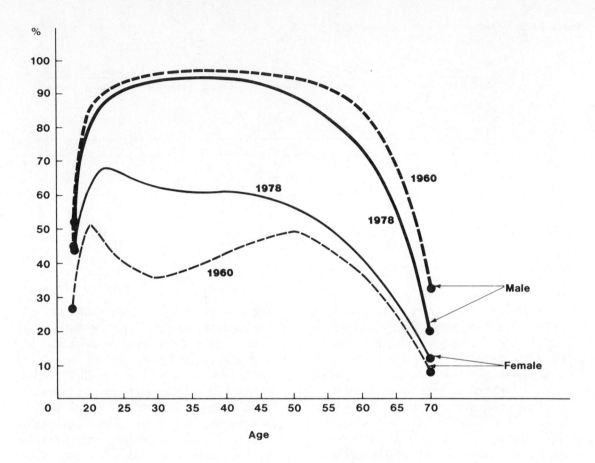

Figure 14-1.

LABOR-FORCE PARTICIPATION RATES, BY AGE
AND GENDER, 1960 AND 1978

SOURCE: U.S. Department of Labor, *Monthly Labor
Review.*

had less than a full high-school education;
half had finished high school; and over 25%
received at least some college education. The
first percentage is falling rapidly, and the latter is rising.

The incentive to seek work in the market responds to the wages offered. As the
supply curve *SS* in Figure 14–5 shows, at
higher wage rates more people enter the labor force or work longer hours, but at very
high wages and higher incomes people may
offer a smaller total amount of labor as they
seek more leisure or as fewer wives work because their husbands earn more. Whether
we have reached that reversed arc of the
curve is unknown. Nevertheless, one way the
amount of labor supplied is reduced is by reducing the number of hours people prefer to
work in a week; in the last hundred years it

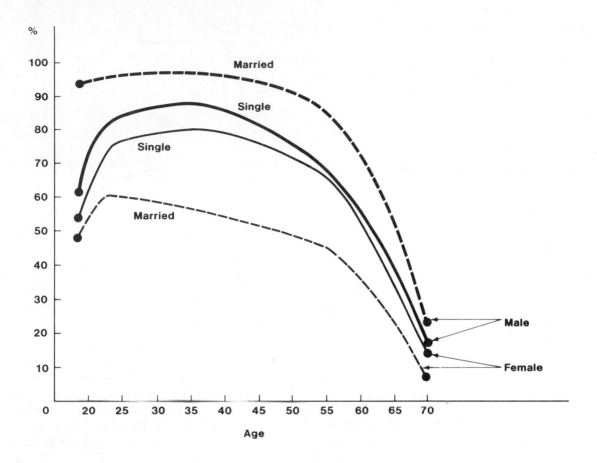

Figure 14-2.

LABOR-FORCE PARTICIPATION, BY AGE
AND MARITAL STATUS, 1978

SOURCE: U.S. Department of Labor, *Monthly Labor Review.*

has gradually fallen from 60 hours to 40, where it has stayed for nearly the past 50 years. Also, of the 40 hours, more is now devoted to leisure time while at the work site—coffee breaks, rest periods, and so forth.

To properly analyze how the wage rate affects the amount of labor supplied, we should note two distinctions. The first is between a temporary rise, say for a weekend or for a couple of months, and a permanent rise in wage rates: A temporary increase does not increase wealth as much as a permanent increase in future earnings. The second distinction is between the supply of labor to one employer and the supply to the economy as a whole: With permanently higher wages the amount supplied in the total economy may decrease, whereas the amount supplied may increase to any sector in which wages

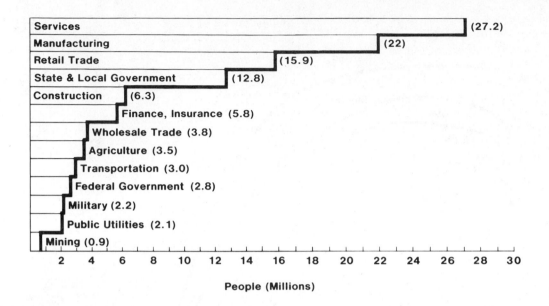

People (Millions)

Figure 14-3.

NUMBER OF PEOPLE WORKING, BY TYPE
OF ACTIVITY, 1980

The *services* category includes workers in amusement
and entertainment, recreation, travel and hotels,
education, and health.
SOURCE: U.S. Department of Labor, *Monthly
Labor Review.*

rise more than in other sectors.

If there is plenty of work to be done,
why is 40% of the adult population not in
the labor-market force? Presumably the market rewards are not attractive enough, or, reversing the point of view, nonmarket opportunities are too attractive. A large fraction
are women, and some men, whose productivity in the home is greater than in the market.
When asked why they refuse to join the labor-market force, they gave the responses recorded in Table 14–3.

Never Too Few Jobs

The overriding fact of scarcity means that
more goods are desired than are produced. It
follows that there are too many, not too few,
jobs and tasks still available! *The problem
that every person faces is to discover which
is the most valuable rather than to wastefully
work on inferior jobs.* Roads could be improved; more police protection and more national defense would be useful; more houses
could be built; more food could be grown by
cultivating and irrigating more, land; more

mechanics could be employed by service stations; more teachers could teach smaller classes—and so on *ad infinitum*. We must explore and estimate which ones are most valuable and what their value is likely to be. That is not easy or riskless. The preceding comments may seem strange, but they do not mean the unemployed have no sensible reason to be unemployed nor that unemployment is wasteful. The issues are more complicated, as we shall see later.

DEMAND FOR LABOR

As repeatedly emphasized, the demand for productive resources reflects the producers' estimates of the consumers' future value of their services and products. This is as true for labor as it is for land and machinery. Most productive activity is organized by business firms, in which the employers act as predictors and guarantors of that ultimate valuation by consumers. Employers compete for productive inputs according to their estimate of what the inputs will contribute toward the predicted ultimate consumption values of products. They estimate what is called the *marginal productivity* of inputs— the increase in value of products because of

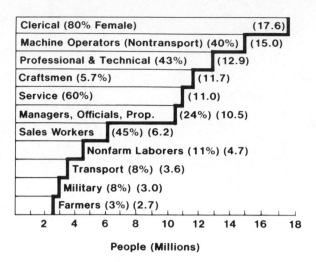

Figure 14-4.

NUMBER OF PEOPLE WORKING, BY SKILL, 1980

SOURCE: U.S. Department of Labor, *Monthly Labor Review.*

Table 14-3 REASONS FOR NOT BEING IN LABOR FORCE (NUMBER OF PEOPLE IN MILLIONS)

	Total	Male	Female	White	Black
Not in Labor Force	58.5	16.6	41.9	51.1	7.4
Do not want job now because:	53.1	14.9	38.2	47.1	6.1
In school	6.1	3.1	3.1	5.0	1.2
Ill or disabled	4.5	2.4	2.1	3.7	.8
Keeping house	29.5	.3	29.2	26.9	2.6
Retired	9.3	7.2	2.1	8.5	.8
Want job but not looking because:	5.3	1.7	3.6	4.0	1.3
In school	1.3	.7	.7	1.0	.4
Ill	.7	.3	.4	.5	.2
Keeping house	1.3	.03	1.2	.9	.3
Think acceptable job cannot be found	.8	.3	.5	.6	.3
Other reasons	1.1	.3	.8	.9	.2

Source: *U.S. Department of Labor*

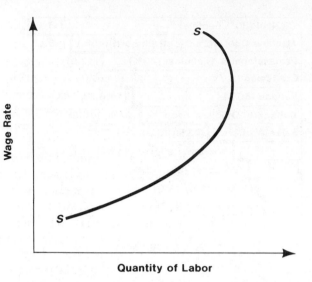

Figure 14-5.

SUPPLY OF LABOR SERVICES

Higher wage rates attract more labor; but at very high wage rates (per hour), workers may be less willing to offer more labor. However, the amount supplied to any one industry or firm will always increase at higher wage rates as labor is attracted away from other industries or firms.

the employment of one more unit of input. And not surprisingly, more inputs increase the *total* output but decrease the *marginal value* of product. The relationship between the quantity of any type of input employed and the marginal value product is typified by a downward-sloping line, as in Figure 14-6. The principle is the same as that in the fishing boat example of Chapter 8 in which the marginal product declined with more people fishing on the boat. As a result of this relationship, at higher wages less labor inputs would be demanded, and at lower wages more would be demanded—just as for the demand for all other goods.

The determination of the quantity of each type of input to be used in a firm is dependent on the input's marginal productivity schedule and its wage or price for its services. A firm will use that amount of each input at which the marginal product is equal to the input's price. That is, a firm's *demand* for an input depends on that input's marginal productivity.

What affects this marginal productivity *schedule*? In general, the greater the number of other cooperating, *complementary* inputs or units of equipment, the higher the marginal product schedule of a given kind of input. For example, the larger the store and its inventory, and the quantity of sales equipment, and the higher the quality of goods that can be sold, the higher the marginal productivity schedule of sales clerks. The marginal productivity schedule of engineers in a firm will be higher as the quantity of complementary capital equipment with which they can work increases.

But some capital equipment may be a close substitute for an input and therefore lower the marginal productivity schedule. So no generalization can be made about the effects of more or less capital equipment on the demand for any given kind of labor services. Terms like *capital equipment* and *labor* are too broad to be useful ways to characterize all types of inputs. For one thing, labor includes too vast a variety of types of people and talents, some being close substitutes, such as young men for middle-aged men, others being complements, such as secretaries for executives. Capital equipment also includes a variety of types of equipment, some closely substitutable, such as word processors for typewriters and for typists, and some being complementary, such as elevators and building space. Nevertheless, the schedule of marginal productivities for any particular type of input depends also on the amount, quality, and type of other jointly used inputs.

But whatever its position, one thing is sure—the schedule is characterized by decreasing marginal products at larger amounts of the input. Hence a good working rule is that the amount demanded is larger the lower the price, and is smaller the higher its price because the amount of each input demanded is that amount at which its marginal product equals its wage or rental price.

DEMAND AND SUPPLY OF LABOR SERVICES

"Labor is not a commodity" is a union battle cry. But labor *services* are bought and sold daily in the market. What *is* different is the market procedure: the personal involvement among persons at work.[2] Although personal relations are significant in determining negotiating procedures, contractual forms, and working arrangements, the forces of demand and supply operate. Labor service is a commodity.

---

[2]The ban against selling all one's future services for a single advance payment does not prevent a person from converting some future earnings into present wealth. One can borrow now to buy a house and car and repay out of the future income. In this way, part of future earnings are exchanged for present goods. Without the right to borrow or to mortgage wealth as security or to buy on the installment plan, people would be at a greater disadvantage in adjusting consumption to the present wealth value of future earnings.

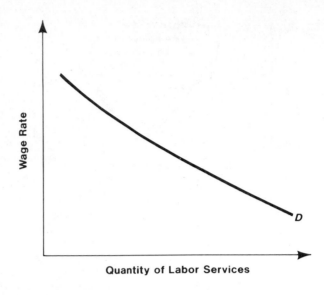

Figure 14-6.

DEMAND FOR LABOR SERVICES

At higher wage rates less labor is demanded and only higher-valued goods and services are produced. At lower wage rates more labor is demanded and more lower-valued goods and services are produced.

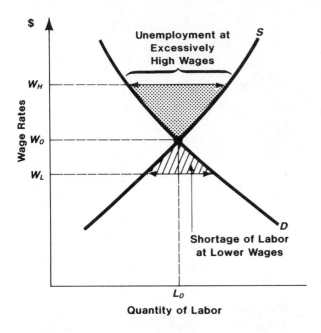

Figure 14-7.

EFFECTS OF FIXING WAGES ABOVE OR BELOW
MARKET-CLEARING WAGE

If wage is set at W_H, higher than market-clearing W_O,
there will be some unemployment. If wage is fixed
at W_L, employers will be unable to get all the labor
they want.

However, this does not mean that all
wages are set by demand and supply in open
competition. Some wages may be set arbitrarily or by political fiat or by the sheer
power of some groups to control the allowable wage rates. Nevertheless, the effects of
even those arbitrary wage rates on the
amount of employment and working conditions can be perceived by demand and supply analysis.

Competition among workers for employment keeps wages low enough for all
willing to work at that wage to be employed, whereas competition among employers pulls wages up high enough to get the
marginal product at that number of employees. That market-clearing, equilibrium wage
rate is the result of competition among employers (actual and potential) for workers
and competition among workers for the better jobs. Because people can leave when
they know of more attractive jobs, to retain
employees an employer must match offers of
other employers. An employer who gives
periodic wage and salary reviews and grants
pay raises without forcing employees to first
seek other offers will not have to pay higher
wages. Instead, by anticipating market
search by employees and competition from
other employers, the employer will have
more willing employees than if all the job-
opportunity comparisons are made by the
employees.

If the wage were arbitrarily set above
the open-market wage rate, job seekers
would exceed the number demanded. If the
wage were artificially held down by some
law, there would be a shortage of workers.
We shall later give real examples of such
cases.

If the demand schedule were raised (that
is, if the marginal productivities of labor
were raised), the wage rate would be competed up. On the other hand, any increased supply of labor in this market would depress
wages, because with more workers the marginal productivity is low. Figure 14-7 will

Table 14-4 ESTIMATED AVERAGE ANNUAL EARNINGS IN VARIOUS TASKS, BY GENDER, IN 1980
(IN THOUSANDS OF DOLLARS)

Occupation	Male	Female	Occupation	Male	Female
Physicians	$52	$23	Telephone linemen	$16	—
Dentists	45	14	Meat cutters	16	$ 7.5
Lawyers	39	20	Auto assemblers	16	—
Optometrists	36	14	Coal miners	16	—
Airline pilots	36	—	Surveyors	16	—
Physicists	31	20	Chemical lab technicians	15	—
Dental hygienists	30	16	Legal secretaries	15	12
Sales managers	30	27	Truck drivers	15	—
Chemical engineers	30	22	Registered nurses	15	13
Economists	30	17	Airline stewardesses	—	13
Architects	28	15	Cabinetmakers	14	—
Administrators	28	22	Secretaries	—	11
Pharmacists	27	21	(Homemakers, housewives)	—	11*
Union officials	23	—	Dieticians	—	10
Accountants	22	13	Upholsterers	13	—
Librarians	22	14	Typists	13	8
Tool & die machinists	22	—	Bank tellers	12	8
Insurance agents	22	—	Bartenders	12	6
Firemen	21	—	Sales clerks	12	7.5
Electricians	21	—	File clerks	11	6
Plumbers	19	—	Nurse's aides	10	6
Urban transport motormen	19	—	Gardeners	7.5	—
Postal clerks	19	—	Cashiers	6.6	5
Carpenters	16	—			

*Value of services—at market cost—estimated and reported by U.S. Social Security Administration and Cornell University.

Source: U.S. Dept. of Labor, *Monthly Labor Review*; U.S. Dept. of Commerce, *Statistical Abstract of the United States.*

help you to understand the remainder of this chapter and the next.

Income Differences

Table 14-4 shows some 1981 average salaries by occupation and sex. The range among the average of different occupations exceeds 10 to 1, from over $50,000 to less than $5000. Within *each* occupation the range of salaries far exceeds 10 to 1. Is it better to be a very good gardener or a mediocre doctor? Actors, musicians, and entertainers have a sensationally wide income range, from millions down to practically nothing, and the average is probably very low indeed.

RELATIVE DEMAND AND SUPPLY

If more first-class musical talent were available and the ability to read or compute were relatively rare, secretaries would get higher salaries than fine musicians. If the number of doctors somehow became enormous, their wages would fall below those of secretaries, because with that many doctors the marginal value of doctors would be very low.

People seek as much training (investment in human capital) as the prospective rewards justify. If anyone could borrow and invest now for clearly perceived higher future earnings resulting from the training, anyone could invest in profitable education. This would not equalize earnings among people, because people's talents differ, but all could fully exploit their talents. However, not everyone can do this. In our legal system and courts, it is not deemed desirable to enforce debts incurred by minors, so lenders are wary of educational loans to young people. Even for adults, enforcement of repayment—or availability of good security—is difficult.

CHANCE-TAKING DIFFERENTIALS

Some people are more willing to give up a surer but narrower range of prospective wages for the risky prospect of earning a higher wage. An architect who gives up a secure job designing conventional buildings and tries to create desirable new designs may end up very much richer or poorer. These choices result in large differences in lifetime earnings within the same occupation.

DIFFERENCES IN PRODUCTIVITIES

Do earnings differences exceed differences in productivities? It has been argued as follows: "When the president of General Products, who is paid $500,000 a year, retires, someone now getting far less will take his place at that high salary. Is that high salary a function of the *position* or of differences in abilities?" In fact it depends on both. The expected productivity of an input affects what it is offered. The associated value of capital or wealth that a manager controls affects the marginal productivity. For example, consider the differences in results between two managers, one with the ability to make correct decisions 5% more often than the other. Roughly speaking, if a 5% superiority is worth about $50,000 in a $1 million business

but only about $5000 in a $100,000 business, then the larger business would gain more with the superior manager than would the small company. On the other hand, because two low-level employees (say typists) who differed by 5% in their ability would not affect the firm's wealth as much as those at the top, the value of the difference in their talents would not be so great. This is why wages for nonmanagerial skills will tend to be independent of the size of the firm, whereas the salaries and abilities of the better top managers will be larger and correlated with the size of the company. The explanation is not that the big companies have more wealth and "deep pockets" and therefore can pay the skilled manager more; instead, superior managers are worth more in bigger than in smaller firms. So competition among firms will raise wages of superior managers in those highly sensitive positions.

MONEY AND NONMONEY WAGE DIFFERENCES

Jobs differ in more than just money earned: The personality and behavior of the employer, health hazards, type of work, job amenities, location, and congeniality of fellow workers are some other features. Money wage differentials that offset these nonmoney differences are called *equalizing*, or *compensating, wage differences*. Differences in nonmoney employment conditions can persist indefinitely if costs of equalizing those conditions exceed the compensating difference in money wages. For example, if getting people to work in the heat raises the wage they must be paid by less than the cost of air conditioning, money wage differentials will persist.

Employees' characteristics also differ. Courteous, pleasant, cooperative, congenial, and accommodating employees provide employers with benefits. If two people are equally productive of wealth at equal wages, the brighter, more pleasant, better-dressed person with a better-modulated voice would be preferred. Desirable qualities will get a higher wage. Higher pay to the attractive person is the same thing as lower pay to the less attractive. Differences in money wages, then, provide employment opportunities for less attractive or less able employees, just as do differences in working conditions. (Question: If differences among employers and working conditions are considered acceptable reasons for employees' discrimination in choice of employers, why do federal laws declare employer discrimination illegal?)

Specific versus General on-the-Job Training A large amount of on-the-job training is provided in business firms. Such training can differ greatly in its applicability to other jobs. Training that is specifically useful to only the current employer is not a source of higher future income in any job with some other employer, so no employee will pay for that, since the employer could later refuse to compensate him. The employee couldn't get paid elsewhere for that specific skill. So the employer must pay for it and will do so if the employee can be restrained from quitting soon after he receives that training. General training is that which is useful with other employers, too. For example, the military services "give" on-the-job training useful in general civilian life with many employers. The employee pays for the general education by accepting lower money wages during training, as during an apprenticeship. The employee is being rewarded with the general training that makes him more productive to any other employer.

Observed Differences in Personal Income and Wealth

Many people view differences of income among people as the result of a division of a *predetermined, fixed* total income, as if my income can increase only if yours is reduced. In fact, the aggregate is created largely by individual contributions. Furthermore, whether the resulting *pattern* of personal wealth is fair and equitable or should be more equal cannot be answered, because the meanings of *fair, equitable,* and *equal* are unclear (which may be why the terms are so popular). One could ask whether the *processes* determining how productive and wealthy a person is and how much the person gets for his or her work lead to larger incomes, to less social friction, or to larger or smaller differences in income.

To illustrate the difficulty in assessing what an "equal distribution" would be, what would you think if some people offered more to Magic Johnson to play more basketball or to Liza Minnelli to sing more, thereby enabling them to be richer than other people? The result would not be a redistribution of some fixed total of income, but an increase in the total. The fans get more of what they want produced, and Johnson and Minnelli each have more income because they rendered more of the highly valued services.

If you argue that no one should inherit more than others, what made Magic Johnson so talented and coordinated and Minnelli so vocal and vivacious? Parents endow their children in many ways other than with buildings, lands, or goods (any or all of which could be taxed away): in genetic inheritance, in giving them knowledge, and in seeing that their abilities are developed by education. Jewish emphasis, for example, on mastering personal skills may be a survival trait developed during a long history in which nonhuman wealth was confiscated. What about your inherited intelligence, color, sex, and abilities? If you object to the inheritance (but not to the giving?) of physical marketable wealth as unfair and unearned, is it any less unfair if it is instead redistributed by taxation? Economic analysis offers no answer.

It may be argued that the existence of a

few very, very wealthy people in a sea of poor people is unjustifiable. Does that mean that their wealth should not have existed? Or should have been given to the poorer as it was produced? If the latter, would there have been incentive to produce the wealth in the first place? We have no complete answers to these queries. We pose them to prevent the facile presumption that answers are obvious, or easy, or even possible.

Socialists say that socialism leads to more equal wealths and incomes and more freedom. The evidence does not support the contention. Top political authorities have special privileges, access to the state's wealth, and power over the lives of other people through the police power of the government—something that the wealthy in a private-property economy lack.

GEOGRAPHICAL DIFFERENCES

Earnings differ among geographical regions and between urban and suburban areas. Workers in areas with high costs of living must have sufficiently high marginal productivity if they are to be paid enough to be attracted to those higher-cost areas. Higher wages in Alaska are due to the higher marginal productivity of the small number of workers there. The workers are producing a service with a value great enough to offset the higher costs of providing these people with the quality of life sufficient to attract them.

If wages and income affect the supply of labor, we ought to observe labor moving from lower-wage areas to higher-wage areas. And we do. Conversely, we should observe capital goods and factories moving toward the lower-wage areas. And we do. Nationwide, the movement of *people* is predominantly to areas with higher wages; counties that have grown in total population are those with higher median family incomes, whereas counties that have lost population

through migration are those with lower incomes.[3]

FAMILY INCOME DIFFERENCES

Table 14-5 classifies families according to income. In 1980 less than one-third of families earned annual incomes over $25,000; less than 10% earned over $40,000. To give you some perspective, the average annual income of economics professors is now over $25,000. Your college's president, if you are at a state university, is most likely in the $50,000-and-over category. As the table shows, U.S. families in the bottom 20% obtained about 7% of after-tax national income, while the families in the top 20% obtained about 40% of the after-tax national income. The middle 60% obtained over 52% of that income. Table 14-6 compares income distribution in the United States with those of Sweden and Russia, often regarded as leaders in income equality. All incomes are after-tax and after-income transfers through subsidies. The similarities in the table are remarkable. Even these data overstate the degree of income differences within a country due to factors to be considered shortly.

Patterns by Family Size Table 14-7 presents 1980 median annual incomes according to size and composition of family. (The median is that which separates the top from the bottom half: Exactly as many families have incomes larger than the median as have incomes lower than the median.)

---

[3]Data reported by Gladys K. Bowles and James D. Tarver, "The Composition of New Migration among Counties in the United States, 1950–1960," *Agricultural Economics Research*, U.S. Department of Agriculture, January 1966. From 1950 to 1960, counties with the lowest median family incomes (under $5000) had a net loss of over 28% of their population. Those with $6000–7500 median family incomes gained 11%. The migration was greater for younger people. No doubt labor is attracted by higher-wage areas and repelled from the lower-wage areas.

Table 14-5 PERCENTAGE DISTRIBUTION OF TYPES OF ANNUAL INCOME, BY FAMILY INCOME CLASSES (UNITED STATES, 1972, EXPRESSED IN 1982 DOLLARS)

	Percent of National Total of Sources of Income in Each Income Class				
Income Class	Household Units	Property Income	Receipts of Government Transfers	Labor Earnings Income	All Income
$ 0–10,000	17	4	19	2	4
10,000–15,000	10	5	12	4	5
15,000–20,000	17	9	15	11	11
20,000–27,500	26	16	18	26	25
27,500–45,000	23	26	19	36	34
45,000 and over	7	40	17	21	21
	100%	100%	100%	100%	100%

Source: U.S. Bureau of the Census, *Current Population Reports*, Series P-60 No. 90, and Lowell Galloway, "The Folklore of Unemployment and Poverty," 1975.

Table 14-6 PERSONAL INCOME SHARES BY QUINTILE: UNITED STATES, SWEDEN, AND THE SOVIET UNION (AFTER TAXES AND SUBSIDIES)

Income Units	United States	Sweden	Soviet Union
Lowest 20%	7%	8%	8%
Middle 60%	53	56	55
Highest 20%	40	36	37
	100%	100%	100%
Highest 5%	15.9	12.9	14.0

Source: L. Galloway, "Folklore of Income Distribution," in S. Pejovich, ed., *Governmental Controls and the Free Market*. College Station: Texas A & M University Press, 1976, Chapter 2. Based on data from Bureau of Economic Analysis of U.S. Commerce Dept. and foreign sources.

Table 14-7 EARNINGS BY TYPES OF FAMILIES, 1980

Family Categories (in Millions)	Median Year-Round Earnings
14 Husband and wife only	$17,500
12 Three persons	19,000
11 Four persons	20,000
10 Five or more persons	21,000
47	
8 Female family head	11,000
55 million	

Source: U.S. Bureau of Labor Statistics, *Monthly Labor Bulletins*

Why Incomes Differ

AGE-RELATED INCOME DIFFERENCES

So far we have been thinking of differences in money plus nonmoney incomes as if they really were differences. But there are some differences that are deceptive. For example, the income of a person varies over one's life. Any income as of a particular year will not necessarily be typical of the average over one's lifetime. Unfortunately, most data on incomes are measures of income of *one* year. Therefore if we use the data on incomes at one year of several people, some of whom are older and some of whom are just beginning their careers, their difference in incomes at any one time will reflect not only differences in lifetime earnings but also in age-related income levels. The older people earn more than young beginners, but over their lifetimes the earnings could be equal.

If every person had the same lifetime pattern of income, rising until about age 50 or 60, but the population comprised people of different ages, then recorded individual incomes in any one year would be unequal because of age-related differences in incomes. The younger would have smaller earnings than the middle-aged; yet lifetime incomes would be equal.

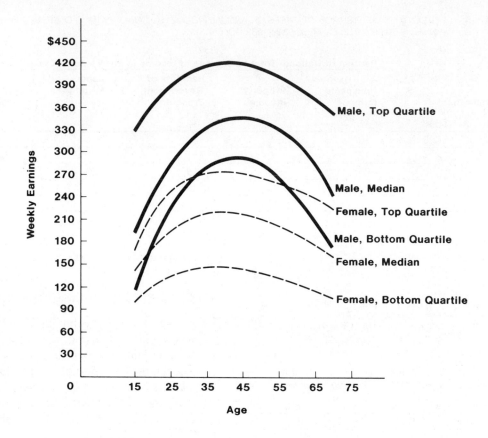

Figure 14-8.

DIFFERENCES IN WEEKLY EARNINGS, BY AGE

SOURCE: U.S. Department of Labor, *Monthly Labor Review.*

Figure 14–8 depicts the observed age-related patterns of weekly incomes for the top quarter, the middle half, and the bottom quarter for males and also for females. For everyone's income in 1980, without regard to age, the differences between the averages of the top and bottom quarters is about $230 per week (between $180 and $410). But for the same age and sex, say at age 50, the range is smaller by some 33%, about $150 per week. Because earnings vary with age, at any time there will always be some poorer people—the young and the elderly—even if everyone had equal lifetime earnings.

An interesting question is how many people in, say, the bottom quarter of the population at any given moment are there solely because of the age-related differences in incomes, and how many are the result of persisting differences in lifetime incomes. It has been estimated *that if everyone had equal lifetime earnings* (though each person's income moved from low at youth to peaks in middle age, then declined), the bottom 25% of the population (mostly the young and elderly) would appear to earn only 20% instead of the age-adjusted lifetime average that equals 25% of the national income of that year. Similarly, the top 25% of the income earners in any one year would account for 35% of the total national income in that year instead of an age-adjusted 25%. Hence, only to the extent that the lowest quarter in any one year earns less than about 20% to 25% of national income and the top quintile earns more than 35% to 45% of national income should one look for differences in skills and productivity among people. In fact, the data indicate that the bottom quarter of people accounts in any one year for only about 15% of national income instead of the age-corrected 25%. Clearly, the observed differences are not all explained solely by the age pattern.

The age effect on income is greater for males than for women during the younger ages. This difference reflects in part the tendency of women to take shorter work spells than men and to invest less in job-related skills.

INVESTMENT
AND INCOME DISPERSION

Another source of the effect of age on income is investment. Some people save more and invest at an early age in property, personal knowledge, and skills. Later they have higher incomes than those who consumed more earlier. This increases income dispersion at the *older* ages. People differ in how they prefer to pace their patterns of consumption over time. Medical doctors, college teachers, and scientists with advanced postgraduate degrees have larger earnings late in life because they consumed less and invested

Table 14-8   MEDIAN FAMILY INCOME BY ETHNIC GROUP, UNITED STATES, 1980

Racial or Ethnic Group	Median Family Income
Japanese	$24,000
Chinese	22,500
White	20,000
Filipino	18,500
Cuban	17,000
Mexican	13,000
Puerto Rican	12,000
Black	11,500

Source: U.S. Bureau of the Census, *Decennial Census of 1970,* adjusted to 1980.

more when younger. A high-school graduate who saved two-thirds of his or her income for about seven years, as some doctors must in their education, would accumulate a respectable amount by age 25.[4]

ETHNIC INCOME DIFFERENCES
REFLECT AGE EFFECT

Income differences among ethnic groups are grossly deceptive because of the very different average ages of income earners. For example, census data indicate differences like those in Table 14–8. The high-income ethnic groups happen to have more older people in their working population, which reflects the effect of time and experience on income.

The average age of blacks in the labor force is much younger than for whites. Therefore, the lower average income of blacks reflects some effect of lower age. Similarly, the average age of Puerto Ricans and

---

[4]If $16,000 a year is earned for seven years (and $10,000 is saved each year), at 8%, a wealth of about $90,000 will accumulate in seven years. This would yield an annuity for 30 years of over $10,000 a year. Will your college education do as well for you? On the average, it is about a toss-up.

Mexican-Americans is lower than for other groups and explains part of the differences in average incomes. Furthermore, if some ethnic group tends to invest more in college education, delaying its years of earnings, and earns more later at older ages, the differences in any one year will overstate the income differences due to any ethnic-related ability. The lifetime differences may be either nonexistent or less than the difference at any one time or for any one age group. None of our analysis explains why one ethnic group invests more in education for later, higher earnings while the other opts for earlier and flatter curves of lifetime in earnings. Nor does it explain any cultural differences that are manifest in different attitudes toward work in the market. What it does reveal, however, is that comparisons of crude data, not corrected for effects of age, formal education, time in work force, and geographic location, are grossly deceptive.

MONEY INCOME DIFFERENCES BETWEEN MALES AND FEMALES

On average, women employees earn money wage incomes about two-thirds the size of men's. But when the observed differences are adjusted for effects of experience in the work force, training, types of work performed, and marital status, the difference attributable to prejudice is greatly reduced or eliminated.[5]

How much of the unwillingness of women to forsake their opportunities of higher-valued domestic productivity accounts for less work in the labor-market force is unknown. It has been said that many women have not entered the market work force because of prejudice against women. But that kind of explanation is of little help. For example, if it *were* prejudice, whose prejudice is it? Why would male employers forsake the profits that could be achieved by hiring equally productive women at lower wages? We do know of two important factors that help explain female-male differences. Women's wages relative to men's *declined* between the late 1940s and about 1970, though they had been increasing prior to World War II. A simple explanation is that after the war women were marrying at an earlier age and having more children. Their average time of work experience was decreasing. But in the 1960s this marriage-age and birth trend reversed. As to be expected, accompanying that reversal was a *rise* in average duration of female work experience and income relative to men's. When adjusted for marriage and differences in work experience, the facts indicate that women in their thirties during the 1970s who have worked continuously since high school or college earned slightly more than single men. In sum, the basic factors explaining female-male differentials appear to be the effects of the female's childbearing productivity and work in the household on her work experience—not employer prejudice and discrimination.

CHOICE OF RISK

Chance events create transiently high incomes in some years and lower ones in others, and contribute to the differences among people's earnings in any *one* year and also over a lifetime. Because people have imperfect foresight, there is no way to avoid that. The question is, "Who will bear the uncertainty?" We can share the risk by averaging over everyone. Or some people can pay others to bear a larger share of the risk. That is one reason self-employed people have a

[5]One study, by J. Mincer and S. Polachek, "Family Investments in Human Capital: Earnings of Women," *Journal of Political Economy*, Vol. 82, no. 2, Part II, March/April 1974, pp. S76–S108, indicates the difference would be reduced to one-sixth. Another study of salaries in college teaching indicates that women with backgrounds and records equal to men get more.

greater dispersion of income over their lifetimes *and* in any year at any one age than do salaried employees, who choose not to bear as much of the enterprise's risk.

MARKET AND NONMARKET INCOME

As explained earlier, real income includes more than money income. Some people get more income in nonmonetary form (for example, farmers versus city dwellers). Some people prefer more leisure; a teacher with three months' absence from teaching has a smaller money income but more time for travel. And as stated earlier, the services of homemakers are excluded from typical money income measures. For these reasons, recorded money incomes fail to encompass full real incomes.

INCOME FROM PROPERTY VERSUS PERSONAL LABOR

Differences in ownership of property are not a primary cause of interpersonal differences in income. Total income from property accounts for about only 10% of total recorded national income. The dominant factor is the difference in earned income from human services—wages, salaries, and self-employment. Finally, government taxes and subsidies redistribute some income. An estimate of the effects of all these is listed in Table 14-5. The similarity of the percentages in the two columns, Labor Earnings Income and All Income, indicate that differences in human earnings are the overwhelmingly dominant source of income differences.

LAND OWNERSHIP AND INCOME DISTRIBUTION

A nontrivial source of income is natural resources: land, and its minerals and water. How much of national income is attributable to the owners of natural resources? Suppose their owners were merely collecting rents for use of those goods and were doing nothing else, so that what they get someone else does not get. Since about 10% of national income appears to be attributable to nonhuman wealth, and of that about 30% is land and its components, we arrive at about 3% as the share of national income going to land and mineral owners. (About 40% of land in the United States is government-owned, most of it the least valuable land.)

It is sometimes argued that if the land and natural resources were owned by everyone equally, incomes would be much more equal. If all of that income from land and natural resources were given to the bottom 15% of income earners in any one year, their average income would equal that of the next 20% above them. That does not come close to equality. But the rationale for this redistribution is further undermined by two facts. First, *current* landowners did not acquire those rights by taking them away from the rest of us (no matter how the rights may have been acquired a couple of centuries ago). The current holders, or their parents, almost all bought it from someone else. Hence, that a large share of the land is held by a very few people does not mean the wealth of the rest of the public is smaller by that amount.

Second, the present and future income derivable from land depends on how well it is used and maintained. Giving everyone an equal right to land (and insisting they keep that right) will affect how the land is used and cared for. If no one can sell the land, incentives to improve it for a capital gain or to transfer it to a higher valuing user are reduced, which tends to reduce the income producing power of the land.

In a few unusual countries, such as Oman and Kuwait, the land is so poor except for containing oil—and labor incomes are so small, the value of the natural resource (oil) is an enormous proportion of the income of these countries.

The Poor

Even though the poorest 10% of income receivers in the United States are enormously richer than most of the population in India, China, Peru, or Tanzania (that is, richer than about 80% of the world's population), they are said to be in poverty.

What does **poverty** mean? In the United States, one criterion (used by the Social Security Administration), adjusted for family size, ages of the family members, and the locality, has the poverty-household income in 1982 varying from about $4000 for a single person to $5500 for a two-person and $8500 for a four-person urban household. (What it may mean in other countries is probably a very much lower level of income.)

The proportion of the population in poverty in any one year in the United States has decreased since 1950 from about one-third to one-tenth, and certainly had long been decreasing before that. For the reasons already given, the number in poverty in any one year overstates the fraction that remains there. First, as explained, personal incomes fluctuate; in some years the income can fall into the poverty category, while in other years it is above it. Second, about one-third of the families in the poverty group are elderly, who because of short life expectancy are consuming more than their income.[6] And many college students will be counted in the poverty group if only current earnings are counted. Third, recent immigrants (for example, Cubans and Asians) constitute disproportionately high but *temporary* membership in the poverty group—a characteristic of most immigrants in their initial years in the United States.

Emphasis must be placed on the *temporary*, initial low-income status of immigrants. In fact, male immigrants in their first year make substantially less (about 20%) than the average native U.S. male. But after 10 years in the United States the immigrants reach equality of income, and after 15 years they *exceed* the average of native-born U.S. males of equal schooling. This increase from an initial temporary low income is common to virtually all immigrant groups regardless of country of origin. An intriguing side fact is that first-generation sons of foreign parentage earn 5% more than the sons of U.S. native-born parents and 8% more if only the father is foreign-born. (Were U.S.-born girls more able than foreign-born girls to select the more promising bachelor immigrants as husbands?)

Who, then, tends to remain in the poverty group? Undoubtedly most important is the sad fact that some people are mentally or physically incapable of producing a significant income. Or some with normal capacities lack the drive and responsibility or training to produce and save toward normal contingencies. Families whose primary source of income is from a woman, an aged person, a farmer, a black, or one lacking a high-school education are heavily represented in the persistent poor.

WELFARE AND ALLEVIATION OF POVERTY

Not every low-income earner receives the same corrective or alleviative aid. Family responsibility for relatives is a prime source of aid. Whereas voluntary charitable aid is distributed according to personal judgments about the merits of each case, political agents cannot display such personal discrimination. Tax-financed redistributions of income and wealth are part of all governments' activities. Graduated income and inheritance taxes take

---

[6]Some give all their wealth to their children to qualify for welfare, relying upon their children also to assure them of support for consumption. A person with a life expectancy of five years and a wealth of $20,000 would report an income of perhaps $1000, although he could consume at the rate of about $6000 a year for five years. Should such a person be considered *long-term* poor?

a larger portion from higher incomes. For example, it has been estimated that for families with annual incomes of under $4000, federal and local taxes take over 40% of income, compared to about 25% for middle-income families and 45% for very high income families with $50,000 and over. But interpersonal transfers of wealth by taxes and subsidies (social security payments, welfare, and unemployment compensation) yield the under-$4000 families an estimated *net increase* of 80% of their pretax income. The group earning over $50,000 has been estimated to experience a net decrease of about 45%.

Unfortunately, that comparison is defective because it does not include all government services. If some of those services are distributed to the higher-income or politically powerful groups in amounts greater than their taxes, they would be aided and the poor hurt. Some government services *are* received in greater amounts by the richer groups—for example, publicly subsidized golf courses, and better schools, parks, colleges, and roads in richer residential areas. Without better data, no definitive answer can be given about the overall effects of government taxes and expenditures.

Government welfare activities are intended to relieve the indigent by transferring wealth and by encouraging recipients to increase their abilities or rehabilitate themselves. Some argue that many of the poor have not worked as diligently and been as careful in saving income as others who are not poor. Others argue that the poor are poor for reasons not of their own making: They argue that poverty is the social byproduct of a complex, highly interdependent, dynamic economy, and conclude that responsibility for alleviating this poverty therefore rests primarily with society. Both arguments are defective. The first does not imply that nothing should be done for (or to?) those who may be so irresponsible as to be poor. The second is defective in that even more poor existed when society was less complex, inter-

dependent, and dynamic; furthermore, everyone—rich and poor alike—lives in that kind of society. More germane is what kind of aid to give—in what form, how much, and under what conditions.

Automatic money aid to very low income groups has been proposed. One form, known as the reverse, or negative, income tax, would give money to those earning less than a specified standard of income. This has been proposed as a substitute for the entire welfare system, which uses additional criteria for deciding whom to aid. The negative income tax plan would be less expensive to administer, but would it contain the purported remedial elements of the current welfare system?

To strike more directly at one cause of low income, more appropriate education has been proposed. High-school education has not generally provided significant vocational training for those not continuing to college. More on-the-job training could be subsidized by taxes if such vocational training is not given in the public schools. Exempting teenagers from the minimum-wage law would permit on-the-job training to be part of their pay, because teenagers' services to employers while learning are often worth less than the money they must be paid by law under the minimum-wage requirement. In this case the training cost would be borne by the teenager rather than by taxes on the rest of society, as is done for nonvocational education.

Unemployment and Poverty?

Surprisingly, unemployment is not a cause of poverty or low-income status. Unemployment affects incomes temporarily during the period of unemployment. Because Chapter 17 investigates the causes and extent of unemployment, we note here only that unemployment, for example, of carpenters, construction workers, or auto or steel workers, does not push them into poverty levels. That unemployment which is caused by the uncertainties of weather and building-completion dates results in higher wages per hour actually worked. In many industries layoffs are a recurring phenomenon, so they can be expected, but when they will occur cannot always be predicted accurately. Their anticipation forces employers to offer more to offset those temporary intervals.

Unemployment has a minor effect on incomes and wealth, and cuts across all levels of income earners—some of the very rich (entertainers, skilled mechanics, and lawyers) as well as the poor. When it occurs the unemployed find themselves in a lower-income group for a while. But over half of the unemployment spells are shorter than two months and, furthermore, are not periods of loss of total income. It should not be surprising, then, that spells of unemployment are not a significant factor pushing people into the poverty category, or into substantially lower lifetime wealth. More details are given in Chapter 17.

Social Security System

An important element altering the pattern of incomes is the Social Security System—more accurately known as the Old Age, Survivors, Disability, and Health Insurance Program (OASDHI), instituted in 1936. People above the age of 65 receive annually an amount that is based partly on their earlier earnings and payments to the Social Security System. The funds paid out in any year are obtained from taxes on the incomes of the currently nonretired people. Initially the recipients were so few that the tax on the nonretired was more than sufficient, and a surplus was accumulated.

That sort of intergenerational wealth transfer could continue if the younger working population increased enough to more than match the increasing number of retired people. Since the earlier contributions are now (1982) exhausted, heavier taxes must be levied (22% of income earned), or promised benefits reduced, or the retirement age deferred. But the Social Security System has induced a very substantial number of people to retire earlier.

Technological Progress and Jobs and Wages

Although opposed by some labor groups, adoption of production-increasing inventions is a source of increased wealth, easier work, and higher real incomes, and makes a larger population possible. The ox-drawn plow was a great technological advance over the use of human pulling power. The people who lost their jobs pulling plows turned to what formerly were less important tasks, like collecting more wood and building more stone fences. When the tractor replaced the horse and several plowmen, people were released to produce other things. With the new machines, labor's marginal productivity in the old jobs was reduced below that in tasks formerly left undone. Technological progress creates new types of jobs. There will always be plenty of jobs—in fact, more than can *ever* be filled. We repeat, there are not too few but *too many* jobs! The problem is comparing and deciding which to perform and which to leave unperformed. Inventions, automation, and progress make us richer, but they do not eliminate the persisting problem of predicting the highest valued of the remaining tasks.

To discern the employment and income effects of technological progress, we distinguish three groups of people. Consider the rise of television: (1) Some people get higher wages because they produce more in TV with the new equipment and programs.

They benefit doubly—from higher income and from lower prices of improved products. (2) Some other people have incomes that do not depend on TV. They benefit from the lower costs of home entertainment, without any loss of income. (3) Some people are displaced by the advent of TV and transfer to next-best jobs. This class can be further divided into three subcategories: (a) Some are better off on net, because they gain from being able to use television as a consumer. (b) Of the remainder who do not reap a gain, even after considering all the effects of this particular innovation, some are nevertheless better off than if *all* progress were stopped. They gain through the lower prices and quality improvements to consumers—despite their income loss. (c) Some employees and owners of outmoded equipment suffer such severe reductions in demand for their services that, even after taking into account the gains from TV and from all technological improvements that will occur during the rest of their lives, they are worse off. This is more characteristic of older people in radio than of the younger.

As yet, we are unable to predict for any invention how many people, let alone who, will fall into each class. Even afterward it is often impossible to tell, because other changes obscure the effects. For example, did the invention of the typewriter increase or decrease the demand for secretaries? The discovery of oil may have attracted labor from coal mines into oil well drilling, refining, and pipeline work, so that the wages of coal miners *increased* despite the negative effect of oil on the demand for coal. Inventions not only affect the productivity of workers in the affected jobs, they attract workers, thus raising wages elsewhere. Spectacular examples are the railroad and the automobile, which lowered costs of transportation; as a result, transport increased, as did the demand for workers to provide materials for transportation. Canalmen, livery-stable operators, and buggy-whip makers shifted to better-paying jobs in the new transportation industry. New machines sometimes reduce the costs of products so much that the increased amount demanded raises the demand for labor in that job (for example, typewriters and computers).

COMPENSATION PRINCIPLE

Out of the net gain from technological progress, the whole community could compensate displaced and reallocated workers for any loss. This is a logically airtight possibility, because the increased value of output exceeds the losses of the displaced factors. However, innovations are too extensive to identify each and every displaced factor and to determine who loses how much. How would we know how much to pay a person who claims to be displaced by the introduction of electronic computers? How could we be sure that some easy, low-paying job has not been taken—in the expectation of receiving a payment large enough to make up the difference? Only if people's incentives were not changed by the compensation principle, and if there were no prohibitive costs in discovering who gained or lost how much, would that compensation system be feasible. Nevertheless, compensation is not ignored. Today, people pay taxes for a program to retrain and relocate workers.[7] But if labor were

---

[7]This aid is proposed, however, not only for those whose incomes are cut by competition from new, more productive equipment, but for any laborer who lives in an area where there is a general decline in demand for services—whatever the reason. A displaced worker in a prosperous *area* is not eligible.

The Trade Expansion Act of 1962 gives the president additional powers to negotiate for tariff reduction and, when injury from increased imports can be demonstrated, provides for "trade adjustment assistance" for both business firms (through technical assistance, loans, tax relief) and workers (through special unemployment benefits, retraining, loans for moving to jobs in different communities).

compensated, why not also owners of nonhuman assets? If compensation were paid *out of taxes* for every change in value resulting from innovation, the general public would be the risk bearer, through taxes from which government services would be financed.

Summary

1. About 80% of the value of marketed goods and services goes to income for human labor. The remainder pays for the services of nonhuman capital goods.

2. Payment for the use of a capital good is called *rent* if the good is used by someone other than its owner, and is called *interest* if the good is money. Earnings from the use of a capital good by its owner are called *implicit rent*. Income earned by a firm is paid out to its owners, the stockholders, as *dividends*.

3. A *capitalist* advances payment to labor to make goods that will yield services later, at which time the capitalist hopes to be repaid for depreciation and interest on the goods' earlier costs.

4. Unemployment results not from there being too few jobs but from too many. People investigate and evaluate alternative jobs to determine which is best, rather than taking the first seen alternative.

5. Demand for labor (or for any input) reflects the marginal productivities of different amounts supplied. The schedule of marginal productivities for any given input depends upon the types of other resources that can be used jointly. Some jointly used inputs, called *complements,* raise that input's marginal productivity schedule, and some, called *substitutes,* lower it. *All* joint inputs are substitutes in the sense that having more of one will in part offset having less of the other.

6. About 60% of the U.S. adult population is in the market labor force, 80% of the males and 50% of the females. The male labor-force participation rate has been decreasing; that of females has been increasing. Also de-creasing are the rates for those under age 20 and those over 55 (the latter primarily because of Social Security payments).

7. At very high wage rates the total labor force participation rate in the U.S. may be reduced as people seek more leisure by working fewer hours or leave the work force because their spouses earn more.

8. Wage rates, like the prices of any other goods, are determined by demand and supply market forces.

9. Ricardian rent, which is the amount by which a higher wage exceeds a lower wage for the same productive activity, is a payment for superior talents or abilities; or for willingness to undertake riskier tasks, or to work and live in certain regions; or for the costs of training and education.

10. If all annual incomes were measured at the same instant, the differences among them would be related to how income earners differ in age, sex, geographic area, money vs. nonmoney incomes, ethnic background, past investment in personal training, variances between the highest and lowest wages in any occupation, transient variations of income over time, and talents and abilities.

11. When people's earnings are summed over their lifetimes they are much closer to equal than is suggested by the income differences among people of different ages in any one year.

12. Between 1950 and 1980 the proportion of people usually described as being poor has decreased from a third to a tenth of the U.S. population.

13. Governmental redistribution of income has tended to raise the real incomes of the poor relative to those of the richer.

14. The Social Security System finances old-age retirement benefits by taxing current income earners; the amount paid to a retiree is partly dependent upon the retiree's pre-retirement Social Security taxes and income.

15. Unemployment is not the reason that some people are poor.

16. Technological advances increase real output and would make everyone better off either by lowering the costs of purchases or by raising incomes. But some losses do occur to those whom the advance displaces to lower-paying jobs. Those displaced could, in principle, be compensated, because the total social gains exceed their losses, but for a variety of reasons they are rarely compensated.

Questions

1. "In the open market, wages are driven down to the subsistence level." That is the iron law of wages. What is meant by "the subsistence level"?

2. "My doctor charges me a high fee because he has to cover the high cost of his education and equipment. On the other hand, my golfing teacher also charges me a high fee, even though his education is practically absent." Is either one cheating or fooling me? Explain.

3. "Elizabeth Taylor was paid over $5 million for making a film. Yet Glenda Jackson could have taken her place for, say, $1 million. There must be something wrong with the movie industry." Using marginal-productivity theory, explain how it can be sensible to pay Elizabeth Taylor that much more.

4. A candidate for the office of U.S. Senator proposed that employees be given time off with pay to promote political campaigns of their favored candidates.
   a. Tell under what circumstances you as an employer would not care if this were done. (Hint: Remember, there is more than the money pay that attracts employees to a job.)
   b. Who would be paying for the time off?

5. A law is passed requiring each employer to provide hospitalization and premature retirement benefits for his employees who have "heart attacks."
   a. Who will benefit by such a law?
   b. Who will be hurt?
   c. Who will pay the costs? (In answering, first consider the same questions if a law were passed requiring employers to pay for all the housing costs of redhaired employees. Explain why if you were a redhead you would be smart to dye your hair black. Similarly, if you had a heart condition, why would you try to keep it a secret? Does the employer pay for these services—in the sense that his wealth is lower as a consequence of the law? If he doesn't, who does?)

6. Some employment contracts provide the employee with the following: paid time off for jury duty, funerals of relatives, voting, sickness, and vacations; free parking space and work clothes; retirement; two weeks' severance pay; seniority rights over new employees; no discharge for union activities; no discharge if job is displaced by new machinery.
   a. Suppose you were to offer to work for some employer who did not give any of these provisions and who insisted on the right to fire or discharge you at any time for any reason whatsoever. Would you consider working for him at the same take-home pay as for the other employer?
   b. Would the employer be willing to pay you a higher take-home salary for an employment contract without all those provisions listed earlier?
   c. In the light of your answers to the preceding questions, who do you think pays for those fringe benefits listed earlier?

7. The National Teachers Federation, a teachers' union, advocates a single salary scale—wherein every teacher, regardless of specialty, gets the same salary in his first year of teaching, with salary thereafter tied strictly to years of service. Who would benefit and who would suffer if that were made universal: Men or women? Blacks or whites? Superior or inferior teachers? Mathematics or physical-education teachers?

8. Laws have been passed designed to prohibit employers from discriminating among potential employees according to race, religion, and, in some instances, age. Why are there no laws prohibiting employees from similarly discriminating among employers for whom they choose to work?

*9. Minimum-wage laws prevent relatively untrained people, especially teenagers and blacks, from getting jobs. To overcome this the federal government is going to subsidize employers for hiring these less-trained people. The rationale is that the workers hired at the minimum legal wage, though not that productive, will learn on the job and in time become productive enough to warrant that wage. In the meantime, the employer, receiving a subsidy of an amount equal to the difference between the worker's productivity and the wage paid the worker, is providing on-the-job education. Show how this amounts to facilitating a privately operated educational system, with choice by students of the private "school" they will attend.

*10. At many colleges students are gaining membership on committees that appoint or fire faculty members. The faculty usually contends that employment is a matter best judged by qualified people like faculty members. Students contend that the faculty chosen affects their lives and hence they should have a say in the matter. (1) The authors say that neither faculty nor students should have the authority to hire or fire faculty. (2) Moreover, students already have more power than the faculty. Explain in what sense (2) is correct; then defend as best you can the preference expressed by the authors in sentence (1).

11. Black capitalism is often advocated. Black capitalism might mean either (a) that blacks will borrow only from black savers, or (b) that blacks will buy only or primarily from black merchants. Would blacks be benefited or harmed?

Chapter 15
Labor-Market Institutions

As we saw in the last chapter, labor services, like other goods, are allocated and priced according to the laws of demand and supply. But although labor services are sold, their sources, human beings, are not sold as if they were machines (except in a slave economy). Because the social relationships between buyers and sellers of labor services differ from those between buyers and sellers of goods, important differences in marketing, negotiating and contractual forms have evolved. Among the adaptations are **labor unions**: coalitions of a firm's employees with collective contracts covering them all. Also, legal regulations of the conditions of employment (such as minimum-wage and fair-employment laws) are in force. In this chapter we analyze unions and these regulations.

Labor Unions

Labor unions have existed for a long time, often despite being declared illegal as "criminal conspiracies," as they were in England and France at the time of the French Revolution. Although such anticonspiracy laws may have been directed against the threat of violence in strikes launched to restrict open competition for jobs and wages by labor, they also abolished even the right to form a union. By 1830 the English anticonspiracy laws had been repealed and the right to strike was tacitly recognized. In the United States in 1842 the Massachusetts Supreme Court rendered a precedent-setting decision in *Commonwealth* v. *Hunt* declaring unions to be legal. In almost all communist countries—or at least those behind the Iron Curtain—the right to form a union, let alone to strike, is denied.

In the United States only about 22 million employees, 22% of the labor force, are in unions. In some jobs virtually every employee is a union member (longshoremen, transport workers, construction workers), and

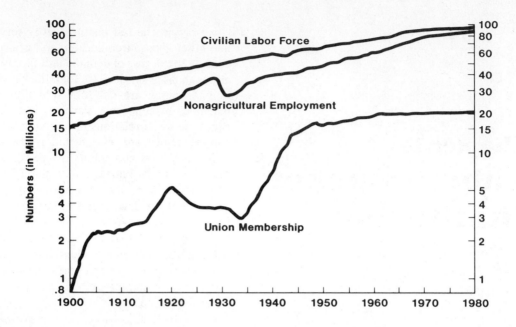

Figure 15-1.

CIVILIAN LABOR FORCE, EMPLOYEES IN
NONAGRICULTURAL ESTABLISHMENTS, AND TRADE
UNION MEMBERSHIP, 1900–1980

SOURCE: L. Troy, *Trade Union Membership, 1897–1962*
(New York: National Bureau of Economic Research,
1965). Updated, *U.S. Statistical Abstract.*

in others nearly none (chemists, typists, engineers, clerks, economists). Figure 15-1 charts union membership against the total U.S. civilian labor force throughout this country. Figure 15-2 shows the percentage of the civilian labor force belonging to unions. The dramatic increase in union membership during the late 1930s has been attributed primarily to legislation (such as the Wagner Act, passed in 1935) compelling employers to negotiate with a union if a majority of the employees so vote. Federal labor laws are administered in large part by the National Labor Relations Board (NLRB).

National unions are federations of many separate chartered *locals.* The local, the membership in a small geographical area

such as a city or county, has the power to apply membership rules and approve and monitor contracts. For example, although the national federation has a constitution asserting that membership is open to all regardless of race or creed, the local members set the actual admission standards, which often discriminate according to ethnic background, age, and sex. Discrimination is especially common in craft unions.

Craft unions are those whose members are skilled in the same craft. **Industrial unions** are those composed of people in one industry (defined in terms of product) regardless of their individual skills. For example, the carpenters' union is a craft union, whereas the steel workers' union is an industrial union containing members with different skills in the steel industry. Most craft unions are allied in a national *federation*, the American Federation of Labor (AFL), and most industrial unions are in the Congress of Industrial Organizations (CIO). A few national unions such as the Teamsters and the coal miners belong to neither. The AFL and the CIO have a joint top-level council called the

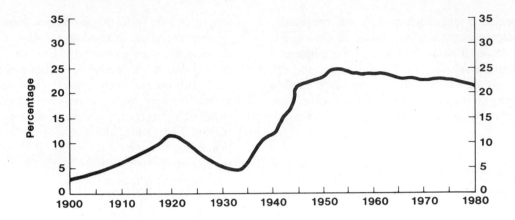

Figure 15-2.

PERCENT OF UNION MEMBERSHIP IN THE
CIVILIAN LABOR FORCE

SOURCE: L. Troy, *Trade Union Membership, 1897–1962*
(New York: National Bureau of Economic Research,
1965). Updated, *U.S. Statistical Abstract.*

AFL-CIO. One of its purposes is to define the jurisdictions of its member unions to reduce rivalry among them, about, for example, whether an electrical fixture may be installed by a carpenter or an electrical worker.

The *local*'s officers, usually elected by the local membership, maintain membership rolls, monitor contract terms, and administer routine affairs such as pension funds and shop grievances. A *shop steward*, a union member in the firm, helps to avoid or settle grievances, much as an agent acts as an intermediary between two contracting parties. Safety rules, working hours, interpretations of vacation policy, and "goofing" on the job are a few of the perennial sources of misunderstanding and dispute that a shop steward can alleviate. Union activity is financed by initiation fees and monthly dues (usually less than $100).

Some firms are *closed shops*: Only union members can apply for and get jobs. Some are *union shops*: New employees must become union members, or at least pay union fees, if they are to retain their jobs. *Open shops* do not require union membership.

A **boycott** is a *concerted* refusal by some group to do business with a certain firm, with the intent to persuade the firm's operators to respond to the boycotters' demands. Sometimes, other firms that do business with the boycotted firm will also be boycotted—a

secondary boycott. The **strike**, which is the ultimate weapon to influence the employer, consists of two necessary parts: Employees stop work *and* prevent other people from replacing them. Without the ability to prevent others from negotiating for the vacated jobs, a strike would merely be a mass resignation.

The right to strike has had its ups and downs. At times it was prohibited as an interference with a nonstriker's access to labor markets. At other times police have permitted pickets to block the entry of others. In 1932 the Norris-LaGuardia Act effectively restricted the power of the courts to issue orders, *injunctions*, prohibiting a union from engaging in strikes, picketing, and certain types of boycotts. But the Taft-Hartley Act of 1947 permitted the president to prohibit any strike that would create a "national emergency." Section 14–b of the act permitted states to ban union shops. Approximately 20 states have passed "right-to-work" laws, which make it illegal to require union membership as a condition for applying for or keeping a job.[1] Such laws do not necessarily increase every worker's range of choice. For example, if some firm and all its employees wanted a union shop, the state right-to-work law would prevent it. On the other hand, a group of employees cannot force other employees to join a union.

Employee/Employer Bargaining Power

Often it is said that individually employees lack sufficient **bargaining power** and so must accept wage offers that are lower than a demanded wage. This is the argument used in favor of **collective bargaining**: the requirement that an employer negotiate wages with all the employees as a group rather than as individuals. But what forces General Motors to pay the wages it does? The answer is that if General Motors offers lower wages than other employers, it will get fewer employees, so its employees get a wage that is at least as high as their services are worth to other employers. An important truth is that employers compete against other employers, and employees against other employees—not employees against employers, as folklore says. It is the availability of higher-valued alternatives, not the ability to bargain collectively, that increases bargaining power.

Labor-Union Objectives

"The high wages of the American worker are a result of a strong labor-union movement." If only it were true. Higher income for all workers in poor countries would be easy: Un-

---

[1]The Taft-Hartley Act is under attack from unions, and almost every year attempts are made in Congress to repeal it by prohibiting any state from requiring open shops in all places of employment.

ionize and strike for higher wages. However, neither economic reasoning nor factual evidence supports the quoted claim. If a community has more natural resources and capital equipment, high educational levels, skilled workers, and a system for organizing productive activity, productivity will be higher. That, and nothing else, is the foundation of high wages and income. But can unions contribute to higher productivity and thereby raise wages or improve employment conditions? Yes.

Agents of a union within any firm can smooth grievance procedures and can monitor working relationships among employers, supervisors, and employees, much as real estate agents serve as negotiators between sellers and buyers to ensure more effective fulfillment of contracts. That is why union agents monitor an employer's provision of promised working conditions, fringe benefits, security, insurance, retirement, and the like. If an employer supplies less in the way of pensions, vacations, or medical insurance than was promised, no one employee might discover that fact until it was too late to seek a remedy—because unlike weekly or monthly wages, these forms of pay are to be received as services *in the future*. Thus, if the employer's performance in the interim were closely monitored, the employee would be surer to get the promised future benefits. Similarly, unions can monitor the performance of the employees themselves. Possibly the most important function of unions, then, is to improve general productivity by improving contract negotiation and fulfillment between employers and the multitude of employees.

This monitoring of performance is so valuable that almost every big firm whose employees are not members of a *labor* union will create a *company* union, operated by the firm for its employees. A company union reduces grievances by more efficiently monitoring for employees the employer's promised performance of agreements—and by monitoring the employees' performance.

If an employer and the agents of a labor union are unable to resolve a dispute, they sometimes hire an outsider as an *arbitrator* to suggest mutually acceptable terms (though neither party necessarily agrees to accept the terms). No law requires employers and employees to submit disputes to an arbitrator for a binding settlement, but about 90% of labor-union contracts provide for some kind of arbitration.

If enforcing the employer's performance of a contract by punishing violations were the only purpose of union strikes, few employers would oppose unions. The monitoring of promised performance does not produce the spectacular situations that are created by another attribute of unions: going on strike, disrupting the firm's business, and preventing other workers from competing for union members' jobs. This ability to strike to restrict the labor-services market, or monopolize it, is the reason employers fear labor unions.

Do Unions Raise Union Wages?

Not all union bargaining, backed up by the threat of a strike, is necessarily designed to achieve wages higher than would be obtained in an open market. Suppose, for instance, an employment contract were signed two years ago, and since that time wages, because of general inflation, have risen 15%. To retain, as well as improve, the work force in the face of better wages elsewhere, the employer may be ready to offer a pay raise of 20%, but initially offers 15%. Union officials, also expecting to get 20%, first demand 25%. After a ritual of bargaining, the terms come out to be 20%, and the union claims it has raised wages. However, neither the employer nor the union set the final wage rate: The employer pays the wage that must be paid to retain employees, and the union

members accept the offer unless they are prepared to face a loss of job opportunities from this employer, who will be unable to hire so many at a higher wage.

Some unions have raised their hourly wage rates above those on the open market; many others have had no detectable effect on their wage rates. The best estimates are that the effect on the *average* union member's income has been to raise it 10% to 15% above that of equivalent nonunion workers.[2] But this apparent superiority may have been achieved because nonunion wages are made lower than they otherwise would be, because fewer people are hired at that higher union wage. The displaced workers then move into the nonunion labor market, where by enlarging the supply they lower the average wage. Some unions have had greater effect; for example, the income of union coal miners was estimated to be about 50% higher than that of nonunion miners, though fewer were employed at those wages, and nonunion wages were reduced.

Our earlier economic analysis, summarized here in Figure 15–3, suggests three primary ways to raise wages:

1. Raise the productivity and hence the competitive demand for labor (panel A of the figure).

2. Restrict the supply of labor (panel B).

3. Impose higher wage rates despite the resulting reduced amount of employment (panel C).

1. Although some unions may try to help raise the demand for labor (the marginal productivity schedule), there is little evidence of significant success. However, insofar as the union serves as an efficient monitor of the

---

[2]See H. G. Lewis, *Unions and Relative Wages in the United States* (Chicago: University of Chicago Press, 1963).

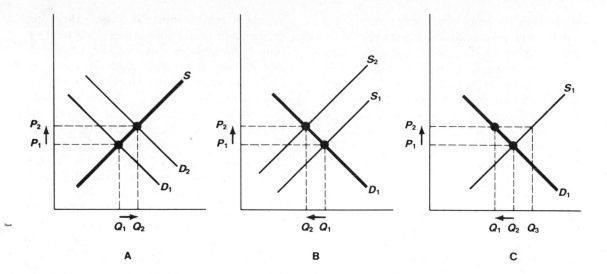

Figure 15-3.

ALTERNATIVE BASIC MEANS OF AFFECTING
WAGE RATES AND EMPLOYMENT

Panel A shows that an increase in demand for labor will
increase wage rates from P_1 to P_2 and employment from
Q_1 to Q_2.

Panel B shows that a decrease in supply will
increase wage rates but not employment. The problem is
how to exclude some people from the market in order to
reduce supply. Immigration restrictions, licensing, entry
qualifications (education, age, sex, residence) are some
of the means.

Panel C shows that an arbitrarily higher wage rate
negotiated without a change in demand or supply will
leave displaced workers whose presence may be
sufficiently strong to restrain the possibility of pushing
up wage rates. The problem is how to prevent new
entrants and displaced workers from undercutting
the agreed-upon wage rate. Jobs can be rationed
or shared by spreading reduced work over all
members, as the musicians' union does.

employer's promises, the *full wages* (that is,
including nonmoney components) are higher.

2. The supply in some cases is effectively limited by restricting admission to certain
unions or professional groups: longshoremen,
plumbers, doctors, certified public accountants, electricians, projectionists, linotypists,
and butchers, to name a few. Apprenticeship
requirements, compulsory licensing, and limits on membership are examples of devices
for restricting entry to restrain supply.

3. By exercising sufficient restrictive
power, the union or professional group may
impose wages higher than the competitive
level. The fewer available jobs at that higher
wage will have to be rationed among the
larger number of applicants. Employers in
the industry who cannot survive at the higher imposed wages do not replace equipment.
Output diminishes until the smaller supply
results in higher prices to cover the higher
wages of the fewer employees. Displaced employees shift to less-valuable jobs at wages
lower than they otherwise would have
earned, and the increased competition for
those jobs among displaced workers pushes
those wages still lower. The national income
is smaller.

Because wages increase only for those

employees who retain their jobs at the higher wage, strikes and imposed higher wage rates cannot raise the wages of employees *in general*. For labor, as for any other good, the higher the price (here wage rates), the smaller is the quantity demanded.

There is a way in which a union can get a *short-lived* increase in wages for all its members. This can happen if an employer has some resources and equipment that are useful *only* in this present firm (that is, the resources are *specific* to the firm). Higher wages would absorb most of the revenue that would have gone to these firm-specific resources. These resources, having lower alternative use value elsewhere, simply couldn't get any more than the residual after the necessary *general* inputs are paid. To take a simple example, if a union of peach pickers were to strike at the moment the peaches were ready to be harvested, it could demand a wage so high as to absorb all the value of the ripened peaches. After all, unpicked peaches would be worthless. The farmer would have no better alternative than to pay up to as much as the entire value of the peach crop to get them picked, because the costs of growing the peaches and bringing them to harvest ripeness have already been incurred.

This action expropriates the *quasi-rent* of the employer's investment, the realization of which depends on having a labor force at the competitive market wage rate, no higher. That quasi-rent of the peach crop will be lost to the employer if the peach pickers can demand the value of the crop as the price of picking it. This threat, if believed to be likely, would prevent investing in growing peaches. That fear is one reason that farmers are so strongly opposed to unions. In some other industries, such as steel, the productive resources and product don't wither away, so there is much less possibility of destroying so much of the employer's investment in specific resources.

Obviously, this expropriative tactic is not likely to be repeated with any employer. No employer would ever again agree to a contract with those employees or that union—as is seen in the grape growers' strong resistance to unions that do not have a reliable record of not engaging in that tactic. In any event, although this tactic is not a lasting source of higher wages (unlike the first-mentioned method of imposing higher long-term wages at the cost of fewer jobs), it sometimes leads to spectacular strikes. As a result people often think that striking to raise wages above their competitive levels is the only function of the union—thereby overlooking the important monitoring function explained earlier.

THE STRIKE AS A MARKET RESTRICTION

It is a tribute to the intelligence and economic acumen of union leaders that they know that the right to strike is crucial to a strong union. To be effective the strike must, as already emphasized, succeed in preventing other people from competing for the jobs.

When a union prevents nonunion workers from working for less than the wages it seeks, does it differ from the medical profession, which prevents a free market for medical services? One difference is that the medical profession has *more successfully* defended its actions, in the name of higher quality of (a smaller quantity of) medical service. That it also enables doctors to get higher wages is not a difference. The second difference is that the medical profession does not have to rely on strikes and private intimidation of competitors who would sell their services at lower prices. Instead, it has a licensing law which is enforced by arrest, and possible prosecution, of the competitor. If laws prohibit the sale of workers' services by anyone except a "licensed" (union) person, or prohibit training except in approved schools, then the union can keep the supply small and wages higher. Were the public police force available, gangsters and hoodlums, the specialists in intimidation, would be of less value. All union officials would be as free of the "undesirable elements" as are the officers of the medical and legal associations and public utilities, to name only a few closed monopolies. There is no apparent reason why the people who seek to collude or to eliminate competitors should only be, for example, tobacco growers, milk producers, liquor sellers, taxi owners, lawyers, morticians, doctors, teachers, and radio and television station owners, rather than teamsters, carpenters, auto assemblers, retail clerks, and dock workers.

JOB RATIONING
IN RESTRICTED LABOR MARKETS

Because the amount of labor supplied exceeds the number of jobs available at a wage higher than its open-market level, those jobs must be rationed in accord with some non-wage criteria. One procedure is to have a seniority system, whereby job security is proportional to the number of years already on that job. The employees with less seniority get the temporary, seasonal jobs; when demand is low they are the first to go, thus protecting employees with seniority. Another method is work sharing, limiting the number of days a person can work, so that more people can be hired to produce the same output (at the same productive rate).

Jobs may be rationed through restrictions on union membership (such as by larger initiation fees or by more rigid or narrower standards applying to race, age, sex, education, experience, and probationary membership). "Unethical' job-seeking conduct (for example, advertising) prejudicial to the senior employed members of the union (whether it be the American Medical Association, the American Bar Association, the Teamsters, or the longshoremen) can warrant expulsion. An alternative, publicized reason for these restrictions is protection from shoddy work

by less competent workers.

Protests by blacks and women against these criteria for union membership and jobs have persuaded national union officials to try to change the situation. But local unions decide admission, and complaints still abound. And as long as membership is limited or wages exceed the market competitive level, economic analysis tells us that more discrimination on bases other than wages is necessary in deciding who shall obtain the jobs.

If the union is strong enough to raise wages and restrict access to jobs, it may also be able to impose some other employment conditions, such as "featherbedding", or "tie-ins" whereby an employer must pay laborers more than they otherwise would be paid. Hod carriers, for example, once refused to carry premixed concrete unless paid part of the employer's cost savings; typesetters required newspapers to set duplicate type if preset type forms were submitted by advertisers; building and movie production codes specify unnecessarily expensive labor-using techniques; standby local musicians must be hired when touring orchestras perform locally. All are expressions of legal monopoly power deriving from the power to strike effectively, and all extract some of the quasi-rent of the employer's specific resources.

PUBLIC UTILITIES
AND GOVERNMENT BUREAUS
VULNERABLE TO MONOPOLY
RENT TO EMPLOYEES

There remains still another source of higher wages to a strong union. Public utilities are legal monopolies whose prices are regulated to prevent them from charging the full monopoly price. But when faced with union demands, public utilities, whether privately owned or government-owned, can more easily yield to union wage demands because they can draw on potential monopoly rent. The regulatory commission may allow the public utility to raise prices to transfer to its employees any monopoly rent the utility can still expropriate from the public. Examples are transit systems, whether bus, taxi, or rail.

A similar situation arises when public employees strike against governments, again, withholding services *and preventing anyone else from replacing them*. When they do so and succeed, they in effect use government power to tax the public to finance their demands. (We know of no analysis that determines how much of such taxation the public will tolerate.) Of course, the higher the wages the greater will be the number of people seeking some of those jobs, whether they be firefighters, police officers, garbage collectors, teachers, or bus drivers. One restraint on higher tax-supported wage is competition among cities and among states. People and industry move to locales where taxes and utility costs are comparatively low. Why then do some state legislatures and city councils encourage and even require unions for public employees? Ask your political science instructor, but only after you try examining the economic interests of politicians to see whether they get a better hold on political office, income, and power by votes from government employees whom they have benefited. Again, note that nothing in the preceding pages suggests that people shouldn't act as they do.

Airline pilots had great success in getting high wages when the airlines were *legal* monopolies (before 1980). Some of their demands were met from airline monopoly earnings protected and authorized by regulatory commissions; some other portion was obtained by expropriating the quasi-rent of the airlines' specific investment values in aircraft.

UNION ACQUISITION AND DISPOSITION OF CLOSED-MARKET MONOPOLY RENT

It is not true that all the value expropriated from an employer by a strong union will go to the employees. For example, suppose that a union agent *could* raise the wage rate in a firm to $15 an hour by contrived restrictions on the number of permissible job applicants. If the union agent chose to hold specified wages down to $10 an hour, employers would be prepared to pay up to $5 an hour extra to get employees. An employer might then be persuaded to pay the extra $5 per hour to the agent responsible for assigning union workers to employers. Or the employer might offer that $5 to a pension and welfare fund—managed by the union agent. The union agent could demand or accept payments for favoring the short-handed employer. In effect, the payment made by the employer is not paid entirely to the workers. Employers reluctant to follow the suggestions of such an agent will discover they get very few employees.

An especially notorious monopoly rent to union officers (as, for example, those in the Teamsters Union) arises from their management of union funds for pensions, health, and recreation. If the officers invest those funds at lower than normal interest rates, the favored borrowers will offer to pay the difference to union officers as favors, commissions, or business purchases from favored firms with which the officers' union is associated.

The equity and morality of this "sharing" by union officials is not simple. Union organizers can claim they accomplished the closed-market monopoly status for the members and deserve to be rewarded with larger salaries, expense accounts, vacation resorts, and better homes. Economics contains no ethical criteria by which to judge this. It merely reveals.

Another beneficiary of imposed increases in wage rates is, surprisingly, some employers, in particular those whose competitors tend to use more of the higher-wage workers and thus have higher costs and a harder time surviving. The employer who uses fewer of the higher-wage workers thereby has lower costs and can underprice the others. For example, household movers who primarily use low-wage labor will suffer more from imposed higher wages than those employers who use bigger trucks with power equipment to move objects.

DIFFICULTY OF MAINTAINING LONG-LASTING MONOPOLY RENT

Monopoly rent is not easy for any business or union to maintain. Even if all carpenters joined forces to make the monopoly industry-wide, product competition would be effective, because of substitutability. Plaster, steel, cement, glass, and other building materials can partially displace carpenters' products. Even doctors' attempts to raise fees are partly restrained by the availability of proprietary (nonprescription) drugs, advice of friends, Christian Science, self-diagnosis and self-care, faith healers, and the like.

UNION MONOPOLY VERSUS EMPLOYER MONOPOLY

Union monopoly power is often said to countervail the monopoly power of industry. But in all but one set of circumstances this proposition is false. The steel industry is a group of independently owned firms—just as a union is a group of independent workers. Yet there is a fundamental difference: Access to any customer is open to all steel producers, of which there are more than 1000. And no restrictions are imposed on expansion of capacity or on new entrants. But only *one* union can exist for any class of employees and act as its exclusive bargaining agent. In this one crucial difference lies the error of thinking that employers constitute a monopoly that requires a countervailing union monopoly. Not even for purposes of negotiating with a common "antagonist," such as a labor union, is it possible for the steel companies to avoid open-market competition. Thus, that

unions are necessary because only a labor monopoly can bargain effectively with a producer monopoly is an empty assertion unless the employer is also an actual monopoly, as is a public utility.

Legal Restrictions on Open Markets for Labor

Some laws affecting the labor market are commonly viewed not as restrictions on the free-market labor but instead as a means of correcting perceived ills. However, their effects are often quite different from publicly espoused intentions.

MINIMUM-WAGE LAWS

Minimum-wage laws prohibit employment at less than some stated wage per hour. Federal law currently (1982) specifies a minimum wage of $3.35 an hour. Whenever wages exceed the free-market rate, the quantity of labor demanded is less than is offered.[3] Those

---

[3]Except possibly in what is called a *monopsonistic* market, a market in which one firm makes up such a significant part of the total demand for labor that to add employees it must offer higher wages for new and old employees. The graph in this footnote shows a rising labor-supply curve (WW) to the firm. This curve is also the firm's average-wage curve. The marginal-wage-cost curve (MWC), the height of which shows the increase in the *total wage bill* for one more employee, lies above the average-wage curve, because the higher wage for the new employee must also be paid to all other employees. The intersection of the labor-demand curve (DD) with MWC indicates the wealth-maximizing employment (E_0) at which the wages paid each person are W_0, indicated by the average-wage curve. To hire one more employee would increase total costs by the height of the MWC curve but would yield a marginal product indicated by the demand curve (DD). (This employing firm, though large relative to the supply of labor, is not the only employer. It must pay all its employees the same higher wage or they will leave and work for other employers.)

If a minimum uniform wage, higher than W_0, is now imposed at W_1, the firm could hire as many emwho cannot get work at that legal minimum wage may seek to work instead as private, independent contractors to their former employer, taking a lower income by asking a *contract price* equivalent to the old wage.

---

ployees as it wished at a *constant* wage rate out to where the horizontal line W_1 intersects with WW. Each extra employee (out to that limit) would increase the firm's total wage bill only by the wages paid that new employee. In effect, line W_1 becomes the average-wage schedule, and the marginal cost of more labor is therefore *equal* to the constant uniform wage already paid each employee. It would pay the employer to hire out to where the line W_1 intersects the labor-demand curve. In the graph, this employment rate at the higher constant wage W_1 is greater than with a rising wage for successive employees that must also be paid to existing employees. Imposing a *uniform* wage increases both the wage rate and the employment rate.

So far so good. But three factors are often overlooked. First, the higher wage rate will raise the firm's *total* costs of operation, reducing its output as price must be raised and thus reducing employment. Second, employers faced with a rising labor-supply curve (WW) are often able to confine the higher wage to the new employee only: The old employee has no better option in any event, whether or not the new employee is hired; special fringe benefits or job classifications permit differential wages among employees. Third, a few employers make up a large enough percentage of the market for labor to have significant long-term effects on wages by individually varying their rates of employment. Over the long term, then, the flow of workers from other employers and areas makes this case of little significance.

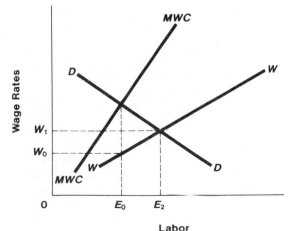

Or, an employee could continue to work at the higher wage but provide more of the capital equipment to the employer at a lower price than the true cost. For example, say a person was holding a job as a taxi driver at $3 per hour, or $120 for a 40-hour week. Suppose a minimum wage of $3.35 per hour is imposed, coming to $134 for a 40-hour week. The worker displaced by the employer's demanding less labor at that wage could rent the taxi from that employer at a weekly rental of, say, $14 a week (offering, that is, a sort of reverse tie-in).

People whose services normally are not worth the legal minimum hourly wage may obtain jobs when demands temporarily rise to make their hire worth that wage rate. But these will be temporary jobs: These workers' vulnerability to the vagaries of general business fluctuations is heightened.

Full wages, like full prices, contain more than money payments. Partially offsetting the employment effects of minimum-wage laws are adjustments in work conditions not controlled by the law: for example, the extent of health care and on-the-job training, length of vacation, number of sick days, tolerance of tardiness and use of company mail or telephones, number of coffee breaks, length of lunches, cleanliness of restrooms, provision of parking space, safety precautions, and air conditioning. Employees will accept jobs with less of these nonmonetary features to reduce the employer's full costs of hiring them.

The groups most severely exposed to all these effects are teenagers, blacks, women, and the aged.[4] It is hard to refute the charge that the minimum wage laws are devices perpetrated by white, middle-aged, male chauvinists. As a wit wrote, "A $5 industrial

---

[4] It follows that because the minimum-wage laws do not very effectively cover paid household help, a large portion of which is provided by black women, the law hits harder at black men than women.

minimum wage would go a long way toward perpetuating the family farm."

EQUAL PAY FOR EQUAL WORK

Wage differences often reflect differences in employees' abilities and in working conditions, yet such compensating differences in wages are not always welcomed. One of the classic methods of trying to eliminate them is to try to apply the maxim "equal pay for equal work"—on the presumption that equal work is easy to identify and that nonmonetary differences among services by employees or by employers should not count.

The person who has what some people consider to be inferior features dislikes being paid less for the same work, even though the wage difference is what enables the person to offset a personal nonmonetary disadvantage. Popular people complain that compensating wage differences allow those less popular to compete for jobs. Men may be hired because an employer prefers them as workers, but that preference is made more expensive by the excess over the lower wages the employer could have paid for equally valuable work by women. The employer pays more to hire men. Males cleverly advocate equal pay for equal work—of course, at the higher wages paid to men. The effect is to protect men's employment by reducing the opportunity for women to underbid the men.

This analysis extends to geographical differences in pay. Because of differences in the supplies of labor, wages for similar labor are lower in the South than in the North, and lower in Puerto Rico than in the United States. Northern employees can protect their wage rates from the competition of lower-wage southern labor, and U.S. laborers protect their higher wage rates from Puerto Rican labor, by means of the "equal pay for equal work" and minimum-wage laws, which remove the reason employers would relocate to those locales.

FAIR-EMPLOYMENT LAWS

Because laws requiring uniform pay or minimum wages transform expressions of discrimination from differences in wages to selection of employees by their nonmonetary attributes, pressure mounts for **fair-employment laws**, which prohibit employers from choosing employees on the basis of any nonwage criterion ruled unethical—usually race, creed, age, and sex. These laws are difficult to enforce. How can it be determined what is motivating an employer? Furthermore, employers become reluctant to observe the spirit of the law in their hiring practices if they believe it will be more difficult to dismiss those whose services are unsatisfactory, because they could be accused of discrimination. Fair-employment laws impose burdens on *employees*: If Armenians prefer to work with Armenians, Catholics with Catholics, blacks with blacks, or Mormons with Mormons, these laws make that illegal.

HOURS AND SAFETY LEGISLATION

Several other laws affect labor-market operations. For example, laws specify the minimum ages and maximum hours of work for children and women. A federal government agency, the Occupational Safety and Health Agency (OSHA), requires employers to maintain safe working conditions. It should not be entirely surprising, if you have learned your economic analysis well, that the rate of reported accidents on jobs may be unaffected, or increased, by that law. (As we saw in an earlier chapter, studies of the effects of higher automobile safety standards show similar results. Automobile accidents became more frequent.) The apparent results do not prove that the laws are undesirable; instead they indicate that actual effects often differ from intended effects because, where safer systems and devices are used, people act less carefully.

IMMIGRATION RESTRICTIONS

For the past century, immigration into the United States has been restricted. Although it is unwise to admit a desire to create barriers against competition from one's fellow Americans, it is ancient and honorable to bar foreigners. Current favorite targets are the temporary migrant farm workers from Mexico, who are either excluded outright or prevented from working in the United States at wages low enough to induce people to employ them but much higher than those in Mexico. Also, many *products* of foreign workers cannot be imported.

Closed Monopsony: Buyers Close a Market to Competing Buyers

Closed monopsony is analogous to closed monopoly in that it means the exclusion of competitors, the difference being that in a monopsony other buyers rather than other sellers are excluded. Just as *employees* are *sellers* of labor, *employers* are *buyers* of it. Some employers are anxious to restrict competing employers from bidding up wages, to keep them below what would have been their open-market levels. Some have had spectacular successes, as we will see shortly. And some of the successes have been widely regarded as socially desirable.

But most public attention is drawn to the relatively *ineffective* attempts. For example, when asked to name cases in which employers have "ganged up" on employees, people usually cite such phenomena as: "*yellow-dog*" *contracts*, employment contracts whereby the employee agrees not to join a union; *sweatshops*, by which are meant shops where employers pay low wages (but lower than what?); and *child labor*, the employment of children considered too young to be working. The chief argument against child labor has been that children should be in school learning to be more productive. But it is hardly ever noticed that the decrease in child labor over the last hundred years is the result of the decline in farming as a percentage of total employment, because child labor was mostly farm labor. And currently, the higher incomes of parents reduce the pressure for supplementing incomes by child labor.

We turn now to three possibly surprising examples of effective monopsony—collusive actions by employers against employees. They affect over half the young men and some of the women in the U.S. labor force.

HOSPITAL INTERNS

All states require that candidates for medical practice successfully undergo supervised training and be licensed before they can practice. Membership in a medical association is also required if a doctor is to capture the greater income available from practice in a first-class hospital (unless it is part of a medical school). Suppose the association prohibited hospitals from paying interns (medical-school graduates undergoing a formal period of acquiring experience) more than $2000 a month, whereas with open competition among hospitals the rate would be higher—say, $3000. The price agreement is enforced by the threat that any hospital in violation could be punished by withdrawal of its "Class-A" certification, without which it can't attract good doctors. The gains from secret violations—which are very likely to be detected—would be much smaller than the consequences of the possible punishment. The reduced costs are appropriated by doctors in the form of higher medical and hospital incomes.

COLLEGE ATHLETES AND THE NCAA

Colleges maintain an effective but not publicly understood collusion to depress the wages of college athletes. When intercollegiate football became a substantial source of college income, football players received money inducements—in effect, wages—to attend a particular college. Some college administrators decried that as "professionalism." Amateurism was considered to be more virtuous. Yet, with an eye on the football income, administrators were dismayed that competition among schools was raising athletes' "wages" and reducing net income to the college.

An agreement, called an athletic code, to restrict wages was reached through the National Collegiate Athletic Association (NCAA). Not surprisingly, colleges cleverly switched to such offers as athletic "scholarships," "free" room and board, travel to college, payments for little or no outside work, jobs for relatives, clothes, and the like. These methods of competition came about because of the agreement restricting money wages. At identical, limited money offers, the distinguished colleges would get the best athletes. The less distinguished colleges *in metropolitan areas* (with large potential gate receipts) resorted to covert offers. To choose one example from hundreds: Two decades ago, and again in 1982, two California schools, the University of California, Los Angeles, and the University of Southern California, were caught cheating and were fined $100,000 and prohibited from playing in postseason bowl games (the games that are the most profitable). Tennis, basketball, track, and baseball teams—members of which had received no "unethical" payments—were banned from national tournaments.

The professional football and basketball leagues have been made to refrain from bidding for college athletes until after their class graduates. This is not true for baseball and tennis athletes, who have no financial value to the university. The NCAA has restrained its financially useful student athletes from being able to sell their talents to the professional leagues until after the colleges get four years of their service at controlled wages. In contrast, colleges pay students competitive market wages as waiters, ushers, computer programmers, and research assistants. Such is the meaning and effect of the NCAA code of "honorable" athletic behavior.

How could collusion to restrict wages survive in the face of the great advantages of cheating? After all, if television and radio networks tried to suppress performers' wages, other networks could profitably be organized to take advantage of the reduced wages. What preserves the collegiate collusion?

Any college violating the athletic code could lose its *academic* accreditation. Any college put on probation or expelled from the NCAA would find it more expensive to recruit faculty and students. Even the national fraternity Phi Beta Kappa refused to authorize chapters at colleges that gave "disproportionate" athletic scholarships. The survival of the college could be threatened. Why does the present accreditation group have power to prevent the formation of a new accreditation system? A very important reason is that colleges are not self-supporting. No school could get subsidies from the state or major philanthropic foundations without official accreditation by the *present* accreditation group—which has powerful influence on the government and the charitable foundations. We have finally arrived at the source of the value of membership in the NCAA and related organizations: subsidized colleges. The NCAA was not created to restrict the pay of football players. It was set up for other purposes, but once its greater value for these other purposes could be denied to a nonmember, it became an effective enforcement agency of a successful cartel.

MILITARY DRAFT

The most spectacular and successful collusion by employers against employees is the military draft. From World War I into the 1970s the United States has obtained enlisted men by a draft. (And since 1980, 18-year-old males have been required to *register* with the government, although there is no formal draft.) A draftee must work at tasks and at wages set by Congress—lest he lose valuable citizenship rights. Young men may be required to work at less than market wages in the military, though there is no law that requires them to do so as police officers, firefighters, astronauts, garbage collectors, generals, admirals, or politicians. A draft is a tax on young males paid *in kind*, just as the old medieval kings drafted labor to build palaces and roads. The old, the smarter, those who married early and had children, and women avoid that tax.

Recently, when the military moved toward an all-volunteer status, the wages were increased in order to attract people. If the wages aren't maintained high enough relative to civilian occupations, the draft will probably be used again. Without a draft, explicit money taxes must be levied on all who would bear the burden of national defense; the true, hitherto hidden costs of the draft are then revealed. But it is also true that for any specified military capability, those costs are *lower* than under a draft. (Recall what happened in our three-person economy in Chapter 7 when the wrong people were drafted into producing various goods. The total possible output became smaller. And so it is with the draft.) Without the draft the total explicit monetary tax bill is larger, but the real cost is smaller. And without the draft, the military must pay *more attention* (not pay more costs) to the true costs of labor and seek economical means of providing defense services. Drastic recombinations of inputs occur, according to the marginal product and specialization principles outlined earlier. Most obvious is greater reliance on civilian employees to provide services not related to combat or training for it. Custodial, food, and sanitation work around military camps is provided by labor cheaper than that of strong young men who are of greater value as soldiers or in other work. Enlistment turnover rates and training costs decrease. In short, lower-cost methods are forced into use.

If every male has an obligation to defend his country, it does not follow that everyone should do so in the same way—by a tax in the form of military service, which is what those who claim an obligation from only young men are really contending. Specialization in military service is just as sensible as in supplying food, clothing, and domestic police protection.

Let it be noted that the Union Army in the Civil War—a war that used a far greater proportion of our young men, with higher fatality rates than in any subsequent war, and one in which the men fought with unexcelled valor—was *not* a draft army. It was purchased in the open market: Men were drafted, yes, but every draftee had the right to hire someone to take his place, usually by paying that other person a lump sum. The draft was a means of *assigning the tax* among the young men. Once taxed, a man could either pay the amount necessary to buy a substitute or could work it out in the Union Army. Those who served did so in the cold calculation of the amount of the tax.

Summary

1. Though wages for labor services respond to market forces as do the prices of any other good, the sale of labor services differs in involving personal relations to a much greater degree.

2. Labor unions have three dominant functions: to facilitate contract negotiation, to monitor employee performance, and to restrict competition by other labor.

3. Unions can raise full wages insofar as they act as efficient employee agents in contract negotiation and enforcement.

4. Unions can raise wages of some union members if they can monopolize the supply of employees available to employers. Not all union members gain, because less labor is demanded at the higher wage. Nonunion employees face competition from the displaced union members, who by adding to the supply of nonunion workers lower nonunion wages.

5. A strike is a concerted refusal by employees to work and a denial of the access of other potential employees to the employer.

6. Government employees who strike and successfully monopolize the supply of potential employees to a government are using the power to levy taxes to obtain their monopoly wages.

7. Minimum-wage laws that raise wage rates above competitive levels increase the incidence of unemployment for the lowest-earning employees. Laws enforcing equal pay for equal work often harm those intended to be helped.

8. A cartel agreement among buyers of a good to restrain their competition for that good is called a monopsony cartel. Examples of such cases have been found among some hospitals, colleges (competing for student athletes), and the military.

Questions

*1. Coalitions of employees called unions permit the members to have an agent to monitor the employer's fulfillment of promised services and working conditions for employees. Employers welcome that kind of intermediary to smooth relations and give greater assurance to employees. Indeed, if the employees don't form their own union, the employer creates a personnel representative to perform similar services. If the preceding is true, and it is, then why do employers oppose unions?

2. "In a society where there has not been an adjustment of wages to the savings of time afforded by the use of new techniques, and where such savings may result in an oversupply of labor, an agreement among laborers to prevent such conditions has a lawful labor objective." (Decision by Superior Court Judge Martin Caughlin, San Bernardino, California, in case of *Orange Belt Chapter of Painting and Decorating Contractors v. AFL-CIO Painters District Council 48*, July 1958.) Suppose the introduction of spray and roller painting methods reduced the amount of man hours in painting a house to 50% of its former level.

  a. Does the above decision mean that wages should be doubled? Or that the laborers can force the houseowner to hire as many hours of labor with the new technique as with the old?

  b. What does it mean?

3. "Technically speaking, any labor union is a monopoly in the limited sense that it eliminates competition between workingmen for the available jobs in a particular plant or industry. After all, all unions are combinations of workingmen to increase, by concerted economic action, their wages, i.e., the price at which the employer will be able to purchase their labor."(Arthur Goldberg, Justice, Supreme Court of the United States, and formerly Secretary of the Department of Labor and counsel for the United Steelworkers; quoted from *AFL-CIO: Labor United*, New York, McGraw-Hill, 1956, p. 157.) Why did he write *"technically speaking"* and "in the *limited* sense"? Is there some other mode of speaking and is there an unlimited sense of monopoly? Does a monopoly (closed or open?) eliminate competition? What does it eliminate and how?

4. "The steelworkers' union and the U.S. Steel Corporation are both monopolies." In terms of the closed and open monopoly distinction, is that correct?

5. You work for a television manufacturer as a welder, and two unions contend for recognition as the sole bargaining unit for welders. One, a "craft" union, would be composed only of welders; the other, an "industrial" union, would admit all employees who work for television manufacturers.

  a. In which type of union do you think you will be able more effectively to raise your wages by imposing apprenticeship conditions and other devices to restrict the number of people who can seek jobs in competition with you?

b. Which union do you think will be more able to impose a wage-rate increase upon the employer without first restricting union membership? Explain why.

*6. The National Association for the Advancement of Colored People contends that the building-trade craft unions (among others) discriminate against blacks. The national-headquarter officials of each union reply that the local unions in each city are autonomous and determine membership. The charter provides that there will be no discrimination. The unions reply variously that no qualified blacks have applied, that a new member must be nominated by three members in good standing, that they do have some blacks, that they use a quota system to ensure that all groups are equally represented, and that the present time, when even the white members are unemployed, is not a feasible time to increase entry rates. Given that the craft union has the power to determine who and how many may join the union, some system of choice is necessary—if the number is to be restricted in order to maintain wages above the open-market level.

a. What criteria for selection do you think should be used and declared defensible? Explain why.

b. Would you recommend a quota system? Why?

*7. "Plumbers' and steamfitters' union local 2 of New York has no Negroes, and 80–95 percent of the members are the sons of existing or former members." (News story from New York Times, August 2, 1963.) What explanation can you offer for this?

8. a. Labor groups were strong advocates of raising barriers to immigration in the nineteenth century. Employers objected. Why?

b. Labor groups were less enthusiastic for tariffs (taxes on imported goods), but some were in favor of them. Why?

9. Walter Reuther, former head of the auto workers' union, contended that automobile producers should lower their prices to benefit the public.

a. Why did he not propose that the current

tax (tariff) of 12% on importation of foreign cars be abolished as a means of increasing domestic supply?

b. Why do you think Reuther wanted lower prices for products produced by members of his union?

10. Some employers welcome the growth of powerful unions that will be able to raise wages and control the number of employees admitted to the union. Why? In answering, show why some employers would be hurt by the elimination of effective unions (even ignoring the conflict in trying to eliminate the union).

*11. "Any craft union that has to resort to the strike to get higher wages is not being operated efficiently. It should instead concentrate on control of apprenticeship rules and admissions in order to assure high-quality, reliable, skilled union members. And it will incidentally thereby achieve its higher wages in a peaceful, democratic way." Explain what the speaker, a highly successful union leader, meant.

12. As a beginning lawyer, would you benefit if fees for the following were set by the bar association: drawing up someone's will, serving as an executor of an estate, arranging for a divorce?

13. A representative of the Congress of Racial Equality advocated raising the minimum legal wage in order to help blacks get higher wages.

a. Would blacks benefit from a higher minimum wage?

b. Would it reduce or increase discriminatory hiring?

14. "The higher the legally constrained minimum-wage rate, the greater the amount of unemployment of unskilled workers." Is this correct? Explain.

15. If in some town the minimum wage rate for taxi-driver employees were raised to $5 an hour, what would happen to the ratio of cabs driven by the owners to cabs driven by employees of cab owners? Why?

16. You are an immigrant. Would you prefer laws insisting on equal pay for equal work, minimum-wage laws, apprentice laws, or strong unions that have been effective in raising wages above the open-market level? Explain.

17. As a summer-job-seeking college student, are your chances of getting a job increased or decreased if the wages you can get in a cannery, summer resort, factory, and so on, are set by a union comprised of current full-time employees? Why?

18. As a college-age babysitter, would you benefit if an association of babysitters were organized and a minimum wage of $3.50 an hour enforced? Why?

19. "If an enterprise cannot survive except by paying wages of 75¢ or $1 an hour, I am perfectly willing for it to go out of business. I do not believe that such an enterprise is worth saving at that price. It does more harm than good, socially and economically. It is not an asset; it is a liability. So if this kind of business is killed by a minimum wage of $1.25, I for one will not be sorry." (George Meany, Hearings before Subcommittee on Labor Standards, 86th Congress, 2nd Session, 1960, p. 36 of Part 1 of printed hearings.)

    a. How does this statement differ from one that says, "Any person who cannot produce a product worth at least $1.25 an hour should not be allowed to work as an employee"?

    b. Explain why Meany did not suggest that a business that paid wages of $5 an hour was an even greater liability to the community.

20. "The National and American Football Leagues have finally gotten together and agreed to have a common draft of college players. The draft will eliminate those utterly ridiculous $600,000 bonuses that were paid to untried muscular meatballs from the college campuses. The peace pact will also put a stop to the alarming movement to tamper with the legal property of other clubs (i.e., bid players away from other leagues). The peace pact is welcome. If the cost is high, a continuation of the warfare would have been costlier." (Sportswriter Arthur Daley, *New York Times,* June 9, 1966.)

"Pete Gogolak, the star American Football League placekicker, said today he thought player salaries would not suffer because of the merger of the two leagues. He said, 'The new players who stood to get big bonuses because of the competition between the two leagues may get hurt, but I think the salaries of the other, older players will remain high.' Gogolak had played out his option with the American League Buffalo Bills and then signed with the National League Giants at a salary believed to be $32,000." (News item from *New York Times,* June 9, 1966.)

"The common draft, now agreed to by the two leagues, will drastically cut bonus payments and should appease the colleges who have railed against the in-season solicitation and premature signing of college players attributable to the scramble for talent." (Sportswriter J. M. Sheehan, *New York Times,* June 9, 1966.)

    a. To which two of the three writers just quoted would you give a flunking grade in economics? Explain why.

    b. If General Electric, Westinghouse, and other electrical companies could get together and have a common draft of graduating engineers, would engineers' salaries suffer? Why?

    c. If General Electric, Westinghouse, and other electrical companies could get together and have a common draft of college students at a salary of $100 a month and could compel chosen students to work for them or face jail and loss of citizenship, do you think the draft would be regarded as defensible and in the social interest? Reconcile your answer with the existence of the Air Force, Army, and Navy common draft.

Chapter 16
Wealth: Saving and Investing

Wealth is more than machinery, buildings, fertile land, sheltered harbors, rivers, and good climate. To know that the *non*human wealth of the United States has a market value of over $3 trillion is to know only part of our wealth. *People* are wealth, too; and so are cultural values and mores, customs, and etiquette, all of which enable us to be more productive.

Natural resources have to be converted to useful form by the application of effort and knowledge. In this country, the prairie was forbidding until the pioneers sweated over it with the plow. For eons the Indians tolerated New England's rocky soil, severe winters, and short summers, but it was the colonial settlers' knowledge and work that increased the soil's productivity.

Other forms of wealth are a stable government, a reliable judicial process, and respect for property rights and the certainty of their continuance. Because these are not marketed separately, their value is not measurable directly but, rather, is measured in the value of goods sold. For example, people are willing to pay higher rents for premises in cities or neighborhoods with low crime rates.

In the mid-nineteenth century, the U.S. government did not hold land appropriated from the Indians for the "benefit of all the people." During the westward advance people were able to claim and use the land as private property. They could sell it or borrow against it; they could "profiteer," reselling the land at enormous gains in value; they didn't have to stay on the land to obtain the value of their development (as one must today in foreign countries that ban absentee landlords or even the right to sell land, such as Mexico, Iran, Egypt, and India). Landowners were able to realize, or capture, the capital value of the future consequences of their actions and investments. The capitalist system was operating, coordinating people's activities (as we analyzed in the early chapters) by price incentives.

Could a socialist economy achieve greater wealth than a capitalist economy? Undoubtedly a government can compel a higher *proportion* of income to be put into savings than might be done voluntarily. The issues are whether a higher rate is desirable on those terms, whether the savings will be invested as productively, and whether the income itself would be as large. Debaters wax eloquent and emotional, but the evidence is not yet conclusive.

Note the words of a man who, over a period of 14 years, was first a vice-president of the International Bank of Reconstruction and Development and then was president of the International Finance Corporation:

Let us briefly examine some of the frequently cited causes of underdevelopment. It is often claimed that geography and natural resources are determining. They are of course important. . . . But resources lie inert and have no economic worth except as people bring them into use. It is easy to attribute the progress of the United States to its wide expanse and abundant physical resources. However, other areas—in Latin America, Africa, Asia—have comparable natural wealth, but most of it is still untouched. On the other hand, there are countries in Western Europe with limited fertile land and meager mineral deposits, yet they have achieved high levels of economic life. . . .

Perhaps most often lack of capital is blamed. In the first place, there is in most developing countries more potential capital than is admitted. But large amounts are kept outside, because of political instability. . . . Or it is invested in often underproductive land, low priority buildings, or otherwise hoarded. . . . Over the postwar period immense sums have been made available to the developing areas. Some of these funds have been well applied and have produced sound results, others have not. . . . If [money] is applied to uneconomic purposes, or if good projects are poorly planned and executed, the results will be minus, not plus. The effective spending of large funds requires experience, competence, honesty and organization. Lacking any of these factors, large injections of capital into developing countries can cause more harm than good. The test of how much additional capital is required for development is how much a country can effectively apply within any given period, not how much others are willing to supply.

It is popular in many quarters to charge colonialism with lack of development in territories which have been dependent. This argument seems less persuasive when we observe that a number of countries which have been their own masters for long periods are no further advanced.

I am, therefore, forced to the conclusion that economic development or lack of it is primarily due to differences in people—in their attitudes, customs, traditions and the consequent differences in their political, social and religious institutions.[1]

Sources of Wealth

Those (whether people or nations) who wish to increase wealth must do their own saving. First, one can build up wealth from gifts if not all of the aid is used for current consumption.

A second method of increasing wealth is to save and invest more. But how? For a

---

[1]Robert L. Garner, International Finance Corporation, *Summary Proceedings, 1961 Annual Meeting of the Board of Governors*, September 21, 1961, pp. 4–6. Or see the Nobel Prize lecture by Nobel laureate T. W. Schultz, 1979.

country as a whole, investment might be made by the government, financed by taxes, in the belief that private owners of wealth refuse to invest enough. But higher taxes, by reducing income, reduce private saving. Furthermore, to escape the tax, people will invest in ways that yield more nontaxable or nonmonetary income. For example, in the United States homeowners are not taxed on the income (real services) from their homes, whereas money income from investments that would be used to pay for rental of apartments or houses is taxed.

Third, political authorities may increase investment in a particular kind of wealth—namely knowledge—by funding education and research, on the presumption that patent and copyright protections give insufficient incentives to private parties to invest in the discovery of new knowledge on a sufficient scale. But this remains a presumption, because patents and copyrights are available, and because it is impossible to define a *best* rate of invention or discovery of ideas.

A fourth method of increasing wealth is to reduce the costs of channeling savings into the most profitable appearing investments. Just as the costs of distributing food from farmers to consumers are reduced by an extensive network of middlemen, so wealth is increased by an extensive network of specialized financial intermediaries collecting funds from millions of savers and channeling them to better investment prospects.

A fifth way is to make it more likely that the profits of investment will go to the investor. If the rights to profits are threatened or weakened, the incentive to invest is reduced. Price controls and political regulation reduce security. In many countries the security of one's rights in property is unreliable; the reputations of the governments of Argentina, Brazil, Chile, Iran, Indonesia, Kenya, Egypt, Mexico, and Algeria in this respect are not on a par with those of Switzerland, the United States, Japan, and Malaysia, to name a few. (Both lists could be longer.)

Property Rights, Growth, and Conservation

It is often argued that we should safeguard our wealth by *politically* restricting the exploitation of our natural resources such as forests, seashores, fertile lands, oil, and iron ore. This argument fails either to comprehend the meaning of wealth or to recognize that using goods *can* convert them into even more valuable forms of wealth. As explained in Chapter 6, if a tree is more valuable for future lumber than current lumber, the *present* capital value of the live tree exceeds the value of the current lumber in the felled tree. The tree will not be cut now, because lumber now would yield less income than the growth of the standing tree. By comparing the present values of the two uses we discover which will give the greater wealth. Thus, it cannot be said that the private-property, open-market system tends to cut trees—or use its other resources—too fast. It does conserve them by capitalizing into the present value of the live tree its highest valued uses, whether as lumber or as a natural object giving recreation through its beauty, or in any other use.

But there are circumstances in which people cut down trees even though their live value exceeds the current value of the lumber. If no one owns the tree, one way to capture its value as private property is to cut and take the wood. If there is no private ownership of the live tree, no one will have the wealth incentives—or the legal power—to preserve it (rather than cut it prematurely in order to establish rights to the lumber). Or, if land whose use is affected by trees is not owned by anyone, the beneficial effect of a tree on the land's value will not be heeded accurately. Forests in many parts of England and China were prematurely destroyed because no one owned them. First come, first served. Not personal greed but *lack of well-defined, marketable property rights* was responsible for this wasteful use of resources.

This same analysis can be applied to fish and game, which, until caught, belong to no one. Someone who had enforceable ownership rights to the live fish would have the incentive and ability to prevent premature fishing or overfishing.[2] As a substitute for enforceable private-property rights, governments have sometimes managed to reach agreements enforcing limits on catches. Similarly, as long as no one owns the rights to present and future uses of lakes, rivers, or underground water supplies, people have less incentive to use water in its most valuable ways. Instead, being the first to use it is equivalent to possessing it. Garbage is dumped in an unowned lake because the lost value of the otherwise cleaner water is not thrust upon any one person with sufficient rights or self-serving incentives to control pollution. Because most (although not all) major lakes are not held as private property, they are excessively polluted.[3]

Water is not generally allocated by private-property rights. Often the first user of a source of water establishes his or her rights to the water. An aqueduct costing billions of dollars was prematurely built to move water from Northern California to Southern California. In fact, the construction of that aqueduct was basically an exceedingly costly way of establishing Southern California's *rights* to *future* water from Northern California. Petroleum was once considered unowned until taken out of the ground. To remove the incentive to pump oil just to get title to it, rights to subsurface oil were assigned to the owners of the land on which it was drilled.

Let's try to better understand some circumstances in which people miscalculate or inadequately heed costs because they cannot be made to bear the full costs of their actions. A paper mill is a heavy user of water. If a paper mill produces paper worth $10, at a perceived cost of $6, but also pollutes and reduces the water's value by $5, then the total costs ($6 + $5) exceed the $10 value of the paper. Wealth is in fact destroyed. But if the fouled water is reduced in value only by $2, then the paper worth $10 is produced at a total cost, or sacrificed value, of $8—a net social gain of $2. Activity that is profitable after its full costs are accounted is **economic growth** in that people get what is worth more to them than they otherwise would have had.

One way of measuring growth is to make the calculation of costs clearer, and one way of encouraging growth rather than decline is to make people directly bear the costs of their actions. Conservationists, we will presume, are trying to ensure that all costs and all values produced by some activity are fully and accurately assessed, even for unowned resources. Because some resources are not owned, it is often proposed that government agencies should assess the values of *all* effects. One way to impress the value on the user is to make him pay a fee (a price) equivalent to the presumed loss of value; that is, the user purchases a right to pollute. To *prohibit* all use of a resource—be it air, water, or seashore—would eliminate some benefits that exceed the damage to the resource. Yet some laws controlling air pollution and some court decisions prohibit *any* pollution of air in areas newly coming into use, regardless of the benefits that would be obtained by some fouling of the air. That reduces welfare just as effectively as overuse of the air. Fortunately, some legislators and courts instead

---

[2]Walter Cronkite (or his writers) said this overfishing was a failure or weakness of capitalism; it is, on the contrary, a *failure to apply* capitalism to fish in the ocean.

[3]One of the authors of this text owned land adjoining Lake Arrowhead and also land on the Mediterranean Sea. Arrowhead is owned by a private corporation. He dumped sewage in the Mediterranean but not in the lake. Why was he "responsible" at the lake and not at the sea?

weigh the loss in value in one resource against the benefits obtainable thereby.[4]

Investment Activity

INVESTING BY
CONVERTING INCOME INTO WEALTH

Wealth is produced in many ways. We can convert currently consumable goods to sources of future services. For example, we convert fresh milk to cheese, apples to cider, pork to bacon, grain to whiskey, grapes to wine, olives to olive oil. Or we can produce goods that are more durable: steel instead of wood buildings, concrete instead of blacktop roads, diamond-tipped instead of metal-tipped phonograph needles, pipelines instead of trucks.

We have talked of saving and of investing, but a person who saves is accumulating wealth, that is, is investing. *Saving is investing,* but the two words describe different aspects of the process of increasing wealth. **Saving** applies to the *nonconsumption* of income, whereas **investing** applies to the use of the unconsumed income to create more future income.

NET PRODUCTIVITY
OF INVESTMENT ACTIVITY

As explained in Chapter 6, a dollar of current income invested rather than consumed often yields *more* than a dollar of future income. That miraculous gain is called the **net productivity of investment**. Plant a seed today and next year, after allowing for costs,

have more than one seed. This net productivity of investment converts—directly or indirectly—energy or material to more desirable forms.

A Measure of the Net Productivity of Investment If we devote one unit of current income today to obtaining future income, and we thereby get 1.15 units a year hence, the gain is .15 units in one year. If for an amount A invested today we obtain a year later an amount $A(1 + g)$, we define g to be the *net productivity (in percentage)* of investment per year. (In our example, $g = 15\%$ per year.)

We never know in advance what g will be; everyone who invests must gamble. Yet almost all of us make investments of one type or another—in education, buildings, cars, and business. We "bet" (by sacrificing current consumption or going into debt to others who lend us current income) that the future product will be *sufficiently* greater than the present sacrifice.

Profitable Investment Profitable investments are those that yield an increase of wealth at a rate (g) that is *more* than the rate of interest, i. For example, if the interest rate is 5% and you invest $1 now, a payoff of anything more than $1.05 in one year would mean your investment was profitable.[5]

Say that you, and only you, are confident that your investment will yield more than the present investment cost plus the interest, and that within two months other people also become persuaded. They bid up the value of your asset above the sum of your cost and accumulated interest. That excess is an immediate *profit*. But do not conclude that an investor would prefer that the rest of the market react quickly to his or her

---

[4]An economist once shocked his beginning students by remarking that the most valuable use of Lake Erie may be as a seaway for ore freighters, or as a sewer for industrial waste, rather than as a swimming pool for those living next to the lake. It's a matter of which use—and to what extent each use—provides the greatest benefits.

---

[5]On the other hand, the relative increase in future steady *income* flow (not wealth) from a *unit* increase of current investment—$dY_{(t+1)}/dI_{(t)}$—is called the *marginal efficiency* of investment.

activity. The more slowly others react, the longer the investor escapes their imitative competition.

Higher Rates of Investment out of Current Income Tend to Reduce g   The net productivity of investment (g) depends upon factors such as our legal institutions, property laws, the state of international relations, knowledge of the laws of nature, the availability of markets, and mental talents. But one factor particularly affects g: the rate of current income directed into investment. Each unit of increase in investment yields a smaller *net marginal product*. Why? To name one reason, less appropriate resources must be diverted from current consumption to investment. Recall from Chapter 8 that the higher the rate of production, the higher is the cost. Similarly, successive increments of the future gain have increasing present costs—which is an indirect way of saying that higher rates of investment yield lower net marginal gains.

Demand for Investment: The Most Profitable Pace of Investment

How does a person or an economy decide how much to invest or save from current income, and how much investment is demanded? To answer we examine the demand and supply relationships between the pace of an activity and its value and cost (see Figure 16–1). The upward slope of the *SS* curve indicates that the amount of current income people are willing to save (to divert from current consumption to the accumulation of wealth) rises with the different offered rates of return on the vertical axis. The *demand* schedule for investment is derived from the relationship between the rate of investment and g, the net marginal productivity of in-

vestment, which, as we have seen, decreases as investment increases. In Figure 16–1, the investment-demand curve (*DD*) shows for each interest rate the largest rate of investment that people think will yield—on the *marginal* dollar of investment—a rate of return (g) at least equal to that interest rate. The lower the interest rate, the larger is the most profitable rate of investment.

A lower interest rate should not be thought of as merely reducing interest costs to the borrowers of a given investment. Because interest costs are only a small portion of the total borrowed investment, many people mistakenly conclude that a lower interest rate has little effect on costs and profitability, and hence on the rate of investment. They forget that a lower *market* rate of interest increases the *present values of the future income of capital goods relative to the current costs of production*. Current services are used to produce longer-lived capital goods that yield *future* income. Thus, when interest rates fall, the prices of capital goods rise, and a higher rate of investment becomes profitable for a wider range of capital goods.

We can illustrate this principle. Suppose a concrete building costing $750 to build would yield $100 a year net for nine years. Its g is about 4%. (See Table 6–3. At 4%, 7.44 × $100 = $744, close to $750.) At a 5% interest rate, the building's present capital value would be only $711, less than its cost of $750; the building would not be a profitable investment. But at a 3% interest rate, the building's present value would be about $780; the investment would be profitable. (Check our calculations by reference to the data in Table 6–3.)

Lending

Anyone can save some of today's income and lend it to someone in exchange for a promise of more future income. The lender usually gets a **promissory note** or a **bond** as evidence of the claim to future payment. Saving and lending do not necessarily result in the production of wealth: A borrower may use the loan to create capital goods or may instead increase consumption by the amount loaned, say, by using it to take a vacation.

You may think that a person can borrow some wealth rather than income, such as by borrowing a house or a car or money. But all that the borrower gets is the income—that is, the service—from that asset.

The *DD* curve reflects what the public believes are *feasible* investment returns. The *SS* curve reflects how much people would be willing to save in anticipation of that rate of return. Decisions about how much to save and decisions about exactly which specific investments to make are in large part made by different people. Therefore, markets and intermediaries coordinate the two activities, saving-lending and investing-producing. A shift in either the savings or investment schedule affects not only the interest rate but also possibly, and seriously, total income and aggregate employment.

COORDINATING INVESTING AND SAVING DECISIONS

Every person has unique personal *DD* and *SS* curves of investment capabilities and savings propensity. In Figure 16–1, the community *DD* and *SS* curves represent summations of the curves of all individuals. Competition moves the interest rate toward an equilibrium at which the amount of income that people believe they can profitably invest is equated to the savings they are willing to provide.

It would be a mistake to think that this adjustment occurs in just one special market. There is no one market for savings or investment. Instead, those activities are guided in several markets: the lending and borrowing markets, the capital-goods markets, and markets for current production.

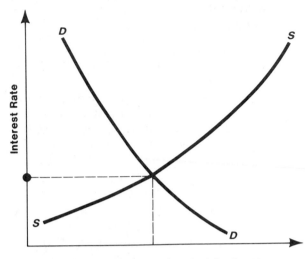

Rate of Investment and of Saving

Figure 16-1.

RELATION OF DEMANDS FOR INVESTING AND SUPPLY OF SAVINGS TO INTEREST RATE

The lower the interest rate of the economy, the greater the most profitable rate of investment that people believe is feasible, shown by the *DD* curve. The lower the interest rate, the lower the rate of saving that people are willing to incur, illustrated by the *SS* curve. The market-determined interest rate is the rate at which the profitable amount of investment equals the amount of savings supplied.

BUYING AND SELLING CAPITAL GOODS

There are several markets in which claims to capital goods, money, and current services are continually redistributed: In *retail markets* money is traded for goods; in *bond markets* claims to future amounts of money are traded for money now; in *stock markets* claims to corporate capital goods are traded for money now; and in *real estate markets* land and buildings are traded for money. By enabling people to revise their holdings of given amounts or kinds of assets, these markets make people more willing to accumulate any one kind of wealth. For example, if I could never sell a house once I had built it, I would be less likely to build one.

INTERDEPENDENCE OF BOND AND STOCK MARKET PRICES

Suppose the explicit interest rate in the *lending*, or bond, market were 5%, and that in the *stock* market some stocks expected to yield $10 a year for the indefinite future were priced at $333, a yield of 3%. In that case, you could sell the stock for $333 and lend the proceeds, by buying bonds, at 5% in the loan market, thereby getting $16.65 a year instead of $10. For that reason, no one would offer $333 for that stock if elsewhere they could get $16.65 by lending the $333 at 5%. The stock's price would fall, raising the stock's realizable rate from 3% toward 5%. The possibility of *arbitrage* between the markets—by selling in one and lending in the other—brings their yield rates together.

Similar adjustments take place between countries. A higher interest rate economy will borrow from a lower interest rate economy, as when South American countries borrow from the United States. And a higher interest rate country will sell goods yielding future services to a lower interest rate country in exchange for current income.

Prices of common stocks change not only because of changes in interest rates but also because of changing anticipations about the future. But those factors that cause changes in future income prospects cannot always be separated from those that change the interest rate, because their effects are the same: changes in prices of stocks. Therefore, we usually study interest rates by looking at bond markets, where the future payments are less uncertain. If stock prices fall while bond prices stay steady or rise, the cause of the fall in stock prices is likely to have been a deterioration in future income prospects rather than a rise in the interest rate. Regardless of the reason for a drop in stock prices, the effect on capital-goods production is quick.

WHY THE BOND MARKET IS A KEY MARKET

Because almost all exchange occurs through the medium of money rather than by barter, people revise the timing of their income or consumption streams not by trading this good now for that good later but by trading money now for money later. Hence, almost all revisions in investment prospects and in willingness to save will affect borrowing and lending of money for which interest rates are most explicitly expressed. That is why factors affecting the rates of interest and investment are often analyzed through their effects on the demand and supply of loanable funds in the money markets. It is also why people tend to refer very misleadingly to interest as the price of money. Interest is more accurately called the price of *borrowing* or of *credit*.

Increase in Propensity to Save If preferences for *future income* increase relative to *present consumption*, the *SS* curve shifts to the right, with two results. First, the supply of loanable funds increases, lowering the interest rate to the competing borrowers. Second, the prices of assets will rise, because assets are means of getting more future income. For example, the prices of such long-lived assets as steel and concrete buildings will rise relative to those of wood; young, rapidly growing animals will rise in value relative to older, slower growing ones. Because a yearling steer grows at a higher percentage rate than an old steer, every pound of a yearling represents a greater percentage increase of future beef than does that of older, slower growing steers. The demand and price of yearlings will rise relative to that of older steers; fewer yearlings will be slaughtered, so the price of veal will rise relative to that of beef.

Consider another example. Suppose the community initially places the value of $710 on each of two goods, one yielding an annuity of $100 for nine years, the other of $200 for four years. Both annuities imply a 5% interest rate (which you can *and should* check by using the data in Table 6–3). If the community's preference changes in favor of longer annuities, the nine-year annuity will increase in value more than the other. For example, if the present value of the nine-year, $100-per-year sequence were to rise to $779 and the four-year stream to $744 (both up from $710), the interest rate would be 3%, down from 5% (check this, too). Production of the longer-lived goods will be relatively more profitable. The interest rate affects production, as can be seen in the fact that prices of longer-lived assets have risen relative to current service costs. House prices, for example, have risen relative to rental rates and costs.

Increase in Productivity of Investment

Suppose there is an increase in the perceived *feasibility* of producing wealth profitably: New inventions, cheaper refrigeration, and more durable, rust-resistant metals are examples of ways to enable more future consumption per dollar of present investments. The *DD* curve of Figure 16–1 shifts to the right, for there is an increased demand to borrow

current (money) income. Thus, the supply of bonds increases and the price of bonds falls—that is, the interest rate rises, rationing available savings to the most profitable investment prospects. (Otherwise, nonprice rationing would occur wherein allocation would be less heavily influenced by marketable profitability, as we have already studied.)

Increased Stock of Capital Goods

What would happen if, say, by a gift from a foreign country or by accumulation over the years, the stock of capital goods increased? That increased stock means an increase in current *and* future income. If the increase is most in capital goods yielding greater, more distant future services, the interest rate would be higher than if the increase were in capital goods yielding near-term services. Why? A larger ratio of future relative to present income makes people willing to trade more of that future income for rights to present income: If you learn you will have more income in the future than you had formerly expected, you will immediately borrow against your future. If, on the other hand, the increased stock of capital goods yields a higher proportion of present consumption services than future services, the interest rate would be reduced. (Why?) Thus, the mere fact of an increase in a country's stock of capital goods does not tell us whether the interest rate will rise or fall.

Prospects of Reduced Future Yields

Take a more difficult case. Suppose people begin to believe that future yields of existing or producible assets will deteriorate; the *DD* schedule shifts to the left. The first to have this belief will try to sell their common stocks or capital goods to others before the belief is confirmed by ensuing events or becomes more broadly shared. Their efforts to sell will depress stock prices, as well as the prices of capital goods such as buildings and land. Investment will be reduced, because lower prices of common stock and capital goods make it less profitable. People will switch to assets whose future yields are not expected to deteriorate so much, such as bonds or money. Interest rates in the bond markets will decline, in effect raising bond prices.

The process is not pleasant, because the future, in our example, is less pleasant. Investment-goods producers (and others) experience transient unemployment and must shift to new jobs with lower incomes. Savings are reduced. So *both* the *DD* and the *SS* curves shift to the left. Caught in a squeeze of falling asset prices and reduced income and the necessity of paying off debts, firms will seek to borrow money to tide them over the "adjustment." During this "liquidity" adjustment (more liquidity often means having a larger fraction of wealth held in money), the interest rate in the loan markets is pushed up *temporarily*. (Why?)

We can see, then, that adjustment of the interest rate pervades every market and all exchanges. And a shift in the investment-demand schedule can also shift the savings-supply schedule. Events that change the demand for—that is, the profitability of—investment and capital goods have broad effects that are not confined to one small market. The consequences are more widespread than a change in the demand for tires, wheat, or almost any other good. The interest rate reflects relative demand for *all* types of goods capable of rendering services in the future. And because rights to present and future income can be traded in many markets, the interest rate will affect many markets, with effects on aggregate incomes. Recessions can result.

THE SEVERAL "FACES" OF THE INTEREST RATE

It is now evident that the term *interest rate* is applied to different concepts:

1. Net marginal productivity of invest-

ment, *g*: the net rate of increase in wealth from a dollar more of investment.

2. Personal valuation of future income relative to present consumption, measured as the amount of future income that is valued as equal to one dollar of consumption now.

3. The *rate of interest on credit*: the return on loans (that is, bonds or promissory notes).

4. The implicit relationship between present prices of capital goods and their future income streams (explained in Chapter 6). If interest rate in the second sense (personal valuation) is less than that of the third (rate of interest on credit), consumption will be reduced and saving will increase; if the second is less than the first, investment will increase. Interest rates in all these senses are brought toward equality in the various markets and goods. When all are equal, the common value is the interest rate. If any are different, then arbitrage (the simultaneous buying and selling in different markets) will push them toward equality. This explains why the interest rate is referred to variously as the price of *current consumption*, the price of *credit*, the price of *savings*, the price of *loans*, the *rate of time preference*, the *net rate of investment productivity*, and the *price of money*. Properly interpreted, it is a measure of all these things in equilibrium. But, again, because the most easily perceived and measured rate is the one in the market for *secure* (that is, riskless) bonds, that is the one by which "the" interest rate is usually measured.

Figure 16–2 provides historical perspective by showing long-term interest rates (on 10- to 20-year secure bonds) during the past century. Some swings in that rate were the result of anticipations of long-term movements in the price level associated with infla-

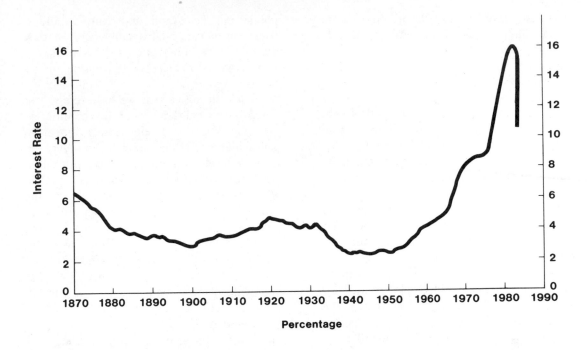

Figure 16-2.

LONG-TERM (10–20 YEAR) NOMINAL INTEREST RATES
OF CORPORATE BONDS (THE HIGHEST GRADE BONDS)

The long-term interest rate has varied over a wide range
for various, not entirely explicable, reasons. We
conjecture that the recent peak at nearly 16% was
in anticipation of a rising price level in the future,
which induced lenders both to insist on a higher
money rate and to be willing to pay more in
money terms if prices are going to rise in
the future.

SOURCE: National Bureau of Economic Research.

tion, or of government monetary policy, or of
changes in business conditions. We shall explain later how these affect the rate of interest.

NOMINAL INTEREST: EXPLICIT RATE AND IMPLICIT YIELD

We know the stated, or explicit, interest rate
of a loan—say, 6% per year—may not be its
implicit rate (also called its *effective* rate).
Recall that if you lend $900 for a promise
that $1000 will be repaid in one year with a
zero interest rate explicitly stipulated in the
written terms of the loan, you are actually
being promised a return of 11.1% *implicit* interest: ($1000 − $900)/$900 = 11.1%. If the
loan is repaid when due, you will also have
realized, or collected, that implicit interest
rate. At the time the loan is made the *implicit* promised *yield* is 11.1% per year, taking
into account not only the explicit rate—here
0.0%—but also the difference between the
amount loaned and the amount due later.
You can see that the implicit rate differs

from the explicit rate if the present amount loaned differs from the principal amount to be repaid. In general, for a *one*-year loan, the *implicit*, or effective, yield *i* is given by the following formula:

$$i = [(Ar + A)/P] - 1$$

where A is the principal, the amount of debt on which the explicit interest is to be paid and the amount of debt to be repaid when the loan is due; r is the interest rate explicitly stipulated in the loan agreement; and P is the present amount paid or loaned.

For example, suppose you buy a bond promising an explicit 5% interest per year on a principal amount of $1000, due and payable in one year. Assume the present price, the amount you pay now, for that bond is $900. The *implicit* yield is [($50 + $1000)/ $900] − 1 = .167, or 16.7% per year. If the present price had been $1000, the implicit yield would equal the explicit yield, 5%.

In referring to an interest rate, we shall usually mean the implicit rather than the explicit rate. And if the loan is paid on schedule, the implicit yield will be the *realized* yield on that loan.

OTHER COSTS INCLUDED IN THE INTEREST RATE

Risk Some debts give very high assurance that the borrower will pay interest and principal promptly. Currently, U.S. government bonds are as high in quality as any available, because the government can use the police to reinforce its ability to collect taxes from which to pay its debts.[6] (It can also "collect" taxes by creating money, as we explain in Chapter 19.) Bonds issued by private firms, such as General Motors, American Tele-

phone and Telegraph, and Santa Fe Industries, are of very high quality because they are almost certain to be paid when due. A vast range of riskier bonds *promise* higher yields.

You will notice that we have referred to "promised yields" and not to the interest rate. Superficially, riskier bonds appear to pay a higher rate of interest. However, the promised return includes a risk premium. Suppose a potential borrower of $100 offers 5% interest per year, and you regard the probability of repayment as being only one-half. To make that an attractive proposition, you could offer to lend him $50 for his promise to repay $105 in one year. Under this arrangement, there is a probability of .5 that you will get $105 and an equal probability that you will get nothing. *On the average* you would get $52.50, which would be equivalent to 5% on your loan of $50, though the *promised* yield on the $50 loan is 110%. For example, on the New York Bond Exchange in mid-1981, Trans World Airlines three-year, $1000, 10% bonds could be purchased for about $880, which promised the purchaser an implicit yield of about 14% annually; Chrysler 30-year, 8⅞% bonds could be purchased for about $45, giving an implicit yield annually of about 24%, if paid; whereas U.S. Government 10-year, 7% bonds could be purchased for about $600, giving a promised implicit yield of about 14% annually. All these bonds promised to pay the stipulated interest annually and the $1000 principal when due.

A test of the validity of this risk interpretation is provided by events in the bonds markets. If differences in risk account for differences in promised yield, then when a business firm has improved prospects of meeting its debt obligations promptly, the price of its outstanding bonds should rise. And they do.

I may know I will repay a debt when due, but does the lender know it? Some borrowers call the loan market imperfect because *they* cannot borrow on the same terms

---

[6]Evidence of the importance of the ability to collect taxes is that government bonds repayable only from receipts of particular projects (such as toll roads) are of lower quality than "general" tax-supported bonds and promise higher yields.

as their neighbor; and some complain that they cannot borrow at all. The lender sees differences among borrowers in the prospects of prompt repayment without extra costs being imposed on the lender. You should not expect a lender to tell you rudely that your promises are too risky. A banker says, "I'm sorry, we just don't have any funds to lend now." The banker is tactful—and misleading. A tactless banker could have said, "We think the prospect of your repaying is not high enough. We specialize in loans to people with better credit prospects. To lend to you, we feel that we should ask 25% instead of 19% to help cover the costs of the collection problems and other activities in defaulted loans. Go to lenders who specialize in higher risks and are better prepared to handle your type of defaults."

Transaction Costs The costs of engaging in the business of assembling savings to be loaned to borrowers and negotiating the transactions must, as in any other business, be covered by the firm's revenues—here, the interest received for loans. This is usually included in what is called interest, just as a risk premium was.

Expected Inflation As explained in Chapter 6, if inflation (a general rise in prices) occurs and is expected to persist in future rises, the effect is to raise the nominal (dollar) interest rate above the real interest rate (that is, unchanged in value relative to goods). Recall, for example, that if you were to lend $100 for one year at 10% per year, and if in a year all prices were correctly expected to double, you would suffer a loss in real purchasing power. You will get back $110, which at the new prices buys only as much as $55 at the old prices. You are being offered a negative *real* interest rate of *minus* 45%! The nominal rate is 10% per year, but the real rate is −45% per year. Using more likely numbers, if inflation continues at the rate of 8% per year, a loan that promises 10% in nominal (dollar) interest is promising

the lender only about 2% in real interest. (All this assumes that the principal and promised interest are actually paid as promised.) The promised *real* rate depends on what is expected to happen to price levels. (Don't confuse the *promised* real rate with the *realized* real rate. The *realized* real rate depends on what is actually repaid and what actually happens to the price level.) The basic rate is the same for everyone at a given time; but differences in other items, such as risks and transaction and collection costs, make the total "interest" rate different among borrowers.

Interest Rate and Quantity versus Change in Quantity of Money

Often it is said that increases in the quantity of money lower the interest rate. However, twice as much money means twice as high wages and prices of goods, land, and stocks. In *money* terms there will be twice as much debt and twice as much wealth, income, savings, and investment—but no lasting change in interest rates or in real quantities.

The belief that the quantity of money affects the rate of interest usually arises from the failure to distinguish between money and credit. Money, as we know, is what people generally use in exchanges: coin, currency (paper money), and checkable deposits. Credit, on the other hand, is a claim to wealth from some other person. (It is the other side of the debt.) Money and credit are confused because when people borrow or go into debt, they do so by borrowing *money* as an intermediary to getting other goods. In effect, they borrow other goods by obtaining the right to use some goods in the interim until repayment is made. Interest is a repayment for that right to *use* the asset *in the interim*—whether it be money, a house, a car, or a book.

As we shall see in Chapter 19, creating more money raises all prices and does not reduce the interest rate. That interest rate depends on the willingness of some people to save and to lend, or grant credit, relative to the demands by other people to use that current income by borrowing it. That demand and supply for current income in exchange for future income sets the rate of interest. It is not determined by the quantity of money, which affects the price level. Do not make the mistake of confusing money with credit.

Nevertheless, it is true that *changes* in the quantity of money can raise interest rates—not directly, however, but because of the way in which newly created money might first be spent. And expectations that the quantity of money will change can change the nominal interest rate, although not the real rate. We now explain these two subtle points.

To see the effects of how *new money is initially spent*, suppose a counterfeiter created more money and proceeded to spend it on fine wines, fine cars, and clothes—with the result that there was an interim increase in the demand and prices for fine wines, fine cars, and clothes, but no increase in interest rates. Now suppose, instead, that our counterfeiter was dull and used this new money only to buy bonds. That would immediately push up the price of existing bonds—that is, lower the interest rate. The creator of the new money, being a member of the community, has shifted the community's demand for future income relative to present income by those bond purchases.

It so happens (as explained in Chapter 19) that the usual process of legally increasing the quantity of money is almost always associated with an initial purchase of bonds and promissory notes. Lower interest on the bonds—equal to higher prices—results not from creating more money but from the initial increase in the demand for bonds relative to other goods. Thus, although you will frequently read that *increased* money leads to transiently lower interest rates, it is only because that *new* money is *first* spent for bonds. If, however, increasing money leads to *anticipation* of further increases of money creation and more inflation, interest rates will be increased.

Though an increased supply of money may first be used to purchase bonds (that is, to lend), thereby raising bond prices and lowering interest rates, that increased stock of money will be chasing the same amount of goods and will lead to higher price levels. If a continuing increase in the stock of money is expected, creating anticipations of continuing future inflation, people are less willing to lend money at such low current nominal interest rates, but others are *more* willing to borrow. The nominal interest rates will be bid upward to adjust for the reduced future purchasing power of money at the higher future price level. Hence, interest rates can be driven down by increasing the money supply to lend more now, if the public can be persuaded that there will be no accompanying increase in the inflation rate. What do you think are the chances of continuing to fool the public in that way after their experience of the past decade? In fact, during the past decade borrowers and lenders have an excellent record of accurately predicting the inflation rate for *one* year ahead, as is evidenced by the extent to which changes in interest rates on one-year loans have closely matched the next year's inflation rate. But longer-range forecasts have underestimated the longer range results—at least up till 1982.

Competition in the Capital Markets

SPECIALIZATION OF BORROWERS AND LENDERS

People who save are not generally the people who select and direct investment. Savers (say, families) rely on business firms to decide which capital goods to make. Coordinating these groups—savers and producers of capital goods—is a complex network of *financial intermediaries* (jargon for middlemen) who compete to obtain savings from savers and channel them to capital-goods producers or to consumer-borrowers. Some financial intermediaries are especially knowledgeable about borrowers' credit worthiness and their likely demands for funds; other intermediaries specialize only in serving savers and rely on other intermediaries to direct savings to the best investors and borrowers. The main financial intermediaries are commercial banks, investment banks, savings and loan institutions, commercial credit and consumer loan companies, pension funds, insurance companies (insurance premiums are partly savings as well as payments for insured risks), stock investment funds, bond markets, and stock exchanges with their host of brokerage houses. All help make the economy more productive and richer than if each saver had to search out and evaluate each ultimate investment or borrower.

Financial intermediaries also reconcile the desires of savers, investors, borrowers, and lenders about the contract terms. If lenders want to lend on the *short* term—say, for less than one year—but borrowers want to borrow on *long*-term (say, 10-year) contracts or bonds, the intermediaries borrow on the short term from the savers-lenders and in turn lend the funds to the borrowers-investors on long-term contracts. For example, a savings and loan bank permits its depositors (savers) to draw out funds with very short notice while it lends on long-term mortgages. The operators of the bank anticipate, correctly, that the day-to-day desposits and withdrawals of savers will just about balance with no large, unexpected net drain of funds. That permits the institution to use the funds for long-term bonds—usually by paying lower interest rates for the collected funds. Their costs of intermediation are *lower* than the costs lenders and borrowers would incur if they tried to operate without specialized intermediaries.

The importance of financial intermediaries can be shown by noting a few of the stages in making, selling, and owning an automobile. The auto maker's employees and suppliers want to be paid now so that they can consume now, even before the cars are completed and sold to consumers. If the firm's owners were to finance the work—that is, pay now and collect later—they would have to defer their own consumption and bear all the risks. Instead, they seek a lender to finance the current production. Automobile manufacturers borrow by selling bonds to the public and to institutions, such as insurance companies, that channel public savings. They also borrow from commercial banks to carry them over periods of low seasonal sales. Car retailers finance their inventories and equipment by borrowing from commercial banks, finance companies, and commercial credit companies. The ordinary consumer has little occasion to deal directly with some of these financial intermediaries. Yet, because they exist, the car dealer can carry a bigger inventory, allowing the consumer to inspect a larger variety of cars and get quicker delivery with lower credit costs.

The typical consumer, who borrows to pay for the car, is likely to deal with a consumer credit company, either directly or indirectly, through the car dealer who attends to details of the loan. Consumers may borrow from a credit union at their place of work, because the credit union is already relatively well acquainted with each employee's personal situation and the prospects of repayment. Or the consumers may borrow directly from a neighborhood bank or from an insurance company with which they have a policy.

As goods pass from producer to final consumer, the successive costs are financed by a series of different lenders with special knowledge about successive participants. An excellent index of a country's wealth and productivity is the sophistication and complexity of its financial intermediary institutions. These reduce the costs of saving and productive investment—the key to economic development. In authoritarian, government-directed economies the rate of saving and the form of investment are controlled by political processes, whereas in private-enterprise societies decisions about savings and investment are made by private individuals.

NEGOTIABILITY OF BONDS

Lenders who may want to change their minds about deferring consumption until a bond is repaid can sell the bond to someone else, who will instead defer consumption. This salability is known as *negotiability* or, sometimes, as liquidity. Lenders (that is, bond buyers) are willing to accept lower interest for greater liquidity. However, some borrowers may offer to pay more to make their debts nontransferable. The original lender might be more considerate and lenient in the event of difficulty in repaying a debt, especially for consumer loans.

Negotiability of bonds is facilitated by bond brokers and by the New York Bond Exchange, a formal, privately owned market where the bonds of well-known, financially sound American corporations can be bought and sold from people who earlier lent money to the corporation, or from those who subsequently bought bonds from the original lender.[7] A large portion of bond resales, however, takes place away from the New York Bond Exchange, through bond brokers or dealers. Much like used-car dealers, they maintain small inventories of outstanding bonds of well-known corporations, but they know other people from whom any particular bond can be bought—at a price. These security brokers, relying on telephones and computers, are known as "over-the-counter" security dealers; they do not operate through a single, formal exchange like the New York Bond Exchange.

None of these bond market transactions transfers money to the original borrower, and therefore some people erroneously think these markets serve no useful purpose to *original* borrowers or lenders. But used-bond markets are as important to saving and lending as the used-car market is to the production and sale of new cars. How many people would buy cars if they could never sell them but had to keep them until they were junked? Because these markets facilitate the transfer of bonds, more people are willing to hold bonds. The initial flow of savings to investors is made cheaper. Negotiability of bonds also permits people to be more discriminating in selecting among risks.

Legal Restraints on Access to Loan and Capital Markets

Interest has been variously condemned or legally prohibited. Aristotle asserted that money is "sterile," so that no interest should be paid for money loans. Yet interest was paid before and after Aristotle's condemnation, despite religious dogma and other sources of objections, because the demand for savings was greater than the supply at a zero price. Until about the sixteenth century, Christian theology condemned usury as a venial sin. Christians conveniently borrowed from Jews, whose religion placed no severe ban on taking interest from gentiles. In fact, the Papacy itself charged a positive interest—though under the name of "fees," "gratuities," or anything but "interest" or "usury." In the Middle Ages, lords had claims to payments from

---

[7]Prices and amounts of bonds exchanged on the major organized exchanges are reported in the financial pages of major newspapers and in stockbrokers' offices. Prices are reported as 100% of the principal. Thus a price of 98 is a price of 98% of the principal of the bond, almost always $1000.

users of land. Sometimes the lord wanted to sell to the Church his rights to future rents. Suppose an annuity of rents was expected to run for at least 50 years. For what price could it be sold? A 50-year annuity of $1 a year would be sold to the Church for less than $50. Thus, in buying lands, the Church was charging a positive rate of interest—unless it paid a unit price equal to the expected, *undiscounted* sum of the future annuity payments. And it never did that, as far as we know.

INTEREST-RATE CEILINGS AND USURY

Economic behavior has insidious ways of circumventing laws. It took the Church about 1000 years to lift the ban against interest on loans—but many governments still decree "unreasonably" high (usurious) rates of interest illegal. In most states of the United States, rates over 10 or 15% were called usurious and illegal. (But many such laws were quickly repealed during the past decade, when market rates rose to over 15%!)

Lenders who make risky loans at high interest rates, in the hope of averaging an acceptable return, resort to legal fictions. Pawnshops, for example, lend to strangers of dubious credit at a rate of 30% per year—not by a loan, but by a "purchase and repurchase" agreement: You sell your camera to the pawnbroker for $100 (which is less than its market value) and simultaneously obtain the right to buy it back in one year for $130, to cover the risk, interest, storage, and transaction costs. Rather than helping high-risk borrowers who would normally pay high rates, laws that limit the interest rates increase the costs of borrowing to poor people by forcing them to use more expensive sources of funds—or prevent them from borrowing at all.

LIMITS TO BORROWING

Because some consumers go "too far" into debt, apparently *everyone* should be con-

trolled. That would seem to be the logic behind laws restricting the behavior of borrowers. Or perhaps, although it's permissible to borrow for a house, doctor bills, or business equipment, it is impermissible to enjoy consumption before one has earned all the costs. A generation ago, consumer installment loans were condemned by extensive publicity compaigns and restricted by legislation. But the desirability of consuming while earning replaced the old-fashioned virtue of high consumption only in one's old age, after sufficient savings had been accumulated. Today, installment buying is an accepted, sophisticated convenience—which has brought the specialized loan market to the young as well as to the elderly.

Individuals can be prevented from "excessive" indebtedness not only as consumers but also as investors. The Federal Reserve Board limits the amount a person may borrow from a security dealer against the stocks and bonds the borrower owns. Why? Not to protect the borrower if the stock should fall, but instead to prevent stock prices from being bid up higher—as it is incorrectly thought they would be if people could buy shares with lower down payments. The power to control credit suggests that the members of the Federal Reserve Board can better judge what the prices of common stocks should be than can investors in an open market. (If they could, they could get very rich, very fast!) In any event, the evidence and economic analysis both say that the board's restrictions do not affect stock prices in any systematic way. Moreover, it is easy to foil the debt limit, because money is fungible. Borrow from a banker (instead of the security broker), using the stock you are about to buy as the pledged security. Your banker can lend you money but not for the express purpose of buying more stock. The money you get from the banker can be used to pay some other bills, and the money you otherwise would have used to pay those bills is released for stock purchases.

Whether controls on the stock market are proper cannot be settled by simply weighing whether or not they promote profitable investments and diminish the number of unprofitable ones, or by counting the number of dishonest security dealers or promoters. There is also the question whether we ought to be allowed to make whatever investment choices we want to make, through whatever agency we choose, as long as we pay for the resources used. Whether we invest foolishly is a decision we might consider ours to make. Who is right?

Personal Investment Principles

It is well and good to talk about investment and wealth in general, but both take particular forms. Consider, for example, a widow who finds herself with a small fortune of, say, $100,000. In what form should she keep that wealth to provide herself with an income and perhaps a legacy for her children? What should a young father do to accumulate a fund for retirement?

DIVIDENDS OR CAPITAL-GAIN STOCKS?

Should these people buy for income from dividends or for appreciation of capital value? Except for tax purposes, this question is pointless. Why? Because business firms either reinvest their net income in the firm or use part of it to pay dividends to stockholders. Companies that pay dividends do not themselves reinvest all of their earnings, whereas companies that do not pay dividends reinvest all their earnings for the stockholders. But with either kind of stock, you can consume the same amount. If the company pays dividends, you can yourself reinvest the unconsumed dividends. If the company rein-

vests the earnings instead of paying dividends, you can sell some of your appreciated stock (appreciated to reflect the reinvested earnings) or borrow against it and consume as much as you would have if the dividends had been paid.

For example, suppose you have 10,000 shares in a company that earn $1 per share annually. Assume the stock is now selling for $10 a share; your wealth is $100,000. If the company were paying dividends of $1, the stock price would stay at $10. You receive $10,000 annually, which you can consume, and at year-end you still have $100,000. If, however, the corporation reinvests the earnings, the stock will rise in value by $1, to $11 at year-end. You can sell 909 shares of the stock at year-end for $11 each and consume the $10,000 proceeds, and you will have 9091 shares left worth $11, or $100,000 in total. In both cases, the amount you can consume and the amount of wealth you have left are nearly the same.[8]

---

[8]*Nearly* because your income taxes are affected differently. If you are in a tax bracket paying over 25% of the highest dollar earned, you might be well advised to hold nondividend stocks and to realize the income in the form of capital-value proceeds by selling stocks. This is an idiosyncrasy of our tax laws that puts a lower maximum tax on capital gains. There is another difference: The cost of selling some shares is not negligible.

At this point it may occur to you to wonder why any business firm would ever pay dividends, which are taxed more heavily than the capital-value gains which would occur as the firm invested the dividends instead of paying out stock. Going further, it might even seem irrational for a business firm to pay dividends instead of paying off its debt. Thus, if a firm didn't pay dividends but instead invested them, stockholders could finance their consumption by selling some shares of their growing wealth. Closer analysis suggests the following answer: If dividends were not paid, either people would incur transactions costs of selling off a few shares each month, or they would incur borrowing costs to finance consumption between times of selling some shares. If it costs less for the corporation than it does for the individual stockholder to borrow, we can see that stockholders should use the firm as a cheaper intermediary to borrow, letting the firm pay out dividends frequently during the year to reduce the individual stockholder's need to borrow.

HOW MUCH RISK
OF VARIANCE IN VALUE?

Any investor must decide whether to invest in assets (we use common stocks as our example) that are volatile or those that are called blue chips. *Volatile* stocks have a wider range of potential future values (say, plus or minus 30%) in a year; *blue chips* promise a smaller range (say, plus or minus 15%). But both types, measured by their past performance throughout this century, have almost the same 12% average return. But you cannot expect exactly the *average* yield every year on every stock. Buying a volatile stock gives you a greater chance of being farther above or below the average at the end of the year than buying a smaller-variance stock. In return for that extra risk, the larger-variance stock has on *average* a slightly higher yield.

You can achieve near certainty (zero variance) in what your future dollar wealth will be by holding high-grade, short-term bonds or savings deposits. However, these give a small expected average gain. You must decide how much variance—that is, how much risk—to expose your wealth to. Against which unpredictable future events do you want protection? In this book we cannot explain how to compute the tradeoff rate between risk and expected average rate of return. But we can alert you that there *is* a tradeoff.

WHAT ARE THE
MEAN AND VARIATION
OF STOCK PRICE CHANGES?

If, from the years 1926 through 1980, you chose one year at random and then took one stock at random from the New York and American stock exchanges and the principal over-the-counter markets, how much would your investment have changed in value during that one average year? The *average* of all such changes would have been such that $1 grew to about $1.13 (counting the increased

value of the stock plus any dividends paid out). You can be almost sure you would not experience exactly that average. What is the dispersion around that mean within which your stock would probably have fallen? In 90% of the cases, your initial wealth of $1 would have been between about 50¢ and $2 at the end of the year. In 50% of the cases, it would have been about 80¢ and $1.25.

Figure 16-3 shows these approximate ranges of potential loss or gain, which we shall call *probability intervals*. All three panels in the figure show the performances of 1-, 2-, 8-, and 16-stock portfolios and a portfolio consisting of all the stocks on the New York Stock Exchange. The top panel shows the estimated .9 and .5 probability intervals, or ranges, of the different numbers of randomly selected stocks for *one* year. (The shorter, thicker bars represent the .5 probability intervals; the longer, thinner ones, the .9 intervals.) The successively narrower intervals for both .9 and .5, that result as increasing numbers of randomly selected stocks are included in the portfolio, are shown as successively shorter lines. The one-year average of an eight-stock portfolio shows a narrower .9 probability interval, of about .6 to 1.7, than does the one-stock or two-stock portfolio. And if every stock on the New York Stock Exchange were held in your portfolio, the .9 probability interval would be about .75 to 1.5.

If the investment made by random selection were maintained for 5 and 10 years, what are the resultant average wealth ratios and the .9 and .5 probability intervals? The *average* increase in wealth over 5 years was 1.9 (an invested $1 would be worth $1.90) and for 10 years was 2.8. As one might expect, the probability intervals are greater for the longer-term investments, although successively larger portfolios narrow the probability intervals substantially. That the intervals with only a 16-stock portfolio are nearly as narrow as for the whole market is surpris-

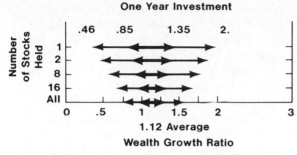

One Year Investment

1.12 Average
Wealth Growth Ratio

(Note Horizontal Scale Is Larger for 5 and 10 years)

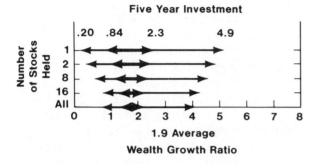

Five Year Investment

1.9 Average
Wealth Growth Ratio

Ten Year Investment

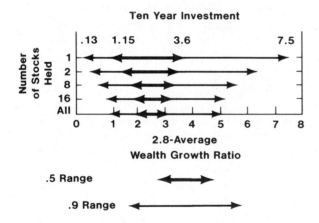

2.8-Average
Wealth Growth Ratio

Figure 16-3.

INVESTMENT WEALTH RANGES FOR .9 AND .5
PROBABILITIES FOR PORTFOLIOS OF 1, 2, 8, 16, AND
ALL STOCKS ON THE NEW YORK STOCK EXCHANGE
(1926–1980)

SOURCE: Through 1966, Lawrence Fisher and James H.
Lorie, "Some Studies of Variability on Returns on
Investments in Common Stocks," *Journal of Business*
(April 1970), pp. 99–134. Data for 1967 through 1980
were included by the authors.

ing to many people who think one must hold
many stocks to be well diversified.

RANDOM SELECTION
WITHIN VARIANCE CLASS BECAUSE
OF INFORMATION EFFICIENCY

Once you have identified the high- and low-
variance stocks from inspection of past behavior, which ones in each set should you
buy? A very good first rule is to do what we
did in the previous section: Pick at random,
especially if you buy only stocks sold in the
major stock markets. Any stocks that *were*
good buys will have already been bid up to
where they are no better than previous bad
buys, whose prices have been allowed to fall
until they are equally good buys. The publicized prices of trades on the open market
provide us innocents the equivalent of stock
evaluation. For the market prices reveal the
best opinions of the insiders (the professionals) and everyone else. The best opinion may
be lousy, but unless you think you have access to *better*, or *secret*, information and can
evaluate it better than anyone else who also
has it, you had better accept the existing
market price as an unbiased reflection of the
worth of various stocks. *Competition among
buyers and sellers makes all stocks equally
good buys when measured against their expected future performance.*

In Chapter 6 we investigated the theo-
retical rationale for these propositions, the
confirming evidence for which is overwhelming. Not only do they apply to stock market
prices but apparently also to all assets and
securities; it simply means that other people
(the market) leave no sure-fire, or above-
average, prospects of gains above the normal
interest growth. The prospect of a gain or a
loss in each period is independent of any *pri-
or* price change. Drawing charts of past stock
prices to predict future prices is unprofitable,
however popular it may be. Popularity is not
profitability. Unless you have inside informa-

tion that no one else has, pick the stocks at random!

Still better is to first classify stocks on the basis of how closely their returns correlate or move with the other stocks in the market in general. Some stock prices tend to move more and some less than the market as a whole; that is, some tend to show more *covariability* than others. Almost every stock brokerage company provides information about the covariability of each stock with the behavior of the market as a whole. Although computing covariability is a more expensive method of forming portfolios of stocks, it promises a smaller uncertainty around an average expected return than does completely random selection. Nevertheless, even correlating random selection to covariability does not affect the propositions that (1) current price equals the average of the future price, and (2) no detectable past patterns in stock prices can predict future patterns, despite what some brokers contend when talking of "peaks," "floors," "support points," "momentum," "rebounds," "technical reactions," "profit taking," or other such nonsense.

The above propositions reflect the ability of people in the stock exchanges to make available to the public, almost instantly and at extremely low cost, the best information and evaluations by the many stock analysts and investment counselors. You pay a commission to use the exchange, which in part reflects the expenses of providing faster, more complete information about present stock prices. But there is no point in paying for that information twice, once as commission and again as a fee to an investment counselor or to mutual funds that will only reproduce that information.[9]

---

[9]An extensive study showed that of the mutual funds, those funds did best that spent the least for research and commissions in changing stockholdings—thereby having the lowest expense ratio and hence the highest growth. W. F. Sharpe, "Mutual Fund Performance," *Journal of Business*, 39, Supplement (January 1966), pp. 119–39).

Your stockbroker, security analyst, or investment counselor is not worthless. Each reduces the costs of access to the securities market. All of them can tell you about the covariability of each corporation's stock with the stock market as a whole, and they will take care of securities you have purchased. Those are significant functions. They can also provide information to facilitate *diversification* of risks, so that with as few as from 7 to 12 stocks you can reduce the variance of your portfolio performance to close to that of a very large portfolio. (We have not written about diversification and its principles, which are beyond the scope of this book; but everything said above is compatible with them.)

Summary

1. Several conditions favor the growth of wealth: savings that are plentiful and thus available at low interest rates; explicit and secure property rights in wealth; and profitable investments that are readily perceivable and exploitable by investors. Growth of wealth is also aided by institutions for organizing, coordinating, and directing the flow of savings to investors.

2. Conservation, as preservation of resources in their initial form, is not necessarily a means of preserving or increasing wealth. Conversion of resources to goods or of goods to other forms of wealth can be more valuable.

3. Investment and saving each have curves on the demand and supply schedule: The saving schedule represents the *willingness* of people, at various rates of interest, to divert current income from current consumption to accumulate wealth. The investment schedule shows the amounts of current income that *could be profitably* diverted from consumption at various rates of interest. Thus, saving is positively related to the interest rate, whereas investment is negatively related. The investment schedule is often

called the demand for savings; the savings schedule is often called the supply of savings.

4. There is no single market for saving and investment. Rather, there are several: the loan markets, the capital-goods markets, and the production-activity markets.

5. The greater people's preference for future income relative to present income or consumption, the more willing they are to save, an increase in the saving-supply schedule. The result of more saving is a lower rate of interest. If the profitability of investment opportunities is perceived to increase, there is an increase in the investment demand schedule, which results in a higher rate of investment and a higher interest rate.

6. Because both the supply and the demand schedules involve the interest rate, it is reasonable to believe that the interest rate adjusts to equate the rate of profitable investing with the rate of intended saving. It does, but both saving and investing also affect, and are affected by, other variables, such as wealth, income, and expectations about the future.

7. The effects of an increased stock of wealth on the rates of interest and investment depend on the *kind* of wealth that is increased.

8. The market-clearing interest rate reveals several variables: the perceived net marginal productivity of investment, the personal value of present consumption relative to wealth or future income, the rate of return on loans, and the relative prices of capital goods and consumer goods.

9. *Increases* in the quantity of money will transiently affect the interest rate because the new money is usually first spent to buy bonds. But the *total* quantity of money will not in itself affect the interest rate, affecting instead the price level.

10. The nominal interest rate includes the real interest rate and the expected rate of change in the price level. An expected increase in the stock of money leads to expectations of inflation: higher prices of *all* goods and services. This expectation increases *current* interest rates and dominates the money increase.

11. In addition to the pure interest, the quoted interest yields usually include a risk allowance (riskier loans require a higher explicit yield) and an allowance for the costs of negotiating the loan, as well as an inflation adjustment if inflation is expected.

12. The implicit interest yield on a one-year bond is $i = [(Ar + A)/P] - 1$, where A is the principal amount and r is the stipulated interest rate, both due at the end of the year, and P is the present price of that bond.

13. The capital market for lending and borrowing is a complex network of specialized intermediaries between savers and investors.

14. Negotiability is the legal right of the owner of a bond (who is thereby a lender, or creditor) to sell the bond to someone else. Bond exchanges facilitate negotiability; they also facilitate borrowing, because lenders regard negotiability of bonds as a desirable attribute.

15. Like many markets, the lending market is not entirely open and free of restrictions, such as those on interest rates, extent of borrowing, and length of loans. These restrictions are supposed to protect borrowers and lenders from their own excessive optimism. They do protect one class of borrowers or lenders from open-market competition of other borrowers and lenders.

16. All common stocks on the stock market, when adjusted for anticipated degree of risk, have almost the same expected average gain. If any were thought to have greater expected gain after adjustment for risk, the current price would be bid up to reflect that and thereby eliminate any abnormal gain from a current purchase of that stock, as extensive evidence in security and commodity markets verifies.

17. The present market prices of stocks and bonds reflect all publicly available information about future earnings. Past prices are ir-

relevant for distinguishing more- from less-promising stocks. Trying to predict future prices by plotting the past prices of common stocks to try to detect "bottoms" or "tops" or patterns is a worthless activity. Analysts who contend that it is not have not been able to prove that contention. Competition to estimate future economic events prevents anyone from being able to predict better than the group. No one has displayed the *ability* to do that—only, occasionally, the *luck* to make a "correct" forecast.

Questions

*1. In a public park an apple tree yields excellent apples. These may be picked by the public, but not more than one apple per person at a time. When will apples be picked? Why? If the American buffalo had been owned by someone, do you think the buffalo would now be so nearly exterminated? Why?

Do you think seals and whales would be faced with extinction if some person or group were able to buy, as private property, the right to catch whales and seals? Why?

*2. You are an unborn spirit offered your choice of country in which to be born. In country A all land is owned by its users; absentee landlordism is forbidden. The land cannot be mortgaged by the owner. Everyone is born with rights to use certain parcels of land and these cannot be taken away or contracted to others. In country B, absentee landlordism is legal. All land is privately owned and either used by the owner or rented to the highest-paying tenants. Land can be sold or mortgaged. Private-property rights are strictly enforced for everyone. Many people do not own land at all. Into which country will you request that you be born? Why?

*3. "Extending the three-mile limit now in force for American territorial waters out to 1000 miles would help to conserve sea resources." Explain why. Why not extend the territorial claims out to half way across the ocean up to the territorial claims of other countries, as has been done in the North Sea for oil rights? What would that do to the doctrine of the "freedom of the seas"? What does the doctrine of freedom of the seas do to the efficient use of ocean resources?

4. a. Why will a person who has salable property rights in an enterprise for which he is making decisions be more influenced by the longer-run effects of his decisions than if he did not have salable property rights in the enterprise?

*b. Does this difference in type of property rights induce a systematic difference in the kinds of decisions made by government employees, as contrasted to employees of a privately owned enterprise—even if both are engaged in the same kind of activity (production of power)? Explain why the influence of the salable capital value of property rights will or will not make a difference in decisions.

5. Drying grapes to convert them to raisins is investing. Why is this investing, since it merely changes one form of consumption good to another form?

6. Instead of playing bridge, a man works around the house painting and refinishing the walls. Explain why this is a form of investment.

7. By giving up $100 of present income for $105 of consumption rights available in one year, a person gets what g?

8. "Roundabout, more capitalistic methods of production are always more productive than direct methods using less capital equipment. Therefore, any country that wants to develop should start increasing the amount of capital goods it has." Evaluate.

9. A man plants a seed for a tree. The rent for the land on which the seed is planted is 50¢ per year. In addition to that cost, there are other costs—spraying, watering, fire protection, taxes—to be paid over the years. In the table below, the present value of all those costs is indicated in column 4. The tree, if cut and converted to lumber at the end of the ages indicated, will yield lumber worth the amount indicated in the second column. The third column gives the *present* value of that future potential lumber, at 10% rate of interest. Some of the entries are not presented.

a. Compute the missing values.

b. Find the age at which the tree should be

cut to provide the maximum *present* value of that tree.

c. What is that maximum present value?
d. How much is a newly planted tree worth?
e. Suppose that the value of the tree rises relative to current lumber prices. What would this imply about the rate of interest?
* f. If no one owned the tree, and it could be cut by anyone who wanted to use the lumber, when would it be cut?

(1) Age	(2) Lumber Value	(3) Present Capital Value of Lumber	(4) Present Value of Costs	(5) Present Value of Profit If Cut at Age Indicated
0	$ 0	$ 0	$5.00	$−5.00
5	1	0.62	5.70	−5.08
10	4	1.54	6.20	−4.66
15	11	2.63	6.50	−3.87
20	25	—	6.60	—
25	60	5.54	6.80	−1.26
30	140	—	6.82	—
35	260	9.25	6.95	+2.30
40	450	—	6.96	—
45	650	8.91	6.97	+1.94
50	800	6.80	6.98	−0.18

10. Some whiskeys improve with age. The following table lists the consumption value of a barrel of whiskey at various ages. For example, if the whiskey is removed from its aging vat and sold now to consumers for current consumption, it will sell for $100. If sold in 10 years, it will fetch $250 for *consumption.*

a. How much will the vat of whiskey be worth right now (at 10%) if it is to be held until the end of the second year before being bottled and sold?
b. For what length of time should one expect to keep the whiskey in the vat for a maximum present value? (Hint: How much is it worth paying for the whiskey now if it is to be held for five years? For ten years?)
*c. If no one owned the vat of whiskey, how long would it remain unconsumed?

*d. Suppose it were owned but could not be sold; how long would it be kept before consumption?

Consumption Date	Consumption Value	Consumption Date	Consumption Value
Now	$100	6	$205
1 year	120	7	220
2	140	8	230
3	160	9	240
4	175	10	250
5	190		

*11. Goods differ in their rate of yield of consumption services, or in their "durability." Pine lumber naturally deteriorates more rapidly than redwood. If demand for future consumption rights should *rise relative* to present consumption rights, would pine or redwood experience the greater rise in present price? Show why this is expressible as a fall in the rate of interest. (Hint: The interest rate is the exchange rate between present and future consumption rights.)

12. Changes in the rate of interest are detectable in the changes in the structure of relative prices of various types of goods.

a. If the price of raisins (relative to grapes), of prunes (relative to plums), of whiskey (relative to corn), of cider (relative to apples) should rise, would that mean a change in the rate of interest? In what direction?
b. What effect would that have on the profitability of producing raisins, prunes, whiskey, and so on?
c. Ultimately, what effect would the revised production have on the relative values (for example, of raisins and grapes)? What effect would that have on the rate of interest?

13. In a certain country the only productive goods are "rabbits." Either the rabbits are eaten, or the rabbits increase at the rate of 20% per year.

a. If there are 1 million rabbits in the community at the first of the year, what is the income of the community (measuring the income in rabbit units)?
*b. What will be the rate of interest in that community?
*c. What is the maximum possible growth?

*14. "A rise in the profitability of constructing houses and buildings tends to push up the rate of interest." Why?

15. The propositions on costs in Chapter 10 imply that the demand curve for investment is negatively sloped with respect to the rate of interest—that is, that higher *rates* of investment will be less profitable. Why is this implied by the earlier propositions on behavior of costs?

16. "If savings is defined as an increase in wealth and if investment is defined as an increase in wealth, then savings by definition is always equal to investment; for it is merely the same thing looked at from the point of view of two different people." Since this statement is correct, how is it possible to speak of equilibrating the rate of investment and the rate of savings?

*17. "The most important fact about saving and investment is that they are done by different people and for different reasons."
    a. Is that why savings must be equilibrated to investment via a demand for investment and a supply for savings function? Why not?
    b. Suppose that everyone who invested had to do his own saving and could not lend or borrow or buy capital goods from other people. Would that destroy the principles of demand-and-supply analysis for growth of wealth? Why?

18. The rate of interest helps to equilibrate investing and savings, and the demand for borrowing and the supply of savings; it is the relative premium of price of current consumption rights over future consumption rights; it is the price of money; and it equates the demand and supply of assets. Explain how it is all these things at once.

19. Suppose the world were going to last for just two years and you have wealth of $100.
    a. If the interest rate is zero, what is the income available in each of the next two years?
    b. If the interest rate is 10%, what is the income of each period (again assuming a two-year life to the world)?
    c. If the interest rate is 10% but the world is going to last for an indefinitely long peri-

od, what is the maximum annual maintainable rate of consumption?

20. You are a visitor in some underdeveloped country in which all lending and borrowing are effectively prohibited.
    a. Is there a rate of interest?
    b. If so, where could you get data to compute it?
    c. How could you tell when it changes?

21. "Large corporations have so much of their own funds that they do not have to borrow in the capital-funds markets in order to make new investments. They are therefore immune to interest rates in the capital markets so that their investments are not screened as are those of investors seeking funds in the capital markets." Explain the error in that analysis.

22. "Most states have restrictions upon the rate of interest that may be contracted for in the absence of special authorization for higher rates. The most common maximum contract rates are 6% and 8% a year, but a few states permit contract rates as high as 12%. Loans to corporations are generally exempt."
    a. Who is helped and who is hurt by these laws if they are effective?
    *b. Do you think they have any effect on the rate of interest?
    *c. What do you think happened when interest rates on excellent bonds exceeded 10% in 1974?

23. You propose to buy a house for $20,000. You have $3000 in cash now, so you seek to borrow $17,000 from a lender at 5% rate of interest. We say 5% because the government of the state in which you live has agreed to guarantee the loan on your house since you are a veteran. The law will guarantee your loan so long as the lender does not get over 5%. Unfortunately, no one will lend to you at that rate because 6% is available elsewhere. But you are clever enough to find a lender who will lend to you at 5%, *after* you make the following proposal: If he will lend you $17,000 at 5% (which is, let's say, 1% less than the 6% rate he could get elsewhere—and thereby costs him $170 a year interest otherwise available; that is, 1% of $17,000 is $170 per year), you will buy from him insurance on the house and on

your car and life. In doing this, you may or may not realize that you could have bought the same insurance at a lower rate or more conveniently elsewhere.

    a. Why do you make this agreement with him?

    b. Is he being "unfair" or "unscrupulous" or "unethical"? Are you?

  *c. Who is aided or hurt if such tie-in agreements are prohibited?

    d. Do you think they can really be totally prohibited by laws? Why?

24. You are trying to decide which of two stocks to buy. One has been falling in price during the past month, but the other one has been rising steadily during the month. Which one should you buy on the basis of that information?

*25. A retired person has $100,000 to invest in stocks and expects an income of about $10,000 annually because interest rates are about 10%. If you advise him to buy stocks that pay out no earnings as dividends, he complains that he will have no income. How would you explain to him that he does have an income of 10%?

*26. If you were a Jew in an Arab country, or an Asian in Africa, or an Englishman in Indonesia, or an American in Argentina, or a Moslem in India, would you invest for your son in personal human capital or in physical capital? Why?

*27. Distinguish between conservation of specific resources and the growth of wealth. Is conservation of specific resources an efficient way to increase the productive wealth of the community?

*28. "In a socialist state it is difficult for the state to own the producers' goods that are involved in artistic creativity—the human brain and body. Consequently musicians, artists, au-
thors, and poets will be more able to behave in deviant, unorthodox, nonnationalistic ways than those whose earnings are more dependent upon state-owned resources—machines, factories, land, and so on. In a capitalistic system this difference would not be present."

    a. What premises underlie the propositions?

    b. Would your preference for one system over another be influenced by the validity of those propositions? Why?

*29. In Russia and China, two socialist states in which most producers' goods (goods with which you can earn a living) are owned by the government, targets are assigned to factories in terms of the total value of the output (not profits) they are supposed to produce. Plant managers are told to accomplish and overfulfill targets as much as possible. Prices are set by law.

    a. Is it desirable to have these targets overfulfilled?

    b. Is it more desirable to state a target for each particular good in terms of total value of output than in terms of maximizing profits? What are the differences in performance that will be induced?

    c. Which criterion is more likely to provide a more effective incentive for the manager?

*30. Assume that you are a member of a minority group in some country and have reason to doubt that your private-property rights would be enforced and respected in that community.

    a. In what forms of capital would you invest?

    b. What kinds of skills (as forms of accumulations of wealth) would you encourage for your children?

    c. Do you know of any evidence of such actual behavior by minority groups?

Chapter 17
Unemployment and Idle Resources

In our economy there always seems to be a great number of people who are unemployed: They are without a wage-paying job but are seeking one. Who are the unemployed? And why does **unemployment** occur? One answer to the first question is also an answer to the second: The unemployed are those who are between jobs or who are first-time job seekers and, rather than taking the first job offered them, choose to remain without one while searching longer for the best alternative. That interval of search and evaluation called unemployment is an economical way to examine and compare the many jobs that have at least some value to society.

Many of those seeking their first job are just out of school or college, or are housewives deciding to seek work for money wages; some retired people reenter the job market seeking part-time work. But why are some people *between* jobs? Obviously, many leave one job to find another that is more personally satisfying in its tasks or surroundings, or the like. But others are between jobs because of changes in the market for goods and services: When the demand for some product declines and the demand for another increases, producers and workers must adapt; resources must be transferred from producing the good of which less is demanded to making more of the other. People must investigate and evaluate the many opportunities and decide which is best. That takes some time. Over 50% of those who become unemployed select their new jobs within two months. Only about 5% to 10% continue evaluating for six months or more.

Unemployment, then, is not caused by the absence of jobs, as is commonly thought, but rather by the evaluative activities of those between jobs or those looking for their first job. This is true not only of labor but of machinery as well. What would be a better way to determine what to do next when a current job pays too little to be worth doing?

This interpretation of unemployment—that it is caused not by a shortage of jobs but by passage between, or to, jobs—though correct, may seem surprising, but recall our analysis in Chapter 14: Because of the perpetual condition of scarcity of goods and services, there is always more work to be done, but which of the many tasks is the best one to do is not instantly discoverable. When demands shift, we must examine and evaluate opportunities. Seen as a way in which we effectively adapt to unforeseeable changes, the unemployment of resources is, then, not necessarily wasteful. Indeed, consider how great the costs would be if you were *never* allowed to be unemployed after changes in demand or supply. You would not be allowed to quit and spend a month discovering and evaluating other options. It is unlikely that while working at the old job you could instantly, and at no cost, find the best of alternative jobs and *know* that you have found it. Unemployment is not simply *job* seeking; it is job-*information* seeking.

No college graduate knows everything about every potential employer and vice versa. Employment offers differ in both monetary and nonmonetary features of different jobs. Accepting a first offer reduces the probability of finding the highest paid job. The more firms investigated, the greater is the probability of finding a better job. The greater the difference is believed to be among potential wage offers and working conditions, the greater the amount of search it pays to perform.

Because the gain from extra search diminishes, there is a limit to the sensible length of search. A person should search for and explore wage offers until the expected gain (the present value of a larger future income) for further search no longer exceeds the cost of continued search. And, although probably few persons make detailed calculations, the observed behavior of most job seekers conforms to this practical rule. The

greater the fluctuations in demands or the greater the costs of relocating, the greater is the gain from more extended search, and the greater is the rate of unemployment.

The *employer's* search process is associated with unfilled jobs. An employer whose information and hiring costs were zero would instantly hire the right people at the appropriate wage. But information not being free, an employer who always takes the first available person is less likely to get the best person.[1]

Obviously, *some* unemployment and *some* job vacancies are an inherent, wealth-maximizing feature of a society in which demands change unpredictably and people select their jobs according to open-market competitive prices rather than being assigned to jobs. In the military, everyone always has a job; however, it is not clear this is more desirable than frictional unemployment. If less attention were paid to seeking the most appropriate jobs and workers, it would be easier to keep everyone busy. Avoiding unemployment by making arbitrary work assignments is called **disguised unemployment**, because, although no one is jobless, there is no way of assuring that labor and resources are being used in their most valuable ways. In the Soviet Union and the People's Republic of China people are assigned to jobs by the political authorities: There is no measurable unemployment, but there is assuredly disguised unemployment.

To recognize that unemployment is *an* economical way to respond to changing demands and supplies does not mean it is the

---

[1]The concept of unfilled jobs or vacancies is a dangerously misleading one except when applied to the sort of situation just described, in which an employer maintains a job vacancy long enough to find the best person to fill it. The simple fact of scarcity in this world means that there are innumerable tasks or productive activities that people could perform. So we must ask, *at what wage* is a job unfilled? At higher wages the job—or the offer to employ someone in it—would not exist. At lower wages the number of jobs *offered* increases without limit.

only, or necessarily the best, way, or that it is pleasant. It is not here implied that all sources of changes in demand and supplies are unavoidable or are good things. Indeed, some downward changes in demand and supplies have been caused by mistaken economic policies. Thus, the severity of the Great Depression was the result not of the typical fluctuations that give recessions and recoveries but of mistaken policies that exacerbated the initial recession into a severe, prolonged depression. It is misleading, even if true, to say that the resulting unemployment was "economical." But in the absence of other actions that would have prevented it, the best feasible response for many individuals was to be unemployed for lengthy spells.

In all chapters so far we have analyzed how prices in a private-property, open-market system operate to (a) determine what goods are produced and in what amounts, (b) control consumer demand and allocate those goods among consumers, and (c) affect the income and wealth of the owners and suppliers of productive resources. Though each depends upon the other, we considered each of these activities or consequences of the open market one at a time, assuming, for the sake of simplicity, that the others were fixed or appropriately adjusted. And, indeed, if the market for each good was independently and simultaneously cleared, regardless of what was happening in other markets, the analysis in the preceding chapters would adequately describe how the economic system as a *whole* operates and remains coordinated. But activities in producing and selling various goods are not independent of incomes, prices, and outputs in other markets and industries. So no market achieves fully coordinated adjustments to changes in other markets instantly and without cost.

If demand rose in one market as it fell in another, and if people could instantly know that those demand shifts were not temporary disturbances, and if the productive inputs were immediately shifted from the one to the other, there would be no unemployment and no idle resources. But immediate shifts to some other job are not sensible because of the costs of discovering the best of the other opportunities. These costs of information about the true state of demand and about other opportunities explain a wide class of activity known as **frictional**, or **natural**, **unemployment**: the unemployment of labor and resources that lasts the duration of that search for the best jobs or uses. If virtually all the unemployment in an economy is frictional (natural), which means in our economy that about 3% to 5% of the total work force is between jobs, then the economy is arbitrarily said to be in **full employment**. Frictional unemployment, whether of labor, houses, capital goods, or any good whatsoever, is a way to adjust to foreseen transient, minor, and possibly unfortunate changes in demand and supply.

Numbers of Employed and Unemployed in the United States

Of the 100 million people with gainful employment in the United States in 1982, about 70 million worked full time and 30 million worked part time. Figure 17–1 shows the trends of employment for men and women from just after World War II to 1982. But for a better perspective on the relative extent of job shifting, it is useful to know that stable, long-term employment is characteristic of a large fraction of the U.S. labor force. On average a worker holds a job with the same employer for about eight years. And over a quarter of all workers remain with the same firm for over 20 years. Over 75% of middle-aged workers who have held a job for 10 years will hold the same job another 10 years. Of workers over 30 years of age, almost half the men and about a quarter of the women

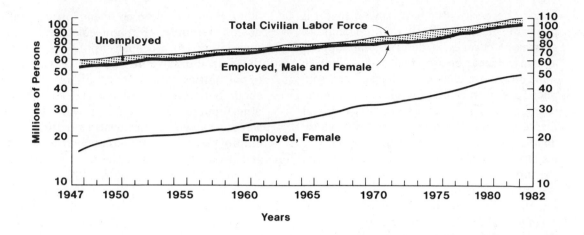

Figure 17-1.

U.S. EMPLOYMENT TRENDS FOR MEN AND WOMEN,
1949 TO 1982

SOURCE: U.S. Department of Commerce, *U.S. Statistical Abstract*, 1981.

will keep their jobs for more than 20 years, and only a quarter of the workers will have jobs that last less than 5 years. Blacks have the same record of job duration as whites. Women have had substantially shorter or more interrupted job tenure than men because of their greater productivity as housewives and mothers—productivity that in the absence of market prices has been vastly undermeasured.

In the United States the unemployed are measured by interviews of about 100,000 adults monthly. People holding jobs but not working because of illness, vacation, or job dispute are not considered unemployed. To be counted as unemployed, one must be "actively" looking for work. However, "actively" looking" can mean as little as asking friends or relatives about some jobs in the preceding four weeks. An examination of who is called unemployed may yield some surprises.

Approximately 10 million workers changed jobs during 1980. Every month, *on the average*, approximately one in 20 employees quit or was laid off or dismissed; the same proportion took new jobs or returned to old ones. In this process, over 15 million persons reported themselves unemployed at some time during 1980, although at any one time the number of unemployed averaged about 6 million. Some 3 million were unemployed all through the year, 2 million from one to three months, and 3.5 million from four months to more than six months. Almost 6 million had at least two spells of unemployment. These data reveal a persistent flow of people and resources from job to job, some flowing more quickly than others, and still others experiencing more prolonged unemployment while reassessing their best options or considering possible new occupations. Table 17–1 gives more details.

Table 17-1 UNEMPLOYMENT RATES (PERCENT OF WORK FORCE)

	1960	1965	1970	1975	1980
All Workers	5.5	4.5	4.9	8.4	7.1
White	4.9	4.1	4.5	7.7	6.6
Male	4.8	3.6	4.0	6.5	6.4
Female	5.3	5.0	5.4	7.0	6.8
Married men	3.3	2.2	2.4	5.0	4.0
Nonwhite	10.2	8.1	8.2	14.0	13.3
Teenagers	14.7	14.8	15.3	20.0	17.3

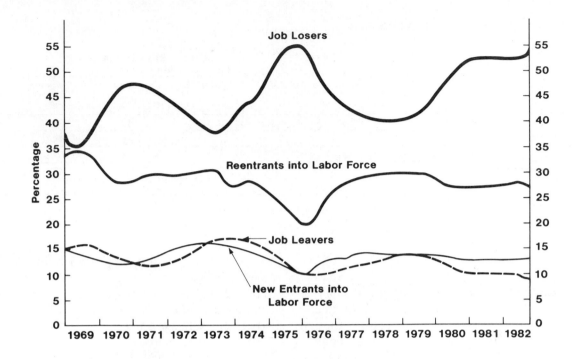

Job Losers

Reentrants into Labor Force

Job Leavers

New Entrants into Labor Force

Figure 17-2.

CATEGORIES OF THE UNEMPLOYED AS PERCENTAGES OF TOTAL UNEMPLOYED, 1969–1981

SOURCE: U.S. Department of Commerce, *U.S. Statistical Abstract*, 1981.

During a **recession**, a period during which output, capital investment, and employment decline, the average unemployment over the whole labor force usually rises from the full-employment rate of around 3% to 5% to about 7% to 9%. Figure 17–2 charts the percentage of reported unemployment for the whole labor force over the past several years. In the years 1932–33, the depth of the Great Depression, it averaged about 15%—though hitting an average of 20% in the worst months.

Who Are the Unemployed?

Certainly unemployment is difficult to define, especially for people near the margin of preference for employed work relative to retirement, schooling, or household productivity. Government studies of the unemployed reveal the anomalous facts that about 35% look for work, 24% keep house, 20% go to school, and 14% are retired. Although sur-

prisingly few are looking for work, people do not sit idly during unemployment.

Over the past decade, an average of close to about 6% of the adult population was unemployed at any one time. Of these, 25% were teenagers and another 25% were of ages 20 through 24. In other words, half of the unemployed are young people 16 to 24 years of age, though that age group represents only about a quarter of the U.S. population of 16 years and over. Half of the unemployed teenagers are, however, in school and are seeking only part-time work. Of teenagers not in school, about 15% are unemployed. Teenagers are a group with transient attachment to the labor force, and their in-

Table 17-2   ENTRIES INTO UNEMPLOYMENT

Source	Percent of Total	Fractions in Each Source of Entry Who Are:		
		Under 25	Men	Women
Laid off (expect recall)	12	20	52	48
Dismissed	33	33	63	37
Job leavers	13	47	45	44
Want temporary work only	13	74	43	57
Left school	7	88	52	48
New entrants to labor force	12	—	—	—
Other	10	—	—	—
	100%			

Source: Robert Hall, *The Nature and Measurement of Unemployment*, National Bureau of Economic Research, Working Paper 252, 1978.

centives to find steady work are less persistent than others'. About 20% of the unemployed young people are blacks, though blacks represent only about 10% of the population. In contrast, in the prime age category—25 through 54 years of age—the unemployment rate has averaged about 4%.

The natural (frictional) rate of unemployment increased in the 1970s because of an increasing fraction of teenagers in the population. Also, more women sought satisfactory work for money wages. In addition, more extensive unemployment and welfare benefits were paid only to those registering themselves as unemployed.

People can become classified as unemployed by any of several routes. Some have been temporarily laid off and are expecting recall; others have been dismissed or have quit. About half of those becoming unemployed are job losers, and for half of these the job losses are temporary layoffs. A quarter of the unemployed are those who are reentering the labor force after withdrawing earlier for family or educational reasons. About 10% of the unemployed are those who are entering the work force for the first time. Some are teenagers, high-school graduates entering the work force and sampling various jobs in their

search for the most appropriate job. In their job sampling, they frequently enter and leave the ranks of the unemployed until they settle into some more permanent job in their mid-twenties. Others, especially women and retired people, more commonly are seeking temporary work only and are counted as unemployed between jobs or while looking for the best job. Table 17–2 gives the relative importance of the different sources of entry into unemployment for the year 1976. Figure 17–3 charts the percentage of unemployment for the labor force as a whole over the past 30-odd years.

In a 1977 study of unemployment, it was discovered that only 40% of those who claimed to be unemployed, and were counted as such (7 million persons, 7% of the work force), were considered by some other adult in the sampled household to *be* unemployed. More surprising was that only about one-third of those counted as unemployed reported that they had in fact satisfied one criterion of being officially counted as unemployed: seeking an acceptable job during the preceding four weeks. Most of the remaining two-thirds who claimed to be unemployed were going to school, keeping house, or were more or less retired. This suggests that many who, when asked, say they are unemployed make "better" use of their time than actively seeking work: In effect, they let the satisfactory

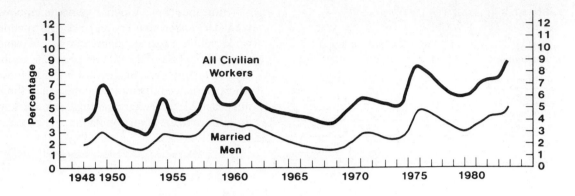

Figure 17-3.

PERCENTAGES OF REPORTED UNEMPLOYMENT, 1948–1981

SOURCE: U.S. Department of Commerce, *Survey of Business*, various issues.

job find them. Unemployment, then, is extremely difficult to define in ways that satisfy everyone.

LENGTH OF UNEMPLOYMENT

In 1978 about one-third of the unemployed experienced more than one spell of unemployment. For example, in the construction industry, workers move from job to job and in the interim may be briefly classified as unemployed. The temporary nature of some jobs or specific tasks implies a higher frequency of unemployment. Thus, a 1978 study of construction-industry workers (5% of the total work force at that time) showed that they accounted for almost 20% of the people who had more than one spell of unemployment. As you would expect, the average spell was shorter for them than for those with only one spell. Fifteen weeks was the average length of spell for the single-spell unemployed; nine weeks per spell was the average for those with two spells, and about seven weeks for those with more than two spells in the year. Sixty percent were reemployed in less than a month, with another 20% within 5 to 10 weeks; at the other extreme, 3% were unemployed for over 6 months. For the construction workers the average duration of a spell was about 6 to 7 weeks.

(Because unemployment data are collected once a month, people with very short spells, say, of a week or so, are less likely to be unemployed at the date of observation. This leads to an underestimation of the number of people actually unemployed during the month but to overestimation of the average length of the spells of unemployment, since the shortest ones are more likely to be omitted.)

The best data available suggest lengths of unemployment like those given in Table 17-3. Approximately half the spells are less than five weeks, and almost 75% are less than three months, increasing during recessions. The average length varied from as low as nine weeks to as high as 16 weeks during the 1970s.

UNEMPLOYMENT AND INCOME

What is known about the relationship between unemployment and income? One thing is that the unemployed do not have very low incomes. In 1980 the average family income of households in which a person was

Table 17-3   LENGTH OF UNEMPLOYMENT

Length of Unemployment	Percent of Unemployed				
	1960	1965	1970	1975	1980
Less than 5 weeks	45	50	52	35	43
5–10 weeks	21	29	23	20	23
11–14 weeks	9	8	8	10	9
15–26 weeks	13	10	8	15	13
26+ weeks	12	10	8	20	11
Average duration, weeks	13	12	9	14	12

Source: U.S. Statistical Abstract, 1981.

unemployed was over $19,000. And for 40% it was over $20,000. The average annual income of *all* families was about $29,000 (the median was about $21,000). About 20% of the unemployed were in families below the poverty line. However, the average income of female-headed households that experienced unemployment was only $8,500, though 8% were above $20,000. Even after correcting to a per capita basis, since such households are relatively small, the average per capita is lower than for male or multiple-employee households.

Of the unemployed living alone, almost 75% earned less than $10,000. But over half the unemployed who are teenagers live with families that have incomes exceeding $20,000, with an average of almost $25,000. Only about 16% lived in families below the poverty line. For the unemployed black teenager, the average family income was over $17,000; one-third were below the poverty line. Individuals reporting more than six months of unemployment lived in households with an average income of $16,000, while a bit less than 30% were below the poverty line.

To what extent does unemployment tend to lower one's earnings? For the auto and steel workers who were unemployed in some year, family income averaged about $21,000 in that year, while families with no reported unemployment averaged $28,000. Over

a lifetime the effect is much less since unemployment does not occur every year. For construction workers the comparable figures are $19,000 and $26,000. Not all of the difference can be attributed to unemployment, because more of those who experienced unemployment (such as those under age 24) have wage rates that are lower than the average of the adult population.

Trends in Unemployment

The unemployment rate has increased during the past 30 years. One reason is that teenagers, with a high rate, have become a larger proportion of the labor force, thereby raising the overall rate even though the rate may not have increased for any particular group. But there has been a small upward trend in unemployment for everyone except people over 55, where the trend is essentially zero. Also, the increased proportion of multiworker families permits greater flexibility in the search for new employment opportunities. The greater the fraction of such families in the work force, the greater will be the average extent of unemployment. Both of these forces reflect change in labor-force composition rather than changes in the effectiveness of the economic system to maintain high employment.

But some things have contributed to greater unemployment even without any change in the composition of the labor force. Greater and longer-lasting unemployment benefits applied to a wider range of industries have contributed to the upward trend. Also, more welfare payments are contingent on persons being classified as unemployed. Further, the minimum-wage laws have reduced employment of the very young and have increased their sensitivity to business-cycle changes. All these factors—the change in demographic composition, the benefits receivable when unemployed, and the minimum-wage laws—have been estimated to have raised the average unemployment rate about two to three percentage points over the last three decades, from around 3%–4% to about 5%–6%.

DEMOGRAPHIC FACTORS IN UNEMPLOYMENT

The percentage of the work force that is unemployed varies not only over time with changing business conditions but also according to such characteristics as age, gender, color, and general skills. Typically, the statistically reported unemployment rate among married men 25 to 65 years of age is less than 3%, whereas for unskilled, nonwhite teenagers it exceeds 10%.

Why do unemployment rates differ according to gender, age, and color? It might be thought that teenagers, women, and nonwhites are not trained for the jobs available, but that assumption is incorrect because insufficient training would explain only why they are paid less per hour than adult, white males.[2] Then why are the unemployed not working at the tasks they can do? Because some would rather not work at the wages offered for the available jobs, and others have not yet decided what is the best job. Some people may have so little wage-earning capability for the best-known job that they prefer not to work for wages, yet say they are "unemployed." But why do sufficiently pro-

---

[2] Statements about unskilled or untrained people or people with skills that do not correspond to job requirements are misleading. That would have an effect only if wages had to be uniform for all workers and if there were *no* value for *any* of the services that could be provided by low-skilled people. (Again, remember that economic analysis does not make recommendations or pass judgments. We are not implying that nothing should or can be done to alleviate the situation, or that the existing situation is desirable. The doctor who traces your back pain to your wearing high-heeled shoes is not saying that you deserve it, or that nothing should or can be done to prevent or alleviate it.)

ductive teenagers or nonwhite adults experience such high unemployment rates? As already noted, teenagers quit jobs more readily than others in their evaluative search for careers. Another factor is the minimum-wage law, which prevents employers from hiring unproven teenagers at wages low enough to reflect their low productivity and to distribute the job-training costs to the teenagers. When demands shift, the teenagers are the first to go, because they cannot adjust their wages below the legal minimum. For blacks, another factor has been their high rate of migration from agricultural areas into cities. As a result a large number are engaged in extensive job-opportunity search and evaluation; hence a large fraction of young and mobile blacks will show up often as unemployed.

COSTS OF CHANGING JOBS

Evaluating the available jobs is time-consuming, taking up most of the average two-month search. Lost income during that time represents a small percentage of what a person makes during an average 5-year job, usually less than the costs of selling a house, a car, a piece of land, or even a share of stock, which range from 1% to 10% of the good's value. This does not mean that unemployment is not a source of increased anxiety for the job seeker during those two months but rather, in purely economic terms, that the costs of the job search are lower than the job seeker's state of mind might suggest. Moreover, unemployment insurance and welfare payments reduce the cost of the search still further.

The subject of monetary aid for the unemployed can arouse intense emotions in people. Some unemployment compensation is an insurance payment to the unemployed person, who had paid annual premiums while employed. Yet a large number of the unemployed receive relief payments unrelated to any unemployment insurance premiums they may have paid. This relief increases people's tendency to enter the ranks of official unemployment and to stay longer. In some instances the unemployment insurance payments, welfare payments, and reduced tax obligations reduce the loss of income for six months of unemployment to hardly more than 10% to 20% of full-employment income. If one then calculates a value of leisure or of not working, the costs of a spell of unemployment are greatly reduced.

OTHER TYPES OF UNEMPLOYMENT

Some people are excluded from particular jobs by restrictive apprenticeships or licensing laws. They call themselves unemployed electricians, musicians, meat cutters, projectionists, or bricklayers. Some of these people will remain "unemployed" until they either become independent owner-contractors or shift to other, less productive occupations without such entry restrictions.

Another category of the unemployed is made up of people who take employment only when demand for their services is high enough to warrant the high wages that would attract them. Some housewives work only during seasonally high demands for certain types of labor—in grape picking, fruit packing, or clerking at the Christmas season. The rest of the year they prefer not to work at the lower-valued jobs they could obtain. People in short-lived projects such as movies, plays, or housing construction are commonly called unemployed between projects—especially if they have qualified for unemployment benefits. For example, at any one time over 80% of the members of the Screen Actors Guild in Hollywood are classified as unemployed—as they must be to qualify for unemployment and some union and government welfare benefits.

Changes in Structural and Aggregate Demand

STRUCTURAL UNEMPLOYMENT

Although the economy as a whole may be stable or even growing as the general demand for goods increases, certain changes can occur in particular markets or occupations that reduce the demand for labor in those areas. The demand for some goods may fall, while the demand for others may so increase that resources are bid away from the production of goods for which demand is growing slowly or not at all; or, new production techniques may make different types of labor more valuable than they had been in some uses and less valuable than they had been in other uses. These changes in the demand for, or supply of, labor, if they persist or exist on a large scale, are called *structural shifts*. As a consequence of them, people and resources whose services fall in value must accept lower wages and rents or must shift to other jobs, or possibly do both. This change initiates unemployment called *structural unemployment*.

DECREASE IN AGGREGATE DEMAND

Figure 17–4 shows graphically the percentage of 172 major industries expanding their use of labor at the same time. The percentage fluctuates, rarely reaching 100% or zero %, usually staying within the range of about 20% to 80%. Rarely are less than 20% or more than 80% of these industries expanding their employment at the same time. (Expansions and contractions among *firms* within an industry show a similar pattern.)

If the line in Figure 17–4 were stable at about 50%, it would suggest a relatively steady *aggregate*, or national, demand for labor, with the various industries expanding or contracting independently of one another but generally balancing their labor demands

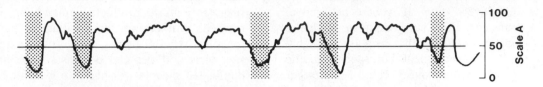

Scale A

1957 58 59 60 61 62 63 64 65 66 67 68 69 70 71 72 73 74 75 76 77 78 79 80 81

relative to one another at that aggregate demand.

If demand for one good falls and another rises, resources will transfer to other equally good activities relatively quickly. But if *general* demand (one correlated over many products) decreases, then a more difficult adjustment and searching process follows. Say you are an auto worker and demand for cars has fallen. You can retain your job only if you cut your wages to practically zero—unless all other inputs to auto manufacturing also cut their prices at the same time by, say, 10%, in which case taking a 10% wage cut would enable you to keep your job. But do suppliers of steel, tires, fabrics, copper, plastics, and transport all *immediately* know that demand has *also* fallen elsewhere, so that they too will have reason to quickly adjust prices for their products (which would permit you to retain your job with only a 10% wage cut)? No.

No firm can instantly know whether a decrease in demand for its goods is transient or persisting, whether or not it extends across the economy as an aggregate decrease in demand. Nor do the employees know. If the shift were known to be a transient, reversible one, the buffer inventory would perform its function and employment and output would be maintained. If, however, buffer inventories were too expensive to maintain, the output would be reduced and employees temporarily laid off.

No one employer can quickly know whether a decrease in demand, transient or permanent, applies only to the goods of that

Figure 17-4.

CONFORMITY OF EXPANSIONS IN EMPLOYMENT AMONG 172 INDUSTRIES

The curved line shows the percentage at which employment expansions in 172 industries conform to one another. Rarely if ever does employment in all industries expand or contract at the same time. But in some periods most may contract for a while, as in 1957, 1960, 1970, 1974, and 1980, when the curve dips to the lowest percentages of conformity of expansion. It should be expected that normally about half would be expanding and half contracting—as is confirmed by the movement of the curve around the 50% value (the straight line). During periods of low conformity of expansion conformity of *contraction* is high. Such periods are called *recessions* or *depressions* if lasting more than a year. Lightly shaded areas indicate recessions.

SOURCE: U.S. Department of Commerce, *Business Conditions Digest,* monthly.

one firm or to all firms in an industry. Nor can employees know. If it were believed to be transient, the likely response would be temporary layoffs. If the decrease were believed to be permanent but specific to the employer, the employees would leave rather than accept a wage lower than available elsewhere or a long-term or permanent layoff. If the decrease were believed to be industrywide or economywide, employees would be more likely to accept a wage adjustment to keep their jobs, believing the options elsewhere to be no better.

But if, in fact, workers are wrong in their beliefs about the anticipated lengths of demand decreases as the shifts persist and are more general than anticipated, they will find, when refusing to take a wage cut in their firm, that they cannot get other jobs at essentially the same wage, nor as soon as expected. They will be unemployed longer than anticipated, making their unemployment *unanticipated* or *involuntary*. If, however, they could instantly have known that a demand shift was general and persisting, they would have accepted adjusted wages to keep the same jobs. But, of course, they cannot know. Hence we see spells of surprisingly long unemployment, with wage and price rigidity and general unemployment across many industries—that is, recessions.

If demand and supply conditions change, it is conceivable that a new set of market-clearing prices would, *if instantly achieved*, keep everyone employed at their same jobs. However, this would mean that some people and resources would be getting much less than they could get in other jobs. Hence, they accept unemployment and search for and evaluate other opportunities. Therefore, when demand or supply shifts are widespread or large, or are not immediately known to be long-lasting, unemployment increases as resources adjust to the new circumstances, especially if demand decreases have predominated. If demand *increases*

have predominated, job offers will flow from firms for whose products demand has increased. Workers are more willing to move to a clearly better paying job with less extensive search. If demand decreases have predominated, people will begin to look for the next-best job. That is why a general decrease in demand is accompanied by temporary (though not insignificant) disorganizing increases in unemployment. Gradually, over a few months or a year (depending on the reason for the decrease in demand), unemployment is reduced as people discern the new, lower wages and the new best available jobs.

The worker's unwillingness to accept lower wage rates to reflect the prices of other goods does not indicate wage inflexibility. Nothing prevents any worker from showing perfect, instant wage flexibility. One's *notion* of what price can be obtained lags behind the facts; the cost of getting information makes the *state of knowledge* lag behind the actual equilibrating price that would restore employment. It is an *informational stickiness*, or *inflexibility*, or *lag*. People choose not to reduce the price of services, because they think the equilibrating price is higher than it actually is.

Though we have concentrated on people seeking the best employment opportunities, people contemplating opportunities for investment face exactly the same task. They want the *best* opportunities for the investment of their savings. What new buildings or equipment or tasks for employees will be most profitable—if profitable at all? Not surprisingly, even when the willingness to invest is unchanging, the rate of investment will fluctuate. Inventions, plus changes in tastes, production techniques, and the available supplies of various goods (such as reduction of the oil supply in the 1970s), drastically alter the profitability of different investments. Because people scan opportunities rather than investing in the first one that appears profitable, delays and fluctuations occur in the rate of investment and in the demand for resources with which to make the investments.

But it should not be surprising that the search for best options tends to subdue the fluctuations in the general direction of full employment. Though all options may be deteriorating, people will accept the best (though poorer) options available rather than not invest or not work at all. Hence fluctuations in demand and productive opportunities will not move the economy's rate of activity around at random levels without any force toward full employment. Nor will the economy persistently maintain full employment. It will persistently be pushing toward full employment after shocks or changes in demands and supplies have converted formerly profitable arrangements into unprofitable ones.

Fluctuations of Aggregate Demand

Aggregate market demand fluctuates instead of being nearly constant with virtually offsetting shifts from one product to another. Expansions or contractions in one industry or sector set up forces for expansion or contraction in other industries or sectors: An increased or decreased demand for final goods in one industry will increase or decrease the demand for inputs bought from supplier industries. For example, a decreased demand for cars will decrease the demand for steel and a chain of other services, which consequently will amplify the decrease in the demand for cars. That several sectors move in close step should not be surprising.

The aggregate demand for goods receives a particularly serious shock whenever there is a reduction (for reasons we need not go into here) in the supply of money. With less money in the economy, existing prices are too high for the present rate of output to be profitable, but at first nobody knows this. People must conduct an extensive search for the new pattern of market-clearing prices and outputs.

The system that produces money (cash, paper money, and checking accounts) is uniquely critical to the performance of the economy because of its power to exercise **monetary policy**: to manipulate the size of the money supply in order to influence aggregate output and price levels. For example, the controlling agency of the U.S. monetary system, the Board of Governors of the *Federal Reserve System*, permitted large, unexpected decreases in the supply of money in the years 1929 through 1933. That decrease was a significant contributing factor in the Great Depression.

In the early years of the depression, legislation was passed that, however well intended, had the effect of impeding economic recovery. These laws imposed many unprecedented restrictions on price changes and on the access of would-be new producers to the market.[3] But what was done by one government agency was undone, in part, by some other agency. After 1932, the federal government spent newly created money through various public works projects to provide jobs with higher pay than otherwise available. That money was not old money collected from citizens by explicit taxes but was newly printed by the Federal Reserve Bank. The government ran a budget deficit, that is, spent more than it was collecting in taxes. By so doing, the government was exercising **fiscal policy**: the use of government spending or taxation to influence aggregate output and

---

[3]The rate of recovery from 1932 on has been underestimated, because many people were counted as unemployed who were in fact employed on new government projects. We cite this fact not to deny the severity of the depression in 1933, nor to fully explain the slowness of recovery (which has not yet been satisfactorily explained), but to refute the beliefs that forces tending to push the economy toward full employment were absent and that *such severe depressions* are an inherent characteristic of an open-market economy.

employment. But in creating new money to finance the deficit, it was using *monetary* policies. Thus, in the 1930s, the government entered into a new policy role, trying to end the depression by deliberately influencing the magnitude of aggregate demand for goods and services by fiscal and monetary means.

Aggregate demand is influenced less by the amount of government spending and deficit than by how much of that is done with *newly created money*. Increasing taxes to cover increased government spending transfers wealth from private citizens to the political agents, with little effect on the size of aggregate demand. Higher taxes, however, do diminish the incentives to work and to invest, thereby tending to reduce aggregate output. These effects on incentives and output have recently been called the *supply-side* effects of government fiscal policy. Whether government's attempts by fiscal policy and by monetary policy to influence aggregate economic activity have on net been beneficial or harmful is the focus of a raging, unresolved debate. No systematic, reliable, unbiased evidence is available.

Economic Fluctuations and Full Employment

Economic fluctuations (other than those related to seasonal changes in demand or supply of particular goods and services) are not systematic cycles in the sense that high prosperity creates recession. They occur unsystematically. The main characteristics of a recession are decreases in national money income, employment, the aggregate output of goods, the prices of assets and common stocks, profits, and wealth. Most of these characteristics are highly correlated. If the decreases last more than six months the economy may be considered to be in a recession, and it is certain to be so called if they

last a year. Unemployment rates and net business income fluctuate by the largest percentages. If we look at employment rather than *un*employment, the fluctuations are small, because a 3% decrease in employment from 97% to 94% is the same as a 100% increase in *un*employment from 3% to 6%. To some, employment of about 95% to 97% of those who desire employment seems phenomenally good; to others, an unemployment rate of 3% to 5% seems too high.

For reasons given earlier in this chapter, downward shocks causing recessions from full employment are later overcome by market forces tending to restore full employment. One strong piece of evidence is the high normal rate of employment, which is around 94% to 98% most of the time.

Another powerful piece of evidence of the economy's tendency to return to full employment is that the upward recovery is of the same general magnitude as the preceding downward shock. Moreover, the size of a recovery, or interval to the next recession, does not determine the size of the next recession. If it did, it could then be assumed that the system is one in which a "boom" causes a "bust": "What goes up must come down." The economic system does not show that pattern; nor does it simply wander at random with no connection whatever between any declines and rises.

Although the evidence is overwhelming for the tendency toward full employment, speed or rate of recovery can vary. Over the past half century, the actual unemployment recovery rate has averaged about 4% per year. That is, unemployment recovered on average from, say, 8% to 4% or from 7% to 3% in one year, or from 7% to 5% in six months. Sometimes it was faster and sometimes slower, depending in part on factors that initiated the downward shock. The dip in employment because of, say, a widespread strike was followed by a rapid recovery, because almost everyone knew where the best opportunities lay when the strike was over.

But when downswings were caused by broad changes in supply or demand, as when energy supplies changed in 1973, people had to inform themselves more extensively to find the best alternative options for work, investment, and production. That took more time.

Some shocks are so slow to be felt, or are so minor, or impinge on so small a part of the economy that the adjustment is hardly noticed. For example, the rise of television and the decline of radio occurred so gradually that there was no long-lasting unemployment of those formerly employed in radio. The slow rise of the automobile, the airplane, and the electronics industry were all integrated without upsetting the economy. Because they impose greater physical damage, wars sometimes cause greater adjustment problems. But the economy adjusted so quickly from war production to peacetime production in 1946, and after other wars, that its coordinative efficiency must then have seemed adequate to withstand any shock. However, sometimes a succession of unpredicted, novel shocks have caused major impairments in the power of the market system to direct and coordinate the output and allocation of goods—as happened in the Great Depression of the 1930s.

A decrease in aggregate demand, or an *increased* fear of unstable governments and insecurity of property and person, makes investments in existing activities less likely to be profitable. The normal savings flow cannot be as profitably invested until adequate information is obtained about the expected future situation. A substantial portion of resources must shift to new tasks. But which new ones? To what new products? Because of the changed situation, it becomes more worthwhile to investigate alternatives and prospective prices before making any new investment. For example, the quick adjustment after World War II contrasts sharply with the slow recovery after the decline between 1929 and 1932. One difference was that when the war ended, people knew it had ended. But the severe decline in the money supply beginning in 1929 did not end with an official announcement in 1932. Who was to know then that the money supply would really increase? Furthermore, a series of new laws and profound changes in economic institutions after 1932 created more uncertainty about the future, requiring that those wanting to adapt to that future acquire still more information. These facts explain not why the recovery was as slow as it was, but rather why it was slower than the adjustment following World War II, or other recessions before and since.

International Comparisons

International comparisons to the United States (using similar concepts and measurements of unemployment) are not entirely reliable, but they indicate similar behavior in western European countries, Japan, and Australia, with the difference that Japan and Sweden had smaller unemployment rates. Great Britain, Japan, and Germany had substantially lower teenage unemployment rates. The overall average of spells of unemployment was much shorter in the United States, about 11 weeks compared to over 20 weeks for the other countries. Well-validated explanations for these differences have not been identified.

Summary

1. Changes in the demand or supply of goods induce changes in output and in the number and allocation of the employed. In the interim, labor and resources are unemployed while they find their new most-profitable activities.

2. Unemployment—the condition of being

without a wage-paying job and looking for one—can be the most efficient way of finding and evaluating job alternatives and of adapting to unpredictably shifting demands. It is not caused by a lack of jobs, for in a world of scarce goods and services there is no such lack.

3. Unemployment occurs for any one or more of several reasons: (a) legal restraints such as minimum-wage laws that prevent some people from accepting wages that reflect their marginal productivity; (b) restraints that exclude from certain jobs all those who lack required qualifications such as union membership or having undergone an apprenticeship; (c) the willingness of some workers to work only during seasonal peak demands when wages are high; (d) the unwillingness of some people to work at wages that reflect their productive capacities; (e) a shifting of relative demands or supplies that induces a reallocation of jobs, called structural unemployment; (f) a falling aggregate demand requiring that wages and prices be reduced but not immediately perceived as a persisting decrease by workers, who therefore refuse to accept lower wages for their present jobs.

4. The incidence and duration of unemployment depend in part on age and work experience. Teenage newcomers to the work force, experimenting with different types of jobs, take more spells of unemployment than do older people with longer work experience. The average spell of unemployment lasts two months or less. During recessions more people are unemployed and for a longer time.

5. Because information is not free, and because the quicker the adjustment, the higher the costs, reductions in demand are not immediately followed by reduction of prices to new market-clearing levels or by complete adjustment in the employment patterns of all productive resources. Instead, productive resources are unemployed (if labor) or idle (if nonhuman capital goods) while the changed demand and supply conditions are discovered and adjusted to.

6. Decreases and increases in aggregate demand are not well predicted. One cause is a substantial change in the money supply. Other causes may be wars and changes in beliefs about the security of property rights in future investments or in beliefs about political stability.

7. Resources become unemployed to the extent that the decrease in aggregate demand is larger than expected or immediately detected.

8. After recessions and depressions the market economy tends to return to full employment of labor and other productive resources.

Questions

1. The usual criterion of an unemployed person is "not employed by someone else and actively looking for a job." It says nothing about the range of jobs or wages he refuses to consider. What do you think the criterion implicitly assumes to avoid being completely useless?

*2. "A man who loses his job through no fault of his own should not have to bear the losses of unemployment. The government must see to it that he does not." This is a quotation from a campaign speech of a major candidate for governor of California.
   a. Is the candidate proposing that there be no unemployment or that anyone not currently employed should be given an income equivalent to what he was formerly getting?
   b. How can either of these be accomplished?

3. Is a person who loses his job through no fault of his own also unemployed thereafter through no fault of his own? Explain.

*4 "Unemployment is a wonderful privilege. Without it we would all be slaves to tyrants."
   a. Can you interpret this "ridiculous" statement so as to make it not ridiculous? (Hint: There is no unemployment in the military. There is reputed to be none in Russia. Distinguish among the factors that shift demands, those that make job information costly, and the losses of

wealth consequent to those demand shifts and costliness of job information.)

b. Would you prefer to live in a community in which unemployment is forbidden? Why? (Later we shall analyze ways of reducing unemployment without forbidding it.)

5. a. What different kinds of unemployment (with respect to why unemployment exists) do you think it is relevant to distinguish?

*b. Why?

6. Suppose the daily sales of each of 50 firms are determined by a process simulated by the turn of a roulette wheel with numbers from 0 through 30. Further, suppose that the firm will on the next day seek to hire as many employees as the sales of the preceding day. Thus, if sales are 20 on the first day, the firm will seek to hire 20 people on the second day—given the wages of $25 per person per day. If there were 50 firms, the number of employed people would be 50 × 15 = 750 on the average.

a. Would that employment rate stay constant day after day despite the independent additive random process for determining the number of employees demanded at that wage rate?

b. If those who were laid off by one employer took a day to select a new job, would there always be some unemployed?

c. Would there always be some unfilled vacancies?

d. Would the number of unemployed equal vacancies?

e. What would happen to the number of job seekers and to the number of vacancies if the top five numbers on the roulette wheels were erased?

f. What would happen if all the numbers had been increased by 5?

g. The change from day to day in the totals of the 50 firms with an unaltered roulette wheel and the change when the roulette wheel is altered are two different kinds of changes. Which would correspond to a correlated decrease in general aggregate market demand for goods?

*h. How quickly do you think a person would detect a changed wheel, that is, a general demand change?

7. On the average, the cost increment of each extra job investigated increases. Also, on the average, the gain in wages from another job investigated diminishes. If these two propositions are true, then what must be the relation between the increment of gain and the increment of cost in order to conclude that it will pay to always take the first job investigated?

8. Employment agencies charge about 50% to 60% of one month's salary for their services for jobs paying about $600 per month. For jobs paying about $1000, the fee is one month's salary. If this is paid to the employment agency by the employer, does it mean the employer bears the costs? Do you think this fee is too large? Why?

9. Is the analysis of this chapter consistent with the fact that unemployment among blacks is higher than among whites? Does it explain the level of employment at "full employment" or the massive changes in the unemployment rate?

*10. When requesting a Congressional investigation into the methods, charges, and quality of services of private employment agencies, Mr. Abel, president of the United Steelworkers of America, said, "A man or woman should not have to pay—often a large sum—for the privilege of obtaining a job." He also asserted that society and government had an obligation to make it possible for "every willing and able individual to work at or near his highest skill." Evaluate those remarks in the light of economic analysis.

*11. In deciding who is an unemployed person, would you consider the following:

a. Is he now working for someone else as an employee? If his answer is "Yes," would you classify him as unemployed or as employed?

b. He answers "Yes" to the preceding question, but answers "No" to the question "Is your current job your usual kind of work?" He reports that he is working at a service station, while looking for a job as a lathe operator. Would you change the classification?

c. Next he is asked, "Are you willing to take

an available job as a lathe operator at a wage of $5 an hour?" He answers, "No, I used to work for $10 an hour and I'm an experienced operator, not a novice." Is your classification of him still the same? Why?

d. If you do not call him unemployed in the preceding question, then how can you call anyone unemployed? For there are always jobs available at some sufficiently low wage—a wage he would call "ridiculous," "un-American," or "below standard."

12. Almost every year someone proposes that Congress enact legislation "to create more jobs." Of course, it doesn't create jobs, for there are already too many jobs to do and the jobs it presumes to create already exist as useful things to do. What is Congress really being asked to create by that legislation?

13. In almost every city and state during the recent energy flap people were told that unless more energy were conserved or made available, jobs could not be preserved. That statement is of course incorrect. Jobs would in fact be increased by a reduced supply of energy for there would be more work for people to do! What do you suppose people meant, or should have meant, by saying the jobs could not be preserved?

14. "A substantial number of relatively unskilled persons reported that they cannot find work. At the same time, there are many unfilled jobs for relatively skilled people. Apparently, the problem is that there are more unskilled people than unskilled jobs." What is wrong with the reasoning?

15. In feudal England there was no unemployment—only work and leisure. Employment for wages was rare. But the rise of the commercial system introduced markets for labor services and induced peasants to break away from their feudal ties and to sacrifice their feudal security for the hazards of private contractual employment and unemployment. By the sixteenth century employment for money wages was well established (but maximum permissible wage rates were set by government, and potential employers were exhorted not to offer more and were punished if caught).

a. What devices do you think developed as a means of paying more than the maximum-wage ceilings?

b. Why would the government have imposed *maximum* limits to wages?

*16. America was founded partly on "slavery" of white men. In early days immigrants "indentured" themselves, pledging to work for the benefit of a master for seven (or some specified number of) years if the master would finance their way to America. Today, this is illegal.

a. Why?

b. Who gains and who loses if such contracts are prohibited?

*17. "Automation is destroying 300,000 jobs a month." Is destroying jobs socially good or bad? Explain why it does not mean that anyone will be left without a job.

*18. The federal government is taxing and paying for job retraining for those who lose a job.

a. Do you think it should provide an apartment renovation service for people whose apartments become vacant?

b. What is the difference between the two forms of aid?

19. What is the explanation for high unemployment among male blacks, Puerto Ricans, and Mexicans? (Do not answer "low education," "prejudice," or "immobility" because all of those would imply lower wages, not higher unemployment.)

*20.a. In your first job after college would you rather have (1) a lower wage with more assurance of not being laid off during a transient recession in the first year—with an implied understanding on your part that you will not leave until after a year even if you found a better job, or (2) a higher wage with no such assurances?

b. Which preference would imply greater unemployment for you?

c. Who is likely to prefer (1) and who (2)?

Chapter 18
The Domestic and Political Economies

The Nonmarket Domestic Economy

The dominant share of economic activity is conducted through market exchanges; the second-largest source is domestic activity in the home. Domestic activity is also a form of exchange in that husbands and wives agree to do things for each other: They engage in specialization and exchange of services. But because the value of domestic services is given no formal accounting, it is not called a market transaction and is not included in formal measures of national income. If it were, what fraction of the total national income would it make up?

To make a rough estimate, merely ask what it would cost if all the household activity now done by family members without money payment were performed by employees—cooks, cleaners, buyers, designers, nurses, educators, and so on. Most such work is performed by wives. And although no official agencies maintain an accounting of the value of that output, in the tragic circumstances of the death of a young mother, estimates of losses are often made for the purpose of insurance or damages compensation. The resulting valuations in those cases are perhaps surprisingly high to those unaccustomed to thinking of domestic tasks as economic activity. One study used the method of comparing the economic welfare of single persons and married couples with one spouse working in the home: If a man and woman living separately and each earning about $15,000 a year were to marry, and only one continued working for money income while the other worked in the home, the money income had to be only about $20,000 to enable both to have the same economic welfare as before. Thus, for a two-person family with a money income of about $20,000, the value of the household activity amounted to about $10,000 a year.

If in each of the approximately 80 million U.S. households the domestic economic activity were valued at only $10,000, that would amount to $800 billion. The 1982 U.S. net national income from market exchanges amounted to slightly over $3000 billion; adding the uncounted value of domestic activity brings the total to almost $4 trillion. Non-market domestic activity makes up 20% of our net national income, nearly twice as large a percentage as that of the largest market-oriented industry, manufacturing.

Why, then, is that enormous household production, mostly by women and untaxed, largely overlooked in official measures and definitions of our "national income"? Because national income is computed in order to measure fluctuations in market activity and to estimate future tax proceeds. It is presumed that although market-coordinated activity can undergo recessions, there is always full employment in household activity.

Measuring National Income: Value-Added

National market-oriented *output* is not to be confused with market *sales* of all goods and services, because some goods are sold repeatedly in the process of being transformed from raw materials to finished consumer products. Only the *added values* at each step accurately measure the income produced. A simple example clarifies how the values of sales and the value of national income are related, and shows the forms in which that income is earned. Table 18–1 summarizes the tale.

Imagine that a mining firm sells some iron ore to a steel mill for $100. The mining firm pays $70 of that price as wages and pays itself $20 in rent for the land and $5 as dividends and interest on the firm's investment. Additionally, $5 worth of shovels are worn out and must be replaced.

The $100 of iron ore sold to the steel mill is converted into steel, which is sold to a toolmaking firm for $200. The value added by the steel mill is $85. It paid $100 for the steel: $70 for labor, $5 as interest and dividends, $10 for rent of the land, and $15 for tools worn out in the production process.

The steel purchased by the tool factory for $200 is turned into shovels and tools worth $260, from which $40 is paid for labor, $5 for dividends and interest, $5 for rent, and $10 for equipment worn out.

As Table 18–1 shows, the payments of wages, interest and dividends, and rent total $230. These payments go to individuals in their capacity as income earners for their households. Those earnings will be used for consumption or investment. The total value of the finished products sold to consumers is $260, but $30 worth of worn-out equipment has to be replaced from that final output, so the *net* final product is $230. This sum is also the value of earnings by householders in the form of wages, interest and dividends, and rent. As the table shows, these payments represent the value added at each stage. Purchases by one firm from another firm are not measured as **value-added**: Only the value by which the sale price exceeds the purchase price of the good from other firms is counted. (If the purchase price of the good from the firm were included in value-added, that price would be double-counted in the later sale of the products to the next firm.) The sum of the sequence of values added is the net total income of this community, or, in the case of an entire economy, **net national income**. The values added give a measure of national income derived from production, but are also the earnings of householders.

The major part of the economy, then, can be viewed essentially as operating through *firms producing goods* and paying out earned incomes, which go to *households*. The 1981 U.S. Gross National Product (GNP) was about $3.3 trillion, and the net national income (the GNP minus depreciation) was about $3 trillion. Thus, about 10% of the gross national product went to replace depreciated resources used up in production. Figure 18-1 is a circular flow diagram showing how much of recorded national income goes where; it also shows the government as a tax collector, spender, and producer. But it excludes value of services produced in the household and undetected transactions. (Recent estimates are that actual net national in-

Table 18-1   VALUE-ADDED INCOME

| Value of Production (in $) = Earnings Values | | | | | |
Iron Mine		Wages	Rent	Interest & Dividends	Depreciation
Labor	70 Value-	70			
Rent	20 Added		20		
Interest & dividends	5			5	
Depreciation of existing assets	5				5
Gross value	100				

Value of ore sold to steel mill					
Purchased ore	100				
Labor	70 Value-	70			
Rent	10 Added		10		
Interest & dividends	5			5	
Depreciation of existing assets	15				15
Gross value	200				

Value of steel sold to tool factory					
Purchased steel	200				
Labor	40 Value-	40			
Rent	5 Added		5		
Interest & dividends	5			5	
Depreciation of existing assets	10				10
Gross product	260 =	180 +	35 +	15 +	30
Minus depreciation	−30				
Net product	230	Net Income			

Actual U.S. National income (1981)

U.S. Gross National Product—	$3.3 trillion
Minus Depreciation	−0.3 trillion
Net National Product	$3.0 trillion
Per Capita (population: 230 million)	$13,000—or about $6/hr.

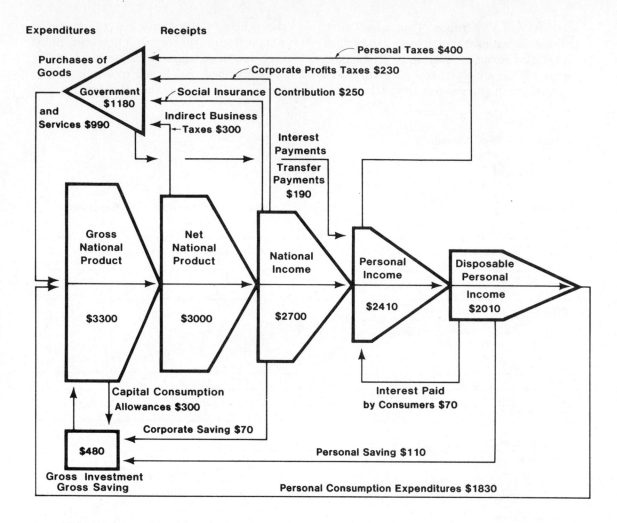

Figure 18-1.

FLOW OF INCOME AND EXPENDITURES (BILLIONS OF DOLLARS), 1981

Gross national product was $2500 billion in 1981 and can be measured as the sum of consumption expenditures, federal and state government purchases of goods and services, and gross investment, the latter including both gross private domestic investment and net exports of goods and services. The difference between gross saving and gross investment reflects primarily a government deficit.

SOURCE: U.S. Department of Commerce.

come is about 20% larger than officially reported because of transactions that are conducted "underground," that is, unreported to authorities—to avoid having to pay taxes.) Figure 18–2 shows the historical path of recorded U.S. national income since the end of World War I.

Economic activity takes place within and among three major components: the home, the market, and government. Total economic activity conducted by federal, state, and local governments amounts to about 10% of the total with approximately 70% of the remainder directed by markets and about 20% per-

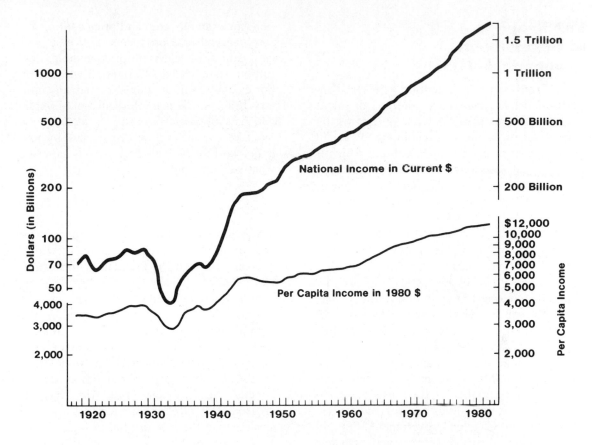

Figure 18-2.

U.S. NATIONAL INCOME IN CURRENT DOLLARS AND
PER CAPITA PERSONAL INCOME IN 1980 DOLLARS

SOURCE: U.S. Statistical Abstract.

formed in households. (Other forms of organizing economic activity, such as clubs, nonprofit groups, cooperatives, and the like, are minor and will not be investigated here.) Of the three components, market activity is the most susceptible to economic analysis; the family (its formation, activities, and internal controls) is susceptible to *some* economic analysis; and government economic activity is the least susceptible to economic analysis. That government economic behavior is less well understood than that of the market economy does not of course imply that either of the two components is more or less desirable than the other. With that provision, let us examine the role of government in the economy.

The Scope of Government Economic Activity

Government is, by definition, the social institution that monopolizes the use, or threat of the use, of physical force to control the behavior of people. It also retains the exclusive power to print money, without which it would not last long. The rights, behavior, and competitive actions that a government allows vary among nations. But without government the state of society would be intolerable, and there could be neither exchange of private-property rights nor such rights. Because security against foreign and domestic aggressors is not adequately organized by private contracts, the military, the police, and the courts are essential. Furthermore, for some resources the highest valued uses cannot be achieved by private-property rights. For example, air, water, and roads usually escape our ability to define and enforce private-property rights in their use. So other means are used—often control by governments. Another role of government is the redistributing of wealth. Government transfers wealth from some people by explicit taxes and uses the proceeds to finance benefits to others.

In several socialist nations, for example, the Soviet Union and the People's Republic of China, the government controls and directs the use of resources that in the United States are guided by private-property and market values. In other nations the apportioning of control over the use of resources falls somewhere in between. It is beyond the scope of economic analysis to attempt to assess the relative merits of the alternative systems. And although virtually any activity is being done by some government agency somewhere in the world, we don't have a clear enough understanding of the avenues of access to government power and its use to explain under what circumstances "this" action (for example, crop and price controls for some agricultural producers, antitrust policies, control of television programming, low-tuition state universities) or "that" action (for example, tuition grants to students, military draft, stock market regulations, public golf courses, social security) is more likely. We can explain a few things, but by and large the best we can do is simply describe what is happening.

EXPENDITURES

The size of government dollar expenditures and revenues in the United States grew dramatically through the first half of this century, when it reached 35% to 40%, of national income. However, looking at the number of dollars spent mismeasures the growth of government. First, the inflation that has occurred during the past decades makes recent expenditures larger in nominal, or dollar, terms than in purchasing power. Second, because the population has increased, the rate of per capita growth is smaller than the rate of total growth. Figure 18-3 shows per capita real expenditures for all levels of U.S. government in the last 30 years, measured in inflation-adjusted dollars equivalent to 1981 prices. Since 1950 the share of national income per capita spent by all governments has been nearly constant.

Each level of government—local, state, and federal—assumes certain responsibilities or shares them with one or both of the other levels in the United States. Education is primarily overseen by local and state governments. Economic activity is regulated by all levels of government, by restricting what consumers can buy or what producers can offer. In general, the more widely the benefits or costs of an action are dispersed over the whole nation, the more likely is the federal government to be involved.

Governments do some things that the market exchange of private-property rights cannot do adequately. The use of roads un-

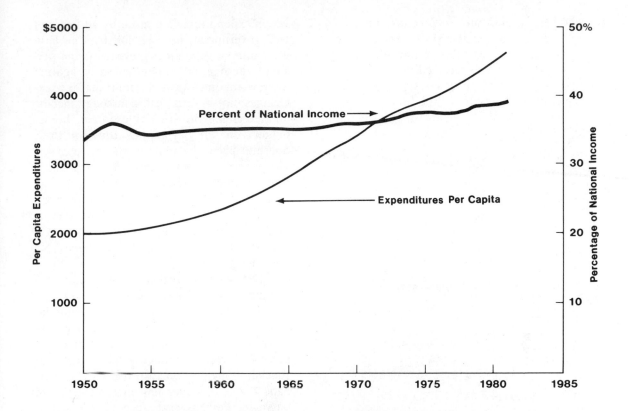

Figure 18-3.

TOTAL EXPENDITURES BY ALL LEVELS OF
GOVERNMENT IN THE UNITED STATES MEASURED AS
DOLLARS PER CAPITA (ADJUSTED TO 1981 DOLLARS)
AND AS PERCENT OF NATIONAL INCOME

SOURCE: U.S. Statistical Abstract.

der a market system would require a forbiddingly complex system of planning, collection, and enforcement devices. Instead, governments levy *tolls* or *taxes* that are actually *prices* for use. A gasoline tax, or at least part of one, is a price for the use of the streets; the amount collected, being proportionate to the amount of gasoline used, is therefore proportionate to the amount of street use. For services that everyone receives and that are not easily assigned, general taxes may be charged, such as for national defense, or, locally, for public library services.

A tax that is really a price charged by the government for services rendered is not easily distinguished from a tax that supplies revenues for general use. However, if a tax, whether it is called that or a fee or a service charge, is determined by measurable use, it is a price. Nevertheless, it is an open question whether the graduated income tax, for example, which taxes higher incomes at higher percentages, constitutes a way of pricing government services received by various taxpayers, or whether it is a result of political power of the many to tax the few.

TAX REVENUES

Table 18-2 shows the source of government per capita tax revenues and the purposes for

Table 18-2

PER CAPITA REVENUES AND EXPENDITURES OF ALL LEVELS OF GOVERNMENT IN UNITED STATES (1982 DOLLARS)

Total Revenue	1960	1970	1980
Taxes	1880	2430	2740
Utility and liquor	70	90	120
Social security	300	400	900
Miscellaneous	250	290	690
Total	$2500	$3210	$4450

Total Expenditures			
National defense	770	880	710
Federal social security	250	370	950
Interest	150	190	360
Education	300	580	730
Highways	150	170	160
Public welfare	70	180	310
Hospitals	60	100	140
Health and sanitation	40	80	130
Police	30	50	70
Fire	20	20	30
Natural resources	60	80	140
Postal services	60	80	90
Farm price supports	50	40	30
Parks and recreation	10	20	40
Housing, urban renewal	20	30	60
Veterans service	60	60	60
Administration	50	70	100
Air, water, transport	30	40	40
Utilities and liquor	60	100	170
Miscellaneous	260	160	250
Total	$2500	$3300	$4570

which expenditures are made by all levels of U.S. government, in 1982 dollars. The largest source of government revenue is the **personal income tax**, levied usually against money income earned from market exchanges, not against real, nonmoney income created domestically. For example, homeowners do not pay money rent for their housing space; the value of the housing service received is not taxed as income. But if someone rents housing space and pays the rent out of dividends received on corporation stock, the income used to pay the rent is taxed. Home ownership rather than rental is encouraged. Was that effect intended? No one knows.

The personal income tax is a *graduated* or **progressive** tax, meaning that the percentage of tax on income increases as income increases. Why does the percentage of tax on marginal incomes increase at higher incomes? Several arguments have been advanced, though no one can really know. Perhaps the rich, being few in number, were outvoted. Perhaps each successive marginal dollar is presumed to be less essential to the rich person's welfare, making it "ethical" or fair that the rich pay more. Perhaps the rich save a larger percentage of income from consumption than others, so that to encourage spending and reduce saving and investing we tax the rich more. Perhaps the rest of the tax structure is biased against the poorer people (taxes on liquor, gasoline, cigarettes, land, and all sales in general), and so the income tax is graduated upward to compensate. Or perhaps because the rich have more wealth, they have more to gain from government protection from foreign and domestic aggressors and, therefore, should pay higher taxes, even disproportionately higher. Take your pick: Any or all of these arguments might have been behind the progressive tax laws.

Whatever its rationale, the graduated income tax is known by analysis and evidence to reduce the incentive to work, reduce the savings available for investment, and encourage more use of nonmarket income. As indicated earlier, there is evidence that as much as 20% of national income is hidden by nonmarket or underground market activity (in which goods are exchanged by barter, or cash is used instead of checking accounts, which can be traced).

In addition to the personal income tax, other major taxes are social security contributions, property (primarily land and buildings) taxes, the corporation income tax, and (as will be explained in the next chapter) an inflation tax on money. It is worth exploring at this point what are the effects of the corporation income tax. Recalling the earlier analysis of what business firms are, it is evident that a corporation tax is a tax on the corporate form of organization. Whose wealth is lowered by the amount of the corporation tax? That is a very difficult question. The tax may be shifted to consumers, if the *number* of corporations can be affected, just as the tax on playing cards would be virtually all shifted to consumers of playing cards, if the supply curve of playing cards were virtually horizontal. The same may be true for the supply of the corporation form of business. But, of course, if a corporation tax were raised or newly imposed, *existing* corporations would lose wealth, just as did the resources specialized to making playing cards in Chapter 10. But because corporations are contractual relations among resource owners, the critical question is: Which owners of which resources in the corporations would lose wealth? The answer is the owners of assets that cannot readily be shifted into doing business under some noncorporate arrangement, resources which probably include a large portion of the existing physical assets of a corporation. But after all is said and done, the available information and evidence as to whose wealth is reduced by the corporation tax is still insufficient to warrant firm conclusions.

Federal taxes are different from state and local taxes, usually for a simple reason. A tax will get no proceeds if people can move away or can easily abandon the taxed activity. A tax on the income of people living on a certain street is easily avoided by moving to a different street. Similarly, a tax on the value of any resource or action can be escaped by moving it to a different government jurisdiction. But an immobile resource is a prime target for taxation. Hence localities (cities and counties) can effectively tax land and building values.

Because federal taxes on incomes cannot be escaped by moving to another state, but state taxes can be, state income taxes are smaller than federal ones and slower to develop. Only when all the several neighboring jurisdictions impose the same or very similar taxes can flight be avoided. Taxes on corporations are federal taxes, because a corporation can readily move its place of business or headquarters while selling nationwide. The correlation between the size of a tax and the inability to escape it, though not perfect, is substantial and helps explain many features of the tax structure.

Because local taxes can be avoided by moving, the federal government practices **revenue sharing**: It levies taxes nationwide and allocates some of the proceeds to local and state governments. However, in so doing, federal government officials also tend to tell local recipients how to spend the money. And if a local government forsakes the funds by refusing to follow the federal directives, it is throwing away an essentially costless gift, because the refusal doesn't reduce the taxes on its own constituents. Thus, the cost-benefit calculations of local groups in determining how much they should be taxed for local benefits is increasingly subjected to federal government decisions. But that usurpation of local autonomy is not entirely unintended, for, by using the overriding power derived from its broader jurisdiction, the federal gov-

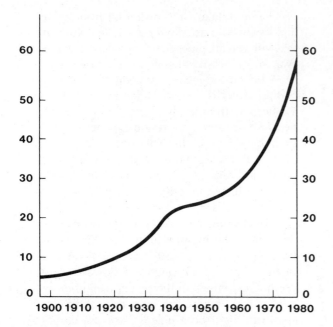

Figure 18-4.

GROWTH IN NUMBER OF U.S. FEDERAL REGULATORY
AGENCIES

SOURCE: *Economic Report of the President*, 1982.

ernment can penalize a local region that refuses to heed the damage it does to other areas, such as by its overuse of water or air or
by its skimping on welfare aid.

REGULATION OF ECONOMIC BEHAVIOR

Although government provides national security, protects life and property, and facilitates valuable uses of some resources, government power has also been used to
suppress the operation of competition in the
marketplace (as several instances examined
in this book have shown) by imposing contrived restrictions on entry. But because government is complex in its formal structure
and diverse in its sources of political power,
its actions are often inconsistent: One branch
or agency of government will *prevent* private
restraints that would reduce competition in
the market while another is *imposing* legal
restraints to reduce competition. There is no
validated theory to explain when government is more likely to prevent or to impose
restraints on competition. All we know is
that both occur.

The economic effect of legislation and
regulation of economic activity need not be
strongly correlated with the amount of money spent. Some regulations can be cheap to
enforce but strong in their effects on economic activity. For example, various regulatory agencies with combined expenditures of
$5 billion have imposed on business and in-
dustry a cost of complying estimated to be
over $100 billion. Thus, one measure of the
U.S. government's role in the economy is the
growing number of regulatory agencies (see
Figure 18-4). Whereas in 1970 there was one
regulatory agency employee for every 2500
people, there is now one for every 800 people, or over three times as many per capita.
Neither the reasons for such growth nor
their consequences have been well identified.

Public Goods and Government Action

In Chapter 5 a **public good** was defined as any good the use of which by one person does not reduce the amount of the good simultaneously available for some other persons. The several users are not "rivals" for use of the good. This characteristic becomes important to the degree in which it is difficult to measure each user's value of its use and to exclude nonpaying users. Not knowing the user's value makes it difficult to know how much of the good is worth producing and to collect funds to cover the production costs.

If we know those values, how much of the public good should be produced? Ideally (as explained in Chapter 5), simply add up the marginal personal use values of all users at the amount available. The sum is the *total* marginal use value. For example, say a television station has three potential viewers, valuing the marginal program respectively at $5, $3, and $2. The total marginal use value is $10. The television program should be produced if the cost is less than $10. A private producer who could collect from only one or two of the viewers would tend not to produce the "right" amount. For this reason, it is often argued that one purpose of organized group action—whether by private clubs (for the use, say, of swimming pools or computers) or by government agencies—is to overcome the undervaluation of goods with public-goods characteristics. These goods are said to include, for example, national defense, parks, public health, and sanitation. Because many goods contain some number of the characteristics of a public good, there are no clear-cut guidelines for saying that government ought to do this or not do that. Thus, it is not known how much public debate about what government should do reflects a genuine concern that public goods be properly valued by their users and how much it conceals a desire to get public subsidies for one's own interest.

Because many goods with the characteristics of a public good are produced by the private sector—television and inventions, for example—a variety of institutions have developed to help measure user values and exclude nonpayers. So, it has been argued, governments should use their tax power to force users to pay. National defense has characteristics of a public good. So also have ideas—hence patents and copyrights to try to reduce free riding. But enforcement is extremely difficult: People who buy books can lend them to others, and people who buy computer software let other people copy the programs without paying the designer.

REDISTRIBUTION OF WEALTH

A major government activity is redistributing wealth and income. Some government actions are designed to enable some people to pay for services they could not otherwise obtain so cheaply through private contractual arrangements—for example, nearby public parks, better roads, sewers, police protection, sanitation, and protection from disease, insect pests, and fire. Other government actions are designed to transfer wealth from some people to others. When all such government wealth-transferring activities are considered, it is highly debatable whether the *net* transfer is from the rich to the poor, as is usually believed to be the case. It may be that wealth is transferred from only *some* of those people who happen to be rich, and it is transferred to others who happen to be poor, not *because* they are poor, but rather because of some particular feature. For example, is a college education at a state university with below-cost tuition a device to aid the poor at the expense of the rich? Or is it a device to aid smart youngsters (most of whom are poorer now only in *current* income) at the expense of others, some of whom went to college but most of whom did not?

Not all government redistribution of wealth is meant to aid the poor. For example, tariffs and restrictions on international trade often hurt rather than aid the poor by raising their costs of goods while aiding higher-income people working in the protected industries. Also, by creating monopolies to get monopoly profits, the government can collect either by operating the monopolies directly (as with liquor stores in some states) or by taxing the monopoly rents obtained by protected, privately operated monopolies (electric, gas, water and transportation). It is not known how much of such redistribution is for some social goal and how much is simply the result of the way political pressures affect decisions. For example, some may argue that it is clear "social policy" to redistribute wealth. Others have contended that the growth of specialization in earning incomes has divided the population into many small, special-interest groups, who have differentiated, concentrated sources of income and thus strong incentives to coalesce politically, to more effectively protect or enhance those incomes. But the evidence is mixed and incomplete.

Government as an Economic Stabilizer

You may wonder why we have not applied our analysis to the compelling question of whether government activities can stabilize the national economy or alleviate recessions. This topic, though very popular, contains more conjecture, unfounded allegations, good intentions, and sheer hope than valid economic analysis. It is highly controversial—meaning no good evidence is available—whether government actions have done more good in cases where they successfully alleviated recessions than harm in those cases where they exacerbated recessions. Some observers and economists argue that by judicious use of fiscal policy—taxes, expenditures, and special benefits to business and the unemployed—recessions have been alleviated, and in some cases they have. Others argue with just as much conviction and evidence that government action is riddled with politics and self-serving objectives which intensify fluctuations and hinder growth. All can cite examples from history to support their claims, but such examples do not constitute reliable, unbiased evidence with which to test some proposition or theory. Perhaps these contradictory claims are equally correct: Government actions have sometimes alleviated recessions and have sometimes surely deepened or prolonged them.

GOVERNMENT DEFICIT

An excess of *government* expenditures over tax revenues is called a *fiscal deficit*, or simply a *deficit* (an excess of tax revenues over expenditures is a surplus). In 1982 the U.S. federal government's deficit was predicted to be $100 billion, though no one can make these predictions with great accuracy. What happens if there is a deficit? The government can sell some of its assets, just as you might sell your second car if your expenditures exceeded your income—unless you could borrow from someone else who would then be spending less while you spend more. That may be worthwhile if the expenditure is, say, an investment in greater future income out of which you can repay the loan principal and interest. Or you may consider present consumption worth more than the future debt and interest repayment. Just as you or a business firm may borrow either for current consumption or for investment that increases future income, so may a government. Governments may borrow to finance investment in roads, public sanitation, and education—worthwhile services not readily salable in a market.

As old investments pay off, the loans are

repaid largely out of the future income—the signs of a productive, prosperous, growing economy. So why all the fuss about budget deficits? If the expenditure is worthwhile, it should be made, whether financed by current taxes or by future taxes to repay borrowing. Only if the expenditure is not worthwhile is the deficit economically undesirable. But it is the expenditure, not the deficit, that is undesirable.

Notice we asked whether government expenditures are *worthwhile*, not "worth more in market values." Why? Because the values of many activities are not measured in marketable prices offered by customers. Hence we used the ambiguous word "worthwhile." How are government actions evaluated and selected as being "worthwhile," given the costs? We don't know, but our not knowing doesn't mean that the process is inferior to how the private sector evaluates actions.

One source of complaint about a government deficit (aside from the key question of whether the expenditures are worthwhile) is the fear that higher interest rates will make it more expensive for some people to borrow, say, to build homes or factories, or buy new cars. They object to competition for loanable funds. But that self-serving argument is not a valid one against government expenditures on worthwhile projects and services that are financed in part by borrowing rather than by current taxation. Still, it may be that interest rates won't rise very much anyway, for two reasons. First, one must look at the total *world* demand for borrowing—by all foreign and domestic private firms and governments—because the U.S. government borrows funds in a capital market that is worldwide. It is difficult to estimate how much a larger U.S. government deficit would raise interest rates in the world capital markets.

Second (and this initially comes as a surprise to many people), if the government borrows more to spend more, that borrowing may simply be the substitute for public borrowing to pay increased taxes. For example, if the government spends an additional $1 billion, it must either tax or borrow (setting aside the idea of printing more money). If taxed, citizens will, in arranging to pay the extra money, borrow more than they otherwise would. The two effects may exactly match each other, so that it makes no difference whether the government borrows or taxes, *given that the $1 billion is going to be spent in either case*. But if one heeds only what the media says in its political-economic reporting, you would think it is the deficit, rather than the size of government expenditures, that counts.

From still another perspective, the private citizen may regard the public debt as an obligation on future tax payments, in the same way as one views private debt. When financing a new car, one would regard the debt as a liability and the car as an asset. If the government borrows, then each citizen has both an increased liability to pay that debt and an asset in whatever the government bought with the expenditures. If the expenditures went for consumption, the repayment cannot be made from any earnings of an asset, exactly as if a private party borrowed for a vacation at Las Vegas. But if the government used the expenditures for a productive investment, the investment would help pay the future debt. Obviously, what counts is not whether the government budget is balanced—that is, with no deficit—but how much is spent and for what. Unfortunately, no extensive research studies have been conducted on this particular issue to measure to what extent one expenditure displaces the other. For the present, one should be very hesitant to jump to the conclusion that the *amount* of the deficit, rather than the size of government expenditures and for what they are made, is what affects the interest rate and the public welfare—a leap of logic that is often made in media reporting of economic affairs.

GOVERNMENT DEBT

The outstanding debt of the U.S. government reflects both present deficits and the cumulative, unrepaid portions of past deficits. When adjusted for inflation that debt, measured per capita, has been nearly constant since about 1950. If everyone held an amount of the debt equal to his or her latent future tax obligations, canceling the debt would result in one claim merely offsetting the other. Of course, that is not the actual situation; so increasing the debt increases the amount of interest to be paid each year, postponing the dispute over what taxes to impose on whom.

Were the government activities financed by borrowing worthwhile? Presumably so, or why would Congress have authorized the expenditures? We are back to the wall. Without a valid, useful theory of governmental behavior, each of you can have your own opinion, which you may share with your political science instructor if you wish.

But perhaps we have overlooked an important reason for concern. Suppose the federal government did what you might do if you had in your basement a secret money machine that printed authentic $100 bills—which you could spend without anyone ever catching on. Heavenly! You, too, would probably run deficits every year and print money rather than sell assets, borrow, or work to earn income. It is a fact that practically every national government (we know of no exceptions) has such a machine and uses it to cover much of its deficit, which brings us to the topic of the next chapter: inflation.

Summary

1. The domestic economy makes up about 20% of the total national income, though it is not counted or reported in measures of national income. Governments account for about 10%, and the market economy for about 70%.

2. National income is the sum of all the *value added* in all productive enterprises.

3. Expenditures and receipts of all levels of government in the United States total to an amount that is between 35% and 40% of the national income. However, because a large proportion of those receipts and expenditures transfers incomes from one person to another, the net value added to national income approximates about 10% of that income.

4. Government, the institution that monopolizes the use of force to set rules and establish rights, also retains the exclusive power to print money.

5. Governments typically transfer wealth from one group to another, and provide services from resources that are inadequately provided by private-property rights as well as control over such resources.

6. Taxes can be not only a means of transferring wealth but also substitutes for prices on services provided by governments. In the United States, the principal federal taxes are the graduated personal income tax, the corporation income tax, the social security tax, and several excise taxes on particular goods. The principal state taxes are income and sales taxes. The principal local taxes are land and sales taxes.

7. Governments are a major provider of public goods.

8. The U.S. government, on average, redistributes wealth from the richer to the poorer.

9. Government stabilization of the economy by the separate or combined use of fiscal and monetary policies is a generally accepted goal. But evidence as to the results of such policies is unclear and controversial, allowing the inference that they have worsened as many situations as they have improved. The truth remains undetected.

10. The effects of government deficits should be distinguished from the effects of (a) greater expenditures (regardless of whether there is a deficit) and from the effects of financing a

deficit by (b) creating new money versus (c) borrowing. Economic analysis suggests that interest rates and economic growth are much more affected by the size and purpose of expenditures than by the size of deficit.

Questions

1. A 10% value added tax could be equivalent to a 10% tax on personal income. Explain.

2. a. Would a tax levied on every transaction between firms be equivalent to an income tax?
   b. What effect would such a tax have on the organization of firms?

3. If a firm sells its products for a price that is more than the cost of materials and labor used, is that excess a profit or a part of value added?

4. "A higher income tax reduces the incentive to work." Evaluate this statement by distinguishing between the average tax and the marginal tax.

5. Your city has a special election to raise taxes to raise police officers' salaries and to increase the size of the police force. Why would some people who advocated higher salaries and a larger police force, which they agree would cost more, oppose higher taxes to cover those costs? (Hint: Money is fungible.)

6. If all tax proceeds go into a general government fund, can it be said that taxes levied for some purpose are being used for that purpose—for example, that gasoline taxes pay for, say, roads rather than for, say, welfare? What kind of data would persuade you that taxes are in fact being assigned to their nominal purposes?

7. If people compare their current net, or after tax, incomes with those of many years ago, would most people conclude that their incomes have risen or fallen?

8. The city of Las Vegas once proposed to abolish its land tax and substitute a tax on sales of goods and services within the city limits. Opponents argued that changing the type of tax would have little or no influence on who bore taxes. Suggest an analysis that supports the opposition argument.

9. Should an increase in taxes that are levied to pay for services rendered to the public be considered an increase in the cost of living?

10. To cover the transitory imbalance between social security revenue and expenditures for the next few years two economists have proposed the federal government sell the national forests to private parties who the economists contend will manage the forests better. Assuming the amount collected would cover the transitional deficit, what premises do you think the economists are using in arguing that private ownership would be beneficial? Aside from that feature, would the sale be a way of covering that transitional deficit without an increase in taxes? If so, how does it do so? If not, why does it not avoid being a tax?

11. Congress passes a law that reduces taxes, thus leaving people with more spendable income. Would the fact that the tax reduction is effective a year from passage rather than immediately make any difference on people's *current* consumption expenditures? Why?

12. "The agency claiming to be the effective government in a social system must have a monopoly in the use of physical force and in the ability to print money." True or false?

*13. Suppose you succeed in leading an army of "liberation." Upon taking office as dictator, you abolish all existing monopoly rights.
   a. Would you then grant new monopoly rights?
   b. If you did, how would that benefit the government (you)?
   c. If you didn't think of granting such rights, who would suggest that you do?

14. "An official Defense Department study reported that the elimination of the draft by raising wages to enlistees would cost about $5–$15 billion annually. Therefore the Defense Department in view of that prohibitive cost is recommending continuance of the draft." (News item from *New York Times*, June 1966.)
   a. Explain why the first sentence is an incorrect assertion.
   b. Would you be willing to assert that raising wages to abolish the draft would *reduce* costs? Why?

Chapter 19
Inflation

Inflation, like death and taxes, appears inescapable. What is inflation? Why does it occur? What are its effects? Can they be avoided?

What Is Inflation?

Inflation is a rise in the cost of living resulting from a *persisting* rise in *all money* prices. Note the three words italicized and consider them in reverse order. It is prices expressed in *money* that have risen. Early in our analysis we emphasized the relativity of all money prices; but with inflation, even if *all* money prices doubled, no relative prices would have changed: Only the dollar, or nominal, prices have risen.

Inflation affects all money prices to the same extent. Therefore, if some prices do rise more than others, other forces are shifting relative demands and supplies so that relative prices are shifting, as they would have even without inflation (Figure 19-1 shows an example). Finally, inflation is a *persisting* rise in all money prices: It is not a single jump in prices. The reason for making this distinction will be explained later.

The rate of inflation is not easily measured. If the dollar prices of gas, sugar, and shoes rise, while those of computers, television sets, and fruit fall, the lower prices tend to offset the higher. People substitute some of the lower-priced goods for some of the higher-priced ones. But we don't know just how much of such substitution would leave people as well off as before: We don't know the new combination that is equally desirable; so we can't compute its dollar cost. And changes in quality add more difficulties: If people switch from black-and-white to color television at three times the price (while black-and-white–TV prices do not change), is it the *cost* of living or the *quality* of living that has risen?

Can we never know, then, whether inflation has occurred? A clue is provided by the

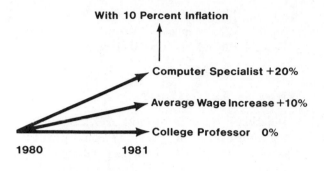

With 10 Percent Inflation

Computer Specialist +20%

Average Wage Increase +10%

College Professor   0%

1980   1981

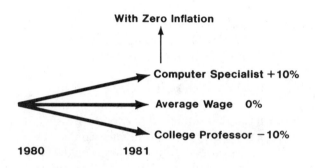

With Zero Inflation

Computer Specialist +10%

Average Wage   0%

College Professor −10%

1980   1981

Figure 19-1.

EFFECT OF INFLATION ON SPREAD OF WAGES AND PRICES

During inflation the college professor's wages appear to lag. But if there had been no inflation the professor's wages would have decreased 10%, because of shifts in relative demands and supplies of various skills.

change in the total money price of a particular *fixed* combination of consumer goods (sometimes called a consumer basket of goods). This method of detecting inflation is based on the assumption that changes in quality and substitution among goods have significantly less effect on prices than inflation has. The U.S. Bureau of Labor Statistics publishes a monthly *Consumer Price Index* (CPI) as an approximation to month-to-month changes in the *dollar* price of a particular basket of goods for average-income people. Figure 19–2 shows the course of such an index over the past 160 years.

We have just seen three factors that affect the accuracy of the figures: First, the number of goods in the sample basket is far from a complete inventory of the economy's goods; second, there may be changes in qualities of goods; third, people may make substitutions toward more lower-priced goods. Allowing for these effects on that fixed combination of consumer goods, a rise of 2% to 3% in the CPI over one year does not necessarily mean that the cost of living has changed. Failing to allow for substitution and quality changes creates an upward bias in the estimate. However, an increase of some 90% within a few years, as happened in the United States from 1941 to 1947, or 100%, as happened from 1968 to 1980, probably is not a measurement defect caused by sampling bias, substitution, or quality changes. Major rises and falls in that index are taken to be useful indicators of inflation and deflation.[1]

An alternative index that reflects a larger range of goods and a wider class of consumers is the **national income deflator**, also computed by the U.S. Department of Commerce. It has usually given a less extreme rate of inflation than the CPI. Until late

---

[1] A major defect of the index is its omission of prices of capital goods (it primarily covers prices of current services). The severity of bias or degree of error resulting from this omission has not yet been determined. Nevertheless, the conventional, though incomplete, measure is commonly cited.

1982, the national income deflator differed from the CPI by not figuring house prices and interest costs as if people were borrowing to buy new houses every year rather than paying a rent (including an implicit rent if the house was owner-occupied). Because the CPI included these two components until 1982, a rise in either interest rates or housing prices caused the index to indicate an exaggerated inflation rate. (If interest rates *fell*, the CPI would exaggerate the fall.) For example, in 1980, when interest rates increased significantly, the CPI showed an annual inflation rate of about 15%, whereas the national income deflator showed one of about 10% (an atypically large difference between the two indexes). This built-in exaggeration was of benefit to people whose incomes are indexed to the CPI, such as social security recipients (who got about $7 billion too much in 1980 because of that difference) and union workers whose wage contracts are tied to the CPI. Furthermore, both indices still fail to allow for the fact that any tax on a good, which raises its price, would suggest inflation, whereas a tax on income would not appear as a higher "price level." These defects and their consequences have long been publicized by the people responsible for computing the CPI and the national income deflator, but correction has been hindered by a tug of war among the affected parties in Congress.

Inflation rates in many other countries have been more pronounced and spectacular than in the United States, as Table 19-1 shows for the years 1963 through 1981.

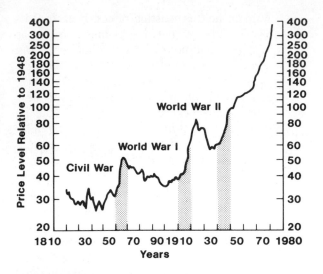

Figure 19-2.

CONSUMER PRICE INDEX, 1820–1982 (1948=100)

SOURCE: U.S. Department of Labor, *Monthly Bulletin.*

What Causes Inflation?

Inflation occurs either when the stock of money increases more than the supply of other goods or when the quantity of goods is reduced without an equivalent reduction in the money supply; in either event the supply of money exceeds the amount that people want to hold at existing prices. If each of us awoke today with twice as much money as yesterday and no less of any other goods and services, we would spend some of the new money for other goods to reduce the excessive proportion of our wealth held as money. The demand expressed for goods would go up, but that would not reduce the *total* holding of money, because spending merely transfers money from one person to another. Instead, prices—and wages—would be "driven," "pushed," "pulled," or "bid" up, and we'd find ourselves wealthier and with more income measured in *dollar terms*. On the average, wealth and income in money terms would be about twice as high as they were, because only then would we want to hold that doubled amount of money. (All firms and families in the United States on average hold money equivalent to about three or four months' income.)

We said that for inflation to occur, a change in the *ratio* of money to the supply of other goods is necessary. Thus, if the stock of other goods were reduced but the stock of money were unchanged, money prices would rise. A natural disaster, such as a drought or a flood, reduces other goods without changing holdings of money. With no less money but fewer other goods, people will spend some of their money in an attempt to replenish stocks of other goods. Because someone else receives what one person spends, prices will be bid up as people try to get more of the smaller supply of other goods. Reducing the stock of other goods, then, is equivalent to increasing the amount of money relative to the supply of other goods; either way, inflation follows.

A significant jump in prices occurred during the Black Death (probably bubonic plague) in England in the fourteenth century.

Table 19-1   ANNUAL PERCENTAGE RATES OF INFLATION BY COUNTRY, 1963–81

Year	Canada	Mexico	Nether- lands	West Germany	Japan	United States	Brazil	United Kingdom	Belgium	Italy	Sweden	Spain	France	Switzer- land
1963	2	1	5	3	4	2	—	3	2	9	2	7	6	4
1964	2	1	6	2	4	2	—	2	4	6	4	11	4	6
1965	4	7	6	3	4	1	25	4	6	4	6	11	2	4
1966	4	4	4	3	4	4	40	4	6	2	6	8	3	2
1967	4	4	6	1	5	3	35	2	2	4	5	8	2	5
1968	4	2	4	1	4	6	28	4	2	1	2	5	5	6
1969	4	4	6	3	4	6	21	6	2	4	2	4	7	4
1970	5	4	5	8	6	4	18	8	5	10	9	5	8	5
1971	4	4	9	8	6	4	17	10	5	8	7	7	7	9
1972	5	6	11	6	6	4	17	10	6	7	7	9	6	10
1973	5	11	9	6	12	6	20	7	6	12	7	11	7	8
1974	12	12	9	6	20	9	31	14	7	20	11	16	11	7
1975	10	16	11	6	8	10	33	28	13	18	11	16	13	8
1976	8	12	9	3	6	6	42	14	8	18	11	17	10	3
1977	6	13	6	4	4	6	45	13	7	16	9	22	9	1
1978	6	12	4	4	5	7	45	10	4	15	10	21	10	4
1979	11	12	6	4	8	8	55	17	4	13	7	16	10	4
1980	11	13	7	5	5	9	100	11	7	18	14	16	13	6
1981	12	15	7	6	3	8	110	11	8	17	9	15	14	5

A substantial percentage of the population died, but the money supply remained unchanged. Wage rates rose spectacularly, as did the prices of other goods, although not nearly as much, because their supply had not decreased as much as the supply of labor had. Survivors got substantial per capita increases in real income, not as a result of inflation but because the population was so reduced relative to the supply of goods. In this case, inflation caused by the *decrease* in population relative to the unchanged stocks of money and other goods was accompanied by a *rise* in living standards for the survivors.

At other times crop failures have left societies with less to eat but no less money. The increased ratio of money to goods resulted in a rise of prices on average, with the greatest rise in food prices. These decreases in real per capita wealth have been called an *effect* of inflation rather than a cause. More precisely, higher prices were the result, not the cause, of a reduced supply of other resources relative to the existing amount of money.

If the stock of money increases at about the same rate as the stock of other goods, inflation is not likely. If the money stock increases more rapidly than the normal growth rate of other goods and population (about 3% per year), inflation occurs. If the growth of output temporarily falls below the normal rate while the money stock continues to grow at that rate, a temporary rise in prices will occur.

But if the money stock persistently grows at a rate substantially higher than the rate at which the output of other goods and the population increase, inflation will continue. From 1965 to 1980 the money stock persistently grew faster than other output; not surprisingly, inflation resulted.

Though many other factors can affect the price level, they rarely induce a *persistingly* rising price level. In all countries in the period 1948–80, the average annual rates of persisting increase in the quantity of money are strongly correlated with increases in prices. The correlation would be even more impressive if we included inflations of the kind that occurred in Germany in 1923, when prices rose by a factor of about 100 billion in one year, while the amount of money increased by a factor of 10 billion. This is equivalent to a doubling of prices every two weeks. Similar episodes occurred in Greece in 1944, in Poland in 1923, in Russia in 1921–23, and in Hungary in 1923 and again in 1946, when prices doubled on average every two or three days.

INCREASING THE STOCK OF MONEY

Never has inflation lasted several years unless there has been a persisting increase in the money stock relative to other goods, and never has the money stock increased without an inflation following, as has been happening in all nations in the last decade. But how and why does the money stock increase so rapidly?

The answer is that governments print and issue money more rapidly than other output grows. But why? It is politically easier to print money to spend than to explicitly levy sufficient taxes to balance government budgets. See Table 19-2. Inflation occurs only because of the last item in the table: creating new money. Changes in any other item could be offset by changes in still others, leaving the amount of newly created money un-

Table 19-2

THE RELATION OF NEW MONEY TO FEDERAL EXPENDITURES AND TAXES, 1981 ($ BILLION)

Expenditures (*E*)	$675	
Tax collection (*T*)	630	
Deficit (*D*)	45	
Financed by borrowing old money from the public (*B*)		$35
Creating new money (*M*)		10
		$45

changed. For example, reducing government expenditures by $25 billion, to $650 billion, while borrowing only $10 billion of old money from the public, would still require that $10 billion of new money be created, which is just as inflationary as when $675 billion was spent. Watch the last item, M:

$$E - T - B = M = 675 - 630 - 35 = 10, \text{ or}$$

$$D - B = M = 45 - 35 = 10.$$

The long sweep of history shows that in virtually every country governments have financed expenditures by creating money at a rate exceeding the nation's growth of output. We now give a general description of this process for the United States.

Our coins are minted and our paper money (called Federal Reserve Notes) printed by the U.S. Treasury and delivered to Federal Reserve Banks, its banking agents. The Board of Governors of the Federal Reserve is authorized by Congress to spend the newly created money to buy government bonds—that is, to lend the money to the U.S. Treasury. Though legally independent of the U.S. government, the Federal Reserve Banks are responsive to it. (Unless the Federal Reserve Banks buy U.S. bonds when the president and Congress "advise," new officials will very likely soon be managing those banks.) So when U.S. Treasury administrators decide to sell some new bonds (borrow money) to finance the government deficit, the Federal Reserve Banks typically buy some of the new U.S. bonds with new money, which is then spent by the government.

Though the institutional details are complex, in essence, the Federal Reserve Bank system issues new money when it lends to the U.S. government in exchange for some promissory notes (U.S. bonds). Of course, those bonds are rarely repaid; when due they are renewed—exchanged for new bonds. The issued money stays in the hands of the public (worn-out bills are exchanged for crispy new ones).

In some other countries the government acts as its own central bank and simply prints and issues new money. That *is* the main task of a central bank. But in the United States, for political reasons that are of more historical than economic relevance, the process is more roundabout and involves *monetizing* government debt by the U.S. Federal Reserve Bank (the "Fed"), which acts as the central bank for the U.S. government.

Thus, financing a government deficit *by creating money* causes inflation. Note that the federal deficit is not itself a cause of inflation, because it doesn't *have* to be financed by the creation of new money. The Federal Reserve could refuse to buy the U.S. bonds from the Treasury and force the government to sell them to the public for already existing money. No new money would be created and no inflation would result, as was demonstrated in years when the Fed did not create new money to finance the deficit and no inflation occurred.

So it is not the existence or size of the government deficit that determines the stock of money or causes inflation. Nor is it the size of total government expenditures, or the size of government, or reductions in taxes. In practice, however, for political reasons, larger government expenditures or reduced taxes will lead to an increased deficit that will almost surely be financed by creating more new money, thereby producing inflation.

Though the preceding has referred to money as if it were all paper money, it also consists of coins and checking accounts. Checking accounts are called *demand deposits*, because checks are payable by your commercial bank on demand. (In 1982 checking account balances were about $320 billion and currency—paper and coins—held by the public about $130 billion, a total of about $450 billion.) Checking accounts increase in very close proportion to paper currency (for reasons explained in "For Further Study" at the end of this chapter). As occurred in 1981, a 10% increase in the stock of new currency issued by the Federal Reserve Banks will lead within a year to a similar percentage increase in the total of the public's checking accounts. The resulting rate of inflation of almost 10%—or of 2% or 3% less because real output and the population also increased by about 2% or 3%—should not have been surprising.

Distinguishing True from Apparent Causes of Inflation

You will hear that foreign aid, agricultural price-support programs, social security, and our space, military, energy, and unemployment and welfare programs are inflationary. But the programs themselves can cause inflation only if they cause an increase in the quantity of money. It is necessary, then, to be careful how one defines cause: Increasing the money supply causes inflation in the sense that inflation is an *unavoidable* consequence of the increase; by contrast, the above-named programs are *not unavoidably* followed by money-supply increases. There *are* alternative modes of financing them— however rarely they are used. The moral is: To identify the true cause of inflation, we must always carefully distinguish between an increase in the money stock and the factors that induced the monetary authorities to increase the money stock.

For example, especially common is the highly plausible belief that a *wage push* or *administered* prices cause inflation: Some wages and prices are increased by a few firms or workers possessing *market power*, and all other wages and prices adjust to the new level. Steel prices or union wage rates are often cited as examples. But there is virtually no factual evidence to support this argument. Nor does economic analysis lead to the possibility that there could be key commodities to whose prices the prices of other goods adjust. For example, an imposed rise in the price of

steel will reduce the amount demanded. Employment in steel mills will fall. Some resources used in steel production will in time shift to the production of other goods, whose prices will fall as supply is increased. The overall price level remains unchanged. There is a rise in the price of steel goods but a fall in the prices of others. However, inflation would occur if the transiently unemployed workers, seeking to regain their old jobs, persuade political authorities to *create new money* to spend for their products. Then the increased quantity of money will increase all prices to match those that had been arbitrarily raised. In this way, the inflation restores the former structure of relative prices by an accommodating monetary policy.

Saying that one particular higher price causes inflation is to confuse consequences with cause. For inflation to occur, the money supply must increase by more than the demand for money. And such an increase must be kept distinct from the *motivation* for increasing it. In our example, the motive was to *assure* continued employment in old jobs even at the higher, newly imposed prices. If government authorities maintain a given level of employment in the *steel* industry by increasing the money supply, then steel could be *called* a key industry. If the government assures full employment for some other group of employees, they too could be called the key group—whether they be teachers, custodians, or actors.

In principle, it is easy to stop inflation: Reduce the growth rate of money. (Like stopping drunkenness—don't drink!) But that would require abandoning the political promises, built into government programs, to maintain full employment in old jobs even for those who ask high prices. If those promises are honored, inflation will surely occur whenever the government prints more money to finance them.

Another fallacy is fostered by government methods of reporting the cost of living.

The reports contain such statements as: "The cost of living rose this month by 1% because of a rise in the prices of eggs, gasoline, and medical services." But the inflation did not occur because those prices rose. Those prices rose because the inflation operates on *all* prices. By reversing cause and effect, such reporting leads people to blame the sellers (or buyers) of those particular goods, as if each month a different set of people or forces acted to cause inflation.

Inflationary Redistribution of Wealth

UNANTICIPATED INFLATION

Odd names are given to describe different *rates* of inflation, such as creeping, galloping, runaway, and hyper-. The rate is in fact of less critical consequence to people than whether the inflation is *anticipated*—that is, correctly foreseen—or *unanticipated*—that is, unforeseen or incorrectly foreseen as to timing, rate, or duration. Loans made before inflation was correctly anticipated will lack upward repayment adjustments that assure the lender the same total purchasing power it had before the inflation. Thus, an unanticipated or higher-than-anticipated inflation transfers wealth (measured as purchasing power) from creditors (lenders) to debtors (borrowers).

Monetary **assets** are claims to a *fixed* number of *dollars* in the future. They take two forms: either money or claims to fixed amounts of money, such as bonds, promissory notes of fixed payment, and constant-dollar retirement pensions. Monetary **liabilities** are the other side of those claims: obligations to pay those fixed amounts of money. **Real assets** and **real liabilities**, respectively, are claims to, and obligations to deliver, goods and services whose dollar prices change with inflation. Owners of real assets do not suffer a loss from inflation, because real asset prices rise with inflation.

For example, consider the effect of a completely *un*anticipated inflation of 10% on a person whose total assets are $100 in cash and $1000 in U.S. bonds yielding 5%—both monetary assets. The price level rises 10%. A year later the $100 in cash has depreciated to the equivalent of $90.90 (= $100/1.10) in real terms. The bond, which pays $1050 (principal plus interest) in one year, will return $954 (= $1050/1.10) of purchasing power—a loss of purchasing power of $105.10 ($9.10 on the cash and $96 on the bond).

But if the same person also owed somebody, say, $1200 at 5% interest, that $60 interest and $1200 principal would be paid with dollars that are 10% less valuable in real purchasing power. The person's obligations would be $1145 (= $1260/1.10) in real terms: a gain of $115 (= $1260 − $1145) in real purchasing power, which is a net gain of $9.90 over the loss of $105.10 on monetary assets. Such a person is a *net* monetary debtor: one who has more monetary liabilities (debts) than monetary assets (credits). If you wonder about the *real* resources owned or owed, they change in dollar terms on average by the amount of the percentage change in price level; thus, on average the person neither gains nor loses from the real assets or liabilities.[2]

A common way to be a net monetary debtor is to buy a house with a large mortgage. Say a person has a $200,000 house with a mortgage of 5% on $100,000 (a monetary debt): The two balance sheets in Table 19–3 show the situation before and after an *unan-*

---

[2]Let R and M be net real and net monetary assets, respectively, and E the initial equity. Thus: $E = R + M$. If E' is the new equity when prices rise by proportion P, then: $E' = PR + M$. Finally, let Q be the proportionate increase in the money value of the equity: $Q = E'/E$. Now, substituting and rearranging,

$$Q = P - (P - 1) M/E.$$

ticipated doubling of the price level. The initial monetary assets (money) are $1000 and real assets (house and land) are $200,000, a total of $201,000. The monetary debt is $100,000. The equity (net wealth value) is $101,000. With an *unanticipated* doubling of prices that doubles the dollar value of the house, the equity increases from $101,000 to $301,000, giving a *real* wealth equity of $301,000/2 = $150,500 in dollars of the original purchasing power, because each dollar is worth half as much as formerly. This is a gain of $49,500 (= $150,500 − $101,000) in terms of original purchasing power dollars. The gain occurs because the inflation rate was not anticipated, and thus the amount to be repaid was not adjusted to protect the lender from its loss of purchasing power.

ANTICIPATED INFLATION

If inflation were correctly anticipated to occur at 10% over the next year, a lender would insist on being paid (and a borrower would be willing to pay) about 10% more dollars to compensate for the 10% depreciation in the purchasing power of dollars. So

Table 19-3

BALANCE SHEETS BEFORE AND AFTER UNANTICIPATED INFLATION FOR A NET MONETARY DEBTOR, SHOWING REAL INCREASE IN EQUITY

Before Inflation

Assets		Liabilities	
Cash	$ 1,000	Debt	$100,000
House	200,000	Equity (Net Wealth)	101,000
	$201,000		$201,000

After Inflation (Doubling of Price Level)

Assets		Liabilities	
Cash	$ 1,000	Debt	$100,000
House	400,000	Equity (Net Wealth)	301,000
	$401,000		$401,000

instead of getting back the normal, say, 5% interest in money, the lender would get back an additional *inflation-adjustment premium* of about 10% more of the *principal* on which the promised interest is to be paid. This inflation adjustment is usually paid as if it were a higher "interest" rate (actually a normal interest *plus* an inflation-adjustment premium). So in this case, the interest on a one-year $100 loan would be expressed at 15.5%. The lender gets back $115.50 (= $100 + $15.50) on the $100 loan. At the new initial price level, the $115.50 is equivalent to $105 in original purchasing power, a 5% real return ($115.50/1.10 = $105). If the extent of the inflation were greater than anticipated, lenders would lose and borrowers gain, because the explicit adjustment in the nominal interest rate would be too low. And the opposite happens if an inflation is of smaller extent than anticipated.

VARIABILITY OF UNFORESEEN INFLATION

If interest rates received on all monetary assets and, conversely, paid on all monetary liabilities were adjusted for a perfectly anticipated inflation rate, there would be no wealth redistributions. A correctly and fully anticipated inflation is an analytical ideal, not a practical possibility. No one knows the future that well. A more realistic situation is that of an incorrectly anticipated inflation during which the inflation rate fluctuates, being higher in some years and lower in others. It seems to be a fact that the higher the long-term average rate of inflation, the greater the year-to-year variations around that average rate. It is that high *variability* and the consequent greater *unpredictability* over the long run that seem to reduce the willingness to lend and borrow as well as to invest, thereby reducing the flow of income into investment and growth of productive capacity, and thus of future production.

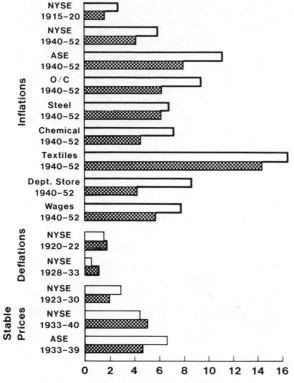

Inflations
- NYSE 1915-20
- NYSE 1940-52
- ASE 1940-52
- O/C 1940-52
- Steel 1940-52
- Chemical 1940-52
- Textiles 1940-52
- Dept. Store 1940-52
- Wages 1940-52

Deflations
- NYSE 1920-22
- NYSE 1928-33

Stable Prices
- NYSE 1923-30
- NYSE 1933-40
- ASE 1933-39

0 2 4 6 8 10 12 14 16

**Market Value Achieved by One Dollar
Invested in Base Year**

☐ Debtors   O/C—Over the Counter
            NYSE—New York Stock Exchange
▨ Creditors ASE—American Stock Exchange

Figure 19-3.

EFFECT OF UNANTICIPATED INFLATION ON MARKET
VALUE OF EQUITY FOR NET MONETARY DEBTOR AND
CREDITOR BUSINESS FIRMS

During every inflation net monetary debtors experienced
an increase in the value of their equity more than
did net monetary creditors. During deflations the
opposite effect occurred. During periods of
stable prices no dominance by either debtors
or creditors was evident. Attempts to
perform the same measurements for
corporations in the 1960s and 1970s
have been thwarted because almost all
business corporations have become
net monetary debtors.

SOURCE: A. Alchian and R. Kessel, "Redistribution of
Wealth through Inflation," *Science*, Vol. 130, No. 3375
(September 4, 1959), p. 538.

WEALTH REDISTRIBUTION FROM UNANTICIPATED INFLATIONS

Substantial evidence collected from inflationary periods of the past 50 years in the United States establishes that the onset of inflations were unanticipated or incorrectly anticipated as to rate and duration, so that wealth was transferred from net monetary creditors to net monetary debtors. Strong evidence is provided by the annual balance-sheet reports of business firms. Firms that were net monetary creditors had a larger total of cash and accounts receivable than they owed in accounts payable and bonds, and those that were net monetary debtors had the opposite balance.

During an inflation, as at any other time, a host of factors affect the fortunes of every business firm—inventions, new products, changes in demands, new management, damage to plant or inventory from fires, and the like. Nevertheless, the transfer of wealth to the net monetary debtor firms should show up in the increased price of a share of common stock *relative* to the stock prices of net monetary creditors.

Because the business firms on the major stock exchanges were roughly divided between net monetary creditors and net monetary debtors between 1915 and 1952, we could test for that wealth-transfer effect. Figure 19-3 presents the results. In every inflation, net monetary debtors did better than net monetary creditors, because the inflation was not anticipated. The opposite effect is observed for deflations. During the episodes of stable prices, there was no significant difference between the two classes.

During the past decade, however, the anticipation of future inflation is evidenced by the higher interest rates (which include an allowance for anticipated inflation). In 1982 interest rates were about 15% on 10-year bonds. Furthermore, almost all business firms are now net monetary debtors. Why they should have shifted so universally is not

But what assurance is there that they would really not inflate the money stock faster? Regrettably, the record is now reliable only for the notorious unreliability of such pronouncements.

Anti-Inflation Monetary Reforms

Once the money stock has increased, one or some combination of these four consequences is inevitable: (1) Price suppression by political controls will prevent people from spending their money and getting what they want at freely negotiable prices. Money and wealth will lose some of their competitive rationing power, because their market exchangeability is restricted. Other forms of competition will be more influential. (2) Higher prices will reduce the real value of money, again with a loss of wealth to money holders. But the role of market competition relative to other forms will not be suppressed. (3) Monetary reform, which is a fancy name for a cancellation of a portion of the money, means money holders will lose. (4) A special tax may be imposed on general wealth (not on money alone), and the money collected as taxes could then be destroyed. But if this kind of general tax could have been imposed, the money probably would not have been created in the first place. The four alternatives are different ways of revealing the reduced value of money. None preserves it.

Transient Effects of Changing Inflation Rate on Employment and Production

A rate of money increase that turns out to be lower than was anticipated will disappoint expectations about demand in the market. The unanticipated slower growth in the demand for goods will result in a *transient* decrease in employment and output, until the public reduces its forecasts of anticipated future demand and correspondingly reduces its prices (as revealed in the inflation-adjusted interest rate). After that, the transient reduction in employment and output will end. The stronger were the anticipations of persisting inflation, the greater and more prolonged will be the transient reductions in output and employment, until the public becomes convinced of the reality of a new inflation-reducing monetary policy.

The episodes in 1970, 1975, and 1980 are instructive. In each, the money increase nearly stopped for almost half a year. Recession set in. Sensitive to public complaints about recession, monetary authorities then reversed themselves to enable the government to embark on recession-combating expenditures by again increasing the money stock. The upturn in demand, output, and prices lasted until the monetary authorities again brought the money growth down from 10% annually to nearly zero. Another transient recession set up new demands for transient recession-combating inflationary measures. Back we went to money increases, and inflation was fired up again. Whether the reduced rate after 1980 will persist remains to be seen.

The awkward feature of an increased money supply is that its effects show up in two stages. First, within a few months there is an increase in output; later, within about a year, prices rise. The "good" output effects precede the "bad" inflation. But when the money growth is restricted, the transient reductions in output and employment come first; later, the rate of inflation decreases. Here the "bad" effects come first. It is difficult to embark on a policy where the bad effects come first, easy to embark on a policy in which the good effects come first. This might be a reason why it is politically hard to stop inflation.

We want to stop inflation. We also want no transient recession as a side effect to ending the inflation, and we want to continue expanding government expenditures beyond explicit tax collections or borrowing from private savings. There is no way to achieve all these. We have to give up some, or we must give up all to some degree.

What Can You Do to Reduce Inflation?

Nothing any person or group can do in a private capacity will reduce or prevent inflation, nor should one try. A refusal to raise prices as a seller or as a competing buyer will reduce your welfare and help no one else by as much as you are hurt. Such is the lesson that should be carried over from the earlier chapters of this book. That may sound selfish and antisocial. In fact, it speeds the discovery of market-clearing prices—with the consequences already developed in the early chapters on exchange and production. It undercuts the errors and political confusion of those who argue that the private citizen should exercise self-restraint and not spend others' money—so the government can spend money at lower prices than the goods are worth to those who are told not to buy so much.

What little you can do is to act in your political capacity to try to deny office to those who would create money to finance government expenditures. That is the *only* way to stop inflation, despite self-serving political oratory and popular media nonsense to the contrary. When the issue is so clearly stated, you may be moved to ask, "Do I want inflation stopped if I must give up some of what the government is doing, or if new explicit taxes must be levied?" The answer may be no, but in any case it will, or should, depend upon evaluating the effects of inflation and possible price controls, and the effects of reduced rates of government activities or new taxes.

Recessions Can Occur During Inflation

Recent recessions in the midst of inflation surprised many people who thought that rising aggregate market demands and prices always stimulated output and avoided recessions. Inflation combined with recession (*stagflation*) persuaded some people that economic analysis such as is presented in this book is wrong. However, recessions during inflation are completely consistent with this economic analysis.

During noninflationary times, if people expect no inflation, investments must yield salable products worth about 5% more than the previous year, if the interest rate is 5%. Otherwise, their full costs will not be covered. If, in the absence of inflation, aggregate demand falls below expectations, recession will set in until a new, expected, lower interest rate is perceived by enough people to induce agreement and discovery of new appropriate prices, for full employment at tasks with the highest earnings prospects.

However, the initial expected inflation rate that was unfulfilled could have been very high, instead of zero. For example, if enough people expect inflation to be 15% per year (with the real interest rate being 5%), any investments or initial outlays must return a sales value that is rising at the rate of 20% a year; otherwise not all costs, including interest, will be covered. If aggregate demand does not rise enough to maintain that expected growth, people will not be selling enough to cover their costs at the developing prices and wage rates. Only after enough people are convinced that the growth in aggregate demand has lagged below that expected rate, and only when enough of them revise expectations, will new prices and wages be negotiated that will restore employment in the best-discerned uses.

To believe that inflation necessarily stimulates output and employment is to think wages and costs lag behind selling prices, so that profits would presumably be increased by any rate of inflation, large or small. But as explained earlier, there is no lag of wage rates behind other prices; nor is there any *contractual rigidity* that makes wage rates in general less mobile, upward or downward, than prices of other goods and services. But there is a lag in *discerning* that the contractual price and wage rates and production activity are not consistent with the new aggregate demands. This information lag is not a result of stupidity or stubbornness, for not every sales fluctuation can be immediately tested to see whether it will persist and whether sales have similarly fluctuated in other segments of the economy. If inventories or sales changes exceed *expectations*, the individual firm will be induced to revise its output. It can't alone change its input prices, because the resources it buys or rents have almost equally valuable uses elsewhere—or so the inputs believe. Not until enough people realize from experience that the deterioration is in *aggregate* demand will they be willing to agree on new prices, wages, and products appropriate to the newly discerned change in demand.

All this can occur during an inflation or in its absence. What count are the differences among the anticipated inflation rate, the actual rate, and the perceived rate, and how quickly people can readjust their beliefs and discover the new appropriate prices and jobs. Indeed, many economists have long warned of the error in believing that higher employment can be sustained simply by raising the rate of inflation.

Lest the preceding analysis suggest that inflation has no effects other than those caused by incorrectly anticipated rates of inflation, it is useful to remember the argument that excessive drinking of alcohol merely disorients a person for a while. Yet, what the person does while drunk may be disastrous. Similarly, in reacting to the fact of inflation, people may want to determine prices and wages by government legislation or regulatory control. But that weakens the role of market exchanges and prices in directing and coordinating the economy. The result is a loss of real income because of inappropriate guides as to what is most valuable to produce. Price controls suppress prices as guides and rewards, replacing them with political persuasion or force. The determination of what and how much to produce, and to whom it is allocated, is removed from individual choice and made more subject to political activity. Society may become more politicized and thus potentially less stable, for in the politicized economy people's behavior is influenced in ways very different from those in the market-exchange economy. Such a conjecture, however, takes us beyond the realm of validated economic analysis. A respect for intellectual integrity and scientific procedure compels us to stop at this point.

And now, gentle readers, you have arrived at the end of this book. We intended your experience with it and your instructor to be pleasant and to improve your understanding of, and ability to use, economic analysis. What did you expect? A pot of gold? Or a money printer?

Summary

1. Inflation is a persistent increase in the level of money prices of all goods. It can be difficult to measure inflation because prices can also be affected by changes in the quality of goods or by consumers' responses to relative price shifts—not to mention the difficulty of ascertaining actual prices.

2. The effects of inflation should be distinguished from the effects of the factors causing inflation.

3. Inflation occurs if the supply of money in-

creases to the point where it exceeds the amount that people, given their existing wealth and income, want to hold. Such an excess is usually caused by an increase in the supply of money, but it may also reflect a reduced demand for money resulting from a loss of real wealth from plague, drought, or other causes of a reduction in the quantity of goods.

4. Every significant inflation (meaning a rate of over 10% in one year) has been caused by an increase in the absolute quantity of money. Reductions in real wealth are usually relatively minor and not persisting.

5. The effects of an inflation depend on how accurately it was anticipated. An unanticipated or incompletely anticipated inflation is one in which the actual rate of inflation differs from what was anticipated.

6. Monetary assets are claims to fixed amounts of money; monetary debts are obligations to pay fixed amounts of money.

7. A net monetary *debtor*, a person with more monetary debts than monetary assets, will obtain a wealth gain from an underanticipated inflation at the expense of net monetary creditors, those who hold more monetary assets than monetary liabilities. Any monetary *creditor* will gain wealth from an overanticipated inflation at the expense of net monetary debtors.

8. Holders of money lose wealth during an inflation (as long as interest is not paid on money) to those whose credit constitutes the money (commercial checking accounts) or to those who issue money (governments).

9. Government, being a very large net monetary debtor, gains wealth from an incompletely anticipated—that is, underanticipated—inflation.

10. A common fallacy is that wage rates usually if not always lag behind the prices of consumer goods. Although extensive evidence lends no support to this proposition, it arises because: (a) specific wages are erroneously compared with the average prices of con-

sumer goods; (b) shifts in relative wages are attributed to inflation; (c) the effects of job changes on income are ignored; (d) the prices of consumer goods are mistakenly thought to always rise before the prices of their components to the producers; and (e) the government's obtaining more of the community's wealth by issuing money and raising prices is erroneously thought to reduce real wages. (The transfer of resources to the government in fact comes from the *wealth* transfer, not from a shift in wages relative to consumer goods.)

11. Inflation does *not* reduce the value of saving. It reduces the real value of monetary wealth, but savings need not be held as monetary wealth.

12. If an inflation is anticipated there is no transfer of wealth from net monetary creditors to net monetary debtors because the interest rate on debts will have been fully adjusted to allow for the rise in price level. Anticipation of inflation does, however, lead to resource distortion because people try to reduce their real money wealth, giving rise to a money shortage that makes exchange more difficult and expensive.

13. Wage and price controls do not reduce the transfer of wealth from net monetary creditors to debtors. The exchange value of money is reduced by restrictions on the right to offer money in the market. (Unanticipated inflation achieves a similar effect.) Suppressing *changes* in price reduces the gains from specialization and exchange; suppressing *prices* enhances the political controls on resource use and allocation.

14. Anti-inflation monetary reforms use taxation to reduce the quantity of money. Such reforms have no effect on the transfer of wealth from net monetary creditors to debtors.

15. If an anticipated inflation is halted or reduced in rate or duration there will be transient reductions in employment and output, because future demand fails to develop as anticipated to cover costs (including the overcommitted interest costs). As anticipa-

tions and costs are revised downward, production and employment return toward their full levels—as long as the revised anticipations are more accurate.

16. By pushing *dollar* incomes into higher brackets of the graduated income tax schedule, where they are taxed at a higher percentage rate, inflation creates an automatic, unlegislated increase in income tax. The tax on capital gains (the gains in the *nominal* values of assets) is similarly increased. To avoid or reduce this inflation tax on money, people increase the relative values of assets that give income in nonmonetary, tax-exempt form, such as by ownership of housing or art works.

17. Because anticipated inflation is a tax on money, people attempt to hold a smaller portion of their income as money. That smaller ratio of *nominal* money to nominal income and wealth reduces the *real* stock of money—creates, that is, a so-called shortage of money. In fact, the excessively rapid increase in the money supply that causes inflation encourages people to hold less money, the value of which will be eroded by the anticipated inflation. The cure for inflation is not creating more money more rapidly, but less.

18. The higher the inflation rate has been, the less predictable have been its future rates. Because of this link between its rate and the unpredictability of future price levels, inflation is economically disruptive: As planning becomes less reliable, investment activity is discouraged; and the introduction of political controls, in a futile attempt to overcome the effects of inflation without stopping its cause, is socially disruptive.

Questions

*1. Almost all consumer price indices for the United States in 1977 reported a rise of about 40% over the price level of 1972.
   a. To test your belief in that—and given an annual income of, say, $10,000—would you rather do all your purchasing from a

1972 Sears (or Ward's) mail-order catalog or from a 1977 one? (If you are tempted to pick the current one because of changes in styles of clothes, suppose the styles were to be altered at no cost.) Which year's catalog would you choose?
   b. Remember, if you choose the current one, you are expressing disbelief in the existence of inflation! How could you reconcile your position—if you choose the current one?

*2. When collecting prices for your cost-of-living survey, you discover that not all customers can buy a good advertised on sale because the limited stock was sold out in the first hour. You discover also that in New York City the rents are controlled; but at the controlled rents apartments are not available to many who would pay the legal price. Why would you not use that legal price as the cost of housing?

*3. "The progressive deterioration in the value of money throughout history is not an accident, and has behind it two great driving forces—the impecuniosity of governments and the superior political influence of the debtor class. . . . The power of taxation by currency depreciation is one which has been inherent in the State. . . . The creation of legal tender has been and is a government's ultimate reserve; and no state or government is likely to decree its own downfall, so long as this instrument still lies at hand unused" (J. M. Keynes, *A Tract on Monetary Reform*, London: Macmillan and Co., Ltd., 1923, p. 9). Explain in more detail what Keynes meant.

*4. It was asserted that if producers of molybdenum responded to increased demand by raising their prices, the effect would be inflationary. Can you spot a fallacy in that argument? (Hint: Remember the discussion of the way meat prices might rise in response to a rise in demand? Suppose that cattle raisers had not asked for a higher price in response to an increased demand. Would that have meant that meat prices to consumers would not have increased?)

*5. If you were asked for the cause of the inflation in Brazil, how would you revise the question?

*6. Suppose that all colleges were forced to pay

professors a minimum salary of $30,000 per year in order to preserve the dignity of professors. Many professors will soon find themselves without jobs. Being of great influence in government, the professors tell the politicians that their salary demands are reasonable and that the basic trouble is insufficient demand. Congress could embark on a program to expand general demand by spending more, financed by creation of more money. If the government assures college professors that they will have full employment without wage cuts elsewhere, is inflation the inevitable consequence? Why?

*7. "Higher interest rates are higher prices and therefore are an element of inflation." Expose the error of that assertion.

*8. A monetary asset is one whose price can change although the asset is a claim to a fixed value in money terms. Give an example.

9. Which of the following are monetary? Which are real? Are they assets or liabilities?
   a. money in the form of checking accounts;
   b. charge account at department store;
   c. prepaid subscription to *New York Times*;
   d. long-term lease for land;
   *e. rental arrangement whereby commercial tenant pays building owner 1% of monthly sales as rent;
   * f. U.S. bonds;
   *g. a share of General Motors common stock;
   *h. house;
   * i. rights to social-security benefits;
   * j. pension rights in a retirement fund;
   *k. teacher's salary.

10. If during an inflation you held all your wealth in the form of real goods, would you gain or lose wealth relative to the price level? (Hint: What else must you know?)

11. Movie actors under the age of 21 are ordered by judges to save a fraction of their weekly earnings and buy U.S. government bonds. They are not allowed to invest that savings in stocks.
   a. If you were a young actor, would you regard this requirement as sound?
   b. If you were a judge, would you regard this requirement as sound?
   c. Can you give any reasons why jurists and the legal system are prone to advise in-

vestments in U.S. government bonds?

*12.a. If in drawing up your will you were arranging for advice to your spouse about investing your life insurance, would you recommend that the funds be invested in bonds or in stocks?
   b. How do the risks from inflation differ in each case?

*13. Show how an inflation that doubles the price level will yield the government more than twice as much in income taxes. (Hint: Estimate the income taxes for a person earning $10,000 a year before the inflation and $70,000 after the inflation.)

14. To test whether average wages lag behind prices of consumer goods, someone examines a 30-year record of price-level increases. Half the time wage rates rose less than the price level; half the time they rose more. He concludes that the wage-lag effect was present half the time. What would you have concluded? (Hint: If someone said a roulette wheel gave odd rather than even numbers, but then on 100 trials half the numbers it gave were odd, would you say the person's assertion was correct half the time or that it was simply wrong? Is this comparable to the wage-lag assertion?)

15. "Wages must lag behind prices because demand first affects selling prices and then filters down to the prices of productive inputs." Evaluate.

16. "If by inflation government increases its share of national income, there is less left for the private sector. Real wages must be smaller simply because available real income is smaller." Even if it is true that the real income left for the private economy is smaller, there is an error in that reasoning. Who loses what the government obtained?

17. a. If you knew that every price was going to rise at the rate of 2% a week, would you try to hold larger or smaller amounts of money relative to your wealth and income?
   b. Would you resort completely to barter to avoid loss of some money wealth every week?
   *c. In 52 weeks how much higher would the

price level be? (Use the tables in Chapter 6 to compute the answer.) Are you therefore not surprised to see why people will still use money even when they know the price level will rise by that amount in one year?

*d. Are you convinced that even at an anticipated rise in prices of 100% per week people would still use money?

e. If people reduce their money balances relative to their wealth and income from, say, one-fourth of their annual income to one-tenth to minimize their loss of wealth from the decreasing value of money, approximately how much would prices jump immediately?

18. Emperor Julian exhorted the merchants of ancient Antioch to practice self-restraint in pricing their wares. Today government leaders exhort industrialists and labor leaders to exercise similar self-restraint. Tomorrow the story will be the same. Why is such exhortation worse than useless?

19. Explain why neither shopping more carefully nor saving more restrains inflation.

20. "Inflation causes price distortions because not all prices are equally responsive to changes in demand. Therefore, a period of rapid inflation causes inefficiencies in the economic system. Evidence of the distortion is clear if one looks at the fact that, during inflations, relative prices change." Would you consider that as evidence for the proposition that inflation causes a change in relative prices? Is there some other reason why you would expect the beginning of an inflation to be associated with greater relative changes in prices more than during the subsequent inflation or during periods when price levels are constant? (Hint: Why did the inflation occur? That is, what events caused the increase in money stock relative to demand for money?)

*21. Suppose that in the years 1978–1981, when people were expecting inflation to continue for the next several years at the rate of about 6% to 9% annually, interest rates on loans were adjusted accordingly, to about 15%. If in the 1980s the inflation is stopped or substantially reduced, who will gain and who will lose? Does your answer suggest that *everyone* would like to see inflation brought down to lower rates?

For Further Study: Creation of Money by Bank Deposits and Loans

Money in the U.S. economy consists predominantly of cash, paper money, and checking accounts in banks. Cash and paper money, also called *currency,* are created solely by the U.S government. Checking accounts—or, more properly, checking account *money*—are created privately in a more complex fashion, to be explained. To avoid common misunderstandings as to exactly what checking account balances are, we examine two ways in which they are created.

Let us assume that a commercial bank (so called to distinguish it from a savings bank, which usually is prohibited by law from offering checking accounts) receives a deposit of new cash from a person who has just received $200 of paper money newly printed by the U.S. Treasury. (The reason for starting with a newly created sum of money will be apparent shortly.) The recipient deposits $100 in this bank as credit toward her checking account balance, which becomes $100 larger. She keeps $100 in coins and paper money for day-to-day use. The deposit leaves unchanged the amount of money held by the public as a whole. Instead of $200 in currency, the public holds $100 in checking accounts and $100 in currency. It has simply exchanged $100 of cash for a $100-larger checking account.

The bank decides that it has more money in its vault than it desires, because not all of it will be wanted by all its depositors at the same time. Some will be writing checks to people who will deposit them at other banks, to which the bank is obligated to transfer currency in the amount of the checks. But at the same time people with checking accounts at other banks are also writing checks, some of which are to depositors in our bank. So a bank will expect to have to pay some currency to other banks as checks are written against it, but it will also be receiving money from other banks against which checks have been written.

Our bank can be confident that during any day as much currency will become owed to other banks as it will be claiming from other banks. Thus, our bank needn't hold currency to equal the value of the checks that will be written against it. Indeed, with a perfectly balanced cross-flow of checks the bank could get by with almost no currency, merely offsetting claims against it with its claims against other banks in what is called the check-clearing process.

The bank, then, may keep an amount of currency equal to only about 20% of its deposits to take care of any outflows that might exceed the inflows during some interval. Thus, of a deposit of $100 in currency into a checking account, the bank will probably want to keep only about $20 in its vault as a *cash working reserve.*

What will it do with the remaining $80? It can lend it to borrowers and get interest. The borrower, however, doesn't want currency but money in a more convenient form—a larger checking account against which the borrower will write a check. That larger checking account was created not by the borrower's deposit of his or her own currency but by the bank. By setting up or increasing the amount in that borrower's checking account, our bank has *created* more checking accounts; it has created money. It now has checking accounts against it of $180 more than before: $100 by the initial deposit of currency and $80 by the loan. (Checking accounts, whether created by an actual deposit of currency or by a bank's lending to a borrower, are called *deposits.*)

When the borrower writes checks against that account and the recipients deposit the checks in other banks, $80 will be owed to those other banks. (For simplicity we assume only one other bank for the moment.) The transfer of the deposit of $80 from the first bank to the second bank creates or enlarges an account there.

Repeat the process. The second bank has $80 in currency and an $80 checking account, against which it estimates it need keep only about 20%, or $16, as a working reserve. The second bank, then, has $64 in excess currency—called *excess reserves.* It lends this to a borrower or client by depositing it in a newly created checking account. The borrower writes a check against that account. Say the people receiving the checks for $64 all deposited them in another bank, a third bank, which now has $64 more in deposits. Of that $64 the third bank keeps 20% ($12.80) as a working reserve and lends out the remainder, $51.20. See Table 19–A.

The third bank finds a borrower to whom it lends $51.20 by creating a checking account. That borrower writes checks for $51.20 which are deposited in still another bank. This fourth bank holds 20% ($10.24) as a working reserve and lends out $40.96. If continued, the sequence of checking accounts newly created through currency deposits and loans is $100 + $80 + $64 + $51.20 + $40.96 + . . ., which will approach $500, or five times the $100 of new currency initially deposited in the first bank.

Thus, the initial creation of $200 of cash or paper currency, $100 of which was held by the public and $100 of which was put in the bank, has enabled the creation, by lending, of checking accounts totaling five times the $100 of new currency deposited. This process indicates why currency is called *high-powered money.*

Table 19-A   CREATION OF MONEY THROUGH CHECKING ACCOUNTS, FROM INITIAL DEPOSIT OF $100 OF NEW CURRENCY

	Bank 1 receives $100.00 in exchange for a checking account of	$100.00
It sets aside $20.00	as reserves and lends $80.00 to borrowers as checking accounts. The borrowers write checks to people who deposit them in Bank 2.	
	Bank 2 has checking accounts that are increased by	80.00
It sets aside $16.00	as reserves and lends $64.00 to borrowers as checking accounts against which the borrowers write checks to people who deposit them in Bank 3.	
	Bank 3 has checking accounts that are increased by	64.00
It sets aside $12.80	as reserves and lends $51.20 to borrowers as checking accounts. The borrowers write checks to people who deposit them in Bank 4.	
	Bank 4 has checking accounts that are increased by	51.20
It sets aside $10.24	as reserves and lends $40.96 to borrowers as checking accounts. The borrowers write checks to people who deposit them in Bank 5.	
	Bank 5 has checking accounts that are increased by	40.96
It sets aside $8.19	as reserves and lends the remaining $32.77 to borrowers as checking accounts. The borrowers write checks to people who deposit them in. . . .	

        .
        .
        .

_____

$100.00
Reserve bank
currency

$500.00
New checking
accounts of
public

Appendix: Using Math and Graphs

A natural question to ask at the outset of one's first course in economics is, "How much mathematics do I need to know to understand economics?" Only arithmetic, and some ability to read charts and graphs and to interpret quantitative relationships between economic magnitudes. So in this appendix we will practice arithmetic, chart reading, and quantitative interpretation, using simple examples that make no attempt to reflect reality.

Imagine we are producing golf tees. To make one tee costs, we assume, $1.00, counting all the needed material, labor, and so on. The costs of producing two, three, four, and more tees per day are shown in Table A-1. The more tees produced in a day, the greater the total cost of that day's output. Two tees cost $1.90, and three cost $2.70. "Total costs" and "tees produced" both change in the same direction. When two magnitudes change in the same direction they are said to have a *positive* relationship. (For example, usually the relation between daily caloric intake and body weight is positive: More of one means more of the other.)

Some relationships are *negative*. For example, whereas up to the age of about 30 years there is a *positive* relationship between

Table A-1   OUTPUT OF TEES AND COSTS

Tees Produced Daily	Total Costs
1	$1.00
2	1.90
3	2.70
4	3.40
5	4.00
6	4.70
7	5.50
8	6.40
9	7.40
10	8.60

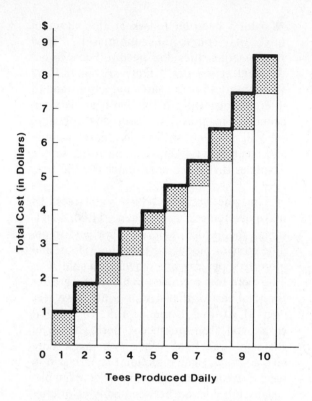

Figure A-1.

BAR CHART SHOWING RELATIONSHIP BETWEEN
TOTAL COST AND OUTPUT OF TEES

Shaded sections denote how much cost increases with
each unit increase in daily output. Relationship between
total cost and tees produced is *positive*, for both
increase (or decrease) together.

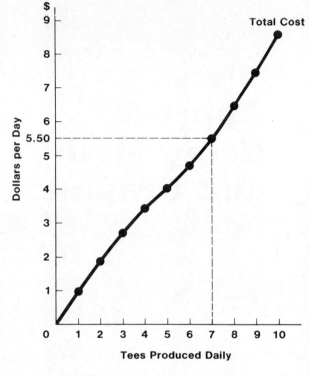

Figure A-2.

LINE CHART SHOWING RELATIONSHIP BETWEEN
TOTAL COST AND OUTPUT

Line chart shows more clearly how total cost varies with
daily output of tees. Height of line at each output
measures daily total cost. Upward slope, called positive
slope, indicates positive relationship.

age and physical strength (the older one gets,
the stronger one gets), from about 30 years
on there is a *negative* relationship: Strength
decreases with age. (Note that neither a positive nor negative relationship is assumed to
imply *causality:* We are *not* saying that a relationship between the changes in two magnitudes means that a change in one *causes* a
change in the other.)

We can use graphs to show relationships
among magnitudes. Figure A-1 portrays the
relationship that we assume between costs of

production and number of tees produced.
The height of each bar indicates *total costs*
of the number of tees to which it corresponds. Each bar has an upper shaded section showing how much higher it is than the
neighboring bar of one less unit of output.
The shaded part of the bar represents the *increment* to total costs that results from producing one more tee. We could draw a
smooth line along the tops of the bars to indicate total costs without showing a lot of
bars, as is done in Figure A-2. You will see
that the line passes through several dots.

The *line* between the dots both guides the eye from point to point and represents the costs of producing fractional amounts. For example, if we produce three tees in two days, our rate of production is 1.5 tees per day. The line in Figure A-2 shows us the costs of producing 1.5 tees a day.

So far we have interpreted a chart by choosing a point on the horizontal axis and then reading up to the line to find the value of the corresponding variable in which we were interested. If we choose five units of tees on the horizontal axis and then read up directly above that point, we see that the cost is $4. But usually we can read a graph the other way, too. Suppose you were told that you could spend $4 producing tees. How many could you produce? To answer, find $4 on the vertical scale, then go horizontally across the chart to the curve (which is what economists call such a line, whether it is in fact curved or is straight) and drop straight down to the horizontal axis to find an output of five tees.

So far we have been using the term *costs* as if it had only one meaning, but there are in fact three kinds of cost: *total, average,* and *marginal. Total* cost includes all the costs of producing tees—materials, labor, and the like. The *average* cost is the total cost per day divided by the number of tees per day. For two tees, the total cost per day, $1.90, divided by 2, is 95¢ per tee. And for five tees the average cost is 80¢. (Compute the average cost of producing five and six tees.)

Marginal cost is the cost of producing one more unit; that is, it is the *difference* between the *total* costs of producing two quantities that differ by one. For five tees a day the total cost is $4.00, and for six tees it is $4.70; the difference, called the *marginal cost,* is 70¢. This is shown in Figure A-1 as the shaded section of the bar for six units.

Marginal cost, then, is the *change* in one variable (here, total cost) associated with a *one* unit change in the other variable (in this case, output of tees). This cost could have

been called the "incremental cost when six are produced rather than five," or the "marginal cost of producing six rather than five," but it is in fact called the "*marginal* cost at, or of, six." Note carefully that it is not the total cost of producing six units ($4.70); nor is it the average cost of producing six units (78¢ per unit). Rather, it is the *increase* in total cost of producing six instead of five units.

We use these concepts extensively throughout this book. Remember: Never use the term *cost* by itself; always identify it as *total, average,* or *marginal.* Thus, if someone asks, "What is the cost of six tees?", you have to ask, What cost? Total, average, or marginal?

Imagine a retail store with four clerks. Total sales are $2000 per day, an average of $500 a day. Some clerks sell more than the average, some less. Add a fifth clerk to the sales force, and sales increase by $200 to $2200. You might conclude that the new clerk is not as productive as the other four. But in fact you might discover that the new

Table A-2   COSTS AND OUTPUT OF TEES

Tees Produced Daily	Costs		
	Total	Average	Marginal
1	$1.00	$1.000	$1.00
2	1.90	.950	.90
3	2.70	.900	.80
4	3.40	.850	.70
5	4.00	.800	.60
6	4.70	.783	.70
7	5.50	.785	.80
8	6.40	.800	.90
9	7.40	.822	1.00
10	8.60	.860	1.20

Total costs increase as number of tees produced daily increases. Average costs are total costs divided by number of tees produced daily. Marginal cost is increase in total costs for one unit of increased output.

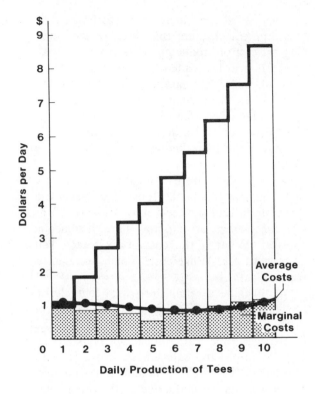

Figure A-3.

BAR CHART OF RELATIONSHIPS AMONG TOTAL, MARGINAL, AND AVERAGE COSTS

Shaded sections show marginal costs. Average costs are shown by line through dots, to avoid cluttering graph. Average costs fall when marginal costs are less than average cost, and rise when marginal cost exceeds average cost.

clerk had $800 of sales, more than for any other clerk. The fifth clerk not only enabled the store to sell $200 more by getting customers who otherwise would have decided not to buy, but also managed to attract customers away from the other clerks.

However, although the clerk's sales were $800, the clerk's *marginal* sales were $200: the *change* in the *total* results of having five clerks rather than four. "Marginal sales" or "marginal costs" or "marginal whatever" must always be interpreted that way—as the *change in total* of one variable as the result of having *one* more of the other variable.

Let us now investigate how magnitudes behave in relation to one another. Notice, in Table A-2, that as output of tees increases, marginal costs at first *decrease,* then beyond a certain point *increase.* After marginal costs begin to increase, between five and six tees, you will notice that so do *average* costs, because once marginal costs exceed average costs they drive up average costs.

Figure A-3 shows these relationships graphically. The bars show the *total* costs of producing a given number of tees per day. The shaded areas at the bottom of the bars (which are exactly the same as those at the top of the bars in Figure A-1) represent the *marginal* costs for each number of tees produced. Notice that marginal costs at first decrease and then increase. Average costs decrease as long as they exceed marginal costs, but increase once marginal costs exceed them. To see how marginal and total costs are related, if you add up the marginal costs at any level of daily production you will see that the total of marginal costs up to and including that level equals total costs at that level.

Figure A-4 gives the same information as Figure A-3, using lines instead of bars. The total cost of seven units of output is shown in three ways: (1) by the *height* of the total cost line at 7; (2) by the *area* under the marginal cost line from the first through the seventh—the sum of the marginal costs; and

(3) by the shaded area of a rectangle whose base is the horizontal axis from 0 through 7 and whose height is the average cost of seven. The average cost of seven ($.785), shown by the height at 7, multiplied by 7 will be the total cost ($5.50, rounded to three figures). Both the area *under the marginal cost curve* and the *rectangular area* formed by the average cost curve height at 7 units represent the total cost.

Let's examine the new data in Table A–3. The first two columns show prices and the number of tees that can be sold at each price. The lower the price, the more that can be sold at that price. Complete the empty spaces in the columns labeled "marginal receipts" and "average receipts"—which you will see is the same as price, because each unit is sold at the same price. Do not be surprised to get some *negative* marginal receipts. And in any event do the arithmetic without worrying much about why the relationship is shown as it is.

On the partially completed graph in Figure A–5, some of the points have already been placed. Put in the rest of the dots for

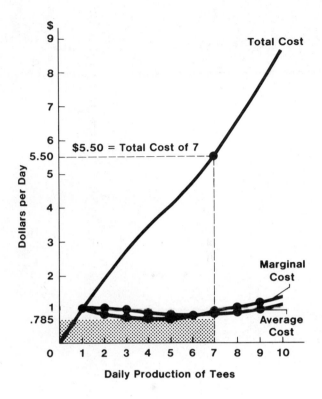

Figure A-4.

LINE CHART SHOWING RELATION OF TOTAL, AVERAGE, AND MARGINAL COST TO RATE OF OUTPUT

Rectangular area with height at average cost and base at output rate is measure of total cost. Area under marginal cost curve is also measure of total cost.

Table A-3   SALES PRICE AND NUMBER OF TEES SOLD DAILY

Tees Sold	Price of Tee	Sales Receipts or Revenue (Dollars)		
		Total	Marginal	Average
1	$10	$10	—	10
2	9	18	+8	9
3	8	24	+6	—
4	7	28	—	—
5	6	30	—	—
6	5	30	—	—
7	4	28	−2	—
8	3	24	—	—
9	2	18	—	—
10	1	10	—	—

Complete the table and plot the results in Figure A–5. Negative marginal sales receipts indicate that total sales receipts diminish at lower price despite increased number sold. Sales receipts are typically called "revenue."

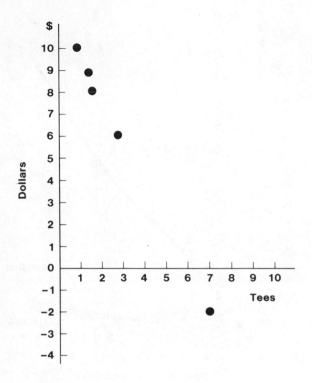

Figure A-5.

EXERCISE GRAPH FOR RECEIPTS—UNITS-SOLD
RELATIONSHIP

You are to complete set of dots and draw lines of
average costs and marginal costs. Relationship of price
and units sold is negative. Is relationship between total
sales receipts positive, negative, or both?

the average receipts and for the marginal receipts and connect the points in each set
with a smooth line. Then draw in the *two*
alternative areas representing total receipts
for four tees at a price of $7. Do the same for
eight tees at a price of $3. Which has the
larger area?

Finally, some algebra. If you put $100 in
a bank that pays interest at the rate of 5%
per year, at the end of one year you will have
$105. At the end of two years you will have
earned another 5% of the $105 with which
you ended the first year, so you will have 5%
of $105 added to the $105, a total of $110.25.
How can this be written in algebraic form?
At the end of the first year you will have
$100 + ($100 X .05) = $105 which can be
written as $100(1.05) = $105. At the end of
the second year, the amount is multiplied
again by 1.05. Therefore the initial amount
of $100 will in two years be $100(1.05)(1.05)
= $110.25 which can be written as $100
$(1.05)^2$. This is what is meant by compounded interest—here compounded once a year
for two years. The initial investment is increased by 5% by the end of the first year
and then that entire amount (initial principal
plus accumulated interest) earns interest the
next year and grows by another 5%, or by
the multiple 1.05. Succinctly, it grows to
100(1.05)^2$ = $110.25. In three years it will
grow to $100(1.05)(1.05)(1.05) or 100(1.05)^3$
which is $115.76. In 10 years it will be
100(1.05)^{10}$ which is $162.89.

Suppose you want to have $150 in six
years at 5% interest compounded annually.
How much must you invest *now* so that the
value will grow to $150 in six years? The an-
swer is obtained by noting that a present
amount, *P*, will grow in six years at 5% interest compounded annually to $P(1.05)^6 = F$,
where *F* denotes some future amount. In the
example we have $P(1.05)^6$ = $150. So divid-
ing through by $(1.05)^6$ we have P = $150/
$(1.05)^6$ = $150/1.34 = $111.93. Of course,
computing the value of $(1.05)^6$ is tedious, but
don't worry. You won't have to, because we

have tables in which to look up the answer.

You have now demonstrated adequate knowledge of arithmetic graphics and algebra. If some of the concepts still seem a little unfamiliar, don't worry. So long as you understand them, later exercises will make them easier to use.

Answers to Selected Questions

Chapter 1

1. False. It is because people are reasonable and act in accord with their interest that there are economic problems and wars.

2. a. Highest valued.
   b. Expressed in a common denominator or measure of value.
   c. In general, no. Not if more than one thing could have been produced—including leisure.

4. The first statement is true, but the second is wrong. The value of an hour is the highest valued use one could have made of that hour. Hence the cost of an act taking an hour is the value of the best alternative action forsaken during that hour. (A common, though not always accurate, measure of the value of time is the earnings one could have obtained during the time.)

5. Costs are not the undesirable consequences of an act; they are the highest valued forsaken opportunity.

6. All costs are private. Social costs are simply the total of all private costs. If a person performing an action does not bear all the costs of that action, then the social costs exceed the total of the costs the person bears (because some of the costs are borne by other people). An equality of private with social costs means all costs of a decision are borne by the decision maker.

7. William the Conqueror, Julius Caesar, Napoleon Bonaparte. You can add scores of others easily.

8. a. Promises to raise or lower taxes (affect other people's wealth) in order to benefit those who vote for you. But the politician can't offer to sell services as a business person can.
   b. Will letters of recommendation help you get a better grade in this course? Does your past record influence the teacher of this course in making grades? Does the wealth of your parents?

9. a. Yes.
   b. We know of no institution with the dominant power of coercive violence that is not the government in any country. Government is an institution for enforcing certain rules and procedures for resolving interpersonal conflicts of interest. The making and enforcement of laws and the judicial settlement of disputes are behaviors that support the propositions. (Note that the second statement says government is an agency, not the only agency. For example, many social disputes are resolved by social ostracism, and by agreement to use an arbitrator.)

10. The only kinds of competition made illegal by private-property rights are competition by violence and involuntary dispossession of goods deemed to be private property. Socialism prohibits competition in the form of offering types of services and goods that individuals privately prefer, without having to obtain authorization of government officials for propriety of producing the services. These are merely examples of types of competition that are ruled out—not a complete chronicle, and certainly not an evaluation of the desirability of the various types.

11. a. Until you define what "socially preferred" means, you cannot answer this question. We don't have a definition to offer.

b. We do not know what socially preferred means. For example, does it mean that a majority prefer it, or that the most important people prefer it, or that everyone prefers it, or that the speaker thinks everyone should prefer it, or that he or she prefers it? Beware of any expression referring to the preference of a group.

13. a. No.
b. Since scarcity is present in socialism—as in capitalism: Competition for control of resources is inescapable. In socialism more is in the form of political avenues of competition.
c. Competition is the interpersonal striving for more of what is scarce and desired—by production, by purchase, by striving for political power, and so on. Cooperation is a joint activity with mutual striving for a common end.

14. These questions will be answered in the course of study. The query is intended to whet your interest in what is coming.

15. a. They are different—because these all involve social, interpersonal interactions. As such, one person's behavior with respect to these characteristics or attributes will affect other people, and their responses to that person's behavior will vary accordingly. Their response and their ability to influence the person's actions will depend upon whether or not there is private property—for reasons we shall see as we progress through the book.
b. Nothing like this question to kill a discussion! (Remember, evidence does not consist of one's unique personal memories.)

16. All societies use force and compulsion. The pertinent issue is: What kinds of coercion and force do various economic, political, and social systems use? The capitalist system uses the force of self-interest; it is coldly impersonal in its market effects; it is a severe and unforgiving taskmaster. He who produces at a loss is forced out of business into some other tasks, perhaps with less compassion than under a socialist dictator, who could spread the loss over other people. More sensible than the question of which system

uses less force is the question of what effects the various kinds of forces (incentives, rewards, signals, orders, and penalties) have on the economic, cultural, and political behavior. For example, how are freedom of speech, job mobility, social fluidity, individual dignity, religious worship, search for the truth, and so on, affected? The effects on all the various goals of a person must be considered.

Not even reference to the use of the rule of law versus the rule of arbitrary dictators is a basis for ultimate judgment. Here, too, the question is: What law and what rules will be enforced by the ruling law—the rule of private-property rights, the rule of socialism, or some other?

Differences are implied about the kinds of opportunities or "freedoms" provided to individuals living under each system. The implications are that an open-market system gives individuals a greater range of consumption patterns or goods from which to choose. Whether it is "good" that individuals should have such a range of options to explore is a question that economic theory cannot answer. A greater range of choice can be regarded as a greater range of temptation, risk, error, regret, and deviant behavior. Just as a parent restrains his children's choices for their own good, we may prefer to restrain the choices of adults because everyone retains some childlike impulses. Whether you wish to regard one system or the other as giving more freedom depends upon your meaning of "freedom." In one sense, freedom can include protection from the costs of resisting temptation and from making unfortunate choices; in another sense freedom might include the right to bear those costs and to make those choices and explore tempting alternatives. Whatever your interpretation, the implications derived from economic theory about the factual consequences of different allocative systems will be helpful in forming a judgment.

17. The cost of building the boats was the next most valuable alternative use of the builders' time. If the boat builders were slaves their owner bore that cost; if the builders were freemen they bore that cost. Therefore, it was not slave labor versus the labor of freemen that made the boat building cheaper. What changed the manner of building boats, if indeed less labor was involved, was the higher alternative value of use of that

labor, slave or free. This, .of course, does not mean that slavery is not worse than freedom; it means instead that the difference between slavery and freedom has no effect on the cost of activities but rather determines who bears the costs.

Chapter 2

1. a. Each has a common goal.
   b. We're sure he has more goals.
   c. No, quite the opposite, because it's a matter of *more* of some goals relative to *less* of other goals. It's not a matter of first fulfilling one goal and then turning to the next.

2. Individuals, not abstract things called colleges, make decisions.

3. Yes; no.

4. By definition of a free good, no one wants *more* of a good that is so plentiful as to be free. But we do want the amount we have. Only if we don't want *more* is it a free good. The question tends to confuse *more* or *less* of a good with all or none. Life is almost entirely a choice of more or less, not all or none.

6. The first statement contains no implication about any thought process. It would also apply to rocks and water obeying the law of gravity. The second statement suggests some mental calculation and choice among alternative possible actions. Economics does not have to assume the second statement as a basis for its theory, despite common arguments that it does.

7. It is.

8. a. One artichoke is worth 5 steaks, or 1 steak has a marginal personal value of .2 artichokes given that I have option A or B.
   b. Between B and C my personal marginal value of artichokes is 6 steaks, greater than between A and B, because I have fewer artichokes at B or C than at A.
   c. Increases the amount of meat that expresses the personal marginal value of artichokes, because I have fewer artichokes (and more meat).

9. The first statement means that *more* of one

goal is achieved at the cost of having *less* of another. The second statement means that goals do not exclude each other.

10. Correct in that increased proximity to perfection costs something and the increase may not be worth the extra cost. For example, removing every typographical error from this book may cost more than a book with no typographical errors is worth.

11.

Personal Value		Revenue	
Total	Marginal	Total	Marginal
2.00	2.00	$2.00	$2.00
3.90	1.90	3.80	1.80
5.70	1.80	5.40	1.60
7.40	1.70	6.80	1.40
9.00	1.60	8.00	1.20
10.50	1.50	9.00	1.00
11.90	1.40	9.80	.80
13.20	1.30	10.40	.60
14.40	1.20	10.80	.40
15.50	1.10	11.00	.20

12. a. Yes.
    b. Yes.
    c. He buys a second unit at a price of $1.90 when he could have bought only one at that price of $1.90 if he wanted to. The fact that he chooses to pay $1.90 to get the second one means it is worth at least that amount to him. The value of one more unit is measured by what one is willing to give up to get one more. The fact that he pays $1.80 more now at the lower price than formerly doesn't mean he pays only $1.80 more *than the price of one* to get a second unit. He saves 10¢ on the price cut, but the second unit costs him $1.90 more *than if he buys just one.*

13. The person adjusts rate of *consumption* or *rate* of purchase over time, not the *amount* purchased at a given moment.

14. The person increases rate of use or replaces items more quickly.

15. True.

16. 18,250 gallons.

17. No. I take longer vacations.

18. First is rate; second and third are stocks.

19. a. Sell 3 at $2; 2 at $9, 1 at $8. Buy 1 at $6; 2 at $5, and so on.
    b. Would buy 4 more to have a total of 8.

20. a. No such thing as basic need. We would use more and we could also get by with less security. It's a matter of what price we are willing to pay, and a matter of more or less, not all or none.
    b. We "need" more of everything that is not free. The amount of any economic good we choose to have is a function of its price. To say our children need more schools ignores what we propose to give up to get more schools.
    c. It depends upon the price, whether it is good enough to have at the price. If this says simply that more is better than less, O.K. Otherwise, it seems to deny relevance of alternatives.
    d. Same as comment to b.

21. See answer to preceding question.

23. Difference is that price is ignored in determining how many golf courses would be demanded ("needed").

25. Because as price is reduced to sell more, all prior units bring in less revenue, and that reduction offsets part of revenues on the extra unit sold at the new lower price.

26. To right of and above.

27. All except g. (Why?)

28. a. Correct.
    b. Correct.
    c. It is conventional to call this an increase in amount demanded, not an increase in demand—the latter referring to a shift in the whole demand relationship.

29. It is the *ratio* of *percentage* change in quantity in response to a *small percentage* change in price.

30. Demands *a* and *b* have the same elasticity at any common price. But the elasticities of *a* and *b* decrease at lower prices. Demand *c* has a lower elasticity at any price than demands *a* or *b*, and its elasticity decreases at lower prices. Hint of reason: The slope of *b* is greater than of *a*, but the quantity at any price is proportionally greater also. Demand *c* has the same slope as *b*, but its quantities are larger at any price. Hence for any small price cut, the absolute change in the amount demanded on lines *c* and *b* is the same, but for *c* the increase is a smaller percentage of the amount demanded (at that price).

31. a. True. Economic theory says they would. Compare cars in countries with higher gasoline prices. How about extent to which automatic transmissions, which impose higher fuel consumption, would be used?
    b. Reduced gas consumption.
    c. Three years.

32. Whatever provides the impulse, the lower the price of the item, the greater is the probability the impulse to buy will result in a purchase; the higher the price, the lower the probability. Habitual buying is consistent with knowing the price from prior purchases and having settled on a consumption plan that is generally repeated over time. However, let the price of some of the consumption goods rise and the habit will be revised. Inconsistent behavior would be behavior that did not conform to that just outlined.

33. Yes, to all.

34. a. No.
    b. The negative relationship between price and amount demanded.

35. It is a fall in the price of candy in ice-cream units. Candy is cheaper relative to ice cream than formerly.

36. The law of demand does not say that every person will instantly respond to every price change no matter how slight. It says a sufficiently high price will induce an immediate response, and it also says that the longer the time allowed, the greater will be the response. In the case at hand, some people will respond quickly though some will not. Even for a small price rise the *aggregate* amount demanded will respond because some people will respond. In time all will respond to a sufficiently large price rise.

37. The higher prices of the high-quality dwellings reduce the amount demanded. Given the

law of demand, it is possible to reduce the amount people demand so that it does not exceed the amount available.

38. a. Demand increases. Schedule shifts upward.
    b. Can't tell. Milk production may be so important a source of your income that you consume more when its price rises (despite the higher price, because you are wealthier). But you consume less than if your wealth had increased for other reasons and without a rise in milk prices.

39. Hiring babysitters at, say, $1 an hour and staying out for four hours will cost $4. Add the cost of two movie tickets at $1 each, and compare that total cost of $6 with the cost of going to the $4 theater. The $4 theater costs a *total* of $12 ($8 + $4) and movies cost a total of $6 ($2 + $4). Taking all costs into account, the $4 theater ticket costs only twice as much as the $1 movie ticket for parents who must pay babysitters. The theater then costs twice as much, but if a couple has no children and no babysitter fee, the theater will cost $8 and the movie $2—a ratio of 4 to 1: theatergoing is relatively more expensive in real terms, that is, in terms of other goods given up. (Testing this would be a fine term project if you have lots of time to collect data.)

40. If T_1/T_2 is less than P_1/P_2,

$$\frac{P_1 + T_1}{P_2 + T_2} \text{ will be less than } \frac{P_1}{P_2}.$$

Therefore, the price (including transport) of goods in the more distant market will be lower relative to the price of good 2 in the more distant market. More of good 1 will be demanded than of 2 relative to that in the domestic market because the relative price of good 1 is lower in the distant market.

41. Welfare change is not measured by total market value of entire crop. If demand elasticity is less than one, bigger supply will lower total *market* value (total market revenue) while total personal value is increasing because of larger supply. Do not confuse total personal use value with total market exchange value (market sales revenue). Former is closer to welfare criterion.

42. What does "invaluable" mean? We are reminded of a news item. "This priceless four-strand necklace is now in the possession of Mrs. Lovely, who bought it for $85,000." Rarely do we find such an incongruous juxtaposition of obvious inconsistencies. However, in fairness to those who often use the term "priceless," we suspect they usually mean that the priceless good is not reproducible. Thus, a Grecian urn or an original Dufy cannot be replaced at any price if destroyed. At the same time, one should be careful not to think it can't be bought at a finite price, or that a nonreproducible item is necessarily valuable.

Chapter 3

1. No. It does not imply what is good, bad, better, or worse. It implies what will be observed in the real world.

2. Denies none. Power over other people is a goal or good.

3. a. If it is supposed to mean that one area had more of some good than it wanted—that is, could possibly use at all—the statement is wrong. And we can't think of anything else it might mean.
   b. We propose that the relative supplies were different so that relative values were different, leading to mutually preferred exchange and reallocation of goods among Mediterranean and Baltic people.

4. It assumes that the middleman performs no service to consumers or producers by making exchange easier and less expensive than otherwise, and that therefore he can be eliminated without someone else's having to perform the service in which he specialized.

5. Middlemen facilitate exchange and specialization, while "do-it-yourself" is a reduction of specialization and exchange or a case of doing middlemen's activities by oneself.

6. a. No. Middlemen perform services for householders more cheaply than consumers could. And middlemen are paid by consumers; the purchase price paid to the farmer is not therefore reduced. In fact, if middlemen's services save consumers enough to make them want more of the

farmers' goods, the purchase price paid to the farmer can be raised.

   b. Not necessarily, because that might be the result of no middlemen's services to consumers. The farmer would get all of the price paid by the consumer, but that price would be less than if middlemen performed those services more efficiently than the consumer could.

7. All are denials of open markets.

8. a. Yes, unless all consumers could agree to pay me more than the one seller to whom I gave the monopoly right. (In principle they could always pay more than the monopolist would gain.)

   b. The one who helped me most to get elected or offered me the most.

   c. No. Their monopoly rents are partly used to aid (pay?) politicians and are also dependent on political favors and support.

   d. Once in office, people create favored monopoly privileges by prohibiting entry of competitors. As we shall learn later, consumers lose more than the monopolies gain. But the ability of the monopoly party to pay the politician exceeds that of consumers, who have more difficulty in arranging payment because there are so many consumers, each with a small amount involved.

9. See answer to 7. Those who restrict it gain, but their gain is less than the loss imposed on others.

11. Free speech means a right to speak or communicate with others who are willing to listen, free of government intervention or prohibition. It is not a right to take the resources of other people for purposes of communication with other people. To use college property without the permission of the college authorities for speech is not a right of free speech; it is simply appropriation of property as if the property were free for the taking. Nor is it a denial of free speech if a college or anyone else denies the use of resources under its or his control which others would like to use for the purposes of communication; it is instead a denial to others of resources to use in ways they would like. This does not mean that

colleges ought to refuse to allow use of their resources for communication of popular or unpopular ideas; it is simply a clarification of the difference between free speech and the proposition that resources are "free" to anyone for the taking so long as they will be used for communication.

12. Because it is easily recognizable, and it is portable, divisible, and durable. If it were more plentiful, many things would be gold plated—automobiles, airplanes, dishes, appliances, and the like. Gold, then, being corrosion resistant, has many valuable uses, making it an excellent medium of exchange and store of value.

Chapter 4

1. a. 0, 1, 2, 4, 6, 8, 9, 11, 13, 15 for prices from $10 through $1.

   b. Four to A and two to B.

   c. Shortage.

   d. Surplus.

   e. By a change in price.

2. a. $7.

   b. Three to each.

   c. Shortage.

   d. Remove price control.

3. Yes. Demanders compete with one another—in the free market, by price. Any resource that has more than one use is being competed for by more than one demander. Thus, its supply to any one user is determined by how the price offered by that demander induces other demanders to move back up their demand curves to smaller quantities, thereby releasing more resources to that one demander. Figures 3–1, 3–2, and 4–4 illustrate this rationale.

4. a. Yes. It is true for all goods.

   b. We have yet to find one.

5. The first law of demand relates purchase rate to price. Law of demand and supply states that price is at the intersection of supply and demand. The former law holds generally; the latter does not hold always, especially when prices are controlled by law.

6. Yes, for it does advance the argument (analysis?) to grasp the meaning of scarcity and to understand that economics says nothing about which goods ought to be allocated via the exchange-market form of competition. We leave it

to you to try to figure out why the "degree of scarcity" should affect the form of competition that should determine how a scarce resource is allocated among alternative uses and users. We can't.

7. In brief, how price affects amounts demanded and amounts supplied is ignored. Past equality of supply and demand (through the late 1970s on the graph) reflects the simple fact that *price* was allowed to adjust up or down so as to equate *amounts* demanded with amount supplied. No particular amount demanded can be projected for a given year unless some particular price is projected for that year. A higher projected price would reduce the amount demanded and raise the amount supplied, thus raising the supply line and lowering the demand line to keep them equal. An appropriate path of price over the future will affect the amounts demanded and the amounts supplied so as to keep the two equated. All the diagram says is that price will be kept too low, whereas in the past it was allowed to equate the amounts demanded and supplied. For any good, every such projected future imbalance of amounts demanded (probably mislabeled "needs," "requirements," or " demand") with amounts supplied (probably mislabeled "supply," "availabilities," "stocks") is merely a prediction that price will not be allowed to move to equate them—as it has in the past. Beware of being fooled by such worthless diagrams.

8. They probably use the phrase "heavy buying" to mean increased demand, or at least so we hope.

9. Shopping several sellers is better because alternatives are what sellers must beat. See A. Jung, "Price Variations among Automobile Dealers," *The Journal of Business,* October 1959, pp. 315–325.

10. Holding down the wholesale price of cattle to the meat processors increases the spread between purchase price and selling price for the processors. The price to consumers, which is not controlled, would rise anyway. The wealth that would have been available to cattle growers is instead given to the cattle processors.

11. Price controls do not increase the probability that lower-income groups will get more housing. They may get less (and over time, because con-

trols affect the production of housing, housing quality and quantity will deteriorate). Outcome depends more upon possession of nonpecuniary attributes that now play a greater role in allocative decision.

12. Scarcity is pervasive. A reduced supply is not a shortage. A reduced supply is a reduction in the amount available—pictured as a shift of the supply curve to the left. What people call shortages are simply the result of prices that are kept too low. Confusing these three different concepts helps create imaginary problems.

14. A vertical supply curve means that the amount supplied is fixed, unresponsive to price. Thus, price falls by the full amount of the demand fall. If the amount demanded is to remain unchanged from before, the price must fall by the full change in the marginal use value at the existing amount. Competition among sellers will reduce the price to that lower level.

15. The curve implies that although price will fall, it falls by less than the fall in demand, for the following reasons. As price falls, resources that are mobile will move to next best paying jobs. Reduced output will prevent price from falling by full reduction in marginal use value, because at smaller amounts the marginal use value is higher.

16. If demand falls, inputs will not accept a lower price, because they can move elsewhere to obtain the initial rates of pay. If demand rises, higher prices for this output will be thwarted by an influx of resources from elsewhere at no rise in costs. That is what is implied or described by depicting the supply situation by a horizontal line.

17. The person currently owning the rights to the drama would bear the tax. The resources used to make the series have already been incurred, and no expenditures or new resources are required to maintain the tape. (In fact, there are some storage costs and costs of projection or broadcast, so price could not fall below those costs, or the tape not only would not be shown, it would not be preserved.)

19. The belief that money or market-exchange value is the sole criterion of allocation is widespread, deeply ingrained, and incorrect. Money is

not the only criterion; that much has already been established by our analysis. (That it ought to be or ought not to be is not the issue.) Only if the options are equivalent in *all* other respects do money costs become the *sole* criterion, simply because cost is the only one that, in this case, makes any difference. On the other hand, if money costs were equal, then only other attributes would be relevant.

When I dine in a restaurant, I select my dinner not only according to prices but also according to what the item is. I never tell the waitress to bring me the cheapest items only. The taste, nutrition, and looks of the items are considered. Similarly, when buying a suit, I take into account style, feel, looks, and fit, as well as the price. Nor for national security do we buy the cheapest weapon regardless of what it will or will not do, nor the most modern, expensive weapon simply because it is the most expensive or modern.

20. According to this criticism, we are all so influenced by our interest in our economic wealth that other criteria are dominated. However, the exchanging of goods does not make it difficult for anyone to be influenced by the artistic, social, humanitarian, or cultural uses to which that person can put his or her goods and services.

Saying that only "lowbrow" products sell well seems to suggest that this is a result of the market-value system. But that system, although effectively revealing and enforcing the lowbrow tastes and desires of the public, does not create those tastes. Actors, writers, and artists are frustrated because other people don't want as much "quality" as they would like to provide at the prices they would like to get. Or putting it "selfishly," the artists must admit that the income they can get from "low-quality" work is so high that they prefer to produce low-quality plays and get a big income rather than produce high-quality plays and live with a lower income. In this case, it is also the artists' and actors' own tastes for more wealth, not merely that of the public, that precludes quality.

21. True.

22. Both. Choice is an act of discrimination.

23. All.

24. The sale price, if goods were available at that price at time of sale. Price means exchange prices, not hoped-for price.

25. Because monetary competition is precluded, allocation of price-controlled goods is likely to enhance political and government influence and authority, either directly, as government agencies assume economic control, or indirectly as demanders compete politically to satisfy their demand for price-controlled goods.

29. You should disagree. A higher price permits a reallocation of existing goods—a reallocation that would not occur in the absence of higher prices. The point is to note that higher prices do have a consequence—reallocation—and that personal preferences should not blind one to that fact.

30. All contain rent, so far as existence is concerned.

31. Yes. Land would still exist at a lower price, but particular use is determined by full payment received. The person who gets to use it must pay at least what it would be worth to the next highest valuing user, so the rent paid is a cost to the person who gets to use it.

Chapter 5

2. a. Yes.
   b. Yes, and it pays not to cut rent to get an immediate occupant (because the cost of immediate occupancy is greater than the rent cut would be worth).

4. Tolls on bridges; parking meters; tollways.

5. Yes, this could be so. Although it is not possible to know what is necessarily better, the total cost of providing parking space could be cheaper if it were not policed as carefully as a park-for-pay lot. A free lot would impose the costs on those who purchase from the persons who provide the free parking lot, but not on those who use the lot without doing any business with the providers of the parking space.

6. A is suing for property rights to uncongested streets. Under current law this kind of right seems not to be recognized. Presume we would rule against blocking construction. What do you say?

8. If you define access to sunlight as an aspect

of land ownership, then it is a strengthening of private-property rights.

9. a. Either way.
   b. No.

10. Not true. To remove all risk of accidents costs more than it's worth.

11. a. No rights were being curtailed. Instead, rights are being defined and allocated for the first time.
   b. No, they were being defined and specified.

12. Nader ignores the social gains provided by activities that produce smog and pollution as a by-product. Just as automobiles and airplanes produce death; just as travel takes up land for roads; just as making sheet steel involves less of other desirable things like leisure, quiet, and rest; just as oil wells create some smell in their vicinity—so all productive activity involves some undesirable by-products. All of these "pollutions" of our environment are part of the costs of production and could be avoided if we were willing to have a less convenient, more Spartan life. We should not look only at costs and think that something is wrong with those economic activities that involve the largest costs, for they may also yield the greatest benefits. Relieving one's self in the river may be less valuable than the value of output from a factory that creates equivalent pollution and may be avoidable at lower cost. Similarly, smoggers are producing other services in the process, whereas muggers produce no social service.

The complaint that Nader should develop is that governments and courts have not introduced a system of making people pay for the right to pollute—a system that would induce people to pollute *less if* the gains obtained from activities that yield pollution are worth less than the damage from pollution. Just as we could produce less oil or less paper by having less pollution of air and streams, there is a tradeoff between more or less clean air or water and more or less of other desirable goods. Efforts to calculate that tradeoff rate and to induce the pollution costs to be taken into account by a system of prices for the right to pollute (by fines) rather than with zero prices or absolute prohibitions (infinitely high prices) are what Nader might more usefully recommend.

13. a. Camp sites are not privately owned.
   b. Less space per person.

14. a. Privately owned. More of proceeds go to identifiable owner.
   c. Privately owned course.

15. Seats are allocated first come, first served, rather than sold to worshipers—except in some churches, where a person donates a large sum and is given a special pew as a token of appreciation.

18. In 1972 the U.S. Supreme Court declared that *the dichotomy between personal liberties and property rights is a false one. Property does not have rights. People have rights. The right to enjoy property without unlawful deprivation, no less than the right to speak or the right to travel, is in truth a "personal" right. . . . a fundamental interdependence exists between the personal right to liberty and the personal right in property.*

19. Ignores *prices* at which government goods are distributed. Price of such goods is so low as to create a shortage: an *appearance* that there is an insufficient amount.

20. Depends upon extent to which you want to give parents authority to determine allocation of funds to family members.

22. Building and nonfaculty purposes gain and faculty also gains to the extent salaries are raised more than they otherwise would have been. Money that would be spent for faculty salary increases can be spent for other purposes.

26. As many as people want to use or create. There is no objective test to determine the right number.

27. (c) is correct.

28. The theater cannot house everyone: Each spectator displaces someone on the outside who would enter were there room.

30. a. No.
   b. No.
   c. Probably not.

31. If good is already produced, exclusion benefits no one.

32. True.

34. The laws of demand, expressing general prop-

ositions about human preferences, hold in any kind of economy. So does competition of one kind or another. But the probability that open-market prices will be permitted to direct production and allocation is much lower in a socialist system.

35. A disinterested economist estimated that reliance on smaller cars resulted in one extra death for every $2.5 million saved in fuel costs. No reliable estimates of the tradeoffs among safety, pollution, and fuel costs seem to have been made prior to enactment of the legislation. It is worth noting the economist's additional remarks: "... there are serious doubts that significant health effects are associated with levels of photochemical smog currently prevailing in even the most polluted cities. Certainly, the health effects are small compared to those for suspended particulates and sulfur dioxides, which come primarily from stationary sources. This is a case where the secondary effects [increased automobile manufacturing costs and greater danger] amplify a conclusion evident from the primary effects: health effects do not justify the most stringent controls mandated by Congress." The essential point is to realize that there are always tradeoffs; we should estimate them dispassionately. And it is worth recalling our analysis in Chapter 4 of the effects of smog control on land values. (Source: Lester Lave, "Conflicting Objectives in Regulating the Automobile," *Science,* 212, 22 May 1981, pp. 893–899.)

Chapter 6

1. ($385 − $350)/$350 = .10; 10%.

2. $250(1 + .07)^3 = $306.25. Would double in about 10 years (72/7 = 10.3).

3. Refer to Table 6–1, present value of $1. At 10% the present value of $1 deferred one year is now $.9091. Therefore, the present value of $220 deferred one year is $220 × .9091 = $200.

5. $1702; $2500 ÷ (1.08)^5. Tables have only three-digit accuracy. Use Table 6–1.

6. $1158; $2500 ÷ (1.08)^{10}. Use Table 6–1.

7. $2580. Use Table 6–3.

8. $267.

9. 4.35 × $50 = $217.50.

10. a. $1440.
b. $80,000.

11. It depends on the interest rate. At 10% the $20 higher operating cost for each of 10 years has a present value of $61.40, so machine A, which would avoid that extra cost of $61.40 but costs only $60 more to buy, would barely be cheaper. At 12% B would be cheaper. Indeed, at rates above 11% B would be cheaper. At lower rates A is cheaper. Clearly the extent to which it pays to economize on operating (energy?) costs depends on the rate of interest and the difference in purchase price of the equipment.

14. Yes. With a higher interest rate you still buy other resources equivalent to your house, but if fire has caused the loss you can buy only half a house or equivalent type of resource. In both cases you do suffer a loss relative to some other resources, but loss is more general in case of fire.

15. a. $10,000 plus interest on $5000 for last six days of the year.
b. No.
c. $500.

16. Very probably "yes" for college students.

17. Fall, because future expected receipts fall.

18. $5000.

19. $1000, and it will stay at that value.

20. Pay $40,000 now and $1000 a year rent. And with the accumulated value of lower *initial* difference you will have in 50 years more than the value of the house and land at that future time.

21. $5 million at 3% annually; while market rate is 10% it is equivalent to a subsidy of 7% of $5 million annually. Present value of that $350,000 subsidy for 25 years is over $3 million, which is a taxpayer-financed gift of about $3000 to each of the 1000 employees.

23. Increase in value of holdings is the income. Stocks that do not pay out any earnings as dividends will grow in value by 10% because all the earnings are reinvested in the company. If non-dividend-paying stock is bought, some of the more valuable shares can be sold at the end of the year, equivalent to the reinvested earnings, and the person still ends up with $100,000 in wealth. If the stocks are those on which all earnings are paid out and nothing is reinvested, the person would collect dividends and have stocks that did not grow in value. In either case the person has $10,000 to spend while ending up with $100,000.

The correct way to view the gains from investment is to sum the dividends paid out and the increase in market value of the stock. The sum of those two, however divided, is the earnings. Taxes aside, it makes no difference in what form that earning accrues to the owner of the stock.

Chapter 7

1. a. $5 for 1st oats, $10 for 2nd oats, $15 for 3rd oats, and so on.
   b. Four bushels.

2. A choice means an opportunity among two or more options. The most valuable of the forsaken options is the cost of the one taken.

3. True.

4. Hours of labor have alternative uses. Hours cannot be used. Hence best *forsaken* use *value* of an hour is the cost of any hour of use of labor.

5. Production is efficient if the output of one of the possible products is maximized for stated amounts of the other products. Or production is efficient if there is no waste of potential output: if an increase in output of one of the products can be achieved only by reducing the output of some other product.

6. a. 2 by A, 4 by B.
   b. Yes.
   c. 1–10 units of Y per X is Y price of X.

7. a. 2 X and 12.4 Y by A; and 4 X and 6.4 Y by B.
   b. Yes.
   c. 2 X by B, none by A.

8. b. A is lower marginal cost producer up to three units.
   c. Producer B.
   d. At any ratio below 1.

9. Not necessarily correct. Losing firm may have higher price than profitable firm.

10. Suggests you will be poorer and engage more in "do-it-yourself." Reduced opportunity to trade limits extent to which gains from trade can be achieved.

11. We believe all are returns to superior productivity rather than monopoly-protected incomes. We know of no evidence that any have power to exclude competition by methods not related to superior performance.

12. B loses compared to what he or she would have been able to purchase had C been able to produce Y and sell to A. A keeps wealth compared to what he would have had if C had open access to markets. That C lives on an island across the Pacific rather than on the North American continent has no effect on the analysis.

13. Losers are consumers of the product that would be produced by the newcomer. Frustrated would-be newcomer also is worse off. Examples are taxis, interstate airlines, liquor stores, high tariffs on imports.

14. Yes. The law delays entry.

15. Confuses (1) wealth transfer from existing doctors to patients, because of increased supply of doctors, with (2) social increase in value of extra medical care.

16. Speed of entry of new resources and their similarity to existing resources.

17. A subsistence economy is one in which people consume what they produce. Specialization means people produce more of a good than they consume, and consume more of other goods than they produce. Specialization also means that producers do not produce complete consumer goods but instead concentrate on components or portions of assembly tasks.

18. No. It merely assumes that existing knowledge can be used and subjected to performance tests. Assumes no restrictions on rights to purchase or exchange knowledge. Knowledge is a valuable (economic) resource. To assume it is free is, for example, to deny that schools exist and that teachers perform a useful or desired service. A substantial fraction of our wealth is devoted to gathering information of one kind or another.

19. Private-property rights plus knowledge of the market prices of various feasible crops.

20. a. All exchange benefits *both* parties.
    b. Yes.

21. Private property, market exchange, and observance of contracts.

22. Don't know. His wealth does depend on other people's demands for services obtainable from his wealth.

23. a. Large.
    b. Greater variety of relative talents and training so that differences in people's abilities are more common. Further, the larger market enables a person to sell more of a special output at profitable prices.
    c. Greater concentration of time on same repeated subtasks. For example, hair-shearing for poodles only; specialists in color TV only; architects specializing only in certain types of buildings; greater number of specialty shops.

25. Capitalist society does not restrain production. Production for profit is production for higher-*valued* uses—not just anything for any *use*. Einstein didn't seem to understand what *value* and *costs* meant or how they affected profitability.

26. a. Usually production is used to mean only activity that is not illegal. We wish we knew of a better answer. The question helps to reveal the hidden normative content of concepts that at first seem to be objective and free of ethical presuppositions.

27. How much steel is "needed" depends on costs. Imports are not costs. Capacity is a variable, not a fixed number. Present values are ignored in three-year calculation. "Need for steel" and "shortage" of dollars are rhetoric. India could not "afford" to produce at a higher cost than the cost of importing steel.

28. No. Ignores the possibility of monopoly rent.

30. The self-sufficiency is not, but the increased wealth from the discovered oil is.

Chapter 8

1. It is more difficult to assess the performance of each member.

2. a. Because marginal product, though decreasing, still may exceed marginal cost.

b. Private-property rights that are enforceable and transferable. Also political controls where private rights are enforceable.
   c. That at which marginal product value equals marginal cost.

4. All except full house in movie, and possibly customers in store during sale.

5. a. The number that maximized the average take. With three in each boat, 33 boats (with two on 2 boats).
   b. 7⅓ fish (net of the boat cost of ⅔ fish per person per day).
   c. Price would be two fish. $7.33/2 = 3.67$ boats per day.

7. Socialism does not permit discretionary selection of wealth holdings by each individual. Profits and losses are borne in accord with taxes, rights to use government resources, and powers of political office.

8. No. Future rental value may be affected.

9. a. Resources are said to be specialized *to each other* if the behavior or service of one of them significantly affects the value achievable by the other relative to its next best uses.
   c. If resource A is specialized to resource B, it will need to be owned by the owner of B.

10. The value of houses in the town will depend on the mine operations. Hence employees who own land and houses near the mine will have a large portion of their wealth specific to the mine owner and hence dependent on the owner's behavior. Renting instead of owning spares the employee from having to have so much wealth dependent on the mine.

11. a. Suppose you had one piece of paper and were told to maximize your use of that paper. What would you do? Is it clear now that the expression has no meaning or that it means anything you want it to mean? Usage is not something you maximize; for usage is not measurable in a single-dimensional sense. In international radio-communications conferences, the statement sounded good to many radio and electronic engineers working for the FCC and for the State Department—pre-

cisely because it lets them interpret radio uses however they wish to. It's like having your parents tell you to maximize your time at college.

12. a. The owners of the enterprise: the people who promised payments to the employed inputs.
    b. The owners: the people who promised payments to the employed inputs and who invested in and own the resources specialized to that firm's activities.
    c. If promises exceed revenues, the enterprise will shut down, leaving a smaller supply and higher price for the remaining firms, which may then be able to cover their costs. If promises are less than the firm's sales receipts, competition by imitators to reap similar gains will raise promised payments to responsible inputs and will increase the output, thereby pushing costs up to revenues.

13. The desire for greater wealth and the competition among actual and potential employers for those resources that give greater rather than less wealth.

14. Ratios of final consumer goods purchased would change, thus redirecting use of inputs toward those outputs whose input ratios are more efficient at the new prices.

15. Labor used to make typewriters is substituted for the typist. Substitution of capital for labor is misleading because it ignores labor used to make machines.

16. a. Yes. Equipment on the bus for a laborer on the bus.
    b. Yes. Labor off the bus for labor on the bus.
    c. Yes. Total labor is reallocated in its tasks. No labor is released from work force, since that labor is used to produce more of other goods—except to the extent that some now choose a bit more leisure (as total output is larger).

18. No. Unlimited number of jobs available; only those are filled which are highest-value jobs, given present knowledge and resources. New inventions induce labor to seek and move to best of other unfilled jobs. The labor moves to a less valuable job. But at the same time the total wealth of the community is increased. The displaced person, as explained in the text, has no assurance of realizing a net gain from the particular innovation which displaces his most profitable job opportunities; but he does gain from most other innovations that do not displace his job.

19. No. People are released from some kinds of work so they can do some other productive work—of which there is always some as long as scarcity exists.

20. a. Fixity of ratios of kinds of inputs in the final product says absolutely nothing about the ratios in which those inputs will be used to produce the good.

21. a. Power mowers and equipment, smaller gardens.
    b. Sellers of power equipment, cement surfaces, plastic flowers, and the like.

22. Compares value of what is produced with the cost, rather than merely minimizing cost of what may not be worth even that cost.

23. Can't tell. Depends on costs.

24. Inadequate because it doesn't necessarily maximize difference between value of the total thrust and the cost of getting it.

25. Can't tell. This tells us nothing about cost. We presume new method is technologically or technically efficient, in that no more could be obtained as output for given amount of specified inputs. But this doesn't tell us output is worth the input.

26. Same as answer to question 24.

27. b. To include exchange efficiency. Values of outputs are being included as judged by what people will pay in an exchange system. Thus, efficiency is broadened to include deciding *how much* of *what* to produce, rather than merely the cheapest way to produce an arbitrary output.

Chapter 9

1. Yes, because I am investing in my friend's managerial talents.

2. No to all questions.

3. a. No. In ordinary circumstances we would expect stability.

   b. Should the typical voter or minority groups be able to turn out the governor of their state? It is precisely in order to prevent every single person from making his own will count that voting systems are utilized.

   c. It means a majority controls through the medium of a minority of the stockholders to whom a majority gives its votes, as the Congress constitutes a minority of the American public, being only some 537 people representing 200 million.

4. Depends on what is meant by "very few." Annually many corporations show decreases in the value of their common stock. Approximately 30% to 40% of all corporations report losses for the year, although the firms reporting losses are not always the same. Since 1916 the percentage has always been above 20% and has been over 50% in several years. For all reporting corporations the aggregate earnings (after taxes) normally run about five times that of the losses. For more details consult *Statistics of Income*, U.S. Treasury, issued annually.

5. a. Wealth constraints are different in the two classes of cases.

   b. The former, because of reduced possibility of personally capturing capitalized value of improvements of new management—as can be done in private corporations through purchase and sale of common stock.

6. a. Probably not.
   b. No.

7. The engineer is specific to the other assets; the secretary and guard are not.

8. Yes. Her services are now recognized by the market for teachers to be more valuable. That increase is a profit.

9. No. They are borne by different people more in accord with political power.

10. Disagree. Paper profits usually refer to an increase in value of some asset that a person has not yet sold in exchange for money. But they are real profits that one continues to keep in the form of the asset whose price has risen.

11. Suppose only the president of the company knew the secret and also owned some shares. He would be less willing to sell at the old price and would be willing to buy more shares. In other words, his demand to hold shares increases and thus affects market demand. Certainly several people in the company knew the secret and several also owned stock in the company. Price would rise because their own demand to hold the stock had increased in the light of the secret developments.

12. No one would pay anything for a losing business—that is expected to continue losing. (1) Buyers are more optimistic about how they can manage the business. Or, (2) the business is really not a "losing business" but instead had already invested more than was worthwhile, in light of subsequent returns. So new buyers bid a sufficiently low price for the business so that on that lower price they will be able to cover those costs out of the future returns. In this case there is no point in selling the business, because the loss from the prior inopportune investment is not avoided by the sale of the business. The lower sale price of the business will make that loss explicit in the accounting records, without really changing anything.

13. That everyone has an incentive to lie and cheat is not denied. But is the ability to get away with it affected by the ease of competitors' making counterclaims? The question has only to be posed to be answered. A newspaper will be more careful with the truth if it knows that other news media can challenge its veracity. Politicians are more cautious if they know opponents can challenge their statements. Witnesses in court are more careful with statements of facts if they know they will be cross-examined. The easier it is for all to enter the market of ideas, the more counterclaims and different interpretations of events will be offered. The open market offers more incentives to disprove the claims and to submit counterclaims. That is why it is a good rule to talk to a Ford salesperson if you want the truth about Chevrolets, and conversely.

14. No. The only remaining source for their profits is risk taking: bearing risks others chose not to bear. That is a service. In prospecting for

oil, some will lose and some may win. And some of us do not have to commit our wealth to that risky venture. Still, if we want more oil, the "lucky" investors who bear the risks relieve us of that risk. For that function they are allowed, under private-property rights, to obtain profits. As for taxing them away, that depends on your desire to have risks borne selectively and voluntarily, on your willingness not to renege on general agreement to let lucky ones keep wealth, and on attitudes toward differences in wealth among people.

15. The *corporate form* of organizing our productive work.

16. False. The second sentence is not logically implied by the first. See the analysis in the chapter relating size of profits realized by high-risk, large-investment industries and entry incentive and realized profit rates by *successful* firms.

Chapter 10

1. Marginal revenue is about 61⅜ per share; total revenue difference is (61,500 − $30,812.50) = $30,687.50 for 500 shares change in sales. This is $61.37 per share. Elasticity is very large.

2. Yes. Increase in supply by any one seller has a trivial effect on price.

3. Ignores demand by consumer. "What number is 50% larger than 15?" "If the grocer's selling price to consumers was 50% over his own buying price of 15¢, what is the price to consumers?"

4. c. $6.75.
   d. $7.00.

5. Marginal costs along with marginal revenue indicate maximum wealth-maximizing output, while average costs in relation to price indicate whether the profits are positive or negative.

6. Two different programs, each with different costs.

8. a. Between $21.00 and $22.00.
   b. Close to 770 units.
   c. Shortage with waiting or rationing.
   d. Yes; profits are being earned.
   e. Over $7.00, because of answer to part g.
   f. Contract.
   g. Costs will rise as price of resources re-

sponsible for lower costs are bid up by new entrants seeking those resources. Profits will be absorbed into their costs.

9. Resources will be increased in production of X until extra value of output of X falls to $5.

10. Not "consumer sovereignty" but "individual sovereignty" is more accurate. Individuals make choices as consumers (buyers) and as producers (sellers). An individual expresses choices about working conditions as much as about consumption goods. If mining is unpleasant compared to cutting timber, so that individuals are more willing to work at the latter rather than the former, the amount of lumber relative to coal will be larger than if individual preferences as producers were reversed.

Because there are so many other people, each of us is usually powerless to affect output or market demand in a significant way. This does not mean we cannot choose among alternative purchases or products to produce. Nevertheless, because we cannot significantly change the range of offers made to us, each open market producer thinks the consumer (a personification of the market) is sovereign, while the consumer erroneously thinks that producers (personification of supply) decide what consumers can have.

11. We are using here a possibly inaccurate theory of behavior under government control. No validated theory for that behavior is available.

12. a. Reduce the output.
    b. At first, if output is not reduced but taxes are paid, the wealth of peanut growers will fall. Higher marginal costs indicate a lower output as the new wealth-maximizing output. Or some who formerly made a profit or broke even will now have a loss and be induced to abandon or reduce peanut production.
    c. Reduced supply, shown by shift of supply curve to left, implies higher price.
    d. Land will fall in value only to the extent it was worth more for peanut growing than for next-best use.
    h. Peanut consumers.

13. a. Nothing noticeable.
    b. Nothing noticeable, since the one producer yields a trivial part of industry supply.

c. This taxed producer will lose wealth of resources specialized to growing peanuts on his farm. Other peanut producers are unaffected.

d. See answer to c.

14. Nothing is implied about that.

15. b. Output of each firm is at same marginal cost. Each firm sets same price, and marginal cost equal to price (for price-taker) maximizes wealth.

c. At each output the maximum value of all other outputs is achieved.

16. a. Mill B would clean three gallons and Mill C would clean four gallons.

b. B would buy three; C buys four.

c. Worse, since A would have to shut down, although producing an output worth more than the clean water obtained by stopping production.

d. No, in sense that total value of output (of all goods and services including cleaner water) would be lower.

e. Marginal cost equals value of extra output.

f. Yes. Would probably reduce it.

g. "Excessive use" is analytically more useful meaning.

17. a. Down to a price of 70¢.

b. $5000 (= 90¢ − 40¢ × 1000 units).

Chapter 11

2. a.

Price	Quantity	Revenue		
		Total	Marginal	Average
$20	2	$ 40		$20
19	3	57	$17	19
18	4	72	15	18
17	5	85	13	17
16	6	96	11	16
15	7	105	9	15
14	8	112	7	14
13	9	117	5	13
12	10	120	3	12
11	11	121	1	11
10	12	120	−1	10
9	13	117	−3	9

b. It goes to intramarginal purchasers as a lower price. For example, between a price of $18 and $19 with sales of four and three units, respectively, the marginal revenue, $15, is less than the average revenue, $18, by $3. This amount is distributed to buyers of the three units by a price that is $1 lower than formerly.

c. Seven units.

d. $15.

e. Yes. See f.

f. Having smaller profits than if price were set at $16.

3. A higher price of tickets would have reduced the amount demanded; *but* if the demand were inelastic the proceeds would have been greater, even with some seats unsold for every performance. In any event, the sell-out indicates the price was probably too low and should be raised; the producer has less revenue than he could have had.

5. b. Yes.

c. It is, when I do it. How about you?

9. Price that maximizes their wealth depends on demand, not on their own desire for more wealth. Prices three times as high would, in the opinion of sellers, yield smaller wealth or profits.

10. a. Lower it by $5.

b. Price is $15 or $14. Output is $6 or $7.

c. $90 − $57 = $33.

11. a. Nothing.

b. Reduced by $5 to $28.

12. a. Price searcher; an open-market monopolist.

13. In the sense that it indicates the amounts of the good that the productive resources would be willing to provide through the intermediary of the businessperson. But it does not present the supply schedule of the amounts actually forthcoming at each potential selling price of the good, because the intermediary businessperson is heeding marginal revenue rather than price (average revenue). Instead it is the schedule of amounts at each marginal revenue. If marginal revenue is essentially equal to price or close to price, the marginal cost schedule will approximate the supply schedule and no significant difference will exist between price and marginal costs.

14. a. Either $5 or $6.
    b. $7.
    c. None. It is the wealth-maximizing price.

16. *Pre*purchase service and information to potential customers are often provided by retailers selling goods with a manufacturer's trade name. The retailer also affects the degree of service or quality of the item (by fitting it well or adjusting it or repairing it at the retailer's own expense). The retailer will cover costs in the initial purchase price if he or she does a good job. Protecting the retailer's ability to cover the costs of prepurchase service requires that the customer who obtains such services from the retailer be obliged to buy the product, if he or she decides to buy, from that retailer. But if *other* retailers could capture the customer *after* the customer has obtained prepurchase service at that retailer's expense, then no retailer would be willing to provide that prepurchase (or postpurchase warranty) service.

   Another reason for exclusive territories is to enable the retailer to obtain a higher share of the sales proceeds. That extra profitability of handling a manufacturer's product will be lost if the manufacturer discontinues that retailer as the manufacturer's exclusive outlet. The threat of that loss of future profits will induce the retailer to provide services that help the manufacturer compete with other manufacturers. Thus in both the above situations, exclusive territories (or even retail price maintenance) can serve to enhance intermanufacturer competition and benefit the customer, despite its superficial appearance of being a device to restrict competition. In fact, it restricts the kind of competition that would be self-defeating in withholding better service and products from customers.

17. Folklore suggests that with fewer large, nationwide or international corporations producing a large share of the U.S. sales, consumers have a smaller range of purchase options. That is wrong: Consumers now have *more* alternative suppliers. If, for example, there were 1000 small towns each with five sellers, every one of whom, like every buyer, did business only in that one town, there would be 5000 different business firms, but each buyer had only five from which to choose. Cheap, fast transportation and communication covering larger areas allow each firm and buyer

to do business in a larger number of towns. The number of business firms could be cut to, say, 40, and if each firm and consumer were now able to trade in half the markets, each buyer would face, on average, 20 possible sellers. In fact, transportation and communication have so improved that today the average consumer undoubtedly has more options from more suppliers.

19. a. The seller need cover only marginal costs with marginal revenue, but marginal revenues are not the same as price.
    b. As long as initial difference in marginal revenue (at equal prices) exceeds transport cost, it will pay to ship to lower-priced market.
    c. No.

20. Yes, they are discriminatory. Depends on who you are.

21. No.

22. a. He'll sell four units and retail price will be $17.
    b. This is known as the problem of successive monopoly distortion. Your instructor will probably explain this in more advanced courses.

23. a. $7 to A; $5 to B. Total receipts are $38.
    b. $6 to both. Total receipts are $36.
    c. Eight units. Sell five to A at $6; three to B at $4. Net earners are $26 (= $42 − $16).

Chapter 12

1. a. Slightly more than 10¢. Call it 10¢ for subsequent computations.
   b. Between 65¢ and 67¢. Call it 67¢ for subsequent computations.
   c. Each would sell 10 units at 67¢ each, for $6.70 daily.
   d. Formerly received (10¢ × 20 units) = $2 daily. Each gets $4.70 more.

2. Government agencies enforcing laws against collusions concentrate on collusions against government. Second, government uses a system of sealed bid, publicly opened. This is ideal for preventing secret price cutting or evasion of collusion by colluding firms.

4. Collusion connotes elements of deception in seeking to negotiate exchanges in the pretense that the sellers are acting as independent competitors. If buyers knew sellers were in agreement, they would be alerted to each seller's incentive not to bid as he otherwise would. Without the element of secrecy, buyers are aware of lack of competition among sellers as, for example, among the two salespersons of the same firm. The pretense of competing in price and quality is designed to induce the buyer to think he or she is already obtaining advantages of competition among sellers.

With open collusion, such as mergers, there is no pretense. Buyers are not deceived and can then obtain offers from other independent sellers. Open agreements not to compete are not deceptive and consequently are much less effective in open markets. Partnerships, being open, are not deceptive, hence do not connote elements of collusion. Element of deception is undesirable.

Competition connotes interpersonal striving about who will get what of existing resources, whereas cooperation connotes joint action to increase total stock of wealth to be distributed. Some actions do both at the same time. Thus, exchange with specialization is both competitive and cooperative in increasing wealth as well as in allocating it.

5. a. Team owners are able to sign new players at lower wages, because other owners agree not to compete for these players. The team owner's problem is to pay just enough to induce the newcomer to play; the owner does not have to compete against other owners. The competition is transferred to that of determining the initial assignments of newcomers to each team—by giving the lowest-standing team first choice of the newcomers (high school graduates) and the next-lowest team the next choice. This is the "draft." Although this assignment system is alleged to help equalize team abilities, it does not; players are subsequently sold to other teams, at prices far in excess of that paid the newcomers.

The better athletes suffer. Since it is impossible to know in advance precisely how good an athlete will be, the initial sign-up price will be lower to reflect that uncertainty. There is a stipulation in all contracts that wages cannot be cut "rapidly," so those who turn out to be poorer than expected will be overpaid for a substantial time. Those who turn out better than expected will be underpaid thereafter, because other team owners will not bid for their services by offering the player the higher wage, but will instead pay the team owner to get that player.

b. Perhaps this explains why we call these "sports" rather than "businesses." No business could do this. It is a much tougher, and still unsolved, task to explain why other businesses cannot do what sports can do. The existence of laws restricting business firms does not explain why.

Chapter 13

1. a. To control secret violations of sales of a homogeneous product.

b. The law compelled them to join.

4. a. We think students can discriminate as ably as any other group you would suggest. To the argument that students are prone to take snap, popular, "theatrical" courses, we ask, "What is bad about popular, theatrical courses if the course is nevertheless good?" To say that students select snap courses (meaning courses that are easy—not because teaching is good but because course content is trivial) is to provoke the question as to why students do that. To say they are lazy is to presume that they should not be lazy or that only hard-working students should attend a class—a rather presumptive judgment. More germane is the question of why students who are able and motivated to go to college should nevertheless sacrifice "good" courses for the sake of an easy grade. Does it suggest something about the criteria imposed on the students by the college administrators? What?

6. a. The best—by definition, because the students can select from the entire world, rather than just within one state.

7. b. As any of these groups, we would oppose the development proposed.

8. Distinguish between open-market price searchers and closed or restricted market access. Closed markets imply higher price.

9. Distinguish between open-market price searchers and closed or restricted markets. Closed markets imply higher prices.

11. Simply a case of monopoly rent.

13. a. We don't know the answer to this question. But it shows the difficulty of deducing collusion from overt behavior.
    b. Newspapers are privately owned and use privately owned resources. Their right to publish is not controlled by government agency.

14. Enhances political power. (Or ask your political science professors.)

16. a. Read G. L. Priest, "The History of the Postal Monopoly," *Journal of Law and Economics*, 18, 1 (April 1975), 33–80.

19. Yes, because extent of exchange and specialization is reduced, with consequent smaller wealth.

21. a. No.
    b. Yes.

Chapter 14

1. Wages are driven down or up to whatever equates the amount of labor demanded at that wage to the number willing to work. This may be so high as to result in real incomes adequate to support a rapidly growing population that is also getting richer per capita, as has been true for the past 500 years in most countries. "Subsistence" doesn't specify what *level* of subsistence.

2. In each case supply of that talent gets that price, whether because of higher costs of creating that talent or because of natural scarcity. Neither one is cheating or fooling.

3. Producer estimated E. Taylor would attract at least $4 million more in box office receipts—a greater marginal productivity by E. Taylor.

4. a. New employers who are yet to enter business wouldn't care.
   b. Employees would compete down monetary wage offers or other nonmonetary features to get those jobs that now offer more desirable selected nonmonetary features. Only if every adjustable feature of a job could be controlled would such imposed requirements be totally effective.

5. a. It will aid people who already are employed and who are going to have heart attacks and who either do not plan to shift to new jobs or who do not appear to be prone to heart attacks.
   b. It will make job shifting more difficult, and will hurt those who reveal a higher probability of heart attacks insofar as they want to change jobs. Will help them as long as they stay with *current* employer (with employer at time of passage of law).
   c. All new employees will bear some of the costs since the heart attack is not perfectly predictable. People with a record of attacks will bear the heaviest cost, since they will not be able to get jobs at as high a wage as formerly.

6. a. Would not. I would want a higher wage.
   b. He would offer higher wage.
   c. Employees.

7. They lose who would have advanced more rapidly because of personal superiority in job performance as judged by superiors. We conjecture those who would have advanced rapidly are men, whites, superior teachers, mathematics teachers—of the characteristics listed in the question. (What is your conjecture? Do we differ in principles of analysis or in estimation of attributes that would lead to more rapid advance?)

8. We don't know. We conjecture that employee discrimination is regarded as acceptable; and would be incapable of being prohibited by any law, in any event.

11. Under (a) black borrowers will be worse off because they are restricting themselves to a smaller supply of loanable funds, with higher interest rates to black savers. Under (b) black suppliers would gain, but as a whole, blacks would

be worse off, for reasons explained in Chapter 8, under both (a) and (b).

Chapter 15

2. a. Ask the judge.
b. Ditto.

3. *Technically* often means "accurately and unambiguously." All monopoly is limited in some sense to some class of goods. Monopoly does not eliminate competition. It eliminates certain forms of competition and increases reliance on other forms. In the present case it reduces the scope of wage-rate competition, but increases relevance of age, seniority, and so on.

4. Yes, except for the important fact that the union is not an open-market monopoly and U.S. Steel is. (With respect to the world open market, both are closed-market monopolies as a result of immigration laws and tariffs and taxes on imports.)

5. a. Craft union of welders.
b. We don't know.

8. a. It would have reduced the number of laborers and raised wage rates.
b. Producers (employers and employees) of goods that could be obtained more cheaply by importation wanted tariffs.

9. a. Members of his union would have to switch to lower-paying jobs.
b. The number of cars purchased by the public would be increased, and if producers responded by producing more cars, the number of employees making cars—and the number of union members paying dues to the union—would be increased. The suggestion also serves as a publicity ploy in preparation for contract bargaining sessions.

10. If the union can eliminate low-wage sources of labor, then firms can be eliminated that would survive with low-wage, low-productivity labor and thus compete against the firms with higher-cost labor.

12. It would be made harder to get business if the fees were uniform among all lawyers. But if fees are set at a point that maximizes net reve-

nue from this kind of business—as in collusive price-setting—the present value of the future receipts may be higher even though present receipts are reduced to younger lawyers (who will get more of higher receipts after they are older, more experienced, and well known).

13. a. Some would. But we conjecture most would not.
b. It would increase revealed discrimination by color, because currently blacks can compete by taking lower wages to get a job. (Do you think a law prohibiting choice of employees by color or race would be effective enough to offset increased incentive to discriminate and would be enough to offset reduced employment on a wage basis?)

14. Those who cannot provide services worth as much as the minimum-wage rate will have to work as self-employed or commission-basis employees. Thus, in saying that a higher minimum wage reduces employment, we meant employment for wages—not productive work as self-employed or commission-basis employees.

15. Increase. Self-employment is a way of evading wage regulation.

16. We would prefer none of those laws, since they restrict the opportunity of an immigrant to compete against more popular types of residents in seeking jobs as employees.

17. Decreased. The union will set wages higher to keep only full-time employees at work, with less interest in casual, seasonal laborers.

18. Depends upon whether parents prefer college-age people or old people for baby sitters. Certainly high school students will suffer, since they are poorer quality and manage to compete by offering to work at lower wages.

19. a. It will aid people who already are employed and who are going to have heart attacks and who either do not plan to shift to new jobs or who do not appear to be prone to heart attacks.
b. It will make job shifting more difficult, and will hurt those who reveal a higher probability of heart attacks insofar as they want to change jobs. Will help them as long as they stay with *current* employer

(with employer at time of passage of law).

20. a. Flunk writers of first two items. Bonuses paid were reflective of estimated value of players to the teams. "Bidding away legal property" in Daley's article is not ridiculous, for what else does one do when he buys something? Does Daley imply there is "theft"? Not if bid away. If a player is not legal property, like a slave, bidding away is neither illegal nor "unethical." Daley seems to be advocating that employers be allowed to hire employees while employees are not allowed to be paid open-market competitive wages.
  b. No. Could pay new firms to enter business and bid away the employees.
  c. Probably not. Cannot reconcile this with draft.

Chapter 16

4. a. Longer-run consequences are, insofar as foreseen, discounted into present capital value of the enterprise and are hence borne by the present owner.

5. It permits more future consumption at the cost of less current consumption.

6. Current consumption is forsaken for future income from the preserved house.

7. 5%.

8. Not all roundabout, capitalistic methods are more productive. But many forms are. So the right forms of capital-goods accumulation will enhance wealth in the future.

9. a. $3.71; $8.02, $9.95, $6.80 for col. (3); —$2.89, + $1.20, + $3.04 for col. (5).
  b. 40 years.
  c. $3.00.
  d. Lower interest rate.
  e. As soon as its lumber value is positive.

10. a. $115.60.
  b. Three years.

12. a. Yes. A fall in the rate of interest.
  b. Increase the profitability.
  c. Reduce the ratio of the price of raisins to grapes. Raise the rate of interest.

13. a. About 200,000 rabbits.

15. Higher rate of investment means a higher rate of production of some goods, and this implies a higher cost per unit of those goods.

16. Investment is defined as that rate of conversion (of present income) to wealth which can be profitable. The function relating these rates to the rate of interest is the investment-demand function. Saving is defined as that rate of conversion of present income to wealth that the community wants to engage in. This desired rate—or the rate at which the community is willing to divert income from current income to wealth accumulation—is a function of the rate of interest (among other things); and this relationship between the saving rate and rate of interest is the supply-of-savings function.

18. See pp. 352–353.

19. a. $50 per year.
  b. $57.80—a 2-year annuity.
  c. $10.00.

20. a. Yes.
  b. Relative prices of capital goods and earnings.
  c. Changed price of capital goods relative to current consumption goods; prices of capital goods relative to earnings.

21. Corporation managers do not have to invest all funds within the corporation. They can invest in other companies; they can lend the money. So long as they consider possible alternative investments, they will use funds within the firm only if to do so looks more profitable, as would be the case if the funds were to be borrowed from the market.

22. a. Among those hurt are people whose credit is so poor that they are unable to borrow at these low rates. Among those helped are the better-credit borrowers, since some funds that would have gone to high-risk borrowers are now diverted to the safer borrowers with a consequent lower interest rate to them; corporations are benefited.

23. a. To evade the 5% interest limit in order to get the guarantee.
  b. Is this economic analysis or name calling?
  d. No. Tie-in sales are literally impossible to

prohibit completely. (Once upon a time there was a man who rented his house, under rent control, at the legal maximum rent to the renter who also had offered to buy his ailing cat for $1000.)

24. Either.

Chapter 17

1. A person should be able to get a job at a salary close to his last salary without a significant cost of finding such a job.

3. No. He chooses not to accept the best alternative job he has so far discovered and is instead looking at more jobs—which is not to say that he is lazy or deserves to be poorer.

5. a. Unemployment from relative demand shifting; from general money demand shifts; from closed markets.

6. a. No. The sum of a random variable, summed over trials (one for each firm), will still be a random variable. Random deviations do not cancel each other exactly.
b. Almost certainly. Very rarely would every firm have bigger sales on the following day.
c. Almost certainly. Very rarely would every firm experience a decrease in sales.
d. No, almost certainly not.
e. Average would be decreased.
f. Average would be increased.
g. The former.

7. Increment of cost exceeds increment of wealth for second job possibility investigated.

8. Costs borne by both—no matter who pays the employment agency. If you think it too large, why don't more people go into the business?

9. It is consistent with it, but how far it goes toward implying that higher rate is not clear. As blacks move to the North away from smaller towns with fewer employers, they find it profitable to engage in a larger scope of search; also, employers find it profitable to engage in more extensive search of these applicants than in a small town. A major factor is also believed to be the minimum-wage rate, which cuts more heavily against less-skilled persons—which is not inconsistent with the analysis of this chapter. Massive unemployment in response to big decreases in general demand is certainly an implication of the analysis and is a powerful piece of evidence supporting the analysis.

12. Demand to employ people at higher wages than now offered in available jobs. This does not mean the current offers in those jobs ought not to be increased by monetary or fiscal policy. They may and they may not be already appropriate; but in any event it is not more jobs that are being created but higher money-wage offers.

13. Productivity in existing jobs would be reduced if cheap energy were available in smaller supply. Indeed, more-expensive (less-available) energy would increase tasks to be done by people. More labor would have to be used, like pushing a lawnmower rather than using a power mower! Remember, jobs are never saved or created by changes in resource availabilities. They are made less or more productive. Labor becomes more or less productive in jobs the more or less other jointly usable resources are available.

14. As in prior questions, there are too many jobs to be filled. The problem is to get productivity and hence wages in each task acceptable to people. Unskilled persons may refuse to work unless they are paid more than they are worth in jobs. The skilled may not be skilled enough for some jobs that could be performed only by very skilled people. I might offer $5 an hour to someone who could keep my computer program working, but no one is skilled enough to do that. Or if they are, they could earn more at other jobs. We can always specify some task that no one is skilled enough to do or offer a wage too low to attract those skills. Though that would mean "unfilled jobs for the more skilled," obviously the wage is too low to attract adequate skills. And at the required wage the job might not be offered.

15. a. Employees were also paid in nonmonetary ways, such as "free" or "low-cost" clothing, food, or housing.
b. Feudal lords wanted people to remain tied to their estates, so they tried to prevent industrial employers from attracting them to more attractive industrial activity.

19. Minimum-wage laws preventing employment of low-productivity labor would strike most heavily against those listed in the question.

Chapter 18

1. See Table 18-1. The value added is equivalent to income earned. Hence a value added tax would be equivalent to a tax on income, if the definition of taxable value added corresponds to that in the table.

2. a. No.
   b. It would encourage firms to integrate into one firm to avoid taxable transactions among themselves.

3. Part of that excess is value added. If larger, then a profit is earned.

4. A higher *marginal* tax bracket (that is, the tax on the extra dollars earned) reduces the supply of labor to the market. But a higher *average* tax rate, if the marginal tax rate is fixed, may increase *or* decrease the supply of labor to the market. Be careful to distinguish between marginal and average taxes.

5. Money is fungible: It can be spent for anything. Thus, money collected to be spent on the police may permit other expenditures to remain undiminished despite such increases, whereas without the tax police expenditures could not be increased unless other expenditures were diminished.

6. Same answer as in above question.

7. Some taxes pay for benefits received by the taxpayer. Hence to treat aftertax income as the only income is to overlook government services. If governments tax more heavily but provide more services, then aftertax incomes will be a deceptive measure of economic welfare.

8. Because land is a resource whose supply is fixed independently of price, the sales tax will increase the cost of living in Las Vegas, and land values will fall commensurately, because land cannot move to other places.

9. No. But in some measures of the cost of living it is nevertheless misleadingly counted.

10. If the public regards government property in trees as part of its wealth—possibly by sales of the cut lumber thereby providing public services without explicit taxes—then people who would otherwise not have paid taxes when the trees were government property would pay higher taxes after the lumber is sold. Selling one's wealth does not eliminate taxes. It reduces the source of one's income.

11. No, because anticipated future events are capitalized into present measures of wealth. If one's present wealth increases, one increases one's current consumption, possibly by borrowing against the future greater aftertax income.

12. True.

14. a. Correct form of statement would be that it would raise the *payments* the federal government would have to record in its budget. Real costs are being paid already by those who are drafted. The income they are sacrificing is the cost, and this cost would be reduced if the draft were eliminated and military personnel were obtained by paying adequate wages to attract men.
   b. You should, because it will. Better assignment of people to jobs in this country—which would be a result of using adequate wages for military personnel—would increase the total productive efficiency and output, thereby reducing the size of our sacrificed output. The draft conceals costs by making federal expenditures lower through the device of compulsory service.

Chapter 19

9. a. Monetary asset to creditor; monetary liability to debtor.
   b. Monetary asset to creditor; monetary liability to debtor.
   c. Real asset to both parties.
   d. Real asset to leaseholder; real liability to lessor; monetary liability to leaseholder and monetary asset to lessor.

10. Are you a net monetary debtor?

11. a. No.
   b. Yes, because legal ethics and principles are concerned only with the nominal val-

ue of the funds and not with their real value, which is relative to changes in price level.

c. Our legal system seems to act on the premise that inflation is not a fact of life, and thus that the nominal value of your investment is all that has to be protected by a prudent trustee.

14. The wage-lag assertion implies a systematic relationship between inflation and wages, not a random one, so if the assertion is correct, lag should be apparent more than half the time. All evidence refutes the existence of a lag.

15. Increased demand does not necessarily first occur for consumer goods. It can be for labor to make buildings, machines, or roads. To think of demand as always having its first impact on final consumer goods is to confuse impact of demand changes with value derivation from consumer goods. Furthermore, recall the discussion in Chapter 4 of the effect of a change in demand for meat.

16. Money holders.

17. a. Smaller.

b. No.
e. By about 250%.

18. It prevents prices from facilitating exchange; it diverts attention from causes to consequences.

19. Neither affects the quantity of money or of real goods and services, or the demand to hold money.

20. The desire to revise the pattern of demand is often a reason for resorting to a policy of money creation. The inflation does not therefore cause the revised price pattern; instead, the revised demand brought about by the new money causes the relative price changes. At least this interpretation is consistent with facts about sources of inflations and observed changes in relative price patterns. The statement that inflation in and of itself causes a dispersion of prices because of price rigidities is not entirely false if regard is given to prices that are fixed by law and can be changed only by appeal to a regulatory agency (as public utilities must). But the assertion is usually more sweeping, and for that there is no supporting evidence.

Glossary

Aggregate demand: The sum of all individual demand schedules.

Aggregate supply: The sum of all individual supply schedules.

Annuity: A series of future annual yields or payments.

Bargaining power: A measure of the ability of parties in negotiations (such as labor unions and employers) to achieve their goals.

Bond: A promise to repay a borrowed amount, or principal, usually with interest, for some specified number of years.

Boycott: A concerted refusal to buy, and an effort to persuade others not to buy, the product of a particular firm.

Business firm: A group of productive resources jointly producing goods and services for sale to others.

Capitalism: Essentially the same system as a market economy.

Capitalist: The individual who makes the wage or rent payments to inputs of production.

Capital gain: An increase in the market value of an asset (usually realized at the time the asset is sold).

Capital goods: Durable goods producing a stream of future goods or services that have some market value at the time of production.

Cartel: A coalition of sellers who conclusively agree to reduce output and raise prices, as well as to restrain entry of new competitors.

Closed shop: A firm in which only union members can be hired.

Collective bargaining: Negotiations on contract terms and working conditions that are conducted by employees as a group—usually through a representative, such as a union official.

Command economy: An economy in which production and distribution of goods and services is organized and directed by a central authority.

Comparative advantage: That productive activity for which one has the lowest marginal cost in terms of other productive activities forgone.

Competition: Rivalry among sellers and among buyers for goods and services, a method of coordinating economic activity through free exchange of productive resources and final goods and services under a system of private property.

Constrained maximum: Maximization of some variable (like output of a good) subject to some constraint (like a given output of another good); the production-possibility boundary represents constrained maximization.

Consumer price index: A measure of changes in money prices of a typical market basket of goods and services for average-income people, compiled by the Bureau of Labor Statistics of the U.S. Department of Labor.

Consumer's surplus: The benefit to a buyer from the purchase of a good; the difference between the buyer's total personal use value of the good and the good's market value.

Copyright: The assignment of an exclusive right to commercial use of written or published material.

Corporation: A business firm that is jointly owned by several people, whose liability is limited to their stock in the firm, and that continues to exist despite death or sale of stock by owners.

Cost: The most valuable forsaken alternative to an act.

Craft union: A labor union whose members are practitioners of a particular skill, like carpentry or bricklaying, though they may work in different industries.

Deficit spending: The spending of more than has been taken in as revenues.

Demand, or demand schedule: A schedule of the different quantities of a good or service an individual is willing and able to buy at various prices.

Depreciation: The predictable reduction in the value of a resource as it deteriorates with use or with aging.

Depression: A decline in production, income, and employment that is more severe, and may be longer lasting, than a recession.

Derived demand: The demand for productive resources derived from demand for the output those resources can produce.

Differential earnings: The earnings to a superior talent or more efficient resource; a Ricardian rent (but *not* a monopoly rent).

Division of labor: The division of production of some output into a number of different tasks in which people specialize.

Dominant firm: A seller controlling a sufficient amount of supply to act as a price searcher, while competitors are price takers of the price established by the dominant firm. The dominant firm controls not only current supply but also sources of expanded supply in the near future.

Earnings: The accounting conception of profits as the margin of revenue over accounting cost, as opposed to economic profits, which are the margin of revenue over economic costs (including a 'normal' profit).

Economic efficiency: The condition of an economy that is operating with productive efficiency (that is, is on the production possibility boundary) and is maximizing consumer welfare such that no change in resource or output allocation could make someone better off without making someone else worse off.

Economic good: A good that is scarce, of which less is available than people want.

Economic growth: Increase in the output of an economy in conditions of full employment.

Economic rent: Any price that is unnecessary to keep a good in existence; hence any price in excess of resource cost. Economic rent may, however, be necessary to allocate goods to their highest-valued uses.

Endowment effect: The effect that change in a good's price has on demand for that good by a person whose income or wealth is partly derived from that good. The endowment effect on quantity purchased moves in the same direction as price.

Equilibrium-sustaining price: The market-clearing price.

Fair-employment laws: Laws regulating the hiring practices of employers, with the stated intent of prohibiting discrimination.

Federal Reserve System: The central banking system created by the U.S. government; the major tool of monetary policy.

First law of demand: At any given price, there is some higher price at which less of a good is demanded.

Fiscal policy: Government use of expenditures and taxation to attempt to alleviate fluctuations in general economic activity.

Free enterprise: Another term for private-property market-exchange system.

Free good: A good (such as air) the availability of which is sufficient to satisfy all wants, even at a zero price. Some goods that are "free" to their consumers, like public education, are not free by this definition.

Frictional unemployment: Unemployment arising from normal shifts in demand and supply in the labor markets. It is an efficient method of adjusting to changing market conditions by searching for the best available alternative employment.

Full employment: The condition in which the entire labor force is working except those who are temporarily between jobs.

Full price: The money price of a good or service plus all other costs incurred in making the purchase, such as time, inconvenience, and the like.

Gains from trade: The difference between seller's or buyer's marginal personal use value for each unit of a good traded and the price of that good.

Good: Anything that someone desires.

Goodwill: A specialized asset of a firm, which earns a rent equal to the excess of the value of the firm over the sum of the value of each of its productive resources were those resources used elsewhere.

Gross national income: National income including wages, rents, profits, interest, and the value of capital equipment used up through depreciation.

Import quotas: Limits on the amount of a good suppliers from other countries are permitted to sell in the country imposing the quota.

Income elasticity of demand: The responsiveness of the quantity of a good demanded to changes in the incomes of buyers of the good; the ratio of the percentage change in quantity demanded to the percentage change in income.

Income release effect: An effect of a lower price, which releases some of the income formerly spent on that good at its higher price. There is usually a negligible effect on demand for the good in question, the released income being spread out over all the goods purchased. The opposite effect occurs when the price of the good increases.

Industrial union: A labor union whose members work in a particular industry, such as steel or automobiles, though there may be numerous different skills practiced by its members.

Inferior good: A good of which less is demanded by an individual as personal income rises, all other things affecting demand for that good remaining unchanged.

Inflation: A persisting increase in all money (nominal) prices; conversely, a decline in the purchasing power of money. All prices rise by the same amount. (Differences in the increase in prices of various goods during inflation reflect changes in relative prices, not differences in the effects of inflation on the prices of different goods.)

Interest: The anticipated rate of growth of wealth were income reinvested; the amount of wealth that could be consumed in a given year without reducing one's stock of wealth below its original value. Hence it is the price of borrowing money.

Investment: Saving or nonconsumption for the purpose of transforming saved resources into productive capital for future use.

Labor-market participation rate: The proportion of the adult population that is in the market labor force (which excludes the nonmarket labor services of the military and of spouses in the household).

Labor union: A coalition of employees of a firm to monitor and affect wages, fringe benefits, employer–employee relations, and working conditions at the firm.

Long run: Either (a) the interval in which all productive resources can be changed to adjust optimally to a given level of output, or (b) a long-lived activity. The two meanings of the term should not be confused.

Long-run period: The period in which all desired adjustments to market conditions have been made, including changes in any and all productive resources and in prices and output.

Marginal cost: The increase in total cost from producing one additional unit of a good or service.

Marginal personal use value: The value a person places on one additional unit of a good, measured as the amount of some other good the person would forsake to get that unit.

Marginal product: The increase in total output from the addition of one unit of some input, with all other inputs used in the production of that good held constant.

Marginal revenue: The change in total revenue (market value) from a good when price is reduced enough to sell exactly one more unit.

Market-clearing price: The market price at which quantity demanded equals quantity supplied. Graphically, it is the point at which the supply and demand curves intersect.

Market economy: An economic system in which individuals have rights to control and use private property and to exchange such property at market prices.

Market period: The period in which the supply of a good is unchanged regardless of the change in the price for which the good can be sold.

Market value: The total value of an amount of a good at its market price: the price of the good times the quantity sold at that price.

Mercantilist system: A system in which access to private property and markets is limited by government to certain individuals.

Merger: The combining of two firms into one, either by one firm's buying the other or by the two being aggregated under common ownership of the original owners, who form the new ownership of the merged firm.

Minimum-wage law: A mandated rate of pay below which employers are forbidden by law to pay employees, whether or not individuals are willing to work at that lower wage.

Monetary policy: Government use of expansion or contraction of the money supply to affect the general level of economic activity.

Money: A costlessly recognized, divisible, storable, and exchangeable good used in virtually every exchange. It serves as a medium of exchange, unit of measure, and store of value.

Monopoly: The presence of a single seller of a good or service legally protected from the entry of potential competitors.

Monopoly distortion: The failure of a monopolist to produce goods for which the value to buyers exceeds the costs of production, because marginal revenue is less than marginal cost for units not produced.

Monopoly rent: The higher income received by a monopolist as a result of the monopoly.

Monopsony: A monopoly held by a buyer rather than a seller.

Multipart pricing: The selling of additional units of a good at successively lower prices as larger quantities are produced but with no lowering of prices of the earlier units.

National Income Deflator: A measure of inflation—usually lower than the Consumer Price Index—calculated according to the rise in money prices of all national income. By including all goods and services it provides a more reliable measure of inflation than CPI, which uses a rigid market basket that does not allow for substitution among goods whose relative prices have changed.

Natural monopoly: A firm whose costs decline as output increases such that one firm is more efficient than two or more could be.

Net National Income: The sum of value added over the entire market economy: the sum of wages, rents, interest, and dividends for the entire economy.

Net of tax: The price of a good a seller receives after taxes on that good have been subtracted.

Net productivity of investment: The increase in future income created by investment today to transform some resource into a more highly valued form for later use, a form more highly valued than the present value of the funds invested.

Nominal price: The amount of money, rather than the amount of other goods, that must be given up to get some of a good. If the value of money is falling, an increase in the nominal price of a good does not necessarily indicate a change in its real or relative price.

Nonprofit corporation: An enterprise, usually nongovernmental, holding assets the return from which is not distributed to any individual (as they are under private-property arrangements) but is reused to further the stated goals of the enterprise.

Obsolescence: Unexpected reduction in the value of a productive resource from unanticipated development of a new, superior competing resource.

Oligopoly: A situation in which each of the few sellers of a good makes pricing and output decisions according to the anticipated responses of other sellers.

Open market: Markets to which all individuals have access without legal or artificial barriers. All individuals are permitted to buy or sell goods or services at market prices.

Opportunity cost: The most valuable alternative that must be forsaken to undertake a given act: cost.

Pareto-optimal allocation: Output allocation such that any change to make someone better off would make someone else worse off.

Parity price: A government-guaranteed minimum price for agricultural output—essentially, a price floor on agricultural products. These are said to bring "parity" with the costs of farm output.

Partnership: A form of proprietorship involving two or more owners, each liable to the extent of their wealth. A partnership dissolves upon the death of a partner.

Patent: Assignment of an exclusive right to commercial use of an invention not previously known. The patent usually has a limited life, and prohibits only the commercial rights to the good or service; private production and consumption aren't limited.

Poverty line: A level of income, chosen by the Social Security Administration, below which families are said to be in poverty. The line is based on family size and includes no in-kind income, such as government-provided medical services or food stamps.

Present value: The current value of the future stream of goods or services that an investment will yield; it is derived by discounting the value of that stream at an appropriate rate of interest.

Price discrimination: Selling goods at different market prices to different groups, reflecting differences in demand among the groups rather than differences in the costs of providing those goods. It is undertaken to capture some of the consumer's surplus that goes to consumers under uniform pricing.

Price elasticity of demand: The responsiveness of the quantity of a good demanded to changes in the price of that good; formally, the ratio of the percentage change in quantity demanded to the percentage change in price.

Price searcher: A seller who affects the price of a good by changing the quantity produced and sold. The seller faces a downward-sloping demand curve, and price exceeds marginal revenue. The seller must search for the profit-maximizing price. A price searcher is said to have market power.

Price taker: A seller whose sales are a small enough portion of the total quantity demanded of the good that the seller's changing the supply will not affect market price. The price taker must sell at whatever price the market determines, rather than searching for a price.

Private property: Economic goods that can be controlled, used, and exchanged by individuals without political restrictions.

Production-possibility boundary: The locus of points describing the maximum amount of one good that can be produced given production levels of a second good with given resources and technology.

Productive efficiency: Production of the maximum output possible at given levels of resources and technology; it is described by the points along the production possibility boundary.

Profit: Any increase in wealth above and beyond that accounted for by investment of savings out of standard income: increases in an economy's stock of wealth that are not anticipated in the market.

Promissory note: A legal contract promising to repay a debt at some point in the future at a stated rate of interest. "Buying debt" is the purchase of a promissory note.

Proprietorship: A business owned by one person who has full liability for all the firm's debts to the extent of his or her entire wealth. The firm ends upon the death of the proprietor.

Public good: A good that can be consumed by any one person without there being less available for others to consume. The value of a public good is thus the sum of the value all individuals who consume the good place on each unit.

Quasi-rent: Any part of a price that does not affect the amount of a good available now but will affect the future amount of that good available; a temporary rent.

Real asset: Any asset (such as land) the real value of which remains unchanged by inflation, although the money value of such assets will change.

Real liability: Any obligation the real value of which is unchanged by inflation, although the dollar value may change.

Real price: The same as relative price.

Real wages: Wages measured against living costs—the actual goods and services that can be purchased with the wage.

Recession: A transient decline in the general level of employment, income, and production from some shock to the economy.

Relative price: The price of a good compared to the price of all other goods. The amount of other goods (other than money, itself a good) that must be given up to get a good. If all money prices change by the same amount (as during inflation), relative prices are unchanged.

Rents: Earnings paid for the services of nonhuman resources, such as land.

Revenue sharing: Distribution of federal tax revenues to state and local governments.

Ricardian rent: The higher return received by a more productive or more efficient resource.

Saving: The nonconsumption of standard income, thus adding to an economy's stock of wealth and increasing that economy's future standard income.

Scarcity: The condition of limited resources relative to unlimited human wants.

Secondary boycott: A boycott against a firm that deals with a firm being boycotted.

Second law of demand: In the long-run, demand is more elastic for any given good as substitutes for that good become more readily apparent and available.

Shortage: An excess of quantity demanded over quantity supplied because the price of a good has not been permitted to rise to its market-clearing level.

Short run: Either (a) the interval in which the stock of productive resources remains fixed, or (b) the time required to make a quick adjustment in the level of output (and cost). The two meanings of the term should not be confused.

Socialist economy: A system in which income-producing goods and durable consumer goods are controlled by the government and are not salable at market-clearing prices.

Specialization: The production of more of a good than one consumes, the unconsumed portion being sold for other goods one wishes to consume.

Speculation: The buying of a good in the hope of making a future profit by a rise in its price.

Standard income: The increase in an economy's wealth, analogous to the interest rate, that the economy can consume in a year without detriment to the original stock of wealth. The market-forecasted sustainable rate of increase in wealth.

Strike: A concerted refusal by employees to work for a particular employer with which a union has a grievance, and to prevent others from taking jobs with the same employer in their absence.

Structural unemployment: Unemployment caused by very large and long-term or permanent shifts in labor demand in a few industries, often forcing those unemployed to accept lower wages or rents in other industries where their skills earned in the declining industry aren't so valuable.

Substitution effect: The effect of a change in price of a good on the quantity of the good demanded; when the price of a good rises, other goods will be substituted for it and the quantity demanded will falls, all other things affecting demand for that good remaining unchanged.

Superior good: A good of which more is purchased by an individual as personal income rises, all other things affecting demand for the good remaining unchanged.

Surplus: An excess of quantity supplied over quantity demanded because the price of a good has not been permitted to fall to its market-clearing level.

Tie-in: Sale of a product on the condition that a different, perhaps unrelated, product be purchased as well.

Total personal use value: The total amount of other goods and services one would be willing to give up to obtain some amount of good.

Unemployment: The absence of employment acceptable to the unemployed in terms of wages and working conditions.

Union shop: A firm in which one need not be a union member to gain employment, but must join the union and pay dues within a specified period after being hired.

Utility-maximization theory: The theory that individuals seek the highest possible satisfaction from the goods and services they consume and from other activities they undertake.

Value added: The value of a product in excess of the cost of materials and services purchased by a firm to make that product. The sum of values added, rather than the value of sales at each step of production, is the proper measure of national income.

Wages: Earnings paid to providers of labor services.

Wealth: The sum of the market value of all goods and services in an economy. (The term physical wealth refers to the collection of an economy's goods, not their value.)

Index

Markup, 194

Marx, Karl, 6, 157

Math, use of, in economics, 429–35

Mercantilist system, defined, 7

Merger(s)
compared with cartels, 270
criticisms of, 273
defined, 270
impediment to effectiveness of, 270

Mexican-Americans, and ethnic income differences, 316

Middlemen
competition among, 50–51
as restricted by law, 51–52
tactics used by, 51–52
use of, 48–50

Money, creation of, 381, 382, 407–8, 425–27

Monopolies
airlines as, 333
ambiguity in defining, 273
competition for, 294–95
government regulation of, 272–73
inefficiency resulting from, 155–56
and labor unions, 332–33
natural, 291
patent and copyright, 292–93
and price discrimination, 255
public utilities as, 291–92
and redistribution of wealth, 398
"shared," 274

Monopoly distortion, 256

Monopoly rents, 263, 288, 293–95, 332–34

Monopsony, 337–39

Montgomery Ward & Company, 214

Multipart pricing
and cost subsidizing, 249–50
distribution of gains in, 249
feasibility of, 250
government view of, 251
inefficiency in, 250
to one customer, 247–49
and public utilities, 250

National Collegiate Athletic Association (NCAA), 338

National Energy Act (1975), 73–75

National income deflator, defined, 404–5

National Labor Relations Board (NLRB), 326

Natural resources. *See* Resources

NCAA (National Collegiate Athletic Association), 338

New York Bond Exchange, 358

NLRB (National Labor Relations Board), 326

Norris-LaGuardia Act (1932), 327

Notes, promissory, 112

OASDHI (Old Age, Survivors, Disability, and Health Insurance Program), 319–20

Obsolescence, defined, 226

Occupational Safety and Health Agency (OSHA), 336

Oil
and government restrictions, 146–47
and OPEC, 265–68
present versus future value of, 124, 268–69
price control of, 73–75
rate of exploration for, 268
reasons for price increases of, 268–70
See also Gasoline

Old Age, Survivors, Disability, and Health Insurance Program (OASDHI), 319–20

Oligopoly, 271–72

OPEC (Organization of Petroleum Exporting Countries), as a cartel, 265–68

Open market(s)
and cartels, 52
and costs of trading, 50–51
ethics of, 52–53
features of, 190–92
freedom provided by, 53–54
middlemen in, 51
misconceptions about, 227
as restricted by law, 51–52
and restrictions on pricing, 72
and use of natural resources, 345
See also Market(s); Orderly market(s)

Opportunism, 170, 171–73

Orderly market(s)
and the dairy industry, 287
defined, 287
and holding crops off the market, 289
and import quotas, 287–88
and price supports, 288
and surpluses, 288–89
See also Market(s); Open market(s)

Orderly market argument, 287

OSHA (Occupational Safety and Health Agency), 336

Outputs
as affected by tax, 219–20
appropriate, 217–18
components of, 224–25
efficient, 3, 141–42
expansion of, 212–13
in joint production, 165–66
measuring, 224–25
with more than two producers, 151–54
response to demand of, 213–14
See also Inputs; Production; Specialization

Pareto, Vilfredo, 76

Pareto-optimal allocation, 76

Parity price, defined, 288

Partnership, defined, 185–86

Patents
defined, 292, 292n
misconceptions about, 293
pooling of, 293
for public goods, 101

Perpetuity, defined, 115

Personal use value
and consumer's surplus, 17–18
curve depicting, 45–48
and expenditures, 17–18
illustrations of, 15
marginal, 14, 71
measurement of, 14–15
and tie-ins, 251
and trade opportunities, 45
versus market value, 18–19

Philanthropy
foreign aid as a form of, 98
nontransferable, 99
public goods as a form of, 99–101
unintentional, 98–99
who gains from, 96–98